John Donne's Religious Imagination:
Essays in Honor of John T. Shawcross

Corporis hæc Animæ sit Syndon Syndon Jesu
Amen.

JOHN DONNE'S RELIGIOUS IMAGINATION

ESSAYS IN HONOR

OF

JOHN T. SHAWCROSS

Edited by
Raymond-Jean Frontain
and
Frances M. Malpezzi

UCA Press
Conway, AR
1995

Library of Congress Cataloging-in-Publication Data

John Donne's religious imagination : essays in honor of John T.
  Shawcross / edited by Raymond-Jean Frontain and Frances M.
  Malpezzi
      448 p. 23 cm.
      Includes bibliographical references and index.
      ISBN 0-944436-23-4 : $42.95
      1. Donne, John, 1572-1631--Religion. 2. Christian poetry,
  English--History and criticism. 3. Christianity and literature--
  England--History--17th century. I. Shawcross, John T.
  II. Frontain, Raymond-Jean. II. Malpezzi, Frances M., 1946-
  PR2248.J65   1995
  821'.3--dc20   94-24000
                                                            CIP

For Raymond A. Frontain and William M. Clements,
"reverend heads" of another sort

Contents

Preface

"When thou hast done, thou hast not done, / For, I have more,"
cautions the speaker of Donne's "A Hymne to God the Father." As so
many of Donne's editors and commentators on his canon have discov-
ered, few warnings have proved more prophetic. Donne's thought is as
elliptical and mercurial as the conceits he has become identified with,
perhaps in no way moreso than in terms of his religious practices and
beliefs.

Donne's religious life—and the imaginative works that his religion
inspired—are among the most troublesome set of paradoxes and prob-
lems to emerge from the English Renaissance. He was born into one of the
most visible and influential of Catholic families, yet he concluded his life
as one of the most visible and influential spokesmen for the Anglican
compromise. Fascinated by the conversion experiences of Saint Paul and
Saint Augustine, and the author both of poems of extraordinary interior-
ity and of prose meditations that betray a pained self-scrutiny, he para-
doxically left little conclusive evidence by which the modern reader or
biographer may chart his spiritual progress with any certainty. He has,
alternately, been accused of guilt-ridden recusancy, been condemned for
gross political expediency, and been lauded for maintaining an extraordi-
nary integrity in a religiously volatile age.

The consequences of such ambiguity are everywhere evident in Donne
criticism. Scholars today divide over whether this poet—theologically
one of the best-read men of his age—was more heavily indebted to native
Protestant traditions of meditation or to continental Catholic models.
Many readers are troubled by the seeming irony that in *Ignatius, His
Conclave* Donne lambasts the founder of the Jesuits for the very casuistry
that the speakers of his *Songs and Sonets* employ with such aplomb.
Identifying even the tone of a poem may prove an insurmountable ob-
stacle: Is the reference to woman as a source of prevenient grace in lines
41-43 of "Elegie: Going to Bed" an act of strategic blasphemy? Or is it the
central dramatic moment in the poem when the male speaker's seem-
ingly chauvinist bravado falters and his real sense of sexual and spiritual
helplessness comes through? Donne's brilliance in this poem may actu-
ally lie in the fact that despite the speaker's use of imperatives and the
seemingly relentless progress of the woman's disrobing, the reader never
learns whether the woman accedes to the speaker's final demand or not.
The poem's resistance to closure is as frustrating to the reader outside the

poem as the speaker's anticipation of being finally delivered of his sexual labor is to him within.

*　　*　　*

Insofar as it was found possible, the essays that follow are organized according to the arrangement of Donne's poems in John Shawcross's edition of the *Complete Poetry* (1967), from which all quotation of the poetry comes as well. The essays on Donne's prose are loosely organized according to the prose works' dates of publication.

The editors would like to express their gratitude to those past and current members of the advisory board of the John Donne Society who generously but shrewdly commented upon the initial versions of these essays. In particular we would like to thank Professors Diana Trevino Benet (New York U), Meg Lota Brown (U of Arizona), Eugene R. Cunnar (New Mexico State U), Robert T. Fallon (La Salle U), Achsah Guibbory (U of Illinois), Dayton W. Haskin (Boston C), Judith Scherer Herz (Concordia U, Montreal), Albert C. Labriola (Duquesne U), Graham Roebuck (McMaster U), Gary A. Stringer (U of Southern Mississippi), Ernest W. Sullivan, II (Texas Tech U), and Claude J. Summers (U of Michigan, Dearborn).

The University of Central Arkansas Faculty Research Council, chaired by Dean Robert M. McLaughlin, provided financial subvention for, among other things, the reprinting of the volume's illustrations. The Arkansas State University Research Reassignment Program supported released time for Frances Malpezzi to work on the volume. Likewise, Professors Charles R. Carr and Terrance B. Kearns provided material assistance and secretarial support from the Arkansas State University and the University of Central Arkansas English departments which they, respectively, chair.

Mrs. Charlene Bland waved her hand over twenty computer disks submitted in a variety of programs and magically deconstructed a Babel of conflicting computer discourses. Dr. Jonathan A. Glenn served as a daily resource during the final editing process: surely there is a place in heaven for those who pity and protect their less fortunate computer brethren!

Finally, the editors acknowledge the good will, unflappable competence, and extraordinary flexibility in creative matters manifested daily by Ms. Kathleen Hart-Sparks, Dr. Jeff Henderson, and Dr. Robert E. Lowrey of the University of Central Arkansas Press in bringing this leviathan of a manuscript to bay.

A Note on Texts and Citations

Unless otherwise noted, all references to Donne's poetry will be from John T. Shawcross, ed., *The Complete Poetry of John Donne*, The Anchor Seventeenth-Century Series (Garden City, NY: Doubleday, 1967); to Donne's *Devotions* from Anthony Raspa, ed., *Devotions upon Emergent Occasions* (Montreal: Mc-Gill Queens U P, 1979, and New York: Oxford U P, 1987); and to Donne's sermons from George R. Potter and Evelyn M. Simpson, eds., *The Sermons of John Donne*, 10 vols. (Berkeley: U of California P, 1953-1962). Only the line numbers of poems, the page numbers of the *Devotions*, and the volume and page number for *Sermons* will be cited parenthetically in the text.

ANQ *American Notes & Queries*
ELH *English Literary History*
ELN *English Language Notes*
ELR *English Literary Renaissance*
HLQ *Huntington Library Quarterly*
JDJ *John Donne Journal*
JEGP *Journal of English and Germanic Philology*
JHI *Journal of the History of Ideas*
JRMMRA *Journal of the Rocky Mountain Medieval and Renaissance Association*
MLQ *Modern Language Quarterly*
MLR *Modern Language Review*
MP *Modern Philology*
N&Q *Notes & Queries*
PLL *Papers on Language and Literature*
PMLA *Publications of the Modern Language Association of America*
PQ *Philological Quarterly*
Ren/Ref *Renaissance and Reformation/Renaissance et Réforme*
RES *Review of English Studies*
SEL *Studies in English Literature*
SP *Studies in Philology*
TSLL *Texas Studies in Literature and Language*
UTQ *University of Toronto Quarterly*

Introduction

"Make all this All": The Religious Operations of John Donne's Imagination

Raymond-Jean Frontain

eligious man's profound nostalgia," writes historian of religion Mircea Eliade, "is to inhabit a 'divine world,' is his desire that his house shall be like the house of the gods, as it was later represented in temples and sanctuaries. In short, this religious nostalgia expresses *the desire to live in a pure and holy cosmos, as it was in the beginning, when it came fresh from the Creator's hands"* (65). On few imaginations has this need pressed more heavily than John Donne's. At times nearly pulverized by the threat of dissolution, Donne expresses in nearly everything he wrote the desire to regain a lost world of primal significance and integrity. His was essentially a religious imagination.

And with reason. His life spanned the particularly troubling transition period in which the hierarchies that, theoretically at least, guaranteed the cohesiveness of the universe were challenged by the "new Philosophy" which called everything into doubt (*First Anniversarie*, line 205), and the analogies which characterize Tillyard's idealized Elizabethan World Picture were all but reduced to a set of poetic cliches.[1] In religion the metaphorically seamless coat of Jesus was rent by squabbling Catholic, Anglican, and Calvinist polemicists, making it painfully difficult for a man of Donne's intellect and religious thirst to conclude with absolute certainty which church was the true Bride of Christ. The Petrarchan idealization of woman as an angelic source of grace and the primary means of the poet-lover's salvation was being challenged increasingly by the portrayal of more realistic mistresses whose eyes were nothing like the sun. Few of his contemporaries were more sensitive to, or more traumatized by, the threat of dissolution implied by such changes than Donne, or motivated by as powerful a sense of loss. He responded with a ferocity of spirit and intellect, determined—imaginatively, at least—to recombine the scattered fragments of the created universe into a coherent and cohesive whole and "make all this All" ("Upon the translation of the Psalmes," line 23). For, however powerful the images of dissolution and jarring disharmony that appear in his writing, they are inevitably absorbed by Donne's relentless search for a stabilizing center and integrated into his assertion of the essential coherence of both the world and his own experience. Most importantly, Donne increasingly came to see poetry not simply as a way of expressing his "nostalgia" for "a pure and holy cosmos, as it was in the beginning, when it came fresh from the Creator's hands," but as a religious activity itself, the most effective way available to him of attempting a return to such a world, and of enabling others to return there as well.

Donne's Erotic Spirituality

To highlight the essentially religious impulse of Donne's imagination, let us consider first his *Elegies* and *Songs and Sonets*, which include some of the most erotically bumptious and strategically blasphemous love lyrics in the English language, and thus appear to be the *least* obviously religious part of his canon.[2] Repeatedly a poem's speaker confronts change, dissolution, and fragmentation: the woman may prove fickle and the lover's own appetites inconstant; beauty is ephemeral and the body—site of love's initial attraction—is fated to decay. Corresponding to a speaker's fear of betrayal, however, is a motivating desire for transcendence that, for the younger Donne, only love seemed able to allow. What makes love a religious experience for Donne, poems like "The Canonization" and "The good-morrow" suggest, is that the intensely private nature of the love experience allows transcendence of worldly, everyday concerns, launching the lovers out of the world of prosperity and display, in which men struggle to improve their estate or mind, into a realm of transcendent meaning. Love, for Donne, is a cohering experience capable of making one little room an everywhere and of enlivening and inspiring the lover with a fulfilling sense of cohesion. In one of the most powerful instances of what J. B. Leishman astutely calls Donne's "single-mindedness,"[3] everything in the world becomes subsumed into love; "Nothing else is"

2

("Sunne Rising," line 22). The lovers who find their ultimate source of meaning in the love experience and make love their god are so completely "centered" as to be worshiped by the less fortunate.

In "The Canonization," for example, the speaker—confronted by a supposedly well-meaning friend who reminds him of the obvious inappropriateness of his embarking on a new love affair—vividly acknowledges the extent to which he has become the victim of time. He is stricken with both palsy and gout; his hair is either badly thinning or beginning to gray; and he has either run through his inheritance or lost it through the machinations of Fortune. But if the poem opens with a frank acknowledgement of the speaker's progressive disintegration, firmly grounding the speaker in the profane world of change, it concludes with gloriously transcendent images of the speaker and his beloved canonized as patterns of love; the lovers and the reader have been projected by poem's end into the realm of the sacred. Through the mysterious alchemical process of the third stanza—which the speaker enters defensively but exits boasting gloriously—the poem enacts the very transcendent power of love. If change signals death, it also signals resurrection and rebirth; the speaker and his beloved, mysteriously transformed or recreated, are eventually to be canonized by love and elevated to the highest sphere. Love removes the speaker from the world of flux in which men frantically seek social and political preferment; by the end of the poem change is no longer threatening but transcendent. "The Canonization," thus, suggests not only the powerful religious drive behind so many of the *Songs and Sonets* but their close relation to the *Anniversaries*.

If, as theologian Paul Tillich argues, "faith is the state of being ultimately concerned" (1) and religion is whatever concerns one ultimately, then it is love's power to reorient the lover in his world that makes love a religious experience. In "The good-morrow," for example, love is figured as a rebirth, as an awakening onto a higher plane of consciousness. "I am come that men might have life, and that they might have it more abundantly," Jesus revealed (John 10: 10, KJV), and the speaker of "The good-morrow" rejoices in discovering the source—albeit non-Christological—of fuller, richer life. Love presents a stable center in a changing world; the lovers are able to stay put while sea-discoverers frantically go off to new worlds and map makers are forced to rechart the dimensions of the known universe. This exclusionary or recentering impulse animates "The Sunne Rising" as well. The sun revolves about the lovers, the speaker boasts; they are the world's stable center. Underlining such glorification of love is the recognition that time is love's great enemy: it abruptly puts an end to a night of lovemaking; it delves wrinkles in the beloved's brow; and the sun's revolution around the earth will presumably continue long after individual lovers are in the grave. Even the Renaissance displacement of the earth-centered universe by Kepler's sun-centered model (one aspect of the "new Philosophy") suggests unsettling change and calls into doubt what had fairly recently been thought stable. But love redeems the speaker and his beloved from the most traumatic of changes and threatened dissolution; it allows them to transcend to a timeless sphere where their joy is intensified and becomes the animating principle of the universe.

Donne's according such power to love makes most moving those poems in which the speaker, facing the loss of transcendence that love allows, is forced to consider how he might sustain the religious feeling. In "A Valediction forbidding mourning" the speaker imaginatively resorts to the famous compass conceit to prove to his lover that physical separation, far from severing their bond, only further purifies their love, allowing them to transcend the limitations that time and space place upon "Dull sublunary lovers love / (Whose soul is sense)." By the end of the poem the circle drawn by the figured compass as the one leg completes its journey home becomes a magic circle, as it were, that both separates the lovers from "the layetie" and protects the lovers' love from "prophanation." Only by such an imaginative act is the speaker able to sustain the feeling of empowering transcendence that he receives through love.

In "A nocturnall upon S. *Lucies* day," however, the speaker must draw upon images of religious "uncreation" in order to figure the emotional reality of the loss of the woman who was "All" to him. Like Shakespeare's Othello, the speaker of "A nocturnall" can only cry that "Chaos is come again" (*Othello* 3.3.92) when he is deprived of the woman who was the cause of his spiritually animating love. If love enlarges the lover's world and focuses its disparate elements into emotional and spiritual coherence, the loss of love causes the world to dissolve around the speaker, shrinking time into the year's shortest day, which threatens to run out on him even as he speaks (it is midnight). The speaker becomes the antithesis of the creating Word of God that first animated the universe; he is "Of the first nothing, the Elixer" (line 29), the alchemical element needed to effect the process of de-creation. The loss of love so shrinks and diminishes the speaker that, like the meditating voice of the *Devotions*, he can be compared to the main eroded or washed away by the tide (*Devotions*, Meditation xvii), plunged back into temporality rather than lifted out of it. The title of the poem, with its emphasis upon the liturgical calendar and upon religious ceremony, makes "A nocturnall" the most religiously grounded of Donne's *Songs and Sonets*. Not coincidentally, it is also the most profound of the love poems, proving in the final analysis to be an un-love poem, one in which the speaker is in danger of falling back into profane creation and destructive temporality.

Little wonder, then, that Donne invests so much imaginative effort in the attempt to construct what T. Anthony Perry has termed an "erotic spirituality"—that is, the recognition that love is not polarized between body and soul, or between the erotic and the spiritual, as it is in Petrarchan and neoplatonic thought, but is capable of uniting the two, the physical being the typological adumbration of the spiritual, in an understanding of human sexuality that depends heavily upon incarnational theology.[4] What does surprise is that poems like "The Extasie" and "The Flea" continue to leave readers uneasy with Donne's conflation of the spiritual and the physical aspects of love into a single moment of intense consciousness, oftentimes into a single image. Donne's speakers talk of religion in sexual terms as easily as they talk of sex in terms of religion—not simply to shock the audience or seduce the addressee as certain influential readers have concluded[5]—but to jar the reader into perceiving the existence of an essentially religious world in which the individual's body and soul cohere, rather than are polarized. In *Satyre III* the speaker's search for the true Church is figured in a witty reversal of the terms of the Petrarchan conceit of woman as an angelic or redemptive force deserving to be worshipped; importing Spenserian allegory into formal verse satire, Donne makes the Church a woman besought by the male lover/believer. Such an operation is all the more shocking in the compressed form of a sonnet which concludes that Christ most loves his spouse when she is "open" to the largest number of men, the speaker's passion a reversal of Jeremiah's or Hosea's dismay that Yahweh's betrothed Israel "is gone up upon every high mountain and under every green tree, and there hath played the harlot" (Jer. 3: 6). Upon reflection, however, the reader's shock should not be caused by the scandalous reference to Christ as sexual cuckold, but by the appropriateness of the conflation.

Indeed, one might argue that the very genius of Donne's greatest love poems lies in their determination to make of love as deeply spiritual an experience as it is erotic. Consider the effect of "Elegie: Going to Bed." Multiple references to theophanic experience, or to the reception of some divine revelation, combine to support the speaker's plea to his mistress that she reveal herself completely to him as she undresses for bed and so allow him to experience an ecstasy that is simultaneously sexual and spiritual. The poem turns upon the parenthetical qualification made within lines 38-43: "Like pictures or like books gay coverings made / For lay-men, are all women thus array'd. / Themselves are mystick books, which only wee / (Whom their imputed grace will dignifie) / Must see reveal'd." The woman is, thus, both a revelation designed for the chosen few and the guardian of that revelation; both the "mystick book" and the superior spirit with power to impute to the speaker the grace necessary to make him worthy of receiving the coveted message. Rather than being "the celebration of simple appetite" or "a pornographic poem . . . intended to arouse in the reader the appetite it describes," as C. S. Lewis claims (102)—that is, a description of a situation in which the woman is verbally manipulated by a chauvinistic voyeur—the poem is a self-consciously powerless but audacious speaker's petition to be permitted the full extent of the woman's revelation. "Knowledge" of her will entail both sexual orgasm and the impartation of a mystical knowledge whose exact nature cannot be specified to the general reader. Indeed, I find little difference between the attempt in "Going to Bed" and that in "The Extasie" to restore the carnality of the Petrarchan woman who remains nonetheless capable of spiritually redeeming the self-consciously needful male except that the elegy's tone is not the quiet, breathless, hushed speaking of religious/sexual mystery; rather, "Going to Bed" has something of the undergraduate's attempt to mask his insecurity with bravado. "Going to Bed" is on a par with the other elegies in which the creation and language theology of the Book of Genesis (whose significance Donne formally analyzed in his *Essays in Divinity*) is used to describe the phallic act—as when the speaker of "Elegie (Natures lay Ideot)" audaciously boasts of having planted knowledge's and life's tree in his mistress's garden of paradise (line 26). "Going to Bed" reflects the mindset of a young man who is frustrated not to have yet discovered the transcendence that he is certain sexual relations must allow him access to if the act is to have meaning, as much as "The Extasie" reflects that of a man who has found transcendence in love.

When the full reach of Donne's erotic spirituality is recognized, the cynicism of poems like "Song: Goe, and catch," "The Indifferent," or "Loves Alchymie" can be fully understood. "What ever dyes, was not mixt equally," the speaker of "The good-morrow" (line 19) recognizes, and the groups of poems in which, as Helen Gardner organizes them, the speaker displays his cynical detachment by bullying and abusing the woman ("Group 1," Gardner li) or suffers painfully from unrequited love ("Group 2," Gardner lii-liii) generally betray the speaker's anxiety at not finding a love that is "mixt equally" and will not die. By wittily boasting of his own, or protesting his lover's infidelity and promiscuity, the speaker seems to denigrate the very coherence that the speakers of Gardner's "Group 3" poems so ardently desire. But as Ilona Bell so persuasively argues, in those *Songs and Sonets* characterized by "lusty frivolity" (117), "the witty, lusty braggadocio" of the speaker is his attempt "to defend himself, to foresee and pre-empt rejection" (116). It is, in essence, the whistling in the dark of a man who fears experiencing the dissolution so poignantly felt upon the loss of the woman who has been All to the speaker in the "Nocturnall" ("I am every dead thing"). Against the threat of such pain the speakers of the more cynical poems assume the mask of bravado to counteract their fear that transcendence will not be sustained, and that love will be reduced to the emblem of faithlessness, change, and spiritual impoverishment. The speaker of "Song: Goe, and catche" claims to be willing to undertake the rigors of "a Pilgrimage" to wonder at "a woman true, and faire" (stanza 2) except that he has no faith in the object of his proferred devotion. As the speaker of "Loves Alchemie" sadly notes, men searching for "that hidden mysterie" and the "centrique happinesse" of love feel particularly betrayed by the absence of fulfillment in love: "So, lovers dreame a rich and long delight,/But get a winter-seeming summers night" (lines 11-12). Rather than allow him to transcend the sullying effects of time, contact with his partner has drawn the speaker all the further into the very realm of mortality that he longs to escape.

Thus, the only language available to describe the transcendence that empowers the speaker in love is religious; for Donne love *is* a religious experience. It allows the speaker to recover "a pure and holy cosmos, as it was in the beginning, when it came fresh from the Creator's hands," except that in the case of the *Songs and Sonets* the lovers are themselves the creators and so deserve to be canonized for love. Even while expressing the seeming misogyny of their speakers, the cynical ferocity of poems like "Loves Alchemie" and "Song: Goe, and catch" reveals the intense longing for other possibilities on the part of their creator. If love allows the speaker to transcend the mortal world into the realm of the sacred, its failure arouses in the hopeful lover the fear that he will be further profaned, imprisoned in a divisive, secular universe, and spiritually deadened.

Sacred Time and Space:
The Operations of a Donne Poem

When William Butler Yeats claims that he would be satisfied at journey's end to dine with Landor and with Donne, I suspect that the conversation he would like to have with Donne, at least, concerned their common perception of how "things fall apart; the centre cannot hold" ("The Second Coming," line 3) and of the ways in which such threat of dissolution can be met and transcended. For Donne and Yeats span the modern world, even though from opposite poles.

The threat of dissolution animates nearly every part of Donne's canon. The *Satyres* depict a world that is morally disintegrating, and there is a sense of the gradual profanation of the world in *Metempsychosis* as the world's soul migrates from "that apple which Eve eate" to Queen Elizabeth, John Calvin, or wherever its final location was to have been. (True to its topic, the poem itself seems unfinished and achieves no firm closure; as in Spenser's *Faerie Queene* and Donne's own *Anniversaries*, incompletion is an essential feature of *Metempsychosis* as text.) The world is literally dissolving in *The First Anniversarie*: color fades, beauty decays, proportion is disfigured, and joy grows as dry as a cinder. The speaker's sense of spiritual fragmentation in *Holy Sonnets* drives him to issue what is perhaps the most pained cry in Western poetry since the *De profundis* psalms,[6] raising in modern criticism (witness Rollin) the question of whether the poems display something pathological. (Significantly, to meet the needs of the speaker's spiritual crisis, Donne adapts the operations of the sonnet—traditionally the vehicle of love expression—to his cause. Love and religion are never far apart in Donne's mind.) Donne's poetry in general is situated between the hope of transcendence through Elizabeth Drury, who is "th'Elixar of this All" (*First Anniversarie*), and the fear of losing one's source of transcendence and becoming oneself "the Elixar of the first nothing" ("A nocturnall").

Indeed, one might go so far as to suggest that it was his fear of dissolution that made *The Lamentations of Jeremy* the only portion of the Bible that, with any certainty, Donne himself translated. Donne's translation raises a number of troubling questions regarding his spiritual and poetic practices. Is it possible that Donne did not feel the pressure to translate into verse some poetic portion of Scripture, as nearly every other poet—and poetaster—of his age did? As his poem praising the Sidneys for their metrical translation indicates, he saw the need for the Psalms to be translated for use in communal devotion. Donne's contemporaries might have wondered if it were not incumbent upon him as Dean of St. Paul's to redeem his earlier amorous verse and harsh satires by making scriptural verse translations, an obvious proof of one's devotion. The inclusion in the 1633 *Poems* of a psalm translation *not* by Donne (and dropped in subsequent editions) might even suggest the discomfort of his executors not to have more of the same to offset the "uncircumcised" poems that had to be printed so "promiscuously" with Donne's sacred ones. That *Lamentations* is the only biblical translation that may with any certainty be ascribed to Donne suggests how crucial its images and operations must have been to him. Presumably this is because, in its depiction of the woman Jerusalem raped, of her children's heads dashed against the stones, and of the city's walls pulled down, it expresses the horror of the world dissolving about the prophet even as he speaks:

> our end is now approached neere,
> Our dayes accomplish'd are, this
> the last day.

Such a passage could just as easily have come from "A nocturnall" or from *The First Anniversarie*. *Lamentations* may be the portion of Scripture which betrays the closest affinity with Donne's own imagination.[7]

God's action of making all this fragmented creation back into its original All—which is basically the action that Mircea Eliade says religious man longs for, to have the world returned to its original pristine state, or for the individual to leave the profane world and transcend to that original purity—is the action that Donne hopes finally to approximate in his poetry. At heart, Donne's writing attempts to reestablish the world infused with transcendent meaning, one in which everything coheres. Donne variously expresses that desire in his poetry as to "launch at paradise, and . . . saile towards home" (*Metempsychosis*, line 57); or to make one little room into an everywhere and thus imaginatively transcend the limits of space and time; and even, in the *Holy Sonnets*, to transcend temporality and defeat death ("Death thou shalt die"). The bumptious search for love's "centrique part" in the love poetry is but a more festive rendering of this same process, and what Donne refers to as his "holy thirsty dropsy" in "Holy Sonnet: Since she whome I lovd" (line 8) might be considered his immoderate, all-consuming thirst for coherence. Donne's imagination constantly seizes upon the ways that human actions can lift men and women outside space, and project them beyond the boundaries of time, launching humankind from the realm of the profane towards the paradise that he considers "home."

Again, Mircea Eliade proves especially helpful in framing discussion of the essentially religious impulse of Donne's imagination, for Eliade's greatest contribution to our understanding of religion is his isolation of the need of religious man to be at the center of the world, to invest himself in sacred time and space.

Donne's poetry repeatedly stakes a claim for physical centrality, thus giving witness to Donne's "centroversion," which is a psychic movement to the center suggesting a psychological process of individuation (see Hartman xii-xiii). John Demaray describes the way in which physical matter was rendered by medieval cartographers "so as to conform to the assumed configurations of spirit."

> The "T-and-O" *mappaemundi* were flat projections with the land masses of Europe, Africa and Asia—the then-known world—contained usually in a circle, but on occasion in an ellipse or even a rectangle, with the Garden of Eden at the top-center of the circle at the farthest point east. Asia, harboring sites including Mt. Sinai, the Dead Sea and Jerusalem, was located in the upper half of the circle; Africa with the city of Babylon, modern Cairo, and the Nile River and Red Sea sites, in the lower right quadrant; and Europe containing Rome on the River Tiber, in the lower left quadrant. The medieval *Mare Internum*, the present Mediterranean Sea, divided the lower half of the circle in the form of an altar-like "T." The Pillars of Hercules, modern Gibralter, which gave access to the Great Ocean surrounding the entire circular land mass was situated in a low position at the base of the "T," while holy Jerusalem was placed, as might be expected, just above the "T" crossbar near or at the spiritual-physical "center" of the earth's round land mass. The holy city was in turn regularly drawn as a circle, bisected by two key streets in the form of a cross, nested within the wider circle of the world. (8)

Such a map would have appealed to Donne's imagination, containing as it does a center of the world towards which one might move symbolically while growing in holiness, yet the further away from that center, the more certainly one is engulfed by chaos. The "dissolution" threatened by flat maps which have no center, or by globes that make everything of equal importance, had to be met imaginatively by the Donnean speaker's reclaiming the center, as it were. "*Paradise* and *Calvarie*, / *Christs* Crosse and *Adams* tree, stood in one place," asserts the speaker of "Hymne to

God my God, in my sicknesse" (lines 21-22; see also *Metempsychosis* lines 77-78), and the desire of the speaker in so many of Donne's poems is to take possession of the physical center of the universe or, if that is impossible, to imaginatively invest the site from which he speaks with central significance.

Thus, love in "The good-morrow" is capable of making one little room an everywhere, and the woman in "The Sunne Rising" is "all states" over which the speaker alone rules. In "Going to Bed," the speaker addresses the woman from "this bed, [which] our temple is." As Eliade puts it, "where the sacred manifests itself in space, *the real unveils itself*, the world comes into existence" (63). Throughout the love poems the beloved woman's body is figured spatially as the center of the universe, her vaginal opening the "centrique part" or source of meaning for the lover. The male speaker is empowered not only by being granted access to it but being allowed control of it, the "Mons Veneris" becoming the *omphalos* or sacred navel of the universe.[8] The speaker of "Elegie: Natures lay Ideot" who boasts of having "planted knowledge and lifes tree in" the woman and thus of having "refin'd" her "into a blis-full paradise" (lines 24-26) mimes the actions of primitive religious peoples who carry about with them the totemic *axis mundi*, which they plant at the center of their camp every evening, thus ensuring that they remain at the center of the world (Eliade, chap. 1). The younger Donne may have been embarrassed by this need and sought to disguise the seriousness of his hunger for transcendence with self-mocking humor, but as the phallic outrageousness of "Natures lay Ideot" shows, sex rarely failed to carry for Donne the biblical connotation of transcendent knowledge.[9]

Indeed, the impulse to put himself at the center of the universe, whether through sexual intercourse or prayer, was so overpowering as to be an obsession for Donne. Donne's poetry is the record of a search for the mysterious centrique part, contact with which makes more "real" an otherwise fragmentary and incoherent existence. This, I believe, is the essential meaning of the journey motif that so dominates Donne's writing. Whether meditating on the progress of a soul to heaven, as in the *Anniversaries* or the poem in praise of the Sidneys; or considering undertaking a "pilgrimage" in "Goe and catche" or actually launching towards paradise and sailing home in *Metempsychosis*; or setting out on his last journey to Germany or anticipating coming to that holy room in which he will be made into music, as in the great hymns—the speaker of a Donne poem seems always setting out in hopes of arriving at a more sacred place.

Likewise, Donne's fascination with concurrent moments and cyclical confluences betrays his intense need to be lifted from profane into sacred time.[10] The Annunciation and Passion falling on the same day, Adam's tree and Christ's cross standing in the same place, his original seal of entwined serpents proving appropriate to his new vocation as minister of the gospel, or his ride westward on business proving inimical to his spiritual salvation: these are more than coincidences, but moments of confluence or congruence in which the speaker recognizes a divine order operating behind the seemingly random circumstances of this world. His best poems record the moments when the veil of change, dissolution and chaos that renders murky the profane world is lifted and the operation of a larger transcendent scheme is revealed. Richard Hughes has noted "Donne's continual excitement over the way events collapse into one another, revealing in a sudden flash a pervasive unity in the world. The work of his maturity is filled with wonder over the marvelous congruences that of a sudden show different places, objects and times rushing together, charismatically asserting a pattern which underlies all experience" (198). Indeed, the meditative process associated with Donne's name might actually be considered the movement of the mind toward the recognition of such wonders, as when in *La Corona* the speaker understands that Mary could simultaneously be the mother, daughter, and bride of Christ; or in "Upon the translation of the Psalmes" the speaker celebrates a series of multiple twinnings that includes Moses and Miriam, Sir Philip Sidney and the Countess of Pembroke, and the twin-tongued flame of inspiration associated with Pentecost. The confluence of event and symbol which suggests an underlying meaning to experience clearly moved Donne deeply.

Thus, the most provocative stance of a Donne poem is one of wonder,[11] which the speaker assumes in the presence of what historian of religion Rudolph Otto (chapter 4) calls the *mysterium tremendum*. This, explains Otto, is something "Wholly Other" that fills the individual with awe at its "absolute unapproachability," the result of which is a self-deprecation that paradoxically inspires the worshiper with the "urgency" or "energy" of the numinous. Thus, when confronted by the powerful renewal that he experiences after growing to love the unnamed woman at his side in bed, the speaker of "The good-morrow" can only "wonder" (line 1) at the profane quality of his existence before that moment. (Similarly, when first able to look upon Britomart's face, Spenser's Arthegall "fell humbly downe vpon his knee, / And of his wonder made religion"; *Faerie Queene* 4.6.22.) Occasionally Donne's lovers are able to inspire wonder in others, as occurs in "The Canonization" and "The Relique." And as Dennis Quinn suggests, in the verse epistles, obsequies, and epicides Donne takes the stance of wonder before the patterns of virtue that Elizabeth Drury and the great ladies of Jacobean England supply (637-39, but see also Lewalski 67).

Just as often, however, the speaker is bereft at the loss of—or at his exclusion from the domain of—the "wonderful," as when he complains of the absence of the *mysterium tremendum* in *Lamentations* and the "Nocturnall." Indeed, the challenge most often faced by the speaker of a Donne poem is how to negotiate the transition from the realm of the profane to the sacred. The meditative action of the *Second Anniversarie* (lines 339 ff.) allows the speaker's "drowsie soule" to look "up, up" and participate in an act of spiritual transcendence even at the moment of the body's dissolution. In general Donne's poems move between the poles of the sacred and the profane, of the coherent and the dissolute. What makes them great is the "urgency" or "energy" (to borrow Otto's words) of their desire to ensure the move from the one realm to the other.

Educated by a Metaphoric God

Donne's poetic development can be mapped in terms of his shift from secular to sacred models—that is, from Ovid, Petrarch and Ronsard, and from Horace, Juvenal, and Persius, to the *"figurative, . . . metaphoricall God"*

> in whose words there is such a height of *figures*, such *voyages*, such *peregrinations* to fetch remote and precious *metaphors*, such *extensions*, such *spreadings*, such *Curtaines* of *Allegories*, such *third Heavens* of *Hyperboles*, so *harmonious eloquutions*, so *retired* and so *reserved expressions*, so *commanding perswasions*, so *perswading commandements*, such *sinewes* even in thy *milke*, and such *things* in thy *words*, as all *prophane Authors*, seeme of the seed of the *Serpent* that *creepes*; thou art the *dove*, that flies. (*Devotions*, Expostulation 19)

Essentially Donne's is a concretic, emblematic imagination.[12] He possessed an eye for transcendent gestures, such as "a bracelet of bright haire about the bone" ("The Relique," line 6) signalling something that does not dissolve, that transcends death and the body's dissolution, that retains love's perfect shape, the circle. As Sharon Cadmon Seelig points out, the metaphysical conceit as perfected by Donne is an attempt to reassert the emblematic nature of the universe. The conceit "is not only a discovery about reality," as criticism traditionally discusses it, but "a claim about the nature of reality" (4), an attempt to hold the physical and spiritual dimensions of human experience together in the face of the Baconian assault on the medieval analogical view of a physical universe infused with cohering meaning. Often the more outrageous the conceit, the more urgent the writer's need to see the physical world as continuing to figure forth the spiritual.

Donne's metaphysical "conceitedness" is perhaps most apparent in "The Crosse," whose speaker protests his sense of a revealed or emblematic world, one inhering with divine meaning if only the human eye can be brought to see it. "The Crosse" reasserts man's need to learn to "read" the emblems that God has written into the universe, a process that makes for an essentially religious response to an increasingly secular and polarized world. This is, likewise, the process that Donne records in his Latin verse epistle to George Herbert. Finally understanding that his original seal of a sheaf of serpents possesses typologically the same spiritual promise as his new seal of an anchor and Christ, the speaker recognizes the emblematic significance of a gloriously coherent universe in which seeming discontinuity is actually evidence of a deeper, more mysterious and "wonder-full" contiguity than human vision is initially capable of penetrating. Samuel Johnson's slam against the metaphysical conceit as violently yoking together the most heterogeneous ideas fails to appreciate how deep was Donne's need to reassert the transcendent and spiritually coherent meaning of the material realm.[13]

Donne's religious writing betrays continued fascination with such configurations in God's patterning of the world as the Annunciation and Passion falling on one day, or Adam's tree and Christ's cross standing in the same place. Such symbolic concresences make for a world of wonder for Donne whose great discovery, Frederick Rowe notes, is that "life had meaning at the moment of conjunction" (221). In "Upon the translation of the Psalmes" God's process of uniting two in one suggests the restoration of the sin-debased world's primal unity. As much in his poetry as in his religious prose, Donne attempts to uncover and reveal such patterns, to "explicate" God's "conceits" as it were.

But above all, it is God's linguistic power—His creation *ex verbo*—that fascinates Donne. God has inscribed emblems or conceits of Himself in His Creation, "The Crosse" reminds its readers; Nature itself is God's poem. The process by which God ensures the continued availability of His Word is described in "Upon the translation of the Psalmes." Indeed, God put His law into song, the speaker of the *First Anniversarie* emphasizes, making God the poet's best model and encouraging Donne to experiment with similar operations and images. In the *Anniversaries* Donne appropriates the voice and vision both of the Old Testament prophet who announces in the *First* the dissolution of the sin-infested world, and of the New Testament prophet of grace and redemption in the *Second*, bearing witness in both poems to the transcendent power of virtue. The significance of this maneuver becomes clear only in comparison with the speaker's terror at the close of *Satyre* II that "my words none drawes / Within the vast reach of th'huge statue lawes" (lines 111-12), where it is not the inefficacy of language in general that the satirist protests, but of *his* language in particular. Yet at the conclusion of the *Second Anniversarie* the speaker is figured as a trumpet that calls people to attend to the model of virtue that is Elizabeth Drury. This shift suggests a renewed sense in Donne of the power of language to re-form an incoherent, dissolving universe. (It was this same renewal, I suspect, that allowed Donne finally to overcome his scruples and become a preacher, the vehicle of the Divine Word.)

The success of Donne's poetic education by a "figurative, . . . metaphoricall God" is best evidenced in "Upon the translation of the Psalmes." The poem contains twenty-eight couplets, the final one of which is cast in identical rhyme, making one of two and poetically imitating the action of the Creator in "mak[ing] all this All" (line 23). By leading his congregation forward in singing praise of the Sidneys, the poet-priest hopes to provoke the moment when the three choirs will join together in one song, and the shattered, otherwise useless parts of the sin-jarred universe will be made to cohere. Donne's poetic "making" repeats the biblical action of creation; it is his own best attempt at re-creating the harmony and coherence of the earthly and heavenly spheres, and thus of ensuring his own and his reader's salvation. The threat of dissolution and fragmentation defeated, the speaker anticipates "translation" at poem's end into sacred time and space.

Conclusion

All his career Donne struggled to find the means of passing from the profane to the sacred realm. Yet the quintessential speaker in Donne's writing straddles two worlds or exists in a strange state of suspended activity. The conclusion of the "Deaths Duell" sermon, for example, illustrates the poetic action of the great religious lyrics. Pointing to the crucifix above the altar upon which a representation of the Savior God hangs in

the agony of sacrifice, the preacher admonishes members of his congrega-
tion to throw themselves across the gulf of sin separating them from
Christ and to hang "in that *blessed dependency*" upon the outstretched
arms of the Savior (*Sermons* 10: 248). Yet in the hymns, the "sinne of feare"
that the arms of Christ will not embrace and hold him, but will allow him
to slide into dark and painful oblivion below, keeps him from approach-
ing God directly. It is as though, even while conscious of the need to take
drastic action, the speakers of the hymns hesitate to act without assurance
that the anticipated action will be effective. The religious poetry records
the paralysis of a spiritual trapeze artist willing to take the death-defying
leap only if he can be certain that someone will catch him in his mid-air
flight. Desire for reassurance that he will be helped to pass from the
profane to the sacred threatens to undermine the very experience of faith.
The speaker's longing to transcend to sacred time and space may actually
entrench him the more deeply in the mortifying realm of the profane.

Thus, the speaker of "A Hymne to Christ, at the Authors last going into
Germany" asserts his willingness to undertake a dangerous journey away
from all that he knows, loves, and finds comfort in on earth, but only after
he requests his Savior's seal on "this bill of my Divorce to All" (line 22)—
an implicit assurance of his getting to the other shore and the payoff, so to
speak, which will justify his sacrifice. Likewise, the speaker of "A Hymne
to God the Father" stands on the shore's end, unable to go much further
under his own power, anticipating having "spunne/My last thred" (stanza
3) even before he has done so. Each stanza of that poem concludes with a
postponement, the final stanza being structured grammatically according
to a condition, the demand in which can only be satisfied in the future. A
complementary image of waiting controls the "Hymne to God my God, in
my sicknesse" where the speaker is in an antechamber preparing for an
audience with his Judge and King that does not occur before the poem's
end. This drama of suspended activity rises to an almost grotesque com-
edy in what editors have concluded is among the last of the *Holy Sonnets*
written, "Show me deare Christ, thy spouse." Here, a spiritual Petrarchan
lover protests his willingness to embrace another man's wife, as presum-
ably he has been invited or commanded to do, only he cannot tell which
of the many available women is she! The allegorical figure of Patience
which comforts the speaker of Milton's sonnet, "When I consider how my
light is spent," would have little power in Donne's spiritual universe; the
assurance that "They also serve who only stand and wait" would be
intolerable to Donne's impatiently suspended speakers.[14]

Donne found in the creating power of religious language his passport across the mysterious border from dissolution to transcendence, his most potentially sacrilegious yet ultimately most devout gesture being his appropriation of a peculiarly biblical use of the imperative mode. The prophet's command "Speak that I may see thee!" suggests the religious power of language in the biblical world: without speech there is no reality; speaking the word bespeaks the world into existence. For biblical Hebrews and Christians alike, language was talismanic, possessing awful creative and destructive powers. Harold Stahmer summarizes the religious significance of language: "early man was unable to look upon his world as symbols, as designations or representations of a higher reality. The words, speech, language, for them was identical with reality, and men partook in the unity of the universe to the extent that they were capable of speech and aware of its dramatic, concrete powers. Against this setting, man does not control speech; rather speech literally seizes a man" (15-16). The Hebrew *davar* signifies both word and event; Yahweh spoke the world into existence in Genesis just as the Word becomes flesh in the Jesus of John's Gospel. Once spoken a word—whether in blessing or in curse—cannot be recalled, as Isaac reminds Esau (Gen. 27: 32-41). Name bestows identity for, as R. A. Wilson notes, in ancient Mesopotamia "the utterance of a name is in itself an act of creation" (qtd. in Stahmer xx). Significantly, traumatic experience which effects a personality transformation results in a change of name, as in the cases of Jacob/Israel and Saul/Paul. The *ruah* or spirit is as much the animating power of the Old Testament universe as the *Logos* is of the New Testament one. Language, thus, is man's only means of approaching the deity and, hopefully, man's call will elicit a divine response.[15] Use of the imperative in biblical texts is, paradoxically, a petitioner's way of using speech to seize other men, and sometimes even the Almighty, and persuading them to work on his behalf.

Donne's poetry, far moreso than that of most of his contemporaries and perhaps even moreso than Milton's, is heavily logocentric. Language is the means by which a highly vulnerable but deeply hopeful petitioner attempts to pass from the dissolute, fragmentary world of the profane to a realm of completeness and transcendence. In his earliest poems, it is true, Donne's wit functions merely as a sort of rhetorical *leger de main*, a linguistic trick by which the speaker is able imaginatively to overcome the threat of impending fragmentation. For the lyric moment that is the poem, a Donne speaker is able to defeat a desired woman's resistance or subvert the threat of a once-beloved woman's faithlessness; he is able, as miraculously as Joshua, to make the sun stand still or to defeat proud death. These are linguistic games that, as Arnold Stein (125-26) notes in his analysis of "The Sunne Rising," not only attempt to control but to create reality.[16] Their linguistic bravura is finally but a whistling in the dark, however; a momentary stay against inevitable confusion.

In Donne's more tonally complex poems, however, the speaker uses all the powers of language available to him to engage the numinous on his own behalf that he may be "translated" from the profane realm to the sacred. In both "Elegie: Going to Bed" and in the *Holy Sonnets*, for example, a speaker provocatively adopts the imperative mode to elicit a salvific response from an all-powerful woman or deity, not with the confidence of primitive, religious man, but precisely because the speaker *lacks* confidence and finds himself in such great need. Testing or pushing the power of language is Donne's final act of hope when threatened by despair, and one can see a growing confidence in the power of his language as Donne matured. The woman whom the speaker commands to disrobe in "Going to Bed" is both the revelation and the guardian of the revelation that will allow him to enter into paradise; the poem, however, is deliberately outrageous, as though the speaker himself is uncertain whether he believes his use of the imperative can work. The *Holy Sonnets* and "Goodfriday," however, are spoken by men so acutely conscious that they are in the process of spiritual disintegration that they actually *command* the "three-person'd God" to batter the *Sonnets* speaker's heart, and *implore* the Saviour to think the rider "worth [His] anger," that they may be saved.

The suspended action of "Going to Bed" is painfully similar to that of Divine Poems, however. Does the woman of the elegy drop her final piece of clothing and allow the speaker the prevenient grace he needs to be able to merit the revelation that she is the guardian of? Likewise, does Christ scourge the speaker of "Goodfriday" after he turns his back? And will Christ seal the speaker's "bill of my Divorce to All" that is comforting and secure in the earthly realm as he leaves for Germany? Will the Father allow the speaker of "A Hymn to God the Father" to pass over the gulf? The poems themselves do not answer these questions, leaving the reader as curiously suspended as the speakers are themselves within the poems. This is the religious power of Donne's imagination: language is his only means of trying to bridge the profane and sacred realms, of trying to provoke an all-powerful woman or deity into giving him the sign that the petitioner's passage will be successful, that grace is forthcoming, that transcendence will be achieved. "Going to Bed" and the Divine Poems are poles apart in many ways, but ultimately they are the products of the same religious imagination, one ferocious in its attempts to "make all this All."[17]

* * *

The great irony of Donne criticism, historically, is that readers, failing to appreciate the anxiety of the liminalized in Donne's poetry, should polarize where he tried so desperately to unify. What many of the essays collected here attempt to do is erase boundaries, too many of which prove artificial or are the constructs of earlier criticism's imagination.

The most persistent of these is one for which Donne himself is partly responsible, the myth of Jack Donne the rake vs. John Donne the divine. Acutely conscious all his life of his spiritual progress, Donne made a practice of having himself painted or sculpted at critical moments, even at the risk of suggesting that his career was more segmented than it actually was. The understanding of a deeply polarized Donne crystallized by Edmund Gosse's *Life and Letters* is but evidence of readers' inability to accept Donne's determination to locate the point of the sacred's convergence with, and reclamation of, the profane. The resulting polarization that afflicts Donne studies is neatly defined by Thomas Yingling's analysis of the different modernist traditions that derive from T. S. Eliot and Hart Crane: "And where Eliot and Crane agreed on a canonical figure— Donne, for instance—we feel they were reading two different texts: Crane reading the discourse of religion in Donne erotically, Eliot reading the erotic in him religiously" (20). The essays by Theresa DiPasquale and Allen Ramsey that follow, however, demonstrate how extensive was Donne's effort to create an erotic spirituality. Sectarian debate over the Eucharist as sign or sacrament, DiPasquale displays, may determine the reading of one of Donne's most ingenious seduction poems, "The Flea." Native English marriage rituals were transformed by Donne's religious imagination in the "Epithalamion made at Lincolnes Inne," Ramsey demonstrates, in order to establish marriage as the emblem for the union of the body and soul, and for eternal life's conquering death, which is the essence of Christian faith.

More troublesome—and perhaps unresolvable—is the issue of Donne's allegiance to emerging Anglican, Roman Catholic, or Calvinist theological traditions and literary models. Did Donne convert from Catholicism to Protestantism sincerely and completely, or expediently and half-heartedly? Does his writing betray an apostate's guilt, a devout convert's sincerity, or a self-interested man's wearing whatever fashion is most likely to get him the attention of the patron he wanted to please at a particular moment? As the essays that follow demonstrate, it is impossible to relegate Donne to any strict category. Dennis Flynn shows in a "biographical prolusion" to the volume's critical essays that Donne's contemporaries accorded him a certain "space of honor" as a member of a Roman Catholic family that suffered religious persecution and exile; his close association with the ancient Catholic nobility continued longer than anyone has heretofore suspected. Clearly, Donne's Catholic heritage was not something that Donne put off entirely, either in his own mind or in the eyes of his contemporaries.

But neither did Donne's Catholic beliefs remain constant. The Mariological litmus test applied by George Klawitter proves provocatively inconclusive. Unlike his recusant contemporaries, Donne betrayed no interest in certain key tenets of Marian belief. Yet, Klawitter shows, Donne's statements regarding the intercessory powers of the Virgin Mary—what modern intellectual historians consider one of the most divisive topics of Reformation debate—do alter significantly from his private, devotional poetry to his very public sermons, suggesting either a significant evolution in his personal theology or a willingness to suppress his private beliefs when speaking in his official capacity as Dean of St. Paul's cathedral.

But even this theory of a difference in public and private modes falters when we realize that, as one of the age's most visible spokespersons for the Anglican Church, Donne might be expected to excoriate Puritans. Yet, as Daniel Doerkson demonstrates, even when he preached from the pulpit of St. Paul's cathedral Donne's attitudes towards Puritans were far more accommodating than has generally been assumed. Indeed, Mary Papazian concludes, in the *Devotions* Donne is far from being the antithesis to John Bunyan that Joan Webber has led a generation of Donne scholars to believe; his generosity concerning theological and literary "things indifferent" proves one of his most salient traits.

Perhaps the only fair way of describing the religious Donne, if a label is finally required, is in terms of what Theresa DiPasquale has called (in private conversation) a "proto-ecumenical Anglicanism"—that is, in terms of his extraordinary aloofness and independence that permitted him to sustain close social relationships with Roman Catholics, to absorb contradictions in his personal beliefs and practices, and to transcend polemical arguments. Donne's writing betrays a highly independent fashioning of a religious self, one continuously in evolution; like Walt Whitman, he is broad and encompasses contradiction.

An analogy with Shakespeare criticism may prove helpful. Addressing the troubling issue of the *Sonnets* as evidence of Shakespeare's own sexuality, Stephen Booth has shrewdly concluded that "William Shakespeare was almost certainly either homosexual, bisexual, or heterosexual" (548). We may just as surely conclude that Donne was either Anglican, Roman Catholic, or Puritan . . . or some indiosyncratic mixture of the three, the balance of which shifted from doctrine to doctrine, or from period to period, not necessarily for reasons of political self-aggrandizement, but to meet the objections of his most recent opponent, countering the opponent's extreme with one of his own as he sought a middle, unified, coherent course. Joshua Scodel shows how carefully Donne sought an individual mean in religious affairs, rejecting the immediate and relatively easy comfort of submitting to either the Roman Catholic Church or the Church of England. Rather, the spiral model described by M. Thomas Hester for "the mindes endeavours" in Renaissance epistemology—an elliptical or spiralling progress that touches on both extremes in order to rise or move forward—might hold for Donne criticism as well. Or, perhaps as Frances M. Malpezzi suggests, rather than debate which religion was Donne's exclusive affiliation, we should read him in terms of general religiousness, for, as Jeffrey Johnson demonstrates, Donne's statements about prayer transcend sectarian divisions, allowing him paradoxically to be at his most public when at his most private.

The arguments of several other essays demonstrate how much of a piece the operations and concerns of Donne's imagination are, transcending both genre considerations and chronology. After isolating the Derridean metaphor of the *pharmikon* in *Ignatius* to reveal how that text's dramatization of conflicting discourses produces unstable meanings denied direct articulation within the text, Julie Yen demonstrates that similar strategies are also used in the *Holy Sonnets* in order to dramatize the difficulties of leading an active Christian life. Paul Harland isolates mirror images in several works on the Passion in order to highlight Donne's awareness of the ego's need to break out of the prison of destructive self-preoccupation into a liberated state of true self-love which best expresses itself in willing and disinterested giving. Joan Hartwig traces the evolution of a symbolic motif from the elegies and satires to "Goodfriday," analyzing how traditional associations of horse and rider with body and soul operate as a basic "grammar" that Donne learned to think and write with. And by demonstrating the unsuspected integrity of a group of sermons, whose redating allows them to be seen as part of a long and rich tradition of meditation on the penitential psalms, Paul Stanwood offers insight into the remarkable consistency of Donne's preaching style.

A last group of essays offers models for reading Donne's specifically religious poetry and prose. Helen Brooks reads "Goodfriday" in terms of the Augustinian theology of time, showing how the three parts of the poem's Ignatian meditation coalesce to form a timeless imaginative experience as the speaker attempts to free himself from the transitory, worldly distractions that fail to satisfy the soul's unmitigated longing for union with God. Catherine Creswell analyzes the Pauline theology of "Batter my heart" in a consideration of how the *Holy Sonnets* revise praise's relation to its object and, in turn, refigure the status of the subject. Joy Linsley analyzes the uneasily resolved theological, emotional, and gender conflicts in "Since she whome I lovd," and concludes that the poem deliberately betrays itself as text in order that the speaker might assert his artistic control over Nature. Kate Frost recovers a number of highly sophisticated contexts for the least-commented upon of Donne's religious poems, showing "Resurrection, imperfect" to be, not incomplete, but a finished poem concerned with unfinished time; in the process she not only suggests the critical processes by which authorial intentionality can be recovered, but displays how Donne used his art to transform the imperfect, mortal universe into a Christ-filled cosmos. And Jeanne Shami analyzes the highly polemical uses made of Donne's sermons in recent criticism, offering in effect a theory of how to read a sermon.

Essentially, what these essays *in toto* reveal is how much of a piece Donne's work was. If his Drydenian chase caused him to make some peculiar and spirited digressions, it still had a single beast in view, one we may name Coherency. Donne's is a religious imagination which ultimately transcended sectarian limitations, even if sectarian causes were part of the initial impulse of a particular poem or sermon. Donne's integrity lies in his striving to make all this All.

Notes

[1] While Charles Coffin's *John Donne and the New Philosophy* (1937) has been corrected and superseded in many regards, it remains the best overview of Donne vis à vis the radical changes in ontology and epistemology that his age experienced. I am equally indebted to more recent studies of Donne's "interior career," most notably John Carey's analysis of the psycho-artistic consequences of what he terms Donne's "apostasy," but more in terms of help they offer in refining areas of disagreement.

[2] Cleanth Brooks and Murray Roston, among others, anticipate me in discussing the integrity of the religious impulse in Donne's erotic verse. For evidence of the critical problem that continues to exist, however, see the representative statements summarized in note 5 below.

[3] Leishman's remarks, offered in a discussion of lines 21-22 of "The Sunne Rising," bear repeating in full in as much as they comment indirectly on what, later in this essay, we will see Eliade call the enhancement of reality in religious experience: "what distinguishes Donne's serious love poetry is not merely its seriousness but its single-mindedness. 'Nothing else is'. Everything except their love for one another is shadowy and unsubstantial: everything else, one might almost say, exists for him only in so far as it can be related to this. He does not use this experience as a mere starting-point, as a means for investigating and interpreting other experiences: all other experiences, all other universes of discourse, all his ingenious analogies, all his so-called metaphysics, are valuable to him only in so far as they help him to feel and comprehend more clearly and more intensely the essential this-ness of this experience" (214).

[4] The most engaging discussion of this typology remains Kathryn Kremen's, which notes that "In the songs and sonnets Donne presents the resurrection of the body in sexual love as a prefiguration and 'remembrancer' of the 'hypostaticall union' of man and God in Christ in heaven, which sanctions this figural incorporation of the eschatological into the erotic" (122). Kremen's thesis is that for Donne "the eschatological and the erotic incorporate each other" (90-91). Unfortunately Margaret Miles does not include Donne in her survey of "female nakedness and religious meaning in the Christian West." Donne's association of the woman's nakedness with divine revelation in "Going to Bed" challenges Miles's conclusion that female nakedness is presented almost invariably "as symbol of sin, sexual lust, and dangerous evil" (81).

[5] Among the more emphatic readings of this aspect of Donne are Pierre Legouis's argument that the speaker of "The Extasie" is "an idle dilettante" who, like Molière's Don Juan, "can call on Heaven when convenient and cloak his wicked designs [of sexual seduction] in religious cant" (61-71); N. J. C. Andreasen's

conclusion that the prevalence of religious imagery in an erotic poem signals Donne's own highly conservative "Christian sense of the moral repulsiveness of lust" (80); John Carey's assumption that theological niceties, when "thrust into a bawdy poem [like 'Going to Bed'], typify the defensive and derisive treatment of religion which . . . Donne's apostasy [in forsaking Roman Catholicism] prompted" (106); and R. V. Young's using lines 39-43 of "Going to Bed" to undermine the proponents of a specifically Protestant poetic, insisting that the doctrine of imputed righteousness is being "ridiculed" by Donne rather than sincerely and creatively appropriated (33-34). C. S. Lewis's comments on the same poem are quoted below.

⁶ Indeed, Mary Ann Radzinowicz specifically links Donne's *Holy Sonnets* to the "anima mea" psalms.

⁷ Gosse identified *Sermons* 10: 9, preached on Lamentations 3:1, as the sermon which Walton declared to have been the first which Donne preached after his wife's burial in August 1617, but Simpson dates this sermon as having been preached after 25 April 1624. Whatever the circumstances of its transmission, its reliance upon the verse, "I am the man which have affliction seene" (Donne's translation), suggests the emblematic presentation of a depleted self common to "A nocturnall" and the *First Anniversarie*. See also *Sermons* 4: 9, preached on 5 November 1622, the anniversary of the Gunpowder Plot, which takes Lamentations 4: 20 as its text.

⁸ On the *omphalos*, see Eliade 43-45.

⁹ In ancient Hebrew, *yada* signals both knowledge of a person and sexual intercourse with a person; hence the still-current euphemism "to know someone in the biblical sense."

¹⁰ On Donne and the immersion in sacred time, see Paul Stanwood and A. B. Chambers.

¹¹ On Donne and wonder, see Dennis Quinn and Richard Klause.

¹² As Frederick Rowe observes, "Donne was excited by the emblematic concentration of meaning, by an idea caught up in some conjunction of circumstances, or in some material thing that made thought tangible, apprehensible. His endeavour to compress meaning into the smallest space was not just an exercise in ingenuity, though he could play at this better than most and occasionally did; it was his response to truth, which came to him incarnate, and which he expressed in emblems and images and conceits" (73).

¹³ Bettie Anne Doebler's summary of Ruth Wallerstein's teaching on the conceit as presenting a unified world (iv-v) is appropriate in this regard, but the best discussion continues to be Roston, chap. 1.

¹⁴ Donne is the great poet of the liminal. In "A nocturnall," as the speaker prepares towards meeting the Lucie figure, it is midnight, the border between

two days; in "A Valediction forbidding mourning" the speaker is on the verge of departure; the *Anniversaries* record the passage from one realm to another. I suspect that this is partly the reason why Donne found preaching sermons so satisfying that he significantly decreased his poetic output. Physically he was elevated above the congregation in the pulpit, but still suspended below heaven, facing west as he faced his congregation, but already having passed over into the sanctuary at the east end of the church. He was thus suspended physically between God and men as he engaged in the act of "translation."

15 Harold Fisch highlights the literary implications of the Hebrew "call and response" theology in his chapters on Psalms and Song of Songs. But see also Sessions and Sobosan.

16 See also Docherty's analysis of the speaker's rhetorical attempt to project himself from profane into sacred time and space in "The Sunne Rising" (32-35).

17 The preceding section of the introduction draws upon and extends the ideas presented in several previously published essays. I am grateful to the various editors for permission to reappropriate portions of the following: "Donne's Biblical Figures: The Integrity of 'To Mr. George Herbert,'" *MP* 81 (1984): 285-89; "Donne's Erotic Spirituality: Ovidian Sexuality and the Language of Christian Revelation in Elegy XIX," *Ball State Forum* 25 (Autumn 1984): 41-54; "Redemption Typology in John Donne's 'Batter My Heart,'" *JRMMRA* 8 (1987): 163-76; "Moses, Dante, and the *Visio Dei* of Donne's 'Going to Bed,'" *ANQ* 6 (Jan. 1993): 13-17; "'With Holy Importunitie, with a Pious Impudencie': John Donne's Attempts to Provoke Election," *JRMMRA* 13 (1992): 85-102; and "Donne's Emblematic Imagination: Vision and Reformation of the Self in 'The Crosse,'" *Publications of the Arkansas Philological Assoc.* 20 (Spring 1994): 27-51.

Works Cited

Andreasen, N. J. C. *John Donne: Conservative Revolutionary*. Princeton: Princeton U P, 1967.

Bell, Ilona. "The Role of the Lady in Donne's *Songs and Sonets*." *SEL* 23 (1983): 113-29.

Booth, Stephen, ed. *Shakespeare's Sonnets*. New Haven: Yale U P, 1977.

Brooks, Cleanth. *The Well Wrought Urn: Studies in the Structure of Poetry*. New York: Harcourt, Brace and World, 1947.

Carey, John. *John Donne: Life, Mind, and Art*. New York: Oxford U P, 1981.

Chambers, A. B. "*La Corona*: Philosophic, Sacred, and Poetic Uses of Time." *New Essays on Donne*. Ed. Gary A. Stringer. Salzburg: Salzburg Studies in English

Literature, 1977. 140-72.

Coffin, Charles Monroe. *John Donne and the New Philosophy*. 1937. New York: Humanities P, 1958.

Demaray, John G. *Cosmos and Representation: Dante, Spenser, Milton and the Transformation of Renaissance Heroic Poetry*. Pittsburgh: Duquesne UP, 1991.

Docherty, Thomas. *John Donne, Undone*. London: Methuen, 1986.

Doebler, Bettie Anne. *The Quickening Seed: Death in the Sermons of John Donne*. Elizabethan and Renaissance Studies 30. Salzburg: Institut fur Englische Sprache und Literatur, 1974.

Eliade, Mircea. *The Sacred and the Profane: The Nature of Religion*. Trans. Willard R. Trask. New York: Harper Torchbacks, 1961.

Fisch, Harold. *Poetry with a Purpose: Biblical Poetics and Interpretation*. Bloomington: Indiana U P, 1988.

Gardner, Helen. "General Introduction." John Donne. *The Elegies and The Songs and Sonnets*. Oxford: Clarendon P, 1965. xvii-lxii.

Gosse, Edmund. *The Life and Letters of John Donne*. 1899. 2 vols. Gloucester, MA: Peter Smith, 1959.

Hartman, Geoffrey. *Wordsworth's Poetry*. New Haven: Yale UP, 1958.

Hughes, Richard E. *The Progress of the Soul: The Interior Career of John Donne*. New York: William Morrow, 1968.

Klause, John L. "Donne and the Wonderful." *ELR* 17 (Winter 1987): 41-66.

Kremen, Kathryn R. *The Imagination of the Resurrection: The Poetic Continuity of a Religious Motif in Donne, Blake, and Yeats*. Lewisburg, PA: Bucknell UP, 1972.

Legouis, Pierre. *Donne the Craftsman*. 1928. New York: Russell and Russell, 1962.

Leishman, J. B. *The Monarch of Wit: An Analytical and Comparative Study of the Poetry of John Donne*. Sixth ed. Rpt. New York: Harper and Row, 1966.

Lewalski, Barbara K. "Donne's Poetry of Compliment: The Speaker's Stance and the Topoi of Praise." *Seventeenth-Century Imagery*. Ed. Earl Miner. Berkeley: U of California P, 1971. 45-67.

Lewis, C. S. "Donne and Love Poetry in the Seventeenth Century." *Seventeenth-Century English Poetry: Modern Essays in Criticism*. Ed. William R. Keast. New York: Oxford U P, 1962.

Miles, Margaret R. *Carnal Knowing: Female Nakedness and Religious Meaning in the Christian West*. 1989. New York: Vintage, 1991.

Otto, Rudolph. *The Idea of the Holy*. Trans. John W. Harvey. Second ed. London: Oxford UP, 1950.

Perry, T. Anthony. *Erotic Spirituality: The Integrative Tradition from Leone Ebreo to John Donne*. University: U of Alabama P, 1980.

Quinn, Dennis. "Donne and the Wane of Wonder." *ELH* 36 (1969): 626-47.

Radzinowicz, Mary Ann. "'Anima Mea' Psalms and John Donne's Religious

Poetry." *"Bright Shootes of Everlastingnesse": The Seventeenth-Century Religious Lyric.* Ed. Claude J. Summers and Ted-Larry Pebworth. Columbia: U of Missouri P, 1987. 40-58.

Rollin, Roger B. "'Fantastique Ague': The Holy Sonnets and Religious Melancholy." *The Eagle and the Dove: Reassessing John Donne.* Ed. Claude Summers and Ted-Larry Pebworth. Columbia: U of Missouri P, 1986. 131-46.

Roston, Murray. *The Soul of Wit: A Study of John Donne.* Oxford: Clarendon P, 1974.

Rowe, Frederick A. *I Launch at Paradise: A Consideration of John Donne, Poet and Preacher.* London: Epworth P, 1964.

Seelig, Sharon Cameron. *The Shadow of Eternity: Belief and Structure in Herbert, Vaughan, and Traherne.* Lexington: U P of Kentucky, 1981.

Sessions, William A. "Abandonment and the English Religious Lyric in the Seventeenth Century." *"Bright Shootes of Everlastingnesse": The Seventeenth-Century Religious Lyric.* Ed. Claude J. Summers and Ted-Larry Pebworth. Columbia: U of Missouri P, 1986. 1-19.

Sherwood, Terry G. *Fulfilling the Circle: A Study of John Donne's Thought.* Toronto: U of Toronto P, 1984.

Sobosan, Jeffrey G. "Call and Response,—The Vision of God in John Donne and George Herbert." *Religious Studies* 13 (1977): 395-407.

Stahmer, Harold. *"Speak That I May See Thee!": The Religious Significance of Language.* New York: Macmillan, 1968.

Stanwood, Paul G. "Time and Liturgy in Donne, Crashaw, and T. S. Eliot." *Mosaic* 12 (Winter 1979): 91-105.

Stein, Arnold. *John Donne's Lyrics: The Eloquence of Action.* 1962. New York: Octagon, 1980.

Tillich, Paul. *Dynamics of Faith.* New York: Harper Torchbacks, 1958.

Yingling, Thomas E. *Hart Crane and the Homosexual Text.* Chicago: U of Chicago P, 1990.

Young, R. V. "Donne's Holy Sonnets and the Theology of Grace." *"Bright Shootes of Everlastingnesse": The Seventeenth-Century Religious Lyric.* Ed. Claude J. Summers and Ted-Larry Pebworth. Columbia: U of Missouri P, 1987. 20-39.

A Biographical Prolusion to Study of Donne's Religious Imagination

Dennis Flynn

wo passages Donne wrote about three months after his marriage imply that, even at this late date, he had to imagine going into religious exile among other prospects. On 1 March 1602, after his release from imprisonment in the Fleet, Donne wrote to his outraged father-in-law, Sir George More, concerning his own predicament:

> I should wrong you as much againe as I did, if I should think you sought
> to destroy me, but though I be not hedlongly destroyd, I languish and
> rust dangerously. From seeking preferments abrode, my love and con-
> science restrains me; from hoping for them here my Lord's disgracings
> cut me of. (Kempe 339)

The words "seeking preferments abrode" do not mean that Donne might seek work in some branch of English foreign service. Mentioning "con-science" as a restraint, Donne rather declines to seek *Catholic* preferment in *exile*. By stressing his "conscience" in this way, Donne evidently in-tends, as in other letters to his new father-in-law, to mollify More's baleful view of him as "loving a corrupt religion" (Kempe 334).

To his former employer, Lord Keeper Sir Thomas Egerton, Donne wrote more circumstantially on the very same day:

> It ys late now for me (but that necessity, as yt hath continually an

autumne and a wytheringe, so yt hath ever a springe, and must put forth,) to beginne that course, w'ch some yeares past I purposd to travaile, though I could now do yt, not much disadvantageously. I have some bridle upon me now more, more than then, by my marriadge of this gentlewoman; in providing for whom I can and wyll show myself very honest, though not so fortunate. To seek preferment here with any but your Lordship were a madness. (Kempe 341-42)

Donne's reference to "that course, w'ch some yeares past I purposd to travaile," seems pretty clearly to parallel "seeking preferments abrode" in the letter to More: twice on the same day he juxtaposes a possibly advantageous (if otherwise unattractive) religious exile and the utterly hopeless, even insane prospect of seeking preferment in England under present circumstances.

In mentioning "that course, w'ch some yeares past I purposd to travaile," Donne alludes to a series of events and situations that have not generally been recognized in Donne studies. As a consequence of the Elizabethan Privy Council's religious policy, and its resistance by members of Donne's family, in January 1585 Donne had traveled to Paris for a period of religious exile arranged by his mother and his uncle. The trip eventuated in his witnessing the siege of Antwerp and in other travels on the continent before he returned to England during 1587.[1] Like other Elizabethan gentry and nobility who in the 1580s traveled for religious reasons, Donne remained reticent about these events and situations throughout his life. But evidence of them does appear in various places and in various ways, sometimes between lines we have read without noticing.

Thus a distinct though unobtrusive quality of these passages from the marriage letters is the nonchalance Donne uses in assuring More that he is restrained from "seeking preferments abrode" and Egerton that it is probably too late to resume "that course, w'ch some yeares past I purposd to travaile." Donne writes as if, from their points of view, there were a natural logic about exile in his situation; as if, after his recent imprisonment and disgrace, exile were an option to be expected and understood, although properly to be declined (as Donne does decline it).

Imprisonment and exile were and were to be frequently occurring themes in Donne's imagination. In his poems (e.g., in "La Corona," "Oh my blacke Soule," "A Litanie," "The Lamentations of Jeremy," and the *Anniversaries*, to mention only religious poetry) and in his letters and sermons, references to exile and imprisonment abound. This proliferation of imagery seems rooted in some fundamental quarter of the poet's experience, revisited again and again, holding for him and his original readers some meaning we should seek out and make our own.

For example, the casual quality of Donne's references to exile in these letters to More and Egerton suggests his sense that these men for some reason afforded him a space in which he might choose exile, even if they would disapprove, and even though he no longer had any such intention. In any case, to judge from Donne's rhetorical tone, More and Egerton must have understood Donne in some way that would have made his references to exile seem to them neither surprising nor anomalous. But if More and Egerton shared such an understanding of Donne and his possibilities in 1602, theirs was an understanding far from the images of Donne familiar to us in the twentieth century.

That we have not shared their understanding may have resulted in part from our lack of the kinds of information about Donne readily available to his contemporaries. Gaps have existed and still exist in our knowledge largely because certain information was thought too obvious or too insignificant or too sensitive to be mentioned in writing and saved. But it cannot be simply that we have lacked evidence, a lack in itself frustrating. Beyond the frustrating silence of the past is the additional, more radical frustration at realizing that even when the past has spoken (as in these passages from the marriage letters) our own inclination or disposition to recognize or to seek new evidence has somehow been damped or conditioned or limited. Many scholarly traditions, by now amounting to habits of thought, have continually (if only partly intentionally) shaped our assumptions in such a way as to place certain kinds of questions beyond the pale, questions we have assumed need not or should not be asked. Why were More and Egerton expecting that Donne might be imagining religious exile? The work of understanding Donne consists in asking such questions in order to discover new evidence.

1

After this much as prologue, my purpose is to represent two contexts tending to influence Donne's religious imagination—his lineage and his social circle. Both lineage and social circle were primary elements of the context in which More and Egerton understood Donne; both were factors shaping Donne's character in ways that have been less apparent to us than to his contemporaries; and both were topics associated in poignant ways with the notions of imprisonment and religious exile.

Our problems in understanding Donne's lineage and social circle grow from the single root of our acknowledged tendency to read old texts in terms that suit our way of looking at things but do not take account of cultural differences that separate us from the past. As historians Mervyn James and Kristen Neuschel have noted, sixteenth-century European cultures such as Donne's differ from ours partly because they were "honor" cultures, in which the concept of honor had far greater social significance, influencing the course of people's deeds and words. I am proposing that the space More and Egerton apparently afforded Donne, suggested by references to exile in his letters, was a space of honor to which we need to pay attention.

This space of honor was understood by More, Egerton, and others as connected to Donne's lineage and social circle in ways so obvious that they did not even need mention among his contemporaries, for whom Donne's lineage and social circle were called to mind, automatically and poignantly, by the notions of imprisonment and exile. One particular such association was with Sir Thomas More's imprisonment and judicial murder, overshadowing other examples. But in the wake of this immeasurable disaster for the family Donne's great-granduncle Judge William Rastell, his grandfather John Heywood, and his uncles Ellis and Jasper Heywood—all international celebrities—all had died in exile, only the most illustrious of a dozen men *and women* of Donne's extended family "not much disadvantageously" to have sought "preferments abrode" in the decades following More's death.

William Rastell went twice into exile—first at the imposition of the Book of Common Prayer under King Edward and a second time after the policies of the Elizabethan Privy Council became clear and undeniable. His uncompromising rejection of Protestantism in England, intended to reiterate and renew in others the steadfastness of Sir Thomas More, firmly fixed religious exile as part of the pattern of alternatives presently faced by all members of the family until Donne's time. Judge Rastell tried to define the tone of the family's life in exile when he singled out young Bartholomew More, a grandson of the Lord Chancellor, who was living in Belgium in 1564. Rastell makes a point in his will of stipulating that Bartholomew's inheritance is conditional on his "not passing over to live in England until England is reconciled fully to the Catholic faith and church." If Bartholomew does not remain in exile, or if (as Rastell further stipulates) he "declines into some heretical opinion," his annuity is to be given away to charity (Bang 246-48).[2]

By the time Rastell died in 1566, religious exile was still not subject to new statutory financial penalty. Rastell's way of life at Louvain, like that of other exiled family members in the 1560s and earlier, was still a comparatively comfortable, intellectual life centering in the academic community of the University. Though illegal, their exile was felt as an inconvenience they had prepared for prudently, a sojourn merely until such time as political and religious instability subsided and England reasonably returned to the ordinary religious practice of Christendom. During the time of King Edward, Ellis Heywood, whom Rastell later made his main heir and executor, had led a similar existence in Italy as secretary to the noble exile Cardinal Reginald Pole. After the accession of Queen Elizabeth, Ellis and his parents, John and Joan Heywood, joined Rastell in Belgium; Jasper Heywood had gone into exile somewhat earlier and was a Jesuit academic stationed in Bavaria.

However, following the failed Northern Rising of 1569-70, the Privy Council, dismayed at a sharp increase in emigration by rebellious and otherwise disaffected Catholics, took steps in Parliament to prevent their becoming a destabilizing threat from abroad. Among several anti-Catholic bills passed within a year of Donne's birth was "An Acte agaynst Fugytyves over the Sea," which bore directly on the members of Donne's family, making inevitable the loss of their rents and properties if they did not return from exile. John Heywood, before his flight to Belgium, had designated his new son-in-law, John Donne the elder, to manage his affairs, collecting rents in England and for the next few years forwarding them to Heywood on the continent. Within three months of passage of the "Acte agaynst Fugytyves," Donne would be required to make a complete report detailing any role he had played in Heywood's affairs. Should he be found involved (even *ex post facto*) in secret dealings with a fugitive, he could be prosecuted. Moreover, the bill ordained that if such a fugitive did not himself return to England within six months, all his property would be forfeit to the Crown. Arrangements such as Heywood had made with Donne were rendered void, and the Privy Council was empowered to form commissions of inquiry to settle the cases of fugitives and their suspected accomplices (*Statutes* 4 [part 1]: 531-34).

John Donne the elder apparently saw the trend of events and was not willing to incur a fine and imprisonment; but neither was he willing to comply with the law, meekly losing all of his stewardship. Before the fugitives bill had even been debated in Parliament, he began to take steps to defend himself. First he stopped forwarding Heywood's rents, turning over their collection to his sister-in-law, the widow Elizabeth Marven, a smaller and much less tempting target for prosecution. At about the same time Donne seems also to have arranged a way to hold onto a lease of lands at Romney Marsh in Kent, by far the most valuable of all Heywood's properties. His exact procedure is not clear, but somehow Donne managed affairs so that Roger Manwood, the Privy Council's commissioner investigating Heywood's holdings in Kent, himself (perhaps unknowingly) purchased the lease from Heywood and then in turn sold it to Donne. Not only did this tend to veil Donne's culpability in having direct dealings with a fugitive; it also interposed as a middle man the supposedly disinterested investigator of the whole business (Reed 69). What is not clear is whether Manwood was completely aware of the nature of this transaction. If so, he acted consistently with what we know of his capacity for corrupt practice. If not, he had been duped into dealing with a fugitive; and he was a dangerous man for the elder Donne to have crossed.

As matters now stood, the Romney Marsh lands alone among the family's former holdings seemed secure. The problem was that if Donne forwarded any money to John Heywood he might himself again become liable to prosecution. There seemed no way Heywood could benefit, but he began to try various shifts to avoid loss of all his revenues. Having sent word through an agent of the Privy Council that he remained loyal to the Queen and wanted to return to England to clear his name, Heywood further wrote cleverly to his old Court friend, Lord Treasurer Burghley's wife, Mildred Cooke Cecil, to ask with seeming naivety for her husband's help in retaining whatever part of the property was still not yet disposed of. Heywood also complained slyly that he had been swindled out of a lease by his son-in-law. The return of properties passing through the grasp of the Crown was of course out of the question, but within a few weeks, at Lady Burghley's request, the Lord Treasurer did order Donne (illegally) to send Heywood his arrearages on the Romney Marsh lease (Reed 238). Heywood, for his part, never returned to England. Wise as serpents, mild as doves, Heywood and Donne were thus able to make the most of a bad situation.

Then suddenly, when his oldest son was not yet four and his wife pregnant with their seventh child, John Donne the elder fell sick and died. The elder Donne's sudden death in his early forties would not give us pause were it not for a puzzling reference to Roger Manwood years later in the younger Donne's satirical, annotated bibliography, *The Courtier's Library of Rare Books Not for Sale*. Among the fictitious book titles listed here is "*Manuale justiciarorum*, continens plurimas confessiones veneficarum Manwoodo judici exhibitas, et ab illo abstergendis postea natibus et evacuationibus adhibitas . . . "—i. e. "*A Manual for Justices of the Peace*, comprising many confessions of poisoners, evidence produced before Justice Manwood and applied by him in wiping himself . . ." (*Courtier's Library* 35). The cryptic point of this, Donne's single known reference to Manwood, is perhaps discovered if we consider that the commissioner could be embarrassed sufficiently by his dealings with Donne's father to have exacted a fierce revenge. Manwood's biographer notes his reputation "as a proud and cruel man" and goes on to observe that, "on the evidence of victims of his activities, the stories are so many and so consistent that the verdict must go against him" (Pickering 15-16). Moreover, Donne evidently regarded Manwood "with a degree of contempt that may well have been based on a sense of family injury" (Bald 34). The family here as in other situations had resisted government efforts to punish them for their religion; but as far as we know the family's exiles remained steadfast as a matter of honor in not returning to conform to Anglicanism.

By 1602 Donne thus still had numerous relations living in Belgium, though the first generation of emigres were all dead. Such details of Donne's lineage have not seemed especially relevant in his biographers' handling of the marriage letters to More and Egerton. But the letters in their references to exile do suggest Donne's presumption that More and Egerton would be inclined to feel an unspoken connection between his family's religious history and his situation in 1602. The problem of Donne's lineage for Donne studies is then to appreciate the fact that, as a member of a group directly afflicted by enormous and penetrating social developments, Donne wrote out of an experience that his contemporaries *could* not ignore, that therefore never ceased to dominate *his* outlook, and that may appear as an element in anything he wrote. We should no more separate study of Donne's life and writings from his and his family's religious persecution and exile than we would separate study of the writings of Solzhenitsyn or Wiesel from theirs.

2

A second context tending to influence Donne's religious imagination is one that has been given comparatively less attention, though I believe it will prove more and more central in Donne studies. This is the context of Donne's social circle—more specifically the context of his and his family's association with the ancient Catholic nobility. We have long known several signposts pointing to this association from different angles. One that I have been staring at for several years is Donne's 1591 portrait, which I have argued should be interpreted as an emblem of honor.[3] This signpost points back in time toward the 1580s, toward the "some yeares past" Donne speaks of in his letter to Egerton.

Another such signpost long known to students of Donne is his name on the list of processioners mourning Sir Thomas Egerton the younger at Chester in 1599. In the funeral procession Donne "occupied a position of considerable honour," preceding only a herald of arms and the Bishop of Chester before the bier itself, and "bearing the sword of his dead friend" (Bald 106). How did Donne come by such a position of honor? Given the socially symbolic heraldry of a formal funeral, it is anachronistic to suppose that Donne's position in the procession expresses merely his having been the close chum of the deceased. Especially impressive is his carrying the dead man's sword, a most central and poignant emblem of the concept of honor. It must remind us of that earlier emblem, the sword Donne holds up by its hilt in his 1591 portrait, eight years before the funeral. For reasons not yet entirely clear to us, Donne's contemporaries apparently regarded him not as a desperately ambitious, place-seeking, social-climbing son of a hardware salesman, but as a person of remarkable honor.

Yet another signpost that should receive attention is the fact that Henry Percy, ninth Earl of Northumberland, happened to carry Donne's letter to Sir George More imparting the confirmation of rumor about Donne's clandestine wedding to Ann More. People seem to have assumed that the Earl was just an acquaintance doing Donne a favor; R. C. Bald thought the key to explaining the incident was simply that Northumberland's estate at Petworth was not too far from More's at Losely. That an Earl should *serve* as a letter carrier did not seem strange to Bald (134). But this incident too involves the concept of honor and is crucial to our understanding not only the wedding but much else about Donne. In what context can we place this seemingly isolated incident?

Donne's relationship with the ninth Earl of Northumberland, including their long association during the reign of James I, through most of which Northumberland languished in prison in the Tower of London, stemmed from their families' involvement at the Tudor Court going back two generations to the period following the death of Sir Thomas More. In particular, the children of John Heywood—Ellis, Jasper, and also Elizabeth Heywood, Donne's mother—grew up at Court and were educated along with the children of the ancient Catholic nobility, among them Henry Percy, later eighth Earl of Northumberland and the father of Donne's friend. By the time Donne approached adolescence, the eighth Earl was the most powerful member of the English nobility sympathetic to Catholicism. The Privy Council, mindful of Northumberland's political acumen and energy as well as of his sympathies, had confined him to his Sussex estate. As a consequence, the Earl's son Lord Henry Percy, eight years older than Donne, had already by the age of sixteen begun to play an active role in his father's most secret and dangerous political activities.

Ostensibly traveling in France for educational reasons, by the early 1580s Lord Percy was actually facilitating his father's dealings with English Catholic exiles and with elements of the French Court. The Earl and his son were already deep in undeclared conflict with the Elizabethan regime when in 1581 they provided for Jasper Heywood's triumphant return from twenty years of exile to emerge as a Jesuit missionary in England. Disembarking from a coal barge returning from France to Newcastle (the port of entry controlled by the Earl as Captain of Tynemouth Castle), Heywood descended on London from the North, out of Percy country, "in coach accompanied with many and in costly apparel."[4] Heywood's missionary work quickly eventuated in a campaign at Oxford and Cambridge designed to make the two universities "perpetual aqueducts" through which would pass young English Catholic gentry and nobility bound for religious exile. Working with Heywood and the Catholic embassies in London, Northumberland sought to coordinate the flight of these young men with nascent plans being formed by such powers in France as Henri Lorraine, Duc de Guise, for the so-called "Enterprise of England."

But in late 1582 Northumberland came under more careful scrutiny by the Privy Council after discovery, along with other inculpating evidence, of Lord Percy's dealings in Paris with such dangerous exiles as Charles Paget and Thomas Morgan. The Earl now thought best to recall Lord Percy from France and also to take other defensive measures, including the spiritual step of a formal reconciliation to Catholicism in the spring of 1583 at the hands of Jasper Heywood. These developments may well have led to the first meeting of Donne and Lord Percy.

Throughout the rest of 1583 Northumberland sought to cover his tracks, busily shifting associates who were potential witnesses against him into France, assisted by his son, who traveled back and forth across the Channel disguised and using an alias. But the Privy Council looked ever more determinedly to expose the Earl's activities, especially after they found his name mentioned on some papers discussing the "Enterprise"—papers found among the possessions of Francis Throckmorton, one of Mary Stuart's couriers. Northumberland was now relieved of his post as Captain of Tynemouth Castle and then imprisoned in the Tower, soon to be joined by Heywood. They remained fellow prisoners until

January 1585, when Heywood was deported to France.

It was at this point that Donne traveled into exile to join his uncle at Paris ("that course, w'ch some yeares past I purposd to travel"). Lord Percy too had again come to Paris, where he was staying with two of his younger brothers. It was a time of excitement for the English Catholic community in exile, mainly because, with the pending fall of Antwerp to Spanish forces, the anticipated invasion of England seemed imminent. Largely because of the efforts of Heywood and Northumberland, sons of the gentry and nobility had been flocking across the Channel fòr several months; and many of these looked to serve as officers or gentlemen volunteers with some 400 English deserters, earlier sent covertly by the Privy Council to fight for the Dutch, but now in the pay of Alessandro Farnese, Prince of Parma. Joined to Parma's army with proper officers, these men would provide an English contingent to spearhead the invasion.[5]

Donne had arrived in Paris on 23 February and was still there at least through mid-March. On 20 March Parma ordered to Paris, from his camp at the siege of Antwerp, one William Tresham, commissioned as a Captain in Parma's army. Tresham, cadet son of a strongly Catholic family, had formerly been a gentleman-in-waiting at the Elizabethan Court but had fled England in fear of persecution late in the 1570s. Since then he had, like other English Catholic nobility and gentry, awaited impatiently the onset of an "Enterprise." The purpose of Tresham's commission was expressly to provide leadership for the band of English deserters encamped at Antwerp and for the expectant fugitives scattered in French and Belgian exile (Persons 125-27).[6] From Paris before Easter 1585, Tresham traveled north with a group of such noble and gentle recruits to the English Catholic seminary at Eu, founded by the Duc de Guise in part to serve as a bivouac and staging area for the "Enterprise." From Eu, Tresham and his men proceeded toward Antwerp.

Knowing or sensing the imminent danger of invasion, the Privy Council in the next few weeks ordered extraordinary measures to guard "all the creekes and portes" on the southeast coast and to watch "all suspected places of or costs to prevent the landinge of all dangerouse psons." On 9 June, agents of the Privy Council at the port of Southampton arrested and interrogated Francis Middleton, "a verie suspected person, as wee thinke, and a badde instrument," whom they discovered posing as a French merchant on board a ship bound from Dieppe. Middleton and his family were Percy followers and also had long-standing connections with other Catholic nobility, including the Treshams. Middleton confessed that until the fall of 1584, the time of Tresham's commissioning, he had served Tresham. After Michaelmas 1584 he had returned to England but had again illegally left the country, this time significantly through the Earl of Northumberland's old bailiwick at Tynemouth, traveling thence after Easter to join the "Enterprise" at Eu, "wher he understood ther were divers English gentlemen in a house erected for the Englishe traitors. . . . And beinge further examined of the gents ther, he confesseth that ther was at Ewe in the same house, ii of the Lord Vauses sonnes, the wch he had seene before at Sr Thomas Tresams house, being once his servaunt, but he knew none of the rest that were ther, being as hee thinketh xxx in nomber at the least" (Thomas West and James Paget to the Privy Council, 9 June 1585, and the Examination of Francis Middleton, 9 June 1585; Public Record Office SP12/179/10 and 10.I). Faced with this testimony, the Privy Council had little difficulty divining that Middleton had been carrying intelligence of activities on the continent to Northumberland and to his supporters in the north of England. During Easter he had evidently returned to the continent in order to meet Tresham at Eu. No doubt he was now withholding information Northumberland would want kept especially secret. The thirty "English gentlemen" Middleton declined to identify, I believe, had included Donne and very possibly one or more of Northumberland's sons, most probably Lord Henry Percy, who became Donne's lifelong friend. At some point after Easter 1585 they had all arrived at Parma's encampment near Antwerp.

Northumberland meanwhile remained in the Tower on suspicion of treason. But because of the Earl's wily maneuvers the Privy Council still lacked the kind of evidence that would convict him before a jury of his peers. Nevertheless, on 20 June 1585, just a few days after Middleton's testimony, Northumberland's official keepers in the Tower were discharged of their responsibilities and replaced by a man named Thomas Bailiffe, a servant of the Privy Councilor Sir Christopher Hatton. Within a few hours, just after midnight in the early morning of 21 June, Bailiffe reported finding the prisoner dead on his bed, shot three times in the chest with a pistol. A surgeon supervised by Henry Carey, Lord Hunsdon, performed an autopsy on the corpse, removing the bullets from the Earl's chest, "his heart," according to Hunsdon, "pearced and torne in divers lobes or pieces, three of his ribbes broken, the Chine bone of his backe cut almost in sunder" ([Walsingham] 19).

Two days later, "by her Maiesties special commandement," this enormity was the subject of an unusual proceeding in the Star Chamber. Presiding was the Lord Chancellor, Sir Thomas Bromley, who opened the hearing by declaring that Northumberland had "most wickedly destroied and murdered himselfe" ([Walsingham] sig. A3). A parade of Privy Councilors and other government spokesmen then advanced various charges against the Earl, among them that he had been steeped in treasons for the past fifteen years, most recently in the plotting of Francis Throckmorton and other Catholics for the "Enterprise."

Following these preambles came the main portion of the hearing. Sir Roger Manwood, now Lord Chief Baron of the Exchequer, gave details about the Earl's last night, including the coroner's report and an explanation of the replacement of Northumberland's customary keepers by Hatton's servant Bailiffe. Manwood also gave a lengthy explanation of the background and sequence of events on the night in question. Although no witnesses were produced, Manwood read from depositions to explain how the Earl had obtained a gun and why he had used it.

Finally Sir Christopher Hatton himself, "who (as it seemed) had bene specially employed by her Maiesty" in this case, reviewed the course of royal policy toward Northumberland and concluded that his hard-hearted refusal to confess his treason had been the formal cause of his suicide, since "God by his iust iudgment, had for his sinnes and ingratitude taken from him his Spirit of grace, and delivered him over to the enemie of his soule, who brought him to that most dreadful & horrible end, whereunto he is come" ([Walsingham] 22).

No one who knew Northumberland believed these representations in Star Chamber. Foremost among the skeptics was Lord Percy, for years afterward blackly resentful and humiliated about the suspicious circumstances of his father's death.[7] Lord Francis Russell, who had earlier been appointed to replace Northumberland as Captain of Tynemouth Castle, had the unenviable task of publicizing the reported suicide among the stunned residents of Percy country. Suppressing his own perplexity he wrote to Sir Francis Walsingham: "for the manner of my Lo. of Northumberlands death yt will hardlie be beleived in this Countrie to be as you have written, yet I ame ffullie persuaded, and have psuaded divers that yt was no otherwise" (Russell to Walsingham, 26 June 1585; P. R. O., SP15/29/21). Despite the efforts of such as Russell, disbelief was so rampant that the Council decided to issue an extraordinary pamphlet defending the Star Chamber verdict and speculating that the Earl's suicide followed from a desperate wish to avoid attainder and the ruin of his family.

The author of this *True and Summarie Reporte* (probably Walsingham) stipulates at the outset his purpose to convince skeptics;[8] but the coincidence of the shooting with the replacement of Northumberland's customary keepers inevitably tended to confirm people's suspicion that Northumberland had been murdered. Moreover, an obvious doubt was posed by the conflict between the coroner's report, that the three bullets fired into the Earl's chest had torn his heart apart and virtually severed his spinal column, and the statement that Hatton's servant Bailiffe had heard Northumberland still groaning behind a barricaded cell-door a half hour to forty-five minutes after the sound of the gunshot.[9]

According to a pamphlet published by Catholic exiles at Cologne late in 1585, in answer to Walsingham's *True and Summarie Reporte*, Northumberland's death was a cold-blooded murder by the Privy Council. As evidence the pamphlet cites the report of Dr. Edward Atslowe that a short time prior to the Earl's death, his life had already been attempted unsuccessfully. Atslowe had treated the Earl during his imprisonment in the Tower for an apparent illness but had concluded that these symptoms actually resulted from a slow-working poison (*Crudelitatis*, sigs. C6v-C7).[10] If as is likely this incident was brought to the attention of the authorities, no participant at the Star Chamber hearing saw fit to mention it. But Atslowe's story would be remembered for years by Lord Percy and those close to him, including John Donne.

3

To conclude, in Donne's time (as Mervyn James has written) "Honour was established, not primarily by the skill with which events and situations were manipulated with a view to a successful outcome, important though this might be to confirm and enhance standing and status, but by the determined 'steadfastness' with which they were confronted" (23). In light of this observation we may find a partial explanation for the apparent place of honor accorded Donne by his contemporaries in the events and situations I have been outlining. Honor inhered in these events and situations even in the view of contemporaries who always had opposed or who had come to reject the idea of the "Enterprise," as indeed by 1602 had Donne and the ninth Earl of Northumberland themselves.

Throughout his life Donne's association with Northumberland and with other members of the ancient Catholic nobility was an honor association with a social class whose power can be seen to have been in decline, doomed to eclipse by the political skill and power of Tudor politicians. This defeat, poignantly felt in individual cases as death in prison or in exile, did not for an honor culture detract from the value of steadfastness shown. As Kristen Neuschel has written, "Fighting, particularly in rebellion against the crown, was an overt act that did not escape the notice of contemporary observers eager to bestow praise and blame" (71). Either praise or blame thus constituted an acknowledgement of honor for Donne's contemporaries, often in unspoken ways that are sometimes difficult for us to read out of context in the texts that remain to us.

In us our individualism is so ripe that, compared to sixteenth-century Europeans, we tend to feel life is determined less by noble principle and more by material interests. Moreover, religion's role in human affairs has diverged markedly in democratic society from its traditional role in Donne's society. In the twentieth century religion's social significance, including our sense of its role in forming character, has seemed much reduced—especially in comparison to economic factors—and has seemed in its diminished significance to spring largely from our experience of the kind of religion we call "organized," an experience sixteenth-century Englishmen would not readily have understood. Samuel Johnson observed in the eighteenth century that converts from "Popery" to Protestantism endure a "laceration of mind" that casts in doubt their sincerity and reliability (Boswell 426). This is not a point likely to have been made by any twentieth-century writer, inclined to link personal substance to money and power rather than to religious belief. Dr. Johnson, a self-conscious Protestant who used the term "Popery" with undertones of distaste if not contempt, was nevertheless more sensitive than religiously tolerant modern writers to this "laceration of mind" that was a common experience among Elizabethans.

In Donne's time, the change of religions seemed not merely a superstructure on the economic base, but incomparably the most important social trend affecting people's lives. Rightly or wrongly—whether resistant or enthusiastic, even if indifferent—those in the sixteenth century who considered the nature of their time never doubted or disputed that (not the rise of the middle class, but) a general deprivation of the Catholic sacraments was creating in England a new order of social experience.

Notes

A version of this essay was presented at the Seventh Annual Conference of the John Donne Society at the University of Southern Mississippi—Gulfport on February 18, 1992.

[1] On these travels see my "Donne and the Ancient Catholic Nobility" and "Jasper Mayne's Translation of Donne's Latin Epigrams."

[2] Another document, dated 2 October 1572 at Dillingen, certifies that Bartholomew's inheritance had become Ellis Heywood's to dispose of; whether because of Bartholomew's death or violating Rastell's conditions is not specified (Bang 243-44). Bartholomew More "died in his Youth" (Chauncy 2: 447).

[3] See also my "Donne's First Portrait: Some Biographical Clues."

4. On Heywood's work in England see my "The English Mission of Jasper Heywood, S. J."

[5] On these plans for an invasion see Hicks, *An Elizabethan Problem*, 6-7; and *Letters and Memorials of Father Robert Persons, S. J.* lii-lv. On the English deserters see the letter of the Spanish Ambassador Bernardino Mendoza to King Philip, 30 August 1582 (Hume 3: 398).

[6] The commission itself was enclosed with the letter of Alessandro Farnese, Prince of Parma, to Robert Persons, 20 March 1585 (Roman Archives of the Jesuits, Fondo Gesuitico 651/640).

[7] See Henry Percy, Earl of Northumberland, to Sir George Carew, June 1587, referring darkly to "my present discontent" (Brewer 444). See also Paul Crushe to William Cecil, Baron of Burghley, March 1592, where Burghley's spy reports that his influence with Northumberland is being solicited by a Catholic (Thomas Pigott of Buckinghamshire) in a plot to "seduce" the young Earl to Catholicism. Northumberland, Crushe writes, is already "verie well affected to the Sea of Rome" and "continueth muche discontented for his father death" (Public Record Office, SP12/241/112). Beginning in the late 1580s the ninth Earl had become a notorious malcontent and member of the so-called "School of Night," ostensibly interested in magic, alchemy, and obscure literature. That others as well, years later, rejected the story of Northumberland's suicide is shown by a letter from Sir Walter Raleigh to Sir Robert Cecil in 1601, advising him to crush the Earl of Essex (then under arrest by the Privy Council) without fear of revenge: "For After-revenges, fear them not. For your own Father, that was esteemed to be the Contriver of *Norfolk's* Ruin, yet his Son followeth your Father's Son, and loveth him. Humours of Men succeed not, but grow by Occasions, and Accidents of Tyme and Power. *Somerset* made no Revenge on the Duke of *Northumberland's* Heares. *Northumberland* that now is, thinks not of *Hatton's* Issue" (Murdin 811-12).

[8] The preface tells us that the author, "falling in companie with divers persons

at sundrie times, aswell about the citie of London as abroade," has heard "many men" tell the story of Northumberland's death "as, that the Earle had bene uniustly detained in prison without proofe or just cause of suspition of treason; and, that he had bene murdered by devise and practice of some great enemies, and not destroied by himselfe" ([Walsingham] sig A3v). According to Bernardino Mendoza, Spanish ambassador to England until 1583, Walsingham wrote the pamphlet. See Mendoza to King Philip II of Spain, 16 July 1585; Hume 3: 542).

⁹ According to Manwood, the sound of the shot from inside the Earl's cell was first heard by Bailiffe, who called through the door to Northumberland. Hearing no answer, after some time elapsed Bailiffe sent an old man to rouse Sir Owen Hopton, Lieutenant of the Tower. (Manwood's statement at the hearing is that Hopton was awakened at about a quarter to one.) In the meantime, while waiting for Hopton's appearance, Bailiffe reportedly heard two groans coming from the dead man's cell, then silence. With Hopton's arrival they broke down the door ([Walsingham] 14-15).

¹⁰ Mendoza also mentions this story (Mendoza to King Philip, 16 July 1585; Hume 3: 542), as does Charles Paget: "The Earl of Northumberland was once poisoned before, but cured by Doctor Atslowe, and that not taking place, 'he is payed home with a dagge'" (Charles Paget to Queen Mary of Scotland, 18 July 1585; Bain 8: 28-29).

Works Cited

Bald, R. C. *John Donne: A Life*. Oxford: Oxford UP, 1970.

Bain, Joseph and William K. Boyd, eds. *Calendar of the State Papers Relating to Scotland and Mary, Queen of Scots*. 13 vols. Edinburgh: H. M. General Register House, 1898-1969.

Bang, W. "Acta Anglo-Lovaniensia." *Englische Studien* 38 (1907): 246-48.

Boswell, James. *Life of Johnson*. London: Oxford UP, 1969.

Brewer, J. S. and William Bullen, eds. *Calendar of the Carew Manuscripts, 1575-1588*. London: Longmans, Green, Reader, and Dyer, 1868.

Chauncy, Henry. *The Historical Antiquities of Hertfordshire*. 2 vols. London: J. M. Mullinger, 1826.

Crudelitatis Calvinianae Exempla Duo Recentissima Ex Anglia. [Cologne]: n.p., 1585.

Donne, John. *The Courtier's Library, or Catalogus LibrorumAulicorum Incomparabilium et Non Vendibilium*. Ed. Evelyn Simpson. London: Nonesuch Press, 1930.

Flynn, Dennis. "Donne and the Ancient Catholic Nobility." *ELR* 19 (1989): 305-23.

_____. "Donne's First Portrait: Some Biographical Clues." *Bulletin of Research in the Humanities* 82 (1979): 7-17.

_____. "The English Mission of Jasper Heywood, S. J." *Archivum Historicum Societatis Iesu* 54 (1985): 45-76.

_____. "Jasper Mayne's Translation of Donne's Latin Epigrams." *JDJ* 3 (1984): 121-30.

Hicks, Leo. *An Elizabethan Problem*. London: Burns and Oates, 1964.

_____, ed. *Letters and Memorials of Father Robert Persons, S. J.* London: Catholic Record Society, 1942.

Hume, Martin A. S., ed. *Calendar of Letters and State Papers Relating to English Affairs Preserved Principally in the Archives of Simancas.* 4 vols. Nendeln: Kraus Reprints, 1971.

James, Mervyn. *English Politics and the Concept of Honour, 1485-1612*. London: Past & Present Society, 1978.

Kempe, A. J., ed. *The Loseley Manuscripts*. London: John Murray, 1835.

Murdin, William, ed. *A Collection of State Papers . . . 1571-1596*. London: William Bowyer, 1759.

Neuschel, Kristen. *Word of Honour*. Ithaca: Cornell U P, 1989.

Persons, Robert. "Punti per la Missione d'Inghilterra." *Miscellanea IV*. London: Catholic Record Society, 1907.

Pickering, M. R. "Manwood, Roger." *The House of Commons, 1558-1603*. Ed. P. W. Hasler. 3 vols. London: Her Majesty's Stationery Office, 1981. 3: 15-17.

Reed, A. W. *Early Tudor Drama*. London: Methuen, 1926.

The Statutes of the Realm. 11 vols. London: Dawsons of Pall Mall, 1963.

[Walsingham, Sir Francis]. *A True and Summarie Reporte of the Declaration of Some Part of the Earl of Northumberlands Treasons*. London: C. Barker, 1585.

John Donne and
the Religious Politics
of the Mean

Joshua Scodel

ohn Donne transforms the notion of the ethical mean, which was
central to his contemporaries' defense of the religiopolitical *status
quo*, in order to articulate a new ideological vision. The early
modern English elite generally adopted the Aristotelian identification of
virtue with the mean between excess and deficiency and legitimized the
established church as the mean between Catholicism and radical Protes-
tantism.[1] Donne's spirited and independent engagement with classical
and patristic thought gave him a vital critical distance, however, from his
culture's dominant habits of mind. Donne composed "Satire III" during a
period of religious crisis circa 1596, after he had abandoned the Catholi-
cism of his parents but before he joined the English church.[2] Transforming
both Aristotelian ethics and Pyrrhonist skepticism, the satire spurns the
English church's self-description in order to advocate a skeptical inquiry
as the true religious mean, situated between rash acceptance and rejection
of any of the rival, state-sponsored Christian denominations. As a minis-
ter of the church of England, Donne came to celebrate the national church
as the proper mean, but in his sermons he also adapted in idiosyncratic
ways both classical and Augustinian conceptions of the mean so that he
could embrace the English church without wholly relinquishing his com-
mitment to the individual's quest for religious truth.

Donne's unique deployment of the mean illuminates the relationship
between early modern subjectivity and cultural institutions. New histori-

cists and cultural materialists have portrayed Renaissance persons as subjects indelibly shaped by cultural forces rather than the autonomous selves that some Renaissance figures and some Burckhardtian critics have celebrated. Stephen Greenblatt, for example, discovers no instances of "pure unfettered subjectivity" in the English Renaissance but only "human subject[s]" who are "remarkably unfree" (256). Donne's search for a middle way between the wholesale acceptance or rejection of prevailing religious norms invites us to rethink the binary opposition between autonomy and subjection and to examine the kinds of middle ground that some Renaissance figures themselves sought to articulate.[3]

1

Horace's satires provided the Renaissance with influential treatments of the ethical mean (*Satires* 1.1, 1.2, 2.2; see also *Epistles* 1.10, 1.18; *Ode* 2.10), and "Satire III" is one of three poems in which Donne imitates Horatian satire by invoking the mean. Unlike Horace, however, Donne does not treat the mean as an unproblematic norm. Near the end of both his second and his fourth satires, he uses the mean-extremes polarity to treat issues or characters peripheral to the central issues that he confronts. Both passages allude nostalgically to Horace's secure stance, evoking a stable moral vision unavailable to Donne and incapable of explaining the most powerful evil forces of his world.[4] By contrast, in "Satire III" Donne repeatedly transforms the mean in order to make it applicable to his search for "true religion" in a dangerous and bewildering world of secular temptations and rival religious sects.

In the first verse paragraph of "Satire III" (lines 1-42), Donne first seeks a mean of proper emotional response as he confronts mankind's sinful neglect of religion and then boldly transforms the Aristotelian mean of courage in order to advocate brave spiritual battle against sin. The poem opens with a burst of intense but conflicting emotions as the poet confronts mankind's sinfulness: "Kinde pitty chokes my spleene; brave scorn forbids / Those teares to issue which swell my eye-lids" (lines 1-2). In the third line, "I must not laugh, nor weepe sinnes, and be wise," the poet admonishes himself to control his strong feelings with an allusion to an ancient satiric topos concerning the proper response to the flaws of mankind. Juvenal's *Satire* 10 commends both Democritus's laughter and Heraclitus's weeping as wise responses to human frailties. Juvenal presents laughter as more natural, however, thus implicitly associating his poem's stance with Democritus (lines 28-53).[5] In "Satire IV," Donne similarly adopts the Democritean attitude when he claims that a fop would make even laugh (line 197). In one of his paradoxes, all of which were probably written during the same period as the satires, Donne also expresses a preference for laughter but notes that both responses are extreme: "The extremity of laughing, yea of weeping . . . hath beene accoumpted wisdome: and *Democritus* and *Heraclitus* the lovers of these extremes have beene called lovers of wisdome" (*Paradoxes* 15).[6] "Satire III," by contrast, deviates from both Juvenal and other Donnean works by suggesting that true wisdom will avoid such emotional extremes.

Donne's rejection of laughter and weeping sounds Stoic. Seneca argues that the wise man should "calmly" accept human faults without either laughing or weeping because he should not trouble himself with others' misfortunes (*De tranquillitate animi* 15.2-5). Seeking passionless detachment from the foolish world, the Stoics advised suppressing the emotions rather than bringing them to the mean, as Aristotle recommended (see Seneca, *Epistulae morales* 85.3-5 and 116.1). Yet like many of his contemporaries, Donne the satirist is more Aristotelian than Stoic regarding the emotions.[7] He does not seek Stoic impassivity. Though he wants to avoid the extremes of laughter or weeping, he does not suggest that his "pitty" and "scorn" are themselves improper.

Donne's question, "Can railing then cure these worne maladies?" (line 4), fully reveals that the poet seeks not Stoic detachment but rather an efficacious and therefore morally justifiable expression of emotion. "Railing" recalls Juvenal's most familiar stance, the angry abuse that stems from "indignatio" (*Satire* 1, line 79; see Knox 190-92). Yet Donne does not simply vent his rage in a Juvenalian outburst; instead he weighs the propriety of giving expression to his anger. His sense that expressing rage might be the best response to sin runs counter to Stoic but not to Aristotelian norms. Seneca argues that both Heraclitus's weeping and Democritus's laughter are better responses to folly than anger, the most violent emotion (*De ira* 2.10.5). Aristotle, by contrast, argues that there is a mean of virtuous anger (*Nicomachean Ethics* 4.5). It is not clear what the implied answer is to Donne's question concerning "railing," or whether the rest of the verse paragraph is to be interpreted as virtuous "railing" or not. It is clear, however, that Donne desires not to suppress but rather to regulate his emotions properly as he confronts mankind's sins.

The rest of the verse paragraph continues to stress the dangers of extremism by depicting mankind's sins as Aristotelian extremes. Complaining that men neglect "our Mistresse faire Religion" in favor of secular pursuits (line 5), the poet berates as a "desperate coward" (line 29) a "thou" who represents both himself and his fellow men. Donne often contrasts reckless desperation and cowardice as dual extremes opposed to courage. One Donnean paradox begins by noting that "extreames are equally removed from the meane: So that headlong desperatnes asmuch [*sic*] offends true valor, as backward cowardise"; another claims that "betweene cowardise and despayre valor is ingendred" (*Paradoxes* 9, 21 [cf. "The Calme," line 44]). The satire's oxymoronic "desperate coward" is a new version of Aristotle's rash man. Although Aristotle contrasts rashness and cowardice as excess and defect on either side of courage, his detailed analysis of the rash man breaks down the distinction between these extremes by arguing that rash men are generally "rash cowards" (*thrasudeiloi, Nicomachean Ethics* 3.7.9).[8] The rash man "pretends to courage which he does not possess," is overly bold in situations that are not truly threatening, but is unable to endure truly frightening ones (*Nicomachean Ethics* 3.7.8-9). Donne's "desperate coward" similarly collapses the distinction between the two extremes: he "seeme[s] bold" in recklessly fighting in "forbidden warres" but is afraid to fight the spiritual battle "appointed" by God (lines 29, 32).[9]

Donne's list of various kinds of "desperate coward" underscores their extremism. Reversing conventional depictions of military men as boldly active and lovers as meekly passive in order to emphasize the mad excesses of both, Donne opens with a soldier who entombs himself in "ships woodden Sepulchers," thus making himself a "prey," and ends with a gallant amorist who attacks others with sword or "poysonous words" (lines 18, 28). The imagery of hot and cold used to describe the middle figures, the explorers and buccaneers, also emphasizes their extremism, which ancient and Renaissance texts often describe in terms of the contraries of hot and cold.[10] In a sonnet lamenting his own sinful mixture of opposite extremes, "Oh, to vex me, contraryes meete," Donne laments that he is "ridlingly distemperd, cold and hott" (line 7). The explorers and adventurers who use their internal "fire to thaw the ice / Of frozen North discoveries" (lines 21-22) and endure "fires of Spaine, and the'line" by being "thrise / Colder then Salamanders" (lines 22-24) seek out drastic situations in order to license their lack of moderation.

As he proceeds, Donne transforms the Aristotelian mean of courage by adapting a patristic revision of Aristotelian ethics. Aristotle argues that the courageous man has the proper amount of fear and can therefore face the most terrifying thing, death in battle (*Nicomachean Ethics* 3.7.5; 3.6.6-10; see also Leighton, Pears). In his *Divinae institutiones*, Lactantius agrees with the Aristotelians as opposed to the Stoics that virtue depends upon the proper regulation rather than the eradication of emotions such as fear. The Latin father claims, however, that only Christians are able to control their emotions properly by attuning them to God's order (see Perrin 489-93). He argues that the Christian's fear of God is in fact "greatest courage" ("summa . . . fortitudo") because it enables the Christian to face all calamities bravely (6.17). Adapting Lactantius's claim, Donne asserts that the "feare" of damnation is "great courage" (lines 15-16) and that the God-fearing, courageous Christian dares to confront and combat what are truly the most terrifying things, the spiritual "foes" of mankind, the infernal triad of the devil, world, and flesh (lines 33-42).

Donne wholly rejects the conventional association of courage with military valor upon which Aristotle relies. In a paradox asserting that "only Cowards dare dye," Donne argues from the Aristotelian premise that courage is a mean between recklessness and cowardice to a radically non-Aristotelian conclusion. While Aristotle distinguishes between the brave man's willingness to die in battle and the coward's desire to escape from life through suicide (*Nicomachean Ethics* 3.7.13), Donne's paradox deflates the traditional norm of military heroism by condemning all who court death as simultaneously reckless and cowardly suicides: whoever "run[s] to death unimportun'd" incurs "condemn'd desperatnes" and whoever "dares dye to escape . . . anguishes" is a coward unwilling to endure the "warfare" of life (*Paradoxes* 9-10). In "Satire III" Donne broadens his rejection of traditional concepts of valor by condemning as rash and cowardly suicides all who risk killing or being killed in secular strife rather than fight the spiritual war demanded by God. Such people seek suicide in a deeper sense than Aristotle envisioned. They court damnation, the "death" of their souls (compare Grierson 2:114).

Donne's image of the truly courageous man as one who would "stand / Sentinell in his [God's] worlds garrison" (lines 30-31) suggests how closely he identifies the "desperate coward" with the reckless and cowardly suicide. The image recalls Saint Paul's Christian soldier, who "stands" firm against his spiritual foes (Ephesians 6:11-17); expanding on Paul, Christian handbooks from Lactantius's *Divinae institutiones* (7.27) to Erasmus's *Enchiridion militis christianis* (*Opera* 5. 4) warn that failure to persevere as a *miles Christianus* causes the "death" of one's soul.[11] Donne's image also evokes a classical topos based on an influential mistranslation of a passage in Plato's *Phaedo*. Refusing to commit suicide, Socrates argues that man dwells in a "prison" (*phroura* 62b) that he has no right to leave until God bids him to do so; ancient and Renaissance readers often gave *phroura* the contextually implausible meaning of "garrison."[12] In critiques of suicide based directly or indirectly on this passage, Cicero (*De senectute* 20.73), John of Salisbury (143), Erasmus (*Colloquia* 253), Spenser (126 [*FQ* 1.9.41]), and Montaigne (253) all compare man to a soldier who cannot quit his garrison without divine permission.[13]

The classical refusal of suicide is balanced by a refusal to cling to life. In the *Phaedo* Socrates refuses to avoid death by renouncing his philosophic mission, just as he refuses to embrace death (61c). In *De senectute* Cicero introduces the prohibition of suicide by noting that old men should no more avidly seek than violently reject continued life (20.72). Donne christianizes this classical ideal of equilibrium as a standing guard in spiritual battle, a religious mean between the excess of attacking in "forbidden" wars and the defect of retreating from the "appointed" battle. In *Pseudo-Martyr* (1610), Donne suggests once more that such a stationary position is a religious mean. Attacking the Jesuits' supposed pursuit of martyrdom as a reckless impetus to suicide, Donne notes,

> The way to triumph in secular Armies, was not to be slaine in the Battell, but to have kept the station. . . . As it was in the Romane Armies, so it ought to be taught in the Romane Church, *Ius legionis facile: Non sequi, non fugere.* For we must neither pursue persecution so forwardly, that our naturall preservation be neglected, nor runne away from it so farre, that Gods cause be scandaliz'd, and his Honour diminished. (*Pseudo-Martyr* sig. E1)

The satire's Christian sentry is Donne's earlier version of the "easy law of the legion"— "Not to pursue, not to flee"—that saves men from suicidal extremes.

2

While the first verse paragraph identifies religious devotion with the courage to fight traditional Christian enemies, the second verse paragraph identifies it with the courage to seek true Christianity in a world of warring, state-imposed sects. Those who simply accept one of the national churches provide Donne with satiric examples of how not to seek true religion. Some of the satiric portraits have Juvenalian models, but their careful arrangement recalls Horatian depictions of opposite deviations from the mean rather than Juvenal's looser mode of progression. Donne first presents a triad of characters who embrace Roman Catholicism, Genevan Calvinism, and the English church. Because the English church considered itself the mean between the excessive and deficient ceremonialism that it ascribed, respectively, to Catholicism and radical Protestantism, readers might have expected Donne to attack the first two characters' extremism and then praise the third's embrace of the English middle way. After satirizing the first two figures as extremes, however, Donne pointedly refuses to treat the third as the mean. Mirrheus chooses Catholicism, Crants his Calvinism on the basis of opposing "humors" (line 53) or irrational preferences for various contraries—old versus young, ornamented versus plain, courtly versus rustic. Their respective attachments to the "ragges" of a "thousand yeares agoe" (lines 46-47) and to a "yong" (line 51) religion recall the contrast between what the Elizabethan prayer book describes as those "addicted to their old customs" and those "so newfangled that they would innovate all things" (*Book of Common Prayer* 19). Yet by comparing Mirrheus's fondness for Roman "ragges" with Englishmen's fawning at a monarch's "statecloth" (lines 47-48) and Crants's love for Genevan "plaine" simplicity to a "lecherous" preference for "country drudges" (lines 51, 53-54), Donne associates deviations from the supposed mean of the English church with two extremes of English social life: the slavish life at court, which Donne attacks at length in "Satire IV," and the brutish rustic life, where one "suck[s] on countrey pleasures, childishly," to quote "The good-morrow" (line 3). Moreover, Graius, the third figure, does not avoid extremes by staying "at home" (line 55) in the English church but instead mixes them through a perverse embrace of contraries. Impressionable and subservient, he obeys corrupt elders, preachers who act simultaneously like "Godfathers" and "bauds," and laws "Still new like fashions" (lines 56-57, 59), religious statutes that are as young as Crants's church and as devoid of substance as Mirrheus's rags. The name "Graius," the Latin for "a Greek," recalls Juvenal's depiction of the typical Greek as an empty sycophant who not only does whatever his patron commands but also derives his opinions and even his facial expressions from his patron (*Satire* 3, lines 73-80, 100-106). Donne's allusion suggests that the typical English conformist, who thinks precisely what the authorities "bid him thinke" (line 57), has not attained a virtuous mean but instead has forfeited his very identity to the powers that be.

The first triad thus fails to locate a positive model. Having disposed of prevailing approaches to religious allegiance, Donne begins afresh with a second, unconventional triad composed of extreme figures who reject and accept all the religious sects plus the poet's vision of the true mean adumbrated in the poem's final exhortative section. Unlike the preceding characters, the two extreme figures in this second triad, Phrygius and Graccus, do not evade the problem posed by religious diversity through superficial preferences for the various national churches:

> Carelesse Phrygius doth abhorre
> All, because all cannot be good, as one
> Knowing some women whores, dares marry none.
> Graccus loves all as one, and thinkes that so
> As women do in divers countries goe
> In divers habits, yet are still one kinde;
> So doth, so is Religion; and this blind-
> nesse too much light breeds. . . . (lines 62-69)

Insofar as Graccus and Phrygius have genuine reasons for their views, they approach what Donne will reveal as the proper stance. Yet they reason themselves into opposite extremes. Phrygius is spiritually deficient in joining "none" while Graccus is excessive in regarding "all" sects as valid.[14] Donne deepens his attack, moreover, by suggesting that both figures actually combine rather than avoid opposite extremes.

Phrygius is "carelesse" primarily in the sense of "heedless" or "reckless." He responds to the diversity of churches and the evident impurity of some with a rash decision to have "none."[15] His "abhorre[nce]" implies dread as much as hatred, however, and he is not only rash but also cowardly in giving up the search for "true religion" out of excessive fear. Donne's comparison of Phrygius to one who "dares marry none" indeed makes him a "desperate coward" like those who "dare" to neglect religion in the first verse paragraph or those who "dare dye" in Donne's paradox concerning suicides: he rashly denies himself the possibility of finding salvation within a true church because he is overly afraid of the possibility of being damned by the choice of a false one.

The philosophical resonance of the epithet "carelesse" reveals the self-defeating nature of Phrygius's stance. Richard Strier has suggested that "careless" evokes *ataraxia* or tranquillity, the ancient philosophical ideal of being without care. Though Phrygius is too fearful actually to *be* "carelesse" in this sense, he clearly *seeks* personal tranquillity by avoiding religious commitment. *Ataraxia* was the goal of the major Hellenistic philosophical sects, Stoicism, Skepticism, and Epicureanism, all of which advocated ways of detaching oneself from the world and thereby gaining tranquility. We have seen Donne eschew Stoic calm at the very opening of the verse, and the satiric portrait of Phrygius completes the poet's rejection of the ancient escapist ideal. Phrygius represents both a kind of Skepticism and a kind of Epicureanism, which the erotic analogy links as parallel and equally vain attempts to attain tranquillity by suppressing the desire for knowledge, whether cognitive or erotic. Responding to the epistemological uncertainty caused by the diversity of philosophical sects, the ancient Skeptics sought tranquillity by eschewing all doctrines; Phrygius responds to the diversity of religious sects by avoiding all churches. Epicureans sought tranquillity by avoiding pain and pleasures that could cause pain, such as erotic love; they consequently did not marry.[16] Donne's erotic analogy suggests that like the Epicureans, Phrygius seeks to avert possible pain by refusing to marry a (spiritual) mistress.[17]

Donne's Graccus, by contrast, is described as a religious libertine: loving all sects, like all women, equally much and therefore equally little. Like Phrygius, he is both excessive and deficient: by "too much light," by seeking to be too enlightened or by blithely accepting the supposed "light" of all denominations, Graccus falls into "blindness," the inability to distinguish the light of "true religion." Since "breeds" activates the latent sense of "light" as "wanton, unchaste" (*OED* 14b), the claim that "too much light breeds" Graccus's "blindness" recalls the Renaissance commonplace that sexual excess causes blindness and thereby suggests a physical analogue for Graccus's combination of spiritual excess and defect.[18]

Like Phrygius, though in an opposite way, Graccus avoids difficult but necessary choices. By accepting all religious sects as valid on the grounds that, like women, they are still "one kinde" despite their "divers habits" (line 67), he avoids the superficial choices of the first three figures but evades the problem recognized by Phrygius, who "knows some women are whores." Donne bids his reader seek "*true* religion," not religion as such; and to be *a* "Religion" is not necessarily to be a "true religion" any more than to be a woman is necessarily to be an honest one. In "The Indifferent," one of Donne's libertine lyrics, the speaker claims he can love any kind of woman as long as "she be not true" and not "binde" him to reciprocal fidelity (lines 9, 16). As a secular Graccus, Donne realizes that erotic license is irreconcilable with norms of truth and troth.

A pun reenforces Graccus's self-serving suppression of crucial distinctions. Aristotle defines virtues and vices as *hexeis*, normally translated into Latin as *habitus* and in Renaissance English as "habits." In several poems Donne uses "habit" and its cognates in the Aristotelian sense (see "To Sir Henry Wotton" [Here's no more newes], line 3; "To Sir Henry Wotton" [Sir, more then kisses], lines 25-26; and "Oh, to vex me, contraryes meet," line 3.) In the elegy "On his Mistris," Donne puns on the two senses of "habit" when he begs his beloved not to follow him as a disguised page and not to "change / Thy bodies habite, nor mindes" (lines 27-28); "habite" applies to mind as well as body, constitutive ethical dispositions as well as superficial appearances. The similar pun on "habits" in "Satire III" undercuts Graccus's love of all churches: while the dressing of a church or woman may not matter, their "divers habits" in the sense of divergent dispositions define them as good or bad.

The names Phrygius and Graccus recall "effeminate" men attacked in Juvenal's *Satire* 2: 82-116. By evoking Juvenal's practitioners of the "Phrygian mode" (self-castration) and transvestite-bride Gracchus, Donne suggests that Phrygius's spiritual cowardice makes him "less" than a man and that Graccus's spiritual libertinism is "womanish" in its labile excess.[19] Hence he advocates seeking a mean position between Phrygian abstention and Graccus's promiscuity. His claim that "thou / Of force must one, and forc'd but one allow" (lines 69-70) demands that his reader seek a mean between Phrygius's and Graccus's numerical extremes of "none" and "all." The seeker must find the one true religion rather than remaining content with none, like Phrygius, and even under the force of persecution, he must not concede the validity of more than one religion, like Graccus.

3

Yet the poet promotes a mean position based, like Phrygian irreligion, on ancient Skepticism.[20] Donne's exhortation "Be busie to seeke her, beleeve mee this, / Hee's not of none, nor worst, that seekes the best" (lines 74-75), his command that one "doubt wisely" (line 77), and his claim that "To stand inquiring right, is not to stray" (line 78) all use the vocabulary of Pyrrhonist Skepticism. Pyrrhonists were variously called "inquirers" (skeptikoi) and "seekers" (zêtêtikoi) because they professed to search ceaselessly for the truth and "doubters" (aporêtikoi) because they doubted all dogmatic claims (Sextus Empiricus 2 [*Outlines of Pyrrhonism* 1.3-4]; see also Laertius 675 [9.70]). There is a crucial difference, however, between Phrygius's skeptical position and the one that Donne recommends.

The relationship between two major elements in Pyrrhonism has puzzled commentators. For Sextus Empiricus, *ataraxia* is the Skeptic's goal, and his means to that end is *epochê*, the suspension of all opinions. Sextus also, however, presents the Skeptic as continuing to investigate both sides of any issue on the grounds that future resolution of the issue is theoretically possible. Myles Burnyeat observes that the Pyrrhonist treats as "an open question whether *p* or not-*p* is the case" without "actually *wondering* whether *p* or not-*p* is the case, for that might induce anxiety" (139; compare Lloyd 168). The Pyrrhonist must be in some sense satisfied that no answers are forthcoming in order for his inquiring thoughts to come to a state of rest. Burnyeat argues that the Pyrrhonist in fact holds an impossible position, for insofar as he is satisfied that he will gain no answers he has in fact become a negative dogmatist like the Academic Skeptic, who professed to know that one could know nothing (139-41). Donne avoids this dilemma by splitting the Skeptical position: on the one hand is the negative example of Phrygius, who in quest of *ataraxia* holds himself back from any religious dogma in a state of *epochê* that is the practical equivalent of negative dogmatism; on the other hand is the position recommended by the poet, continued inquiry on the grounds that thus far there is no proof of any given church's validity. Donne's portrait of fearful Phrygius suggests, however, that *epochê* cannot actually confer *ataraxia*. By exhorting himself and his reader to "Be busie to seeke" the true church, furthermore, Donne signifies his rejection of the very goal of classical tranquillity, which was associated with *otium* rather than *negotium*, ease rather than business. By proceeding to compare the inquiring mind's "indeavours" to "bodies paines" (lines 86-87), Donne differentiates the rigor of his skeptical inquiry not only from Phrygius's Epicurean avoidance of pain but also from a Skepticism compatible with such Epicureanism. Donne further underscores the distinction in gender terms, for his exhortation that the male inquirer struggle hard to "reach" and "winne" the feminine figure of Truth (lines 79-82) sharply opposes his "masculine" urge to Phrygius's "effeminate" dread of the female. Thus Donne sets Phrygius's permanent suspension and desired tranquillity against his own ideal of temporary suspension and vigorous, passionate seeking. His litotes—"Hee's not of none, nor worst, that seekes the best" (line 75)—asserts that to persevere in the skeptical search for the true church is already to belong, in some sense, to the community of true believers. Such a claim reveals how much Donne wishes to avoid Phrygius's spiritual isolation.

Donne thus presents the proper religious stance not only as a quantitative mean between Graccus's "all" and Phrygius's "none" but also as a skeptical mean between the extremes of positive and negative dogmatism: the seeker must neither rashly believe that he has already found the one true church, as the first three satiric figures do, nor rashly despair of

the search, as Phrygius does. Lines 76-79 recapitulate the satire's move-
ment from a triad consisting of the major churches' positions to one
consisting of two extremes and the authentic mean of skeptical inquiry:
"To'adore, or scorne an image, or protest, / May all be bad; doubt wisely;
in strange way / To stand inquiring right, is not to stray; / To sleepe, or
runne wrong, is." Donne's first triad hypothesizes that all the major
churches' views concerning images might be in error: the Catholics'
reverence; the Calvinist and radical Swiss reformers' iconoclasm; and the
intermediate positions of the Lutherans, the original "protestants," and of
the Elizabethan church, which self-consciously sought a "middle way"
concerning images (see Eire 54-105; Phillips 111-39). Though such a possi-
bility is hard to reconcile with the poet's firm conviction that one can
eventually find the true church, Donne stresses that he is not advocating
the easy adoption of a state-authorized compromise but a more funda-
mental conception of the mean between dogmas. The exhortation to
"stand inquiring right" appropriately recalls the Christian of the first
verse paragraph who adheres to the mean by "stand[ing] / Sentinell,"
and Donne contrasts his skeptical mean with the two extremes of "sleep,"
that is, shirking the quest for true religion, and "runn[ing] wrong," that is,
recklessly embracing a particular church or all churches. While Donne's
warning against spiritual sleep echoes Pauline admonitions like "Let us
not sleep, as do others" (1 Thessalonians 5:6), his warning against run-
ning recalls classical, patristic, and humanist attacks on rash behavior
that misses the mean. Horace claims that fools who seek to avoid a vice
"run" ("currunt") into its opposite (*Satire* 1.2.24); Augustine criticizes
ignorant men who wrongly "run" ("perverse . . . currant") from one
extreme to the other (*De genesi ad litteram* 9.8); Boethius attacks a theolo-
gian who "has run" ("cucurrit") from one heretical extreme to its equally
heretical contrary (*Liber de persona* 5); and the Tudor translator of Erasmus'
Adages notes the human "tendency to runne to[o] farre" in redressing
abuses of the church (Taverner sig. ciiiv).[21] Donne's descriptions of
"runn[ing] away" from spiritual perfection in *Pseudo-Martyr* and of "run-
ning to death unimportun'd" in his paradoxes similarly associate run-
ning with foolish extremism.

Donne's conception of a skeptical mean is not wholly unique. Sextus
Empiricus provided a lead in contrasting three schools of philosophy,
dogmatists who claim to have discovered the truth, Academic Skeptics
who assert that it cannot be apprehended, and Pyrrhonists, who go on
inquiring (1-2 [*Outlines of Pyrrhonism* 1.1-4]). While Sextus does not relate
the middle position of the ostensibly open-minded Pyrrhonists to the

mean, Renaissance thinkers both before and after Donne did make the connection. Montaigne, the most famous Renaissance Pyrrhonist, conflates Sextus Empiricus's contrast with the Aristotelian scheme: castigating dogmatists who attribute to the human mind "a capacity for all things" and Academics who argue that that it is "capable of nothing," Montaigne claims that both kinds of philosophers espouse "extreme[s]" (792). In the *Novum Organum* Francis Bacon similarly presents his form of skeptical scientific inquiry as the mean between dogmatic and Academic "extremes," the "presumption of pronouncing on everything, and the despair of comprehending anything" (4:39; see Scodel, "Mediocrities" 115-18). Like Montaigne and Bacon, Donne associates skeptical inquiry with a mean between all and nothing and between the rash belief that one has the truth and despair that one can ever attain it. He differs sharply from both, however, in applying the skeptical mean to the investigation of religion. Montaigne mixed a Pyrrhonist attitude toward reason with a fideistic acquiescence in Catholic dogma (Penelhum in Burnyeat 296-97). Bacon excluded matters of faith from his inquiry (see, for example, Bacon 1:175-76). Donne, by contrast, collapses the distinction between philosophy and faith by setting both "true religion" and "Truth" itself as the goal of his simultaneously philosophical and religious inquirer.

4

Donne ends "Satire III" explaining how to "Keepe the'truth which thou hast found" (line 89), whatever it might turn out to be. Yet Donne's directives continue to employ the notion of a skeptical mean. Holding fast to the truth requires a distancing from opposite extremes similar to the skeptical stance of "inquiring right." The Pyrrhonist suspends belief by opposing every dogmatic argument with a contradictory argument of apparently "equal strength," pitting arguments from authority against one another.[22] Donne adapts this skeptical method to argue that the individual must not relinquish true religion by accepting either of the extreme "contraries" espoused by opposing (pseudo-)authorities: "Is not this excuse for mere contraries, / Equally strong? cannot both sides say so?" (lines 98-99).[23]

Donne denies that men "stand / In so ill case" (lines 89-90) that temporal rulers can dictate the religious choices of their subjects. There is no legitimate authority besides God, he argues, in spiritual matters; rulers deserve obedience only in temporal affairs. Commentators have noted that Donne here draws upon a strand within Protestant thought contesting state control over religious beliefs (Allen 103; Milgate 147; Strier 307-8). It has not been noticed, however, that Donne follows this Protestant strand by adapting the Aristotelian mean to the issue of proper obedience. In 1523 Luther argued that temporal authorities, who must acquire neither "too little" nor "too much" power, had no jurisdiction over religious faith (104); in 1556 John Ponet claimed that subjects, who must eschew "to muche" as well as "to littel" obedience, were answerable to God rather than temporal rulers in religious matters (C8r, D2v-D3r; compare Goodman 148-49). While Donne's first verse paragraph exhorts men to "know" the traditional enemies of mankind (line 33), the end of his poem exhorts men to "know" the limits of earthly power: "That thou mayest rightly'obey power, her bounds know; / Those past, her nature, 'and name is chang'd; to be / Then humble to her is idolatrie" (lines 100-102). Returning to the theory of the mean in order to challenge state control over men's consciences, Donne recalls the famous description of the mean in Horace's first satire, which notes "fixed bounds" (certi fines) beyond which one must not stray (lines 106-7). Donne's claim that exceeding "bounds" changes the "nature and name" closely resembles the assertion in one of his paradoxes that "exces . . . changes the natures and the names" of things (*Paradoxes* 2). Just as near the beginning of "Satire III" Donne suggests that excess changes courage into recklessness, so near the poem's end he claims that excess turns virtuous obedience into sinful idolatry. Donne does not spell out the objective change in the nature of "power" when rulers exceed their "bounds"—the transformation of legitimate authority into tyranny—but instead focuses on the subjective consequences for the ruled—the change in the "nature and name" of a subject's obedience. He thereby underscores that for a subject to recognize the "bounds" of power entails his knowing the proper mean of response.

Donne ends with a powerful image of the dangers that subjects incur when they exceed their proper obedience:

> As streames are, Power is; those blest flowers that dwell
> At the rough streames calme head, thrive and do well,
> But having left their roots, and themselves given
> To the streames tyrannous rage, alas are driven
> Through mills, and rockes, and woods, and at last, almost
> Consum'd in going, in the sea are lost:
> So perish Soules, which more chuse mens unjust
> Power from God claym'd, then God himselfe to trust. (lines 103-10)

The poem returns to rash and cowardly suicides, souls that recklessly seek destruction because they fear to "stand" in their appointed station. The image of flowers and the stream is complex. The flowers who "perish" by giving themselves to the "streames tyrannous rage" represent souls who submit to a temporal power that exceeds its legitimate authority by claiming spiritual dominion. The image of a stream's flow suggests that rulers' movement from the proper rule of the "calme head" to the tyrannic excess of the "rough streame" is all too natural in the fallen world.[24] Yet Donne's strikingly unnatural image of flowers, which normally have no power of self-motion, willfully leaving "their roots" suggests that persons who submit to tyranny perversely abandon and exceed their natural human capacities and dispositions. The initial positive image of the "blest flowers" that "thrive" at the "calme head" implies that human beings can be nurtured rather than destroyed by worldly authority simply by remaining in their natural place, aware of the proper minimum and maximum "bounds" of their obedience. Donne thus envisions both the objective inevitability of tyrannic excess and the subjective freedom of individuals, who can flourish by recognizing only legitimate rule or (conversely) can destroy themselves by accepting tyranny. Trusting in God as their spiritual master, and consequently aware of the limits on the allegiance they owe temporal powers, the blessed thrive. Instead of using the concept of the mean to defend the church and state of the Elizabethan settlement, Donne uses it to promote individuals' independence, but not isolation, as they seek and preserve the truth. In such an active, masculinist poem, it is striking that Donne ends with the passive and—according to Renaissance connotations of gender—feminized image of souls as flowers. He clearly wishes to persuade himself and his readers that after successfully completing the painful struggle for truth, it will be easy for individuals to maintain the truth, the mean, and their own "blest" souls.

Jonathan Dollimore has argued that the most important Renaissance thinkers, far from promoting individualism, "decentered" man. Adducing Donne as an example of the "corrosive skepticism" of a period that undermined conceptions of the free individual as much as cultural institutions, Dollimore cites "Oh, to vex me, contraryes meet" and other texts to exemplify Donne's sense of the "fragmentation of the self" (179-81). The portrayal of suicidal extremism in "Satire III" certainly reveals this sense of fragmentation, but the satire also uses skepticism re-constructively to imagine a self finally saved from self-destructive extremes. The poem's skepticism is not "corrosive" because it is limited. While Donne questions the validity of any given ecclesiastical and political formation, he does not doubt God's ultimate benevolence and man's eventual ability to find his proper place in the world. Dependent on God as he seeks a beneficent relationship to the world, the free, inquiring self that Donne invokes and thereby seeks to create is neither Dollimore's "decentered" subject nor the fully autonomous person imagined by the Enlightenment but rather a distinctive early modern *tertium quid.*

5

Donne eventually chose, of course, to join the church of England, and as a minister he not only celebrated it as the proper mean between Catholicism and radical Protestantism but also came to deny his own satire's rejection of the state's right to control religious belief.[25] Nevertheless, in his later religious writings Donne continues to adapt and transform both skepticism and the mean in order to sustain the individual's quest for religious truth. Both imaginative rhetoric and strained logic reveal his determination to curb rather than wholly renounce the ideal of the independent seeker of "true religion" in "Satire III."[26]

After becoming a communicant of the national church, Donne's attitude toward his earlier period of indecision regarding the "true religion" has its ambiguities. His claim in *Pseudo-Martyr* that he used "no inordinate hast[e], nor precipitation" in joining a church suggests unequivocal retrospective approval of his stance as a cautious "seeker" in "Satire III" (*Pseudo-Martyr* sig. B2r). A sermon of 1624 seems to recall the exhortation to "stand inquiring right" in "Satire III" when it distinguishes between sinful falling and innocent standing: "a man may stand upon the way, and inquire, and then proceed in the way, if he be right, or to the [sc. right] way, if he be wrong" (*Sermons* 6:69). Yet by this date Donne was ambivalent about such a "stand," noting that "too apt" a propensity "to conceive scruples" often "stops, and retards" the finding of the proper path (*Sermons* 6: 69). Donne thus suggests the difficulty of determining whether such a "stand" is prudent moderation that prevents one from religious error, or excessive caution that retards religious progress. Did his own avoidance of "inordinate hast[e]" in joining the church remain a prudent mean in his own mind or had it become for him an example of the opposite extreme of inordinate slowness? It is impossible to say with certainty.

Yet Donne the minister continually sought to distinguish the true Christian from the easy-going conformist and to require from the sincere conformist some of the skeptical seeker's commitment to "inquiring right."

In a 1617 sermon, which begins by noting that the Biblical authors use "phrases" and "allusions" from their former professions (*Sermons* 1: 236), the preacher borrows phrases from the verse satirist in describing how to seek and find Christ:

> But where are we likeliest to find him? . . . Thou must not so think him in heaven, as that thou canst not have immediate accesse to him without intercession of others, nor so beyond Sea, as to seek him in a forrein Church, either where the Church is but an Antiquaries Cabinet, full of rags and fragments of antiquity, but nothing fit for that use for which it was first made, or where it is so new a built house with bare walls, that it is yet unfurnished of such Ceremonies as should make it comly and reverend; Christ is at home with thee, he is at home within thee, and there is the neerest way to find him. (*Sermons* 1:246)

The passage echoes "Satire III"—"Seeke true religion. O where?" (line 43)—with its two satiric extremes of Mirrheus, who loves Catholic "ragges," and Crants, who loves a reformed church that is "yong" and "unhansome."[27] But in place of the satiric portrait of Graius, who complacently and timorously "stays still at home," Donne proclaims to his audience that "Christ is at home with thee, he is at home within thee, and there is the neerest way to find him." The passage suggests how markedly the true believer's being in the church differs from Graius's conformism: while Graius simply relies on the authorities "at home" rather than searching for true religion, Donne asserts that Christ is "at home" in such a way that the members of the church must still seek in order to find him. While Graius lost all integrity by simply acquiescing in doctrine "at home," in the national church, the sermon's repetition of the phrase gives it a crucial double sense that encompasses the believer's own "private" conscience as well as the national church.[28] Steeping himself in the emphasis of his favorite church father, St. Augustine, on God's presence in the human soul in the years following "Satire III," Donne now stresses that the believer must "seek" for Christ not only in the church's authority but also within: while the claim that Christ is "with thee" presumably refers to his presence in the church, the claim that Christ is "within thee" emphatically reminds the audience of his presence—waiting to be found—within the individual believer.[29]

Donne begins the *Essays in Divinity*, his allegorizing commentary on sections of Genesis and Exodus that he probably completed in late 1614 shortly before his ordination (Bald 298-300), with a defense of individual religious inquiry. Associating proper religious "Studiousnesse" with *"Temperance,"* he distinguishes it from two vicious extremes—"a groveling, frozen, and stupid Humility, as should quench the activity of our understanding, or make us neglect the Search," on the one hand, and "curiosity" that "transgresses" the "'bounds'" of human knowledge, on the other (*Essays* 5). Yet because Donne wishes to justify a desire for ever increasing religious knowledge, the condemnation of deficiency, the "stupid Humility" of a Graius, is lengthier and more impassioned than the attack on excess. The minsterial Donne urged his lay audience to engage in a similar search but shifted the emphasis, insisting that the layperson avoid excess by deferring to ecclesiastical authority. While in the *Essays* Donne lauded Daniel as a *"Vir Desideriorum"* (Daniel 10:12) and cited St. Paul's exhortation to "Desire . . . better gifts" (1 Corinthians 12: 31) (5-6), in a 1621 sermon Donne adduces the same Scriptural passages but replaces the earlier argument that one should desire ever more religious knowledge with a warning that the laity content themselves with knowing less than their ministers:

> To beleeve implicitly as the Church beleeves, and know nothing, is not enough; know thy foundations . . . [but] so much knowledge is not required in thee in those things, as in them, whose profession it is to teach them; be content to leave a roome stil for the Apostle[']s *Aemulamini charismata meliora*, desire better gifts; and ever think it a title of dignity which the Angel gave *Daniel*, to be *Vir desideriorum*; To have still some farther object of thy desires. Do not thinke thou wantest all, because thou hast not all. . . . For there is an over-fulnesse of knowledge, which forces a vomit. (*Sermons* 3:239-40)

As in the *Essays*, Donne suggests a mean between the defect of unthinking faith and the excess of superfluous curiosity,[30] yet the preacher offers a paradoxical argument for limiting the quest for knowledge. He advises his audience to retain "some farther object of . . . desires," that is, to desire that their desires not be wholly fulfilled—so that they can humbly preserve their desires as desires! The passage's logical contortions reveal the conflict between Donne's deep, long-standing commitment to religious search and his commitment to ecclesiastical authority as a cleric of the national church. Donne simultaneously glorifies and attempts to control the individual's religious search—moderating not only his audience's desire to seek and know but also (retroactively) the desires of Donne the free-thinking satirist and the (lay) theological speculator.

In a sermon addressed to Charles I in April 1627, Donne again tempers the ideal of the skeptical inquirer that "Satire III" celebrates. He represents the church as a mean between Catholic denial of the freedom to read and interpret the Bible for oneself and more radical Protestant assertions of such freedom. Unlike Roman Catholics, Donne declares, his hearers have "Christian liberty" to read the Scriptures "at home," but "at Church" are "taught to use that liberty modestly, to establish their faith upon places of Scripture that are plain, and to suspend their judgement upon obscurer places, till they may, by due meanes, preaching or conference, receive farther satisfaction therein, from them, who are thereunto authorized by God in his Church" (*Sermons* 7:401). Donne once more emphasizes both the private "home" and the national church, but he firmly subordinates the first to the second.[31] He applies the language of Pyrrhonist skepticism, in which he had articulated the individual's religious inquiry in "Satire III," to urge the individual's deference to authority: like the Pyrrhonist with his *epoché*, believers "at home" may "suspend their judgement," but only until the religious authorities "at Church" teach the truth. Donne the minister thus suggests a mean position far less radical than that of the satirist: while the latter trusted wholly in individual judgment and completely rejected arguments from authority, the former proclaims that the individual believer must neither wholly rely upon his judgment nor wholly abdicate it (as Graius does) but rather must be ready to "receive . . . satisfaction" from those in authority, that is, be open to persuasion by the authorities' rational arguments.[32]

The 1627 sermon not only describes Donne's sense of the lay believer's complex relation to ecclesiastical authority but also embodies his conception of the conscientious minister's own complex relation to ecclesiastical superiors. The sermon was addressed to the supreme head of the church, Charles I, but Donne's emphasis on both the layman's reading of Scripture and the preaching of the Word suggests Donne's distance from the Arminian or Laudian faction supported by the king, which promoted ecclesiastical authority and ritual mystery at the expense of both the layman's faith and of preaching.[33] The king and William Laud, then bishop of London, reprimanded Donne for his sermon, at least partly for seeming to gravitate against the Arminian position and toward the Calvinist views of the out-of-favor Archbishop of Canterbury George Abbot. While Donne denied following Abbot, his sermon clearly adapts the notion of the mean to articulate an anti-Arminian view of the proper direction of the church. In one section Donne chastises fellow preachers for their invidious centrism: "All Divines that have their *soules* and *con-*

sciences, so disposed, *as their Libraries may bee*, (At that end stand Papists, and at that end Protestants, and he comes in the middle, as neare one as the other) . . . have a brackish taste . . . in comming so neare the Sea of Rome" (*Sermons* 7: 398). Here Donne rejects as a pernicious "middle" position the attempt to maintain an even course between Catholics and Protestants, and in so doing he suggests that the Laudian faction has made a mockery of the ideal of religious moderation. In the 1620s the Laudians attempted to modify the church's long-standing and virulent "antipopery." In 1624 Richard Montagu argued in print that the Roman church was a true though unsound church and rejected as unproven the long-standing Protestant identification of the pope with the Antichrist. While he and his fellow Arminians insisted that they vehemently opposed Catholic superstitions, their outraged Calvinist opponents attacked their milder attitude toward Rome as proof of their Catholic leanings, accusing the Arminians of being "papists" or of trying to straddle the fence between Catholicism and sound Protestantism (Hill 1-41; Tyacke 55-56, 149, and *passim*.). In 1626 attacks on Montagu, Daniel Featley accused him of "halt[ing] downright between two religions" (i.e., Roman Catholicism and Protestantism) (50), and Francis Rous similarly described Montagu's position as a "double-faced thing that looks to two Religions at once" (105-6). That same year, Charles I issued a proclamation, written with Laud's aid, banning further controversy concerning Montagu's opinions and thus repressing the growing opposition to the Arminian leanings of the church (Tyacke 77). Despite the royal proclamation, Donne's 1627 sermon suggests his own anti-Arminianism by attacking a position he, like Featley and Rous, describes as a pernicious "middle" between Catholicism and Protestantism.[34] Throughout his sermons Donne portrays a staunchly Protestant Church of England situated between the extremes of Catholics and *radical* Protestants, whom Donne variously dubbed *"Puritans"* (*Sermons* 1: 186-87, 219), *"Separatist[s]"* (*Sermons* 5:150), or *"Schmisatike[s]"* (*Sermons* 8:135). The Arminian churchman who "comes in the middle" travesties Donne's favorite image of the religious mean between Catholics and radical Protestants, one of the "middle road" or *via media* between left and right deviations that he and his contemporaries derived from Augustine.[35] Donne's 1627 Christmas sermon suggests how to apply the image correctly when it describes the "moderate, and middle wayes" of "the Reformed Church" in which "we should . . . walk," avoiding the "left hand" of Catholic "superstition, and Idolatry" as well as the right hand of "inordinate [i.e., "Puritan"] zeal" (*Sermons* 8: 135-6).[36]

Later in the April 1627 sermon, however, Donne counters the pernicious mean of the Arminian with a strikingly new image of the church's proper middle path. Here he recalls the skeptic inquirer of "Satire III," who avoids the vicious extremes of positive and negative dogmatism as he "seekes the best." The church figures both as a normative mean between extremes and a provisional, open-ended midpoint on the way to the best position:

> From extream to extream, from east to west, the *Angels* themselves cannot come, but by passing the middle way between; from that extream impurity, in which Antichrist had damped the Church of God, to that intemerate purity, in which Christ had constituted his Church, the most Angelicall Reformers cannot come, but by touching, yea, and stepping upon some things, in the way. He that is come to any end, remembers when he was not at the middle way; he was not there as soon as he set out. It is the posture reserved for heaven, to sit down, at the right hand of God; Here our consolation is, that God reaches out his hand to the receiving of those who come towards him; And nearer to him, and to the institutions of his Christ, can no Church, no not of the *Reformation*, be said to have come, then ours does. (*Sermons* 7: 409)

Donne contrasts the true path of the church with that of temporizing Arminian ministers: far from being "too near" the Catholic church, Donne's church is "nearer," so he declares, to Christ's original institution than any other "Reformation" church. Donne's reference to the "Antichrist" as the corrupter of the church strongly suggests the traditional identification, contested by the Arminians, of the Pope with the Antichrist, and Donne's reference to the Antichrist's "damp[ing]" of the church sardonically recalls his earlier pun on "the Sea of Rome." David Norbrook has argued for construing Donne's admission of the church's imperfections and of its "moving towards a state of greater purity" as his declaration of sympathy with the "Puritan" desire for further reformation of the church in the face of the Arminians' movement in the opposite direction (23-24). Yet the positive "middle way" in the sermon is no unambiguous endorsement of a "Puritan" urge for greater "purity." While only an intermediate stage in the journey *from* a bad "extream" to a supremely virtuous "extream," this "middle way" nevertheless retains, by dint of Donne's rhetoric, the traditional normative resonance of the "middle way" as the virtuous path *between* two vicious extremes. Donne has in effect boldly conflated two different aspects of the Augustinian conceptualization of the proper Christian "way"—as the necessarily imperfect, incomplete journey to Christ and as the via media between aberrant extremes. Augustine admonishes the Christian *viatores* to be discontented with their current state so that they can continue onward to perfection; mixes praise and exhortation by reminding them that they have already completed part—but only part— of the journey; urges that only the humble and charitable can walk aright; consoles them with the thought that it is better to limp on the right path than to run beyond it; and assures them that Christ offers them his guiding "hand."[37] Donne's church behaves like Augustine's Christian *viator*, registering both how far she has come and how much still remains ahead, humbly trudging onward to receive the helping "hand" of God. Thus the church's arrival at the "middle way" on the path to perfection may be reconceived, on an Augustinian calculus, as evidence that she is keeping to the normative "middle way." Donne's observation that even angels must pass through the "middle way" implies that those who seek the "intemerate perfection" of Christ more aggressively or quickly than the English church in fact deviate from the normative "middle way" of humility into proud excess by foolishly attempting to outdo the angels instead of behaving with proper moderation as "Angelicall" human beings guided by God.[38]

Donne's reliance on paronomasia reveals both the creative daring and vulnerable logic of his depiction of the church's "middle way" as both imperfect and normative. The analogy to angelic motion used by Donne to underscore that the church should proceed with humble moderation is based on nothing stronger than a witty pun. Scholastic angelology licenses Donne's claim that the angels must go "from extream to extream . . . by passing the middle way between." Describing angelic locomotion, Aquinas argues that an angel who moves "from one extreme to another" ("de uno extremo . . . ad alium") necessarily passes "by the mean" ("per medium") (*Summa Theologiae* 1-1, q. 53, a. 2); here the terms "extreme" and "mean" refer to spatial locations and have nothing to do with ethical "extremes" and "means." Donne, however, plays on the ethical resonances of Scholastic vocabulary to tease from angels' mode of travel an ethical lesson concerning the "middle way" between "extremes." Similarly, the phrase "intemerate purity" strengthens the call for humble moderation by evoking, as a quasi-pun, "intemperate purity," which suggests both that Christ's "extream" purity differs from human virtues that reside in the mean in not being "temperate" in the sense of "tempered" (*OED*, s.v., "temperate," 7), and that, consequently, the attempt fully to attain this "extream" perfection would be proudly "intemperate" for mere human beings.

With his unique vision of the church's "middle way," Donne distances himself from both the Arminians and their "Puritan" critics, noting (like the "Puritans") the church's "imperfections" while suggesting that more radical Reformation (as the "Puritans" suggested) risks dangerous extremism.[39] Like the layman who must desire more knowledge but not to have his desires wholly fulfilled, lest he become over-full, the church must desire perfection (as the "Puritans" did) but also humbly recognize that such desires cannot be wholly satisfied. In "Satire III" Donne had proclaimed the need of the individual to search for the "best" church; in the sermon he transfers the search for the "best" church onto the church of England itself, and he thereby defends it as an institution against those individuals who would search beyond it.

The 1627 sermon is not the first instance of Donne's claim that the church of England is normative precisely because it both struggles against its own imperfections while recognizing their inevitability. In a sermon of 1616/1617, Donne urges that one imitate God's "exact purity" so that one may all the "more studiously endeavor the amendment" of "extreme and enormous fouleness and impurity" (*Sermons* 1:185). Yet such imitation must proceed in the awareness that "absolute pureness cannot be attained to *In via*, It is reserved for us *In Patria*" (*Sermons* 1:189). In chastizing both Roman Catholics and schismatics for "their fantasie[s]" of perfection (*Sermons* 1:186), Donne suggests that the members of the English church are on the proper middle path precisely because they are aware of their unavoidable imperfections. In a sermon of 1629, Donne claims that he "wil endeavour to be pure, as my Father in heaven is pure, as far as any Puritan" but goes on to criticize the person who thinks himself already pure and who rejects the national church because he foolishly "imagines a Church that shall be defective in nothing" (*Sermons* 9:166, 169).

In the April 1627 sermon Donne hints that he knows he is being controversial about the church's via media. Annabel Patterson notes Donne's desire to emphasize his "evenhandedness" throughout the sermon (110-11). Donne begins his sermon by noting that a preacher cannot be "over-timorous" nor "over-venturous" in preaching the word: he can neither subtract from nor add to Scripture (*Sermons* 7:394-95). He warns against subjects who "speake evill of Superiours" (*Sermons* 7:408) but notes that kings must beware of flatterers (7:411). He thus suggests that he himself hews to a mean of courage, between cowardice and recklessness, and of benevolent candor, between flattery and detraction.[40] This personal application of the mean captures some of the independent spirit of Donne's early satire: Donne invokes the mean not simply to celebrate authority but also, as in "Satire III," to establish the proper relation of the individual to it.

Patterson plausibly argues that Charles I disliked the sermon and reprimanded Donne primarily because of the sermon's two allusions to the Catholicism of Charles I's wife, Henrietta Maria. The most explicit occurs within a passage concerning the proper attitude toward English "Church-government" that introduces Donne's description of the English church as the imperfect but normative "middle way":

> The Church is the spouse of Christ: Noble husbands do not easily admit defamations of their wives. Very religious Kings may have had wives, that may have retained some tincture, some impressions of errour, which they may have sucked in their infancy, from another Church, and yet would be loth, those wives should be publikely traduced to be Heretiques, or passionately proclaimed to be Idolaters for all that. A Church may lacke something of exact perfection, and yet that Church should not be said to be a supporter of Antichrist, or a limme of the beast, or a thirster after the cup of *Babylon*, for all that. (*Sermons* 7:409)

This passage, Patterson notes, represents Donne's attempt to forge a compromise between Charles I and his "Puritan" critics, who violently attacked the Catholic queen as a menace to the church and as a symbol of the "popish" tendencies of Charles I and his Laudian church hierarchy (110).[41] By declaring that Henrietta Maria should not be "publicly traduced" or "passionately" denounced as a heretic while himself gently noting the queen's "errour," Donne attempts to articulate the mean of tactful honesty, between flattery and defamation.[42] This act of mediation is closely linked in Donne's mind, however, to the church as via media, for Donne inserts his allusion to the queen's Catholicism as a digression within his discussion of the proper attitude toward the English church. By defending the church but conceding it may have flaws, Donne suggests that one should neither defame the church (as more radical Protestants have done), nor flatter it by denying all imperfections (as the king would wish?). Donne reveals his self-conscious moderation by forging a rhetorical parallel between his views of the proper attitude toward the English church, on the one hand, and of the proper attitude toward Henrietta Maria's Catholicism, on the other. Transforming the Arminian argument that one should not identify Catholicism with the church of Antichrist by applying it to the defense of the English church, Donne distances himself from the Arminians (even as he attacks his church's more radical Protestant critics). By also defending Henrietta Maria, a Catholic, from violent defamation, he suggests his own personal mean of integrity, defending an individual Catholic, the queen, as the legitimate though flawed consort of the legitimate sovereign but rejecting and "correcting" the Arminians' defense of the Catholic church itself.[43]

Thus the defense of the church of England as the via media in the 1627 sermon is closely bound up with Donne's own claims to adhere to a mean that allows him a certain critical distance from the very church he represents and upholds. The link between Donne's depiction of the national church and his assertions of both allegiance and independence is strengthened by an echo in the sermon of a personal prayer from Donne's *Essays in Divinity*. As he contemplated criticizing aspects of his monarch and his church, Donne had good reason to think back to this prayer, which begins with the request that he be enabled to balance his spiritual and earthly duties:

> let my Soul's Creatures have that temper and Harmony, that they be not by a misdevout consideration of the next life, stupidly and trecherously negligent of the offices and duties which thou enjoynest amongst us in this life; nor so anxious in these, that the other (which is our better business, though this also must be attended) be the less endeavoured.

He immediately proceeds to associate this proper "temper" of earthly and spiritual concerns with the "mean way":

> Thou hast, O God, denyed even to Angells, the ability of arriving from one Extreme to another, without passing the mean way between. Nor can we pass from the prison of our Mothers womb, to thy palace, but we must walk (in that pace whereto thou hast enabled us) through the street of this life' . . . let me . . . so esteem opinion, that I despise not others thoughts of me, since most men are such, as most men think they be: nor so reverence it, that I make it alwayes the rule of my Actions. (*Essays* 37-38)

The "mean way" is a temporary path from "prison" to "palace," from bad to good, but to "walk" in this "mean way" at the "pace" God has determined is the proper behavior of man, a simultaneously earthly and spiritual creature. "Walking" in the "mean way" therefore has the normative status of the Aristotelian ethical mean and the Augustinian via media. In 1627 Donne's sense of his mission as a preacher, with obligations to God's word but also to the earthly head of his church, prompted him to recall this prayer, with its sense of the inextricability of the "middle way" from the balancing of one's spiritual goals with one's earthly state, which must be neither over- nor under-valued.

The professedly moderate movement from bad to good that Donne wishes for himself and his church respectively in the *Essays* and in the 1627 sermon recall the seeker's cautious inquiry in "Satire III" even as they move from that position toward greater deference to the world and its institutions. While in "Satire III" Donne transformed and endowed with intense religious significance both Aristotelian ethics and skeptical epistemology in order to articulate his personal vision of the true religious mean, the religious prose Donne composed after joining the English church draws eclectically and idiosyncratically upon classical, patristic, and Scholastic formulations in order to outline a less radical but still independent vision of the proper religious mean. This later vision allows Donne to embrace the church of England without wholly relinquishing his sense of himself and all sincere believers as questing individuals, "Vir[i] desideriorum" still "seek[ing] the best" even after they had supposedly found it—"at home" in both senses of that phrase.[44]

Notes

[1] On the English church's self-understanding as the mean between Catholicism and radical Protestantism, see George and George 375-418; and Lake, *Anglicans and Puritans?* 17-24, 111-12, and 157-60. George and George mainly treat the Jacobean and Caroline church, while Lake analyzes Elizabethan developments.

[2] I am indebted to the discussions of the young Donne in Bald 19-79; Marotti 3-133.

[3] In a recent discussion of Renaissance individualism, Kerrigan and Braden note Jacob Burckhardt's own awareness of the social determinants of Renaissance selfhood and urge that one attend to the "paradoxes" of the early modern self rather than choose between the binary opposites of pure freedom or total subjection (3-35 and 223, n. 27). Discussing contemporary conceptions of the self, Taylor similarly argues for "situated freedom" as an alternative to the "polarized debates" between those who posit a wholly "disengaged subject" and those who

repudiate the concept of individual freedom altogether (514-15 and *passim*).

⁴ The brief passage in "Satire II" celebrating a mean of country hospitality and attacking the extremes of Bacchanalian excess and monk-like fasts (lines 102-9) escapes rather than confronts the poem's urban universe of hack poets and corrupt lawyers, figures all too close and threatening to the urban satirist. The comic passage in "Satire IV" mocking a fop and a *miles gloriosus* "in the other extreme" (line 220) does not address the real dangers of court life depicted in the satire—its oppressive power, spies, and capacity for contaminating all who encounter it.

⁵ Hester (56) notes the Juvenalian model but argues that Donne follows rather than deviates, as I contend, from Juvenalian norms.

⁶ I agree with Carey that the paradoxes are no mere witticisms but sceptical exercises that freed Donne from conventional views (236). The paradoxes offer the most fruitful parallels to "Satire III."

⁷ For Elizabethan arguments that the passions must be moderated rather than suppressed in Stoic fashion, see Purpus 13-31.

⁸ Donne would have found Aristotle's oxymoronic coinage "thrasudeiloi" rendered literally as "audaces timidi" or "timidaudaces" in Renaissance Latin versions of the *Nicomachean Ethics*; see, for example, the translations of Feliciano (67); and Riccobono (132).

⁹ Donne's collapse of opposite extremes is facilitated by his designation of the rash man (Aristotle's *ho thrasus*) as a "desperate" man. Though "desperate" in Renaissance English often means "reckless" (*OED* II.4), its root meaning of "having lost hope" suggests cowardice. Aristotle argues that cowards are "without hope" (*duselpis, Nicomachean Ethics* 3.7.11). When Donne himself treats desperation in a strictly theological context, he considers it a form of cowardice: see, for example, the letter to Sir Henry Goodyer, composed circa 1612 (Gosse 2:9). "Desperate cowardice" is thus pleonastic as well as oxymoronic.

¹⁰ For an example from classical satire, see Persius 3.107-18; and for a discussion of Renaissance love poets' comparisons of their immoderate emotional states to hot and cold, see Forster 16-17.

¹¹ Donne's image of the Christian soldier's avoiding the suicidal extremes of the "desperate coward" may have been particularly influenced by Erasmus's exhortation in the *Enchiridion* that the *miles Christianus* hew to a middle course ("medius cursus") between presumption and despair (*Opera* 5.6). In an oft-reprinted Tudor translation of the *Enchiridion*, these two dangerous extremes sound close to those collapsed by Donne's "desperate coward": the Christian soldier must "kepe a meane course," neither becoming "rechelesse" nor losing his "courage" (*Enchiridion . . . An English Verrsion* 41).

¹² On the translations of Plato's *phroura* and their influence, see Courcelle;

Powell 247-48. Ficino's Plato translation maintains the ambiguity by rendering *phroura* as "custodia" (*Divini Platonis opera omnia* 37), which can mean either "prison" or "garrison."

[13] Lewis links the Platonic and Spenserian passages to Donne's lines (25-26). Milgate cites John of Salisbury's work, about which Donne composed a paradox, as a source for Donne's lines (142). All the passages were well known.

[14] I agree with Strier's argument that Phrygius and Graccus exemplify more reasonable positions than the first three figures (295-99), but I find Phrygius and Graccus far more flawed than Strier contends. For a striking present-day parallel to Donne's rejection of Phrygius's "none" and Graccus's "all" as extreme responses to the diversity of religious positions, see Rescher's critique of the radical sceptic's "none" and the syncretist's "all" as inadequate responses to the diversity of contemporary philosophical doctrines (241-60).

[15] Donne's "Satire IV" treats the "rough carelessenesse" (line 221) of a braggart soldier as a reckless unconcern for others: "Whose cloak his spurres teare; whom he spits on / He cares not" (222-23). Phrygius has a reckless unconcern for himself.

[16] A textual crux in Diogenes Laertius (10.119), as emended by the great Renaissance scholar Isaac Casaubon and some modern editors, records Epicurus's warning against marriage; see Laertius 782 (text) and 119 (notes). For ancient attacks on the Epicureans' rejection of marriage, see Epictetus 294; Clement of Alexandria 87v; and for discussion of the ancient testimony, see Chilton.

[17] I discuss Donne's further association of Phrygius's spiritual deficiency with an Epicurean avoidance of love by means of a pun on "carelesse" as "loveless" in Scodel, "Medium" 490-1.

[18] For Renaissance assertions that lust and lechery cause blindness, see Elton 111-12. The notion is at least as early as pseudo-Aristotle, *Problems* 4.3. Strier notes the suggestion of promiscuity in Donne's use of "light" but considers it strangely undeveloped.

[19] For an extensive discussion of the significance of these names, see Scodel, "Medium" 492-94. On the traditional association of sexual libertinism with effeminacy, see the opening of Donne's epigram "The Jughler"—"Thou call'st me'effeminat, for I love womens joyes"—and the citations in Scodel, "Medium" 494 n. 53.

[20] Several critics have discussed Pyrrhonism's influence on Donne's thought in general and on "Satire III" in particular: see Bredvold 193-232; Carey 231-60; Strier; and Wiley 120-36. Critics have not explored my concern, however, the relationship between Donne's scepticism and his use of the mean.

[21] See also the claim in the 1606 translation of Pierre Charron's *De la Sagesse* that the mob "runne[s] alwaies one contrary to another" (cited in Patrides 134).

[22] The Greek term is "isostheneia"; Henri Éstienne's standard Renaissance Greek and Latin edition translates it literally as "aequa potentia" (Sextus Empiricus, 3, 18-19, 40 [*Outlines of Pyrrhonism* 1.8, 88-90, 202]).

[23] "Contraries" is the English term for the most extreme form of opposites as defined in Aristotle, *Metaphysics* 10.3.

[24] Overly influenced by the satire's final cuplet, some critics have interpreted the "calme head" of the stream as referring to God rather than to human power that maintains its legitimacy by avoiding excess (e.g., Hester 6971; Strier 310). Donne introduces the image of the stream with an assertion concerning the proper "bounds" of *human* authority. Cf. Donne's declaration in "Satire V" that the "greatest and fairest" ruler, Elizabeth I, is not aware of, and is therefore not responsible for, the excesses of her judicial officers; echoing the image in "Satire III" of properly restrained versus excessive human power, Donne compares the queen to the "calme head" of the turbulent Thames (lines 28-30). For a reading of the final image of "Satire III" that resembles mine, see also Moore 49.

[25] On Donne the minister's celebration of the English church as the mean, see William Mueller 148-63. Donne the minister asserts that the church should use persuasion rather than legal compulsion in proselytizing "where there is nothing in consideration, but Religion merely." The qualification sharply distinguishes the minister's views from those of the satirist, for the preacher defends the anti-popish laws on the grounds that apostasy from the national church is also "treason" (Donne, *Sermons* 7:156-57; 4:135-36, 4:301).

[26] For a learned and sensitive discussion of the continuities in Donne's religious views, see Baker-Smith 404-432. Baker-Smith underemphasizes, however, the changes in Donne's views.

[27] I am indebted to Marla Lunderberg for calling my attention to these echoes of "Satire III."

[28] One may compare "at home" in the second sense to Donne's use of the phrase to evoke Stoic retirement into the self in his epistles to Sir Henry Wotton ("Sir, more then kisses") and to Rowland Woodward ("Like one who'in her third widdowhood"): Donne bids Wotton be his own "home, and in thy selfe dwell" like the snail who "still is at home" (lines 49-50), and advises Woodward to stay "at home" and "to thy selfe be'approv'd" (lines 29, 34). Donne the minister christianizes this sense of being "at home" by associating it with Christ's indwelling presence.

[29] On Donne's debt to the inward turn of Augustinian spirituality, see Baker-Smith 411; and Janel Mueller 30-32. Simpson notes the "remarkable intensity" with which Donne the preacher studied Augustine (5).

[30] See also Donne's discussion of the "extreames" of "Implicite Beliefe" and "Curiosity" and of false "satisfaction" and "restlesse. . . desire" in two undated

sermons (*Sermons* 3: 329-30, 5:276-77). Baker-Smith notes Donne's worries about "excessive passivity" and "excessive self-reliance" (414).

[31] One of Donne's undated sermons similarly warns against simply trusting in one's faith "at home" and neglecting to worship Christ "in his Church" (*Sermons* 5: 276).

[32] In 1623, Donne dwells upon the the duty of preachers to "satisfie" the "reason" of "Implicite . . . ignorant beleevers" who rest in "easinesse in beleeving" (*Sermons* 4: 351). Ministers must convince their congregation with rational argument, and their auditors must be open to such persuasion.

[33] On the rise of the Arminian movement, I am indebted to Tyacke and the modifications of Tyacke in Lake, "Calvinism and the English church, 1570-1635." See also the chapter on "the restraint of preaching in Davies 126-171. Norbrook discusses Donne's emphasis on preaching as an anti-Laudian gesture (24).

[34] See also Joseph Hall's early attack on Laud for striving to remain "betweene" Catholics and Protestants (cited in Tyacke 64); and Abbot's claim that the Arminians espoused a "hotch potch of religion" derived from both Lutherans and "papists" (cited in Lake 53-54).

[35] In his sermons on the Psalms and on the Gospel of John (14:6), Augustine combined the Scriptural images of the righteous "way" with the classical doctrine of the mean to produce the most influential patristic images of the via media: Augustine notes that one must walk in the Christian "via[m] media[m]" without deviating into sins on the left or the right, such as despair or presumption (*Patrologia Latina* 37:1151, 1839 and 38:778). Augustine also frequently uses the image of sailing "in medio" between the extremes of Scylla and Charybdis to describe the orthodox position as opposed to heresies that exceed or fall short of Christian truth; see the texts and discussions in Berrouard 204-5, 226-27, and 471-72. The image of the via media became widespread in the Reformation when the major rival churches, including the English church, promoed themselves as the "middle way" between (variously described) extremes (Bainton 46-50). Donne's treatment of the via media is directly indebted to Augustine, however, whose sermons on the Psalms Donne especially admired (see Simpson 5).

[36] See also Donne's 1625 description of the "way to heaven" as the "straight" path of those who deviate neither to "the left hand" of "Temporizings" (i.e., compromising with Catholicism) nor "the right hand" of "over-vehement zeale" (*Sermons* 7:244) .

[37] I draw upon various discussions of the Christian "via" in Augustine's *Enarrationes in Psalmos* and *Sermones* in *Patrologia Latina* 36:326, 37:1092, 1838-39, and 38:777-78, 926. Donne cites Augustine on the necessary imperfections of the church on earth in an undated sermon (*Sermons* 5:125-26).

[38] In a 1622 sermon, Donne warns that the desire for "heavenly purity" on

earth must be tempered by the awareness that until they are "glorified" in heaven human beings are not "equall" to the angels (*Sermons* 4:301); the 1627 sermon implicitly rebukes those who wish not simply to equal but rather to *outdo* the angels in purity.

[39] In sermons of 1629 and 1630 Donne continues to suggest the need for a middle position between Arminians and "Puritans" when he complains that true "Protestant" behavior is often mischaracterized as either "Papist" or "Puritan" by the rival factions within the church (9:166, 217).

[40] On the mean between flattery and inordinate criticism, see Aristotle, *Nicomachean Ethics* 2.7.13, 46; and the extended discussion in Plutarch's essay, "How to Discerne a Flatterer from a Friend," in Plutarch 105-16. Patterson describes Donne's "uneasy" stance "on the indeterminate edge between cowardice and courage" (111); Donne would have hoped that it was interpreted rather as the difficult stance of courage between cowardice and recklessness.

[41] Patterson expands on the suggestions of the editors of Donne's sermons (7:41-42), and Bald (492). See also Donne's earlier condemnation of a preacher's concerning himself with the disposition of a court, including the ruler's "Wife," rather than with the Gospel message he should deliver (*Sermons* 7: 397).

[42] Patterson interprets Donne to be arguing that the queen was not to be publicly criticized but to be privately disciplined (110). Since Donne makes no explicit mention of private approaches and is himself publicly, however obliquely, noting Henrietta Maria's "errour," I think the distinction is rather between inordinate criticism and well-meaning candor (whether public or private).

[43] Donne's juxtaposition of his defenses of the English church and of the Catholic queen misled Hill into treating the passage as an Arminian defense of the Roman Catholic church (Hill 36). Donne may have deliberately created the possibility of this misunderstanding in order both to express and obscure his dissent from the Arminian views of his royal auditor, but he makes clear to the attentive that he is defending the English rather than Roman Catholic church by following immediately with the passage discussed above contrasting the imperfect but improving English church and the " impurity" of the church corrupted by Antichrist. Six weeks after his reprimand from the king, Donne enunciated the Arminian line concerning the Pope but greatly tempered it with traditional antipapal rhetoric: in his May 13, 1627 sermon he calls the pope "the man of sin . . . that pretends to be. . . . a *Hyper-Christus*" and warns the Pope that he "take heed" of the title of "*Antichrist*" that "some are apt enough to give him, however he deserve it" (*Sermons* 7:448). While the concluding clause espouses the Arminian line that there was no proof of the Pope's being Antichrist, all that precedes suggests Donne's sympathies with the traditional identification: the description of the Pope as "the man of sin" of 2 Thes. 2:3-9, who was conventionally identi-

fied with the Antichrist (Hill 4); the witty alternative coinage *"Hyper-Christus"*; the rhetorical warning to an absent Pope not to prove correct those who accuse him of being the Antichrist; and the ambiguous phrase "apt enough," which hovers between a neutral description and commendation of those who make the traditional identification. Donne continued to chart a personal middle course between the powerful Arminian faction and its opponents.

⁴⁴ This essay is part of a work-in-progress on conflicting conceptions of the mean in early modern England. Sections 1-4 are a revised and shortened version of portions of "The Medium is the Message: Donne's 'Satire 3,' 'To Sir Henry Wotton (Sir, more than kisses),' and the Ideologies of the Mean," *MP* 90 (1993): 479-511. I have profited from suggestions of participants at the Faculty Colloquium and the Renaissance Workshop of the University of Chicago's English Department and at the 1992 MLA Convention, where I delivered earlier versions of this essay. I am also grateful to Raymond-Jean Frontain, Achsah Guibbory, Frances Malpezzi, Janel Mueller, Michael Murrin, and Richard Strier for incisive criticism of various drafts.

Works Cited

Allen, D. C. "Two Notes on John Donne." *MLN* 65 (1950): 102-3.

Aquinas, St. Thomas. *Summa Theologiae*. 5 vols. Madrid: Biblioteca de Autores Cristianos, 1961-65.

Aristotle. *Metaphysics*. Trans. Hugh Tredennick. 2 vols. Cambridge, MA: Loeb Classical Library, 1933-35.

————. *Nicomachean Ethics*. Trans. H. Rackham. Cambridge, MA: Loeb Classical Library, 1956.

Aristotle (pseudo-). *Problems*. Trans. W. S. Hett. 2 vols. Cambridge, MA: Loeb Classical Library, 1936-37.

Augustine, St. *De genesi ad litteram*. Vol. 34 of *Patrologiae Cursus Completus, Series Latina*. Ed. J. P. Migne. 221 vols. Paris, 1878-90. 246-486.

————. *Enarrationes in Psalmos*. Vols. 36-37 of *Patrologiae Cursus Completus, Series Latina*. Ed. J. P. Migne. 221 vols. Paris, 1878-90.

————. *Sermones*. Vols. 38-39 of *Patrologiae Cursus Completus, Series Latina*. Ed. J. P. Migne. 221 vols. Paris, 1878-90.

Bacon, Francis. *The Works of Francis Bacon*. Ed. James Spedding, R. L. Ellis and D.D. Heath. 7 vols. London, 1857-59.

Bainton, Roland. "Luther and the *Via Media* at the Marburg Colloquy." *Studies on the Reformation*. Boston: Beacon, 1963. 46-50.

Baker-Smith, Dominic. "John Donne's *Critique of True Religion*." *John Donne: Essays in Celebration*. Ed. A. J. Smith. London: Methuen, 1972. 404-432.

Bald, R. C. *John Donne: A Life*. Oxford: Clarendon P, 1970.

Berrouard, M.-F., ed. *Homalies sur 1' évangile de saint Jean 34-43.* Oeuvres de Saint Augustin 73a. Paris: Etudes Augustiniennes, 1988.

Boethius. *Liber de Persona et Duabus Natures.* Vol. 64 of *Patrologiae Cursus Completus, Series Latina.* Ed. J. P. Migne. 221 vols. Paris, 1878-90. 1337-54.

The Book of Common Prayer, 1559: The Elizabethan Prayer Book. Ed. John E. Booty. Charlottesville: UP of Virginia, 1976.

Bredvold, Louis I. "The Religious Thought of Donne in Relation to Medieval and Later Traditions." *Studies in Shakespeare, Milton and Donne by Members of the English Department of the University of Michigan.* New York: Haskell House, 1964. 193-232.

Burnyeat, Myles. "Can the Skeptic Live his Skepticism?" *The Skeptical Tradition.* Ed. Myles Burnyeat. Berkeley: U of Califomia P, 1983. 117-48.

Carey, John. *John Donne: Life, Mind and Art.* London: Faber, 1981.

Chilton, C. W. "Did Epicurus Approve of Marriage? A Study of Diogenes Laertius X, 119." *Phronesis* 5 (1960): 71-74.

Cicero. *De senectute, De amicitia, De divinatione.* Trans. W. A. Falconer. Cambridge, MA: Loeb Classical Library, 1923.

Clement of Alexandria. *Clementis Alexandri . . . omnia . . . opera.* Trans. Gentianus Aurelianus. Basle, 1556.

Courcelle, Pierre. "Tradition Platonicienne et Traditions Chrétiennes du Corps-Prison *(Phédon* 62b; *Cratyle* 400c.*)." Revue des études latines* 43 (1965): 406-443.

Davies, Julian.*The Caroline Captivity of the Church: Charles I and the Remoulding of Anglicanism, 1625-1641.* Oxford: Clarendon P, 1992.

Dollimore, Jonathan. *Radical Tragedy: Religion, Ideology and Power in the Drama of Shakespeare and His Contemporaries.* Chicago: U of Chicago P, 1984.

Donne, John. *Essays in Divinity.* Ed. Evelyn M. Simpson. Oxford: Clarendon P, 1952.

_____. *Paradoxes and Problems.* Ed. Helen Peters. Oxford: Clarendon P, 1980.

_____. *Pseudo-Martyr.* London, 1610.

Eire, Carlos M. N. *War against the Idols: The Reformation of Worship from Erasmus to Calvin.* Cambridge: Cambridge UP, 1986.

Elton, William R. *King Lear and the Gods.* San Marino: Huntington Library, 1966.

Epictetus. *Epicteti stoici philosophi enchiridion.* Trans. Angelo Poliziano and Jacob Schegk. Geneva, 1594.

Erasmus, Desiderius. *Colloquia.* Ed. L.-E. Halkin, F. Bierlaire, and R. Hoven. Amsterdam: North-Holland Publishing, 1972.

_____. *Enchiridion militia christiani.* Vol. 5 of *Desiderii Erasmi . . . opera omnia.* Ed. Jean Leclerc. 10 vols. Leiden, 1703-1706.

_____. *Enchiridion Militis Christiana: An English Verrsion.* Ed. Anne M. O'Donnell. Early English Text Society. Oxford: Oxford UP, 1981.

Featley, Daniel. *Pelagius Redivius.* London, 1626.

Feliciano, Giovanni Bemardo, trans. *Aristotelis Stagiritae moralia Nicomachia . . . [Nicomachean Ethics.* By Aristotle.] 1541. Paris, 1543.

Ficino, Marsilio, tr. *Divini Platonis opera omnia.* By Plato. Leiden, 1590.

Forster, Leonard. *The Icy Fire: Five Studies in European Petrarchism.* Cambridge: Cambridge UP, 1969.

George, Charles H., and Katherine George. *The Protestant Mind of the English Reformation, 1570-1640.* Princeton: Princeton UP, 1961.

Goodman, Christopher. *How Superior Powers Oght to be Obeyd* (1557). Pref. Charles H. McIlwain. New York: Facsimile Text Society, 1931.

Gosse, Edmund. *The Life and Letters of John Donne.* 2 vols. 1899. Gloucester: Peter Smith, 1959.

Greenblatt, Stephen. *Renaissance Self-Fashioning, from More to Shakespeare.* Chicago: U of ChicagoP, 1983.

Grierson, H. J. C., ed. *The Poems of John Donne.* 2 vols. Oxford: Oxford UP, 1912.

Hester, M. Thomas. *Kinde Pitty and Brave Scorn: John Donne's Satyres.* Durham: Duke UP, 1982.

Hill, Christopher.*Antichrist in Seventeenth-Century England.* Oxford: Oxford UP, 1971.

Horace. *The Odes and Epodes.* Trans. C. E. Bennett. Rev. ed. Cambridge, MA: Loeb Classical Library, 1968.

_____. *Satires, Epistles, and Ars poetica.* Trans. H. Rushton Fairclough. Cambridge, MA: Loeb Classical Library, 1926.

John of Salisbury. *Frivolities of Courtiers and Footprints of Philosophers.* Ed. and Trans. Joseph B. Pike. Minneapolis: U of Minnesota P, 1938.

Juvenal. *Juvenal and Perseus.* Trans. G. G. Ramsey. Cambridge, MA: Loeb Classical Library, 1961.

Kerrigan, William, and Gordon Braden. *The Idea of the Renaissance.* Baltimore: Johns Hopkins UP, 1989.

Knox, Norman. *The Word Irony and Its Context, 1500-1755.* Durham: Duke UP, 1961.

Lactantius. *Divinae institutiones.* Vol. 6 of *Patrologiae Cursus Completus,* Series Latina. Ed. J. P. Migne. 221 vols. Paris, 1878-90. 111-822.

Laertius, Diogenes. *De vitis, dogmatis . . . clarorum philosophorum.* Trans. Henri Estienne with Isaac Casaubon's notes. Geneva, 1593.

Lake, Peter. *Anglicans and Puritans?: Presbyterianism and English Conformist Thought from Whitgift to Hooker.* London: Unwin Hyman, 1988.

_____. "Calvinism and the English Church, 1570-1635." *Past and Present* 114

(1987): 32-76.

Leighton, Stephen R. "Aristotle's Courageous Passions." *Phronesis* 33 (1988): 76-99.

Lewis, C.S. *The Discarded Image: An Introduction to Medieval and Renaissance Literature.* Cambridge: Cambridge UP, 1964.

Lloyd, G. E. R. *The Revolutions of Wisdom: Studies in the Claims and Practice of Ancient Greek Science.* Berkeley: U of California P, 1987.

Luther, Martin. *Temporal Authority: To What Extent it Should be Obeyed* (1523). Trans. J. J. Schindel, rev. Walther I. Brandt. Vol. 45 of *Luther's Works.* Ed. Walther I. Brandt. General ed. Jaroslav Pelikan and Helmut T. Lehmann. Philadelphia: Muhlenberg P, 1955. 75-130.

Marotti, Arthur. *John Donne, Coterie Poet.* Madison: U of Wisconsin P, 1986.

Milgate, W., ed. *The Satires, Epigrams and Verse Letters.* By John Donne. Oxford: Clarendon P, 1967.

Montaigne, Michel de. *The Complete Essays of Michel de Montaigne.* Trans. Donald M. Frame. Palo Alto: Stanford UP, 1958.

Moore, Thomas V."Donne's Use of Uncertainty as a Vital Force in ' Satyre III.'" *MP* 67 (1969): 41-49.

Mueller, Janel, ed. *Donne's Prebend Sermons.* Cambridge, MA: Harvard UP, 1971.

Mueller, William R. *John Donne: Preacher.* Princeton: Princeton UP, 1962.

Norbrook, David. "The Monarchy of Wit and the Republic of Letters: Donne's Politics." *Soliciting Interpretation: Literary Theory and Seventeenth-Century English Poetry.* Ed. Elizabeth D. Harvey and Katharine Eisaman Maus. Chicago: U of Chicago P, 1990. 3-36.

Patrides, C. A. "'The Beast with Many Heads': Views on the Multitude." *Premises and Motifs in Renaissance Thought and Literature.* Princeton: Princeton UP, 1982. 124-36.

Patterson, Annabel. *Censorship and Interpretation: The Conditions of Writing and Reading in Early Modern England.* Madison: U of Wisconsin P, 1984.

Pears, David. "Courage as a Mean." *Essays on Aristotle's Ethics.* Ed. Amélie Oksenberg Rorty. Berkeley: U of California P, 1980. 171-88.

Penelhum, Terence. "Skepticism and Fideism," in *The Skeptical Tradition.* Ed. Myles Burnyeat. Berkeley: U of California P, 1983. 287-318.

Perrin, Michel. *L'Homme antique et chretien: l'anthropologie de Lactance (250-325).* Paris: Beauchesne, 1981.

Persius. *Juvenal and Persius.* Trans. G. G. Ramsey. Cambridge, MA: Loeb Classical Library, 1961.

Phillips, John. *The Reformation of Images: The Destruction of Art in England, 1535-1660.* Berkeley: U of California P, 1973.

Plato. *Euthyphro, Apology, Crito, Phaedo, Phaedrus.* Trans. H. N. Fowler. Cambridge, MA: Loeb Classical Library, 1914.

Plutarch. *The Philosophie, comonlie called, The Morals.* Trans. Philemon Holland. London, 1603.

Ponet, John. *A Short Treatise of Politike Power* (1556). Reproduced in Winthrop S. Hudson. *John Ponet, Advocate of Limited Monarchy.* Chicago: U of Chicago P, 1942.

Powell, J. G. F., ed. *Cato maior.* By Cicero. Cambridge: Cambridge UP, 1988.

Purpus, Jean R. "The Moral Philosophy of Book II of Spenser's *Faerie Queene.*" Diss. U of California at Los Angeles, 1946.

Rescher, Nicholas. *The Strife of Systems: An Essay on the Grounds and Implications of Philosophical Diversity.* Pittsburgh: U of Pittsburgh P, 1985.

Riccobono, Antonio, trans. *Aristotelis ethicorum ad Nicomachum libri decem.* [*Nicomachean Ethics.* By Aristotle.] 1593. Frankfurt, 1596.

Rous, Francis. *Testa Veritatis.* London, 1626.

Scodel, Joshua. "'Mediocrities'and'Extremities':Francis Bacon and the Aristotelian Mean." *Creative Imitation: New Essays on Renaissance Literature.* Ed. David Quint et al. Binghamton, NY: Medieval and Renaissance Texts and Studies, 1992. 89-126.

_____. "The Medium is the Message: Donne's 'Satire 3,' 'To Sir Henry Wotton (Sir, more than kisses),'and the Ideologies of the Mean." *MP* 90 (1993): 479-511.

Seneca. *De ira.* Vol. I of *Moral Essays.* Trans. John W. Basore. 3 vols. Cambridge, MA: Loeb Classical Library, 1928-35. 106-355.

_____. *De tranquillitate animi.* Vol. 2 of *Moral Essays.* Trans. John W. Basore, 3 vols. Cambridge, MA: Loeb Classical Library, 1928-35. 202-285.

Sextus Empiricus. *Sexti Empirici opera* . . . Ed. and trans. Henri Estienne. 1562. Geneva,1621.

Simpson, Evelyn M., ed. *John Donne's Sermons on the Psalms and Gospels.* Berkeley: U of California P, 1963.

Spenser, Edmund. *The Faerie Queene.* Ed. A. C. Hamilton. London: Longman, 1977.

Strier, Richard. "Radical Donne: 'Satire Ill.'" *ELH* 60 (1993): 283-322.

Tavemer, Richard, trans. *Proverbs or Adages.* By Desiderius Erasmus. London, 1569.

Taylor, Charles. *Sources of the Self: The Making of the Modern Identity.* Cambridge, MA: Harvard UP, 1989.

Tyacke, Nicholas. *Anti-Calvinists, The Rise of English Arminianism, 1590-1640.* Oxford: Clarendon P, 1987.

Wiley, Margaret L. *TheSubtle Knot: Creative Scepticism in Seventeenth-Century England.* Cambridge, MA: Harvard UP, 1952

Receiving a Sexual Sacrament: "The Flea" as Profane Eucharist

Theresa M. DiPasquale

n a funeral elegy printed in the 1633 edition of Donne's *Poems*, Jasper Mayne urges would-be lovers to take Donne's erotic poetry as their model:

> From this Muse learne to Court, whose power could move
> A Cloystred coldnesse, or a Vestall love,
> And would convey such errands to their eare,
> That Ladies knew no oddes to grant and heare. (45-48)

Mayne praises Donne's "masculine perswasive force" ("Elegy: On his Mistris" 4) by drawing images from the master's own seduction poetry. The image of "Cloystred coldnesse," for example, reminds us of "The Flea," in which the speaker argues that he and his lady are "cloysterd in these living walls of Jet" (15).[1] The allusion fails, however, to capture the wit with which Donne applies his religious imagination to the business of seduction. In "The Flea," the cloister image is of the seducer's own making, and he puts it to his own erotic uses; it is a weapon in his arsenal, not—as in Mayne's allusion—a metaphor for the female chastity he has under siege. According to Mayne's rather conventional conceit, Donne's rhetoric is powerful enough to burst through the convent wall and melt the snowy virtue of a nun. Donne's speaker, however, addresses not a Carmelite in full habit, but an English girl who lives at home with her "grudg[ing]" parents; and his wit is too finely honed, too specific, to describe the chastity of an Anglican virgin as "Cloystred coldnesse."

Indeed, as M. Thomas Hester argues in a recent article, the denominational affiliations of the speaker and the lady help to determine the shape of the courtship drama. Using Reformation and Counter-Reformation treatises on the controversy over the Eucharist, Hester argues that the speaker in "The Flea" "appropriates the precise lexicon and paradigms of the current theological debate" in which Catholics and Protestants sought to define the word "This" (*Hoc*) as it functions in the all-important assertion, "*Hoc est corpus meum.*" The speaker signals the analogy between his argument and the Eucharist debate "by the reiteration of 'this' (six times in the first line nines)"; and as the argument unfolds, the "'Catholic' exegete" elevates before "his 'Protesting' lady" a quasi-eucharistic sign, telling her that, in essence, *Hoc est corpus nostrum* (Hester 377). For Hester, however, the lady's triumphant gesture upon killing the flea "*marks . . .* the death of the speaker's carnal hopes," for her purpled nail shows "the absence of mystery or miracle in his sexual metonymy," and she is thus able simply to deny "the real sacrifice" of her virginity (Hester 381). According to Hester's reading, then, the poem "traces its own failure" as sexual persuasion, "unless . . . she is to be seduced by the rigor of an erect wit" (377). This phallic image puts a Donnean edge on the Christian concept of redeemed reason (compare Sidney's reference to "erected wit" in the *Defence of Poesy* [217]); and the argument of "The Flea" does depend upon the keenness of that edge.

But Hester's metaphor remains insufficient, for the seductiveness of the speaker's theological wit is a function not of its rigor, but of its delightful flexibility. The poem, I would argue, functions simultaneously on each of several mutually contradictory levels; for, by inscribing the speaker's argument in eucharistically charged language, Donne has insured that his signs and verbal gestures will be as polyvalent and as open to debate as the signs and gestures of the sacrament. The Lord's Supper is for one Christian an efficacious sacrifice, for another a merely symbolic action, and for yet another a dynamic event that takes place in the heart of the individual receiver; in the same way, "The Flea" may be read as a Petrarchan tribute, a libertine entrapment, or a true lover's persuasion. The poet assigns a given set of responses to the lady in the white spaces between the stanzas and—in so doing—sets up the shifting strategies the speaker makes in response to "her." But it is the reader of the poem who decides the lady's final answer in the white space following the third stanza and—in so doing—defines the effectiveness and significance of the speaker's argument as a whole. In short, the outcome of the seduction is—as any undergraduate will tell you—"left up to the reader."

Interpretations of the Eucharist are, nevertheless, always guided by theologians' readings of authoritative scriptural and patristic texts; indeed, they often allude to the importance of discovering Christ's authorial intention in the words of institution.[2] The options open to the reader of "The Flea" are similarly delimited by what John Shawcross calls the "author's text" (*Intentionality* 3-4). In the poem, Donne directs reader response not only by using the language of theological debate, but also through his choice of the flea-poem sub-genre and his reworking of that lyric type as seduction-poem (in which the speaker addresses a lady) rather than as envious apostrophe (in which the flea itself is addressed).[3]

In the analysis that follows, I explore two different ways of reading the seduction as successful; each depends upon a different reading of the images and arguments presented to the lady who is the "reader" within the text. The first is an anti-Petrarchan, libertine reading, based upon the principles of radical iconoclasm; the second is a response rooted in an Anglican semiotic, which finds in the speaker's signs and gestures an invitation to genuine erotic communion. I argue, moreover, that this second way of reading the poem helps to explain some intriguing parallels between the woman in the lyric and Ann More Donne as her witty husband constructs her in a letter.

However one approaches the text, the lover's strategy suggests from the start that he wishes to anticipate "reader response," for he tailors his approach to suit his lady's wit and temperament. Clearly, she is a resourceful and practical-minded opponent, not to be impressed by helpless longing or ingenious postures of despair. Thus, the speaker's opening gambit employs neither elaborate Petrarchan compliments—which many of Donne's speakers decry as inherently self-defeating[4]—nor the despairingly lascivious alternative of the conventional flea poem, in which an unrequited lover fantasizes about being the flea in his mistress' cleavage (see Wilson, Brumble). Instead, Donne's speaker addresses the lady directly and attempts to dispense with at least one of her reasons for resisting his advances: the fear of pregnancy. As Hester (379) points out, the lover jokingly alludes both to the Annunciation miracle and to Renaissance theories of conception when he points to the flea as the virgin womb in which "two bloods" are "mingled" without "sinne," or "shame," or "losse of maidenhead." Though *it* "swells with one blood made of two," she needn't fear that her own womb will, for "this, alas, is more then wee would doe" (9).[5]

The lady could, if she had a mind to, play along with this mock-Christian miracle of virginal conception; but she is not impressed. The flea and the argument are both pests; and in the white space between the first and second stanzas, she moves to crush them. The speaker intervenes quickly; but the way in which he does so seems to make matters worse. Leaving behind the argumentative stance and demonstrative terminology of the polemical theologian, the speaker adopts the pleading, prayerful accents of a worshiper:

> Oh stay, three lives in one flea spare,
> Where wee almost, yea more then maryed are.
> This flea is you and I, and this
> Our mariage bed, and mariage temple is;
> Though parents grudge, and you, w'are met,
> And cloysterd in these living walls of Jet.
> > Though use make you apt to kill mee,
> > Let not to that, selfe murder added bee,
> > And sacrilege, three sinnes in killing three. (10-18)

The speaker here indulges in the Petrarchan hyperbole which he so carefully avoided in the first stanza; he claims to be slain by the lady's cruelty and defines his desire as a holy devotion.[6] At the same time, his phrasing and his choice of imagery lends that devotion a distinctly Catholic character. Indeed, the second stanza puts the erotic theology of the first into full-blown liturgical practice; the speaker consecrates and elevates the flea: "This flea *is*"—hoc est—"you and I"! The literalism of his hocus-pocus cannot but exacerbate the lady's irritation.[7] And as for the "living walls of Jet": what self-respecting Protestant lady would submit to being "cloysterd" anywhere? In Tudor England, the speaker's insistence that the flea is a monastery practically ensures that its walls will be razed, even as his pleading tone, his exaggerated reverence, and his tribute to her "killing" powers virtually solicit the "cruel" response that is *de rigeur* for ladies addressed in the Petrarchan mode.

But the speaker's shift in tone serves a purpose: he began by eschewing the self-defeating language of Petrarchan courtship which "destroyes it selfe with its owne shade" (as Donne puts it in a verse epistle "To the Countesse of Huntingdon" [34]); but if his insectile signifier is to die, he wants it to die as the embodiment of such definitively frustrated and frustrating discourse. Thus, speaking in the persecuted tones of what Donne elsewhere dubs "whining Poëtry" ("The triple Foole" 3), the speaker reifies and venerates the sign, insisting that violence done to it will be a "sacrilege" (18). The lady responds to his papistical-sounding nonsense with an iconoclast's righteous violence and acts upon the implicit dare; by the start of the third stanza, she has demolished the jet walls of the idolatrous "temple."[8]

In response to her action, he at first assumes a stance of shocked indignation: "Wherein could this flea guilty bee," he asks, "Except in that drop which it suckt from thee?" (21-22) His question evokes a logic reminiscent of Hooker's conservative response to iconoclastic zeal. Arguing against the destruction of medieval cathedrals and churches, Hooker concedes that things previously put to idolatrous uses may have to be abolished or extinguished, but he stresses that such action cannot be considered a punishment of the thing destroyed (*Laws* V.xvii.3).

But the lady's action and attitudes clearly render such distinctions moot. She is flush with the excitement of iconoclastic zeal. In his study of Renaissance iconoclasm, Gilman recounts the story of a Lancashire boy who, when urged by a radical Protestant schoolmaster "to mock the images in the chapel, . . . seized a sword from the image of St. George and broke it over the saint's head, shouting, 'Let me see now how thou canst fight again!'" (8). The thrill of exposing an idol's impotence exhilarates the lady of the poem in much the same way, and the speaker can hear the ringing defiance and mockery in her voice: "thou triumph'st, and saist that thou / Find'st not thy selfe, nor mee the weaker now" (23-24).

At the very moment when she is sure that she has defeated him, however, he once again shifts ground. Though he previously identified the signifier with the signified, claiming that it would be "selfe murder" for her to kill the symbol which represented her, he now admits—with Protestant care—that the reality is a thing separate from the sign; her violence destroyed only the signifier, not the thing it represented. If she wants to be an iconoclast, he goes on to stress, she must be consistent; for she too has been treating a sign as though it were the very thing it signified:

> thou
> Find'st not thy selfe, nor mee the weaker now;
> Tis true, then learne how false, feares bee;
> Just so much honor, when thou yeeld'st to mee,
> Will wast, as this flea's death tooke life from thee.
> (23-27)

A woman's honor, his analogy implies, is the reality for which sexual abstinence—physical chastity—is but a tangible sign. An intact "maidenhead" is not the "honor" with which tradition equates it; and because there is such a gap between signifier and signified, the destruction of the sign will not affect the underlying truth. The devil can quote scripture, and a lover Augustine: the sacrament is one thing, its virtue is another.[9]

Read this way, "The Flea" is a voluptuous worldling's "Theatre for Fastidious Mistresses"; its emblems exhort a virgin to break her own most precious icon. The lady (or the reader of the poem, deciding for her) may leave it at that. She may sleep with her suitor on the understanding that tangible seals mean nothing; agreeing that the flea's death is an empty occurrence, she need attribute no significance to the "death" of her virginity. As we have seen in Mayne's verse tribute to Donne, a seventeenth-century reader was clearly capable of eliding the poet's success with the speaker's triumph. And for a significant number of twentieth-century readers, too, the seduction seems a *fait accompli*. Critics who choose to eschew the role of resisting reader, who enjoy the sheer pleasure of surrendering to Donne's wit, afford the lady at least as much latitude and argue that she will indeed yield to the speaker's "irresistible conclusion that the loss of maidenhood is nothing more than a flea bite."[10]

Other readers, however, see in the speaker's argument something beyond the desire for meaningless fun. As Arthur Marotti notes, Donne's lyric differs from most erotic persuasions in mentioning marriage at all (93). And its theological imagery, gamesome though it is, does more than teach a lesson in iconoclasm. Rather, the speaker's blasphemous analogies preach a sexual-salvation-history with a Protestant flavor. The flea is set up as the incarnate union of the lover and his lady even as Jesus is the incarnate union of God and Man. And if the speaker offers it to be a sign of their oneness, the covenant between them can be fully accomplished— as in the case of Christ's Atonement—only through the *shedding* of the "one blood made of two." The killing of Jesus was the consummate sin, yet it was the only means to reconcile God and man. Similarly, it is "sacrilege" for the lady to "[Purple her] naile in blood of innocence," yet that nail of crucifixion proves instrumental in the lover's plan to make her his own.

It is here that a distinctly Protestant appeal comes into play: the Reformers rejected the Catholic conception of the Mass as a sacrifice offered by the priest because they held that Jesus' death on Calvary was the only sacrifice and could not be repeated or continued in the eucharist.[11] Similarly, the flea has served as Paschal-erotic Victim, and its spilt "blood of innocence" cancels all guilt: "[This is] the effect of his bloodshed, that sinne be not imputed unto us" (Calvin II.xvii.4). Thus, the lady's yielding will be no holocaust and no sin, but an erotic *communion*.

The analogy between sexual yielding and Protestant eucharist is set up by the poem's movement: it starts with static gazing upon an elevated sign and shifts to the un"wast"ed use of that sign; this sequence recalls the Protestant response to visual adoration of the eucharist, which for many Catholics had replaced the taking of communion.[12] The Elizabethan "Homilie of the worthy receiving and reverend esteeming of the Sacrament" urges believers not to hold back from participation in the meal "although it seeme of small vertue to some" but rather to seek the "fruition and union" of the eucharistic banquet in which they may "sucke the sweetnesse of everlasting salvation" (*Certaine Sermons* 197, 199, 200):

> To this, his commandement forceth us. . . . To this, his promise entiseth . . . So then of necessity we must be our selves partakers . . . and not beholders. (198)

The speaker of the poem also feels "enticed" to do more than just look. Though Neoplatonic lovers may vilify sexual "partaking" as an act of "small vertue," he presses forward to "sucke the sweetnesse" of a "fruition and union" which can save him from the death of frustration conventionally suffered by Petrarchan lovers. He wishes to avoid the folly of stupefied gazing—so mockingly repudiated in "Elegy XIX"—and become one of those who "taste whole joys," as the speaker of the elegy puts it.

The lady moves things in the right direction by handling the sign (none too gently) rather than merely "Marke[ing]" it as the speaker first asked her. But physical violence done to outward signs does *not*, he hopes to convince her, destroy what they represent. Renaissance Protestants stressed that Christ's body is not chewed up, swallowed, and digested along with the bread; the homily on the Sacrament explains that it is "a ghostly substance" which believers "receive . . . with the hand of [the] heart" (*Certaine Sermons* 200-201). The speaker of "The Flea" wants the lady to think in the same way of her "honor"—that "ghostly" or intangible signified which she has so closely identified with the tangible signifier called "maidenhead." Though he never directly promises to receive her honor into his keeping, he hopes to convince her that its substance will not be lost and "wast"ed when her hymen breaks. Thus, the ambiguous syntax of the penultimate line gives the impression that "yeeld'st" is a transitive verb with "honor" as its direct object: "Just so much honor, when thou yeeld'st to mee," he says, and we expect to hear next what will happen after she has yielded "just so much honor" to him. Of course, "honor" turns out to be the subject of the completed sentence, "yeeld'st" intransitive, and the "when . . . " clause parenthetical, but even after we hear the speaker's statement in full, the impression remains: her honor will not be *wasted on him* because it will not be wasted *by* him when she yields.[13] He may want to consume her virginity, but as a semiotic sophisticate, he knows the difference between sign and signified, between defloration and dishonor, between giving over and giving in.

Thus, if the lady of the poem wishes to be married in fact as well as in flea, she may grant her lover's request on conditions his own imagery suggests. She may insist that he receive her eucharistic virginity—and the honor it signifies—with the reverence and faithfulness of a devout communicant who receives "with the hand of the heart." If she does so, she will be committing herself to him. For in conveying himself through the eucharist, Christ confirms that he will never abandon the faithful believer; as Calvin puts it, he "doth . . . so communicate his body to us, that he is made throughly one with us" (IV.xvii.38). In the same way, the lady who conveys her honor as she yields her body assures the lover to whom she entrusts them that she will never absent herself from him. The female speaker of another Donne poem makes the point eloquently: "I faine would *stay*," says the woman in "Breake of day," for "I [love] my heart and honor so, / That I would not from him, that had them, goe" (10, 11-12; emphasis mine).

But it is a very worried lady who speaks those lines, and her "aubade" reminds us of the dangers involved in yielding. Having surrendered body, heart, and honor to her lover, the Renaissance mistress must fear that he will abandon her and take everything *but* her body with him. Will the lady of "The Flea" risk such danger? Clearly, she still has the option of refusing altogether; she can point out that what the speaker says about his spurious private symbol has no bearing on the socially determined relation between the sign of virginity and the substance of honor.[14] Will she allow her lover to consume that sign? Will she convey to him that substance?

If she is anything like the woman Donne married, she may. The lady's scruples and anxieties do not necessarily imply that the speaker's love is unrequited. "Though parents grudge, and you, w'are met," he says; and as Marotti points out, "the progression from 'parents' to 'you' to 'we' . . .

places the woman rhetorically, emotionally, and morally between the disapproving parents and the importunate suitor" (94).[15] This is precisely the situation in which Ann More, Donne's own beloved, found herself; and as Edward LeComte argues, Ann may have escaped the impasse by consummating her relationship with Jack before the clandestine ceremony in which they took their vows. LeComte consults two key documents: a letter Donne wrote to his father-in-law on 2 February 1602 [New Style], in which he claims that their wedding took place "about three weeks before Christmas" 1601, and a record of the court's decision on the secret marriage's validity, dated 27 April 1602. Noting the vagueness and inconsistency of the dates cited in these documents, and considering seventeenth-century attitudes toward clandestine marriage, LeComte speculates on the actual "sequence of events":

> Ann and John, after a separation of many months, found each other irresistible when at last they met again several times in the fall of 1601. They had made solemn promises to each other, and looked forward to marrying. Physical union was not an evasion of, but a way into, marriage: it strengthened their legal claims on each other. So, with the dissolution of Parliament on 19 December, Ann was taken back by her father to Loseley, neither a virgin nor a bride. In January, it probably was, the girl sent word to her lover in London that she had reason to believe she was pregnant. Thereupon, . . . she escaped from her father long enough for a secret ceremony. [Donne], when at last he had to inform Sir George More, predated the marriage so that the couple's first child, Constance, would be born nine months afterwards, not seven or eight. (20)[16]

The marriage did not stay secret for long—a pregnancy would help explain that fact—and Donne found himself in a very delicate situation. Hoping to placate his father-in-law, he composed the aforementioned letter. In it, he confesses that he and Ann married in December, but claims that they had committed themselves to one another even before the ceremony; his spurious argument recalls the one advanced in "The Flea." Comparing the lovers' precontract to a building with a strong foundation, Donne argues in the letter that their private engagement was—like the flea as "marriage temple"—too holy to be torn down: "So long since as her being at York House this had *foundacion*, and so much then of promise and contract *built* upon yt, as withowt violence to conscience might not be shaken" (*Selected Prose* 113; emphases mine). He then intercedes for Ann as the poem's speaker does for the flea, begging "that she may not to her danger feele the terror of your *sodaine* anger"; Donne fears that his father-in-law will, like the lady of the poem, react with "cruell and sodaine" violence. But he can't leave it at that; with the same saucy impudence displayed by the speaker of the poem, he goes on to stress that, "Though parents grudge, . . . [they] *are* met":

> I know no passion can alter your reason and wisdome, to which I adventure to commend these particulers; that yt is irremediably donne; that if yow incense my Lord [Egerton, Donne's employer] yow destroy her and me; [and] that yt is easye to give us happines . . . (113)

"[I]t is irremediably donne"; the marriage is consummated, and Ann More is now, quite irreversibly, Ann Donne. Like the speaker of the poem, the bridegroom argues that the union he defends is a *fait accompli* and points out "How little" it would take for the addressee to make him happy. But he does so, like the speaker of the poem, partly to keep the potential benefactor from "killing three": himself, his spouse, and—if LeComte is right—their unborn child.

Surely Janet Halley is right to caution readers against the hope that they can know the "real" Ann More Donne through the textual constructions of her husband.[17] But the parallels between these two texts—one a dramatic lyric and the other a petitionary letter—can lead us to a clearer appreciation for the lady who speaks in eloquent silence between the stanzas of "The Flea," and for the poet's intentions in devising her. The intention of Donne's letter to George More is clear: he wants his father-in-law's blessing (and with it his financial assistance); he wishes to defuse More's anger, to persuade him to endorse the union. He thus describes and defends Ann as a young woman who has, heroically, risked everything for the sake of mutual commitment: "We both knew the obligacions that lay upon us, and we adventurd equally" (113). In the poem, Donne invites the reader to view the exchange between the speaker and the lady in a similar light, to see that, if the young lady of "The Flea" chooses to take seriously the quasi-eucharistic signs which her lover offers, she, too, will "adventure equally" and convert "what we would *doe*" to an act "irremediably *donne*." She will embrace her lover's sacramental imagery and insist that the gift of her virginity be considered no less binding than a precontract.

As critics of the poem, we can insist on no one reading, no one way of taking the sacrament; readers will continue to decide for themselves.[18]

But we cannot avoid envisioning a range of specific outcomes from chaste denial to playful submission or reasoned acquiescence, and the speaker does seem set on excluding the possibility of outright refusal. As Baumlin notes, "the poem erects logically and morally specious arguments that the skeptical reader, taking the addressee's part, must seek to refute" (242), but it "cannot be fully defeated, for its arguments resist a reader's resistance, refusing to deconstruct" (244).

Calvin explains the effectiveness of sacramental grace in terms that may explain such stubborn persistence: a sacrament is like a rhetorical persuasion, he asserts, and the operation of the Holy Spirit ensures that its rhetoric cannot fail. It guarantees that the signs presented to the faithful *will* take effect, for it prepares their hearts to receive them (*Institutes* IV.xiv.9-10). In the sacramental persuasions of erotic love, a successful seduction presupposes the influence of another inward flame: the spirit of mutual desire. If that is present, it will—to borrow Calvin's wording—"truly bring to passe that the hearer . . . will obey the selfe same counsels which otherwise he wold have laughed to scorne" (*Institutes* IV.xiv.10). Such predestinate wooing, such preaching to the converted, is—Donne argues in one of his verse epistles—the only kind a man should attempt: "Man's better part consists of purer fire, / And findes it selfe allow'd, ere it desire," he says ("That unripe side of earth" 59-60). Perhaps it is this logic which underlies "The Flea," with its confident allusion to a future "When"—not "if"—the lady yields.

Notes

[1] Mayne's elegy, which includes a number of verbal echoes of Donne's work, begins by asking, "Who shall presume to mourn thee, Donne, unlesse / He could his teares *in thy expressions* dresse[?]" (1-2; emphasis mine). It seems likely, then, that the cloister image is a conscious allusion.

[2] See Calvin's acknowledgment that "before that we goe any further, we must entreate of the selfe institution of Christe: specially because this is the most

glorious obiection that our adversaries have, that we departe from the woordes of Christe. Therefore that we may be discharged . . . our fittest beginnyng shall be at the exposition of the woordes" (*Institutes* IV. xvii. 20).

³ A lyric, as Shawcross explains, is "a briefer poem in which the author intends to produce a successful literary creation by specific chosen techniques, devices, form, language, strategy, and the like in an ultimately competitive spirit for evaluation by the readers. It implies a fictive voice that may appear to be an authorial one, and that may owe its substance to an authorial voice; it is a fictive voice speaking to an auditor, implied or also fictive, who always also is the reader" (*Intentionality* 86). "The Flea" clearly provides ample opportunity for the reader to identify with the lady who is the fictive auditor; and there is no doubt that the battle-ready speaker bears a strong resemblance to Donne himself as he enters the flea-poem arena in a "competitive" attempt to rework and outdo previous lyrics of that type. In order to judge the poet's attempt "successful" while insisting that the seduction attempt fails, a reader will thus find it necessary to cling very closely to a condemnation of the intentional fallacy.

⁴ See "To the Countesse of Huntingdon" ("That unripe side of earth . . ."), in which the speaker claims that he "Who first look'd sad, griev'd, pin'd, and shew'd his paine, / Was he that first taught women, to disdaine" (35-36) or "The Triple Foole," in which the folly of unrequited love is doubled through the composition of "whining Poëtry" that expresses the emotion.

⁵The sighing note of the interpolated "alas," somewhat out of keeping with the matter-of-fact tone he has maintained up until this point, anticipates the more emotional argument of the second stanza. In implying, subtly, that he would actually prefer it if they *could* have a child together; he cunningly evokes an attitude of commitment without avowing it. Only a Donnean speaker could manage to say, "Don't worry, you won't get pregnant" and sound, at the same time, as if he were singing, "Would you marry me anyway? Would you have my baby?"

⁶See Brumble (150) on Donne's adaptation of Petrarchan convention in stanza two.

⁷Brumble (150) notes the movement from mere analogy in stanza one to more literal claims in the second stanza.

⁸ See also Gilman on Donne's ambivalence toward images and the frequent recurrence in his poetry of what the speaker of "Witchcraft by a Picture" calls "pictures made and mard." Gilman does not discuss "The Flea."

⁹ Augustine makes this assertion—"[A]liud est Sacramentum, aliud virtus Sacramenti"—in his "Tractates on the Gospel of John" (XXVI.11).

¹⁰The quotation is from James Winny (126), who is one of seven twentieth-century critics noted by Laurence Perrine in an "annotated list of critics who

believe that the seduction-attempt in 'The Flea' is successful" (16); the list also includes Helen Gardner and Patricia Meyer Spacks. Perrine blasts their readings as unfounded, insisting that the evidence provided "in the poem . . . favors the inference that this attempt on the young lady's virginity is as unsuccessful as those that have preceded it" (6). For Perrine, the poem dramatizes a witty game— as sexually fruitless as any Petrarchan ritual—played "for the 'fun' of the thing" by a perennially unrequited lover and his definitively coy mistress (7); but recent criticism of the poem—Perrine's list extends only through 1970—has persisted in taking the speaker's rhetoric considerably more seriously. See, for example, Baumlin's argument as discussed below, and Docherty's observation that "Prediction is tantamount to the generation of factuality in this poem" (59).

[11] See, for example Luther's "A Treatise on the New Testament" (*Works* 35: 94-101) and "The Babylonian Captivity of the Church" (*Works* 36: 51-55).

[12] See, for example, Calvin: "They consecrate an host, as they call it, which they may carie about in pompe, which they may shew foorth in a common gazing to be loked upon, worshipped, and called upon" (*Institutes* IV. xvii. 37). For a concise explanation of medieval Catholic "communion through the eyes," see the section entitled "The Gaze that Saves" in Emminghaus's second chapter.

[13] See also Donne's insistence that we must "apply [Christ's] bloud . . . shed for us, by those meanes which God in his Church presents to us," since not to do so would be a "wastfull wantonnesse" (*Sermons* 3: 162-163).

[14] See also Rajan's argument (809) that the *Songs and Sonets* invite resistance, that they evoke a response much like the one Donne solicited for the *Paradoxes and Problems* when he described them as "swaggerers" and "alarums to truth."

[15] Marotti concludes that the poem pits "a shame morality that views loss of virginity before marriage as a woman's greatest dishonor . . . against a personalist morality that regards the intention of commitment (and marriage) as largely legitimizing the premarital intercourse of mutual lovers" (94).

[16] As LeComte notes, the exact dates of Constance's birth and baptism are not known.

[17] Because Donne's *Songs and Sonets* cannot be dated with any certainty, the parallels between the poem and the letter cannot be applied to a biographical account of the poet, either; but as Shawcross stresses, such applications tend, at any rate, to limit rather than enrich our understanding of Donne's lyrics (see "Poetry, Personal and Impersonal"). What I am exploring in this reading, then, is not "The Flea" as biographical document, but rather the parallel between the rhetorical project Donne undertook in the letter and the lyric project he undertook in "The Flea."

[18] The letter to George More, for its part, did not persuade its addressee; far from convincing Ann's father to bless the match, Donne's rhetoric seems, under-

standably, to have incensed him further—just as the speaker's argument provokes the lady to extreme measures in the first two stanzas of "The Flea." When Donne wrote to Sir George again on 11 February, it was from the Fleet Prison, where he was held for a brief period after having been dismissed from Egerton's service.

Works Cited

Augustine. "Tractates on the Gospel of John." *Patrologia cursus completus* 35. Ed. J. P. Migne. Paris: 1878-1890.

Baumlin, James S. *John Donne and the Rhetorics of Renaissance Discourse.* Columbia: U of Missouri P, 1991.

Brumble, H. David, III. "John Donne's 'The Flea': Some Implications of the Encyclopedic and Poetic Flea Traditions." *Critical Q* 15 (1973): 147-154.

Calvin, John. *The Institution of the Christian Religion.* Trans. Thomas Norton. London: Thomas Vautrollier for Humfrey Toy, 1578.

Certaine Sermons or Homilies Appointed to be Read in Churches In the Time of Queen Elizabeth I (1547-1571). A Facsimile Reproduction of the Edition of 1623. Intr. by Mary Ellen Rickey and Thomas B. Stroup. Gainesville, FL: Scholars' Facsimiles and Reprints, 1968.

Docherty, Thomas. *John Donne Undone.* London: Methuen, 1986.

Donne, John. *Selected Prose.* Chosen by Evelyn Simpson. Ed. Helen Gardner and Timothy Healy. Oxford: Clarendon P, 1967.

Emminghaus, Johannes H. *The Eucharist: Essence, Form, Celebration.* Trans. Matthew J. O'Connell. Collegeville, MN: Liturgical P, 1978.

Gardner, Helen, ed. "General Introduction." *John Donne: The Elegies and The Songs and Sonnets.* Oxford: Clarendon P, 1965. xvii-lxii.

Gilman, Ernest B. *Iconoclasm and Poetry in the English Reformation: Down Went Dagon.* Chicago: U of Chicago P, 1986.

Halley, Janet E. "Textual Intercourse: Anne Donne, John Donne, and the Sexual Poetics of Textual Exchange." *Seeking the Woman in Late Medieval and Renaissance Writings: Essays in Feminist Contextual Criticism.* Ed. Sheila Fisher and Janet E. Halley. Knoxville: U of Tennessee P, 1989. 187-206.

Hester, M. Thomas. "'this cannot be said': A Preface to the Reader of Donne's Lyrics." *Christianity and Literature* 39 (1990): 365-385.

Hooker, Richard. *The Works of that Learned and Judicious Divine Mr. Richard Hooker.* Ed. John Keble. 7th. ed. Rev. by R. W. Church and F. Paget. 3 vols. Oxford: Clarendon P, 1888.

LeComte, Edward. "Jack Donne: From Rake to Husband."*Just So Much Honor:*

Essays Commemorating the Four-Hundredth Anniversary of the Birth of John Donne.
Ed. Peter Amadeus Fiore. University Park: Pennsylvania State UP, 1972. 9-32.

Luther, Martin. "The Babylonian Captivity of the Church." Trans. A. T. W.
Steinhauser and Rev. by Frederick C. Ahrens and Abel Ross Wentz. *Works.* 36.
Ed. Abel Ross Wentz. Philadelphia: Muhlenberg P, 1959.

_____. "A Treatise on the New Testament, that is, the Holy Mass."
Trans. Jeremiah J. Schindel. Rev. by E. Theodore Bachmann. *Works.* 35. Ed.
Theodore Bachmann. Philadelphia: Muhlenberg P, 1960.

Marotti, Arthur. *John Donne, Coterie Poet.* Madison: U of Wisconsin P, 1986.

Mayne, Jasper. "On Dr. Donnes death: By Mr. Mayne of Christ-Church in Ox-
ford." *Poems, By J.D. with Elegies on the Authors Death.* London: Printed by M.F.
for John Marriot, 1633. Facs. ed. Menston, England: Scolar P, 1970. 393-396.

Perrine, Laurence. "Explicating Donne: 'The Apparition' and 'The Flea'." *College
Literature* 17 (1990): 1-20.

Rajan, Tilottama. "'Nothing Sooner Broke': Donne's *Songs and Sonets* as Self-
Consuming Artifact." *ELH* 49 (1982): 805-828.

Shawcross, John T. *Intentionality and the New Traditionalism: Some Liminal Means to
Literary Revisionism.* University Park: Pennsylvania State UP, 1991.

_____. "Poetry, Personal and Impersonal: The Case of Donne." *The
Eagle and the Dove: Reassessing John Donne.* Ed. Claude J. Summers and Ted-
Larry Pebworth. Columbia: U of Missouri P, 1986. 53-66.

Sidney, Philip. *Sir Philip Sidney.* Ed. Katherine Duncan-Jones. Oxford: Oxford UP,
1989.

Spacks, Patricia Meyer. "In Search of Sincerity." *College English* 29 (1968): 591-602.

Wilson, David B. "*La Puce de Madame Desroches* and John Donne's 'The Flea.'"
Neuphilologische Mitteilungen 72 (1971): 297-301.

Winny, James. *A Preface to Donne.* New York: Scribners, 1970.

Donne's "Epithalamion made at Lincolnes Inne": The Religious and Literary Context

Allen Ramsey

God is Love, *and the* Holy Ghost *is amorous in his* Metaphors; *everie where his* Scriptures *abound with the notions of* Love, *of* Spouse, *and* Husband, *and* Marriadge Songs, *and* Marriadge Supper, *and* Marriadge-Bedde. *(Sermons 7:87)*

If so little has been written on "Epithalamion made at Lincolnes Inne," the poem may be neglected because so little is known about it. Critics tend to agree that Donne wrote the poem during his early years at Lincoln's Inn, around 1595, rather than during his later years, around 1613, when he was a reader there--but there is no evidence to support that position. And not only is the date of composition unclear, but the principals of the marriage are a mystery, and Donne's motives for writing the poem are unknown. Finally, to judge from published comments, the poem is either totally unremarkable or unacceptably coarse. The most thorough examination of the poem has been made by Heather Dubrow, who concludes that it is "seriously flawed" and has "lapses in taste" (157). David Novarr conjectures that the poem is a parody on the grounds that Donne couldn't have been serious.

In fact, on the surface, "Lincolnes Inne" is uneven in that its tone shifts rather abruptly from festive to somber. It may be unremarkable, too, if it conforms slavishly to some of the conventions of the genre. Besides celebrating a wedding, it has a narrative voice and a refrain not unlike Spenser's in his "Epithalamion." The imperative mood creates the dignified tone of epideictic rhetoric: "Leave, leave, faire Bride, your solitary bed" (2). In keeping with the genre, Donne makes the chronology of the wedding day the organizing principle of the lyric. In rapid succession, the narrator makes the familiar call to the bride to rise from her chaste bed; he calls to the "Daughters of London" (13) to "Help" (17) the bride, the "Sonnes" (26) to "shine" (31) and to "bring" (31) the bride to the Temple. In the fourth stanza the narrator tells the Temple gates to "hold" (38) the bride and groom in its "sacred bosome" (38). In the fifth stanza the narrator returns to the theme of time, in keeping with the impatient urge to rush to the wedding bed. The sun "sweates" (54) and, passing noon, gallops down the western slope. In stanza six, the evening star "is rose" (61), and the musicians are told to rest. But in the last two stanzas the poem deviates (in tone, at least) from the expected closure. Rather than a celebratory tone in the seventh stanza, the nuptial bed is described as a place where the sacrifice of virginity will occur. Finally, in a solemn tone, the sacrificial image is extended to remind the bride that this life is spent so that a better one may follow.

This brief summary suggests some of the conventions of the genre, but its simplicity may be deceiving. Although writers looked back to Catullus for classical guidelines, two other considerations are less visible. First, England had its own conventions accompanying marriage rites, drawn apparently from classical tradition, but naturalized into a secular, native English ritual. The most promising literary guide is Chapter 26 of George Puttenham's *The Arte of English Poesie* (often ascribed to his brother Richard), "The maner of rejoysings at mariages and weddings." In this chapter Puttenham is both historian and literary critic, giving us a commentary upon English wedding customs as well as shedding light upon the English epithalamion as a celebration of a social and religious ritual. With Puttenham as cultural historian, coinciding as his commentary does with the poetic career of John Donne, one gains access to the cultural background to the English epithalamic tradition.

Additionally, while the tradition recorded by Puttenham is secular, the design of Donne's religious imagination is imprinted upon this poem. Unlike those who have faulted the poem for its indecorum and coarseness, I suggest the dissonant tone in the poem is justifiable when set in its historical and religious milieu. To illustrate how generic expectations distort interpretation, one need only turn to Novarr's response to the first three lines of stanza four:

Thy two-leav'd gates faire Temple' unfold,
And these two in thy sacred bosome hold,
   Till, mystically joyn'd, but one they bee. [37-39]

Of this image Professor Novarr says that "Such gross stress on the procreative capacities of a church admits of no allegorical interpretation" (259). As I shall argue in the following pages, when taken in the context of the poem, the term "mystically joyn'd" reveals something more. Louis L. Martz, in his classic study *The Poetry of Meditation*, points out that meditation leads to union with God, an experience that is "open to all, including the married," and that such contemplation leads to the "Mystical Union" that Louis de Blois describes in his *Institutio Spiritualis* (Martz 18). While the discipline of meditative exercises is not part of Donne's epithalamion, the significance of "one" spans Donne's religious and secular poetry. In brief, "mystical" union in the work of John Donne cannot be dismissed as "gross stress."

The influence of these two forces in the poem, then--the presence of a native English tradition permeating the contemporary wedding ceremony and the pattern of Christian imagery created by Donne's religious imagination--produces the dissonances that induce Novarr to conclude the poem is a parody, on the one hand, and Dubrow to conclude that Donne "was more liable to occasional blunders in 1595 than in 1613" (157), on the other. It will be my contention that these two elements, although creating disparate moods, are appropriate to the metaphysical sensibility and reflect the religious imagination of the mature phase of Donne's poetic career. It should be said here that, although Puttenham's secular interests are distant from Donne's intensely Christian conscience, their concern intersects on the same object--the bride. Specifically, in contrast with the celebratory acclaim accorded the bridal party in typical Renaissance wedding treatises, both Puttenham and Donne find the locus of the marital experience to be the anguish of the bride. For Puttenham, the bride is a virtual victim, a pawn who perpetuates family geneologies and estates. For John Donne, in the "Epithalamion made at Lincolnes Inne," a young woman stands at the threshhold of marriage, frightened and alone, but her plight is alleviated by the promise of a Christian marriage.

1

In the first Book of *The Arte of English Poesie*, Puttenham writes "Of

Poets and Poesie," but he devotes a number of chapters to occasions for poetry. Chapter 13, for example, examines the ways in which poetry condemned "vice and the common abuses" (24); chapter 15 explains "In what forme of Poesie the evill and outragious behaviours of Princes were reprehended" (26). These motives for poetry justified its value, declaring virtuous an activity that had been questioned at least since Plato and Aristotle. In this, Puttenham's widened scope encompassed the occasions for poetry, a purpose which overlaps with his apology. Thus, chapter 25 celebrates the birth of children, "specially to Princes" (40) and progresses to the "rejoysings at mariages and weddings" of chapter 26. Matrimony is called the "occasion of children" (40), not only for princes, but for all people. The poetic rejoicings that it inspires, called *Epithalamies* by Puttenham, were executed in ballad form at the door of the bride and groom and sung "very sweetely by Musitians" (41). The song tradition- ally was divided "by breaches into three partes to serve for three severall fits or times to be song" (41)[1]. The first "songs were very loude and shrill" (41) to drown the noise made by the newlyweds. Puttenham apologizes for stating what might be taken as "licentious speach," but he emerges a true antiquarian in detailing the meaning behind the ritual. Since there were in olden times within the bedchamber "skreeking & outcry of the young damosell feeling the first forces of her stiffe & rigorous young man" (41), it was proper for "old nurses (appointed to that service) to suppresse the noise by casting of pottes full of nuttes round about the chamber upon the hard floore or pavemet, for they used no mattes nor rushes as we doe now" (41). Puttenham identifies the epithalamion as a substitute for those antiquated practices, since the epithalamion presum- ably has the wedding guests "occupied what with Musicke" (41). Puttenham concludes that the first breach (or division) was intended "to congratulate the first acquaintance and meeting of the young couple" (41). The parents of the bride and groom, meanwhile, sat within listening distance of the progressing activities,

> allowing of their parents good discretions in making the match, the[n] afterward to sound cherfully to the onset and first encounters of that amorous battaile, to declare the co[m]fort of childre[n], & encrease of love by that meane cheifly caused: the bride shewing her self every waies well disposed [41].

Puttenham's detailed account of the ritualized first hours of the wed- ding night provides a reminder of two crucial factors underlying the

English Christian marriage: it was arranged by parents who often held enormous stakes in the fortunes of the parties involved, and it was matter-of-factly a mandate springing from Genesis 9:1 to procreate in order to populate the earth and increase the saints in heaven[2]. Additional specific pragmatic demands to perpetuate the family blood and, preferably, name, were also no small matter, as Shakespeare's first 17 sonnets well illustrate. John Donne himself lost five of twelve children, attesting to the hard realities of perpetuation in the seventeenth century.

The second part of the epithalamic ritual, says Puttenham, began around midnight, when the musicians arrived at the chamber door, because "the ballade was to refresh the faint and weried bodies and spirits," since "the first embracementes never bred barnes . . . but onley made passage for children" (42). Thus, the "second assaultes," Puttenham states bluntly, were "apt to avance the purpose of procreation" (42). Although merriment is implied in this late night refresher, it is devoid of the sniggering associated with the shivaree, comparing more with a dash of cold water to the face of the pugilist between rounds. In short, the ballad called "epithalamie" is wholly secular and almost solemnly functional.

The third "breach" of the epithalamion transpired when "it was faire broad day" (42); the bride emerges "no more as a virgine, but as a wife" (42)--or, as Donne's epithalamion has it, when she has "put on perfection" and taken "a womans name." As "dinner time" arrives, the bride must show herself "very demurely" to exhibit her well being. At that time, the musicians again appear to present "a Psalme of new applausions" (42), or approval, sealing this marriage which has been legitimized by consummation of the sex act and solemnized by the surrender of the precious maidenhead. Although Puttenham spices this festive occasion "with twentie maner of sweet kisses" (42), the seriousness of the ritual cannot be disguised: the musicians' applausions celebrate

> that they had either of them so well behaved them selves that night, the husband to rob his spouse of her maidenhead *and save her life*, the bride so lustely to satisfie her husbandes love and scape *with so litle daunger of her person* [42, emphasis added].

For all the ostensible merriment of marriage there is no joke embedded in Puttenham's description. Without the manuals of the age of Freud, the business of marriage embodied enough ignorance, pain and, at times, apparently, terror to make Puttenham's term "inviolable wedlocke" (143) sound as joyless as funeral rites.

Appropriately, Puttenham closes his discussion of the epithalamion by calling the event a "ceremony," (43) manifestly a process

> omitted when men maried widowes or such as had tasted the frutes of love before, (we call them well experienced young women) in whom there was no *feare of daunger to their persons*, or of any outcry at all, at the time of those terrible approches [43, emphasis added].

The English tradition of the marriage ritual is extremely different, then, if the bride was a widow or divorcee (as was the case with Donne's epithalamion to Frances Howard's marriage to the Earl of Somerset) rather than a virgin--and the epithalamion itself reflected that difference.

2

The "Epithalamion made at Lincolnes Inne" makes the bride the poem's subject and, indeed, hardly acknowledges that there is a groom. Broadly, the poem conforms to Puttenham's criteria for the epithalamion, but Donne is innovative in his approach, especially in bringing to the poem the timely language of the religious significance of the occasion. The opening stanza, while introducing the standard motif that expresses the urge to hasten the clock, asserts that the bride is a virgin. The tension between the push towards marriage, with its "perfection" of one flesh in consummated marriage, as opposed to the resistant forces urging the bride to retain the innocence of virginal childhood, is captured in lines 4-5 in referring to the maiden's bed,

> It nourseth sadnesse, and your bodies print,
> Like to a grave, the yielding downe doth dint,

and these disparate emotions set the tone of the poem.

Donne returns to images of the grave on two more occasions in the poem, but it is here that a mood of wistful loss builds to the most beautiful lines of the poem:

> Loe, in yon path which store of straw'd flowers graceth,
> The sober virgin paceth;

Except my sight faile, 'tis no other thing;
Weep not nor blush, here is no griefe nor shame.
To day put on perfection,and a womans name. (32-36)

These lines by themselves assure that this poem is no parody. Rather,
they make realistic the plight of a bride in Renaissance England as de-
scribed by Puttenham. The compassion Donne shows for the bride sug-
gests that she was a personal friend whose anguish and/or fear provoked
the poet's sympathy. Donne's candor also explains the refrain, a device
whose repetition makes manifest the Christian mystery of marriage: we
are born half a person and only through marriage are we made whole,
exemplified by Adam and Eve in becoming two people, one flesh. This is
the Christian explanation and consolation for every woman's charge to
serve her master's pleasure in bed and perpetuate the family line at the
risk of her own life. The divergent moods of triumphing over death in the
face of danger reverberate through the poem.

Stanzas two, three and four turn from the solemn isolation of the bride
and adopt a jocular tone about this marriage; the poet assumes the
ceremonial epideictic stance: "Daughters of London . . . And you frolique
Patricians" (13, 25). Appropriately, the allusions are classical—"Daugh-
ters . . . Patricians . . . Senators"—with reference to Flora and
Hermaphroditus interspersed. This segment of the poem appears to have
topical references, as has been noted (Ousby 135, 141), and Donne's
rhetorical strategy supports this position: the stanzas present the comic
relief of the poem at the expense of the groom and his peers. Stanza two
alludes to the English practice—ritual—of assessing the net worth of the
bride. No matter how crass the practice may seem today, a felicitous
financial settlement would be cause for celebration. The epideictic stance
of the persona allows the poet to turn an eye toward "Our Golden Mines"
(14), the bride's peers, who are also likely to present themselves and their
wealth to the town's bachelors.[3] The wittiness of the "mine" conceit is
enriched by the dual nature of riches: calling the bride a "jewell" joins
"wealth" with "beauty" by yoking it with floral imagery; the juncture
makes the word convey wealth *and* beauty: "As gay as Flora, and as rich
as Inde" (22).

The third stanza turns the joke upon the friends of the groom. The title
of the poem ostensibly alludes to the groom and the masculine world of
the Inns of Court, and stanzas three and four give point to the topicality.
Since the poem flatters and comforts the bride (and is apparently directed
to the bride and her family), Donne can easily make the groom the butt of

his joke, particularly if the groom was one of Donne's peers at Lincoln's Inn. Still in the epidiectic mode, the poet in a convoluted conceit calls upon the "frolique" (25) students to "shine" (31) upon this wedding. The "Sonnes of these Senators" also bring wealth to the marriage arrangement—but Donne expands the mockery by lining up three comic accusations in rapid succession: They are "painted courtiers," hoarders ("barrels") of other's "wits" and a strange combination of "study and play," made thereby into "Hermaphrodits" (30). Explicitly stated, the groom is one of them: "Yee of those fellowships whereof hee's one" (29). As Ousby points out, the line "leads us to believe that at some point Donne had a real groom in mind" (141). It follows that Donne had a real bride in mind, too. In searching for Donne's purpose, it is significant that the bride is addressed directly (most notably in the refrain) while the groom is referred to in the third person.

The joke is soon over: With a sudden turn in mood, the poet, still using the imperative voice of the epidiectic persona, directs these young men to bring the bridegroom to the "Temple" (31). Professor Shawcross points out in his notes to the poem that Donne may be alluding to the Inner Temple or Middle Temple (403). Indeed, stanzas three and four allude to people and places in the immediate area. The renowned Lincoln's Inn Fields, adjacent to Lincoln's Inn, survive to this day. Although Donne does not get so specific as to document in detail the familiar environs of Lincoln's Inn, the vivid description of the Temple grounds stands out partly because of the emphatic "This Bridegroom to the Temple bring" (31). This command makes an interesting connection with the locale of the Inns of Court since "yon path which store of straw'd flowers graceth" (32) provides a provocative image for Donne's readers to summon up in relation to the adjoining Lincoln's Inn. Just down Chancery Lane toward the Thames stand the Inner Temple, the Gateway and the Temple Church. The Gateway (finished in 1610) is a three-story tunnelled archway leading to the Temple Church. The Temple Church (built 1160-85), a common haunt of the students in the Inns of Court, would have been familiar to Donne's peers. The striking images, even today, include the tombs of the Templars, dating from the thirteenth century, with the ten effigies of the knights set across the floor of the Temple Church[4].

The gates become the climactic conceit for the topical segment of the poem. Stanza four provides the transition from the topical allusions back to the broader epithalamic conventions, but in doing so, the poet joins the bride and groom "mystically" (39), like the two locking leaves of the Temple Gate. These lines resume the epithalamic progression toward the wedding, since the second reference to the Temple (37) has the couple joined at last in "thy sacred bosome" (38). Gayle Edward Wilson has traced the etymology of the term "sarcophagus" as a "flesh-eating tomb" (73) to explain the nature of the womb/tomb configuration. It would seem that if Donne wished to evoke a Greek derivation from the term "sarcophagus," he would have used the word in the poem.[5] Still, the direction of Wilson's argument seems correct in seeing the morbidity of the passage as "a witty way of satisfying the epithalamic convention of wishing the bride and groom a long life" (73). If the topical allusion is intended, as I have suggested, the word "thy" in lines 37, 38 and 40 has "Temple" (37) as its referent: the "leane and hunger-starved wombe [of the Temple]/Long time expect their bodies and their tombe" (40-41). The imagery is entirely appropriate if, as I have suggested, the Temple Church, with its prominent sarcophagi, is the topical allusion.

The sexual implication of the "two-leav'd gates" (37) has been discussed by Ousby and Novarr. The extended image of the temple as a womb, however, wherein the bride and groom are "mystically joyn'd, but one they bee" (39), embodies a major theological concept in Donne's work. The scope of this inspiration is suggested in two wedding sermons, each of which elucidates the principle of union. On November 19, 1627, Donne preached a sermon at the marriage of the Lady Mary, daughter of the Earl of Bridgewater, to the eldest son of Lord Herbert of "Castle-iland" (*Sermons* 8: 94). Deliberating upon the theological nature of marriage, Donne states that a marriage in the church is, in addition to joining two people in marriage, a mysterious wedding to the Church itself:

> But Mariage amongst Christians, is herein *Magnum mysterium*, A Sacrament in such a sense; a mysterious signification of the *union of the soule* with Christ; when both persons professe the Christian Religion, in *generall*, there arises some signification of that spirituall union: But when they both professe Christ in *one* forme, in one Church, in one Religion, and that, the right; then, as by the *Civill* Contract, there is an union of their *estates*, and *persons*, so, as that they two are made one, so by this *Sacramentall*, this mysterious union, these two, thus be made one, between themselves, are also made one with Christ himself; by the *Civill* union, common to all people, they are made *Eadem caro*, The same flesh with one another; By this mysterious, this Sacramentall, this significative union, they are made *Idem Spiritus cum Domino*; The same Spirit with the Lord. (*Sermons* 8: 104)

In an earlier sermon of 1621, Donne more specifically identifies a marriage as a tripartite event: the secular marriage (the predestined matching of one man with one woman); the marriage of the soul to Christ "in his eternall decree"; and "our third and last marriage, our eternall mariage in the triumphant Church" (*Sermons* 3: 253).

These explications from sermons six years apart—both given on the occasion of a wedding—breathe life into stanza four of Donne's epithalamion, typifying the Christian background that infuses the poem. As discussed above, the gates of the church open and the bride and groom enter, where they are "mystically joyn'd" (39). There, the womb of the temple enfolds them, and, with the bride and groom eternally married both in and to the Church, the temple will

> Long time expect their bodies and their tombe,
>   Long after their owne parents fatten thee. (41-42)

Inherent in this ostensibly gloomy pronouncement is the poet's benediction that the wedding couple will long outlive their parents, but underlying the promise of a long life is the more optimistic promise of eternal marriage to the Church. While this vividly emphasizes death, since Donne, as Ousby puts it, "sees the skull beneath the skin of even a bride and groom" (135), still, the inspiration of Donne's religious imagination gives the marriage victory over fleeting Time—which produces the dissonance in the epithalamion (the maiden hesitant to move toward wedlock while the sun hastens down the Westward slope toward the bedding of the bride). Thus, while the wedding ceremony states "till death do you part," for Donne the tripartite Christian marriage is ultimately the bedrock of eternal life, making the conquest of death the triumphant promise of Christian faith.

The words beginning stanza five—"Oh winter dayes" (49)—make a clear break with the topicality of the preceding stanzas and lead the reader back to the standard epithalamic topic of Time. Echoing Spenser, Donne urges the sun to "gallop" (58) down the western sky. The rest of the poem moves directly toward the wedding bed, but stanza six pauses to make explicit reference to the native epithalamic tradition as described by Puttenham:

> Release your strings
> Musicians, and dancers take some truce
> With these your pleasing labours. [63-65]

In alluding to the process directing the traditional English wedding, Donne makes a felicitous connection with the term "perfection" in the refrain: the dancers need not continue their "pleasing labours" (65) because extensive practice ("use") causes weariness as much as (or, instead of) "perfection" (66). The term "perfection" repeated in the refrain—to "put on perfection"—connects the festivities in the hall to the "other labours" (70) of the bedchamber—the tradition being that the festivities of the guests will obliterate the noises in the bedchamber, as Puttenham indicates.

The closing lines of the poem give poignant emphasis to the ritual preparatory to procreation. The bride is disrobed and the gown set aside to transmute the bed into a grave for virginity, reborn as a cradle (80). The exchange is repeated in the final stanza. Shawcross annotates line 86, "That this life for a better should be spent," to refer "to the belief that sexual intercourse reduced one's life-span" (173). The word "spent," like "die," subsumes that meaning, but the context of the poem allows at least two *additional* readings.

> Even like a faithfull man content,
> That this life for a better should be spent [85-86]

suggests that the benefits of marriage for a woman are no different than those for her spouse: that is, it would be better to spend this (married) life in celibacy (even though it is better to marry than to burn). The line following—"So, shee a mothers rich stile doth preferre" (87)—extends the equation to imply that the bride's "rich" life as a mother and wife is a luxury that properly should be sacrificed for chastity. The image of a sacrificial lamb, "when tenderly / The priest comes on his knees t'embowell her" (89-90), provides a religious context which carries forward the Christian argument for chasity, thus unifying the conceit. This reading compares with Puttenham's secular assertion that the bedding of the bride is painful, but has its rewards for the families involved in perpetuating the family estates.

A second application for this passage makes "this life" refer to the life the bride has enjoyed up to the wedding day. Then, just as "a faithful man" is "content," so being a faithful mother will be a better life than that of the innocence of youth prior to marriage. This extends the burden of Donne's attempt to convince the bride that she need feel neither "griefe nor shame" (35) about getting married.

Thus, taken in the context of Christian thought the thematic direction of these lines is lucid. David Novarr complains that the lamb image "is not wittily lascivious; it is grossly cruel" (252). Ousby disagrees, saying that metaphysical poetry typically generates connotations that must be ignored (134). She adds, however, that Donne's sacrificial image fails "in a way that is also characteristic of metaphysical imagery; the connotations jar too much, the tingling of the glass is out of control" (134). The error in both of these appraisals lies in their neglect of Donne's religious imagination—a glaring oversight, considering the image is explicitly a priest on his knees before a sacrificial lamb. Although the lamb is a standard emblem in Christian teaching, a single passage from Donne's sermon preached at the wedding of Mistress Margaret Washington, at the church of St. Clement Danes, May 30, 1621, illustrates how Donne's poetic language in "Lincolnes Inne" is anchored in religious imagery and meets the standards of decorum as they apply specifically to the wedding ceremony:

> And in this third mariage, the persons are, the Lamb and my soul; *The mariage of the Lamb is come, and blessed are they that are called to the mariage Supper of the Lamb.* . . . That Lamb who was *brought to the slaughter and opened not his mouth,* and I who have opened my mouth and poured out imprecations and curses upon men, and execrations and blasphemies against God upon every occasion; That Lamb who *was slain from the beginning,* and I who was slain by him who *was a murderer from the beginning;* That *Lamb which took away the sins of the world,* and I who brought more sins into the world, then any sacrifice but the blood of this Lamb could take away: This Lamb and I (these are the Persons) shall meet and mary; there is the Action. (*Sermons* 3: 253)

Although Donne's application of the lamb image in this wedding sermon differs from that of the "Epithalamion made at Lincolnes Inne," it puts to rest the contention that one should consider the conceit either "grossly cruel" or "the tingling of the glass." Rather, the image draws upon orthodox Christian doctrine, appropriate to both the religious imagery found in Donne's secular poetry and the jarring images of the religious poems. Unlike the extreme images of, say, Robert Southwell's "The Burning Babe," Donne's sacrificial lamb is a conventional image that would inevitably stir the religious imagination of Donne's audience. In the sermon, as in the epithalamion, the image of the slaughtered lamb is at once poetic and religious.

Seen in this light, the sacrificial lamb of lines 89-90 extends the thought of the previous stanza, where the virgin's girdle is set aside for a "pleasing sacrifice":

> Thy virgins girdle now untie,
> And in thy nuptiall bed (loves alter) lye
> A pleasing sacrifice. [73-75]

The bed, like the temple of stanza 4, provides a grave—here replaced by the cradle, which produces the eternity of procreation. Winfried Schleiner draws attention to the distinction between high and low metaphor to demonstrate that Donne willingly violated decorum if it made a sermon more convincing. Finally, she cites Donne's own words, found in his sermon "Preached to the King," dated "Probably February 11, 1626/ 27" (*Sermons* 7: 369): "No metaphor, no comparison is too high, none too low, too triviall, to imprint in you a sense of Gods everlasting goodnesse towards you" (24). In both the church and the wedding bed, then, the bride puts on perfection and a (married) woman's name. To John Donne and his audience, the sacrificial lamb presents the promise of Christianity, as delineated in the sermon preached to the Lady Mary, daughter of Bridgewater: in consummating the marriage, the sacrifice of virginity embraces a divine mystery, the tripartite promise of eternal lif—through the resurrection, through procreation and through the marriage with Christ.

3

George Puttenham's attempt to record the English wedding tradition was published as literary criticism, falling as it does between the occasion of rejoicing at the nativity of the prince's children and the occasions for epigrams. The sense of chapter 26 is that an epithalamion had a functional value that determined its form. That is, while literary in nature, it was sociological in provenance. Puttenham assures the reader that the poet is "to celebrate by his poeme the chearefull day of mariages" (40); it is the "highest & holiest, of any ceremonie apperteining to *man*" (40, emphasis mine). The gender-specific reference no doubt referred to some unspecified degree to the human race, but Puttenham asserts that the ballads called *Epithalamies* celebrate "the bedding of the bride" (41), not the groom. Other "Musicks" occurred during the wedding celebration, but these were not "epithalamies," since they contributed nothing to disguising the sounds of the "amorous battaile" (41).

The bridge from Puttenham to Donne is found in the disconsolate state of the bride. Donne does not pattern his poem specifically into three "breaches," starting with the introduction to the bedchamber, returning at midnight to refresh the bride and groom, and concluding in "faire broad day" (42), nor is there solid evidence that Donne used Puttenham as a direct source (as Shakespeare used Holinshed, for example). But "Lincolnes Inne" shares the spirit of suffering, the native tradition secularized as artifact in Puttenham's work, but transmogrified into triumphant suffering through the religious imagination of Donne's Christian learning. Puttenham compares the bride to "all virgins tender & weake, & unexpert" (41); the noise in the house is intended to "diminish the noise of the laughing lamenting spouse" (41)—meaning the bride. In the morning the bride should emerge to show herself, "whether she were the same woman or a changeling, or dead or alive, or maimed by any accident nocturnall" (42)—and other dangers as already quoted in this essay. Donne encourages her to "put on perfection, and a womans name." Puttenham says the bride should come forward, "no more as a virgin, but as a wife" (42). Donne makes specific reference to Puttenham's epithalamic ritual in stanza six: "Release your strings / Musicians, and dancers take some truce" (63-4). He points out as well that she "goes a maid, who, least [lest] she [re]turne the same, / To night puts on perfection, and a womans name" (71-2). Donne's "better state" is "a cradle" (80), having sacrificed "this [virgin] life for a better" (86) one—motherhood—while eternal life is not excluded. In lines 93-94 Donne also makes a startling reference to himself, as if he is one of the wedding celebrants outside the bedchamber—

> This Sun will love so dearely
> Her rest, that long, long we shall want her sight

—a reference which makes him not merely a member of the wedding party, but one of many placed strategically at the moment of the epithalamic ritual when the third breach is about to occur.[6] The penultimate line of the poem, moreover, brings home with climactic force the suasion inherent in Donne's description of the sacrifice the maiden is making to become an adult: "Wonders are wrought, for shee which had no maime" (95). If one turns to Ovid or Catullus, the line provokes laughter or malice. But this is an English wedding poem, and when turning to Puttenham we find him saying that "her parents and kinsfolkes" look at the emerging bride to see "whether she were the same woman or a changeling, dead or alive, or maimed" (42). The difference between the scene described by Puttenham and that by Donne is that Puttenham's bride could be any English maiden. The "sober virgin" (33) of Donne's poem, it would seem, stepped down a flowered path leading to a specific English wedding into the throes of a sacrificial wedding bed in a community so familiar and vivid that the title identified the occasion and the principals involved.

Finally, one returns not to Puttenham, but to Donne. Donne's wedding sermons dwell upon the religious mandates of marriage; the power of the religious imagination pervades the metaphoric language, the iconography, the poetic imagery that made this great preacher a poet for all time. While the stolid realism of Puttenham's treatise validates the seriousness of the secular transaction of marriage, the energy of "The Epithalamion made at Lincolnes Inne" is generated largely by Donne's religious inspiration. When the gates of the "faire Temple unfold" (37), taking the bride and groom into "thy sacred bosome" (38), they are there mystically joined, not only like the two leaves at the entrance to the womb, but also like the "mysterious . . . *union of the soule* with Christ" (*Sermons* 8: 104).

Notes

[1] I have preserved the original spellings in quotations except to modernize the long "f" with "s" and "u" with "v."

[2] In concluding his "Epithalamion," Edmund Spenser, too, sounds a note of supplication for the bounty of progeny:

> And ye high heauens, the temple of the gods,
> . . . .
> And all ye powers which in the same remayne,
> More then we men can fayne,
> Poure out your blessing on vs plentiously,
> And happy influence vpon vs raine,
> That we may raise a large posterity,
> Which from the earth, which they may long possesse,
> With lasting happinesse,

> Vp to your haughty pallaces may mount,
> And for the guerdon of theyr glorious merit
> May heauenly tabernacles there inherit,
> Of blessed Saints for to increase the count. (409, 413-23)

[3] The topical allusions in stanzas 2-4 call attention to two separate but related topics: the status of the English bride at the turn of the century and the date of composition of the poem. The prevailing tendency has been to date the poem around 1595. If written in 1595, the poem coincides with the appearance of *Romeo and Juliet*, a play that gives comic attention to a young man who is in love with love but turns tragic when a family decides a marriage of convenience is preferable. The year 1595 is also the year often cited as the time when the Earl of Southampton was being pressured to marry properly (and is thought by some to be the subject of Shakespeare's sonnets). The year of the sonnets and *Romeo and Juliet*, however, does not argue for an early date of composition, since the marriage of convenience as a tragic plot device was being explored on the stage until the theaters were closed in 1642. For example, the Duchess is exploited by her brothers in *The Duchess of Malfi*, Rowland Lacy is pressured to marry in his rank in *The Shoemaker's Holiday*, and a marriage of convenience is urged in the subplot of Heywood's *A Woman Killed with Kindness*. These events show that marriages of convenience were being questioned and, in theater, challenged. This essay notes that the information available does not assure early composition of the poem. On the other hand, construction of the Inner Temple Gates in 1610 may provide a terminal date for the poem. I suggest further that, since the epithalamion resonates with the imagery and tone of Donne's sermons, a later rather than an earlier date deserves serious consideration.

[4] The burden of my discussion does not depend upon any particular gates, at Lincoln's Inn or elsewhere. The renowned Inner Temple Gateway provided a vivid vehicle to provoke the imagination of Donne's audience. Whether the reference is to those gates, the gates to one of the churches in the Inns of Court or to fictive gates is, ultimately, irrelevant. The topicality of the poem, however, invites examination of the possibilities attendant upon the local scene identified in the title of the poem, particularly since Donne uses the term "Temple" twice and the Inner Temple Gates lead to Temple Church--where, as suggested in lines 38-39, the bride and groom are joined.

[5] This image makes another connection with *Romeo and Juliet*. In the final scene of the play Romeo uses the womb/tomb wordplay in referring to the Capulet mausoleum, calling it a "maw," a mouth which consumes flesh. The figure, however, was a common one in the Renaissance.

[6] The lines ". . . O light / Of heaven . . . / This Sun will love so dearely" (91-93)

renders inevitably the sun/Son pun, but in this context the image bears mention. Extended, the penultimate line "Shee which had no maime" (95) invites association with the Virgin.

Works Cited

Dubrow, Heather. *A Happier Eden: The Politics of Marriage in the Stuart Epithalamium.* Ithaca: Cornell UP, 1990.

Martz, Louis L. *The Poetry of Meditation: A Study in English Religious Literature of the Seventeenth Century.* New Haven: Yale UP, 1954.

Novarr, David. "Donne's 'Epithalamion Made at Lincolnes Inn': Context and Date." RES 7 (1956): 250-63.

Ousby, Heather Dubrow. "Donne's 'Epithalamion made at Lincolnes Inne': An Alternative Interpretation." *SEL* 16 (1976): 131-43.

Puttenham, George. *The Arte of English Poesie* (1589). Menston: Scolar, 1968.

Schleiner, Winfried. *The Imagery of John Donne's Sermons.* Providence: Brown UP, 1970.

Shakespeare, William. *Romeo and Juliet. The Riverside Shakespeare.* Ed. G. Blakemore Evans, et al. Boston: Houghton, 1974. 1055-99.

Spenser, Edmund. "Epithalamion." *Spenser: Poetical Works.* Ed. J. C. Smith and E. De Selincourt. London: Oxford UP, 1966. 579-84.

Wilson, Gayle Edward. "Donne's Sarcophagal Imagery in 'Epithalamion made at Lincolnes Inne,' vv. 37-42." *ANQ* 18.4 (Dec. 1979): 72-73.

The Shape of "the mindes indeavours": Donne's First Anniversarie

M. Thomas Hester

he structure of Donne's *The First Anniversarie. An Anatomy of the World* has been the subject of considerable critical debate. But from O. B. Hardison's study of its genre to Barbara Lewalski's discussion of its symbolic design this debate has attended almost exclusively on the rhetorical structure of the poem. Certainly, as Rosemond Tuve illustrated many years ago, such a concern is appropriate to Renaissance poetry, the near identification of oratory and poetry in the age being so prominent. Nevertheless, in support of these views one additional feature of the structure of the poem should be examined: its *metaphoric* shape. Such a perspective provides several insights into the central meanings of the poem–specifically, by showing that the speaker of the poem has a much more positive or optimistic attitude towards man's condition and the value of his own art than studies of the poem's rhetoric have intimated or claimed.

The jeremiadic speaker of the *Anatomy* himself reminds us that the metaphoric shape of the poem derives from the central metaphor of neo-Pythagorean aesthetics and Renaissance cosmology–the planes of correspondence in the macro-microcosm. More specifically, the speaker's attitude towards his mosaic "office" and anatomical endeavors is clarified by observation of the shape of thought in Donne's initial elegy for Elizabeth

Drury. Like Dante's allegorical search for Beatrice as traced by John Freccero ("Dante's Pilgrim"), the metaphoric shape of thought in *The First Anniversarie* is that of a spiral. At the conclusion of the poem, although the speaker remains where he had begun–at the graveside of a dead girl lamenting her death and the larger significances of her death–not only has Elizabeth Drury been transformed into an "Idea"[1] which resides now in heaven, but the speaker himself has advanced to a stage where he can now affirm that leap of faith which will initiate *The Second Anniversary*. In addition to being emblematic of what Louis Martz has called "a mind caught in a deadly oscillation, caught in a narrowing gyre that ends in the grave" ("Donne's Anniversaries Revisited" 40), the poem's structure figures forth a mind in a widening gyre that ascends beyond this world to the circumference of *Sapientia*. The organization of the poem is, in one sense, as one reader suggests, "strictly logical, beginning with man whose Fall was the root of all the evils described, then taking up the ever-widening ramifications of that Fall throughout the world and the universe" (Lewalski 262). But this does not mean that the poem is merely "analytic rather than progressive" (Lewalski 261-62) or that "the direction of the poem [is] toward the grave" (Martz 37). Rather, the formulaic character of the poem-as-meditation and the melancholic mood of the poem-as-satire (as explained by Martz) should not overshadow the speaker's "progress" in the poem. In his creative transformation of a dead girl into a living "Idea" he does *ascend*, from a focus on that corpse in that grave to a vision of the boundaries of the known universe. Just how Donne's speaker has "progressed" through this first elegy and just what that "progress" implies is clarified by recollection of the shape of his meditations and the significances of the spiral as an emblem of "The mindes indeavours" in medieval and Renaissance epistemology.

The application of the spiral motions of the universe, as thoroughly traced by Freccero, has a long and significant history. The most famous example of this metaphor is in the *Commedia*, in which the wanderings and ascent of Dante's pilgrim are figured as spiral motion. The ultimate source of such a view is probably the myth of the soul in Plato's *Timaeus*, which posits correspondence between the revolutions of the universe and the human soul. In Plato's exposition, the analogy compares (1) the circular motion of the celestial realm with the perfected human reason, (2) the rectilinear motion of matter with irrational human behavior and animal activity, and (3) the spiral motion of the planets with the motions of the rational soul. As phrased by Pseudo-Dionysius the Aeropagite, man is capable of three intellectual movements: "*circular*, when the human mind enters within itself and contemplates the Supreme Being; *linear*, when the human mind concentrates on external things; *spiral*, when 'the knowledge of divine things illuminates it, not by way of intuition or in unity, but thanks to discursive reasons, so to speak, by complex and progressive steps'" (as cited in Freccero, "Dante's Pilgrim" 175). This same correspondence, Freccero points out, is reiterated in the writings of Philo Judeaus, the commentaries on the *Timaeus* by Chalcidius, the scholarship of Albertus Magnus, Boethius' *Consolation of Philosophy*, St. Bonaventura's *Itinerarius mentis in Deum*, and St. Thomas' *Summa Theologica*.

In the Renaissance, Petrarch's attempt to discover an allegorical *figura* for the motions of his spiritual "progress" is representative of the vitality of this epistemological motif. In his "Ascent of Mont Ventoux," as recorded in his popular *Le Familiari* (Basel, 1581), the Italian humanist describes his difficult trek up the "steep and almost inaccessible pile of rocky material" by ceaseless "striving" after a "daring attempt" had proved unsuccessful. "At last," he records, "I felt utterly disgusted, began to regret my perplexing error, and decided to attempt the heights with a wholehearted effort." His journey up the mountain, he explains, took him around and around the summit, up and down valleys, as he gradually progressed up the peak. "Frustrated in [his] hopes" at one point, he pondered the allegorical significances of his journey:

> There I leaped in my winged thoughts from things corporeal to what is incorporeal and addressed my self in words like these: "What you have experienced today while climbing this mountain happens to you, you must know, and to many others who are making their way toward the blessed life. It is not easily understood by us men, because the motions of the body lie open, while those of mind are invisible and hidden. The life we call blessed is located on a *high peak*. 'A narrow way,' they say, leads up to it. . . . On the highest summit is set the end of all, the goal towards which our pilgrimage is directed . . . ; having *strayed* in error, you must either ascend to the summit of the blessed life under the heavy burden of *hard striving*, ill deferred, or *lie* prostrate in your slothfulness in the valleys of your sins. If 'darkness and the shadow of death' find you there . . . –you must pass the eternal night in incessant torments."

Such an understanding renewed his vigor and aided his eventual success, he explains, and at the conclusion of his letter, "turn[ing his] inner eye toward [him]self" again, he writes:

Silently I thought over how greatly mortal men lack counsel who, *neglecting the noblest part of themselves* in empty *parading*, look without for what can be found within. I admired the *nobility of the mind*, had it not voluntarily degenerated and *strayed* from the primordial state of its origin, converting into disgrace what God had given to be its honor. . . . How intensely ought we to exert our strength to get under foot not a higher spot of earth but the passions which are puffed up by early instincts. (Petrarch 36-46, emphasis mine)

The inscription of man's ascent to (or towards) Truth as spiral motion is prominent in many of Donne's poems prior to *The First Anniversarie* as well. The emblematic description of the "huge hill [of] Truth" in "Satyre III" (79-84), for example, relies on this topos, recommending the pilgrim's progress "about . . . and about, . . . th'hills suddennes" (81-2) as an exemplary alternative to the fugacious mental motions of modern "devotion." This monitory survey of the types of "mindes indeavours" (87) required by "our Mistresse faire Religion" (5) describes various mental activities in terms of motion. Failures in devotion are evident by the mere physical motions of Elizabethan adventurers who exert their brutish nature in seeking only "golde" across the flat "map" of the physical world; the mere "humoral" motions of sectarian amorists who follow only the dictates of their emotions are described as equally serpentine or rectilinear. To these failures is proposed the spiral motion of the pilgrim of Truth in his ascent to where "Truth stands." Both thematically and metrically, "Satyre III" describes this motion as the only activity "worthy' of all our Soules" (6) energies—in accordance with traditional descriptions of the rational soul's motions as the harmony of man's body *and* soul, the emblem of his human perfection as a creature of rectilinear duration and the circle of eternity.

One of Donne's most famous "metaphysical conceits"—the figure of the souls of parted lovers as "stiff twin compasses" in "A Valediction: forbidding Mourning"—repeats the basic shape of the earlier emblem in "Satyre III." Here the spiral is figured as mutual lovers' souls which exist simultaneously in the world of durative, rectilinear space and the eternality of "just" circular spacelessness because of their love:

> If they be two, they are two so
> As stiffe twin compasses are two,
> Thy soule the fixt foot, makes no show
> To move, but doth, if the'other doe.

....

Such wilt thou be to mee, who must
Like th'other foot, obliquely runne.
Thy firmnes makes my circle just,
And makes me end, where I begunne. (25-28, 33-36)

As Freccero points out, the combination of circular and linear movement in this image "comprises the dynamism of humanity. With its whirling motion, the compass synthesizes the linear extension of time and space with the circularity of eternity" ("Donne's 'Valediction'" 336f.). The lovers can "suffer" the vicissitudes and separation of rectilinear motion (the speaker's departure) because of the eternal circularity of their spiritual commitment; thus, the "motions" of mutual lovers' souls are identical in design to those of the pilgrim pursuing "our Mistresse faire Religion." It was in direct contrast to sectarian fools who choose their religious "love" for the wrong reasons, we might remember, that the example of the pilgrim of Truth was offered in the earlier poem.

It should not be surprising, then, that Donne's fullest presentation of the mind's pursuit of something commensurate with man's capacity for love, in *The First Anniversarie*, is also structured as a spiral. This poem *does* demonstrate, in one sense, how human reason comes to understand the "limits of reason," but such a perspective should not obviate the signifi-cance of the "pattern" of thought by which Donne's speaker reaches that conclusion. The central action of the poem is also the search for a female figure "worthy' of all our Soules devotion," and again the movement of the lover-anatomist's quest is figured as simultaneous rectilinear and circular motion. In one sense, his vision ascends a straight line: he begins with the spatially "lowest" form in the universe of the poem, mankind, and gradually progresses through the various planes of correspondence in the macro-microcosm, until he arrives finally at the *circumference* of eternity and the boundary of human reason. But this is a *vertical* line–an ascent.

In its *ascent*, his mind focuses first on the "sicknesse" of man's body: "so in length is man / Contracted to an inch" (135-36), he laments, incapable of health, strength, or even survival because of the loss of his "heart." He then anatomizes the next cosmic level–"the worlds whole frame" (191)–and finds it equally "Quite out of joynt" (192) because of a "generall sicknesse" (240). The next observation renders the same general conclusion: "the worlds subtilst immateriall parts / Feele this consuming wound" (247-48), suffering the same iron age degeneration as the lower levels of universal being: "the Sunne [cannot] / Perfit a Circle" (268-69). The entire "worlds proportion disfigur'd is" (302). The ascent of the poet's vision to the cosmic level reaffirms the same conclusion about universal decay: "art is lost, and correspondence too" (396).

Rhetorically, then, the poet's meditations have seemingly only worked elaborations on the single theme of universal degeneration: *contemptus mundi*. As Frank Manley urges, "the overall movement [of the poem] is downward to decay. Its ultimate discovery is a universe of death" (48). Such a conclusion seems supported, in fact, by the occasional lapses of control that the speaker suffers (Martz, "Revisited"). In this sense the anatomist's argument provides dramatic example of the fallen and flawed workings of the rational soul: the interruption of the smooth movement through the three powers of human thought by digressions and even on occasion by the dropping of the meditation-eulogy-moral pattern (the speaker's attempt to re-create the Image of God in the fallen human sensibility) provides a dramatic example of a human mind "striv[ing] about . . . and about" in its attempt to "Reache [the] Truth" ("Satyre III") of the human condition.

At the conclusion of his ascent from the "heart" of man to the "body" of the cosmos in pursuit of the risen soul of "Mistres Elizabeth Drury," however, Donne's speaker himself has re-traced the path that her de-parted soul took in "abandon[ing]" the fallen world. But the journey of the anatomist in this poem is not futile, for by following the dictates of reason he has discovered not only reason's limitations but also, as the eulogies and morals make clear, the need for and values of faith. The benefits and advantages of his initial pursuit of Elizabeth Drury are evident, in fact, when we realize that once again this progress has been figured as a spiraling ascent: as the speaker's mind has moved rectilin-early from the body of man directly, stage by stage, to the circumference of eternity it has traversed not simply "planes" but actually the *spheres* of Creation. He has scanned the entire body of man, the hemispheres of the globe, and the "trepidatious" circular paths of the cosmos in his search. Therefore, the figurative structure is not just serpentine, vertical, or recti-linear but, more accurately, closer to the workings of a compass which moves from its "just" center to scan the planes and circles of reality in its search for perfection and "rest." In this case the departure which occa-sions the *Valediction* has already occurred: like Astraea, Elizabeth Drury has already left her "lover," the speaker. But the description of the motions of this pursuit as figured in that other love poem is mirrored here, except in this case it is the soul of Elizabeth Drury that makes the speaker's "circle . . . just."

In one sense, of course, the anatomist's progress towards eternity is *merely* circular: he ends up where he began–anatomizing a dead body which has "lost" its soul. At the same time, the very circularity of his "progress" (to borrow the subtitle of the next *Anniversary*) intimates also a cause for some "joy," as P. G. Stanwood has shown. That "joy" will not be envisioned or mentally realized until his *Progress* by faith to the fuller vision of the benefits of heavenly Grace; but, as the conclusion of this poem intimates, the speaker has moved above the "speechlesse" (30), lethargic (24) melancholy with which he began his meditations. By following the path by which her soul "to heaven did clymbe" (8) and therein transforming "the twi-light of her memory" (74) through his Mosaic song (463-64), his poem–his mind–has realized its own (partial) powers of self-regeneration. At the beginning he saw what, he concludes, "a strict grave could do" (471); now he realizes what man-as-a-little-word, an image of *the* Creating Word, can do also:

> Verse hath a middle nature: heaven keepes soules,
> The grave keeps bodies, verse the fame enroules. (473-74)

He has managed only to transform that corpse into an *Idea* "worthy" of man's pursuit; the simultaneous circularity and rectilinearity of his mental progress intimates that he has done all that human reason can do. But the spiraling search through the orbs of fallen reality has at least convinced him of the need for that leap of faith which the next poem dramatizes. Moving outward and upward, from the body of man to the periphery of Heaven, moving forward in time from the Fall to Christ's incarnation, crucifixion, and resurrection (91-170) to the present moment, the speaker's Augustinian movement, in effect, moves backwards also–back to the source of his memory, God. The transformation of "the nightmare landscape of the fallen world [into] a vision of heaven" (Voss 30) is not completed by the end of the poem; but the transformation of "Mistris Elizabeth Drury" into verse, beyond and above the earthly limitations of mere "Chronicle" (460), and the transformation of his own mortality into "A last, and lasting'st peece, a song" (462), suggest that the speaker's re-creation of her involves a re-creation or at least re-assertion of man's fullest and highest humanity. He is still "emprison[ed]" in a world of decay, just as "she is emprison[ed]" in his verse (47); but mentally, he has ascended in pursuit of her beyond the "strict grave" of mortality through the fullest exercise of his rational, creative powers.

George Herbert once questioned whether "all good structure [is] in a winding stair" ("Jordan [I]" 3); for Donne, *The First Anniversarie* exemplifies that not only all "structure" but, indeed, the truth which the human reason can attain is realized in the "winding" ascent of the mind towards God. Both the necessary beauty and the truth about the capabilities of the rational soul, the stairway to Truth and the exemplary motions of the rational soul, are figured in his poems as a spiraling ascent towards its own eternal Image in time. That ascent cannot be completed, of course, without the loving motions of faith, but the metaphoric shape of the *Anatomy* reminds us what the early "Satyre" promised and the next *Anniversary* discloses, that "mysteries / Are like the Sunne, dazling, yet plaine to [the] eyes" of all who "strive" rationally towards the circle of eternal Truth ("Satyre III" 87-88, 83). The rational faculties, Dean Donne later warns in one of his sermons, "though they be not naturally instruments of faith, yet they are susceptible of grace . . . they have much in their nature that by grace they may be made instruments of grace . . . ; do not thinke that because a naturall man cannot doe all, therefore he hath nothing to doe for himself" (*Sermons* 9:85). Man must, as he said in his "Hymne to God," strive to "tune the Instrument" (4) of his rational soul in order to prepare for and respond to the grace of God. That preparation, the tuning, which was traditionally figured as the spiral motion of the soul, is figured forth in the metaphoric shape of *The First Anniversarie*. The poem intimates, then, not just the "gyre" of imperfection in which man's fallen consciousness endlessly spins, but, more accurately, the fuller response and fuller self-expression which natural man can achieve.[2]

Notes

[1] According to Drummond, Donne told Jonson that his poem concerned "the Idea of a Woman and not as she was." See Edward W. Tayler's impressive appraisal of the significance of Jonson's view of the poem.

[2] As John Shawcross has suggested to me, a more positive view of *The First*

Anniversarie allows insight into other central works by Donne: recognition of the spiral "motion" of the rational soul in the *Anatomy* reminds us of the status of "*Metempsychosis* as satire of the progressive thinking which is only rectilinear. Placed in a chronological development this all makes sense: *Satyre III, Metempsychosis, First Anniversarie / Valediction, Devotions*" (private letter, 7 February 1992).

Works Cited

Donne, John. *The Anniversaries*. Ed. Frank Manley. Baltimore: Johns Hopkins UP, 1963.

Freccero, John. "Dante's Pilgrim in a Gyre." *PMLA* 76 (1961): 168-81.

_____. "Donne's 'Valediction: Forbidding Mourning.'" *ELH* 30 (1963): 335-76.

Hardison, O. B. *The Enduring Monument: A Study of the Idea of Praise in Renaissance Theory and Practice*. Chapel Hill: U of North Carolina P, 1962.

Hester, M. Thomas. *Kinde Pitty and Brave Scorn: Donne's Satyres*. Durham: Duke UP, 1982.

_____. "Donne's Hill of Truth." *ELN* 14 (1976): 100-05.

Lewalski, Barbara. *Donne's Anniversaries and the Poetry of Praise: The Creation of a Symbolic Mode*. Princeton UP, 1973.

Martz, Louis L. "Donne's Anniversaries Revisited." *That Subtle Wreath*. Ed. Margaret W. Pepperdine. Decatur, GA: Anges Scott College, 1973. 29-55.

Petrarch. "Ascent of Mont Ventoux." Trans. Hans Nachod. *The Renaissance Philosophy of Man*. Ed. Ernst Cassirer, Paul Oskar Kristeller, John Herman Randall, Jr. Chicago: U of Chicago P, 1948. 36-46.

Stanwood, P. G. "'Essential Joye' in Donne's *Anniversaries*." *TSLL* 13 (1971): 227-38.

Tayler, Edward W. *Donne's Idea of A Woman*. New York: Columbia UP, 1991.

Voss, A. E. "The Structure of Donne's Anniversaries." *English Studies in Africa* 12 (1969): 1-30.

John Donne's Attitude toward the Virgin Mary: The Public versus the Private Voice

George Klawitter

That John Donne had some interest in the Virgin Mary we know from his sermons and poems. As for his private devotion, we can read in Walton that Donne had a painting of Mary that was willed to Christopher Brooke, the friend who had officiated at Donne's secret marriage to Anne More. We also have witness from one book in his personal library, *Miracula Quae ad Invocationem Beatissimae Virginis Mariae*, that Donne followed Marian theology, and we know that Bellarmine, the champion of Roman Catholic mariology, was, according to Walton, his favorite Roman Catholic author (Keynes 262). Indeed, it would be difficult for a man of Donne's litigious character to stay away from a topic so ripe for controversy as the Marian beliefs, but where did his Marian sentiments actually lie? The pronouncements of his public sermons show consistent Protestant orthodoxy regarding Marian matters, but his private devotional poetry does not. Of four Marian dogmas that surface in Donne's poetry, divine motherhood and perpetual virginity were easy for Donne to accept, as they were for Elizabethan and Jacobean Protestants generally; that he ever held to a third doctrine, an immaculate conception for Mary, we cannot tell for certain from his writings, but as for invocation of the Virgin, we have proof positive that Donne underwent a change in faith. Some who study Donne surmise that he changed religions to advance his career, but no study has detailed the specifics of his faith change. The Virgin Mary affords us one avenue to document Donne's spiritual metamorphosis. Given the dating of his poems, we must conclude that in one Marian tenet, John Donne grew from Roman Catholic to Reformer: in 1608 he praises Mary's intercessory powers, but in 1617 he denounces them as spurious. As a young poet, he had no public obligation to endorse a given Marian theology, but as an ordained minister in his final years, he had to embrace orthodox Protestant views in his public life. My primary task here will be to examine those religious poems, as well as Donne's sermons and some recusant Marian poetry contemporary to Donne that may provide a basis of comparison. But first we must survey Marian theology within both the Roman and Reformed traditions, particularly as they deal with the controversial dogmas of immaculate conception and mediatrix, in order to settle Donne within a theological context.

The Theological Tradition

Early Fathers themselves were divided on the quality of Mary's sanctification. Origen, for example, thought she was imperfect. Marian dogma was not officially formulated in the Middle Ages, and only facts deduced from the Bible (e.g., the title "Mother of God," given to her by the Council of Ephesus, and virgin birth) endured. These items were not subject to debate. Discussion over Mary's role in the Church did not accelerate until the fifteenth century when the argumentation between Franciscans and Dominicans became so furious that Pope Sixtus IV in 1482 forbade dispute on the immaculate conception. A feast honoring her conception (not her immaculate conception) began before 700, reached England by 1050, was suppressed under William the Conqueror, and was revived c. 1125, but some interest in her immaculate conception can be dated to 1099 with Anselm's *De conceptu virginali*: "None greater under God could be conceived" (O'Connor 378). An early apologia for her immaculate conception (*De conceptione B. Virginis Mariae*) was written by the English monk Eadmer (c. 1123?), but acceptance of her special conception was not universal: a religious leader as important as Bernard of Clairvaux argued c. 1140 that the Holy Spirit would not be involved in anything so sordid as conception (332-36). Paris theologians, working in the thirteenth-century with a new biological notion that the soul enters the fetus only forty or eighty days after conception, concluded that the human body could be tainted by sin before the soul arrives, an idea that seems bizarre to anyone raised in the Platonic world of flesh/spirit dichotomy. It was an idea, however, that took firm hold on the western world.

Thomas Aquinas accepted the Paris conclusion: "for she was first conceived in the flesh, and afterwards sanctified in the spirit" (2: 3.27.1). His reasons for denying Mary sanctification before animation were two: first, she could not be cleansed before she was rational, and secondly, if she had been conceived immaculate, she would not have needed redemption by her Son, and "this would be derogatory to the dignity of Christ, by reason of his being the universal Saviour of all" (2: 3.27.2). Although there have been some attempts to show that Aquinas was not actually denying what we understand as the immaculate conception, theologians generally accept that the Angelic Doctor rejected Mary's immaculate conception (Shea 301 and Roschini 194-96).

Aquinas had not, however, the final word on the matter. The thirteenth-century Franciscan Duns Scotus suggested a new twist on the theory, much to the satisfaction of ecclesiastics: "Mary had even greater need of a prevenient Mediator lest there be sin to be contracted and lest she contract it" (O'Connor 381). In other words, Mary retained an inclination to sin, a concept later attributed to Cajetan (1469-1534) who first applied the phrase "debitum peccati" to Mary's inherent tendency towards original sin (71-73). After Cajetan, Peter Canisius (d. 1597) became a champion of Mary in his reply to the Reformers, *De Maria virgine incomparabili*, and Renaissance mariology culminated with the work of Francisco Suarez (d. 1617) whose Roman lectures in 1584-85 set forth Church beliefs in Mary's sanctification.

The Protestant theological tradition for Mary begins in Germany. Luther is not always clear on the matter of Mary's conception, but he does give her a role in the Final Judgment where she will be a mediatrix for sinners, coming between them and her angry Son (Moron 41). He repudiates, however, the sentiments of the "Salve Regina" hymn in which Mary is invoked as "mater misericordiae." In the extended Magnificat meditation he wrote on Mary, Luther comments on the need to keep her power in proper perspective:

> It is necessary also to keep within bounds and not make too much of calling her "Queen of Heaven," which is a true-enough name and yet does not make her a goddess who could grant gifts or render aid, as some suppose when they pray and flee to her rather than to God. She gives nothing, God gives all. (21: 327-28)

Mary is not to be counted upon in intercession. This message is clear from Luther, yet he invokes her both at the beginning and end of this gentle treatise: "May the tender Mother of God herself procure for me the spirit of wisdom profitably and thoroughly to expound this song of hers" (21: 298); "May Christ grant us this through the intercession and for the sake of His dear Mother Mary!" (21: 355). It is interesting to note in this apparent contradiction that Luther links Mary both times to God, a linkage that he insists upon in a 1523 treatise, "That Christ was Born a Jew." The context is, however, decidedly more inflammatory than in the tender Magnificat meditation:

> Now just take a look at the perverse lauders of the mother of God. If you ask them why they hold so strongly to the virginity of Mary, they truly could not say. These stupid idolaters do nothing more than to glorify only the mother of God; they extol her for her virginity and practically make a false deity of her. But Scripture does not praise this virginity at all for the sake of the mother; neither was she saved on account of her virginity. Indeed, cursed be this and every other virginity if it exists for its own sake, and accomplishes nothing better than its own profit and praise. (45: 205)

Luther affords Mary a gracious elevation, as long as she is never praised for any gift or virtue in herself: she must always appear in her role as patriarchal servant, a role affirmed also in Luther's 1535 "Lecture on Genesis" (1: 192).

As the Reformation continued its work, we might expect voices less moderate than Luther's to surface. Indeed, Calvin's voice does: he doubts the "Mother of God" title, attributes Original Sin to Mary, rejects any invocation of her, and suppresses in Geneva all festivals in her honor (Maron 42). He is most vitriolic in his "Antidote" of 1548, a reaction to the Council of Trent:

> Ambrosius Catharinus, of the order of the Dominicans, the old antagonist of Luther, blows out his cheeks. I thought that under the confusion to which he was put twenty years ago, he had gone into some obscure corner to hide himself. . . . Those who formerly read the absurdities of Catharinus would not know that that putrid carcase is still breathing, did they not read his harangues delivered in the Council, in which the mother of Christ is called his [Christ's] most faithful associate, and represented as sitting on his throne to obtain grace for us! Many before him [Catharinus] have given loose reins to their impudence, but none I believe was found, while seeking to deck the blessed Virgin with fictitious titles, to call her the associate of Christ. (135)

Published one year after Luther's death, the tract is the first major Protestant response to the Counter-Reformers. More smoke than substance, riddled with "argumentum ad hominem" rhetoric, the attack on Marian devotion is typical of much sixteenth-century bombast on matters theological. As the sixteenth-century turned into the seventeenth, Mary received less and less attention in Protestant thinking, but she never wholly disappeared from Protestant verse, certainly not from Donne's.

Donne's Poetic Marian References
and the Recusant Tradition

Donne's poems are not only *not* uniformly Protestant, but often reflect his recusant background.[1] Six of his poems mention Mary (the *Second Anniversarie* and five of the "divine poems"), and they touch two debatable aspects of Marian belief: Mary as mediatrix and as having been immaculate conception. A third dogma, divine motherhood, accepted by all Christians, is reflected in the occasional piece "The Annuntiation and Passion":

> At once a Sonne is promis'd her, and gone,
> Gabriell gives Christ to her, He her to John;
> Not fully'a mother, Shee's in Orbitie,
> At once receiver and the legacie.(ll. 15-18)

Commenting on the double motherhood of Mary, to Christ at the Annunciation and to John at the foot of the cross, Donne weaves a gentle and unproblematic image that offends no reader, Protestant or Roman Catholic, because mainstream theologians in both traditions had long accepted Mary's divine motherhood. Two stanzas of "La Corona," those titled "Annunciation" and "Nativitie," are also gentle meditations on Mary's motherhood. Like the stanzas in "The Annuntiation and Passion," they are conventional in their Marian images and interesting only for the conceits that Mary is both sister and mother to Christ; she conceived him who conceived her, making her the creator of her creator and the mother of her father. It is all twisted play on the maternal theme that was accepted by Protestants. The poem has been dated to 1609 by Novarr (265).

A decade later another poetic reference to Mary's role in Christian history occurs in the epistolary verses "To Mr. Tilman after he had taken orders," apparently written when Donne read a poem which Tilman had written before ordination, a poem not widely available to scholars until it was described and printed in 1931 (Wood 184-86). Gardner speculates that Donne knew Tilman (Donne, *Divine* 129), but Tilman's verses are of no interest to us here because they do not mention the Virgin Mary. Donne's 54-line poem itself has but a single reference to Mary:

> *Maries* prerogative was to beare Christ, so
> 'Tis preachers to convey him. (ll. 41-42)

The emphasis is simply on Mary's divine motherhood, and the lines contain nothing that would spark a lively debate between Protestants and recusants. Since Tilman was ordained a deacon in December, 1618, and a priest in March, 1620, Donne's poem comes sufficiently late in his poetic career and well into his clerical period so that we should expect nothing but orthodox Protestant sentiment in the piece.

Such is the poetic response of John Donne to Mary's divine motherhood. He did not, of course, live in isolation in the Renaissance and may have known recusant poets who wrote tenderly of the Virgin's maternity, but of the recusants contemporary to Donne of whom we know, few wrote poems on Mary, and some poems, in manuscript tradition only, are difficult to date. But a widely read poet, Abraham Cowley, published in *Sylva* (1636) "A translation of verses upon the B. Virgin, written in Latine by the right worshipfull Dr. A." These are verses that Guiney (344) suggests may be by Alabaster, an attribution that Calhoun (313) agrees with while noting that the lines are not translations of any of the Alabaster Rawlinson manuscript poems. The verses in Cowley stress the divine motherhood and Mary's perpetual virginity. They mention neither her immaculate conception nor her intercessory powers. Rather than being argumentative, the verses are best remembered for their exotic images, particularly the comparison of Mary's womb to a hive (ll. 3, 9-10) and a very graphic description of the unbroken hymen:

> As when soft westwinds strooke the garden Rose,
> A showre of sweeter aire salutes the Nose.
> The breath gives sparing kisses, nor with powre
> Unlocks the Virgin bosome of the flowre.
> Soe th'*Holy Spirit* upon *Marie* blow'd,
> And from her sacred box whole rivers flow'd.
> Yet loos'd not thine eternall chastity,

> Thy Roses folds doe still entangled lie.
> Relieve *Christ* borne from an unbruised wombe,
> So from unbruised barke the odors come. (ll. 39-48)

Prefiguring the elegance of Crashaw's Marian verses, Cowley's lines on Mary attest to his teenage taste (he was eighteen when *Sylva* was published), clearly not the heady doctrinal rhetoric of divines like Donne.

We turn now to the matter of Mary's sinlessness. Donne's *Second Anniversary* (1612) contains what many read as a poetic attack on the theory of Mary's immaculate conception:

> Where thou [the speaker's soul] shalt see the blessed Mother-maid
> Joy in not being that, which men have said.
> Where shee'is exalted more for being good,
> Then for her interest, of mother-hood. (ll. 341-44)

Most commentators are in agreement that the phrase "that, which men have said" refers to Mary's own conception (Grierson 2: 199, Milgate 169, Patrides 364), but the lines are open to other interpretations since Donne does not specify it is Mary's sinlessness that is less important than her divine maternity. In fact, lines 343-44 could very well mean that her freedom from all sin ("being good") merits her more adulation in heaven than her motherhood does. Where does this leave us with "that, which men have said"? It could refer to those heretics who denied virgin birth and insisted that Mary had a human partner in the conception of the redeemer-messiah. The slippery word in either interpretation is "being" (l. 343). If the word refers to being created good, then she is immaculate; if it refers to her doing no evil, then she may have been conceived in sin but lived a blameless life, free from actual sin. Readers may have been too hasty in the past to find Donne suddenly a thorough Protestant as he neared ordination. Jonson, of course, was dismayed by the *Anniversary*'s supposed blasphemy (presumably its apotheosis of Elizabeth Drury) and remarked to Donne, "if it had been written of the Virgin Mary it had been something" (596), and Donne, as far as we know, responded that he was out to describe generic woman in the poem, not a specific woman. Would that we knew what Donne thought of Jonson's appreciation of Mary.

We do know, however, what an earlier poet, a poet in the same religious order as Donne's uncle, Jasper Hayward, thought of the immaculate conception. Robert Southwell, a Jesuit priest and the best known of the Elizabethan recusant poets, was executed at Tyburn on February 21,

1595. He is believed by his editors to have written all of his English poems in the six year period before his arrest in 1592 (Southwell xxiii). One of the earliest poems, as sequenced by the editors, is titled "The Virgine Mariaes conception" and contains the following closing stanza:

> Four only wights bred without fault are namde
> And al the rest conceived were in sinne,
> Without both man and wife was Adam framde,
> Of man, but not of wife did Eve beginne,
> Wife without touch of man Christs mother was
> Of man and wife this babe was bred in grace. (ll. 13-18)

Although Southwell limits the number of persons conceived immaculately to four (Adam, Eve, Mary, Christ), we are not sure he is attributing an immaculate conception to Mary in the traditional definition of the Roman Catholic Church. He seems to be equating sexual contact with the transmission of sin, and thus parentless Adam and motherless Eve are untainted by standard generation. Likewise Mary, who is "wife without touch of men," is considered special, not because her parents did not have sexual contact but because she did not in generating Christ. The doctrine of her immaculate conception is as muddied here as it is in the minds of many twentieth-century Catholics who, when questioned, usually reply that the immaculate conception means that Mary conceived Christ without benefit of a human husband.

Another recusant to write of Mary's special grace is Henry Constable, whose manuscript poems are even harder to date than Southwell's. Grundy (59) notes that Sir Sidney Lee in 1898 dated the *Spirituall Sonnettes* (Harleian MS. 7553) c. 1593, which time period would make them contiguous to both Southwell and the early Donne. Of four poems written "To our Blessed Lady" only the first touches the matter of grace:

> In that (O Queene of queenes) thy byrth was free
> from guylt, which others doth of grace bereave
> when in theyr mothers wombe they lyfe receave:
> God as his sole-borne daughter loved thee.

Of this quatrain Grundy concludes that Constable accepted the doctrine of the immaculate conception (250), but Grundy fails to note that Constable says nothing of Mary's conception, only of her birth. Thus Constable is in very mainstream Protestant belief, accepting, as Aquinas did, that Mary's special condition occurred sometime between her conception and birth, probably at that moment of inanimation which Constable expresses as "when in theyr mothers wombe they lyfe receave," a line which suggests the body is present in the womb before the soul is. Donne may or may not have known these poems in manuscript. He was certainly close enough to the recusant underground via his family to have contact with Southwell's poems, although by 1593 he was already uncertain as to his institutional allegiance as " Satyre III" proves. Constable, who preceded Donne at Lincoln's Inn by a decade and was a court figure writing a pro-Huguenot book in 1589 (*Examen pacifique de la Doctrine des Huguenots*), had chosen the Roman faith in 1591 when he went to France with Essex to assist Henri IV. He remained out of England throughout the 1590s. It is doubtful that Donne would have had access to Constable's religious poems, but the sentiments they express would have been, of course, a reflection of contemporary recusant thought.

One close friend of Donne's who championed in print the immaculate conception is Sir Toby Mathew, who converted to Roman Catholicism in the summer of 1606 (Bald 152) and published *Of the Love of Our Only Lord and Saviour Jesus Christ* in 1622. Mathew, who affirms in the epistle dedicatory both the immaculate conception and the assumption of Mary, devotes chapters 79-94 to Mary, defending her freedom from all sin (487), her mediatorship between Christ and humanity (500), and titles her the "non plus ultra" of purity (544). Although Donne was still in correspondence with Mathew at the time, he had already noted in a 1613 letter to Mathew "that we differ in our wayes [to Heaven], I hope we pardon one another" (Bald 330). Recusant prose, however, was not always as dogmatic as Toby's: John Falconer's *Mirrour of Created Perfection* (1632), for example, is a life of Mary that tends to be more meditative than doctrinal, focusing as it does on what the reader can learn from the acts of the Virgin and applying them to daily living.

One would expect Marian poems in the sonnets of the recusant William Alabaster, but there is only one, "To the Blessed Virgin" (20), the sestet of which manages to praise Mary's divine motherhood, immaculate conception, and perpetual virginity:

> Unspotted morning whom no mist of sin,
> Nor cloud of human mixture did obscure,
> Strange morning that since day hath entered in,
> Before and after doth alike endure. (ll. 9-12)

She is "unspotted" by sin, and her virginity endures even after "day" (Christ) has entered her. Alabaster's poetic career is uncertain, but Story and Gardner conjecture 1598 (Alabaster xxxi) for the English verse; a sizable collection of his Latin poems exists in Bodleian manuscripts Rawl. D 283 and 293, yet to be winnowed. Donne's poetic relationship to Alabaster, if any, has never been considered; their recusant attitudes, of course, would have been touchstones.

One interesting shift in Donne's Marian theology regards Mary as mediatrix. Any development of Donne's attitude on the Blessed Virgin, of course, is indicative of his wrestling with the idea of "woman" in general as mediatrix. Early on, Donne seems obsessed with the "redemptive" woman: in "The Flea" the feminine audience of one has a sacramental quality to her potential love-making, and in Elegy XIX, "Going to Bed," the woman addressed is mockingly endorsed as a source of prevenient grace. Similarly we need only remember the sanctified Elizabeth Drury of the *Anniversaries* to realize what Donne could make of woman-as-sanctifier: the fifteen-year-old girl is evidence of God's intentions for the history of humanity. As Lewalski has suggested, such an extravagant use of figure becomes a kind of "internalized" typology for each individual Christian, "an important literary means to explore the personal spiritual life with profundity and psychological complexity" ("Typological" 81). If such an observation can be allowed regarding a teenager, we should expect from Donne a similar psychic need to frame an image of the Virgin Mary that would square with his developing faith. In 1608 (on dating see Gardner 81 and Baker-Smith 173), Donne penned "A Litanie" which contains very un-Protestant sentiments:

> For that faire blessed Mother-maid,
> Whose flesh redeem'd us; That she-Cherubin,
> Which unlock'd Paradise, and made
> One claime for innocence, and disseiz'd sinne,
> > Whose wombe was a strange heav'n, for there
> > God cloath'd himselfe, and grew,
> Our zealous thankes wee poure. As her deeds were
> Our helpes, so are her prayers; nor can she sue
> In vaine, who hath such titles unto you. (ll. 37-45)

Mary is, quite simply, the finest intercessor possible: "nor can she sue / In vaine." A title for her Donne would later repudiate, "intercessor" is here consequent to her motherhood. Mary, of course, intercedes rather than acts on her own because monotheism necessitates a single source of power (Warner 288), but as if to aggrieve Protestants more, Donne elevates Mary to a superhuman state when he names her in line 38 a "she-Cherubin." Roman R. Dubinski has recently set the poem within a Calvinist and Lutheran context on invocation of the saints and Mary. He notes that the distinctions which the Roman Church attempted to draw between *latria* (worship of God), *hyperdulia* (veneration of Mary), and *dulia* (veneration of the saints) were confused in the minds of ordinary worshippers and barely enforced as dogma by a Church losing the battle with superstition (10). Dubinski, however, striving to set Donne within the mainstream English Church, fails to emphasize the very blatant Roman dogma of Marian intercession that Donne espouses in "A Litanie." He notes that Donne accepts her as "mediator and intercessor in heaven" (21), but he concludes that Donne's "invocations are distinctly Protestant" (23). He argues that Donne in his sermons rejects Marian intercession (15), but he does not recognize the dogmatic contradiction between Donne-the-poet and Donne-the-preacher. Lewalski similarly misses Donne's Roman attitude in her analysis of the "Litanie" stanza: "Mary's office is treated first, but cautiously, and in general rather than personal terms as if Donne were unsure as to just how a Protestant should formulate the claim upon her assistance" (*Protestant* 261). Lewalski then quotes parts of lines 43-44 but does not comment on their obvious acceptance of Marian intercession, and she ignores the final sentiment in the stanza ("nor can she sue / In vaine"), a sentiment that is anything but "cautious" or "unsure" about Mary's continuing role as mediatrix.

In a letter to Henry Goodyer, Donne comments upon the genesis of "A Litanie": "Since my imprisonment in my bed, I have made a meditation in verse which I call a Litany; the word you know imports no other then supplication" (Letters 32). Sickness has a way of returning a rebel to conservatism, and in his illness Donne may have regressed from his personal reformation. Wellington finds in the poem a structure and tone similar to Cranmer's reformed litany of 1544, a possibility that takes Donne's poem closer to English Catholic roots, but Wellington finds nothing particularly Roman in either prayer: "There is little that is not implied in Cranmer's own prayer for the intercession of the Blessed Virgin . . . and nothing whatever that is uniquely Roman" (190). But Wellington's attempt to level the differences between faiths on the basis of Cranmer's piety, official or not, ignores not only the developing English Catholic credo in the later sixteenth century, but also the rhetoric of Donne's seventeenth-century sermons. When Wellington asserts of

Donne's "Litanie" that "the doctrine presented in these stanzas, including the invocation of the Blessed Virgin Mary and the saints, is Catholic in the sense in which Donne himself understood the term and is altogether compatible with the theology of the English Church" (199), he is referring to a young Donne who accepted Mary's intercessory power in 1608 but not the priestly Donne of a decade later. Wellington would have us believe that English Marian theology changed in the early seventeenth-century when in reality only Donne changed.

Reading Donne's early "Litanie" gives a picture of a recusant Donne and gives us pause in face of the later venom in a Donne Christmas sermon (1627): when he rails in that sermon against those who make Mary a "semi-god" or "sesqui-god," he is condemning his younger self. It is difficult, however, to understand how Gardner can read the Marian stanza in "A Litanie" as an attack on the immaculate conception: "Donne, agreeing with Aquinas . . . wittily denies the Immaculate Conception" (Donne, *Divine* 84). Such is Gardner's reading of the phrase "disseiz'd sinne," but to "disseize sin," while it does refer to Mary's being untainted by any actual sin, does not mean she was untainted only by that form of sin. Gardner is too swift to read meaning into the line so she can keep Donne an orthodox Protestant. But the context of the phrase "disseiz'd sinne" is not Protestant, as we have seen, and indeed the phrase "one claime for innocence" would more imply that Mary was innocent once and for all than that she was conceived in sin and later went on to commit no sin herself. Similar misreadings touch a more famous Donne poem.

"Goodfriday, 1613. Riding Westward" is dated in manuscript, and thus it is all the more remarkable for its possible recusant sentiment coming at a time when Donne had long agonized over his religious affiliation and had opted for the established Church. Curiously, only Patrides notes that line 32 contains "one of the most explicit statements of mariolatry in Donne's poetry" (456). ("Mariolatry" is a charged word and means "worship" of the Virgin, not simply the "study" of Mary, "mariology.") But Patrides' claim is debatable. After Donne has explained in the poem his inability to "see Gods face" on this particular holy day, he rues the fact that he cannot see even God's mother:

> If on these things I durst not looke, durst I
> Upon his miserable mother cast mine eye,
> Who was Gods partner here, and furnish'd thus
> Halfe of that Sacrifice, which ransom'd us? (ll. 29-32)

As Patrides reads line 32, Donne credits Mary with a partnership in redemption (a reading he also finds in "A Litanie"), but "Sacrifice" in "Goodfriday" does not refer to redemption: it refers rather to Christ, the "Sacrifice." It is a poetic personification which brings the lines to mean that Mary furnished half of the God-Man "which ransom'd us." Patrides' reading would make Donne's poem very Roman Catholic, a significant interpretation for a poem dated 1613, but if anything, the lines indicate at most Donne's ambivalance concerning Mary's redemptive role, not an explicit verification of her "partnership" in redemption. Gardner (Donne, *Divine* 84) seems likewise misled by the phrase "Gods partner," though she goes on to note that Donne later repudiates such an image in his March 24, 1617, sermon (Potter and Simpson 1: 200).

The Public Voice of Donne's Sermons

Finally, if we hope to appreciate change in Donne's poetry, we must examine the Marian rhetoric of the established divine, Donne in his ecclesiastical career. In the Donne sermons we might expect Donne to treat of the Virgin Mary on her feast days, but of the four sermons we have from him for Candlemas Day, three of them do not mention her. The exception (*Sermons* 7: 13), assigned tentatively by Potter and Simpson to 1626, begins promisingly: "The church, which is the Daughter of God, and Spouse of Christ, celebrates this day, the Purification of the blessed Virgin, the mother of God: and she celebrates this day by the name, vulgarly, of Candlemas day." Unfortunately, the sermon says not one word more about Mary. In the fifteen years he preached, Donne did not spend much sermon time on Mary, and in those instances where he does discuss her, it is to attack her privileging by the Roman Catholic Church, principally on the two topics of intercession and immaculate conception. Early in his church career, in a sermon (March 24, 1617) preached to the Lords of the Council while King James was off visiting Scotland, Donne contrasts Mary with Eve, asserting that "the Virgin Mary had not the same interest in our salvation, as Eve had in our destruction" (1: 200). Salvation depends only upon Christ, not upon anything Mary did: "God forbid any should say, That the Virgin Mary concurred to our good." Although not specifying the intercessory powers of the Virgin, Donne attacks them obliquely, finally asserting she is like "many other blessed women since," who have done much to advance God's glory and are thus "not unfit for spiritual conversation." He seems to be endorsing a kind of meditative colloquy with the Virgin short of eliciting her protection from the divine wrath, but above all he insists she had no part in Christ's redeeming act (Husain 67).

A year after he attacked Mary's intercessory powers, Donne attacks the immaculate conception in no uncertain terms: "He came into the world; it is not 'in mundum,' into so clean a woman as had no sin at all, none contracted from her Parents, no original sin; for so Christ had placed his favours and his honors ill, if he had favoured her most who had no need of him" (1: 307). Donne argues here that the greatest gift to humanity is Redemption: denying Mary the possibility of that Redemption, which eventuality would occur if she had no need of redemption, would deny her humanity's greatest boon. Furthermore, he asks, if she had no sin, why did she die? Death is a consequence of sin. He does grant that she was preserved from "great and infectious sins" (actual sin), but only so that Christ might come "by a clean woman into an unclean world." Donne does not seem to consider the fact that if she were clean by being free of actual sin, she would be even more clean by being free of original sin, but in argumentation one cannot raise issues that undercut the premise. Apparently, Donne feels it important for Mary to be clean, but not totally clean because complete purity would have made her more than human. He does not consider that freedom from actual sin would also make her more pure than most humans.

Six years later, Donne qualifies Mary's position both as mediatrix and as immaculate in a sermon preached at Paul's on Christmas Day, 1624. After comparing Mary to a queen-dowager who "may be in a high ranke, and yet no Soveraigne" (6: 183), demonstrating that Mary may not "command her Son," Donne picks away at Luther's acceptance of the scholastic notion of Mary's soul being free from sin at its "quickning," even though her body was conceived sinful:

> *Luther* was awake, and risen, but he was not readie; Hee had seene light, and looked toward it, but yet saw not so clearely by it, then, when he said, That the blessed Virgin was of a middle condition, betweene Christ, and man; that man hath his conception, and his quickning (by the infusion of the soule) in originall sin; that Christ had it in neither, no sin in his conception, none in his inanimation, in the infusion of his soule; But, saies *Luther*, howsoever it were at the conception, certainly at the inanimation, at the quickning, she was preserved from originall sin. Now, what needs this? may I not say, that I had rather be redeemed by Christ Jesus then bee innocent? rather be beholden to Christs death, for my salvation, then to *Adams* standing in his innocencie? (6: 183)

Donne does not like this "middle condition" that Luther accepted for Mary, keeping her somewhere between Christ's condition of total body-soul preservation and humanity's total body-soul degradation. She is conceived in sin, for Luther, but at her "inanimation," she is pure. Donne's reasoning against Luther is no different from his reasoning six years earlier: to be redeemed by Christ is a greater gift than to be free from Adam's guilt. It is the "felix culpa" theme that resonates throughout literature from Augustine to Graham Greene.

In a later reference to Mary in his sermons (December 25, 1627), Donne again attacks the concept of Mary as mediatrix:

> Wee who worship the onely true God, need not the semi-gods, nor the sesqui-gods of the Roman Church . . . nor any sesqui-god, any that must be more then God, and receive appeales from God, and reverse the decrees of God, which they make the office of the Virgin Mary, whom no man can honour too much, that makes her not God, and they dishonour most, that make her so much more. (8: 143)

Arguing that Mary cannot "reverse the decrees of God" by intercession, Donne continues to be at pains to keep the Virgin human, to prevent her being deified, as the Romans deified their dead emperors, into something that is neither divine nor human, but rather a "semi-god" or "sesqui-god." Mary is not honored by apotheosis, but dishonored. His rhetoric here seems Calvinistic, and if we try to position Donne in his sermons somewhere in the Reformist tradition, we cannot ignore the possibility of his being influenced by Calvinist thought. In his work on the three sermons Donne preached in Heidelberg and at the Hague, Sellin has noted that the Calvinist Constantijn Huygens proclaimed Donne one of the two greatest preachers he had known (Sellin 37).

One problem with the sermons that we must always keep in mind is that Donne did not write them down for publication at the time that he delivered them. Only in his later years did he write out the sermons from his notes. Thus we have no way of telling how much of his early theology he tempered in the process of transcribing his notes. If he had any sentiments that could be perceived as unorthodox in his early preaching career, he would surely have amended them when he came around to set his sermons for the printer. Sermons are a public act. How often a preacher shapes his beliefs to suit an audience or a state religion, we have no way of knowing. For this reason, Donne's private beliefs may be more accurately reflected in his poems than in his sermons. We know that most of Donne's verses were written for private consumption.

Conclusion: The Problem of Historical Context

When we think of the Reformation, we tend to think in terms of violent shifts in religious opinion with intransigent heretics like Nicholas Ridley being burned at the stake by Mary Tudor or priests being ferreted out of country houses by Elizabeth's spies. We are schooled in Henry's confiscation of monastic properties, and we learn that his second daughter caused a scandal at her coronation by stipulating that the host could not be raised at the consecration and by retreating to her pew and refusing communion when Ogelthorpe disobeyed her (McCoy 241). We rely on radical shifts because they make history manageable and colorful, but most history is rather dull, and shifts, for example in religious practice, are usually more window dressing than fact. An Elizabethan Protestant would never attend "Mass," but the church service he loved was barely distinguishable from the Roman Catholic rite. When Henry waffled in his later years on the matter of transubstantiation and softened his insistence on the "real presence" in the bread and wine, his opinion had no immediate effect on what the country yeoman perceived in the Sunday liturgy.

Sovereigns, of course, often set the tone for what was in and what was out in court theology: when Elizabeth, an ardent Protestant, was thirteen she chose to translate Calvin for an exercise; her sister Mary at a similar age, true daughter of a Roman Catholic mother, translated a Latin prayer by Thomas Aquinas (Somerset 10). But in the churches the trickling down of official opinion depended upon the good will of local clergy and the occasional, brutal imposition of proclamations like "An Act Abolishing Diversity of Opinions" (the Six Articles of 1539). When despots need support for their maneuverings and hatred, they often turn to doctrinal niceties as a sure way to fire an audience, and so we may think that mariology was a sticking point in all Renaissance England, but the Virgin Mary retained a warmth in English lay devotion, her feasts celebrated with aplomb, even as court theologians like John Donne chiselled away at the philosophical underpinnings of her eminence in church doctrine. Not underestimating the interest of the ordinary pew occupant in the vagaries of dogma, we should nevertheless appreciate the data of history as we get them: only gradually did the Virgin Mary assume her lowered niche in the Anglican Church, and few of her devotees were startled by, none were executed for protesting, her declension. More people were persecuted for adhering to a belief in purgatory than were hounded for invoking Mary as mediatrix.

From sixteenth-century Protestant preachers the ordinary worshipper received a picture of Mary that emphasized her cooperation with the divine plan. In the hierarchy of good order, Mary was held up to women as a faithful follower of God's plan for the female: "She knew that silence in a woman is a great virtue," preached Hugh Latimer in 1552. "Here may all women learn to follow the example of Mary, to leave their talk and vain speaking and to keep silence" (184-5). To keep women in their appointed place, a model submissive to patriarchal authority was essential, and Mary filled that role perfectly, as long as she did not become the focus of special privilege accorded by an immaculate conception or by a role as divine intercessor. The Protestant attitude on Mary that evolved during the Reformation is as important in its development as the parallel evolution in Roman Catholic theology, and John Donne, one of Renaissance England's most visible theologians, is an important Protestant voice. He was, of course, privy to strong Marian influence in his youth, was raised a recusant in a recusant family, and wrote poetic lines that evidence that influence. When he speaks in the private voice of a worshipper, Donne's poetry suggests that ideas learned early are not easily discarded. But when he speaks in the public voice of the preacher, Donne's sermons reflect orthodox doctrine.[2]

Notes

[1] Very little work has been done on Donne's poetic mariology; see Ferrari 99-110 for the most complete consideration.

[2] This essay is the result of research done at Brown University as part of a 1992 summer seminar directed by Karen Newman.

Works Cited

Alabaster, William. *Sonnets*. Ed. G.M. Story and Helen Gardner. Oxford: Oxford U P, 1959.

Aquinas, Thomas. *Summa Theologica*. 3 vols. New York: Benziger Brothers, 1947.

Baker-Smith, Dominic. "Donne's 'Litanie.'" *RES* 26 (1975): 171-73.

Bernard of Clairvaux. Letter 174. *Patrologiae cursus completus*. Ed. J.P. Migne. 221 vols. Paris: 1878-90. 182: 332-336.

Boyle, R. "Mary, Blessed Virgin." *New Catholic Encyclopedia*. 9:384-386.

Calvin, John. *Selections*. Ed. John Dillenberger. Missoula, MT: Scholars P, 1975.

Carroll, E.R. "Mariology." *New Catholic Encyclopedia*. 9:223-227.

Constable, Henry. *Poems*. Ed. Joan Grundy. Liverpool: Liverpool U P, 1960.

Cowley, Abraham. *Collected Works*. Vol. 1. Ed. Thomas O. Calhoun. Newark: U of Delaware P, 1989.

Donne, John. *Letters to Severall Persons of Honour*. London: 1651.

Dubinski, Roman R. "Donne's 'A Litanie' and the Saints." *Christianity and Literature 41* (Autumn 1991): 5-26.

Falconer, John. *Mirrour of Created Perfection* (1632). Rpt. Yorkshire: Scholar P, 1971.

Ferrari, Ferruccio. *La poesia religiosa inglese del seicento*. Florence: Casa editrice G. D'Anna, 1975.

Gardner, Helen, ed. *John Donne: The Divine Poems*. 2nd ed. Oxford: Clarendon P, 1978

Grierson, Herbert, ed. *John Donne: Poetical Works*. 2 vols. Oxford: Clarendon P, 1912.

Guiney, Louise I. *Recusant Poets*. New York: Sheed and Ward, 1939.

Husain, Itrat. *The Dogmatic and Mystical Theology of John Donne*. New York: Macmillan, 1938.

Jonson, Ben. *Ben Jonson: The Oxford Authors*. Ed. Ian Donaldson. Oxford: Oxford U P, 1985.

Keynes, Geoffrey. *A Bibliography of Dr. John Donne*. 4th ed. Oxford: Clarendon P, 1973.

Latimer, Hugh. *Selected Sermons*. Ed. Allan G. Chester. Charlottesville: U P of Virginia, 1968.

Lewalski, Barbara K. *Protestant Poetics and the Seventeenth Century Religious Lyric*. Princeton: Princeton U P, 1979.

_____. "Typological Symbolism and the 'Progress of the Soul' in Seventeenth-Century Literature." *Literary Uses of Typology*. Ed. Earl Miner. Princeton: Princeton U P, 1977. 79-114.

Luther, Martin. *Works*. 55 vols. Ed. Helmut T. Lehmann. Philadelphia: Muhlenberg P, 1962.

McCoy, Richard C. "'Thou Idol Ceremony': Elizabeth I, The Henriad, and the Rites of the English Monarchy." In Susan Zimmerman and Ronald F. Weisman, eds. *Urban Life in the Renaissance*. Newark: U of Delaware P, 1989. 240-266.

Maron, Gottfried. "Mary in Protestant Theology." *Concilium*. Ed. Hans Kung. New York: Seabury, 1983. 40-47.

Mathew, Sir Tobie. *Of the Love of our Only Lord and Saviour Jesus Christ* (1622). Rpt. London: Scholar P, 1975.

New Catholic Encyclopedia. 18 vols. New York: McGraw Hill, 1967.

Novarr, David. "The Dating of Donne's La Corona." *PQ* 36 (1957): 259-65.

O'Connor, E.D. "Immaculate Conception." *New Catholic Encyclopedia*. 7:378-382.

Patrides, C.A., ed. *John Donne: Complete English Poems*. London: Everyman's Library, 1985.

Roschini, Gabriele. *La Mariologia de San Tommaso*. Roma: Angelo Belardetti, 1950.

Sellin, Paul R. *John Donne and "Calvinist" Views of Grace*. Amsterdam: VU Boekhandel, 1983.

Shea, George W. "Outline History of Mariology in the Middle Ages and Modern Times." *Mariology*. Ed. Juniper B. Carol. Milwaukee: Bruce, 1955. 281-327.

Somerset, Anne. *Elizabeth I*. New York: Knopf, 1991.

Southwell, Robert. *Poems*. Ed. James H. McDonald and Nancy P. Brown. Oxford: Clarendon P, 1967.

Warner, Marina. *Alone of All Her Sex*. New York: Knopf, 1976.

Wellington, James E. "The Litany in Cranmer and Donne." *SP* 68 (1971): 177-99.

Wood, H. Harvey. "A Seventeenth-Century Manuscript of Poems by Donne and Others." *Essays and Studies* 16 (1931): 179-190.

Donne's Transcendent Imagination: The Divine Poems as Hierophantic Experience

Frances Malpezzi

"Thou 'hast light in darke"

In spite of the interest in John Donne's religious imagination that has burgeoned in the second half of this century, the essential nature of his religiosity remains at issue. Since the publication of Louis L. Martz's *The Poetry of Meditation* (1954), scholars have debated whether Donne's influences were largely Catholic and Continental (in the tradition of Ignatian meditation, for example) or decidedly Protestant and English, as Barbara Lewalski argues. Even scholars who agree on the latter, however, do not concur. Some see Donne as a strict Calvinist; others view him as a more moderate Lutheran or even an Arminian.[1] While attempts to locate Donne doctrinally provide a necessary historical framework for reading his works, they do not begin to fathom the religious impulse that underlies them. For the latter we need to turn to the discipline of the history of religions, especially that branch whose methodology explores not the historical contexts of religions but the structures of religious phenomena in order to understand their essence.[2] Lest we "thrust into strait corners of poore wit" a poet whose work is almost as "cornerlesse and infinite" as the God he sought to magnify, we need to understand the way that Donne's religious imagination transcends the particularities and limits of his time and place. Ultimately, Donne is more than a seventeenth-century Protestant writer (with whatever qualifiers we want to attach to Protestant). He is even more than a Christian writer whose values are firmly entrenched in western culture. The additional and broader perspective gained by placing Donne within the context of the history of religions illumines the cross-cultural dimensions of his religious imagination.

An especially useful framework for examining Donne from this perspective is the work of the pre-eminent and pioneering historian of religions, Mircea Eliade. Author of numerous scholarly treatises and editor of the multi-volume *Encyclopedia of Religion*, Eliade bridged the concerns of anthropologists and earlier students of comparative religion.[3] While comparative religion had emphasized the religions of the complex societies of Europe and the Far East, Eliade's study often incorporated nonliterate and tribal societies, the traditional focus of anthropologists. Looking beyond the bases of particular manifestations of religion, Eliade worked to identify what constitutes the religious impulse cross-culturally.

Even the most cursory survey of Donne's work suggests that he conforms to Eliade's definition of *homo religiosus*, the religious human. In synthesizing the concept of the relgious human, Gregory Alles (444) sees Eliade contrasting modes of "existing in and experiencing the world"; Eliade depicts *homo religiosus* as "driven by a desire for being," living "at the center of the world, close to the gods and in the eternal present of the paradigmatic mythic events that make profane duration possible." Eliade makes a clear distinction between the individual whose fundamental orientation is sacred rather than secular and profane:

> Whatever the historical context in which he is placed, *homo religiosus* always believes that there is an absolute reality, *the sacred*, which transcends this world but manifests itself in this world, thereby sanctifying it and making it real. He further believes that life has a sacred origin and that human existence realizes all of its potentialities in proportion as it is religious—that is, participates in reality. . . . By reactualizing sacred history, by imitating the divine behavior, man puts and keeps himself close to the gods—that is, in the real and significant. (*Sacred and Profane* 202)

The recognition that the transcendent reality of the sacred manifests itself in and sanctifies the world, that sacred history can and must be reactualized, is the core of Donne's religious art. In the essay that follows we will see that Donne not only perceived the world as imbued by the sacred, but also clearly believed the principal events of sacred experience, those preserved in Scripture, are repeatable and accessible to humanity. In this fundamental religious paradox the mortal whose life is contracted to a brief span has open and available the vast reaches of the timeless and immutable. This abstraction assumes concrete form in those divine poems which become hierophanies, manifestations of the sacred, their very time and space transformed to the eternal and cosmic.[4]

> *"As perchance, Carvers do not faces make,*
> *But that away, which hid them there, do take."*

Mircea Eliade argues that religious humans are motivated by the belief that "Life is lived on a twofold plane; it takes its course as human existence and, at the same time, shares in a transhuman life, that of the cosmos or the gods" (*Sacred* 167). As a result, everything takes on meaning: "It is his familiar everyday life that is transfigured.... Even the most habitual gesture can signify a spiritual act" (*Sacred* 183). Throughout his devotional writing Donne views the world from this perspective of *homo religiosus*. Yet Donne did more than accept the commonplace of his era that Creation is a book revealing the Creator; rather, he saw the visible and tangible world as saturated with sacred meaning. In a sermon on John 14.20 he asserts that every creature calls man "to a consideration of God":

> Every Ant that he sees, askes him, Where had I this providence, and industry? Every flowre that he sees, asks him, Where had I this beauty, this fragrancy, this medicinall vertue in me? Every creature calls him to consider, what great things God hath done in little subjects. (*Sermons* 9: 237)

The material world is real to Donne because God manifests himself in it. What might seem insignificant when seen through profane eyes resonates with sacred meaning for *homo religiosus*.

In a sermon preached in 1622 on Job 36: 25, Donne expatiates at length on seeing God in his creation. The divine Author reveals himself in his multi-volume work, including in "the Georgics." Donne exhorts his audience to consider "the *Earth*, a farme, a garden, nay seven foot of earth, a grave" as a manifestation of the deity:

> Goe lower; every *worme* in the grave, lower, every *weed* upon the grave, is an abridgement of all; nay lock up all doores and windowes, see nothing but *thy selfe*; nay let thy selfe be locked up in a close prison, that

> thou canst not see thy selfe, and doe but feel thy *pulse*; let thy pulse be
> intermitted, or stupefied, that thou feel not that, and doe but thinke, and
> a *worme*, a *weed*, thy *selfe*, thy *pulse*, thy *thought*, are all testimonies, that
> *All*, this *All*, and all parts thereof, are *Opus*, a *work made*, and *opus ejus*, *his*
> *work*, made by *God*. (4: 167)

Yet Donne concludes it is not only in God's *"works* abroad" that the
Christian may see the Creator, but in adversity, in God's *"working* upon
himself, at home" in the afflictions and corrections the sinner experiences
(4: 173). Human suffering is the greatest testimony of a benign deity, for
the agony of Christ is reflected in the "red glasse" of each individual's
pain (4: 174). Ultimately, all tangible and visible aspects of creation, all
gestures, actions, and human experience are ways of seeing God for
Donne.

This belief in the manifestation of God through His works and through
His working upon us underscores much of Donne's poetry, but is the
particular impetus of "The Crosse." As Donne takes up the iconoclastic
controversy of his age,[5] the speaker concludes he cannot deny the image
of the cross Christ embraced largely because there is no escaping an
image which marks all life, including the indelible and invisible sign
"dew'd" on his soul at Baptism. Whether he looks high or low, at a bird or
a globe, Donne's speaker sees a sacralized universe reflecting divine
reality:

> Looke downe, thou spiest out Crosses in small things;
> Looke up, thou seest birds rais'd on crossed wings;
> All the Globes frame, and spheares, is nothing else
> But the Meridians crossing Parallels. (ll. 21-24)

A small creature and the enormous frame of the world itself equally
signify the glory of God as they form the sign of His cross.

Moreover, like Eliade's *homo religiosus* for whom the "most habitual
gesture can signify a spiritual act," Donne's speaker realizes he need only
stretch his arms or swim to replicate the sign of Christ's redemption:

> Who can deny mee power, and liberty
> To stretch mine armes, and mine owne Crosse to be?
> Swimme, and at every stroake, thou art thy Crosse.(ll. 17-19)

If the physical world is marked by the cross, and if simple human gestures exemplify that cross, then even more so do the cross and the crucifixion become concrete as they assume materiality in each Christian's patient and submissive acceptance of suffering and tribulation. Through affliction, each individual "When Still'd, or purg'd by tribulation" makes the cross a new reality: "For when that Crosse ungrudg'd, unto you stickes, / Then are you to your selfe, a Crucifixe" (ll. 30-32). Samuel Hazo has argued that the image Donne uses of the carver revealing the face already in the wood is an apt metaphor for conveying the theme of the "indispensability of suffering to spiritual perfection":

> Donne pictures the face hewn by the sculptor as having been hidden within the unsculpted wood or stone. The whittling away of the conceal-ing matter by the sculptor, according to Donne, permits the indwelling face to be seen. Tribulation is said to possess this same sculpting power to the extent that it ends to reveal the Christian or indwelling counte-nance or "true" face after purging man of superficialities. (40)

The metaphor is an equally good one for revealing the indwelling of the divine in the material universe. In a world imbued with the sacred, Donne as *homo religiosus* perceives the divine. As poet, he functions like the carver cognizant of the face within the wood; his words whittle through the world to reveal its sanctification.

As the veil was rent in the Temple at the Crucifixion, the piercing eye of *homo religiosus* penetrates the veneer of the mundane to perceive the inherent sanctity of a world that consistently declares the glory of God. *Homo religiosus* sees not *just* a worm, a weed, a bird, or a person with outstretched arms; rather, he sees God in and through these things. *Homo religiosus* not only experiences prosperity or adversity in the daily course of life but recognizes God's workings in these different manifestations of divine goodness and mercy.

While Donne's "The Crosse" demonstrates that all creation, all life is imbued with the immediacy of Christ's crucifixion, other divine poems also exemplify the way *homo religiosus* sees God in his works and in his working upon humankind. The speaker in the sonnet, "I am a little world," looks at the self and sees a microcosm of the carefully crafted macrocosm. Recognizing that his genesis, too, is the work of God, he knows the Creator in the creature. As the repentant sinner asking God to "Powre new seas in mine eyes" (l. 7), he again sees himself as a microcosm of the world flooded and re-created by the power and grace of a benefi-cent deity. The speaker of "Oh my blacke Soule" is aware that even the colors of the spectrum manifest the spiritual realities of sin, contrition, and redemption through Christ's salvific blood. The speaker in "Since she whome I lovd" saw the Creator in his creation, the woman he loved. As "streames do shew the head" (l. 6), she was the emanation from the divine, revealing the Godhead and, through human love, immersing the speaker in the waters of grace that will ultimately carry him to the spiritual intimacy of celestial love. The world of Donne's divine poems is one in which the invisible things of God are manifest in creation, a world in which every gesture, every act—whether it be the cruciform motion of swimming, journeying westward on a Goodfriday, traveling to Germany, or loving a woman—reverberates with sacred meaning.

> *"This treasure then, in grosse, my Soule uplay,*
> *And in my life retaile it every day."*

Although locked in mortal experience, his mundane existence contracted to "a span, / Nay to an inch," *homo religiosus* is able to recognize the spiritual significance of the created universe because he is never far from the sacred events of mythical time. Mircea Eliade makes a crucial distinction between religious and profane individuals in respect to their perspectives on time. The religious human recognizes the circularity and reversibility of sacred time:

> *By its very nature sacred time is reversible* in the sense that, properly speaking, it is a *primordial mythical time made present*. Every religious festival, any liturgical time, represents the reactualization of a sacred event that took place in a mythical past, "in the beginning." Religious participation in a festival implies emerging from ordinary temporal duration and reintegration of the mythical time reactualized by the festival itself. Hence sacred time is indefinitely recoverable, indefinitely repeatable. (*Sacred* 68-69)

As *homo religiosus*, Donne believed the events of sacred history were not relegated to the past but are a part of the sacred present and accessible to every believer. The Nativity of Christ, for example, did not happen once but continues to happen through time, as Donne notes in a sermon on 1 Timothy 1: 15: "He was not born once and no more, but hath a continual, because an eternall generation, and is as much begotten to day, as he was 100. 1000. 1000 millions of generations passed" (*Sermons* 1: 293). So, too, the crucifixion of Christ has an on-going reality as every sinner continues to crucify Christ daily (1: 160; 1: 196).

Donne believed that it was through the faculty of memory that sacred time became accessible. In a sermon on Psalm 38: 8 Donne articulates the way this faculty enables the Christian to move backward and forward through sacred time, from spiritual history to the spiritual future. Sacred myth as it is perserved in scripture is also encapsuled within memory and the pattern of daily existence:

> All knowledge, that seems new to day, says *Plato*, is but a remembring of *that*, which your soul knew before. All instruction, which we can give you to day, is but the remembring you of the mercies of God, which have been *new every morning*. Nay, he that hears no Sermons, he that reads no Scriptures, hath the Bible without book; He hath a *Genesis* in his *memory*; he cannot forget his *Creation*; He hath an *Exodus* in his memory; he cannot forget that God hath delivered him, from some kind of *Egypt*, from some oppression; He hath a *Leviticus* in his memory; hee cannot forget, that God hath proposed to him some Law, some rules to be observed. He hath *all* in his memory, even to the *Revelation*; God hath *revealed* to him, *even at midnight alone*, what shall be his portion, in the next world; And if he dare but remember that nights communication between God and him, he is well-near learned enough. (2: 74)

The integral sacred reality Donne describes here extends far beyond the mere imaginative leap necessary for the Ignatian technique of composition of place. No passive spectator, *homo religiosus* does not simply visualize events distant in the past or future (creation, flood, apocalypse); rather, he repeatedly experiences the spiritually immediate and timeless. Everything from the mythical beginning to the eighth and everlasting day is tropologically engrained in the daily life of the individual and accessible through the faculty of memory.[6]

While Eliade sees believers transcending the profane through liturgy or religious festival, sacred time is also realized through sacred poetry. In many of Donne's poems, the speaker becomes contemporary with sacred events—as do the readers who participate in the poem. For the duration of the poem, as readers articulate the speaker's words, conforming themselves to him, his experience becomes theirs. What Eliade says of myth is equally true of many of Donne's poems:

> What is involved is not a commemoration of mythical events but a reiteration of them. The protagonists of the myth are made present, one

becomes their contemporary. This also implies that one is no longer living in chronological time, but in the primordial Time, the Time when the event *first took place*. This is why we can use the term the "strong time" of myth; it is the prodigious, "sacred" time when something *new, strong, and significant* was manifested. To re-experience that time, to re-enact it as often as possible, to witness again the spectacle of the divine works, to meet with the Supernaturals and relearn their creative lesson is the desire that runs like a pattern through all the ritual reiterations of myths. In short, myths reveal that the World, man, and life have a supernatural origin and history, and that this history is significant, precious, and exemplary. (*Myth and Reality* 19)

This transcendence of the profane and the attendant hierophany provide a recurrent and integral pattern for many Donne poems.

There are two ways in which Donne's poems make sacred time accessible to the reader. First, in depicting and capturing the eternal present of Christian myth, they make the speaker and participatory readers contemporary with these events, placing them in the continuous present of extemporal and sacred reality. And, second, they show how the life of the speaker (hence, every Christian) replicates these events. In the first way, the poem demonstrates the transcendent power of memory, returning us to sacred time; the second shows the sacralization of the profane as the sacred is "made flesh" in the daily life of each individual.

We see the former most dramatically and consistently in the *La Corona* sequence when the speaker (and, through the speaker, the reader) is made contemporary with the main events in the life of Christ from his conception to his Second Coming. Through the use of the present tense, the poem captures the everpresent now of the spiritual history and future of humankind. As A. B. Chambers has remarked, "One of the verbal signs of the perpetual significance of any event in Christ's life is a tendency to use the present tense, not the past (*"La Corona"* 164). In this sonnet sequence readers are returned to the time of the Incarnation as Christ "yeelds himselfe to lye / In prison" in the descent into Mary's womb and human flesh (ll. 19-20). Through language and imagery Donne emphasizes the hypostatic union as the divine Christ consents to become mortal, to assume the limitations and condition of humanity: "Wee are all conceived in close Prison; in our Mothers wombes, we are close Prisoners all" (*Sermons* 2: 197). Mary paradoxically becomes "now / Thy Makers maker, and thy Fathers mother" (ll. 25-26). The present tense and the crucial "now" of l. 25 transport us not simply to the elusive and shadowy realm of the historical past but to the continuous present of mythical time.

So, too, sonnet 3 represents the immediacy of Christ's birth as the speaker and the readers are at "this stall" (l. 6), at the time and place of Christ's nativity. In the same sonnet, the flight into Egypt becomes reality as we "with him into Egypt goe" (l. 41). Sonnet 4 places us with Christ in the temple. As Patrick O'Connell has shown, the speaker in these two sonnets becomes increasingly more involved in the action. While in Sonnet 3 "he attempts, somewhat hesitantly, to discover a place for himself in the events being narrated" (124), in Sonnet 4 "without realizing it, the speaker has been incorporated into the scene, though not by his own efforts. It is not the speaker's search for Christ, but Christ's search for the speaker, that will draw them together" (125-126). Nania and Klemp, focusing on the centrality of this sonnet in the sequence, read it as an emblem for each individual "who is nothing less than a temple of God" (53). Hence, the sonnet takes us beyond witnessing the events of sacred time as some spectacle to be passively viewed but rather leads us to recognize the way in which speaker and reader participate in the major elements (time, place, action) of the continuous mystery of the divine drama.

The sequence then moves from the everpresent reality of the Crucifixion to the future of the speaker's resurrection from the dead to the final sonnet that conflates Christ's Ascension and Second Coming into one apocalyptic now:

> Behold the Highest, parting hence away,
> Lightens the darke clouds, which hee treads upon,
> Nor doth hee by ascending, show alone,
> But first hee, and hee first enters the way.
> (ll. 89-92)

As hierophantic experience, the poem embodies the divine Word in words. In the immediacy of the sacred present, the sonnets reveal Christ, the infant, the teacher, the sacrificial victim; Christ, the "Mild lambe" (l. 94), bleeding for humankind and Christ, the battering "Ramme" (l. 93), opening heaven's gates. The poet, hence, transforms both poem and readers into the womb, the stall, the temple in which Christ dwells.

"The Annuntiation and Passion" also returns the reader to sacred time and space as this occasional poem highlights the concurrent celebration of the Feast of the Annunciation and the Passion which both fell on 25 March in 1608 (Shawcross 354). In the poem the faculty of memory enables the speaker's soul to see the crucial events in the life of Mary from the time she was "scarce fifteene" to "almost fiftie" (l. 14) and hierophantically to reveal Christ, the Tree of Life, the great Cedar of Lebanon "plant it selfe" (l. 8) in the Virgin womb and tomb. In the circularity of sacred time, Christ's conception and death are one in the ever present moment as both repeatedly continue to happen throughout chronological time. Moreover, both the festal and Donne's poetic "Abridgement of Christs story" (l. 20) drive home the point that for fallen humanity birth and death are inseparable:

> This Church, by letting these daies joyne, hath shown
> Death and conception in mankinde is one. (ll. 33-34)

Hence, the poem reflects on the need for both the Incarnation and Passion: the redemption of Adamic nature conceived in sin and born into the ashes of physical and spiritual mortality; because of the Fall for humankind the "womb and the grave are but one point" (*Sermons* 2: 200). The poem, in abridging Christ's (and Mary's) story, not only reminds us of the root cause for these events but asserts their continuing reality in the life of every Christian who should "uplay" this treasure and "retaile it every day" (ll. 45-46). The play on words in the last line is significant. The story is the speaker's (and humanity's) spiritual currency and is, through the constant telling, always to be made spiritually current. The spiritual treasure of salvation history is never depleted and always accessible.[7]

In other poems sacred time and space become accessible not in a transcendence of the profane but in a transformation of it as Donne demonstrates the way spiritual reality is replicated in the daily and mundane life of each Christian, thus sacralizing it.[8] The process is that which Herbert articulated in "The H. Scriptures. II":

> Such are thy secrets, which my life makes good,
> And comments on thee: for in ev'ry thing
> Thy words do finde me out, & parallels bring,
> And in another make me understood. (ll. 9-12)

John Wall has looked at this process as it particularly occurs in the *Holy Sonnets:*

> The goal toward which the speaker in the *Holy Sonnets* works to open
> himself is God's repeating in him in microcosm the universal salvation

> history of mankind. . . . Several of the sonnets invoke the Christ-event,
> which stands at the central point in Christian history, while others
> extend the scope of time in the *Holy Sonnets* to include "the worlds last
> night," the end of time in the coming of God's kingdom. (200)

What I would add to this point is that the process makes sacred time accessible by transforming profane existence. We see the speaker micro-cosmically reflecting the world of the sacred in "I am a little world made cunningly" as he finds his own existence patterned by spiritual history (Guibbory 90; Clark 77-78). For example, he experiences creation—"I am a little world made cunningly" (l. 1); the Fall—the betrayal to "black sinne" and "endlesse night" (l. 3); the Flood and consequent convenant between God and humanity (ll. 5-9; see also Shawcross 347 n. 9). The last five lines of the poem are especially rich. As the speaker recalls how he has burned with lust and envy (l. 11), he begs to be singed by divine rather than carnal fire: "And burne me ô Lord, with a fiery zeale / Of thee'and thy house, which doth in eating heale" (ll. 13-14). This healing blaze which consumes and is consumed (Clark 77) synthesizes images in Scripture from the pillar of fire of Exodus to the fiery vision of Ezekiel to the flame of the Spirit at Pentecost and the apocalyptic destruction of Revelation.

There are other notable examples throughout the body of Donne's poetry of this sacralization of the profane by paralleling worldly experience to that of sacred history. For example, "Spit in my face yee Jewes" demonstrates the reality of the crucifixion for a sinner who realizes the consequence of his impious actions: "I / Crucifie him daily" (ll. 7-8). He realizes he is playing the wrong role in the re-living of the sacred drama and yearns to re-enact that mystery not as the oppressor but as sacrificial victim:

> Spit in my face yee Jewes, and pierce my side,
> Buffet, and scoffe, scourge, and crucifie mee. (ll. 1-2)

In "Thou hast made me" the speaker transcends to the sacred time and space of Christian psychostasis as he eschatologically ponders his sins.[9] The author/speaker of "A Hymne to Christ" re-lives the Old and New Testament. In sailing for Germany, he is Noah embarking in the ark; like the Jewish nation in Exodus, he faces the clouds of God's anger (Shawcross 387 n.5); like Abraham sacrificing his beloved son Isaac, he sacrifices his beloved "Iland" and all he loves, thus also imitating and conforming himself to Christ's sacrifice in his willingness to surrender his "I" land for God. In many of these poems, the speaker recapitulates the experience of the sacred, transforming profane reality. To paraphrase Herbert's "The Bunch of Grapes," their story, the story of sacred myth, pens and sets him down.

One of the best illustrations of the return to sacred time and place both in terms of the assertion of the continuous power of myth and the replication of mythical events in the life of each individual is Donne's "Goodfriday, 1613. Riding Westward," a poem which conjoins the two. An intensely powerful and dramatic poem that has fascinated many,[10] it has been dubbed "the most carefuly and deliberately wrought of all Donne's devotional poems" (Bellette 347). Yet the external action is negligible; its beginning, middle, and end can be summed up in two words: "I ride" (l. 33).[11] The poem gains its impetus not from any directional shift the rider makes but in his transcendence of the profane journey. In the interior action, we have the core of Donne's poem—the dramatic assertion that Christ's death is not limited and fixed to a point in time and space but an omnipresent, continuing reality accessible to humanity.

The journey of the poem is both through time and beyond time. In traveling westward, the speaker, as Patrick O'Connell has argued, reflects the human condition, traveling the way of mortal flesh: "the speaker's ride becomes a journey in time, an image of inexorable passage toward the 'declining West' of death and dissolution" (17). Donne, in a sermon on Genesis 1: 26, makes this traditional association of west and death: "To that west we must all come, to the earth. . . . Our West, our declination is in this, that we are but earth" (9: 49-50). But the speaker, whirled by pleasure or business, also journeys toward spiritual death as his "westward journey becomes a symbol of his movement, under the influence of the flesh and as a prisoner of time, away from the Christ whom he 'should see,' but cannot or will not" (18). His spiritual progress impeded by his worldliness and by the burden of his guilt,[12] he regards the sight of Christ's suffering as a "spectacle of too much weight for mee," a cross too heavy for him to bear. Yet the cross is as inescapable here as in "The Crosse." The speaker ultimately "sees" the crucified Christ. This hierophantic experience central to "Goodfriday," the manifestation of Christ who "hang'st upon the tree" (l. 36) is the result of the speaker's move from the profane reality of the temporal to become one with the paradigmatic events of divine myth: "the very world of the poem is utterly changed by the presence of Another (O'Connell, "'Restore Thine Image'" 24).

While a move to sacred time and space often occurs through ritual, or sometimes festival, in Donne's poem it occurs, as it typically does in his poetry, through the faculty of memory: "Though these things, as I ride, be from mine eye, / They'are present yet unto my memory" (ll. 33-34). Memory functions in terms of Eliade's threshold between the profane and the sacred. When the speaker in Donne's poem enters this plane of existence, becoming one with the sacred time and place of the crucifixion, he is at the center of the universe—replete with an image of the *axis mundi* Eliade finds in most cultural versions of the experience (see as well *Patterns* 3, 99, 227, for example), here the figure of the cross which occurs at the exact center of the poem.

The speaker's anamnestic experience dramatically illustrates the reversibility and circularity of mythic experience: "In its discovery that the redemptive events are 'present yet,' the memory reveals that Christ's death is not limited to the historical past and so unavailable to the speaker" (O'Connell, "'Restore Thine Image'" 24). The speaker is at the very time and place that Christ's blood once made and continues to make "durt of dust" (l. 27). While it might at first seem tasteless or grotesque to sum up salvation with the image of mud, Donne's image is a significant one. The Adamic red earth of the human condition, signified by the physical and spiritual sterility of dust, is moistened and made malleable for effecting the recreation. As God used red earth at the first creation, moistened red earth becomes the stuff of recreation of all humanity in general and the speaker in particular.[13] Present at sacred space, the speaker also becomes the sacred place. His own sterile dust has become reddened mud. At the foot of the cross, his spiritual aridity is moistened by Christ's salvific blood. He is made malleable and recreated.

Thus, the speaker not only is made contemporary with Christ's passion and death, but he is now prepared to replicate Christ's suffering in his own life. In conformity with Christ, he will journey the *via purgativa*, accepting the penitential and purgative affliction meted out by a merciful God. He is not only present at the Crucifixion; he has internalized it as well. In his new attitude toward his westward journey, he has spiritually oriented himself. As the speaker finds Jerusalem and the events of Christ's death "present" to his memory, the poem in part redefines pilgrimage. In the *Enchiridion*, Erasmus questions, "Is it so very important that you make a physical trip to Jerusalem, when in your heart there is a veritable Sodom, an Egypt, a Babylon?" (128). In a very literal-minded way, the speaker of Goodfriday at first perceives his spiritual problem to be a geographical one: If he could just turn around and ride in the opposite direction he would eventually reach the place where he could see the Son of God whose rise and fall saved humankind from eternal darkness. In his heart of hearts, he assures himself, he longs to go to the East, to Jerusalem, where the physical setting of Christ's passion and death would appropriately stimulate his visionary powers. Yet even as he begins to delineate what he would see "There" (l. 11) he gives a sigh of relief that he is about his own busy-ness since that "spectacle" would be too ponderous. Caught up in his mundane affairs and traveling the realm of the profane, he insists devotion is the core of his being yet shuns the ultimate reality of Christ's death. His notion that should he travel east his devotion would be made manifest is misguided. He suggests simply redirecting his body could reorient his values, assumes traveling east to Jerusalem would signal his devotion—as if God could not see the Babylon of worldliness within.

The speaker's error in assuming that such a journey can make up for spiritual deficiency is one Donne was eventually to preach on at Easter in 1630 as he expatiates on the abuse of pilgrimage. Recalling the words of St. Jerome, he asks:

> How many men carry Sepulchres to the Sepulchre, when they carry themselves to Jerusalem? *Non Hierosolymis vixisse*, saies he, To have lived well at Jerusalem is praise-worthy, but not to have lived there. *Non audeo concludere*, I dare not shut up that God, whom the Heavens cannot containe, in a corner of the earth; and Jerusalem is but so. *Et de Britannia, & de Hierosolymis aequaliter patet aula coelestis*, Heaven is as neare England, (saies S. *Hierom*) as it is to Jerusalem. (9: 210)

Donne further draws upon St. Gregory of Nyssen to support his argument:

> Christ never called that, Blessednesse, saies he, to have beene at Jerusalem, nor ever called this Jerusalem the way to Heaven; why any man should do so, when Christ did not, *Qui mentem habet, consideret*, (saies that Father) Let him that is not distracted, consider. (9: 210)

Early in the poem, the speaker, distracted by his pleasure or business, considers a literal journey to the geographical east as an ideal spiritual goal and the antithesis of his westward movement in pursuit of worldly ends. Far from being to his credit, this marks his failure to recognize his proximity to heaven, his inability to realize his accessibility to the divine no matter what his physical location. By the end of the poem, however, the speaker realizes that if his back is turned from that tree planted in the New Jerusalem it is to carry out the penitential lifespan of every mortal—this west is now his business and the ultimate way to undying pleasure.

As the speaker finds the spiritual Jerusalem and as the events of Christ's death become "present" to his memory, the poem redefines pilgrimage, rejecting what might be considered Catholic pilgrimage—a public, often communal, ritualized journey to a specific geographic location—for a sense of pilgrimage that is more in keeping with Protestant spirituality—a private, personal interior journey to a Jerusalem that cannot be found on any map and to an event that is not circumscribed by time. Yet, at the same time, the poem functions as a communal pilgrimage as Donne takes the reader along with him, transcending mundane reality and secular time.

In this 42-line poem Donne has captured and dramatized a transcendent and mysterious experience, as he portrays a worldly speaker who rides into the presence of the crucified Christ. In his return to a sacred time beyond temporality and space far removed from geographic reality, the speaker experiences a hierophany which transforms his life as he recognizes the necessity of conforming his will to God's and conforming himself to the suffering Christ. He not only experiences the accessibility of sacred time and space but realizes the way profane life can be structured by the divine and thus sacralized.

"till we come th'Extemporall song to sing"

As we examine the products of Donne's religious imagination, we see John Donne was no less a minister of the Word in the poetic manifestation of that imagination than when he was in the pulpit. His view of the paradigm of all poetry, the Psalms, reveals a clear analogy between the role of preacher and poet. The correspondence of language and imagery in his Lenten sermon on Ezekiel 33:32 and his "Upon the translation of the Psalmes by Sir Philip Sydney, and the Countesse of Pembroke his Sister" underscores the similarity Donne saw between the psalmist/poet and the minister.[14] Both are instruments for sounding God's love, for tuning souls that have become disharmonious through sin. Like Gabriel, the angel of the Annunciation, ministers and poets are harbingers of the Word made flesh, of that immensity cloistered in the dear womb of the sermon or poem that enables each Christian to experience anew and repeatedly the incarnation of Christ. Patrick O'Connell has argued that for Donne "the paradox of the Incarnation, God in human flesh, undergirds the paradox of religious poetry, the Word in human words. Because the Almighty humbled himself to such an extent as to become human, he can be brought within the confines of human words and art, not by human power but by cooperation with this divine gift" (124). Human language, corrupted and obscured by the Fall, can be redeemed—purified and clarified by the Holy Ghost (or that spirit's poetic surrogate, the Christianized muse Urania) to reveal the light of the divine. Thus, words of the inspired preacher and poet can serve in the worship of the Word. Like sermons incarnationally meant to convey God to humanity,[15] like the Psalms of David meant "to serve the church of God, to the worlds end" (2: 55), like the Sidneyan translation of those psalms meant to "Be as our tuning" (l. 54), religious poetry for Donne is a vehicle for keeping souls in tune with God "till we come th'Extemporall song to sing" (l. 51). Because of this aesthetic, Donne's divine poems are often hierophantic experiences, manifestations of the sacred. Through them Donne not only asserts the sacrality of life, but returns the speaker, and consequently, the reader to the sacred time and/or space of Christian mythology, either making participants in the poem contemporary with divine events and placing them in the presence of the deity or demonstrating the way these events structure, imbue with meaning, and sacralize profane experience.

While precision in regard to Donne's theological stance is crucial for an understanding of the products of his religious imagination, we must also approach his work from a broader perspective. To see Donne operating from the context of *homo religiosus* means to recognize his relationship not only to those seventeenth-century British writers who shared his ideology nor only to Christians such as Augustine who came before him and helped shape his doctrine. It also means recognizing what he has in common with all those who through the centuries and across continents have been moved by the religious impulse. To see beyond the narrowly defined realm of doctrinal tenets, to see Donne's religious imagination in the context of such manifestations from earlier or later cultures by those who do not share his Christian belief system is ultimately to recognize the transcendent power of his poetry and hence its enduring value.

Notes

[1] While it would be difficult to list all the works dealing with this issue here, one might note the following representative examples. R. V. Young nicely sets forth the sides in the theological debate in his introduction in "Donne's Holy Sonnets and the Theology of Grace." Young contends Donne's Holy Sonnets cannot be read as Calvinist or even Protestant expositions of grace. Instead, he finds the poems present a theologically moderate position and concludes that Donne is typical of devotional poets in the period who draw upon various resources, Catholic and Protestant, Medieval and Renaissance. Richard Strier also does not see the sonnets as consistently Calvinist, but he draws a different conclusion than Young: "The pain and confusion in many of the 'Holy Sonnets' is not that of the convinced Calvinist but rather that of a person who would like to be a convinced Calvinist but who is both unable to be so and unable to admit that he is unable to be so" (361). Paul Sellin, on the other hand, presents a strong argument for Donne's Calvinism. Gene Veith labels Donne Arminian in contrast to the Calvinist Herbert, although he qualifies this somewhat by noting the difficulty of pinning down Donne's theological position (119). Others interpret Donne's theological position in the context of secularity. Carey depicts Donne as an apostate who betrayed his faith in pursuit of self-interest and wordly ambition. Marotti examines "the religious transvaluation of the seclar" (253) as he elaborates on the "politically encoded" nature of Donne's religious prose and poety.

[2] "The 'History of Religion' as a Branch of Knowledge" in Eliade's *The Sacred and the Profane* provides a useful overview of the history of this discipline (216-232).

[3] For a treatment of Eliade's role in the development of the history of religions and a survey of his work, see Kitagawa.

[4] For a useful overview of the term, "hierophany," see Eliade and Sullivan's entry in vol. 6 of the *Encyclopedia of Religion*. They note, "The sacred appears in cosmic form as well as in the imaginative life of human beings" (313). It is the latter which is my concern in this essay. Especially important for the context of my argument is their discussion of the impact hierophanies have on space and time (315-316).

[5] For the treatment of "The Crosse" in relationship to the iconoclastic controversy, see Gilman, Hazo, and McQueen.

[6] On the importance of memory in relation to Donne, see Friedman, Guibbory (esp. 88-95), Guite, and Tebeaux.

[7] Such is also the case in a number of Donne's poems. For example, the speaker's direct address to the sun that sleeps while "A better Sun" rises transports us to sacred time in "Resurrection, imperfect." Christ's death and resurrec-

tion are not treated as historical events relegated to the dusty past but as contemporary reality for the speaker (and for readers) who experience the spiritual significance of "these three daies" (l.12). The Resurrrection for the speaker is in the immediacy of "to day" (l. 4). In the *Holy Sonnets*, the first eight lines of "At the round earths imagin'd corners" impel us to the sacred time of Revelation and Judgment as the speaker directs the angelic trumpeters to blow their instruments and the "numberless infinities / Of soules" to rejoin their resurrected bodies (l. 1-4).

[8] For extended studies of the Protestant view that biblical history is recapitulated in the life of the Christian, see both Lewalski and Clark.

[9] For a further elaboration of this, see Malpezzi, "The Weight/lessness of Sin."

[10] Significant readings of "Goodfriday" have been provided by Bellete, Chambers' two essays on the poem, Friedman, Glaser, Goldberg, O'Connell in "'Restore Thine Image,'" Severance, Sherwood, Sicherman, and Sullivan, as well as in the essays by Brooks and Hartwig in this volume.

[11] On the significance of the horse and rider, see Malpezzi's "'As I Ride.'"

[12] On the speaker's guilt, see Sherwood 167.

[13] For associations between Adam, creation, and red earth, see, for example, *Sermons* 2: 78-79; 2: 101; and 9: 49.

[14] For an elaboration on the relationship between this sermon and poem, see Malpezzi, "Christian Poetics." Studies of Donne's aesthetics can be found in Asals, "Davids Successors" and "The Grammar of Redemption," in O'Connell on *La Corona*, and in McGrath.

[15]In "To Mr. Tilman after he had taken orders," the newly ordained minister is described as "new feather'd with coelestial love" (l.22) and reminded:

> *Maries* prerogative was to beare Christ, so
> 'Tis preachers to convey him, for they doe
> As Angels out of cloud, from Pulpits speake. (ll.41-43)

Works Cited

Alles, Gregory D. "*Homo Religiosus.*" *The Encyclopedia of Religion.* Ed. Mircea Eliade. New York: Macmillan, 1987. 6: 442-445.

Asals, Heather. "Davids Successors: Forms of Joy and Art." *Proceedings of the Patristic, Mediaeval and Renaissance Conference* 2 (1977): 31-37.

————. "John Donne and the Grammar of Redemption." *English Studies in Canada* 5.2 (Summer 1979): 125-129.

Bellette, Antony F. "'Little Worlds Made Cunningly': Significant Form in Donne's *Holy Sonnets* and 'Goodfriday, 1613.'" *SP* 72 (1975): 322-347.

Carey, John, *John Donne: Life, Mind and Art.* New York: Oxford UP, 1981.

Chambers, A. B. "' Goodfriday, 1613. Riding Westward' Looking Back." *JDJ* 6.2 (1987): 185-201.

————. "'Goodfriday, 1613 Riding Westward': The Poem and the Tradition." *ELH* 28 (1961): 31-53.

————. "*La Corona*: Philosophic, Sacred, and Poetic Uses of Time." *New Essays on Donne.* Ed. Gary Stringer. Salzburg: U of Salzburg, 1977. 140-172.

Clark, Ira. *Christ Revealed: The History of the Neotypological Lyric of the English Renaissance.* Gainesville: U P of Florida, 1982.

Eliade, Mircea, and Lawrence E. Sullivan. "Hierophany." *The Encyclopedia of Religion.* Ed. Mircea Eliade. New York: Macmillan, 1987. 6: 313-317.

Eliade, Mircea. *Myth and Reality.* Trans. Willard R. Trask. New York: Harper & Row, 1963.

————. *Patterns in Comparative Religion.* Trans. Rosemary Sheed. New York: New American Library, 1958.

————. *The Sacred and the Profane: The Nature of Religion.* Trans. Willard R. Trask. New York: Harcourt, Brace & World, 1959.

Friedman, Donald M. "Memory and the Art of Salvation in Donne's Good Friday Poem." *ELR* 3 (1973): 418-442.

Gilman, Ernest B. *Iconoclasm and Poetry in the English Reformation: Down Went Dagon.* Chicago: U of Chicago P, 1986.

Glaser, Joe. "'Goodfriday, 1613': A Soul's Form." *College Literature* 13.2 (1986): 168-176.

Guibbory, Achsah. *The Map of Time: Seventeenth-Century English Literature and Ideas of Pattern in History.* Urbana: U of Illinois P, 1986.

Guite, A. M. "The Art of Memory and the Art of Salvation: The Centrality of Memory in the Sermons of John Donne and Lancelot Andrewes." *The Seventeenth Century* 4 (1989): 1-17.

Hazo, Samuel. "Donne's Divine Letter." *Essays and Studies in Language and Literature.* Ed. Herbert H. Petit. Duquesne Studies, Philological Series 5. Pittsburgh:

Duquesne UP, 1964. 38-43.

Himelick, Raymond, trans. and ed. *The Enchiridion of Erasmus*. Glouscester, MA: Peter Smith, 1970.

Hutchinson, F. E., ed. *The Works of George Herbert*. 1941. Corrected reprint. Oxford: Clarendon P, 1945.

Kitagawa, Joseph M. "Eliade, Mircea." *The Encyclopedia of Religion*. Ed. Mireca Eliade. New York: Macmillan, 1987. 5: 85-90.

Lewalski, Barbara K. *Prostestant Poetics and the Seventeenth-Century Religious Lyric*. Princeton: Princeton UP, 1979.

Malpezzi, Frances. "'As I Ride': The Beast and His Burden in Donne's 'Goodfriday.'" *Religion & Literature* 24.1 (Spring 1992): 23-31.

_____. "Christian Poetics in Donne's 'Upon the Translation of the Psalmes.'" *Renascence* 32.4 (Summer 1980): 221-228.

_____. "The Weight/lessness of Sin: Donne's 'Thou hast made me' and the Psychostatic Tradition." *South Central R* 4.2 (Summer 1987): 71-77.

Marotti, Arthur F. *John Donne, Coterie Poet*. Madison: U of Wisconsin P, 1966.

Martz, Louis L. *The Poetry of Meditation: A Study in English Religious Literature of the Seventeenth Century*. New Haven: Yale U P, 1954.

McGrath, Lynette. "John Donne's Apology for Poetry." *SEL* 20.1 (Winter 1980): 73-89.

McQueen, William A. "Donne's 'The Crosse.'" *Explicator* 45.3 (Spring 1987): 8-11.

Nania, John, and P. J. Klemp. "John Donne's *La Corona*: A Second Structure." *Ren/ Ref* 2 (1978): 49-54.

O'Connell, Patrick F. "'La Corona': Donne's Ars Poetica Sacra." *The Eagle and the Dove: Reassessing John Donne*. Ed. Claude J. Summers and Ted-Larry Pebworth. Columbia: U of Missouri P, 1986. 119-130.

_____. "'Restore Thine Image': Structure and Theme in Donne's 'Goodfriday.'" *JDJ* 4.1 (1985): 13-28.

Sellin, Paul R. *John Donne and 'Calvinist' Views of Grace*. Amsterdam: VU Boekhandel/Uitgeverij, 1983.

_____. *So Doth, So Is Religion: John Donne and Diplomatic Contexts in the Reformed Netherlands, 1619-1620*. Columbia: U of Missouri P, 1988.

Severance, Sibyl Lutz. "Soul, Sphere, and Structure in 'Goodfriday, 1613. Riding Westward.'" *SP* 84 (1987): 24-41.

Sherwood, Terry G. *Fulfilling the Circle: A Study of John Donne's Thought*. Toronto: U of Toronto P, 1984.

Sicherman, Carol. "Donne's Discoveries." *SEL* 11 (1971): 69-88.

Strier, Richard. "John Donne Awry and Squint: The 'Holy Sonnets,' 1608-1610." *MP* 86.4 (1989): 357-384.

Sullivan, David M. "Riders to the West: 'Goodfriday, 1613." *JDJ* 6.1 (1987): 1-8.

Tebeaux, Elizabeth. "Memory, Reason, and the Quest for Certainty in the *Sermons* of John Donne." *Renascensce* 43 (Spring 1991): 195-213.

Veith, Gene E., Jr. *Reforming Spiritality: The Religion of George Herbert.* Lewisburg: Bucknell U P, 1985.

Wall, John N., Jr. "Donne's Wit of Redemption: The Drama of Prayer in the *Holy Sonnets.*" *SP* 73.2 (April 1976): 189-203.

Young, R. V. "Donne's Holy Sonnets and the Theology of Grace." *"Bright Shootes of Everlastingnesse": The Seventeenth-Century Religious Lyric.* Ed. Claude Summers and Ted-Larry Pebworth. Columbia: U of Missouri P, 1987. 20-39.

"A true transubstantiation": Donne, Self-love, and the Passion

Paul W. Harland

t is a commonplace to say that Donne is obsessed by self, a self that he has to fight, to indulge, and frequently to escape. One of the tell-tale signs of this supposed egotism reveals itself in Donne's frequent use of mirror and reflection imagery, for here the self could indulge its need for introspection. Donne's self-absorption, it has been claimed, limits his ability to sympathize, to pity, to understand with tenderness those who are truly other and not merely versions of his multifaceted self. Three of Donne's poems on Christ's passion—"The Crosse," "What if this present," and "Goodfriday, 1613. Riding Westward"—and related passages from the sermons tell another story, however. These works, replete with the imagery of reflection, enact the drama of the ego breaking out of the prison of destructive self-preoccupation into a liberated state of true self-love which best expresses itself as willing and disinterested giving. Donne's explorations within the self may thus be seen to animate the familiar Renaissance trope that a human being was a little world: to know and to love the self was a method ultimately of knowing and loving the greater world beyond it.[1]

A study of Donne's writings on Christ's passion records the transformation of degenerate self-love into the regenerate variety, a distinction which Donne makes throughout his *Sermons*. The turning of the self inward was the first of sins and remains the underlying substance of all sin. The angels fell on account of self-love: "The Angels fell in love, when there was no object presented, before any thing was created; when there was nothing but God and themselves, they fell in love with themselves, and neglected God, and so fell *in æternum*, for ever" (3: 254). Furthermore, self-love improperly imagines personal wholeness where there is none and thereby denies any need for dependence upon God: "selfe-love cannot be called a distinct sin, but the roote of all sins. . . . To love our selves, to be satisfied in our selves, to finde an omni-sufficiency in our selves, is an intrusion, an usurpation upon God" (4: 330). In Donne's view, even God, complete unto himself, creates the universe so that he may bestow love upon it.

Nevertheless, self-love need not be confining, but may be a necessary component in loving God and humankind. Giving of self demands first the possession of self: "since we are commanded to love our neighbour, as our selves, we must be sure to love our selves so as we should doe" (4: 319). In addition, Donne believes, the genuine love of self unavoidably issues in the love of God; for this reason, Donne enjoins, "doe but love your selves . . . Only that man that loves God, hath the art to love himself; doe but love your selves; for if he love God, he would live eternally with him, and, if he desire that, and indeavour it earnestly, he does truly love himself, and not otherwise" (8: 236). Essentially, the nature of the self and the nature of its loves are transformed by the ultimate object of devotion. As I shall demonstrate, genuine love of the suffering Christ allows the self to transform itself into its best nature, to reflect Christ, and thereby to love itself fully.

Christ's passion, at once the moment of greatest divine judgment and the moment of greatest divine love, tests the human heart and reveals what variety of self-love is sheltered there. The imagined sight of the crucifixion may inspire desperate guilt and self-loathing, or it may prompt the heart to feel pity and compassion. Donne was fully aware of the former tendency, the soul's unhealthy habit, even in the midst of supposed acts of remorse and contrition, to turn inward instead of outward. The degenerate form of self-love is ironically another name for pride, since it exalts personal sin over God's ability to forgive such sin. In "The Crosse," Donne's speaker, after imagining himself denying the crucifixion, acknowledges that the cross is everywhere to be found: it is woven into the very fabric of existence. More importantly, however, he focuses on the human inclination to misconstrue the deformed species of self-interest as true humility:

But, as oft Alchimists doe coyners prove,
So may a selfe-dispising, get selfe-love.
And then as worst surfets, of best meates bee,
Soe is pride, issued from humility,
For, 'tis no child, but monster; therefore Crosse
Your joy in crosses, else, 'tis double losse . . . (lines 37-42)

The secret exaltation in personal adversity is not really a participation in Christ's suffering, but a pseudo-martyrdom, a heightening of the unhealthy experience of self-sufficiency. As such, it deserves to be crossed, to be cancelled so that it might be corrected, made a more accurate type of the antitype of all crosses. When one removes one kind of sorrow, one is able to "Crosse and correct concupiscence of witt" (58), thereby allowing oneself to be transformed by Christ's original cross: "but crosse thy selfe in all. / Then doth the Crosse of Christ worke fruitfully / Within our hearts" (60-62). Suffering *per se* has little value until the heart moves outward in fellow-feeling, in recognition, in compassionate love: "suffering it self is but a stubbornes, and a rigid and stupid standing under an affliction; it is not a humiliation, a bending under Gods hand, if it be not done in charity" (8: 187).

Donne is thus quick to distinguish two forms of *tristitia* frequently confused in the seventeenth century. Ruth Wallerstein defines the difference in sorrows in this way: "Melancholy is at once, to some degree, the inevitable condition of mortal life and the fruit of surrender to the world; and at the same time it is the source of religious awakening" (459). The origin of the dual nature of sadness may be found in the Pauline formulation "godly sorrow worketh repentence to salvation not to be reprented of: but the sorrow of the world worketh death" (2 Cor. 7.10, *KJV*).[2] T. R. Henn, in his discussion of tragedy, records a similar phenomenon. Speaking of the parent of sorrow, fear, Henn places fear under two headings: "the neurotic anxiety of the ego-centric, and the wholesome humility of fear before the unknown" (288). If individual cases of human suffering, some of the many "crosses" that appear in "The Crosse," are shadowy types of Christ's passion, then the ambiguous human response to suffering is most fully revealed as the mind contemplates the crucifixion. Although his critical eye perceives the double potential of sorrow, Donne usually records, in his meditations on the passion, the psychological movement of the sinner from one form to the other. Sound theological reasons exist for this depiction. The human experience of sorrow and joy is really the response to God's acts of judgment and mercy, respectively.

However, in Donne's theology, these two divine acts are not discrete, but continuous:

> as all the Attributes of God, make up but one God (Goodnesse, and Wisdome, and Power are but one God) so Mercy and Justice make up but one act; they doe not onely duly succeed, and second one another, they doe not onely accompany one another, they are not onely together, but they are all one. (10: 183)

The soul that is blessed enough to discern that judgment-mercy is a single act undergoes an experience of sorrow which also includes rejoicing because that soul knows that God's purpose in purgatorial suffering is to restore the divine image to the sinner. The ultimate goal of the Christian is to conform the self to Christ so perfectly that the restored divine image mirrors Christ completely, or *is* Christ ("Crosse" 36). By appropriating all of Christ's acts, the Christian becomes so much like Christ as to be indistinguishable from him. When such conformity occurs, "God shall know no man from his own Sonne, so as not to see the very righteousnesse of his own Sonne upon that man," and "the Angels shall know no man from Christ, so as not to desire to looke upon that mans face, because the most deformed wretch that is there, shall have the very beauty of Christ himselfe" (7: 273).

Donne frequently reminds his congregation in his sermons that one conforms oneself to Christ by mirroring the active, suffering Christ of history, not the glorious Christ of heaven, whose state can only be a matter of speculation in any case. Donne insists that any knowledge that one has of God in this life—through the light of nature, the scriptures, and the church—is "but *In ænigmate*, in an obscure Riddle, a representation" (8: 225). The glass by which one sees God, extraordinarily beneficial as it is, is limited, and does not reveal God's fullness or magnificence. Now one sees through a glass darkly; then, only in heaven, shall one see God face to face. According to Donne, just as ardent believers would seek to "know nothing of Christ, but *him crucifyed* . . . so we seek no other glasse, to see our selves in, but Christ, nor any other thing in this glasse, but his *Humiliation*" (6: 286). The Christ fit for human imitation is the historical Jesus, God reflected partially, but truly: "we looke upon God, in History, in matter of fact, upon things done, and set before our eyes . . . we have a nearer approximation, and vicinity to God in Christ, then any others had, in any representations of their Gods" (7: 316).

The imputation of righteousness whereby the transformation of sinner into Christ takes place is no cosmetic change and only takes place with the active participation of the individual concerned. Donne warns, "No man may take the frame of Christs merit in peeces . . . No man may take his *Agony*, and pensivenesse, and put on that, and say, Christ hath *been sad* for me, and therefore I may be merry. He that puts on Christ, must put him on *all*" (5: 157). For Donne, "to put on Christ" means to put on all of Christ's suffering and joy, his humiliation as well as his exaltation. One of the most profound and disturbing portrayals of what it means to reflect Christ occurs in a sermon on Matthew 4: 18-20. Here the mirror image presents the sinner hanging upon Christ as Christ hangs upon the cross, his arms stretched out to embrace the sinner and the entire world simultaneously:

> when my crosses have carried mee up to my Saviours Crosse, I put my hands into his hands, and hang upon his nailes, I put mine eyes upon his, and wash off all my former unchast looks . . . I put my mouth upon his mouth, and it is I that say, *My God, my God, why has thou forsaken me?* and it is I that recover againe. . . . (2: 300)

This depiction of the sinner reflecting his savior by hanging with him on the cross, graphic as it is, still is but the most significant moment in God's act of judgment-mercy; as a consequence, Donne boldly asserts that even during the crucifixion, Christ knew joy: "The *holy Ghost* calls it a *Ioy (for the Ioy which was set before him hee indured the Crosse)* which was not a *joy* of his reward after his passion, but a joy that filled him even in the middest of those torments, and arose from them" (10: 244).[3] The discerning Christian understands that just as judgment-mercy is one divine act, so sorrow and joy must interpenetrate: "they doe not onely touch and follow one another in a certaine succession, Joy assuredly after sorrow, but they consist together, they are all one, Joy and Sorrow" (4: 343). The soul mirrors Christ when individual afflictions bear the stamp of joyful sorrow or sorrowful joy that is known to Christ.

This mirroring of Christ is the projected end of the struggling soul once it is imputed righteous by Christ's covering of sins and finally glorified.[4] However, the process by which the result is achieved is a complex conversion, a gradual turning.[5] In "The Crosse," "Holy Sonnet IV: What if this present," and "Good Friday, 1613," Donne's speakers all initially betray fear or repulsion when confronted by the sight of the crucifixion, or of its symbol, the cross. The transformation in the speakers' perception marks the change from one kind of self-love to another, and from one kind of sorrow to another.[6] In "What if this present," for example, the speaker conjures up the different aspects of Christ's tormented face and asks himself whether this face, the tongue of which can "adjudge thee unto hell" (7), is able to "thee affright" (4). The expected answer is: of course the face of the world's judge can frighten. But the surprising answer that comes in the sestet reveals a speaker already undergoing regeneration. A passage from a sermon parallels this situation precisely:

> If when thou lookest upon him as the *Lord*, thou findest frowns and wrinkles in his face, apprehensions of him, as of a Judge, and occasions of feare, doe not run away from him, in that apprehension; look upon him in that angle, in that line awhile, and that feare shall bring thee to love; and as he is *Lord*, thou shalt see him in the beauty and lovelinesse of his creatures, in the order and succession of causes, and effects, and in that harmony and musique of the peace between him, and thy soule. (3: 306-07)

The speaker of the holy sonnet has contemplated the face of the Judge who has been judged by the world and finds it horrifying, but the sestet records the regenerate response of one who has looked upon Christ "in that angle" and has thus been brought "to love." In the world's eyes, the macerated face of the once beautiful Christ appears deformed and ugly. However, for the speaker who is able to see the divine intent of redemption behind the ugly crucifixion, the event becomes beautiful:

> No, no; but as in my idolatrie
> I said to all my profane mistresses,
> Beauty, of pitty, foulnesse onely is
> A signe of rigour: so I say to thee,
> To wicked spirits are horrid shapes assign'd,
> This beauteous forme assures a pitious minde. (9-14)

Profound truth comes out of a seducer's argument to his mistress: beauty is a sign of pity; foulness is a sign of rigor or cruelty. The seemingly cruel event of the crucifixion ironically declares a God who takes pity on humankind. Moreover, because the speaker is able to identify the crucifixion as "beauteous," he demonstrates his own "pitious mind." The reader is thus able to recognize the transformation that has taken place in the speaker.[7]

John Carey reduces the significance of the poem's theological underpinnings when he asserts:

> The argument he recalls using for getting girls into bed (that only ugly
> girls are unyielding) was always fatuous, and applied to Christ on the
> cross it is gruesome. We cringe from the blasphemy. . . . [A]ll he can find
> among the dazed, licentious thoughts that have become habitual to him
> is the hideous piffle about pity and pretty faces which the last six lines
> throw up. (47)

First, Carey neglects the possibility that the "profane mistresses" of the
speaker's "idolatrie" might be more than imagined personal liaisons. For
instance, in "A Hymne to Christ, at the Authors last going into Germany,"
the "false mistresses," the "loves" of the poet's "youth," are "Fame, Wit,
Hopes" (24-25). The negative image of the sinner's going whoring after
strange gods, based upon biblical passages like Exodus 34: 15-16 or
Deuteronomy 31: 16, has always been central to the Christian under-
standing of faithfulness and idolatry. Fame, wit, and ambitious hopes of
advancement, or any number of other kinds of devotion which displace
God from primacy in an individual's mind, are likely to be seen by the
world as beautiful, whereas the way of the cross, as St. Paul warned,
would be perceived as mere foolishness, a deformity of order and propor-
tion.[8] Second, the true standard of beauty, in Donne's view, is not Carey's
"girls," but Christ. A horrifying part of viewing the crucifixion lies in
seeing perfection defaced, of participating in a moment "when he whose
face the Angels desire to look on, he who was fairer then the children of
men, as the Prophet speaks, was so marr'd more then any man, as another
Prophet says, *That they hid their faces from him, & despised him* " (4: 130). The
mark of the regenerate soul that the holy sonnet records is that of a
speaker seeing beyond defacement to the true nature of Christ. Simulta-
neously, as Christ pierces through the deformity of sin to recognize his
own image in the speaker, the speaker pierces through the ugliness of the
crucified Christ to see Christ's essential beauty. Both Christ and the
speaker at such a moment know self-love born out of pity, out of compas-
sion. The two mirror one another as the image of God is restored in
humankind. As the same sermon quoted above continues, "look him in
the face in all these respects, of Humiliation, and of Exaltation too; and
then, as a Picture looks upon him, that looks upon it, God upon whom
thou keepest thine Eye, will keep his Eye upon thee" (4: 130).[9]

In fact, as the sinner moves from narrow self-love to a true self-love
that encompasses compassion, an exchange takes place between Christ

and the sinner. Christ suffers in human suffering and takes on the deformity of human sin while humankind's deformity is purged by Christ's righteousness.[10] The exchange is so complete that Donne can declare, "I were a miserable man, if I could accuse Christ of no sin; if I could not prove all my sins his, I were under a heavy condemnation" (3: 214). When one is truly part of the body of Christ, Christ bears all one's sins so that one's own sins are removed. When one has recognized one's part in crucifying Christ and repented of that act, one may make bold to say, "Christ Jesus is the sinner, and not I" (6: 239). The transformation that takes place in the viewing of the passion is one which moves from isolation to compassion and communion. Thus Donne's method of curing the solitary sufferer, a creature described in one sermon as "a languishing wretch in a sordid corner, not onely in a penurious fortune, but in an oppressed conscience" is to imagine Christ's passion in such a way as

> To set Christ Jesus before him, to out-sigh him, out-weepe him, out-bleed him, out-dye him, To transferre all the fasts, all the scornes, all the scourges, all the nailes, all the speares of Christ Jesus upon him, and so, making him the Crucified man in the sight of the Father, because all the actions, and passions of the Son, are appropriated to him, and made his so intirely, as if there were never a soule created but his, To enrich this poore soule, to comfort this sad soule so, as that he shall beleeve, and by beleeving finde all Christ to be his. (8: 246-47)

Narrow concern for personal affliction, narrow self-love, is broadened by concern for Christ's sufferings because when one recognizes Christ as one's own true image, one is able to realize that "Christ does suffer in our sufferings" (6: 221). In terms that "The Crosse" uses, the solitary sufferer's cross has been crossed by Christ's cross.

The appropriation of Christ's passion takes place so that Christ and the sinner are indistinguishable; they mirror one another perfectly:

> we shall so appeare before the Father, as that he shall take us for his owne Christ; we shall beare his name and person; and we shall every one be so accepted, as if every one of us were *all Mankind*; yea, as if we were *he* himselfe. He shall find in all our bodies his *woundes*, in all our mindes, his *Agonies*; in all our hearts, and actions his *obedience*. (5: 159-60)

Christ not only possesses the sinner, even as the sinner possesses Christ;

sinner and Christ are, by the sinner's willing acceptance of the sacrifice, made one: "of the same nature and substance as he" (5: 158; see Gilman, "'To adore or scorn'" 89). In fact, as "The Crosse" makes plain, images do not onely reflect each other; they *are* each other: "Let Crosses, soe, take what hid Christ in thee, / And be his image, or not his, but hee" (35-36). One takes up the crosses, abundantly provided by nature and circumstances, as "The Crosse" shows, so as to imitate Christ, not in a literal or mechnical way, but in order to reincarnate the real presence of Christ in the world. In a variant of the mirror image, Donne insists that the transformative process is not a passive legal exchange, but an active process of learning:

> [Christ's] death is delivered to us, as a *writing,* but not a writing onely in the nature of a peece of *Evidence,* to plead our inheritance by, but a writing in the nature of a Copy, to learne by; It is not only given us to reade, but to write over, and practise; Not onely to tell us *what he* did, but *how we* should do so too. (10: 196)

The reflection of selves, the exchange of selves, and the identification of selves—this cluster of ideas records the release of the self, through pity, into the communion of saints, the Body of Christ itself. When one, afflicted and suffering, as all persons are, catches a glimpse of oneself in Christ's suffering and sees one's personal story there reflected, one's heart is melted by a com-passion, and through this recognition, freed to love this other suffering being.[11] Furthermore, one is granted the ability to enhance the identification, by taking up the other's burden as one's own. In this way, Christ's passion is appropriated and personalized.

The pattern of the devotee merging with the object of devotion was, in Donne's mind, most clearly associated with the conversion of St. Paul. In St. Paul's example, Donne understands that the guilt of one's actions against Christ becomes unbearable unless one realizes that one is incorporated into Christ. One perceives that one is not only crucifier, but crucified; not only afflictor, but afflicted; not only persecutor, but persecuted (see Sherwood, "Conversion Psychology" 119; *Fulfilling the Circle* 116-30). Donne carefully links the familiar imagery of reflection and perception with Christ's accusation against the unconverted Saul; the accusation pours forth from the Body of Christ as Church:

> And these are the two great effects of his guiding us by his eye, that first, his eye turnes us to himselfe, and then turnes us into himselfe; first, his

eye turns ours to him, and then, that makes us all one with himselfe, so, as that our afflictions shall bee put upon his patience, and our dishonours shall be injuries to him; wee cannot be safer then by being his; but thus, we are not onely His, but He; To every Persecutor, in every one of our behalfe, he shall say, *Cur me?* Why persecutest thou me? (9: 368-69)

As Donne reminds, St. Paul's is the only conversion which the Church formally celebrates in its calendar, and thus, his conversion is the type of every Christian conversion. That conversion is essentially the enactment of the paradoxical biblical maxim, "He that findeth his life shall lose it: and he that loseth his life for my sake shall find it" (Matt. 10.39). Losing one's worldly life—recognized in such idols as wit, fame, and hopes of advancement—means gaining a life in the eyes of heaven. Losing one's life, and thereby narrow self-love, means refusing to be identified any longer by one's sins, for through the sinner's repentence, they become the sins of Christ:

> Here was a true Transubstantiation, and a new Sacrament. These few words, *Saul, Saul, why persecutest thou me*, are words of Consecration; After these words, *Saul* was no longer *Saul*, but he was Christ: *Vivit in me Christus*, sayes he, *It is not I that live*, not I that do any thing, *but Christ in me.* (6: 209)

The persecutor of Christ, having become the persecuted Christ, feels even more keenly his afflictions because he has brought them on himself. This process is the very basis for compassion, because one feels another's sufferings as one's own; only by one's merging with the other is compassion complete, since such compassion thereby becomes one's own passion. After his conversion, having already assaulted the Body of Christ, Paul is ever attentive to the healing of its wounds. Donne's moral vision is founded on such a concept, for imputed righteousness—gained by Christ's passion, and understood in the sinner's compassion—must be transformed, transubstantiated, into the substance or actuality of righteousness:

> According to this Rule, St. *Paul*, who had been so vehement a persecutor, had ever his thoughts exercised upon that; and thereupon after his conversion, he fulfils the rest of the sufferings of Christ in his flesh, he suffers most, he makes most mention of his suffering of any of the Apostles. (1: 237)

That the identification of sinners with Christ may be true in every sense, one must imitate Christ in such a manner as to go beyond what Jesus suffered while he walked upon the earth. The imitation of Christ is not merely the creation in private devotion of an inner memorial, but an engagement in the issues and problems that are current in one's time and place. Using the same theme of identification of persecutor and persecuted that animated his discussion of St. Paul's conversion, Donne demonstrates his moral awareness as he invites his auditors to see Christ reflected in the poor, for Christ claimed the poor

> not onely to be his, but to be He, *Saul, Saul,* why persecutest thou me? The poore are He, He is the poore. And so, he that oppresseth the poore, reproaches God, God in his *Orphans,* God in his *Image,* God in the *Members* of his owne Body, God in the *Heirs* of his Kingdome, God in *himself,* in his own person. (8: 287)

As one who remembers his true self as the Christ who lives in him, the regenerate soul, like St. Paul, takes on the difficult consequences of performing acts of righteousness. True self-love is, in fact, a love of the world in its suffering.

By understanding the nature of St. Paul's "transubstantiation," one may more clearly see the basis of Donne's social concern, an area often neglected by critics:

> God hath made all *mankinde* of *one blood,* and all *Christians* of *one calling,* and the sins of every man concern every man, both in that respect, that *I,* that is, *This nature,* is in that man that sins that sin; and *I,* that is *This nature,* is in that Christ, who is wounded by that sin. (2: 122)

This passage echoes the thought and phrasing of Devotion XVII, in which every action of the Church towards any individual "concernes" Donne personally: "No Man is an *Iland,* intire of it selfe; every man is a peece of the *Continent,* a part of the *maine* " (86-87).[12] The island of which Donne speaks is a pun, for if no man is an I-land, a domain of self alone, every man is potentially a Christ, especially if one says with St. Paul: "*It is not I that live,* not I that do any thing, *but Christ in me*" (6: 209). Donne's *I* has been crossed and corrected by Christ's cross.

The pattern, already noted in "The Crosse" and "What if this present," of initial fear and rejection of the crucifixion, based on narrow self-love, followed by a compassion that occurs when self is mirrored in the tortured Christ, may also be detected in "Goodfriday, 1613." The initially suave, cool, assured self is later disturbed and implicated by the scene of the passion that he creates in his memory and imagination.[13] Here the mirror of recognition is the cause of conversion, of the mutual turning of Christ and sinner towards one another; as the speaker explains, the events of the crucifixion "are present yet unto my memory, / For that looks towards them; and thou look'st towards mee, / O Saviour, as thou hang'st upon the tree" (34-36). As we have seen, the divine granting of mercy prompts human mercy:

> So our eyes waite upon God, *till hee have mercy,* that is, while he hath it, and that he may continue his mercy; for it was his mercifull eye that turned ours to him, and it is the same mercy, that we waite upon him. And then, when, as a well made Picture doth alwaies looke upon him, that lookes upon it, this Image of God in our soule, is turned to him, by his turning to it, it is impossible we should doe any foule, any uncomely thing in his presence. (9: 368)

The mercy with which "we waite upon" or attend God is divine mercy, mercy that comes first from God. The prevention of evil and the generation of good works in the world are the final outcome of the merciful recognition of self in the crucified Christ. One of Donne's letters to Sir Henry Goodyer affirms the principle that the sinner's turning to God, that the sinner's mercy, is actually a reflection of God's mercy: "when we get any thing by prayer, he gave us before hand the thing and the petition. . . . [N]othing doth so innocently provoke new graces, as gratitude" (*Letters* 96).

The promptings of mercy cannot be called authentic, however, unless they issue in action in the world. As A. B. Chambers has pointed out, Donne's speaker in "Goodfriday, 1613" ultimately chooses the "longer and harder westward path," rather than the "irrational" desire to achieve an eastward immediate spiritual gratification (347). The poem, however, does not fully reveal the speaker's newly found commitment to the world unless one takes account of the meanings associated with east and west as Donne himself described them. In his two sermons on the text "And God said, let us make man in our image, after our likeness," a text concerned with mirroring, Donne uses the points of the compass as a method of dividing his text and his sermon into four parts. The first sermon's consideration of east and west helps explain the radical "transubstantiation" which has occurred in the poem's speaker. Using familiar symbolic patterns, Donne associates east ("Let us") with the fountain of light and life, with creation, a knowledge of the trinity, and particularly, Christ as *Oriens*; he associates west ("make man") with earth, the human resting place in earth, and thus death and darkness.[14] However, Donne's consideration of human being as earth is neither merely traditional nor gloomy. The earthiness of human life is a reminder of the good one must accomplish in the flesh and in the body politic. Because God is "the Potter," the human vessel must be sanctified:

> God made man of earth, not of ayre, not of fire. Man hath many offices, that appertaine to this world, and whilest he is here, must not withdraw himselfe, from those offices of mutuall society, upon a pretence of zeale, or better serving God in a retired life. A ship will no more come to the harbour without Ballast, then without Sailes; a man will no more get to heaven, without discharging his duties to other men, then without doing them to God himselfe. *Man liveth not by bread onely,* says Christ; But yet he liveth by bread too. Every man must doe the duties; every man must beare the incumbrances of some calling. (9: 63)

In this context, one may now see that the speaker's initial prompting to move eastward could be read as a temptation, "a pretence of zeale," rather than a wholly righteous response. In the metaphor of the sermon, to move eastward would have been like a ship's attempt to sail only with sails, but without ballast. A "retired" devotion which does not perform charitable acts begins to resemble narrow self-love.[15]

The speaker, at the outset of the poem, posited that the intelligence that moved the sphere of man's soul was "devotion" (1). By way of summary of his first of these two sermons, Donne recalls the phrasing of "Goodfriday, 1613": "man hath bodily, and worldly duties to performe; and is not all Spirit in this life. Devotion, is his soule; but he hath a body of discretion, and usefulnesse to invest in some calling" (9: 69). Donne thus affirms that by the reintegration of body and soul one is truly turned towards Christ. By turning his back on the imagined image of the crucifixion and *becoming* the image instead, the speaker reincarnates Christ in the world. By performing his calling and by "discharging his duties to other men," the speaker will be crucified and purged by the world; in such a way, imputed righteousness, recognized through mutual compassion, becomes fulfilled in act, and the speaker may thus fully reflect Christ: "Restore thine Image, so much, by thy grace, / That thou may'st know mee, and I'll turne my face" (41-42). For Donne, martyrdom was not reserved only for causes that were dramatically and self-evidently religious; one was called upon to endure a "Court Martyrdome," an "Exchange-Martyrdome," and a "Bosome-Martyrdome," thereby accepting a "crossing of our own immoderate desires" in every aspect of ordinary daily life (8: 186). The fact that Donne would have been considering the "calling" of holy orders at the time the poem was written lends the work a particular intensity.

The integration of body and soul is, according to Donne, and orthodox Christianity, the basis of human life: "Death is the Divorce of body and soule; Resurrection is the Re-union of body and soule" (6: 71). Thus devotion united to bodily acts of charity is the means by which resurrection takes place. In this way, the darkness of the west loses its pointlessness; thus "West and East . . . are one" and "death doth touch the Resurrection" ("Hymne to God my God, in my sicknesse" 13-15; see also *Sermons* 2: 199). The speaker's earlier anxiety about gazing upon the crucifixion rested upon his bewildered sense that body and soul were disjoint and heaven and earth alienated, that Christ's crucifixion was mere contradiction, not true paradox, wherein seeming contradiction finds resolution. The speaker finds it fearful that the divine "hands which span the Poles" should be "peirc'd with those holes" (21-22), that "endlesse height" should be "Humbled below us," (22-25), and that the "seat of all our Soules" should "Make durt of dust" (26-27). Once, however, the speaker gazes upon the fearful outward "spectacle" (16) awhile, he appropriates it and suffers in the incarnate Christ. Heaven becomes reconciled with earth; soul is reconciled with body; and the seeming contradiction is resolved (see Smith 30-36). The hands which span the earth's poles, he realizes, are stretched out on a cross in order to embrace the world. The true love of self, therefore, is the love of the whole human being, body and soul acting together in the world; it is the love, not of I, but "Christ in me." When the soul sees God, Donne confidently states, the soul is bound to flesh in a new way; the soul will no longer call flesh "her prison, nor her tempter, but her friend, her companion, her wife" (3: 112).

By the end of the poem, transformed by his appropriation of the crucifixion, Donne's speaker realizes the true purpose of riding westward. That purpose is not, as he initially assumed, merely "Pleasure or businesse" (7), excusable because of the inherent waywardness of human nature, but a riding into the world—to his death—a death now ennobled by the fact that it mirrors Christ's crucifixion. The speaker takes up his own cross and mirrors Christ by being willing, through God's grace, to accept the suffering inherent in loving the world compassionately for God's sake. Riding into the world now becomes the means by which he receives his "Corrections," (38) and undergoes sanctification. Ironically, by exposing himself to, and resisting worldly temptation, as Christ did, the speaker invites God to "Burne off" the "rusts" (40) in order to restore the divine image in him. By giving the soul of devotion a body, and thus making it active, he witnesses his own resurrection, reflects God's image, and becomes Christ in the world, or, as Donne has put it, "not onely His, but He" (9: 369). In the process, he moves the devotion of the private self outward:

> And so, for matter of Action, and Protection, come not home to your selves, stay not in your selves, not in a confidence in your owne power, and wisedome, but *Ite*, goe forth, goe forth into Ægypt, goe forth into Babylon, and look who delivered your Predecessors, (predecessors in Affliction, Predecessors in Mercy) and that God, who is *Yesterday, and to day, and the same for ever*, shall doe the same things which he did yester-day, to day, and for ever. (8: 122-23)

The conversion that the speaker has undergone has not taken him off his path; he still rides into the west. Rather, this conversion reveals to the speaker the divine purpose underlying of the westward journey, which until now, he had failed to see. Now he appropriates the cross by taking it up in his own life's circumstances:

> I must not go out of my way to seeke a crosse; for, so it is not mine, nor laid for my taking up. . . . I am bound to take up my Crosse; and that is onely mine which the hand of God hath laid for me, that is, in the way of my Calling, tentations and tribulations incident to that. (2: 301)

Once the speaker has taken up his cross, a cross chosen not arbitrarily or out of false zeal, but suited to his life and selfhood, one that God has placed in his path, then the speaker may be confident that God will recognize him as his own son. Ironically, in taking up his *own* cross, asserting his selfhood in this measured way, he most truly conforms himself to Christ. Then, as the speaker declares, "thou may'st know mee, and I'll turne my face" (42). This willingness to imitate Christ is proof of the intensity of the speaker's newly found love of God, since "we change our selves into that we love most" (9: 373). The object of love has inte-grated itself into the subject, and the nature of self-love has been purified.

As these three poems on the crucifixion and related writings from the sermons show, the world with all its problematic complexity is not to be shunned, for it is by exposure to the world and by the difficult attempt to discriminate good from evil that the image of God is restored within an individual:

> So then the children of God, are the *Marble*, and the *Ivory*, upon which he workes; In them his purpose is, to re-engrave, and restore his Image; and affliction, and the *malignity of man*, and the *deceits of Heretiques*, and the *tentations of the Devill* him selfe, are but his instruments, his tools, to make his Image more discernible, and more durable in us. (3: 193)

Because direct sight of God is denied to humans in the present life, and because fixation on the image of Christ in private devotion alone is a temptation, only the active engagement in the world whereby one reincarnates Christ crucified can restore his image. For Donne, such active engagement reveals the fullest significance of self-love.

Notes

[1] The notion of Donne as self-obsessed and in need of self-escape has been fostered by T. S. Eliot's pronouncements, such as the following: "he belonged to that class of persons . . . who seek refuge in religion from the tumults of a strong emotional temperament which can find no complete satisfaction elsewhere" (352); and by Douglas Bush's authoritative work, as in this remark: "For one thing, there was the actuality, the pressure, and the fascination of life and world which, as man and poet, Donne felt and sought, as a dedicated Christian, to resist and escape from" (325). A recent example of this tendency may be seen in John Carey's work: "His insistence that 'no man is an island,' taken together with the egotism of his writing, illustrate both his urge to blend and the inescapable selfhood which prompted and frustrated it" (279). Carey also links Donne's "egotism" with mirror imagery and lack of pity (95-97, 189, 270, 278).

On the background of mirror imagery and its use by Donne, see Grabes, Wilson, and Gilman (both *The Curious Perspective* and "'To adore; or scorne'"). On Donne's view of the crucifixion, see Baker-Smith and Julia J. Smith. On the microcosm-macrocosm, see Kawasaki and Norford. And on the complex interrelationship between literary self-fashioning and the process of an individual's being fashioned by cultural institutions, see Greenblatt.

[2] Snyder's review of the Fathers and Reformers stresses the difference between redemptive sorrow leading to hope and the purposeless sorrow of the proud.

[3] This sermon, *Deaths Duell*, also reproduces the mirror image of sinner hanging with Christ upon the cross; see 10: 248.

[4] Lewalski carefully describes imputation as the way that God overlooks the actual "wicked state" of the sinner and sees only Christ's merits (*Donne's Anniversaries* 134; *Protestant Poetics* 16-25, 253-82). However, she does not describe the psychological motivation and the social process whereby the sinner actually becomes more like Christ, thereby incarnating Christ in the world.

[5] For a discussion of "turning" as *aversio* and *conversio*, see Sherwood, "Conversion Psychology" and Severance 29.

[6] Peterson cites the Catholic doctrine on religious sorrow: "Sorrow motivated by fear of divine punishment was defined as attrition; sorrow motivated by a hatred of sin itself and a love for God was defined as contrition." Anglican doctrine asserted that fear in itself "is not sufficient for salvation" (314).

[7] Contrast with Gilman, "'To adore, or scorne'" 91: "The horrid shape Donne would *not* see reasserts itself as the image rightly `assign'd' to him, as a reflection of the idolatry that continues to dwell in his heart, and as a judgment upon it."

[8] Hughes (246-47) discusses the tradition of Christian foolishness in "Goodfriday, 1613."

[9] I agree with Bellette's appraisal of this sonnet as "one of the most deeply felt and at the same time one of the most carefully controlled that Donne wrote" (339).

[10] See Norford's distillation of Ernst Cassirer: "If the infinity of the cosmos threatens not only to limit the Ego, but to annihilate it completely, the same infinity also can be the source of the Ego's constant self-evaluation, for the mind is like the world it conceives" (423). This formulation is reminiscent of the idea that God, as source of the fear of damnation is also the source of the fear that leads through self-judging humility to wisdom.

[11] According to Lauritsen (128-29), the moment of self-discovery is the moment when compassion begins.

[12] Another "I-land" echo appears in Donne's "A Hymne to Christ, at the Authors last going into Germany," (8-11).

[13] For a discussion of Donne's view on the imagination as a faculty of the soul, see Harland.

[14] See Goldberg, Friedman, and Sullivan for the connotations of east and west in the poem.

[15] Contrast Goldberg 483: "self-fulfillment resides in the internalization of Christ" (483). O'Connell notes that the reflection of God's image accompanies the speaker's "passage from *cupiditas* to *caritas*" (26).

Works Cited

Baker-Smith, Dominic. "John Donne and the Mysterium Crucis." *English Miscellany* 19 (1968): 65-82.

Bellette, Antony F. "'Little Worlds Made Cunningly': Significant Form in Donne's *Holy Sonnets* and 'Goodfriday, 1613.'" *SP* 72 (1975): 322-47.

Bush, Douglas. *English Literature in the Earlier Seventeenth Century 1600-1660*. 2nd ed. Oxford: Oxford UP, 1962.

Carey, John. John Donne: *Life, Mind and Art*. New York: Oxford UP, 1981.

Chambers, A. B. "'Goodfriday, 1613. Riding Westward': The Poem and the Tradition." *Essential Articles for the Study of John Donne's Poetry*. Ed. John R. Roberts. Hamden, CT: Archon, 1975. 333-48.

Donne, John. *Letters to Severall Persons of Honour*. Ed. Charles Edmund Merrill, Jr. New York: Sturgis, 1910.

Friedman, Donald M. "Memory and the Art of Salvation in Donne's Good Friday Poem." *ELR* 3 (1973): 418-42.

Eliot, T. S. "Lancelot Andrewes." *Selected Essays*. 3rd ed. London: Faber, 1951.

Gilman, Ernest B. *The Curious Perspective: Literary and Pictorial Wit in the Seventeenth Century*. New Haven: Yale UP, 1978.

——————. "'To adore, or scorne an image': Donne and Iconoclastic Controversy." *JDJ* 5 (1986): 62-100.

Goldberg, Jonathan. "Donne's Journey East: Aspects of a Seventeenth-Century Trope." *SP* 68 (1971): 470-83.

Grabes, Herbert. *The Mutable Glass: Mirror-imagery in Titles and Texts of the Middle Ages and English Renaissance*. Trans. Gordon Collier. Cambridge: Cambridge UP, 1982.

Greenblatt, Stephen. *Renaissance Self-Fashioning: From More to Shakespeare*. Chicago: U of Chicago P, 1980.

Harland, Paul W. "Imagination and Affections in John Donne's Preaching." *JDJ* 6 (1987): 33-50.

Henn, T. R. *The Harvest of Tragedy*. New York: Barnes and Noble, 1966.

Hughes, Richard E. *The Progress of the Soul: The Interior Career of John Donne*. New York: Morrow, 1968.

Kawasaki, Toshihiko. "Donne's Microcosm." *Seventeenth-Century Imagery*. Ed. Earl Miner. Berkeley: U of California P, 1971. 25-43.

Lauritsen, John R. "Donne's Satyres: The Drama of Self-Discovery." *SEL* 16 (1976): 117-30.

Lewalski, Barbara Kiefer. *Donne's Anniversaries and the Poetry of Praise: The Creation of a Symbolic Mode.* Princeton: Princeton UP, 1973.

_____. *Protestant Poetics and the Seventeenth-Century Religious Lyric.* Princeton: Princeton UP, 1979.

Norford, Don Parry. "Microcosm and Macrocosm in Seventeenth-Century Literature." *JHI* 38 (1977): 409-28.

O'Connell, Patrick F. "'Restore Thine Image': Structure and Theme in Donne's 'Goodfriday.'" *JDJ* 4 (1985): 13-28.

Peterson, Douglas L. "John Donne's Holy Sonnets and the Anglican Doctrine of Contrition." *Essential Articles for the Study of John Donne's Poetry.* Ed. John R. Roberts. Hamden, CT: Archon, 1975. 313-23.

Severance, Sibyl Lutz. "Soul, Sphere, and Structure in `Goodfriday, 1613. Riding Westward.'" *SP* 84 (1987): 24-41.

Sherwood, Terry G. "Conversion Psychology in John Donne's Good Friday Poem." *Harvard Theological R* 72 (1979): 101-22.

_____. *Fulfilling the Circle: A Study of John Donne's Thought.* Toronto: U of Toronto P, 1984.

Smith, A. J. "No Man Is a Contradiction." *JDJ* 1 (1982): 21-38.

Smith, Julia J. "Donne and the Crucifixion." *MLR* 79 (1984): 513-25.

Snyder, Susan. "The Left Hand of God: Despair in Medieval and Renaissance Tradition." *Studies in the Renaissance* 12 (1965): 18-59.

Sullivan, David M. "Riders to the West: 'Goodfriday, 1613.'" *JDJ* 6 (1987): 1-8.

Wallerstein, Ruth. "To Madness Near Allied: Shaftesbury and His Place in the Design and Thought of *Absalom and Achitophel.*" *HLQ* 6 (1943): 445-71.

Wilson, G. R., Jr. "The Interplay of Perception and Reflection: Mirror Imagery in Donne's Poetry." *SEL* 9 (1969): 107-21.

Turning to See the Sound: Reading the Face of God in Donne's Holy Sonnets

Catherine J. Creswell

When S. Paul was carried up In raptu, *in an extasie,* into Paradise, *that which he gained by this powerfull way of teaching, is not expressed in a* Vidit, *but an* Audivit, *It is not said that he saw, but that he* heard unspeakeable things. — John Donne

When Levinas defines language as contact, he defines it as immediacy, and this has grave consequences. For immediacy is absolute presence—which undermines and overturns everything . . . It is the infiniteness of a presence such that it can no longer be spoken of. . . . In this night there are no longer any terms, there is no longer a relation, no longer a beyond—in this night God himself has annulled himself. . . .

Light breaks forth: the burst of light, the dispersion that resonates or vibrates dazzlingly—and in clarity clamors but does not clarify. The breaking forth of light, the shattering reverberation of a language to which no hearing can be given. —Maurice Blanchot

oward the end of his sermon on 1 Corinthians 13: 12, delivered Easter Sunday 1628, Donne offers a jarring image of the final revelation: "This is our Spheare, . . . and then our *Medium,* our way to see him is *Patefactio sui,* Gods laying himself open, his manifestation, his revelation, his evisceration, and embowelling of himselfe to us, there" (8: 231). Donne's sermon topic is Paul's famous invocation of the apocalyptic turn to God: "For now we see through a Glasse darkly, But then face to face; Now I know in part, But then I shall know, even as also I am knowne" (1 Cor. 13: 12). It is, as the verse is typically read, Paul's celebration of the Word's ultimate manifestation, the confrontation with God "face to face." Within Donne's sermon, however, the Word's final revelation operates less as an enlightening disclosure than as a subjection to vision. The sermon's descriptive account of the Word Incarnate within 1 Corinthians, its opening of the text, proceeds to a forceful violation. Copia, the Renaissance rhetorical practice of praise or exposition through elaborating repetitions, only renders analysis—or, as in the seventeenth-century usage, "anatomie"—literal.

Donne's *Holy Sonnets* often present spiritual consummation as a break-ing of figures: Christ's "pierc'd head" and bloody face of "What if this present were the worlds last night," the open spouse of "Show me deare Christ, thy spouse, so bright and cleare," the speaker of "Batter my heart, three person'd God" who cries to be "batter[ed]" and "ravish[ed]." Thus, readers may find that the visceral description of revelation within the sermon on 1 Corinthians provides nothing more than the shock of recog-nition. In fact, this sermon and the *Holy Sonnets* not only share an interest in the presentation of the Word Incarnate but provide an occasion for Donne to interrogate the ethical implications of praise, the rhetoric in-forming both psalmic and sonnet traditions. For Donne, the Word is paradoxically both the source of light and speech and the outer limit of perception: "The light of glory is such a light . . . That every beam of it, is not all of it" (8:232).[1] The sonnets contemplate this turn "face to face" as a necessary yet distorting—even violent—accommodation of the Word to the order of vision and knowledge. In dramatizing this confrontation with the Word Incarnate, especially as it is elaborated in "Batter my heart," the *Holy Sonnets* revise praise's relation to its object and, in turn, refigure the very status of the subject.

Concerned as they are with the confrontation with the divine, the *Holy Sonnets* would seem to have found their perfect medium in the idealizing poetry of praise. The poetics of epideictic rhetoric draws upon a Pauline-neoplatonic orthodoxy which depicts the world and language as the shadowy reflection of the Logos. In this mutually reflexive system, all creatures are a "glass" for the higher ideality, inevitably reflecting their origin because they partake of what they represent. In like manner, ideal-izing language presents itself as the simulacrum of the specular Logos. In its capacity to reflect or mimetically present, praise imitates that of which it speaks and, in doing so, ultimately bespeaks the transcendent Ideal. Thus, the biblical text becomes not only the words of God but conveys the

Word itself. "Hearing" the Gospel, as Donne argues, gives "some sight" of God's ultimate manifestation, the "perfect sight of all" (*Sermons* 8: 219-20).

This divine self-reflexivity of language ultimately fixes the referentiality of all speech and makes the poetry of praise, as Joel Fineman defines it, the event arising "when mimesis and metaphor meet" (3).[2] Figurative similitude becomes the likeness of iconic representation; each refers to the other, both having as their ultimate source and meaning the visual Ideal. In this manner, George Puttenham will include the highly rhetorical blazon as the prime example of the "icon or resemblance by imagerie or portrait" and offer the allegorical motif as an example of painterly representation.[3] Donne's sermon on 1 Corinthians 13: 12—although with important qualifications—similarly posits a correspondence between rhetorical figures and representational images, language's self-likeness merely participating in the order which binds the "glass of Creatures" to the ideality it reflects:

> The ministery of the Gospell is but as Gods Vizar; for, by such a liberty the Apostle here calls it *aenigma*, a riddle; or, (as *Luther* sayes too) Gods picture; but in the Resurrection, God shall put of [off] that Vizar, and turne away that picture, and shew his own face. (*Sermons* 8: 233)

The trope or "Vizar" ("vizar" or mask suggesting a figure for rhetorical figures themselves) becomes the functional equivalent to the representational "picture." Pauline interpretation unites figurality ("Gods Vizar") with mimetic copy ("Gods picture"), allowing each to serve equally as the veiled form of the Logos. Idealizing language both reflects and is the microcosmic emblem of its visual ideal. Presentation coincides with meaning.

The reflexivity of idealizing language, in turn, binds the praising poet with the object of his praise. This union of praising subject and praised object is depicted in commonplace Renaissance lyric motifs of lovers whose eyes mirror one another's gaze and the sonneteer who finds his beloved's image etched within his heart; however, this union is central as well to the psalmic tradition. As Aquinas writes, "We need to praise God with our lips, not indeed for His sake, but for our own sake, since by praising Him our devotion is aroused toward Him, according to Ps. 49:23: 'The sacrifice of praise shall glorify Me, and there is the way by which I will show him the salvation of God.'"[4] In praising the Word the psalmist participates in its divinely self-reflexive language; thus praise rebounds upon the speaker and the act of praise itself.

For Donne, however, such a poetics may have been more belated and fallen than persuasive. The *Holy Sonnets*, in fact, suggest less an adaptation of the poetics of praise than an iconoclastic skepticism about the truth of images. Donne's rejection of truth as vision, like his rejection of individual revelation, is an insistence upon interpretation over immanent seeing, often thematized as a move toward "hearing" the Word or turning to the "voyce." In the sermon on 1 Corinthians 13: 12—his attack against those who would perceive the Scriptures directly, or who claim through "the light of Nature" or reason to "know God in this life as well as God knew himselfe"—is an insistence that one may only know God verbally or aurally, through scripture and church teachings: "the eare is the Holy Ghosts first doore" (*Sermons* 8: 228).[5] This emphasis upon "hearing" suggests Donne's rejection of the possibility of any direct phenomenal access to truth and marks his turn to the more problematic task of reading.

In their contemplation of the Word Incarnate, the *Holy Sonnets* reflect a similar mistrust of the iconic image. Rather than serve as an emblem of the specular Logos, the figure of Christ within these sonnets remains resolutely verbal and opaque. Like Christ's blood of "Oh my blacke Soule!," "which hath this might / That being red, it dyes red soules to white" (13-14), the truth or efficacy of the figure within the *Holy Sonnets* lies not in its appearance (as blood) but in its interpretation ("being red/ read"). Moreover, the iconoclastic or material figure resists interpretation as mere perception, as mere "seeing" or "unveiling." In these sonnets, truth, whether our "mindes white truth" ("If faithfull soules be alike glorified" 8) or the nature of God, does not offer itself to revelation but makes itself known only across the gap of figures: "By circumstances, and by signes that be / Apparent . . . not immediately" ("If faithfull soules" 6-7).

This skepticism about the truth of figures stems from Donne's reconceptualization of the Word and the status of praise. The ultimate confrontation with God, as Donne characterizes it, is movement away from vision: "as there is *videre & audire, S. John turned to see the sound*" (*Sermons* 8: 221). Paul's rapture into the third heavens, as Donne insists, "is not expressed in a *Vidit*, but an *Audivit*, It is not said that he *saw*, but that he *heard unspeakable things*" (*Sermons* 8: 228). In the sermon, the turn "face to face" is a confrontation not with the Logos as ideality but with the Word as generative, performative command: the initial, initiating decree, "*Dixit, & facta sunt*." As Donne writes,

> Our Regeneration is by his Word; that is, by faith, which comes by hearing. . . . Carry it higher, the Creation was by the word of God; *Dixit, & facta sunt.* . . . Princes are Gods Trumpet, and the Church is Gods Organ, but Christ Jesus is his voyce. (*Sermons* 6: 216-217)

This "dixit" emerges again in the Incarnation. Thus, as Donne argues in his sermon on Matthew 28: 6, it is neither the presence nor the absence of Jesus's body in the tomb that evidences the resurrection, but the angel's decree that "He is risen" (*Sermons* 9: 202-203). Donne marks this turn from God's "Enunciation" to God's "voyce"—the turn from the realm of all phenomena, verbal and empirical, to the performative Word—as a facing "to see the sound" or a "hear[ing] of unspeakable things. " Such a turn is conversion in the root meaning of the word, a "radical" reading which requires not only a passage from the Letter to the Spirit but a move from the mimetic order to that which subtends and initiates it. It is a turn to the "roote and fountaine of all beeing," not to a different order of meaning but to that which creates the distinctions that make meaning possible. Within this context, reading becomes not a clearer seeing but a facing away from the order of presentation itself, a turn from the "light" to the performative "voice."

Where Donne's sermons posit Christ as the performative power of the Word, the *Holy Sonnets* contemplate how to adequately invoke and lend form to God's "voyce." Christ's face in "What if this present" attempts to serve as just such an apocalyptic figure:

What if this present were the worlds last night?
Marke in my heart, O Soule, where thou dost dwell,
The picture of Christ crucified, and tell
Whether that countenance can thee affright,
Teares in his eyes quench the amasing light,
Blood fills his frownes, which from his pierc'd head fell,
And can that tongue adjudge thee unto hell,
Which pray'd forgivenesse for his foes fierce spight?
No, no; but as in my idolatrie
I said to all my profane mistresses,
Beauty, of pitty, foulnesse onely is
A signe of rigour: so I say to thee,
To wicked spirits are horrid shapes assign'd,
This beauteous forme assures a pitious minde.

The blazoned form of Jesus whose eyes, lips, and tongue form the object of the soul's meditation presents a figure that differs from itself. The eyes would seem to possess "amasing light" whose fire is only slaked or satisfied by its tears, yet these eyes are "quench[ed]" or blinded. The face is "pierc'd" and furrowed with "frownes" and yet smooth or "fill[ed]." The blood from his wounds etches the crevices of his face and "fills his frownes," both marking and covering his features. Rather than simulate the visual ideal of which it speaks—that is, rather than reflect and reinforce the poet's eye—this image simultaneously opens itself to the viewer and surpasses sight. Its eyes are a light that does not clarify or make intelligible but which amazes and puts out of thought. This light is neither the specular likeness of the Logos nor its simple opposite, darkness, but a glare that both blinds and is blinded.

Where Donne will write in the sermon on 1 Corinthians 13: 12, "In the Resurrection, God shall put of[f] that Vizar, and turne away that picture, and shew his own face" (*Sermons* 8: 233), Christ's face of "What if this present" resists presentation altogether. Indeed, this face is a trope for the "voyce" that initiates and lies prior to all speech and vision. In contemplating the picture of Christ crucified, the speaker sees not the Light but the divine performative decree figured in the "tongue" whose speech enacts its judgment ("adjudge thee unto hell, / [or] pray'd forgivenesse" [7-8]). The "picture of Christ," that figure which the speaker must "Marke in [his] heart," thus suggests both a picture set before the eye and the act of inscription, an image of the Word as the originary decree, "Dixit, & facta sunt."

As Donne argues in reading Paul's account of theophany, "Now I know in part, but then I shall know, even as also I am knowne," this encounter "face to face" presents not full knowledge but only an accommodation to vision:[6]

> It is *Nota similitudinis, non aequalitatis*; As God knowes me, so I shall know God; but I shall not know God so, as God knowes me. It is not *quantum*, but *sicut*; not as much, but as truly; as the fire does as truly shine, as the Sun shines, though it shine not out so farre, nor to so many purposes. (*Sermons* 8: 235)

The final revelation arrives only through similitude; it is not the Word's unveiling but the Word's appearance *as*. In lifting his vizar to show his face, then, God reveals not His Essence but yet another visage, the figure for the act of presentation itself.[7]

That the originary decree should escape the optics of presentation is consistent with orthodox neoplatonic convention. The depiction of God as a sun inscribed with the Hebrew letters for Yahweh probably best exemplifies this tradition. This image, offered in countless emblem books, thematizes the Word's status as the eclipsed center of the visual order of the universe, the blind spot or gap within the poetics of presentation. However, as is characteristic of Donne, this blind spot (that is, the inscribed eye of the sun) is *not* the iconic image for the specular Word but is itself marked *as figure*. For Donne this apocalyptic face suggests not a divine simulacrum of the Word but a trope or trace of that which grounds and lies outside presentation. Positing the Word as "voyce" or "visage" locates a materiality within the very heart of language. The presentation of the Word both entails a return to the figurative and is marked as such.

In seeking to remove that *"aenigma"* or "riddle" of the Gospel by moving from the Letter to the Spirit, one can only face the performative in its guise as trope. In effect, one can only encounter the originating speech act as riddle. If, however, praise would reflect the originating speech act, it can only do so awry, for it makes the impossible attempt to mirror forth that which grounds and precedes all images, forms, and perceptions. Praise, as a result, possesses an uncertain relation to the Word. Metaphor becomes not truth's heightened presentation but a darkened, indirect reflection. The psalmist may not so much invoke the Word as impose the distortion of his own tropes. And yet such a gesture misses its mark, for the Word both instates and exceeds the "light" of epideictic rhetoric. Perhaps for these reasons Donne will describe God's *Patefactio* as "his evisceration, and embowelling of himselfe to us" (*Sermon* 8: 231); this "voice" can only emerge as a break in the surface of the image, a disruption within the phenomenal or visual order. Able to locate himself, in this turn to the "voice," only in the shattered, self-divided image, the poet in turn remains similarly absented and exiled.

One cannot, it appears, invoke God without imposing the distortion of one's own tropes. Nor can one give "voice" and "face" to that which both instates and disrupts all such figures. This impasse suggests the problem of praise within the *Holy Sonnets*: praise cannot address the very object and origin of its speech. For Donne, particularly within "Batter my heart," this impasse necessitates an inquiry into the ethical implications of praise. In "Batter my heart," the impossible and necessary gesture of praise is dramatized as the confrontation of the "I" of the psalmic tradition with the Word that both grounds and lies outside speech. In invoking the Word, the speaker of "Batter my heart" moves from the figures of praise to the figures of address and in doing so redefines the project of the sonnet and the very status of the subject.

Patricia Parker contemplates the presentation of the Word as figure in her essay "The Metaphorical Plot," arguing that the Incarnation, in its capacity to cleave divisions, effects what she calls the "radical copula" of metaphor. Christ's appearance, according to Paul, collapses all social and theological partitions: "There is neither Jew nor Greek, there is neither bond nor free, there is neither male nor female: for ye are all one in Christ Jesus" (Gal. 3: 28): "For he is our peace, who hath made both one, and hath broken down the middle wall of partition *between us*" (Eph. 2: 14). The ability to elide distinctions is also a function of metaphor as radical equivalency. Rather than convey through the juxtaposition of two terms, the "radical or 'anagogic' metaphor ('A is B')" fuses disparate words, a characteristic that Parker aligns with "descriptions of the Incarnation as the definitive 'copula' or 'copulacion' and of the breaking down of divisions through the Cross" (40).

However, metaphor's collapse of logical distinctions and its disregard for the propriety of words opens it to the "abuses" of catachresis, verbal combinations made not according to meaning but by forced abduction.[8] As Parker writes, such metaphor divorces language from referentiality and evokes "the transportability and unsettling autonomy of names . . . the nightmarish possibility of words taking on a life of their own" (41). Within Renaissance texts, this endlessly self-referring rhetoric is frequently figured as the seductive, excessive, and particularly female body.[9] It is a copia or dilation, the rhetorical practice of partitioning a subject to subsequently elaborate and amplify its parts, that knows no bounds. Rhetoric which has been feminized and associated with Circe impedes meaningful closure, seducing readers with what Augustine would call "the pleasure of the vehicles" (9-10). Within Donne's writing, nevertheless, it is precisely this fleshly and copious trope that serves as the figure of God.

Indeed, the speaker of "Batter my heart" seeks just such a figure and just such a radical union. His praise would not so much reflect an ideal light as invoke the Word as the force that elides differences, that "hath broken down the wall of partition *between us*":

> Batter my heart, three person'd God; for, you
> As yet but knocke, breathe, shine, and seeke to mend;
> That I may rise, and stand, o'erthrow mee,'and bend
> Your force, to breake, blowe, burn and make me new.
> I, like an usurpt towne, to'another due,

Labour to'admit you, but Oh, to no end,
Reason your viceroy in mee, mee should defend,
But is captiv'd, and proves weake or untrue,
Yet dearely'I love you, and would be lov'd faine,
But am betroth'd unto your enemie,
Divorce mee,'untie, or breake that knot againe,
Take mee to you, imprison mee, for I
Except you'enthrall mee, never shall be free,
Nor ever chast, except you ravish mee.

Presenting himself both as an "usurpt towne" and as a beloved's stoney
heart, the speaker in calling for a figure who would lay siege and enter
him invokes the God of the Song of Solomon and the lover-warrior of
countless iconographies, emblem books, and secular lyrics. Indeed, the
figure is so common that Puttenham quotes without comment a lengthy
conceit on the siege of the mistress's heart as his chief example of allegory
(155). Nor can this rather overly-familiar conceit of secular love lyrics be
neatly separated from the poem's biblical allusions, for the Song of Solomon
is the text most frequently cited as the archetype for the tradition of
epideictic rhetoric itself.

Donne's speaker takes the position not of the sonneteer but of the
besieged citadel or mistress. In this respect, he most resembles God's
beloved of Song of Solomon 5, she who is described as a "garden inclosed,"
who invokes the winds to "blow" upon her and yet struggles to give
entrance to her beloved: "I sleep, but my heart waketh: it *is* the voice of
my beloved that knocketh, *saying*, Open to me, my sister, my love" (Song
4: 12, 16, 5: 2).

The chief figure of "Batter my heart" is apostrophe, the trope that
instates figure or personification. Apostrophe, the first-person address to
another who is absent, seeks to "restore metaphorical exchange and
equality" between addressor and addressee (Johnson 188). As such, apos-
trophe seeks to break down barriers of time and space and achieve a
"mystical fusion" of self and other. This figure of address that gives voice
or face to the absent is invoked within the sonnet in order that the speaker
may in turn receive life: "bend / Your force, to breake, blowe, burn and
make me new" (3-4). The power to destroy belonging to a God who
batters, breaks, and burns must be read inversely, this death as the herald
of a new life: "That I may rise, and stand, o'erthrow mee" (3). Such a
reading is in keeping with traditional interpretations of the Song of
Solomon as an allegory of the church's redemption or the "stages of the

conversion of Israel in anticipation of her final salvation" (Pope 182). What such a reading doesn't fully convey is the cumulative effect of the poem's repeated verbs of breaking, an effect which renders the speaker not so much an errant soul but a tightly closed, though penetrable, body.[10]

The poem's images of breaking and burning, in fact, echo Deuteronomy's call for the destruction of idols or the carnal icon. "Batter my heart," thus, not only invokes the Song of Solomon's blazon of God the beloved, but repeats Deuteronomy's injunction against any such image-making:

> And ye shall overthrow their altars, and break their pillars, and burn their groves with fire; and ye shall hew down the graven images of their gods, and destroy the names of them out of that place. . . . Thou shalt surely smite the inhabitants of that city with the edge of the sword, destroying it utterly . . . and shalt burn with fire the city. . . . (Deut. 12: 3, 13: 15, 13: 16)

Noting in Donne's sermon on the verse his emphasis upon Deuteronomy's warning, "Take heed to thyself that thou be not snared" (Deut. 12: 30), Ernest Gilman maintains that, rather than extend the conceits of the poetry of praise, "Batter my heart" "dramatize[s] the conviction that the work of iconoclasm begun historically in Deuteronomy must be completed morally in the heart still drawn to the lure of 'their images'" (79). True praise will not attempt to better reflect its ideal object but will recognize the rhetoric of praise as a potential usurper.

"Batter my heart's" allusions to Deuteronomy, however, do not translate God's force into a "breaking and renewing [of] the spirit" (Gilman 79) but rather return to the rigor of the "old" covenant. Rather than progress from the carnal letter to a moral truth, the speaker figured as a wayward spouse or captive city is rendered a literal stoney icon. God's "purer 'force'" is not a figural translation but a physical battery. It is not the false images of the heart but the heart itself that must be broken, and such breaking will be the destruction reserved for the adulterous worshipers of idols: "Thou shalt break them with a rod of iron; thou shalt dash them in pieces like a potter's vessel" (Ps. 2: 9). Not a restoration of the speaker and the images of praise, "Batter my heart" crosses the Song of Solomon's blazon of God ("His mouth *is* most sweet: yea, he is altogether lovely. This *is* my beloved, and this *is* my friend, O daughters of Jerusalem" [Song 5:16]) with the injunction against images of God. Such a rhetorical crossing does not present a new, truer figure but disavows the figurative speech it instates. It asserts and crosses out the very act of presentation.

Both these biblical passages, nevertheless, have been read as accounts of God's revelation, particularly the giving of the law at Mt. Sinai. Deuteronomy 12: 3 echoes the commandment against graven images as it is elaborated following Moses's receiving the tablets: "Thou shalt not bow down to their gods, nor serve them, nor do after their works: but thou shalt utterly overthrow them, and quite break down their images" (Exod. 23: 24). Within Christian tradition the Song of Solomon is read as a full opening and celebration of God's parts in accord with the Book of Revelation, and within rabbinic readings it is understood to be an historical account of theophany, particularly God's appearance at Mt. Sinai.[11]

But what is the nature of this apocalyptic appearance in the Song of Solomon? In chapter 5, which is the book's most extended narrative, the beloved's encounter with her lover is at once erotic and missed:

> I sleep, but my heart waketh: it *is* the voice of my beloved that knocketh, *saying*, Open to me, my sister, my love, my dove, my undefiled: for my head is filled with dew, *and* my locks with the drops of the night.
> I have put off my coat; how shall I put it on? I have washed my feet; how shall I defile them?
> My beloved put in his hand by the hole *of the door*, and my bowels were moved for him.
> I rose up to open to my beloved; and my hands dropped *with* myrrh, and my fingers *with* sweet smelling myrrh, upon the handles of the lock.
> I opened to my beloved; but my beloved had withdrawn himself, *and* was gone: my soul failed when he spake: I sought him, but I could not find him; I called him but he gave me no answer.
> The watchmen that went about the city found me, they smote me, they wounded me; the keepers of the walls took away my veil from me.
> (Song 5:2-7)

"His hand by the hole *of the door*" and her fingers "upon the handles of the lock" suggest that the door is a figure for a consummation that draws together tangible bodies and enacts a spiritual dilation. Unlike the requirements for worship ("When they go into the tabernacle of the congregation, . . . they shall wash their hands and their feet, that they die not" [Exod. 30: 20-21]), this encounter requires not so much a purification as a re-entrance into the carnal, a putting *on* of the coat of the flesh. Yet this door is a literal barrier: "I opened to my beloved; but my beloved had withdrawn himself, and was gone." This re-entrance into the flesh is not a paradoxical revelation, a defilement that brings spiritual recovery, but, curiously, an unveiling that wounds: "they smote me, they wounded me; the keepers of the walls took away my veil from me." The door is not the opening onto an apocalyptic encounter, "face to face," but marks a revelation that, in fact, may occur only through the partitions of similitudes. The theophany arrives not as a face revealed but as a "voice . . . that knocketh," not in a present speech but in a command that enacts its meaning even in the flesh: "Open to me."

It is perhaps just such a voice and not a face that God reveals in the giving of the law at Mt. Sinai. Rather than see God's form, within the Pentateuch, the gathered were said to have *seen* a "voice": "'And the people saw the thunderings [literally 'voice', 'sound'], and the flaming torches, and the sound [literally 'voice'] of the shofar'" (Exod. 20: 18; the glosses are by Robbins 131).[12] Such hearing, however, may escape perception. As Jill Robbins argues,

> Thus, in retroversion to a voice, in the ethico-figural turn from vision to voice, it may even be necessary to turn away from voice, to "veil the voice." . . . "The people saw the voice," that is, they saw the writing on the tablets. This progressive dephenomenalization—from vision to voice to writing—suggests precisely that what they experienced was not phenomenally accessible. They saw writing on stone (God's "hewing" word); in other words, they were referred to the giving of the law and also implicitly to the activity of study which is given in advance there (and of course in which the *Mekilta*'s commentators are themselves engaged). They were referred to an arche-writing. (131)

The theophany reveals that which inscribes and exceeds unveiling. Or, rather, it does not show but refers to the originary decree in the guise of the "voice," that "fiery word" that hews or instates. Such a conversation with God is described again in Numbers 12: 8: "With him [Moses] will I speak mouth to mouth, even apparently, and not in dark speeches; and the similitude of the Lord shall he behold."

The Song of Solomon eroticizes this encounter—"Let him kiss me with the kisses of his mouth" (Song 1: 2)—yet in doing so suggests that this "mouth" of God is doubly veiled, that it is the figure for the inscription of figures or "God's 'hewing' word." As the figure for the divine decree, that which instates the law and the phenomenal order, it is a figure that exceeds vision, a voice that surpasses hearing. Such a visitation necessarily will have already passed. As the "voice" that inscribes, it creates yet exceeds or breaks that which it speaks. Similarly, the Word's power in "Batter my heart" is to repeatedly "o'erthrow" the figure it instates. Rather than enlivening the speaker by breaking him in order to make him new, the God apostrophized in "Batter my heart" is neither life nor death, spirit nor flesh, but the force that folds these categories in upon one another. The echoing verbs in lines two and four ("knocke, breathe, shine . . . breake, blowe, burn") do not suggest an intensification of the Word's battery but a power that simultaneously breaks and creates. The Word's "knocke" suggests the "beloved that knocketh *saying*, Open to me" and is the "breake" that smashes the heathen's "pillars." It is the call that would arouse and fully open the soul and the directive that hews down rival figures. The speaker's cry for a "breathe" that would "mend . . . and make me new" repeats the gesture of the Song of Solomon: "Awake, O north wind; and come, thou south; blow upon my garden" (Song 4: 16), and yet also invokes the "blowe" that shatters the idolaters and scatters the enemies of the Israelites. Such a force both mends its figures, allowing them to "shine" and reflect the idealizing light of epideictic praise, and "burns . . . with fire."

In fact, the poem's simultaneous allusions to the praise of the Song of Solomon and the injunction of Deuteronomy suggest not a translation of death and the dead letter into "moral" spiritual meaning but a crossing of the epideictic image and the performative decree that overrides the figures it invokes. Such a crossing does not restore the image's truth but suggests that the Word's emergence is precisely that which splits the image and ruptures the divisions necessary to interpretation and meaning. Like the "radical copula" of the Incarnation, the mystic union evoked in "Batter my Heart" cleaves the partitions deliminating type and carnal letter, figure and body, rhetorical dilation and physical penetration. As the wayward spouse, the "usurpt towne," and the enclosed vessel, the speaker presents an image of the "spouse" of the Song of Solomon, yet this image—when reinforced by the repeated injunctions to break—does not clearly present a figure for the soul, for it duplicates Deuteronomy's figures for idolatry: the broken idols, burning groves and cities. The body to be opened mimics the endlessly open figure of rhetoric, the bodily or icon-like trope that would not reflect but usurp and seduce. The speaker would be a figure to be opened and redeemed like the beloved of the Song of Solomon, the type of God's faithful, yet such interpretive dilation is indistinguishable from physical violation. Conversely, the speaker's demand to be literally battered is the demand for the destruction of false icons: "Thou shalt break them with a rod of iron; thou shalt dash them in pieces like a potter's vessel" (Ps. 2: 9). Figurative translation is a force made palpable and thereby indistinguishable from the irrevocable smashing of the fleshly text.

The speaker's apostrophe is his attempt to give voice and form to God so that in turn he might be recovered, that he might enter into conversation and "restore metaphorical exchange and equality" between them. In not seeking an image but a forceful voice, the speaker would mimic the divine decree, yet such a gesture would be a harsh imposition. It would be to give face to that which lies prior to and exceeds presentation. It would be a figure that lays claim, indeed appropriates, the other. Yet such a gesture can only miss its mark. Rather than reflect the divine ideal, the speaker's apostrophe can only address another trope, not an iconic sign but only a chosen figure. This "mouth," this "vizar," this "voice" is the figure for the divine decree.

The open body figures of "Batter my heart," as well as those of Donne's sermon and "What if this present," do not merely thwart reference but split the subject. Like the theophany that appears only as a break in the visual order or presents that which exceeds presentation, these broken bodily images—by appearing only as a likeness that differs from itself—similarly fragment the "I" that identifies or claims them as its own. Perhaps, in this manner, the broken figures of Donne's *Holy Sonnets* evoke what Michael Fried observes in early seventeenth-century painting, particularly Caravaggio's: "calculated aggressions" against conventional representations of the human body that operate not only "to produce a new and stupefyingly powerful experience of the 'real'" but as "a stunning or, worse, a wounding of seeing" (64-65). Sharing in the Jacobean "tactics of shock, violence, perceptual distortion, and physical outrage" (Fried 64), the broken bodily images of the *Holy Sonnets* that culminate in a speaker who must himself be "batter[ed]" and "ravish[ed]" imply not merely an attack against the iconic image of "visual poetics" but a shattering of vision itself.

The God of "Batter my heart," however, is not merely apostrophized but is that which inscribes the possibility of address and presentation. As in the apocalyptic "face" of God or the figure of Christ crucified, the other addressed serves as the source of figures and the figural operation of the poem itself, a transformation that places knowledge, authority or authorship outside the purview of the subject altogether. Indeed, the success of the speaker's own figures only serves to demonstrate their origin elsewhere. The more the speaker would master praise, the more he is dispossessed of his own speech. As in "Batter my heart," praise brings a union that divides the self from itself: "for I / Except you'enthrall mee, never shall be free, / Nor ever chast, except you ravish mee" (12-14).

The more one invokes the Word the more one misdirects, indeed is left bereft of, language. Yet the Word manifests itself only through these doubly veiled figures. The Word as performative decree disrupts and exceeds the very figures it instates; yet it renders itself intelligible—enters the order of phenomena and being—only as a figure. This interpretive impasse, however, indicates not so much a failure of communion as "metaphorical equality and exchange" as the possibility of another relation.

Thus, the *Holy Sonnets'* revision of the poetics of praise functions as an ethical critique. An idealist aesthetics that would posit praise and its object as the shadowy image of its speaker and the Ideal he addresses situates the subject at the intersection of knowledge and being. The clarity of the figure's form coincides thus not only with its meaning but with the subject's perception. Revelation emerges as the subject's knowledge, indeed, even self-knowledge. This reflexive "optics of likeness" subordinates images as the shadowy reflection or object of the subject, attributing to the image what Lacan calls "that belong to me aspect so reminiscent of property" (81). It is this reduction of the image to a relation of the self-same that perhaps motivates Donne's characterization of vision as a violence to the other. This characterization emerges in the sonnets' broken objects of praise and in the portrayal of Revelation within the sermon on 1 Corinthians 13:12 as God's "evisceration."

Rather than giving witness to a failed consummation, the *Holy Sonnets'* breaking of the speaker's figures of identification signals an effort to thwart the subject's power to elide the other. As that which instates and exceeds presentation, the Word of "Batter my heart" forges figures of identification that must be broken. Similarly, the speaker, to avoid a certain violence to the other, must invoke and yet disavow the figures that such an invocation posits. The conceit invoked by the call to "Batter my heart"—the speaker or wayward spouse as captured citadel and the series of opposed assertions it inspires ("Labour . . . to no end / Reason . . . mee should defend / But is captiv'd . . . / Yet dearely'I love you . . . / But am betroth'd . . . ")—does not find closure but turns to another apostrophe: "breake that knot againe" (11). The mystical union may not be a consummation that makes whole but a binding that ceaselessly rends apart. Not so much a failure of apostrophe, this "Labour . . . to no end" evidences an ethical critique that revises praise and recasts the very status of the subject. It is the call for a revelation that would turn from a seeing as knowing, for a praise that would gesture to a space beyond its own tropic light. The *Holy Sonnets'* revision of epideictic rhetoric is the attempt to seek an address that does not appropriate—through identification or any relation of the self—the other.

Notes

[1] Or as Donne writes of the place of God: "[even] the tongues of Angels, the tongues of glorified Saints, shall not be able to expresse what that heaven is; for, even in heaven our faculties shall be finite" (8:231).

[2] As Fineman explains: "To say that mimesis and metaphor meet is, of course, already to speak figuratively. I do so in order to bring out the ways in which traditional poetic and epideictic theory tend regularly to describe both mimesis and metaphor in terms of the same notion of likeness: verisimilar likeness or resemblance in the first case, the likeness of figural comparison and similitude in the second. According to traditional accounts, poetry in general, but praise in particular, joins these two likenesses together in a peculiarly powerful and mutually corroboratory way, as though the likeness of the one were confirmation of— in some respects, the likeness of—the likeness of the other. Hence, according to traditional accounts, the extraordinariness of poetic language, especially as it is exemplified by praise. With metaphor added to it, mimesis becomes more than merely lifeless imitation, just as metaphor, grounded by mimetic reference, is more than extravagant ornamentation" (3). My discussion of the sonnet and the tradition of epideictic rhetoric is indebted to Fineman's study.

[3] Puttenham translates *icon* as "resemblance by imagerie or portrait" because of the word's relation to painting and portraiture, "alluding to the painters terme, who yeldeth to th'eye a visible representation of the thing he describes and painteth in his table." Yet, this painting or describing is not strictly mimetic but one based on any similarity either referential or metaphoric. The painterly icon is a "likening of lively creatures one to another, but also of any other naturall thing, bearing a proportion of similitude, as to liken yealow to gold." Thus, the example Puttenham offers, the iconic verbal portrait of Queen Elizabeth, is the blazon, "wherein we resemble every part of her body to some naturall thing of excellent

perfection," and the allegorical motif, "So we commending her Maijestie for wisedome bewtie and magnonimitie likened her to the Serpent, the Lion and the Angell" (204).

[4] *"Non quidem propter Deum, sed propter ipsum laudantem."* Summa Theologica 2: 1509; cited in Fineman 6.

[5] While in the sermon on 1 Corinthians 13: 12 Donne presents God as "Light," "the roote and fountaine of beeing," he is equally emphatic in rejecting the possibility of knowledge as full, immanent vision. Vision can offer only a provisional understanding. As Donne insists, in this sphere we see "not by direct, but by reflected beames" and perhaps "but a representation onely." Such vision may allow us to see but not fully know: "in the glass, which the Apostle intends, we may see God directly, that is, see directly that there is a God" but "The best knowledge that we have of God here, even by faith, is rather that he knows us, then that we know him" (*Sermons* 8: 222-23, 230). At worst, an insistence upon an immanent, visible truth is a carnal adherence to what can only be known empirically, through "the light of Nature" or reason. It is to succumb to a misleading seduction of the eye, "the devils doore" (*Sermons* 8: 228).

It is through the ear that the Holy Ghost "assists us with Rituall and Ceremoniall things, which we see in the Church" but only by directing the eye not to *see* but to *read*, "when their right use hath first beene taught by preaching" (*Sermons* 8: 228). In this manner, Donne argues elsewhere that communion is not a consumption of Christ's "spectacular" bodily presence but an imbibing that is a "Hearing and . . . Receiving" (*Sermons* 6: 223).

[6] Donne, in fact, argues rather forcefully against the possibility of full revelation:

> neither *Adam* in his extasie in Paradise, nor *Moses* in his conversation in the Mount, nor the other Apostles in the Transfiguration of Christ, nor *S. Paul* in his rapture to the third heavens, saw the Essence of God. . . . Only in heaven shall God proceed to this patefaction. . . . (8: 232)

And yet again, "Even in heaven our faculties shall be finite" (8: 231).

[7] Like the doubled figure for Christ in "What if this present," the term "vizar" indicates opposing terms, suggesting both mask and face. Vizar, the mask or hinged facepiece on a helmet, is a variation of vizard or visor/vizor which is derived from Middle English viser and Old French visiere: "equiv. to *vis* face (see VISAGE)" (*Random House* 1597). Visage, of course, means face or sight and appearance. The *Oxford English Dictionary* makes this double meaning of "vizard" more explicit, indicating that the term means both "a mask" and "a face or countenance suggestive of a mask" and ultimately "a person wearing a visor or

mask"(19: 718). In its figurative usage, "vizard" is associated with the dead letter or empty forms as is suggested by the example from Gosson's *School of Abuse* (1579), "Trueth can never be Falsehoods Visarde" (19: 718; for the word's use in sermons and religious tracts, see 19: 718, definition 2). In this sense, the term suggests not only a mask but a misleading and shifting appearance: "Vice putteth on a vizard, and goeth disguised and covered with goodly shewes that belong onely to vertue." Thus, it has been aligned with that which may be said to defy perception ("vizard" also indicating "a phantasm or spectre") and identified with the vagrant and improper figure: "*spec.* a woman of loose character wearing a mask in public, a prostitute" (19: 718, definition 5). Indicating both a face and a mask, a body and a rhetorical figure, "vizard" collapses the logical divisions that it initiates.

⁸ As Patricia Parker notes, the classical definition of metaphor with its emphasis on location and transgression places it in perilous proximity with catachresis, the "figure of abuse" or the "forced" transfer. Catachresis, a figure that acts as a definitive name, "a merely verbal or monstrous joining," threatens to displace meaning itself, introducing "the grotesque possibility of mistaking a purely verbal entity such as the 'centaur' for a natural one" (39). Such figures distort and preempt referential meaning and, as Parker reminds us, fittingly serve, in the figures of the centaurs and minotaur, as "the emblems of the circles of *forza* or violence" (39) in Dante's *Inferno*. These "figures of abuse," as Parker observes, become increasingly difficult to differentiate from "proper" tropes: "Metaphor in these discussions is always 'on the margins of discourse' (Barbara H. Smith), outside the city walls, and its potential incivility generates concern for its 'mastery' (Aristotle), 'moderation' (Quintilian), or 'proper management' (Blair)" (Parker 39).

⁹ As Nancy Vickers notes, rhetoric for Renaissance writers is the "'feminized' . . . surface" of the text or as Florentine humanist Coluccio Salutati writes, "Medusa is artful eloquence" (Vickers 112, 110). For George Puttenham both the text's "body" and rhetorical adornment are feminine. Figurative speech is akin to the ornate "courtly habillements" of "great Madames of honour" (114). An excessive use of figures, similarly, is a distortion of a feminine body: excess, or misapplied figures "disfigure the stuffe . . . no lesse then if the crimson tainte, which should be laid upon a Ladies lips, or right in the center of her cheekes should by some oversight or mishap be applied to her forhead or chinne" (115). Puttenham also repeatedly associates wordplay—especially riddles, puns, and irony—with seduction. See the discussions of synecdoche, riddles, and the ironic quip (162-163, 157, 159). Similarly, iconoclastic tracts frequently figured the allure of icons as a feminine seduction:

Wherefore as for a man given to lust, to sit downe by a strumpet, is to tempt GOD: So is it likewise to erect an Idole in this pronenesse of mans nature to Idolatrie, nothing but a tempting. . . . Doeth not the worde of GOD call Idolatrie spirituall fornication: Doeth it not call a gylte or painted Idole or Image, a strumpet with a painted face: Bee not the spirituall wickednesses of an Idols inticing, like the flatteries of a wanton harlot. . . . (*Certaine Sermons or Homilies* 61)

See also Parker's discussion of rhetorical dilation and the Romance (10-13).

[10] William Kerrigan makes this point: "Because of the personified 'Reason,' because 'three-person'd God' is named as lover, we recognize that sexual rape is here a metaphor for the forcible entrance of the deity into an otherwise impenetrable soul. But the design of the poem grants extraordinary emphasis to the penetration of a tight body. Insofar as the tropes reach out of local context to describe the climactic invitation, that sexual event acquires the force of a tenor. The intercourse of the speaker and God becomes virtually a 'real' presence in the poem, a final repository of reference—the shore on which the gathering wave of implication finally breaks" (354).

[11] Rabbinic scholars frequently link the closing declaration of Song of Solomon 5 ("This *is* my beloved, and this *is* my friend") with the deictic gesture of the Song of the Sea ("This is my God and I will beautify him" [Exod. 15 :2]). However, the book is as frequently read as an account of God's appearance at Mt. Sinai, "the Song itself as the crown of that great apocalyptic moment when the heavens opened and all of Torah—primordial, written, oral, and yet to be developed—was brought forth" (Green 144).

Thomas Brightman (1600) holds that the Song of Solomon "describes historico-prophetically the condition of the Church, and 'agrees well-nigh in all things with the Revelation of St. John'" (qtd. in *Song of Songs and Coheleth* 70). "For the rabbis," writes Daniel Boyarin, "the *Song of Songs* is the record of an historical theophany and, in particular, the description of the Lover in 5.9-16 is the description of God as He was seen on that occasion" (143). Rabbi Akiba appears to have understood Mt. Sinai to be the setting of the *Song* and, indeed, speaks of it in terms similar to that of the Torah:

Noting that Akiba spoke of the day when the Song of Songs was *given* to Israel, a term otherwise applied only to the Torah itself, Lieberman shows the early rabbis to have believed in the revelation of the Song, spoken by the angels or by God himself and revealed to Israel in a moment of theophany, either at the splitting of the Sea or at the foot of Sinai, one of those two moments when God descended in his chariot and was actually seen by the Community of Israel. (qtd. in Green 143)

[12] These thunderings and trumpet blasts are recognized as God's voice, for upon hearing them the Israelites ask Moses to intercede in receiving the commandments: "Speak thou with us, and we will hear: but let not God speak with us, lest we die" (Exod. 20: 19).

Works Cited

Aquinas, Thomas. *Non quidem propter Deum, sed propter ipum laudantem. Summa Theologica*. 2 vols. Trans. Fathers of the English Dominican Province. New York: Benzinger Brothers, 1947.

Augustine. *On Christian Doctrine*. Trans. D.W. Robertson, Jr. Indianapolis: Bobbs-Merrill, 1983.

Blanchot, Maurice. *The Writing of the Disaster*. Trans. Ann Smock. Lincoln: U of Nebraska P, 1986.

Boyarin, Daniel. "'Language Inscribed by History on the Bodies of Living Beings': Midrash and Martyrdom." *Representations* 25 (Winter 1989): 139-151.

Fineman, Joel. Shakespeare's Perjured Eye: The Invention of Poetic Subjectivity in the Sonnets. Berkeley: U of California P, 1986.

Fried, Michael. *Realism, Writing, and Disfiguration*. Chicago: U of Chicago P, 1987.

Gilman, Ernest B. "'To adore, or scorne an image': Donne and the Iconoclasm Controversy." *JDJ* 5 (1986): 62-100.

Green, Arthur. "The Song of Songs in Early Jewish Mysticism." *The Song of Songs*. Ed. Harold Bloom. New York: Chelsea House, 1988. 141-53.

The Holy Bible. Authorized King James Version. n.p.: World Bible Publishers, n.d.

"Homilie against Perill of Idolatrie (1563)." *Certaine Sermons   or Homilies*. London, 1623. Gainesville, FL: Scholars Facsimiles and Reprints, 1968.

Johnson, Barbara. *A World of Difference*. Baltimore: Johns Hopkins UP, 1987.

Kerrigan, William. "The Fearful Accommodations of John Donne." *ELR* 4 (1974): 337-363.

Lacan, Jacques. *The Four Fundamental Concepts of Psycho-Analysis*. Ed. Jacques-Alain Miller. Trans. Alan Sheridan. New York: Norton, 1981.

Oxford English Dictionary. Oxford: Clarendon, 1989. 20 vols.

Parker, Patricia. *Literary Fat Ladies: Rhetoric, Gender, Property*. London: Methuen, 1987.

Pope, Marvin. *Song of Songs: The Anchor Bible*. Garden City, NY: Doubleday, 1977.

Puttenham, George. *The Arte of English Poesie*. London, 1589.

Random House Dictionary of the English Language. New York: Random House, 1971.

Robbins, Jill. *Prodigal Son/Elder Brother: Interpretation and Alterity in Augustine, Petrarch, Kafka, Levinas.* Chicago: U of Chicago P, 1991.

The Song of Songs and Coheleth. Trans. Christian D. Ginsberg. New York: KTAV Publishing House, 1970.

Vickers, Nancy. "'The blazon of sweet beautys best': Shakespeare's *Lucrece.*" *Shakespeare and the Question of Theory.* Ed. Patricia Parker and Geoffrey Hartman. New York: Methuen, 1985. 95-115.

A Holy Puzzle:
Donne's "Holy Sonnet XVII"

Joy L. Linsley

ohn Donne's "Holy Sonnet XVII" is of central importance in his transition from the poetry of earthly love to that of heavenly love, a number of influential readers concluding that this transition was completed upon the death of his beloved wife Ann.[1] Although only the insecure beginnings of the divine courtship commence in this work, "Since she whome I lovd" may be regarded as a crisis poem in which the speaker attempts to purge himself of the residual elements of a dead Vision of Eros inspired by his wife and seeks to enter the Vision of God.[2] Biographical interest in "Holy Sonnet XVII" is enhanced if Arthur L. Clements and Ilona Bell's observations, based on a renewed interest in the Ann-John Donne relationship, are correct.[3] Little progress, however, has been made in presenting a reading that deals adequately with the complexities of the poem.[4] The reading offered here reveals Donne's subtle analysis of his spiritual problems, points out the theological, emotional, and gender conflicts present in the poem—as well as their uneasy resolution—and suggests a possible artistic motive for Donne's producing such an intriguing and puzzling text.

The ambiguities and obscurities of "Since she whome I lovd" justify the use of a variety of critical approaches—explication, inter-textual studies, reader-response criticism, gender study, and hermeneutics—to provide an evaluative reading of the poem. A close textual reading of line two is in order because of the critical controversies concerning the reading of that line. Texts from Romans and John, moreover, shed light on Donne's scrupulosity in identifying his spiritual state in lines four, 5-8, and line 12. The sacramental water image in lines 5-8 extends a central paradox first suggested in line four, that while the beloved was "here," she inspired the speaker to seek God; now that she is dead, she is one of those "heavenly things" that distract him from direct communion with God. Readers of the sestet agree that the final lines of the poem present the problems Donne and God face in their divine courtship, but a close reading of lines 9-10 is needed in order to establish whether God woos Donne for the sake of Ann's soul or whether other readings of the line are correct. The poet's serious playfulness with gender roles, moreover, is apparent in the sestet, especially in his adoption of the female role. These final lines of the poem also end decisively a gender struggle between Mother Nature and Father God, first suggested in the two opening lines of the poem, and bring into focus Donne's switches from identifications of woman as natural (dangerous), implied in the opening quatrain, to woman as noble (spiritual) in the the second quatrain.

As the poet moves from the rejection of earthly love to the tentative embracing of heavenly love, he employs spiritual and artistic strategies in coping with the loss of the earthly beloved and with dangers posed thereby to his love affair with God; as one critic has suggested, "Donne possessed a metaphysical imagination broad enough to span widely differing aspects of the love experience" (Frontain 41). I would like to argue that the poem is meaningfully obscure. It is a holy puzzle that partly conceals the poet's deep grief and his methods of coping with it.

1

In the first quatrain the speaker announces "her" death, casting this event in ambiguous terms. In stating that she "hath payd her last debt / To Nature" the poet not only establishes the harshness and inevitability, yet naturalness of her fate, but reminds the reader that the condition of human nature is one blighted by original sin. Her passive soul has been seized or "ravished" by some force, presumably God, and taken to heaven "early," before her expected life span was complete (line 3). In these first lines, the reader is drawn into a religious mystery: was her death lacking in drama, a dull event in which she simply paid her human and womanly "debt," as one might pay off a loan? Or was her death more exciting, a divine raping of her soul before its time?

Whether Nature, God, or both is responsible for the removal of the beloved woman, the speaker declares that his mind is now "Wholy in heavenly things . . . sett" (line 4). Such spiritual absorption, one assumes, should create no problem for a man seeking union with God, but, as Donne learned from Saint Paul, this contemplation or love of "heavenly things"—whether of "saints and angels" (line 12) or of a wife dead in heaven—is an obstacle to the perfect love of God. The speaker suffers from scrupulosity, one of the more painful/pleasurable sins. The Donne who tests out God so thoroughly in his "Hymne to God the Father" also finds the "scrupula," that rough, sharp stone, rubbing and irritating his conscience in this poem and implies that this is his problem in line four. In a passage that illuminates the concern of Donne's sonnet, Paul, himself an apostle of scrupulosity, triumphantly defies those powers that seek to separate the Christian from God, betraying his own anxieties, even as he proclaims:

> Who shall separate us from the love of Christ? . . . I am persuaded that neither death, nor life, nor angels, nor principalities, nor powers, nor things present, nor things to come, nor height, nor depth, nor any other creature, shall be able to separate us from the love of God . . . . (Romans 8: 35-39)

As the Pauline text implies, "any other creature" (such as a wife in heaven), as well as "saints and angels" (line 12), has the power to separate the Christian from the love of God. Moreover, Donne alludes to this separating power both in line four and in lines 11-12 of the poem.

E. M. W. Tillyard writes that Donne's poem "does not set his wife in any large human context" (5); but, in placing her death in the universal setting of Nature, the jealous Mother to whom each of us owes a death, Donne broadens and deepens the circumstance of Ann's death. The interpretation preferred here of the controversial line two[5] has been suggested by Faulkner and Daniels, who argue that the antecedent of "hers" is "Nature." Line two thus reads: "to my prosperity, to my state of well-being, and, indeed, to the general well-being of all of Nature, in which she was a good influence, she is now dead." The speaker evokes the pathetic fallacy explicit in the pastoral elegiac tradition when he suggests that Ann's death is a loss to Nature, who must be, as Donne is, deprived of her good influence. He also calls forth the specter of the dangerous woman who, even dead, is capable of separating Donne and God, for another sin Donne seems to fear here is that of Milton's Adam, uxoriousness.

These matters of gender are, however, vaguely suggested in the opening lines of the poem and can be developed fully only in the context of the whole poem. If the first quatrain concentrates on his wife in heaven, the second shifts to the earth when she was "here"—that is, on this earth:[6]

> Here the admyring her my mind did whett
> To seeke thee God: so streames do shew the head,
> But though I have found thee, and thou my thirst hast fed,
> A holy thirsty dropsy melts mee yett. (lines 5-8)

In this quatrain, Ann appears in the guise of the spiritual feminine stereotype:

> beautiful women are seen as ennobling to men who loved them: Dante is led through purgatory by the vision and guidance of Beatrice; Petrarch worships Laura even though he can never possess her. Perhaps it is significant that Beatrice and Laura . . . are exalted by the poets more after death than before. . . . (Ferguson 7)[7]

Identification of Ann with this stereotype is a courtly, gracious compliment to his dead wife, for the speaker acknowledges that his "admiration" or reverence for her "did whett" his "mind," or incite him to seek God.

Drawing on the familiar sacramental symbolism of water, the controlling image of lines 5-6 is that of a stream (Ann) which leads the thirsty seeker to its "head" or source (God). Figuratively drinking of the water of the stream, the speaker experienced an earthly taste of God's love, and his thirst for that love commenced and was to some degree satisfied. His experience with Ann "did whett" his appetite for God in two senses: it incited him to love God, and it did "wet" (drench) him with God's love. With her physical removal in death, he is left with a "holy thirsty dropsy." The phrase may be "rather silly in sound" to Tillyard (5-6), but it expresses Donne's condition precisely: he suffers from an accumulation of fluid and, already swollen with water, his diseased condition demands more water; thus, he has, paradoxically, a "thirsty dropsy." The dropsy is "holy," of course, because the thirst is for God's love. With Ann his earthly water source gone, the disease "melts" or overwhelms him with dismay and grief. Lines 5-8 reinforce the central paradox of the poem that, while she was here, she inspired him to seek God; but now that she is dead, he thinks only of "heavenly things," such as the now heavenly Ann. His thirst for her heavenly love risks further distracting him from experiencing God's love directly. Dead, perhaps more than alive, she remains the "other creature" who separates him from the love of God. Jesus warned the Samaritan woman at the well: "'Everyone who drinks this [earthly] water will be thirsty again. But whoever drinks the water I give him will never be thirsty'" (John 4: 13-14). Donne finds himself in this "thirsty" condition, having drunk from the stream (Ann) rather than directly from the source (God). For all her spiritual qualities, then, both on the earth and in a heavenly afterlife, Ann as daughter of Nature, as woman, is capable of distracting him from his primary task of achieving union with God.

Lines 5-8 may be read as a call to forsake forever the Vision of Eros for the Vision of God. The lines also may be a command to himself to become more "protestant" in his absolute reliance on God and his shunning of any intermediaries between him and God. If so, John Carey is correct in finding signs of Donne's struggle to convert from Roman Catholicism to Anglicanism in this poem, especially in the references to the "saints and angels" (59).[8]

2

In the octave of the sonnet the speaker expresses his condition follow-ing the loss of his spouse; in the sestet he questions himself and offers some rather suspect sympathy to God for the problems God faces in wooing Donne, "suspect" because any sympathy a weak mortal offers an omnipotent God suggests a Romantic irony. "Love" (line 9) refers in a purposefully ambiguous manner to both his wife's love and to God's. "Why," he asks, should he "begg more love" from either Ann (More)[9] or God when God himself woos his soul "for hers; offering all thine"? Not only does the poet yearn for more love, but he acknowledges that God has new worries (lines 11-14). God not only suffers, as formerly, from his "tender jealosy" of "the World, fleshe, yea Devill," which are the tradi-tional foes seeking to seduce Donne. But God must now also be con-cerned lest Donne give his "love to Saints and Angels, things divine." Stampfer writes: "The sonnet thus begins as a formal declaration of mourning, yet settles to a strange courtship dance of two jealous, newfound lovers, the speaker and his God, each jealously demanding love, each fanatically possessive" (276).[10]

But before the reader can fully appreciate the sestet, a satisfactory account of lines 9-10 is necessary. There are at least four plausible read-ings of these lines, but the one preferred here is based on the Westmoreland MS: For the sake of, and in place of, *her* soul God actively woos the poet's soul, offering all His love. The argument is tedious but of some importance. Gardner, following Bennett's lead, alters the punctuation of line 10, rejecting both the Westmoreland manuscript's reading and Grierson's rendering. The lines are read in these two ways:

> But why should I begg more love, when as thou
> Dost wooe my soule for hers; offring all thine.
> ("W" MS, Grierson, and Hayward)

> But why should I begg more Love, when as thou
> Dost woe my soul, for hers offring all thine:
> (Gardner, Bennett, Shawcross).

By removing the semi-colon and inserting the comma, Gardner no longer feels forced to read that God is wooing Donne's soul so that he may join Ann's soul in heaven, an interpretation offered by A. J. Smith that she finds objectionable mainly because in heaven "they neither marry nor are given in marriage" (Gardner, "Another Note"). Gardner paraphrases the lines in this manner: "How can I ask for more love, when Thou art my wooer, who in place of *her* love offers me all *thine*" (*Divine* 179).[11]

One need not, however, alter the Westmoreland MS version of the poem to secure an acceptable reading. We know, for example, that when Donne wrote Ann Donne's epitaph he contemplated some form of marriage after death, even if only in the union of their ashes. The last line of the epitaph states: "Very grievous to tell the husband, once dear to this dear one, plights his ashes to hers, to be joined in this spot in a new matrimony, God willing" (trans. LeComte 171). The biblical injunction, moreover, concerns unions after death, not a situation in which one spouse is dead, the other alive.[12]

That God woos Donne both for God's sake and for Ann's need not imply a marriage in heaven, so much as the continued spiritual influence of the dead Ann's soul on the soul of Donne. This influence, however, constitutes a kind of heavenly interference that deflects him from union with God and therefore is not "good." To use Clements' terms once more, the Vision of Eros (Ann) conflicts with the Vision of God. In "Holy Sonnet VIII," moreover, Donne speculates that his father's soul anxiously watches his son's spiritual progress, presumably hoping for the salvation of his son's soul and reunion with him in heaven. Surely a devoted wife would do as much. As Beatrice in Heaven actively concerns herself with Dante's salvation, so Ann Donne works for the poet's salvation.

3

David Novarr discerns the stakes involved in this poem when he writes that "although Donne says that love of his mistress has led him to love of God, the thrust of the sonnet is to suggest that earthly love is, largely, profane. It dichotomizes earthly love and heavenly; it sets up a competition between them" (125). The subtext of the poem, moreover, expresses a gender based competition, a richer and more complex amplification of the basic competition Novarr notes. The primary gender forces are Mother Nature and Father God. Ann, a sanitized and spiritualized female, rendered safer by the influences of a male God's adoption as a stream of divine influence and a patriarchal ravishing "early" into heaven, still retains elements of the threatening female influence on the spiritual male, an idea presented in section 1 of this essay. The poet himself, who appears to be the plaything of both natural and spiritual forces, nevertheless remains in control of the situation. He claims both the male role (husband of Ann) and the female role (beloved of God) in a spiritual ascent that begins "here" in the poem and ends "there." The poet places God's wooing of him among "heavenly things" (line 4) in that the poet sees his own salvation as one of God's concerns (line 10). A fantasy scene suggests itself, a kind of divine *ménage à trois* with the soul of the live Donne haunting the heavenly scene of God and Ann, waiting for God to woo and win him.

The flat tone of line one suggests that the speaker will make short work of the power of Mother Nature, who has committed a flamboyant offense by demanding of Ann Donne not only death but death in that most female and "natural" of conditions, childbirth. He implies that Nature's conquest is Pyrrhic inasmuch as the dead Ann can do no further "good" for Nature. Moreover, the paying of the "debt," in its reminders of original sin and God's strictures on woman in childbirth, suggests that Ann really owes her death not to Nature but to God. The power clearly lies with God, not Nature, for rather than allowing her simply to die in the span laid out by Nature, God "ravished" the passive Ann "early." And it is Ann, not Donne, whom God has ravished, in spite of the poet's pleas in "Batter My Heart," a situation that possibly accounts for a certain coyness of tone in the last lines of the poem, especially when one takes into account Shawcross's gloss of "ravished" as "transported joyfully."

The speakers in Donne's poems often adopt the feminine role when addressing God;[13] such transsexual artistic switches are common in mystical poetry, and, indeed, as Stampfer points out, in many Christian poems of this period (263).[14] One may, nevertheless, speculate further about this particular reversal of gender roles. Camille Paglia is only articulating a commonplace when she argues that art seeks to oppose nature and that the sexual personae adopted by artists vividly reflect their desires to propitiate or defy Nature. The adoption of the female role by a male artist indicates the desire to signal a more female-like passivity to spiritual forces and an enhanced receptivity to God by dropping the traditional masculine posture for that of the feminine. The reader suspects that such gender switching also indicates a desire to exert control and to assert individualism. Had the reversal occurred earlier in the poem, the reader might suspect that by adopting the female role Donne hopes to emulate and compliment the powerful figure of Mother Nature that informs this poem about death, but this is an improbable reading of the reversal. What looks like a submission to the female forces marshalled against the poet—death, desertion, seduction from the paths of God—becomes, in the final lines of the poem, a victory for man and God. The poet flaunts the limits of Nature's power over him by deserting that gender to which he has been assigned to take on the female role in a courtly, flirtatious lover's speech to God. Donne perhaps emulates the feminine in hopes of inviting seduction, if not ravishment of the kind experienced by Ann, holding back from God in order to chide God for ravishing Ann rather than him. But by offering himself as a female, ready to be ravished by God in these last lines, he signifies God's power over him. The poem thus exalts his masculine God, who, for the conventional Christian, will always defeat the forces of Nature. In a gesture of tribute and humility, he deserts his gender, willing to be "ravished" or "wooed" as God chooses.

4

A final statement about "Since she whome I lovd" concerns Donne's artistic strategies for coping with the loss of his wife and beginning his divine courtship. Donne exercises the power of his poetic imagination over Nature by retaining the memory of his beloved. But he also exerts his artistic power over grief and death by creating a text that is meaningfully and calculatedly difficult—a text that deliberately betrays itself as text with many turns and twists and ambiguities. The reader suspects that he did so as an artistic assertion of his control over Nature: the text that most betrays itself as text is the most un-natural text. The poem is, moreover, very self-protective in that it is written for the few who understand the nature of his loss and who accept his grief for what it is, a grief too deep to express except to those who break through the puzzles of this work. "Since she whom I lovd," then, might profitably be considered as one of Donne's parting poems, a final valediction to the earthly Ann who made that most serious of departures from the speaker, death.

Notes

[1] For example, Doniphan Louthan states: "With the death of his wife . . . Donne turns away from physical and, indeed, romantic love. His mind is wholly set on 'heavenly things'" (125). William Zunder writes: "the rejection [of human love] is quite clear in the sonnet Donne wrote on Ann Donne . . . after her death" (95-96). Claude Summers remarks: "The apocalyptic reading of 'Show me deare Christ,' locating true religion in the life to come, is strengthened by the poem's association with 'Since she whome I lovd,' the Holy Sonnet occasioned by the death of Donne's wife" (81).

[2] Arthur L. Clements defines the Vision of Eros as a subspecie of W. H. Auden's Vision of Kind (Nature) in which the "object" of the visionary embrace "is another human being with whom the mystic shares erotic love," although the true quest remains union with God. He speculates that Donne experienced a conversion, "a radical transformative realization of the true self by means of the Vision of Eros" in his relationship with Ann (21, 57; but see also his introductory discussion 9-12). "The Vision of God is of the transcendent or introvertive type," Clements concludes (10).

[3] Most scholars follow Edmund Gosse's original assumption that the deceased beloved is the poet's wife (2: 92-110). David Novarr's caution that the woman in the sonnet is not necessarily Ann More (115-27) must be kept in mind, however. Clements thinks the Ann-John Donne relationship probably inspired a group of "poems of faithful or true love, usually both physical and spiritual" (57, 241-43), including the following works: "Song: 'Sweetest love, I do not goe,'" "The Computation," "The Expiration,"[Image and Dream], "The Exstasie," "A Feaver," "A Valediction: forbidding Mourning," "A Valediction: of my Name in the Window," "A Valediction: of the Booke," "A Valediction: of weeping," "The Good-Mor-

row," "The Anniversarie," "The Sunne Rising," "The Canonization," "Loves Growth," "Love's Infiniteness," "A Lecture upon the Shadow," "A Noctural upon S. Lucies Day," and "The Dissolution." Bell claims their relationship was more passionate, intellectual, and important in his literary and spiritual develop-ment than "the old-fashioned idealized image" of Donne's love for Ann More (26) articulated, for example, by Grierson: "the simpler and purer, the more ideal and tender of Donne's love-poems" are "the expression of his love for Ann More" (2: xlix).

⁴ E. M. W. Tillyard makes an unfavorable comparison of "Since she whome I lovd" with Milton's poem on his "late espoused saint." He finds Donne's poem lacking in universality and allusiveness; he calls it uncomplimentary to its sub-ject, Ann Donne (2-7). His charges have not been refuted.

⁵ Interpretations of line two are disputed and uncertain; the reference of "hers" cannot be established. Gardner states in her first edition: "The words 'to hers and my good is dead' may amplify the preceding clause: death ends the possibility of doing good to oneself or to another. Or they may point forward: her death is for her good and his, since by it she has entered heaven early, and his affections are now all in heaven" (79). Tillyard does not disagree with Gardner's remarks in the first edition but thinks "hers" refers to her kin; thus, to both her kin's good and to Donne's good she is dead (77). In the second edition, Gardner retains the remarks in the first edition with some minor alterations (154) and adds the basic idea expressed by Tillyard in her own words, rejecting another idea—that "my good" may be a term of affection comparable to "my beloved" (153).

That Donne thought about the good one may no longer accomplish in this world, regardless of the blisses of heaven, is evident: "Howsoever I shall enjoy God myselfe [in heaven] yet I shall be no longer a means, an instrument of the propagation of God's truth amongst others . . . . David considers . . . that in this world he was bound to propagate Gods Truth, and that he could not doe, if God tooke him away by death" (*Sermons* 5: 384. See also "A Feaver" and "A Nocturnall upon S. Lucies Day."

⁶ Novarr speculates that "here" may refer to heaven (123-4).

⁷ Redpath writes: "Donne must have known well enough the expressions of longing for the dead Laura in the *In Morte* series by Petrarch" (297).

⁸ Stampfer also cites line 12 ("Saints and Angels") as an indication of a "Protestant mistrust of overtones of idolatry in the Roman Catholic Church" (276).

⁹ Louthan notes the pun on her maiden name (125).

¹⁰ Roger Rollin speculates that "in the poem's last four lines the speaker's ego unconsciously attempts to defend against anxiety by projecting that anxiety onto God, attributing to the Omniscient some uncertainty as to whether he [the

speaker] will ultimately attain salvation" (145).

[11] Gardner avoids or does not notice the transsexual implications inherent in the substitution of the male God for the female wife, a courtship similar to Shakespeare's Richard III's wooing of Anne over the corpse of her slain husband, Henry VI.

[12] Summers writes that, "read in concert with 'Since she whome I lovd,' 'Show me deare Christ' might be seen as expressing a plaintive death-wish. God having prematurely taken his spouse, the poet pleads to be shown Christ's spouse, an event that will also occasion a mystical reunion with his dead wife, whose soul has been `early into heaven ravished' (l. 3)."

[13] Donne was doubtlessly aware of the tradition that the soul is feminine, but that he consistently followed that tradition cannot be established. In "Holy Sonnet XVIII," for example, he petitions God: "Betray kind husband thy spouse to our sights, / And let myne amorous soule court thy mild Dove" (lines 11-12). The transsexual switch contemplated here, therefore, may be regarded as deliberate.

[14] Many of Stampfer's excellent remarks on the reversal of sexual roles in the Holy Sonnets, especially those on "Batter my heart" (258-65), also apply to "Since she whome I lovd."

Works Cited

Bald, R. C. *John Donne: A Life.* Oxford: Oxford U P, 1970.

Bell, Ilona. "Under Ye Rage of a Hott Sonn & Yr Eyes." *The Eagle and the Dove.* Ed. Claude J. Summers and Ted-Larry Pebworth. Columbia: U of Missouri P, 1986. 25-52.

Carey, John. *John Donne: Life, Mind, and Art.* New York: Oxford U P, 1981.

Clements, Arthur L. *Poetry of Contemplation.* Albany: S U of New York P, 1990.

Faulkner, Eleanor, and Edgar F. Daniels. "Donne's 'Holy Sonnet XVII.'" *Explicator* 34 (1976): item 68.

Ferguson, Mary Anne. *Images of Women in Literature.* 3rd ed. Dallas: Houghton Mifflin, 1981.

Frontain, Raymond-Jean. "Donne's Erotic Spirituality: Ovidian Sexuality and the Language of Christian Revelation in Elegy XIX." *Ball State U Forum* 25 (1984): 41-54.

Gardner, Helen, ed. *John Donne: The Divine Poems.* Oxford: Clarendon P, 1952.

_____, ed. *John Donne: The Divine Poems.* Second ed. Oxford: Clarendon P, 1978.

_____. "Another Note on Donne: 'Since She Whom I lov'd.'" *MLR*

(1957): 564-65.

Gosse, Edmund. *The Life and Letters of John Donne.* 2 vols. London: Heinemann, 1899.

Grierson, Herbert J. C., ed. *The Poems of John Donne.* 2 vols. 1912. Oxford: Oxford U P, 1963.

LeComte, Edward. *Grace to a Witty Sinner.* New York: Walker, 1962

Louthan, Doniphan. *The Poetry of John Donne.* New York: Bookman Associates, 1951.

Novarr, David. *The Disinterred Muse.* Ithaca: Cornell U P, 1980.

Paglia, Camille. *Sexual Personae.* New York: Vintage, 1991.

Redpath, Theodore, ed. *The Songs and Sonnets of John Donne.* Second ed. New York: St. Martin's P, 1983.

Rollin, Roger B. "'Fantastique Ague': The Holy Sonnets and Religious Melancholy." *The Eagle and the Dove.* Ed. Claude J. Summers and Ted-Larry Pebworth. Columbia: U of Missouri P, 1986. 131-46.

Stampfer, Judah. *John Donne and the Metaphysical Gesture.* New York: Funk and Wagnalls, 1970.

Summers, Claude J. "The Bride of the Apocalypse and the Quest for True Religion: Donne, Herbert, and Spenser." *"Bright Shootes of Everlastingness": The Seventeenth-Century Religious Lyric.* Ed. Claude J. Summers and Ted-Larry Pebworth. Columbia: U of Missouri P, 1987. 72-95.

Tillyard, E. M. W. *The Metaphysicals and Milton.* London: Chatto and Windus, 1956.

Zunder, William. *The Poetry of John Donne.* Totowa, NJ: Barnes and Noble, 1982.

"What doth Physicke *profit thee?":*
The Pharmakon *of Praise*
in Donne's
Ignatius His Conclave
and the Holy Sonnets

Julie W. Yen

n his provocative portrait of Donne the ambitious apostate, John Carey reminds us that *Ignatius His Conclave,* published in 1611, was composed at about the same time that most of the *Holy Sonnets* were written, and he goes on to suggest that reading the two texts together might help us better to understand the sonnets: "at the very time when Donne was preparing his ribald attack on Loyola and the Jesuits, . . . his spiritual life—preserved for us in the 'Holy Sonnets'—was shaping and nourishing itself on what they had taught him" (37).[1] Carey's well-known biographical portrait argues that Donne was never fully able to escape his Catholic upbringing, and that *Ignatius His Conclave* is in fact a rebellious "reaction against those he had been taught as a boy to reverence" (20). Arthur Marotti gives further credence to a connection between the polemical prose and the religious verse by a very persuasive account of Donne's sense of frustration and anger in his years of searching for political advancement: "The grief and despair with which Donne's early religious poems are preoccupied (particularly the *Holy Sonnets)* seem to have been rooted . . . *in both* personal piety and secular needs" (247).

I wish to examine this connection more closely by reading these two texts through the metaphor of the *pharmakon,* or "physicke," that is explored in its multivalency of meanings by Derrida in his reading of Plato's *Phaedrus.* When we scrutinize the movement of the *pharmakon,* simultaneously both a poison and a cure, whose presence pervades the text of *Ignatius His Conclave,* we detect within the dramatization of conflicting discourses a play of endless substitutions of meaning. This continuous deferral of meaning produces discursive strategies which allowed Donne simultaneously to critique and practice the art of elaborate praise that was a common part of Renaissance court behaviour. And these strategies of verbal equivocation, I wish to argue, are the same devices that he uses in the *Holy Sonnets* to praise and court God in "prayers, and flattering speaches" ("Oh, to vex me" 10).

1

Donne sets the scene of his satire, Lucifer's hell, in the foreign regions of outer space, thereby giving the reader a sense of defamiliarization that makes her more receptive to dislocations of meaning. Moreover, by seeming to invert matters in the satire, Donne opens up multivalent possibilities of meaning in the texture of his language. When consignment to hell is considered an honor that many vie for, and the secret place in hell the highest honor that self-styled "innovators" like Ignatius, Paracelsus, Copernicus, and Machiavelli fight over, the reader's initial expectations are disrupted; however, the meaning of what subsequently happens there does not simply translate into its opposite—instead, a series of substitutions occurs, setting into play the process of Derridean "supplementarity" in a continual deferral of meaning.

Among the several contenders for the highest position of honor in hell, a place where "[f]or so the truth be lost, it is no matter how" (13), Machiavelli and Ignatius are the loudest and most strenuously aggressive candidates. As Machiavelli arrives at the gate of hell, he sees that Ignatius has already established himself as a dominant figure at the scene. Immediately perceiving the close relationship between Lucifer and Ignatius, and recognizing that Ignatius is in fact "the principall person next to Lucifer," he realizes that it will be to his advantage to ingratiate himself with Ignatius, hoping thereby to "sweeten and mollifie him" (25). Being a crafty tactician, Machiavelli plots to "make Lucifer suspect, that by these honors & specious titles offered to Ignatius, and entertained by him, his owne dignity might bee eclipsed, or clouded" (25). (As the power struggle between the two rivals escalates, Lucifer does begin to worry, about *both* of them, but it takes him a while actually to comprehend the extent to which his position is being threatened.)

Machiavelli proceeds, then, to address both Ignatius and Lucifer as if he has suddenly been seized with a fit of afflatus:

Dread Emperour, and you, his watchfull and diligent Genius, father Ignatius, Arch-chancellor of this Court, and highest Priest of this highest Synagogue (except the primacy of the Romane Church reach also unto this place) let me before I descend to my selfe, a little consider, speake, and admire your stupendious wisedome, and the government of this state. (25)

This hyperbolic praise of Ignatius is qualified, however, with the parenthetical caveat that he can only be considered the highest Priest if he is not competing against the Pope: "except the primacy of the Romane Church reach also unto this place." Whether he hears this ambivalence or not, Ignatius does see through Machiavelli's design to insinuate himself into Lucifer's favor, and ignoring his attempts to lower his defenses, launches a forceful attack on Machiavelli that focuses on his overpraise of their prince:

Durst any man before him, thinke upon this kinde of injurie, and calumnie, as to hope that he should be able to flatter, to catch, to entrap *Lucifer* himselfe? Certainely whosoever flatters any man, and presents him those praises, which in his owne opinion are not due to him, thinkes him inferiour to himselfe and makes account, that he hath taken him prisoner, and triumphs over him. (33)

Charging that Machiavelli's excessive praise of Lucifer is only meant to beguile and "entrap" him, Ignatius advances the idea that flattery is in effect a form of injury, because it puts a man off his guard and enables the flatterer to assume a position of superiority over the object of exorbitant praise. Interestingly, in his criticism of Machiavelli's strategy, Ignatius could not avoid criticizing Lucifer as well, whether he intended to or not, for he has suggested that Lucifer does not deserve the compliments. Furthermore, as soon as Ignatius has criticized Machiavelli, he realizes that he has also been engaged in the process of paying elaborate compliments to Lucifer; moreover, he has gone even further and combined his flattery with self-abasement: "*Ignatius* . . . threw himselfe downe at *Lucifers feet*, and grovelling on the ground adored him" (31). But recovering immediately, he turns around and attempts to adduce positive attributes to the art of flattery:

there may bee, even in flattery, an honest kind of teaching, if Princes, by being told that they are already indued with all vertues necessary for their functions, be thereby taught what those vertues are, and by a facile exhortation excited to endeavour to gaine them. (33)

This immediate reversal of opinion is a manifestation of Donne's strategy of shifting discourses. By having Ignatius make a statement, as Derrida might put it, "under erasure"—that is, simultaneously asserting and disclaiming an opinion—Donne is in essence saying that "the poet nothing affirmeth." Morevoer, when we remember that this speech is put into the mouth of the villain, the instabilities of meaning in the text suddenly arrest the attention of the reader: what does the word "honest" mean in the vocabulary of a character whose meanings the text has thus far taught the reader to invert? Are princes not to be encouraged to acquire the virtues necessary for government? Or is the reader not to trust the text? The concern with the teaching of proper virtues to princes is consonant with the highest humanistic values in the education of a prince. As this line of thinking appears to be fairly straightforward, does this mean that Ignatius, who is "more subtil than the Devill, and the verier Lucifer of the two" (31), is actually capable of honest, good advice to his prince, presenting himself as a cure rather than a poison? But again, before the reader readjusts her perspective once more and stops thinking of Ignatius as the arch-villain in the satire, his argument takes another turn, accusing Machiavelli of the presumption of attempting to instruct Lucifer: "But was it fit that this fellow, should dare either to deride you, or (which is the greater injury) to teach you? Can it be beleeved, that he delivers your praises from his heart . . . ?" (33). Ignatius first questions Machiavelli's sincerity, then further suggests that Machiavelli was in fact mocking Lucifer. Continuing in his attack on his main rival, Ignatius then accuses Machiavelli of having worked against Lucifer's earthly counterpart, the Pope:

all his bookes, and all his deedes, tend onely to this, that thereby a way may be prepared to the ruine & destruction of that part of this Kingdome, which is established at Rome: for what else doth hee endeavour or go about, but to change the forme of common-wealth, and so to deprive the people . . . of all their liberty: & having so destroyed all civility & re-publique, to reduce all states to Monarchies; a name which in secular states, wee doe so much abhor. . . . (55-57)

Proposing that in *Ignatius His Conclave* Donne succeeded in finding a way to "speak ambivalence" (50), Annabel Patterson has recently observed that the above compliment is "astonishingly" ambivalent. Patterson astutely notes that in spite of the surface praise, "the result is a statement that monarchies come into existence by depriving the people 'of all their liberty' . . . , a curious defense of James I and Elizabeth" (51). The indeterminacy in the passage is even more pronounced, it seems to me, when we consider an earlier passage wherein Machiavelli, speaking for himself, is arguing his claims to occupy the preeminent place for innovators in hell:

> I did not onely teach those wayes, by which thorough perfidiousnesse and dissembling of Religion, a man might possesse, and usurpe upon the liberty of free Commonwealths; but also did arme and furnish the people with my instructions, how when they were under this oppression, they might safeliest conspire, and remove a tyrant, or revenge themselves on their Prince. . . . (29)

Juxtaposing Machiavelli's boast and Ignatius' rebuttal, we see that Ignatius has purposely inverted Machiavelli's claim, changing his initial assertion that he had taught men how to usurp the liberty of a free commonwealth to the accusation that he deprived men of their liberty in order to "change the forme of commonwealth" and thereby "reduce all states to *Monarchies.*" And when we further examine Machiavelli's boast about the innovation of his teachings, we notice that his reference to men who have availed themselves of his ways in "dissembling of Religion" is indeterminate. James could choose to read in the first part of the passage praise for his efforts to defend the True Religion and uphold the freedom of the British commonwealth. However, the second part of the passage, in its reference to the sensitive topic of regicide, should also be read as a warning against bad government. James, who expended a great deal of effort in justifying his system of kingship in the *True Law of Free Monarchies, Basilikon Doron,* and other writings, believed that kings not only were personally chosen by God, but also were invested with a large measure of God's own wisdom and authority. In his eyes, the king's right to rule was therefore divine and absolute. However, James's concepts of a sacred monarchy and royal prerogative, as can be expected, did not sit well with his parliaments. And following the recent eruption of the Gunpowder Plot and the assassination of Henri IV, fears of regicide were very real in England. Charles M. Coffin has noted that in 1598 the Spanish Jesuit Juan de Mariana had just published his *De rege et regis institutione,* which "sanctioned the use of force and violence to dispose of princes who were tyrants, namely, princes who resisted the temporal sovereignty of the papacy" (198). And Sydney Anglo further observes that according to popular belief, machiavellism was very closely associated with jesuitism; in fact, it was commonly accepted that "the doctrine of king-killing itself had been developed by the Jesuits from Machiavelli's *Prince* " (381).[2]

These conflicting discourses that surround the acts of flattery invite us to read them through the metaphor of the *pharmakon*, or "physicke," in the terminology of the text. The *pharmakon* simultaneously contains the contrary senses of poison and cure, and its fluidity of meaning gives Donne room for free articulation without definite expression. The metaphor is first introduced into the text with the appearance of Paracelsus the alchemist-physician right before Machiavelli's entrance, as one of the contenders for the highest reward in hell. He also begins his address to Lucifer with elaborate praise and self-abasement: "It were an injurie to thee, o glorious Emperour, if I should deliver before thee, what I have done, as thogh al those things had not proceeded from thee, which seemed to have bin done by me, thy organe and conduit" (21). After crediting Lucifer as the source of his achievements, Paracelsus proceeds to boast that one of the paramount achievements of his alchemical practices is that he has made some poisons undetectable:

> And whereas almost all poysons are so disposed and conditioned by nature, that they offend some of the senses, and so are easily discerned and avoided, I brought it to passe, that that trecherous quality of theirs might bee removed, and so they might safely bee given without suspicion, and yet performe their office as strongly. (21)

By removing the "trecherous" telling smell or taste of poisons, Paracelsus has made drugs "safe," or imperceptible, without losing their toxic quality. Like the *pharmakon*, flattery is also the most effective when it is the most unobtrusive and undetectable.

Paracelsus, like Machiavelli, is also vanquished by Ignatius. Dismissing Paracelsus's claims, Ignatius suggests to Lucifer that physic is useless: "Let me (dread Emperour), have leave to speake truth before thee. . . . what doth Physicke profit thee? Physicke is a soft, & womanish thing" (23). He then dispatches Paracelsus contemptuously:

> Think therefore your selfe well satisfied, if you be admitted to governe in chiefe that Legion of homicide-Phisitians, and of Princes which shall

be made away by poyson in the midst of their sins, and of woemen
tempting by paintings and face-phisicke. (23, 25)

Knowing that Ignatius is the arch villain, we are alert to the fact that we
cannot accept what he says at face value, particularly when he professes
to "speake truth"; however, neither can we simply invert the meaning of
what he says in order to arrive at the "truth" in the text. Ignatius's
declaration that Paracelsus is only fit to govern "homicide-Phisitians" is
probably a facetious reference to the victims of the "remedies" and "easy
cures" that were derived from Paracelsus's "uncertaine, ragged, and
unperfect experiments" (21), and the remark about women's use of cos-
metics as a seductive device is just another facile misogynistic joke com-
mon at the time. But in the reference to "Princes which shall be made
away by poyson in the midst of their sins," contemporary readers may
have been reminded of more than just the assassination of old Hamlet.
Given the current anxieties about regicide and general suspicion of Catho-
lics, they may very well have also heard an echo of the Spanish Jesuit Juan
de Mariana's thoughts about killing a king: "tyrannicide is justified in
anyone by any means, except poison: and even poison may be used so
long as the tyrant is not made to kill himself with it" (qtd. in Coffin 198).

Ignatius describes the *pharmakon* as a "soft, & womanish thing," and
therefore useless and unworthy of attention. But the text also invites the
reader to consider the profits of "physicke," particulary when it might be
translated as a cure or antidote, or used "safely," that is, unobtrusively.
Ignatius himself is described in terms of a *pharmakon* in the text. Over-
whelmed by the threatening presence of both Ignatius and Machiavelli,
Lucifer initially attempts to balance their powers against each other so
that they might cancel each other out and allow him to continue to rule in
peace. Reasoning that "two poysons mingled might doe no harm" (31),
Lucifer had hoped that he could use one poison as the antidote for the
other. But because Ignatius, being "of the same temper as *Lucifer*" (21),
anticipates his plan, Lucifer fails. Moreover, as Lucifer is virtually com-
pelled to make Ignatius *"his Lieutenant, or Legat a latere,* and trusted him
with an absolute power of doing what hee would" (71),[3] it becomes clear
that the profits of "physicke" for Ignatius are obvious: he successfully
gains preferment through effectual flattery. Donne, likewise, as he dexter-
ously compliments his king, appears to have been successful in negotiat-
ing the conflicting discourses of flattery and praise.

In *Ignatius His Conclave,* Donne pays James many compliments, all the
time keeping in mind the fine line that separates the cure of praise from

the poison of flattery. But Donne's praise of James also often sacrifices his loyalty to the King's female predecessor, Elizabeth. Donne praises Elizabeth's wisdom when Ignatius notes that he cannot "call to minde any woman, which either deceived our hope, or scaped our cunning, but *Elizabeth of England*" (85). This praise of Elizabeth, however, is only incidental to a greater compliment that is being paid to James:

> she had put off all affections of woemen. The principau Dignity of which sex, (which is, to be a *Mother)* what reason had she to wish, or affect, since without those *womanish* titles, unworthy of her, of wife, & mother, such an heire was otherwise provided for her, as was not fit to be kept any longer from the inheritance. (85)

This is a backhanded compliment to the Queen: she was not very much of a woman because she did not fulfill the basic roles of womanhood; therefore, she is more and better than a woman, since womanhood is not a particularly desirable condition. But although Elizabeth was not woman enough to produce an heir herself, an heir that was eminently fit to inherit the throne of England was provided for her. James had gained his throne through Elizabeth's failure to produce an heir, in the same way that both Elizabeth and her predecessor, her half-sister Mary, had ascended the throne because of a lack of more direct heirs. Although this comment could be perceived as a criticism of Elizabeth, it would not apply to James because the succession of the Stuart family had already been assured by the birth of Charles. This subtle compliment therefore not only reassured James's anxieties about the succession of the throne, it also reaffirmed the legitimacy of the Stuart family and re-enforced James's theories of royal prerogative and the Divine Right of Kings to rule.

In Ignatius's unwilling adoration of the two monarchs toward the end of the satire, Donne praises both Elizabeth and James:

> when I [Ignatius], who hate them, speake thus much in the honour of these *two Princes*, I finde myselfe caried with the same fury, as those *Beasts* were, which our men say, did sometime adore the *Host* in the *Masse.* For it is against my will, that I pay thus much to the *Manes of Elizabeth* . . . . (85)

In this hyperbolic compliment, Donne's comparison of James and Elizabeth to the Host may seem blasphemous, but he is in fact using a figure of speech that had already been appropriated by James himself. In his address to the Parliament of 1609, James had figured himself as a god:

> The State of Monarchy is the supremest thing upon earth. For Kings are not only God's lieutenants upon earth and sit upon God's throne, but even by God himself they are called Gods. . . . In the Scriptures Kings are called Gods, and so their power after a certain relation compared to the Divine Power. (qtd. in Healy xli)

Moreover, in using the phrase "the *Manes of Elizabeth*" Donne has artfully succeeded in paying James another compliment. James had referred to the "Manes (if I may say so) of my late predecessor" in his *Apology for the Oath of Allegiance* (qtd. in Healy 148). Thus, by echoing James's own words, Donne subtly flatters the King. And once more, Donne has praised James more than Elizabeth.

Ultimately, perhaps Donne's most subtle compliment to the King lies in his imitation of James's discursive practices. Graham Parry has noted that James "used the theatrical metaphor several times in *Basilikon Doron*, and well understood the need in politics for artifice and compelling imagery" (16). In *James I and the Politics of Literature*, Jonathan Goldberg also underscores the King's predilection for ambivalence and suggestion, arguing that King James's own equivocating discourse provided the poets in his court with the language to express what they could not articulate directly:

> Using James's own strategy of equivocation to represent the king, poets could rely on his self-division and self-contradiction to keep him from understanding implications in their language impossible to express directly.Employing royal language, poets turned the tables on the monarch, appropriating power against power by engaging the most radical potential that resides in language, its own multivalent, self-contradictory nature. (116)

In *Ignatius His Conclave*, Donne exploits the potentialities of language as he successfully manipulates conflicting discourses in the practice of courtly equivocation made available by the example of the king. Showing himself to be a "master improviser," to use Stephen Greenblatt's term, Donne places his dangerous comments on the practice of flattery in the mouths of various equivocating characters, cautiously criticizing court behaviour while remaining inside the power system and availing himself of its strategies of discourse. Donne was doubtless often ambivalent about the uses and abuses of elaborate compliment, but understood that it was an inevitable part of Jacobean court life.

2

Today students of Donne's work do not agree on how immediate a role King James may have played in persuading Donne to enter church service, but there is no doubt about the causal relationship between his Catholic background and his failure to secure political advancement. In the *Holy Sonnets* which bear witness to the personal struggles that beset Donne's religious imagination, we can hear his profound frustration and disappointment in a system which chose to ignore a man's obvious intellectual abillities and deny him preferment because of his religious affiliation. Many of the speakers vent their anger and resentment, but also recognize that the supplicant's position does not allow them to make many demands. Some of the speakers resort to the discursive strategies afforded by the *pharmakon* of praise and attempt to court God with "flattering speaches" but ultimately come to the realization that each cure always already carries poisonous side-effects.

The speaker of "Since she whome I lovd," a sonnet that most readers agree was written after Ann's death,[4] figures his spiritual struggles as a continuing disease of discontent: "But though I have found thee, and thou my thirst hast fed, / A holy thirsty dropsy melts mee yett" (7-8). In this late sonnet, according to David Aers and Gunther Kress, the speaker is at peace with himself because Donne had already achieved social success at the time of writing: "the calm assurance and frankness of the poem are connected with the fact that by the time Donne wrote this sonnet (Ann died in 1617) he was well on the path to incorporation in the social world of the establishment" (69). Marotti, however, argues that this speaker has not yet succeeded in reconciling his spiritual and worldly desires; he contends that the poem associates Ann with "the World, fleshe, yea Devill" (14) and construes her as "an obstacle in the way of a wholehearted religious commitment" (279). "Working through mourning in this way," writes Marotti, "involves not simply coming to terms with the loss of a beloved spouse but also, somewhat cruelly, rejecting her along with the secular world with which the poem associates her" (279). Even if we accept the late date of the sonnet, I do not think that the text gives us enough evidence to read in it Donne's rejection of Ann More after her death; I also don't think that the speaker projects the image of a soul at peace with itself after successfully negotiating the conflicting demands of the religious and secular worlds. The assertion in the octave, "Wholy in heavenly things my mind is sett" (4), is undercut by the sestet:

> But why should I begg more Love, when as thou
> Dost woe my soule, for hers offring all thine:
> And dost not only feare least I allow
> My Love to Saints and Angels, things divine,
> But in thy tender jealosy dost doubt
> Least the World, fleshe, yea Devill putt thee out. (9-14)

Unable to reconcile the contrary images of the Old Testatment God of wrath with the New Testament God of mercy, the speaker projects onto God his own emotions of fear, doubt, and jealousy. Speaking of God's "tender jealousy," rather than the tender mercies of familiar biblical language, the speaker reveals a troubled state of mind. The question that opens the sestet, "But why should I begg more Love," is not adequately answered by the end of the poem. Even though intellectually the speaker knows that God has given him all His love, he is also aware that he cannot reciprocate God's complete love because of the necessary imperfection of human faith. By projecting onto God his own fears and doubts, the speaker defers the acknowledgement of human imperfection for the moment and shifts the responsibility for his frustrating condition onto God; however, it is immediately apparent that his position is untenable when he must admit that he thinks God is jealous not only of his love for worldly things, but also of his love for "Saints and Angels, things divine," which are, after all, all part of God. These instabilities in the text reveal the potential poisonous nature of the *pharmakon* metaphor. Seeking a cure for the spiritual disease of despair, the speaker avows that his mind is completely set on God and spiritual matters; however, by the end of the sonnet he is compelled to admit the continued presence of "the World, fleshe, yea Devill" in his life.

The sonnet "O Might those sighes and teares returne againe" also describes religious life as a state of "holy discontent." In the speaker's complaint about having "mourn'd in vaine" (4) and his hope that though his current condition is still unsatisfactory, he may now "Mourne with some fruit" (4), we can hear Donne's ambivalence about his family religion which had cost him the career opportunites that were readily available to other young men like him. Although he has repented his earlier sins of idolatry, his conversion gives him no peace. His indulgence in idolatry had cost him tears and much grief, but that suffering itself had been a sin. And contrary to the reader's expectations, that suffering does not expiate the speaker's sins, but is paradoxically the reason for him to continue suffering: "That sufferance was my sinne, now I repent; / 'Cause I did suffer I must suffer paine" (7-8). The persecution of Catholics had caused Donne and his family much suffering, and Donne continued to pay the price of religious incorrectness. The speaker laments this injustice. Other sinners may also have to face "comming ills," but at least they have enjoyed their pleasures and will have the memory of those "past joyes" (11) to comfort them when their time for suffering comes; his condition allows for "No ease" (13), either before or after his repentance: "for, long, yet vehement griefe hath beene / Th'effect and cause, the punishment and sinne" (13-14).

When another speaker in the *Holy Sonnets* inveighs against his Maker about his perceived injustices, once again we hear Donne the courtier complaining about the injustice of the political system that had consistently refused to reward him:

> If poysonous mineralls, and if that tree,
> Whose fruit threw death on else immortall us,
> If lecherous goats, if serpents envious
> Cannot be damn'd; Alas; why should I bee?
> Why should intent or reason, borne in mee,
> Make sinnes, else equall, in mee, more heinous?
> And mercy being easie, and glorious
> To God, in his sterne wrath, why threatens hee? (1-8)

Others less deserving and less talented had been advanced; why should familial religious convictions which he may no longer have shared keep him from receiving an appointment in James's court? The King handed out favors with apparent ease; why could Donne not receive his rightful share? But with the sudden turn of argument, as the speaker realizes his presumption in arguing with his Maker, "But who am I, that dare dispute with thee?" (9), the question also signals the recognition of a supplicant that he can only rely on divine grace for any hope of gaining success. Any outward show of his anger and frustration would not predispose either God or the King to grant him his suit. The poem ends with the speaker praying for God's mercy.

In "As due by many titles I resigne / My selfe to thee," the speaker's address to God takes on a special resonance when we consider that Donne was working his hardest to win a place in James's court when he was writing these lines:

> I am thy sonne, made with thy selfe to shine,
> Thy servant, whose paines thou hast still repaid,
> Thy sheepe, thine Image, and till I betray'd
> My selfe, a temple of thy Spirit divine. (5-8)

The line "Thy servant, whose paines thou hast still repaid" could be read with Donne's political as well as religious imperatives in mind. It would then take on an ironic meaning: not praise of God expressing dutiful obedience, but veiled criticism of a King who has *not* rewarded faithful service. The reference to self-betrayal would indicate Donne's ambivalence about his religious faith. And the last lines of the poem, "Oh I shall soone despaire, when I doe see / That thou lov'st mankind well, yet wilt not chuse me" (12-13), could very well be giving voice to his political disappointment as well as his religious torment.

The speaker of "Oh my blacke Soule!" recognizes that previous sins have led to his spiritual decay. In the analogy "Thou art like a pilgrim, which abroad hath done / Treason" (3-4), the choice of the word "treason" to express religious betrayal invites the reader to read the poem in political terms. The pivotal line signifying the turn in the argument towards hope, "Yet grace, if thou repent, thou canst not lacke," seems to hold the promise of satisfaction, both the divine grace of mercy as well as the political favor of an appointment; however, the argument immediately takes another turn with very next line: "But who shall give thee that grace to beginne?" (10). As soon as the assurance is voiced it is undercut by doubts. The rest of the sonnet offers no answers, only an exhortation and an overworked paradox:

> Oh make thy selfe with holy mourning blacke,
> And red with blushing, as thou art with sinne;
> Or wash thee in Christs blood, which hath this might
> That being red, it dyes red soules to white. (11-14)

The soul is advised to make itself black with mourning and red with shame, but this advice is superfluous since by the speaker's account at the beginning of the poem, the soul is already both black and red with sin. Realizing the inefficacy of the exhortation, the speaker then proposes the route of salvation through spiritual purification: baptism in the Savior's blood will transform the sinfulness of scarlet souls to white innocence. The facile paradox, however, fails to carry the force of conviction.

Many of the *Holy Sonnets'* speakers attempt to articulate the difficulties of their religious struggles in paradoxes, but these paradoxes characteristically offer no resolution to the speakers' dilemmas. The speaker of "Oh, to vex me" describes his spiritual malaise in contradictory terms: the only constant habit he has been able to form is inconstant devotion and changeable contrition. And he knows no cure for his religious ailment:

> I durst not view heaven yesterday; and to day
> In prayers, and flattering speaches I court God:
> To morrow'I quake with true feare of his rod.
> So my devout fitts come and go away
> Like a fantastique Ague: save that here
> Those are my best dayes, when I shake with feare. (9-14)

He is acutely aware of his sinful nature. At times he may be able temporarily to forget his inherent unworthiness and supplicate God, but his expectation of divine retribution never leaves him. At best, his intermittent faith is periodically beset by feverish tremors: "I shake with feare."

The speaker in "Thou hast made me, And shall thy worke decay?" is also terrified by doubts about his salvation:

> Despaire behind, and death before doth cast
> Such terrour, and my febled flesh doth waste
> By sinne in it, which it t'wards hell doth weigh;
> Onely thou art above, and when towards thee
> By thy leave I can looke, I rise againe. (6-10)

The thought of God temporarily raises him from despair and he even attempts to flatter God by professing his complete dependence on divine mercy, but his self-doubts resurface immediately in the next two lines: "But our old subtle foe so tempteth me, / That not one houre I can my selfe, sustaine" (11-12). In the very next couplet, the speaker lays a claim to God's grace, but once again the paradox in the concluding lines fails to convey the assurance of Christian salvation: "Thy Grace may wing me to prevent his art / And thou like Adamant draw mine iron heart" (13-14). The image the reader is left with is that of the speaker's unregenerate "iron heart." The speaker of "Batter my heart" makes a more overt profession of his devotion to God, "dearely'I love you, and would be lov'd faine" (9), but at the same time must confess that he is still wedded to God's enemy.

The speakers in the *Holy Sonnets* finally fail to find the "profits of physicke," or the cure for religious malaise. Unlike the "crown of prayer and praise" woven in the proper devotion of the *La Corona* speaker, the "prayers and flattering speaches" of the *Holy Sonnets'* speakers gain no assurance of salvation. But following the traces of the *pharmakon* metaphor in the language of the early religious poems allows us to anticipate the discursive strategies that Donne later practices so effectively in his pursuit of secular preferment. The language of both flattery and praise that Donne uses to articulate his hopes and disillusionment about his search for political advancement is not different from the language that he uses to dramatize the difficulty of religious belief in the *Holy Sonnets*. The profits of "physicke" in the secular world, he discovered, could mean gaining political employment; the profits of "physicke" in the religious realm, if also found, likewise could have translated into a cure for spiritual disease.

Notes

[1] Professor Shawcross was the respondent to an early version of this essay, which I read at the Sixth Annual Donne Conference in Gulfport, MS, in 1991. I am grateful for his comments, which helped me to clarify my argument. I would also like to thank Terry Sherwood, Michael Schoenfeldt, and other members of the Donne Society for their valuable suggestions as well.

[2] To better understand the context of these discourses, it is worthwhile to review the contemporary religious controversy centering on the issue of the Oath of Allegiance. The Oath, drawn up in May 1601 by Bancroft "for the better discovering and repressing of Popish Recusants," required all Englishmen to

profess unequivocal loyalty to the throne:

> I do further swer that I do from my heart abhor, detest and abjure, as impiou[s] and heretical, this damnable doctrine and position, that princes which be excommunicated or deprived by the Pope may be deposed or murdered by their subjects or any other whatsoever . . . [qtd. in Healy xx]

The oath was written to underscore the conflict between loyalty to Rome and allegiance to the throne of England, and in its reference to the theories of the Spanish Jesuit Mariana, betrays the fear of regicide that was in the air at the time. Mariana rejected the divine nature of a monarch's sovereignty and condoned the deposition and killing of kings who transgressed the limits of their authority, asserting that once the tyranny of a king is ascertained, "tyrannicide is justified in anyone by any means, except poison: and even poison may be used so long as the tyrant is not made to kill himself with it" (qtd. in Coffin 198).

[3] In a recent contribution to discussion of this text, Dennis Flynn argues that there is a parallel between the Cecil-James relationship and the Ignatius-Lucifer relationship.

[4] See, for example, A. J. Smith: "Donne's wife Ann died in August 1617 at the age of thirty-three, after giving birth to their twelfth child" (635). See also Marotti 279 and Aers and Kress 69-70.

Works Cited

Aers, David, and Gunther Kress. "Vexatious Contraries: A Reading of Donne's Poetry." *Literature, Language and Society in England 1580—1680.* Ed. David Aers, Bob Hodge, and Gunther Kress. Totowa, NJ: Barnes and Noble, 1981.

Anglo, Sydney. "More Machiavellian than Machiavel." *John Donne: Essays in Celebration.* Ed. A. J. Smith. London: Methuen, 1972. 349-384.

Carey, John. *John Donne, Life, Mind and Art.* New York: Oxford UP, 1981.

Coffin, Charles Monroe. *John Donne and the New Philosophy.* New York: Humanities P, 1958.

Derrida, Jacques. "Plato's Pharmacy." *Dissemination.* Trans. Barbara Johnson. London: Athlone P, 1981. 63-94.

Flynn, Dennis. "Donne's *Ignatius His Conclave* and Other Libels on Robert Cecil." *JDJ* 6 (1987): 163-184.

Goldberg, Jonathan. *King James I And the Politics of Literature: Jonson, Shakespeare,*

Donne, and Their Contemporaries. Baltimore: Johns Hopkins UP, 1983.

Greenblatt, Stephen. *Renaissance Self-Fashioning: From More to Shakespeare.* Chicago: U of Chicago P, 1980.

Marotti, Arthur. *John Donne, Coterie Poet.* Madison: U of Wisconsin P, 1986.

Parry, Graham. *The Seventeenth Century: The Intellectual and Cultural Context of English Literature, 1603-1700.* Longman Literature in English Series. New York: Longman, 1989.

Patterson, Annabel. "All Donne." *Soliciting Interpretation: Literary Theory and Seventeenth-Century English Poetry.* Ed. Elizabeth D. Harvey and Katharine Eisaman Maus. Chicago: U of Chicago P, 1990. 37-67.

Magnus Pan Mortuus Est: *A Subtextual and Contextual Reading of Donne's "Resurrection, imperfect"*

Kate Gartner Frost

n recent years the study of the theory and history of literature has taken new and radical turns, sometimes throwing light on individual works and entire areas of study hitherto neglected. But the utility of these approaches, particularly those which denigrate authorial intention, to the study of premodern literature is questionable. This essay aims to demonstrate that the gulf between modern and premodern literature can better be bridged if the earlier literature is first examined in the light of its own poetic practice, one which emphasized the poet's intentional craft. If there are some works which have been neglected due to misogyny or cultural discrimination, there are others which remain unexamined because the audience is at a loss to confront authorial artifice.

One such is "Resurrection, imperfect," perhaps the least studied of John Donne's divine poems because it has generally been perceived as an unfinished effort.[1] But "Resurrection, imperfect" is not incomplete. Rather, it is a finished poem concerned with unfinished time. My reading has convinced me that the poem is connected to the liturgy of Holy Saturday and to the subject of the Harrowing of Hell and Christ's consequent "hasting to heaven" through the levels of the cosmos. In shaping his work the poet drew widely and wittily on the Holy Saturday topos as it was manifested in the premodern disciplines of alchemy, cosmology, mythography, and arithmology. Such connections confirm in Donne a deliberateness in subtextual and schematic artifice which critics have hitherto been reluctant to acknowledge. I believe that the reader who diligently follows the rather convoluted historical paths of intellectual and religious ideas which underly "Resurrection, imperfect" will find a new understanding of the poem. Such a reading will disclose not only the familiar poet of complex surfaces but also the artificer who offers entry into the substructures of his learning and thinking.

That artificer has lately received both attention and defense. In its very title, John Shawcross's *Intentionality and the New Traditionalism* articulates the concerns of many Renaissance scholars, particularly students of difficult and obscure premodern poetic texts like "Resurrection, imperfect." While he acknowledges the possibility of a reader's text, Shawcross emphasizes the poet's text, one which depends upon employment of external knowledge and tradition. In this view the poet is a maker, intent on his art, bringing to bear external concerns with language and tradition on the matter of internal experience. In effect, the poet attempts to form reader response by deliberate craft. The resulting artifact presents its creator's vision in forms which attract the reader to the underlying idea of his invention and which elicit admiration for his learning and his facility in composition (Frost 82). Such a paradigm, orchestrated by such elements of craft as language, tone, and form, "predicates an aesthetic distancing of the author, and, in its recognition and appreciation, some aesthetic distancing for the reader" (Shawcross 120). Success, or lack of it, in the endeavor should primarily be attributed to the poet's skill at his craft, although it also lies in the reader's ability to appreciate the result.

In the seventeenth century, success depended as much on the poet's skill in constructing, as on the reader's ability to perceive, structures which rely on building blocks of imagery, language, ideas, and relationships of parts, often themselves dependent on mathematical proportion. To take the reader into the world of the poem, the poet employs liminal devices that include genre and mode, "image patterns and metaphoric communications, numerological concerns, allusions and imitations, contextualizations in history, [and] authorial presence" (120). The resulting artifact is the ideal construction for the ideal reader, neither of which exists, of course, either today or in the seventeenth century. But the post-Romantic reader is much less likely to cross these thresholds, or even to recognize them, than a seventeenth-century predecessor. This is especially true given changes in education and the modern habit of discursive reading, which, governed by perception of the periodic sentence as the dominant unit of meaning, results in a sequential and linear reading experience. Moreover, the dependence on affective stylistics which accompanied the modern period has diminished the reader's ability to treat premodern literature on its own terms. This reader may develop a distorted or partial vision of the didacticism inherent in the poetry, often assuming that the poem is a spontaneous projection of the author's psyche or that it is chiefly to be used to shed light on present concerns.

Understanding a poem like "Resurrection, imperfect" entails habits and skills unfamiliar to the modern reader, for one must subordinate the custom of deriving total meaning from sequential order to an overview of the work that may entail a perception of its schematic structure and the relation of its contexts and subtexts to that structure. Such a reading entails methods of aesthetic distancing and techniques of verbal recognition that the present day reader must work to acquire. To this end, in order to discover what Donne has "said" in "Resurrection, imperfect," I shall examine the discursive surface text in a process of verbal recognition according to the multiple seventeenth-century meanings and connotations of its language. This exploration of primary definitions and their alternatives reveals not specific references to but rather a fabric of association with the poem's exegetical, cosmological, mythographic, and alchemical contexts. Although such a reading will not stand alone, I maintain that, considering the contextual examinations which precede the reading and the discussion of mathematical and liturgical associations which follows it, my reading will open "Resurrection, imperfect" more fully to the late-twentieth-century reader.

Exegetical, Mythographic, Cosmological, *and Alchemical Contexts*

In his sermons Donne gave frequent and eloquent testimony to his belief in the Resurrection. Consider, for example, his sermon delivered Easter 1623:

> God hath given assurance unto all men (saies S. *Paul* at Athens), *In that he hath raised Christ Iesus from the dead.* In this Christ makes up his circle; in this he is truly *Alpha* and *Omega*, His comming in Paradise in a promise, his comming to Judgement in the clouds, are tied together in the Resurrection: And therefore all the Gospell, all our preaching, is contracted to that one text, *To beare witnesse of the Resurrection.* (4: 355)

The passage echoes some of the contextual concerns of "Resurrection, imperfect" which this essay will explore: Christ's triumph over Satan, Death, and Hell; the conflation of the day of Second Coming with the Resurrection; and the circularity of the Redemption as mirrored in his descending and rising course through the universe. The poem's exegetical, mythographic, cosmological, and alchemical contexts reflect these concerns and, I maintain, indicate that Donne's "unfinished" lyric is composed as a witty play on the subject of incomplete Resurrection.

The exegetical context: To my knowledge, no critical appraisal of "Resurrection, imperfect" has explored exegetical commentary on the Crucifixion on Good Friday, the Entombment on Holy Saturday, and the Resurrection which traditionally occurred at that day's midnight. In so doing, scholarly critics have ignored a rich and enlightening body of discourse. Donne had for use an established tradition of scriptural exegesis surrounding these events, particularly that narrating the liberation of the Old Testament saints, commonly termed the Harrowing of Hell. The topos derives ultimately from the fourth-century Gospel of Nicodemus,[2] which presents Christ's harrowing of Hell, when he broke open its gates, bound Satan and his minions, and liberated the Old Testament saints. The story depends on Matthew 27: 51-53 which describes the rending of the Temple veil, the earthquake, and the rising of the dead in Jerusalem. According to legend, the rock of Calvary split, Christ's blood pouring into the fissure which reached down to Hellgate. The commentary on Matthew 27 by Cornelius à Lapide, the sixteenth-century exegete upon whom Donne drew often, throws light on Donne's exploration of the topos in "Resurrection, imperfect," and provides evidence of the accessibility of the *decensus* to the poet.

Lapide's remarks at first glance offer no surprises. The reference to Matthew 27: 51, *et petrae scissae sunt*, describes first the splitting of Calvary rock under the terrible weight of the Cross. Lapide cites St. Ambrose on the significance of the text: the rock signifies the hard hearts of the Jews, an interpretation which can be found in many commentaries. But his gloss ends on an odd note, quoting Eusebius, who himself cites Plutarch:

> Under the reign of Tiberius, near the island of Pax, there was heard a great voice: 'Great Pan is dead.' And therefore there was a great wailing of many voices [which Eusebius interprets as referring to Lucifer], . . . for he so to speak may be called Pan, who, Christ dying, was so to speak, himself dead, because Christ won from him men to himself, and so to speak to life. (506)[3]

Eusebius's conflating of Christ and Pan has, for him, linguistic validity since the Greek word *pammegas* [πάμμεγας], which means "all-great," when it referred to Pan was altered to *Pan megas* [Πὰν μέγας], "great Pan."[4] In his harrowing of Hell, Christ replaced Pan as *pammegas*, filling the universe with his real presence. Eusebius's is a demonic Pan. But Christ, who by virtue of his Resurrection has become the new Lord of the Universe, has conquered the demon Satan, and Hell, ruled by Death which is now no longer inevitable to the sons of Adam, has become instead the womb of their rebirth by virtue of Christ's liberation.[5] Illuminating the darkness of death and lighting up the shadows of the infernal regions, Christ by his descent into the bowels of the earth and his ascent to the *coelum empyreum* changes the old order of nature, over which no longer Pan but Christ now reigns.[6]

The exegetes go to great lengths to explain just how Christ is the new Lord of Nature, concentrating in particular on Ephesians 4: 9-10, which for them verified the descent into hell: "Now that he ascended, what is it but that hee also descended first into the lower parts of the earth? He that descended, is the same also that ascended up far above all heavens, that he might fill all things" (*Quod ascendit, quid est, nisi quia et descendit primum in inferiores partes terrae? qui descendit, ipse est et qui ascendit super omnes caelos ut impleret omnia*). This central text engendered a good deal of discourse concerning just how much of the universe Christ had penetrated and whether he had reached the foundations of Hell. Conflating Limbo and Hell, Lapide affirms that Christ in fact penetrated Hell, then ascended through the aetherial spheres to the *coelum empyreum*, his feet coming to rest on the topmost of the convex cosmic spheres.[7] Indeed, he now extends beyond the *coelum empyreum* into the vacancy beyond:

> Thus that he might fill all, and that he might be lord of the whole universe and that he might extend his law to the universe, over it all even in vacant space, Christ extends his glory and rule. In short, just as he descended to the lowest part of the earth, ascending above all the Saints and above all the heavens, he occupies his throne of glory. (506)

In effect, "by coming to reign over the fullness of the world" Christ became the new All. In this light, Lapide's citation of the Pan myth in his commentary on Matthew falls into place.[8]

The structure of "Resurrection, imperfect" reflects this exegetical context in that it presents an emblem of the universe at the moment of its loss of the demonic Pan and its penetration and filling by Christ. As the last two lines of the poem demonstrate, an understanding of the Pan topos can contribute significantly to its reading. The mythographic tradition reinforces the exegesis in its emphasis on the spiritualization of the cosmos, embodied in the figure of Pan.

The mythographic context: The myth of cosmic Pan has recently been elucidated by Patricia Merivale, who sees it as stemming initially from the schematically allegorical Stoic tradition (itself derived from the *Timaeus* where the term τὸ πᾶν is used to designate the universe) and the earlier Orphic Hymn to Pan. As the tradition evolved from classical through medieval writers, the Orphic Pan became the ruler and soul of the universe (combining with the Stoic "All" which understands Pan's to be an allegory of the body), his goatish lower part associated with the earth, his upper parts with the utmost reaches of the cosmos, particularly with the sun and the firmament (9-10). The conflation of Christ and Pan passed inextricably into Christian Renaissance tradition, so that Pan was not only god of the woods and the fields, but also, his pastoral attributes marginalized, ruler of the very substance of the universe as "Supreme Governor or 'soul' of the world" (9).[9] By Donne's day, manifesting itself most frequently in allusions to Nature and to cosmological unity and harmony, the figure was as well known, if not perhaps as frequently employed, as that of the Arcadian Pan.[10] Alexander Ross, for example, whose *Mystagogus Poeticus* is a gold mine of seventeenth-century mythological lore, accepts the topos without question. "By Pan," he says, "may be meant the universe as the word πᾶν sheweth" (476). Correspondingly, Ross's interpretations have cosmological implications:

> By [Pan's] sheepeheards crooke in one hand may be meant that providence by which the world is guided; by the seven pipes in his other hand is meant the harmonious motion of the seven planets; he is painted also with winges to shew the swiftnesse of the heavens motion. . . . By Pan some understand the Sun, for his hornes signifie the sun beames; and his crooked staffe may shew the Suns oblique motion in the Zodiac, his long beard represents his beames which he casteth downwards as the hornes, his beames which he darteth upward; with these he illuminates, the upper regions, with those, the lower. (476-77)

In Christian terms, Pan's feet were planted in a world of matter, time and mutability, sensuality and imperfection. Similarly, his horns touched the realm of God: being, form, eternal unchanging perfection. He filled the cosmos from its material foundations to its ethereal limits of pure intellection.[11]

The goal of man's yearning lay in the ultimate reality of heaven, which was beyond sensory knowledge. The universe, God's creation, was essentially good, and hence the word πάν, in Latin *omne*, in English "the all," was associated with divine perfection and with Christ. But the jointure between man and God, once so sweet that God had walked with Adam in the Garden, was fractured by the Fall, and the rupture could be repaired only by direct intervention of the divine. Hence the figure of cosmic dominion was the demonic Pan as replaced by Christ at the *decensus*. Both

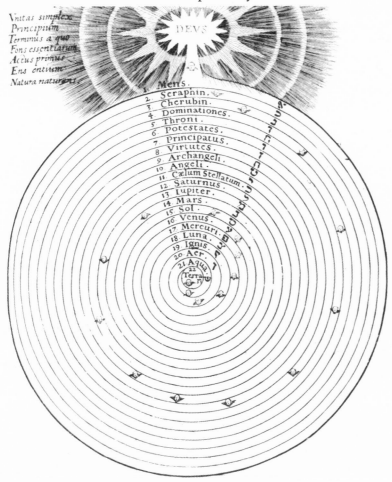

Fig. 1 The levels of the universe. Robert Fludd, Utriusque cosmi . . . historia.

of these Lords of the Universe were closely associated with the mediate Sun, which occupied the point of balance between sense and intellect. In this light, Raymond-Jean Frontain's perception that the two suns of "Resurrection, imperfect" are competitive makes sense, as does his comment that the sun's wound–the eclipse at the Crucifixion–suggests the imperfection of nature as a result of original sin, as opposed to the perfection of supranature which redeemed humankind from that sin and so allows us to 'eclipse' or transcend the natural order of sin and death" (540). When one remembers that sin and death had not always been part of the natural order, the analogy of the fallen world with Pan and of the redeemed cosmos with Christ gains significance. And this significance is strengthened in the light of premodern cosmological theory, which ratifies the evidence of the exegetical and mythographic contexts.

The cosmological context: The universe which Pan filled was finite and stratified. At its center, and hence its lowest point, lay the material, mutable, and imperfect sublunary region of the elements, their strata ranging downward from the ring of fire, through air, water, and earth, to Hell at its center. Above the moon ranged the aetherial world of the planetary spheres, the firmament, the *primum mobile*, and the *coelum empyreum* (the latter often divided into the nine choirs of angels). These strata were visualized in a number of ways: as a division into three, seven, or sometimes fifteen heavens (among other, less prominent schemes), depending on the didactic or poetic intent of the visualizer. That which seems to have the most bearing on "Resurrection, imperfect" counts twenty-three levels from Hell to the *coelum empyreum*. It had ancient roots: the created universe, which ranged from earth through the *primum mobile*, was that bespoken by God at Creation, using the twenty-two letters of the Hebrew alphabet (the twenty-third level of the *coelum empyreum* being beyond human discourse). It was recognized by Dante, for example, who, placing himself and Beatrice at the entry to the sphere of the fixed stars in Canto 22 of the *Paradiso*, is granted there his first sight of Christ (Canto 23). In that same Canto Christ and the Virgin ascend through the *coelum empyreum*. In Donne's own time, Milton, for example, framed the triumphant ascent of Christ through the heavens in twenty-three line blocks of verse (Qvarnström 98-103). The scheme was represented graphically in Robert Fludd's illustration of a twenty-two level material cosmos [Fig. 1].

I shall shortly contend that it is this representation of the cosmos to which "Resurrection, imperfect" structurally refers. The evidence for this contention is to be found not only in the cosmological subtext of the poem, but also in its arithmetical structure, which I shall examine later in this essay, and in its complex alchemical referents. Of the poem's subtexts, the alchemical is at once the most complex and the most revealing. If the reader has followed the contextual evidence I have presented up to this point, particularly the testimony of exegesis, the path through this lore will be marked at least with familiar points.

The alchemical context: The most recent and comprehensive study of Donne's alchemical poetic practice has been made by Eugene Cunnar, who has applied his extensive acquaintance with alchemical lore and language to "Valediction: Forbidding Mourning." Citing Donne's "wide and detailed knowledge of alchemy" (72), Cunnar argues that this knowledge was "much more central to both his intellectual and poetic endeavors than has previously been claimed or demonstrated" (73) and that Donne was, in effect, a spiritual alchemist, an argument with which, in the light of the alchemical subtext of poems like the *Anniversaries*, "Loves Alchemy," and "A Nocturnall upon S. Lucies Day" among others, I find it difficult to disagree. But in the case of "Resurrection, imperfect," despite the poem's obvious alchemical references, critical attention of like caliber has been almost completely lacking. Frontain perhaps rightly ascribes this neglect to the perception of the lyric as an unfinished effort (540), a perception undercut however by the poem's alchemical references.

There is good reason for exploring the alchemical context of "Resurrection, imperfect," for the exegetical and cosmological frameworks which I have already discussed are strongly echoed in the alchemical process.[12] The basic assumption of alchemy was that all matter was unified, and, being possessed of a permanent common soul, was capable of transmutation from its primary form through higher and higher forms to perfection. The alchemist produced this transmutation from the lower to the higher, purifying the flawed (the adept would say "diseased") metals by ridding them of their superfluity of sulphur, which was the fiery impurity in base matter (Holmyard 143). The agent of this transmutation–what we would today call a catalyst–was the medicinal Philosopher's Stone, which cured "diseased" metals and enabled them to rise on the scale of mineral perfection to the element of gold.

Although perfection of the physical was the ancient aim of the opus, by Donne's day the process was more generally applied to the perfection of the human soul, in what is called spiritual or esoteric alchemy. The spiritual adept moved from a state of putrefaction (the *nigredo*) to purity. The process was likened to the Redemption, when at the Resurrection Christ moved up through levels of the cosmos from Hell to Paradise and when at the Second Coming he would descend through those same levels, mirroring the process of volatility and fixation within the orb of the alembic. It is not surprising then that the Harrowing of Hell should have a parallel in the alchemical art, and wide reading in the literature of alchemy reveals the language of the art and of the *discursus* to be organically intermingled.[13] A passage from *An Open Entrance to the Closed Palace of the King*, for example, closely identifies the *decensus/ascensus* motif with the alchemical opus:

> Let your delicate substance remain at the bottom, which is the womb of conception, in the sure hope that after the time appointed by the Creator for this Operation, the spirit will arise in a glorified state, and glorify its body–that it will ascend and be gently circulated from the centre to the heavens, then descend to the centre from the heavens, and take to itself the power of things above and things below. (Waite 2: 192)

The ultimate aim of the opus was the perfection of the subject in a state of incorruptibility and harmony. A figure of this harmony was Great Pan, who, as I have shown, also played a mythographic role in the concept of cosmic order. In the allegorical language of the alchemical art,[14] certain terms stood for chemicals used in the process: the Green Lion, for example, was the compound we now know as ferrous sulphate, used to prepare oil of vitriol (sulphuric acid) a dissolvent of the initial earthy solids (Nicholl 4). Figure 2, a representation of ammonium chloride (in Middle English *sal harmoniak*) recognizably is Pan. Represented variously by a six, seven, or eight-pointed star, it was one of the three basic principles of the Great Work.[15] Salt was the "Soul" of the opus: "Therefore our great Teachers say that ... this fire unites these three things, namely, the Body, Spirit, and Soul,

Fig. 2 Pan as sal harmonica. Anon., 14th century, Biblioteca Mediceo-Laurenziana, Florence, Ms. Ashburn 1166, f.18.

or Sun, Mercury and Salt" (Waite 1: 199). Metaphorically it was associated with birth and resurrection: "He who works without salt will never raise dead bodies" and "the salt Alkali (called by the Sages salt of Ammonia, or vegetable salt) is hidden in the womb of Magnesia" (Waite 2: 107). Moreover, it was associated with the liberation from Hell: "it is the Key which opens the infernal prison house, where sulphur lies in bonds" (Waite 2: 143). All of these associations had a basis in the practical alchemical process, for sal ammonia was a principal agent of the ascent/descent pattern known as alchemical volatility:

> The Salt of the Sages: [its] effect . . . is to fix or volatilize, according as it is prepared and used [and] if extracted by itself without any addition, has power to render all metals volatile by dissolution and putrefaction, and to dissolve quick or liquid silver into the true mercury. (Waite 1: 354-55)

The conflation of Pan with Christ thus takes on an alchemical sense here, for the harmonizing salt was associated with the "mercurial fire" located at the center of the earth. Cunnar describes the effect of its release which

> purified an impure earth or, in terms of man, the soul. This internal mercurial fire was often equated by the alchemists with Christ, his harrowing of hell and overcoming of death, and his resurrection as the *lapis*. The mercurial fire was located at the center of the earth and was considered a point symbolic of God. (88-89)

As Pan, the harmonizing salt of alchemy, in his demonic form spans the cosmos from hell through the upper spheres in an order of progressive immateriality, so Christ, in the spiritual alchemy of the soul, is the mercurial fire that, harrowing Hell, reclaimed the universe at its very center and bound Satan and his minions.

Harmony, proportion, and gradation were essential to the success of the alchemical endeavor. A misstep, a procedure taken out of order, a hurrying of the stages, and suddenly "the potte to breaketh and farewel all is go," as Chaucer's Canon's Yeoman ruefully informs us. But how was one to know whether or not the work was not "go" but successful? The end of the work was determined by very nonscientific methods: by taste (often fatal), by smell (also sometimes fatal, or at least injurious or frightening), or, most often, by perception of color. Generally the process developed in stages from black to white to red. The result of heating in the alembic was usually an oxidized black substance,[16] which was then re-moved from the alembic, pulverized, and albified–that is, washed until it had lost its black color. As always, writers on alchemy could not resist the Christological comparison:

> We may also see an analogy to Christ in the fact that . . . when at length He had given up the ghost, and all the strength forsook His body, so that He went down to the parts below the earth, even there He was pre-served, refreshed, and filled with the quickening power of the eternal Deity, and thus, by the reunion of His spirit with his dead body, quick-ened, raised from the dead, lifted up into heaven, and appointed Lord and King of all. (Waite 1: 102)

By the power of his blood, shed at Calvary for our sins, Christ "changes us imperfect men [and] is a marvellous medicine for all our diseases"; he is, in effect, the whitening tincture (1: 103).[17] This brings us directly to the problematical lines of "Resurrection, imperfect": "Hee was all gold when he lay downe, but rose / All tincture." In the threefold transmutative process the base matter was gradually albified by heating, dissolution, and coction. From the fire emerged the tincture, a white powder, often called the Philosopher's Gold, which imparts its whiteness to everything it is mixed with, purifying and transmuting. In spiritual alchemy, the stage of spiritual gold was achieved by union with Christ, the white tincture.

The stress on color change during the alchemical process throws light on Donne's puzzling lines. In the exegetical tradition, from the wounds and the pierced side of Christ flowed the stream of blood down the cleft of Golgotha to Hell itself. The bloodless body of Christ laid in the grave was likened to the white gold of the process, spiritual now and volatile. By descending to Hell and, like the volatile tincture, ascending to Paradise, Christ laid claim to his Lordship of the Universe. Rising on the third day, "a better sun," he became the red tincture, the Philosopher's Stone, able to multiply his perfection—in Donne's words, to transmute "Leaden and iron wills," "to make even sinful flesh like his." The author of *The Sophic Hydrolith* witnesses the role of Christ as tincture:

> For, as the Philosophical Stone becomes joined to other metals by means of its tincture and enters into an indissoluble union with them, so Christ, our Head, is in constant vital communion with all His members through the ruby tincture of His Blood, and compacts His whole Body into a

242

perfect spiritual building which after God is created in righteousness and true holiness. (Waite 1: 104-05)

Ruth Falk has described Donne's tincture as the "quintessence" (12-14), and Frontain has connected it to the poem's cosmology:

The "old Sun" is incapable of enlightening the human heart, which the "better Sun" harrows even as he did Hell, the light of his grace reducing the darkness of sin until, spiritually converted, men struggle to control their sinful impulses and, spiritually rarified, become more like Christ himself. . . . [T]he "old Sun" in its natural resurrection is but an imperfect copy of the supranatural one, the paradigm of all resurrections. (54)

Frontain's connection is logical and feasible. So too are connections of the alchemical analogy with the poem's exegetical, mythographic, and cosmological contexts. It remains, however, to discover whether the text of the poem confirms these logical and feasible connections. And to the discursive text of Donne's "Resurrection, imperfect" I now turn. A close reading of the poem will, I maintain, ratify the testimony of the contexts, revealing a poem concerned with Christ's triumph over the fallen universe and the sinful human heart.

A Contextual Reading of "Resurrection, Imperfect"

To begin, let us consider the poem's overt structure: a lyric of twenty-two iambic pentameter lines, in a mixture of closed- and open-rimed couplets. The poem's scansion, as usual with Donne, is complex, but it does consist of twenty-two decasyllabic lines. The English is followed by the Latin tag *Desunt caetera*–a trochee (or a spondee) and a dactyl. For the reader who accepts the first foot as a trochee, the effect is a reversal of the poem's meter; for the reader who takes it as a spondee, the effect, more subtle, is to draw attention to the poem's possible circularity, for it opens with a spondee: "Sleep, sleep." That this tag is an integral part of the lyric, or for that matter is even Donne's own composition, is open to debate, and indeed is a central concern of this essay. The manuscript evidence is inconclusive. Included in some manuscripts–the Dolau Cothi, for example–it is excluded in others, among them Puckering, Denigh, and, as Shawcross indicates, Trinity College Dublin and O'Flaherty (*Complete Poetry* 487). Further enlightenment may be forthcoming with the imminent publication of the Donne *Variorum*. Hence acceptance of the tag as integral to the poem's structure is uncertain on textual grounds alone, pending more complete examination of textual evidence. Rather, I believe the contexts which I have discussed in this essay, ratified by the internal evidence produced by an exploration of the poem's linguistic ramifications and by its mathematical structure and liturgical associations, will indicate that the appearance of incompleteness is deliberate and that the Latin tag is a final twist of Donne's wit.

Unlike many of Donne's verses, the surface text of "Resurrection, imperfect" presents no overly difficult problems for the reader. To paraphrase:

> Stay asleep, Sun. You cannot as yet have recovered from your wound of last Friday. Sleep, the world can handle your delay in rising because a better Sun/Son has already arisen today. This Sun, not content like you merely to irradiate the earth's surface, has lighted hell, making its fires grow pale, as your light does ours. The body of this Sun, which walked on earth, is now quickly making its way to heaven, that He might fill all levels of the universe and for these three days become a mine. He was perfect gold when he lay down in the grave, but rose an alchemical tincture, and does not just influence lazy or stubborn wills to do good, but has the power to transform even carnal sinners into his likeness. An overly credulous person who, believing that the soul could be perceived leaving the body, at this grave had seen this body coming out of its shroud, would correctly have thought this body to be a soul, if not of a man, then of all creation. *The rest is lacking.*

Even a literal paraphrase of "Resurrection, imperfect" echoes the poem's contextual concerns: the wounded sun recalls the exegetical commentary on Matthew 27: 51-53. Its replacement by the "better sun" recalls the *descensus*. The mine, the tincture, and the perception of Christ's body as transparent are alchemical references. And the poem's final English statement emphasizes "all creation." But the language of the poem offers us much more, particularly as it relates to the subjects of impregnation and filling, birth and rebirth, body and carnality, harmony and music, cosmological levels and ascent, and arithmetical significance and proportion. Indeed, much of the its language directly parallels that of the exegetes and the alchemical writers.

With these echoes and parallels in mind, I present here six groups of words, unpinned from the poem's text, as they relate to the contextual concerns which I have discussed.

The language of filling, impregnation, birth, rebirth: Consider Ephesians

4: 9-10, "Now that he ascended, what is it but that hee also descended first into the lower parts of the earth? He that descended is the same also that ascended by far above all heavens, that he might fill all things" (*Quod ascendit, quid est, nisi quia et descendit primum in inferiores partes terrae? qui descendit, ipse est et qui ascendit super omnes caelos ut impleret omnia*). This passage, which engendered so much commentary on Christ's descent and ascent through the universe, ends with a most interesting verb: *impleret–* from *implere*, which, according to the *Oxford Latin Dictionary*, means, among other things, "to fill (a space, a container)"; "to fill out, fatten"; "to fulfill, satisfy"; "to make pregnant." Hence, Christ's filling of the universe is one of conjunction and engenderment, birth and rebirth; in his conquering of Death and Satan he has become new Lord of the Universe, and Hell has become a womb for rebirth of the Old Testament dead. One remembers Donne's Whitsunday 1623 Sermon: "That which had power to open Heaven in his descent hither, and to open hell, in his descent thither, to open the wombe of the Virgin in his Incarnation, and the wombe of the Earth in his Resurrection" (*Sermons* 5: 81).

"Resurrection, imperfect" is replete with such imagery. Literally the line "that he might allow / Himselfe unto all stations, and fill all" repeats the matter of Ephesians. But other language connotes a wide range of filling, in the sense of filling a space or vessel, recalling the alchemical process both in its practice and in its metaphorical association with sexual conjunction. There are exegetical associations as well, recalling Christ's wound from which issued the blood filling the fissure of Calvary. Let us begin with the language of filling vessels, as for example line 2: "As yet, the wound thou took'st on Friday last." The expected adverbial use of "yet" according to the *Oxford English Dictionary* is: "hitherto, up to this time, . . . implying expectation or recognized possibility of coming change." But in the sixteenth century, "yet" also took a verbal form: "to pour, shed, infuse"; "to gush forth in a stream, as water, tears, blood"; and, metallurgically, "to (form) an object by running molten metal in a mould; to found," and "to melt down metal." In the line, "yet" is associated with a Friday wound which "thou took'st." "Took," of course, is a past tense of the verb "take," but it is also an obsolete form of "tuck" in a penetrative sense, which was "a blow, a stroke, a tap," and, more concretely, an actual weapon, "a thrusting sword, a rapier." In the light of the exegesis, the "fill all" of line 11 takes on the sense of Ephesians, when we realize that "to fill" is "to pour out (as in filling a vessel)," but also is "to impregnate."

Another verb in proximity to "fill all," which can be associated in a bawdy sense with impregnation, is the "lay" of line 13: "Hee was all gold when he lay down." Of course, as past tense of "lie," the word makes perfect sense, but additional antique meanings strengthen its connections with the contexts. To lay is "to bring low, throw down, overthrow, destroy," "to deposit in the grave; to bury," "to bring to a recumbent position" (as perhaps, in an epithalamic sense, to lay the bride), and even "to bring to bed of a child." All these definitions echo the death, copulation, and birth allusions of the exegesis and the alchemical process. Line 19's "Goe from a body," reflects the same subtle connections: "Go," when spoken of a female, means "To pass (a specified period) in gestation: to be pregnant"; it also means to be "dead; departed from life." So too are the associations of "issue" (line 20): obviously, "offspring, progeny," but also, employed as a verb: "to give birth to."

The language of body, carnality: The entire subject of the *decensus/ascensus*, whether viewed exegetically, mythographically and cosmologically (one remembers Pan as an allegory of the cosmic body in its ascent from gross sensuality to intellectuality), or alchemically in the emphasis on the conjugal union of sulphur and mercury and the putrefaction of the corporeal *material prima*, is intimately joined to flesh and carnality. The account of Matthew and its commentaries emphasize the body of Christ, its wounds and its blood.

The word "body" itself occurs four times in the poem. Its definitions have multiple associations with theology ("the Church of which Christ is the head"), with music ("the resonance box of a musical instrument"), with alchemy ("the vessel in which a substance to be distilled is placed, a retort; a phrase of the astro-alchemists, applied to the seven 'bodies celestial'"), and with cosmology ("the seven bodies terrestial, the seven ancient metals answering to the seven 'heavenly bodies,' that is, the sun, moon, and five old planets"). In the poem the word is associated first, in line 9, with Christ's bodily presence on earth and then, in line 21, is juxtaposed with his soul. In lines 19-20, however, it is associated with the reproductive language cited above: "Goe" and "issuing." Lines 15-16 contain "carnal" references drawn from the vocabulary of Renaissance bawdry: "wills" and "make" and "whole" (taken as wordplay) (Partridge, 143-44, 216, 218). In line 16, the word "flesh" itself appears as sinful flesh transmuted by Christ into his essence.

The language of music and harmony: One of the aims of this essay is to elucidate the emphasis on harmony in the contexts I have examined–Pan as "sal harmoniack," the cosmos as musical scale, and Christ's ascent through it from Hell to the *coelum empyreum*, even the practical application of the conjugal harmony of alchemy, as for example, in the astrological music of Claude Le Jeune and the alchemical music of Michael Maier.[18] Thomas Norton in his *Ordinall of Alchemy* instructed the adept specifically to base the opus on music:

> Combine your elements musically, for two reasons: first, on account of melody, which is based on its own proper harmonies. Join them according to the rules which obtain in music in the proportions which produce musical consonance; for these musical proportions closely resemble the true proportions of Alchemy, at least, as far as the more general aspects of our Art are concerned. (Waite 2: 41)

In his recent study, *Music in Renaissance Magic*, Gary Tomlinson has demonstrated what he calls, following Michel Foucault, the "archeology" of music as it pervaded the magical cosmos. Although he does not touch generally on the subject of alchemy, he reminds us of the ancient association of the cosmic levels with musical tones and cites texts from Agrippa and Ficino which envision the cosmos as monochord and the spirit of man, connected intimately to the harmonic levels of the cosmos, as the vehicle of the soul (61; 106).

The words in the poem associated with music (as "body" above) can refer either to musical instruments or to the techniques of playing them: "rose," in its present tense "an increase in musical pitch or volume," or, as a noun, "the ornamental device inserted in the sound-hole or table of guitar-like instruments." Or they reflect musical rhythm, particularly a pause or sustained note, as in "beare," "stay", and "wait" (line 3), and "dwell" (line 5). Moreover, "rest" appears twice, first on line 3 and again, if one accepts the poem's Latin tag as play of wit, in the English translation of "*caetera*" (according to the *Oxford Latin Dictionary*, from "*ceterus*" "the rest, the remaining part"). Less obvious are possible puns: "soule"/sol (lines 18, 21), "may"/mi (line 3). And one remembers that music generally is noted on a "sheet" (line 20).

*The language of the cosmos:*The various contexts I have presented all relate widely and deeply to cosmological lore, with emphasis on ascent in stages, the pattern of descent as neccessary for ascent, and the movement from carnality to intellectuality in the universe, stabilized by the centric position of the sun. Much of the cosmic allusion in "Resurrection, imperfect" perceptibly reflects these concerns, as with the opening reference to the sun, its repetition perhaps forecasting the division into two suns later in the lyric (and for those taken by Donne's predilection for intricate punning, the use in lines 18 and 21 of "soule," and in line 3 of "wait," used astronomically to refer to the solstice); the references to world, earth, hell, heaven. Other linguistic references are not so obvious to the first glance: "repast," "hasting," and "stations" (astrologically, the apparent standing still of a planet at its apogee or perigee) reiterate the *decensus/ascensus* motif.

The language directly reflecting exegesis and alchemy: Donne's use of the alchemical term "tincture" in "Resurrection imperfect" drew the attention of three critical readers more than fifty years ago, but unfortunately the matter was dropped thereafter.[19] Had they been more versed in "occult" lore, they would have noted more than a single use of alchemical terms. I have already observed the Sun/Son wordplay, but, of course, the "sun" is the ancient alchemical symbol of gold itself. "Repast" of line 1, can mean "having passed beyond," or even "a meal or feast" (and here one thinks of the poem's references to the body of Christ; further references to carnality occur in the use of "presence" on line 8, and even on line 19 of "sepulcher," which could still in Donne's day refer to the church architectural feature for "burial of the reserved sacrament or Real Presence"). The word "repast" was used by Donne himself in this poem, say the editors of the *Oxford English Dictionary*, in the sense of "repair" or "recovery"–a function, one remembers, of the tincture. Others include "yet" (line 12), as we have seen a metallurgic term; "[Hell's] darke fires" (line 7), "the universal solvent of the alchemists"; "pale" (line 8), "to impart a whitish appearance"; "body", as above, "a chemical retort"; "minerall," "a mine," and (here a specific alchemical term) "one of the three varieties of the philosopher's stone"; "tincture" (line 14); "leaden" and "iron" (line 15). Reflecting exegesis in its emphasis on "one" and "all" ("Pan, they say is Christ, for Pan [Πᾶν] is Greek, the same word as *omne*; Christ moreover who is God, is all goodness and *all*, equally "my God and my all" [Lapide 506]), we find "all" (lines 5, 11, [miner*all*] 13, 14);" "one" (lines 17, 18"); "soule"/sole (lines 8, 21), "whole" (line 22).

The language of numerical proportion: The growing body of evidence for Donne's use of arithmetical structures in his poems is generally derived from analysis of numerical substructures in his works, and such an analysis follows. However, I shall attempt first to identify within this short lyric the fabric of language which has connection to numerical structures within the poem itself. My original contention, arrived at some years ago in an investigation of the arithmological structures in Donne's *Devotions Upon Emergent Occasions*, was that "Resurrection, imperfect" embodied structurally a reflection of the twenty-odd levels of the universe discussed above. However, my present reading has revealed that many of the words of Donne's poem in themselves or by wordplay refer to numbers and proportion. I shall list them in the order in which they first occur: "on"/one (lines 2, 6, 9); "alone"/all one (line 14); "to"/two (lines 4, 5, 10, 15); "unto"/one-two (line 11); "three" (line 12); "for"/four, "before"/be-four (lines 4, 12); "not"/naught (lines 1, 5, 22); "have"/halve (lines 1, 9); "even" (line 16); "man"/mean (line 22). These numbers range from zero, one through four, and variants like halves, all, and whole (which, an admitted stretch, can be visualized as a zero). Interestingly, they generally do not go beyond the number four, the number of materiality.[20] If one allows these verbal correspondences then Donne has in effect limited his poem to the mutable human experience.

I wish here to draw attention to the emphasis on ones and twos in the poem. I have dealt with this emphasis elsewhere (Frost 154-57) and here present my thoughts in condensed form. The source is Augustine's commentary on Luke 13 in *De Trinitate* where he emphasizes the numerical ratio of the single to the double which signified the relationship between the single death of Christ to mankind's double death in soul and body: "On this double death of ours our Saviour bestowed His own single death; and to cause both our resurrections, He appointed beforehand and set forth in mystery and type his own resurrection" (891). The ratio was important in harmony (signifying the diapason or octave) and appears in the musical notation and rhythmic figuration of early Gregorian chant.[21] If one accepts this one/two fabric, one should bear in mind as well the exegesis on Ephesians, which featured Christ's rising from earth to take his place with the Father in the *coelum empyreum*, leading with him the souls of the dead.

The Arithmetical Subtext

While the linguistic fabric of Donne's poem reflects, sometimes directly but more often indirectly, the concerns of this essay, it provides no definitive demonstration of my thesis that "Resurrection, imperfect" is a complete lyric, mirroring the structure of the Christ-filled cosmos, finite and stratified, from Hell at its lowest point, through the mutable and imperfect sublunary region of the elements, ranging above it through the aetherial world of the planetary spheres, the firmament, the *primum mobile*, the nine choirs of angels, and finally reaching the *coelum empyreum*. I think, however, that examination of the poem's structure in the light of the arithmological tradition will ratify my contention. Admittedly I have cooked up a kind of word stew in the paragraphs above, one which will provide nourishment primarily for those familiar with premodern language play. However, to temper the concoction for recent students of literature (and of literary theory), I shall now examine, in addition to what Donne said in "Resurrection, imperfect," what he did *not* say in the discursive text, but left for the reader's discovery.

Let us first ask this question: does the poem reflect structurally the contexts I have discussed? To answer this requires first entering the danger zone of Donne's metrical scansion, a foray which may merit opprobrium both from Ben Jonson and the reader. Nevertheless, consider the poem's actual form: twenty-two English decasyllabic lines totalling 220 syllables. (If accepted as part of the poem, the Latin tag, a five-syllable line–a spondee or trochee plus a dactyl–adds five units to the total count.) At the center of the poem the couplet which forms lines 11 and 12 ("Himselfe unto all stations, and fill all, / For these three daies become a minerall") contains verbal allusions to the first four numbers: "unto"– one, two, and "for"–four, "three." Moreover this couplet ends in the exact rime "all." That the numbers four and three are reversed is perhaps significant, for the three of divinity by virtue of Christ's taking his place with the Father has overcome the four of materiality. But perhaps my reading grows too precious here–although I would not put it past Donne, given his intricate mind, to have constructed just such a witty center to the poem.[22]

In fact, he had done it before–that is, if his *Devotions* predate "Resurrection, imperfect," which we presently have no means to ascertain as there is no evidence whether or not Donne's poem postdates 1624. But, as I have shown elsewhere, he formed in this late prose work an extremely witty and complex structure based on the numbers twenty-two and twenty-three, the same numbers which concern him here (Frost 106-60). Based on his number structure in the *Devotions*, I would like to look at possible implications for "Resurrection, imperfect." The number twenty-two, reflected in the poem's English line count, was associated with, not only the levels of the cosmos, but with the human body and the virtue of temperance which brought it into harmony with the cosmos. And the four elements of the human body in turn affected the workings of the soul, so that the connection of spiritual well being with the workings of the universe was very real. The balancing of the humors brought the individual into harmony with the universe (115-17). The number twenty-three, reflected in the poem's line count if one includes the Latin tag, in addition to its association with the cosmic levels, also, among other multiple connections, alluded to the last hour (what we, with our twelve-hour clocks call "the eleventh hour") of the day, the hour before midnight.

In Donne's time it was associated with the Second Coming and, in the hexaemeral tradition, with the moment at the end of the seventh age when Christians awaited day twenty-four, the eighth age of eternity, sometimes termed "the rapture" (130-31). These represented a series of "short time" structural motifs employed by sixteenth- and seventeenth-century poets, most notably Spenser (Hieatt). But the Latin tag, which must be admitted under this scheme, proposes a final turn of wit: for the writer and the reader remain confined still to the twenty-third line, to their mutable sinful worlds where they must call for the risen Christ, the healing tincture. *Desunt caetera* indeed: the rest, eternal rest, is lacking.

Liturgical context

In this essay, despite what might be interpreted as an overly exhaustive examination of the poem's contextual and subtextual concerns, I have not thus far confronted its liturgical implications. When Frontain discusses the problem of the two suns in the poem, he finds that "the 'old Sun' has been eclipsed in strength and vigor by a 'better Sun' . . . youthful and more vigorous [which] actually rose before the elderly planet on Easter Sunday morning" (541). But, as Lapide's gloss on Matthew stresses, Christ rose from Hell to Paradise *body and soul* that he might "fill all." I would suggest, as my final gloss in this essay, that "Resurrection, imperfect" is a poem for Holy Saturday, a poem for Easter vigil. The speaker awaits in the moments before midnight the arrival of an important feast. Those familiar with the traditional Holy Saturday ritual will recognize in the liturgy of that vigil the concerns with which this essay and Donne's poem have been involved.

Imagine Christians assembled on Easter eve: the church void, without light, its altars stripped and icons veiled, its music stilled, and, the Real Presence removed, its doors open to the winds, Christ absent. Among the congregation gathered outside the church are those to be baptised (like the tincture clad in white) and believers who will renew their vows. There the new fire (like the mercurial fire which, harrowing Hell, reclaimed the universe at its very center) is struck from material flint, and the Paschal candle which represents the risen body of Christ, inscribed with his name and with incense grains marking his bleeding wounds, ignited. This candle is carried alone into the darkness of the vacated and hence Godforsaken body of the church (made much more significant if one remembers the ancient architectural patterning of the Christian church after the "body" of God). Reaching the baptistry, the candle is plunged into the newly filled font—an image which conflates the alchemical, exegetical, and carnal images of the subtexts of Donne's poem. The body of the church, structure and membership, begins to be illuminated by this "Christal" light as the flame is passed from person to person. But there is yet no music–the church has been silent since Friday, liturgical signals conveyed by wooden clappers, indicating the absence of the harmonizing Christ from the world. The congregation, like the "whole" of "Resurrection, imperfect," stands awaiting the moment of the Resurrection at midnight, when Christ will be proclaimed as risen and, church bells ringing and music playing, the Christian community will proclaim him as new Lord of the Universe. Like the Old Testament saints so long ago in Hell, the congregation expects their liberation from Satan, Death, and Hell.

This is my conclusion : "Resurrection, imperfect" is a poem of unfinished time. But time in this poem, although it may be perceived as short, is not static. Rather, the speaker and, if the poet has been successful in his craft, the reader progress with Christ from hell up through the cosmos, Christ's body "now / Hasting to Heaven," and they end, presumably, at the Resurrection with Christ's body "issuing from the sheet." The poem stresses that the overly credulous believer, thinking to have seen Christ's "Soule . . . goe from [his] body" is in error: the body seen is "a soule, / . . . of the whole." The whole is Christ risen, body and soul, reclaiming the universe from the demonic Pan and offering to the Christian the same pattern of ascent offered by the exegetes, alchemists, and mythographers, which would follow that of the Old Testament saints liberated from Hell by his Resurrection. In the end speaker and reader face midnight; at the twenty-third hour as the poem ends on the tag *"Desunt caetera"* on line twenty-three, they await their own Resurrection at the Second Coming, as must all believers.

Notes

[1] The distinguished editor of Donne in whose honor I write begins his comments on "Resurrection, imperfect" with the straightforward statement: "The

title refers to the fact that the poem is incomplete" (*Complete Poetry* 353). I hope that I pay Professor Shawcross the compliment of disagreement when I dispute his first note on the poem. My disagreement stems from his gloss on the final English word of the poem: "*whole*: since God is all: see 1 Corinthians 15: 28: 'And when all things shall be subdued unto him, then shall the Son also himself be subject unto him that put all things under him, that God may be all in all.'" I contend that the tension between the supposed imperfection of the poem's form and its stress on Christ as principle of unifying harmony–a stress recognized by the Shawcross note–forms a crux on which the poem's integrity depends.

[2] This in its complete form consists of two parts: the *Acta Pilati* and the *Decensus Christi ad Inferos* which seem to have originated independently at different times, with the *Decensus* the older, perhaps as early as the second or third century, the *Acta* from the late fourth, early fifth (Hulme lxi-lxii). Although the *decensus* has no primary basis in canonical scripture, theological disputes between eastern and western theologians gave rise to intense interest in the subject, and the descent into Hell was formally incorporated into the creed in the middle of the fourth century. Thereafter it became common property of the Christian community, theologian and poet alike. An essential and very popular element of the medieval drama, especially in the Easter cycle mysteries, the subject was the focus of individual plays and scenes within plays, remaining popular until the assault of the Reformation, particularly in England. In England also it could be found frequently in homilies and saints' lives (Hennecke-Schneemelcher lxvii).

[3] Plutarch's elegant narration is worth a read. Epitherses, his grammar teacher, on a voyage to Italy

> embarked on a ship carrying freight and many passengers. It was already evening when, near the Echinodes Islands, the wind dropped, and the ship drifted near Paxi. Almost everybody was awake, and a good many had not finished their after-dinner wine. Suddenly from the island of Paxi was heard the voice of someone loudly calling Thamus, so that all were amazed. Thamus was an Egyptian pilot, not known by name even to many on board. Twice he was called and made no reply, but the third time he answered; and the caller, raising his voice, said, 'When you come opposite to Palodes, announce that Great Pan is dead.' On hearing this, all, said Epithereses, were astounded and reasoned among themselves whether it were better to carry out the order or to refuse to meddle and let the matter go. Under the circumstances Thamus made up his mind that if there should be a breeze, he would sail past and keep quiet, but with no wind and a smooth sea about the place he would announce what he had heard. So, when he came opposite Palodes,

and there was neither wind nor wave, Thamus from the stern, looking toward the land, said the words as he had heard them: 'Great Pan is dead.' Even before he had finished there was a cry of great lamentation, not of one person, but of many, mingled with exclamations of amazement. As many persons were on the vessel, the story was soon spread abroad in Rome, and Thamus was sent for by Tiberius Caesar. Tiberius became so convinced of the truth of the story that he caused an inquiry and investigation to be made about Pan. (5: 401, 403)

That the event occurred in the reign of Tiberius, under whose rule Christ died, lent credence to the legend for Christians, who adapted it to their own ends.

⁴ Says Eusebius: "So far Plutarch. But it is important to observe the time at which he says that the death of the daemon took place. For it was the time of Tiberius, in which our Saviour, making His sojourn among men, is recorded to have been ridding human life from daemons of every kind" (506). Lapide points to agreement by other commentators, citing the sixteenth-century Portugese exegete Barradius: "Pan, they say is Christ, for Pan [Παν] is Greek, the same word as *omne*; Christ moreover who is God, is all goodness and *all*, equally "my God and my all"; the demons deplore his death, because by him through his death their dominion over the earth is destroyed" (506).

⁵ This topos was configured over a long course' of time by the exegetes, beginning with commentary on Matthew 27 and continuing with glosses on a series of prooftexts including, for example: Isaiah 42: 7; Hosea 6: 2, 13: 14; Ephesians 4: 9-10; Hebrews 11: 1; Phillipians 3: 21; 1 Peter 3: 19, 4: 6.

⁶ Donne acknowledges this tradition in a Trinity Sunday Sermon:

> For, *Mutare naturam, nisi qui Dominus naturae est, non potest*: Whosoever is able to change the course of nature, is the Lord of nature; And he that is so, made it; and he that made it, that created it, is God. Nay, *Plus est*, it is more to change the course of Nature, then to make it; for, in the Creation, there was no reluctation of the Creature, for there was no Creature, but to divert Nature out of her setled course, is a conquest upon a resisting adversary, and powerfull in a prescription. (3: 295)

Again, on Whitsunday, possibly in 1623:

> That which had power to open Heaven in his descent hither, and to open hell in his descent thither, to open the wombe of the Virgin in his Incarnation, and the wombe of the Earth in his Resurrection, that which could change the frame of Nature in Miracles . . . cannot be meerely,

absolutely nothing, but the greatest thing that can be conceived. (5: 81)

These passages reverberate with the language of the *decensus* and more particularly with the language of the exegetes: Christ is the new Lord of Nature, he emerges from a second womb at his Resurrection, he has conquered the adversary.

[7] Lapide affirms that the descent is an article of faith, affirmed in the Creed. "Christ," he says,

> ascended most high above all the heavens who lowered himself most deeply and descended to the deep parts of the earth, certainly to hell, and hence he filled the heights and the depths, and in consequence, the middle also and so all: for if Christ had not descended to the Fathers in limbo, [he would not have liberated] the foremost part of the Church, all the thousands of Saints, all who from Adam up to Christ had lived for four thousand years; and therefore he would not have filled all, as the Apostle maintains. (506)

Lapide joins the debate as to whether the descent and ascent were accomplished in body and in spirit. He also poses the questions whether Christ actually penetrated the depths of Hell, and where the progress ended, that is, whether *ascendit super omnes caelos* refers to the topmost sphere of the Ptolemaic universe, to the *coelum empyreum*, or even to the vacant area beyond. In answering, he maintains that the body of Christ truly entered the depths and truly ascended above the heavens (*Christi corpus est, quia in illis est spatiis vacuis*), for although limited in the material universe by dimension, form, and volume, it was not so limited above the material cosmos.

[8] Moreover, he adds a comment which would be intriguing to Donne, concerned as he was with Christian unity: the lesson for Christians in the *decensus/ascensus* is that ascent alone leads to pride, the destroyer of Christian unity. For the Church to be one it must follow Christ, the new All, in first descending through the virtue of humility (506).

[9] Hence, Paulus Marsus, in his late fifteenth-century commentary on Ovid's *Fasti* writes:

> Now what does Pan mean, if not all. Thus the lord of all and of universal nature had died. . . . Truly we are dealing with the Pan of whom better [is said] by Theodosius [Macrobius] when he says [he is] not the lord of the woods, but the ruler of the material substance of the universe. . . . The strength of whose nature forms the essence of universal bodies whether

they are divine or earthly. . . . It is proper for this name to refer to the Sun. (Merivale 13)

[10] References to the Pan topos by Donne's contemporaries are widespread and various. For example: Bacon, *De sapientia Veterum, Liber*: "Pan's horns touch heaven [so] universal forms of nature do reach up to God" (A12r,v); Browne, *Pseudodoxia Epidemica*, specifically mentions Pan in his comments on the cessation of the oracles, adding: "For that they received this blow from Christ, and from no other causes alledged by the Heathens, from oraculous confession they cannot deny" (Zz1v); Cowley, "On the Death of Mr. Crashaw": "And though *Pans Death* long since all *Oracles* breaks, / Yet still in Rhyme the Fiend Apollo speaks" (E3r); E. K., in his gloss on *The Shepheardes Calendar* (May): "By which *Pan*, though of some bee understoode the great Satan, whose kingdome at that time was by Christ conquered, the gates of hell broken up, and death by death delivered to eternall death" (F1r); Marvell, "On the First Anniversary of the Government under Oliver Cromwell": "And all about was heard a Panique groan, / As if that Nature's self were overthrown" (S2v); Milton, "On the Morning of Christ's Nativity": "Full little thought [the shepherds] than, / That the mighty *Pan* / Was kindly com to live with them below" (A3r).

[11] The matter has been eloquently put by S. K. Heninger, who stresses the central place of the sun in the cosmic progression from materiality to pure form:

> "Formality" and "materiality" are different orders of existence, the one increasing in proportion as the other decreases. . . . God and Earth are counterposed, and their opposition continued in the neat balancing of the three angelical hierarchies against the three elements above Earth. Formality and materiality come into exact equilibrium, each equally strong, along a line labeled "the sphere of equality"; and significantly this median position coincides with the sphere of the Sun. Here formality and materiality are in exact balance; the Sun has a component to be perceived by the intellect which is exactly equivalent to its component to be perceived by the senses. (28-29)

[12] The alchemical process, known as "the opus" or "The Great Work," was a real chemical procedure, albeit one grossly imperfect by today's standards. Basically, the alchemist attempted to procure matter at its most primitive state and by a process of reduction, acidification, heating, distilling, and redistilling sought to raise it through the stages of material forms to metallic gold, its ultimate perfection. The work was extremely time-consuming, often taking the better part of a year, and the steps in the process corresponded to the movement of the heavens

through the signs of the zodiac.

The initial matter, what the author of *The Sophic Hydrolith* calls "the earthly Body of the Sun"–often a crude but promising ore, but often too just plain dirt, decaying organic matter, or worse, was mascerated, mixed with "secret fire," and moistened with dew, and the resulting "compost" hermetically sealed in a spherical alembic called the Philocophic Egg and placed in the Athanor, the furnace of the Philosophers. There it was subjected for a period as long as forty days to a constant and gentle heat (Waite 1: 82-83). A repetitive process of evaporation and precipitation (called by the alchemists "volatility" and "fixation") ensued, and, if successful, the process produced in the end the red tincture, a powder productive of the catalytic Philosophers Stone. But with no standards of measurement, no common language of description, no real method of experimentation, and certainly no implemental technology, the effort was always doomed, although its practitioners never stopped trying.

[13] For example, consider two pieces of doggerel from Elias Ashmole's *Theatrum Chemicum Britannicum*. The first is excerpted from George Ripley's *The Compound of Alchymie*:

> For lyke as Sowles after paynys transytory
> Be brought into paradyce where ever ys yoyfull lyfe;
> So shall our *Stone* after hys darknes in Purgatory
> Be purged and joynyd in Elements wythoute stryfe,
> Rejoyse the whytenes and bewty of hys wyfe:
> And passe fro the darknes of Purgatory to lyght
> Of paradyce, in Whytnes *Elyxer* of gret myght. (151)

The second comes from *Bloomefields Blossoms: or, The Campe of Philosophy:*

> The Maistery thou gettest not yet of these *Planets* seven,
> But by a misty meaning knowne only unto us;
> Bring them first to Hell, and afterwards to Heaven:
> Betwixt lyfe and death then thou must discusse,
> Therefore I councell thee that thou worke thus.
> *Dissolve* and *Seperate* them, *Sublime, Fix* and *Congeale*,
> Then hast thou all: therefore doe as I thee tell. (315)

[14] Most detrimental was the inability of the alchemists to describe accurately and fully their art. The reader who for the first time confronts such a treatise is confounded by terms like "the Green Dragon," "the Ouroboros," "the Hermetic

257

Egg," and "the Formula of the Crab," which purported, under the cloak of hermetic silence, to convey alchemical terms, substances, and even whole processes. The illustrations which accompany these are even more mystifying. Often they are grossly sexual and replete with graphic violence and mayhem.

[15] Although it is generally held that the addition of salt (as the principle of uninflammability and fixity) to the principles of sulphur and mercury should be attributed to Paracelsus, in actuality the compound had been perceived through the ages, in the aspect of "Philosophic Salt," as a unifying or harmonizing principle:

> As our Matter, in the philosophical work, after being dissolved into its three parts or principles, must again be coagulated and reduced into its own proper salt, and into *one* essence, which is then called the salt of the Sages.... According to Basil Valentine: "the root of philosophic sulphur, which is a heavenly spirit, is united in the same material with the root of the spiritual and supernatural mercury, and the principle of spiritual salt–out of which is made the Stone. (Waite 1: 99, 14)

[16] The process was variously termed "death," "mortification," or "putrefaction," and the alembic was often referred to as the "tomb" or "coffin" or as "Hell" or "Hades" (Klossowski de Rola 44).

[17] According to the same author:

> As the perfect earthly Stone or Tincture, after its completion extends its quickening efficacy, and the perfecting virtue of its tincture to other imperfect metals, so Christ, that blessed heavenly Stone, extends the quickening influence of His purple Tincture to us, purifying us, and conforming us to the likeness of His perfect and heavenly Body. For, as S. Paul says: (Rom. viii.), He is the first-born among many brethren, as He is also the first-born before all creatures, through whom all things in heaven and earth were created, and reconciled of God. If we who are by Nature impure, imperfect, and mortal, desire to become pure, immortal and perfect, this transmutation can be effected only through the mediation of the Heavenly Corner Stone Jesus Christ, who is the only holy, risen, glorified, heavenly King, both God and man in the unity of *one* Person. (Waite 1: 103)

[18] Jean Antoine de Baïf, who in 1570 founded the Académie de poésie et musique, developed a method of matching musical rhythms to quantitative verse (*musiques mesurées*) which, practically applied by Claude Le Jeune in his music for

the wedding of the Duc de Joyeuse in 1581, produced a "kind of astrological musical magic" (Tomlinson 142). Maier's use of music in *Atalanta Fugiens* is described by Cunnar as "an attempt to relate the stages of the alchemical work to the numerical pattern by which God created the universe" (99). In late years the music of *Atalanta Fugiens* has been performed and recorded. A recent essay by Kay Brainard Slocum demonstrates quite lucidly the cosmic and arithmetical basis to early music.

[19] In 1935, a query appeared in *Notes & Queries* regarding the phrase "All tincture," followed later in the same year by a reply suggesting that the word "tincture" refers not to alchemy but to color (J. 62; Maxwell 104). This is the extent of exploration of the poem in terms of its alchemical context.

[20] I have not taken the "tens" of line 5 into consideration due to the softness of their pronunciation. Line 5 may be interpreted as presenting some wordplay on the number ten—"content," "enlighten"—but I think this may be too clever a reading.

[21] For example, the *Antiphonale missarum*, Laon, MS 238, which dates from about 930, contains chants for the liturgical year composed in a rhythm of long and short notes set in such a two:one proportion.

[22] I am grateful to Raymond-Jean Frontain for pointing out that Donne used this device elsewhere: the concluding couplet of "Upon the translation of the Psalmes" is also an exact rime, as the poet manages poetically to harmonize the various two-in-ones of the poem.

Works Cited

Ashmole, Elias. *Theatrum Chemicum Britannicum* (1652). Repr. Kila, MT: Kessinger, 1991.

Augustine, Saint. *De Trinitate*. 42. *Patrologia Cursus Completus. Series Latina*. Paris: J. P. Migne, 1844-64. 221 vols.

Bacon, Francis. *De Sapientia Veterum, Liber* (1633).

Browne, Sir Thomas. "Of the Cessation of Oracles." *Pseudoxia Epidemica: Or, Enquiries into Very Many Received Tenents, and Commonly Presumed Truths* (1646).

Coudert, Allison. *Alchemy. The Philosopher's Stone*. Boulder, CO: Shambhala, 1980.

Cowley, Abraham. *Poems* (1656).

Cunnar, Eugene. "Donne's 'Valediction Forbidding Mourning' and the Golden Compasses of Alchemical Creation." *Literature and the Occult: Essays in Comparative Literature*. Ed. Luanne Frank. Arlington: U of Texas at Arlington, 1977. 72-110.

Falk, Ruth E. "Donne's *Resurrection, Imperfect*." *Explicator* 17 (1958): item 24.

Frontain, Raymond-Jean. "Donne's Imperfect Resurrection." *PLL* 26 (Fall 1990): 539-45.

Frost, Kate Gartner. *Holy Delight: Typology, Numerology, and Autobiography in Donne's "Devotions Upon Emergent Occasions."* Princeton: Princeton U P, 1990.

Grafton, Anthony. *Defenders of the Text. The Traditions of Scholarship in Age of Science, 1450-1800.* Cambridge: Harvard U P, 1991.

Heninger, S. K. *The Cosmographical Glasse: Renaissance Diagrams of the Universe.* San Marino: Huntington Library, 1977.

Hennecke, Edgar, and Wilhelm Schneemelcher. *New Testament Apocrypha. Vol. 1. Gospels and Related Writings.* Philadelphia: Westminster P, 1963.

Hieatt, Kent. *Short Time's Endless Monument: The Symbolism of the Numbers in Edmund Spenser's "Epithalamion."* New York: Columbia U P, 1960.

Holmyard, E. J. *Alchemy.* Baltimore: Penguin, 1968.

The Holy Bible, Conteyning the Old Testament, and the New (1611).

Hughes, Richard. *The Progress of the Soul: The Interior Career of John Donne.* New York: Morrow, 1968.

Hulme, William Henry, ed. *The Middle English "Harrowing of Hell" and "Gospel of Nicodemus."* Extra Series No. 100. London: EETS, 1907.

J. "All Tincture." *N&Q* 168 (1935): 62.

Klossowski de Rola, Stanislas. *The Secret Art of Alchemy.* New York: Avon Books, 1973.

Lapide, Cornelius à. *Commentari in Omnia Divi Pauli Epistolas.* Antwerp, 1627.

——————. *Commentarius in Scripturam Sacram.* Vol. 5: SS. Matthaeum and Marc. Paris: Ludovicum Vives, 1874.

Marvell, Andrew. *Miscellaneous Poems* (1681).

Maxwell, Herbert and R. S. B. "John Donne's `All Tincture.'" *N&Q* 168 (1935): 104.

Merivale, Patricia. *Pan the Goat God: His Myths in Modern Times.* Cambridge: Harvard U P, 1969.

Milton, John. *Poems* (1645).

Nicholl, Charles. *The Chemical Theatre.* London: Routledge & Kegan Paul, 1980.

Partridge, Eric. *Shakespeare's Bawdy.* New York: Routledge, 1968.

Patrides, C. A., ed. *John Donne. The Complete English Poems.* London: Dent, 1985.

Plutarch. "On the Obsolescence of Oracles." *Moralia.* Cambridge: Harvard U P, 1936. 15 vols.

Puttenham, George. *The Arte of English Poesie* (1589). Fasc. repr. Kent: Kent State U P, 1970.

Qvarnström, Gunnar. *The Enchanted Palace.* Stockholm: Alqvist & Wiksell, 1968.

Rose, H. J. *A Handbook of Greek Mythology.* New York: Dutton, 1950.

Ross, Alexander. *A Critical Edition of Alexander Ross's 1647 Mystagogus Poeticus, or The Muse's Interpreter.* Ed. John R. Glenn. New York: Garland, 1987.

Shawcross, John. *Intentionality and the New Traditionalism. Some Liminal Means to Literary Revisionism.* University Park: Pennsylvania State U P, 1991.

Slocum, Kay Brainard. "*Speculum musicae*: Jacques de Liège and the Art of Musical Number." *Medieval Numerology: A Book of Essays.* New York: Garland, 1993. 11-37.

Smith, A. J., ed. *John Donne. The Complete English Poems.* Harmondsworth: Penguin, 1971.

Spenser, Edmund. *The Shepheards Calendar* (1581).

Tomlinson, Gary. *Music in Renaissance Magic. Toward a Historiography of Others.* Chicago: U of Chicago P, 1993.

Waite, Arthur Edward. *The Hermetic Museum.* York Beach: Samuel Weiser, 1990. 2 vols.

Donnes's Horse and Rider as Body and Soul

Joan Hartwig

he figure of the horse has a major if puzzling place in three of John Donne's poems. " Satyre I," "Elegie 13: Natures lay Ideot," and "Goodfriday, 1613. Riding Westward" share an image of horse and rider that has roots in classical tradition as well as a pervasive history in works of religious imagination, both verbal and visual. Donne's reference to "the wise politique horse" in " Satyre I" is one of the earliest "indisputably authentic notice[s] of Banks' horse yet discovered."[1] The last two lines of "Elegie 13: Natures lay Ideot" compare the speaker's training of his lady only to lose her with the breaker of a colt who, after training him into "a ready horse," leaves him for others to ride. With or without the title, the dramatic episode at the center of "Goodfriday, 1613. Riding Westward" is the physical act of riding a horse, a point also demonstrated by Frances M. Malpezzi.

Usually taken as a curious topical reference, Donne's allusion to Banks' horse in " Satyre I" has received attention as one of the many contemporary references that attest to the horse's notoriety in performing unusual feats.

> But to a grave man, he doth move no more
> Then the wise politique horse would heretofore,
> Or thou O Elephant or Ape wilt doe,
> When any names the King of Spaine to you. (79-82)[2]

Donne's reference, however, is more than an isolated topical allusion. It enhances the reading of the "motley humorist" and the speaker's contest as "a debate" between the body and soul because the horse and rider are traditionally associated with body and soul in discussions of their natures.

Plato, for example, in the *Phaedrus* has Socrates describe the lover's conflict in the soul in terms of a charioteer and his two horses: the good horse, a white steed with black eyes who "needs no whip, being driven by the word of command alone" and the evil horse, "a massive jumble of a creature, with . . . black skin, and grey eyes . . . and hard to control with whip and goad" (103). Although Plato recognizes three parts of the soul, as in Book IX of *The Republic*, "the charioteer and the good horse are so much one in purpose and function that their distinction can hardly be maintained if we seek to go behind the imagery," whereas the evil horse is distinct from the charioteer in being the "headstrong, ruthless character of carnal desire" (Hackforth 107).

In biblical contexts as well, the horse came to be associated with desires of the body in opposition to the desires of the soul (see Rowland 246, 248). Sister Mary Ursula Vogel demonstrates that "by means of the horse-and rider image the threads of the chivalric matter and of the Body-and-Soul legend elements are skillfully interwoven" (11) in the medieval *The Debate between the Body and the Soul*, and that "in medieval religious literature the relating of the body to a horse and the soul to a rider becomes a commonplace" (36).

Without resolving the conflicts of existing readings,[3] viewing the curious reference to Banks' horse as more central to the poem than has heretofore been recognized offers another valid image through which the poem's anecdotal progress makes sense.

The poem's speaker opens with imperatives, "A way" and "Leave me," while he describes that "woodden chest" where he would lie "coffin'd" among "grave Divines . . . Natures Secretary, the Philosopher [Aristotle] . . . jolly Statesmen . . . gathering Chroniclers . . . [and] Giddie fantastique Poëts." Apparently the "fondling motley humorist" appeals to him to join him in the streets of the city, and the speaker rhetorically asks,

> Shall I leave all this constant company,
> And follow headlong, wild uncertaine thee? (11-12)

There is a wry contrast between "this constant company" of the speaker's lettered world and the " wild uncertaine thee" that wishes him to leave the confines of the "woodden chest" and experience the world of the streets. The adjectives attributed to the "thee" who wishes to go out are markedly the attributes of the horse that needs taming and controlling. Given the traditional associations of the rider/trainer of horses as the soul and the horse as the body, the situation is one that undoubtedly has occurred before. Because the speaker/soul knows the resistance of an untrained horse/body to discipline and realizes the necessity to repeat disciplinary lessons, he proceeds to require promises from his companion before accompanying him into the streets.

> First sweare by thy best love in earnest
> (If thou which lov'st all, canst love any best)
> Thou wilt not leave mee in the middle street . . .
> For better or worse take mee, or leave mee:
> To take, and leave mee is adultery. (13-15, 25-26)

Practically speaking, it is difficult for the soul to stay behind if the body chooses to go out, but the assumption of governance by the soul is presumed in such debates (see Vogel 4, 12, 37, 41-63). Therefore, the conditions are the soul's to make and the body's to agree to. The recognition that the body loves "all" without distinction and is probably incapable of constancy, and the requirement of fidelity couched in terms of the marriage vow, suggest that the soul is aware from past experience that the body probably cannot keep a vow of fidelity, but that it is necessary to require a commitment anyway. The soul is exercising its own responsibility in attempting to control the body as they leave the protection of the library's "coffin" and move out into the world of temptations.

Once in the street (66), the soul describes the body's antics with facetiousness if not with disdain. The reference to the "wise politique horse" follows a comparison of the body's actions to that of a fiddler, who "stop[s] lowest" in order to achieve the highest sound, with the body as it bows lowest to "the most brave." Here, the word "brave" connotes "showy" rather than "courageous."

> But to a grave man, he doth move no more
> Then the wise politique horse would heretofore,
> Or thou O Elephant or Ape wilt doe,
> When any names the King of Spaine to you. (79-82)

The elephant and the ape may or may not have accompanied Banks' horse, Morocco, and the show at some point, but all are said to have responded negatively to the naming of the King of Spain.[4]

The two most telling references to Banks and his horse and Spain are from 1596 documents. The first is from Thomas Nashe's "Have with You to Saffron Walden": "For as true as Bankes his horse knowes a Spaniard from an Englishman, . . . so true it is that there are men which have dealt with me in the same humour that heere I shadowe" (quoted in Halliwell-Phillips 52-53). The second, collected by R. Chambers in "Domestic Annals of Scotland," reports in detail many of Morocco's tricks before describing this one: "By a sign given him, he would beck [bow or curtsy] for the King of Scots and for Queen Elizabeth, and when ye spoke of the King of Spain, would both bite and strike at you" (quoted in Atkins 40). If this latter routine is the one Donne has in mind (and it makes sense, given the ironic cast of the satire), the "I" of the poem is describing the erratic behavior of his companion in first, bowing low to a "brave" or flashy person, and then responding unreasonably with animosity to "a grave man," just as the "wise politique horse would heretofore" have done "when any names the King of Spaine." The horse is wise because it can learn routines,[5] and politic because Spain was clearly the enemy of the crown, and so the routine that Banks established with his horse was one that would please the crowd, much the same way that stand-up comedians command a laugh from current audiences by referring to the actions of political opponents, especially in an election year.

The behavior which the "I" of the poem describes following the reference to Banks' horse, may also have a topical connection to that show business "career."

> Now leaps he upright, Joggs me'and cryes, Do'you see
> Yonder well favour'd youth? Which? Oh, 'tis hee
> That dances so divinely; Oh, said I,
> Stand still, must you dance here for company?
> Hee droopt, wee went. (83-87)

The horse rearing, as in "Now leaps he upright," is bound to "jogg" the rider, if we follow through with the associations of the body/soul=horse/rider reading of the poem.[6] Morocco's most famous trick, according to the frequency with which it is reported, was to pick out a particular person from a crowd ("Do'you see / Yonder well favour'd youth? Which?"); and even twentieth-century accounts of the horse that "trotted over Elizabethan and Jacobean literature for sixty years" (Furness 45, n. 50) take up

Shakespeare's phrase in *Love's Labour's Lost*, "the dancing horse."[7]

To train a horse in the way that Banks trained Morocco (and apparently several other horses during his time) is a tedious, repetitive labor, as Gervase Markham details in his *Cavelarice* (1607). Essential to this kind of training is the endless patience and persistence of the trainer to repeat reward and punishment in the face of the horse's resistance to obedience. Yet, once trained, the horse is totally reliable to do what the trainer asks it to do. Likewise, the soul has spent many hours training the body to obey its commands, and in this passage, which is an actual present dialogue between the "I" and the "You," this training manifests itself in the obedience of the "You" to the command and shaming technique of the "I": "Oh, said I, / Stand still, must you dance here for company?" The body responds, as it has been trained to, with subservience, "Hee droopt, wee went." But the victory of the rider/soul over the horse/body is temporary, not lasting out the line, because temptations are many on the streets of London.

In his own sermon "Preached at St. Pauls on Midsommer day. 1622" Donne says:

> It is a lesse miracle to raise a man from a *sick bed*, then to hold a man from a *wanton bed*, a litentious bed; lesse to overcome and quench his fever, then to quench his lust. . . . For, certainly, he that uses no *fasting*, no *discipline*, no *mortification*, exposes himselfe to many dangers in himselfe, and to a cheape and vulgar estimation amongst others. *Caro mea jumentum meum*, says S. *Augustine*, my body is the horse I ride. (4: 152)[8]

Predictably, by the end of the poem, the body has given in to harlotry, "At last his Love he in a windowe spies / And like light dew exhal'd, he flings from mee / Violently ravish'd to his lechery." The similarities between circumstances in the poem and the description in Plato's *Phaedrus* are close enough to warrant quoting:

> We divided each soul into three parts, two being like steeds and the third like a charioteer . . . when the driver beholds the person of the beloved, and causes a sensation of warmth to suffuse the whole soul, he begins to experience a tickling or pricking of desire; and the obedient steed, constrained now as always by modesty, refrains from leaping upon the beloved; but his fellow, heeding no more the driver's goad or whip, leaps and dashes on, sorely troubling his companion and his driver, and forcing them to approach the loved one and remind him of

the delights of love's commerce. For a while they struggle, indignant that he should force them to a monstrous and forbidden act; but at last, finding no end to their evil plight, they yield and agree to do his bidding. (103-104)

Thus, in Donne's poem as well, the soul must allow the body its ravishment and humiliation despite conscience, modesty, and awareness of virtue. The ultimate victory, however, is the soul's when the body, having spent itself in lust and quarreling, returns home "And constantly a while must keepe his bed." The puns on "constancy" and "keeping to bed" are capable of turning around again on the speaker of the poem, but, for the moment, the last triumph is his. The body cannot make its way alone without the rider of its passions. One more lesson in the training of the horse/body has failed, but the rider/soul will try again.

The disciplinary measure of a trainer/rider of horses takes another turn in "Elegie 13: Natures lay Ideot." Although the notion of the soul as rider has given way to lustful man as rider in this poem, Donne draws upon the same idiom of secularized amatory horsemanship that informs Sir Philip Sidney's famous sonnet:

> I on my horse, and Love on me, doth try
> Our horsemanships, while by strange work I prove
> A horseman to my horse, a horse to Love,
> And now man's wrongs in me, poor beast, descry.
> The reins wherewith my rider doth me tie
> Are humbled thoughts, which bit of reverence move,
> Curb'd in with fear, but with gilt boss above
> Of hope, which makes it seem fair to the eye;
> The wand is will; thou, fancy, saddle art,
> Girt fast by memory; and while I spur
> My horse, he spurs with sharp desire my heart;
> He sits me fast, however I do stir;
> And now hath made me to his hand so right
> That in the manage myself takes delight. (49)

Not nearly so graceful as Sidney's Astrophil, Donne's speaker is nonetheless caught in the position of being ridden rather than of riding. The single thread of development that overwhelms this poem's recognitions is that of the *praeceptor amoris* who has taught a backward pupil exceedingly well: "I taught thee"; "I had not taught thee then"; "who have . . .

refin'd thee"; "I planted knowledge and lifes tree in thee." The similarity between the master's teaching his pupil and a trainer's shaping a colt to function in the trainer's world is self-evident. If it were not, Donne's last two lines force the poem to specify the similitude.

> Must I alas
> ... breake a colts force
> And leave him then, beeing made a ready horse?[9]

Thomas Blundeville, in *The Foure Chiefest Offices belonging to Horseman-ship*, details the care with which one must teach a horse different skills:

> I thinke it therefore now meet to shew you what the horse hath to learn for his part, and also what order you shall keepe in breaking him: for if a horse be taught unorderlie, hee shall neuer be perfect in anie thing. As for example, if you (as some men doe for lacke of skil) would use to gallop your horse, before he can stoppe well in his trot: or to runne him, before he can stop well in his gallop: or to manege him with a sweift gallop, before he can stop, advance, and turne readilie on both handes, you shall marre him for euer. (12 recto)

Donne's description of how the speaker has "taught thee to love" details an equal care with the social skills, with "the Alphabet / Of Flowers" and how they may be used to code messages, with the appropriate language to be employed in witty discourse, as well as "with amorous delicacies." All of these skills that the speaker has taught his lover are deceitful skills with which she can betray her husband; and, now that she has proved herself a perfect pupil, she can also use these skills to betray her teacher with other lovers. His lamentation over having taught her too well for the benefit of others, when read in the context of training a colt in the ways of horsemanship, resembles the lamentation of Richard II at the end of Shakespeare's play after he learns that Bolingbroke has ridden his favorite horse in the coronation procession, and is told that the horse went "so proudly as if he disdained the ground."

> So proud that Bolingbroke was on his back!
> That jade hath eat bread from my royal hand;
> This hand hath made him proud with clapping him.
> Would he not stumble? would he not fall down,

> Since pride must have a fall, and break the neck
> Of that proud man that did usurp his back? [5.5.84-89]

Similarly, Donne's speaker feels the offense of betrayal, after having trained his pupil so assiduously.

> Thy graces and good words my creatures bee,
> I planted knowledge and lifes tree in thee,
> Which Oh, shall strangers taste? Must I alas
> Frame and enamell Plate, and drinke in glasse?
> Chafe waxe for others seales? breake a colts force
> And leave him then, beeing made a ready horse?

Unlike Richard, who realizes that he should not "rail" at the horse for allowing another man to ride him, "Since thou, created to be awed by man, / Wast born to bear" (5.5.91-92), Donne's speaker's last note is chagrined. He has wasted all of his training and refining because he will not be the sole rider of this colt.

Richard's metaphorical use of the horse and rider relates to the the state and its king, a traditional association, whereas Donne's metaphorical usage connects with an equally old, but different association. Beryl Rowland points out the long history of the association between horses and women in her essay on Chaucer's use of the horse and rider figure. Rowland observes that "Mediaeval didactic writers make frequent use of the analogy of a woman to a horse . . . under the influence of the Christian Church the significance of the figure appears to harden: the horse is equated with the body or with Woman, the evil repository of sex; the rider is the soul or Man" (248, 246; see also Hartwig).

Donne's speaker in "Natures lay Ideot" draws easily upon the misogynist background of the figure's associations, especially since all of the man's, or rider's, efforts have come to a frustrating conclusion for him. The woman, or the colt, has learned too well, and has moved on to use and display her skills with others now that she has that knowledge. The poem's conclusion actually retroacts upon the opening caustic address. Initially, "Natures lay Ideot" seems to address the object of the speaker's anger, his former pupil, but by the end of the poem it describes the speaker himself. What could be more naive than to have thought that teaching the woman, or the colt, "sophistries" of love, that initiating her into the "mystique language of the eye [and] hand," was to own her and her actions thenceforth? Only an uninitiate in "ars amatoria" could be such an *idiotes*.[10]

The third poem in which Donne uses the horse and rider figure as an integral part of the poem's meaning is "Goodfriday, 1613. Riding Westward." The speaker of the poem is in motion—he likens it to the motion of the spheres—riding westward on horseback. Everything that he says or thinks on this particular day is governed in the literal, physical sense by his being a rider of a horse (as he says in l. 33: "Though these things, *as I ride*, be from mine eye" [my emphasis]). The scholastic hypothesis that opens the poem, "Let mans Soule be a Spheare," insists on the cosmic significance of this westward motion.[11] This intellectual proposition sets up an analogy between the "intelligence" that moves the spheres and "devotion" as they lose directive authority to "foreign motions," unnatural to the form of the spheres and the soul. "Pleasure and business" become the passionate horse (recalling Plato's *Phaedrus*) that moves man from his spiritual direction, whirling the soul away from its "own" motion.

As so often happens with Donne, his intellectual framework which seems rigorously logical at the beginning, proceeds to the *appearance* of consequence. "Hence is't," the speaker says, "that I am carryed towards the West." The hypothesis does not move to this conclusion in a logical way, but the power of the analogy between the soul and the intelligence which guides the spheres makes the logical gap seem insignificant.[12] Part of the convincing effect of the concluding "Hence" derives from the fact that the speaker is "carryed" towards the West. He is passively being taken away from that which he would, or which his soul would, address, the East and the Crucifixion. The rider is not in control. Seen from the traditional association of the rider as soul and the horse as body, this suggests a failing on the part of the soul. The soul as rider is obliged to correct the errant and willful nature of the horse. On this day, a most crucial day, the rider has not exerted its controlling power.[13]

Yet, in another sense, the soul directs the rider's imagination to recreate the vision of the Crucifixion in powerful detail, vivid in the physical presence not only of God in Christ but also of "his miserable mother." What the literal eye does not look on, the mind's eye recreates, which is appropriate to meditative practice. Thus the rider is able to control his horse in a figurative sense and contemplate "devotionally" that transforming event which is the soul's "business" on this day. In so doing, the act of riding westward becomes the same thing as looking eastward, just as death and life become the same thing through the Crucifixion and Resurrection (see Goldberg). Lucas Cranach the Elder's painting, "The Crucifixion, with the Converted Centurion, mounted" [1529] could al-

MAROCCUS EXTATICUS,

OR

BANKES

BAY HORSE IN A TRANCE.

A DISCOURSE SET DOWNE IN A MERRY DIALOGUE BETWEEN
BANKES AND HIS BEAST: ANATOMIZING SOME ABUSES
AND BAD TRICKES OF THIS AGE.

WRITTEN AND INTITULED TO MINE HOST OF THE BELSAVAGE,
AND ALL HIS HONEST GUESTS.

BY JOHN DANDO, THE WIER-DRAWER OF HADLEY,
AND HARRIE RUNT, HEAD OSTLER
OF BESOMES INNE.

Printed for Cuthbert Burby.

1595.

Fig. 1 Title page, Maroccus Extaticus (1595)
Courtesy of the Folger Shakespeare Library

271

*Fig. 2 Lucas Cranach, The Crucifixion, with the
Converted Centurion, mounted (1529)
Courtesy of the National Gallery of Art*

Fig. 3 Hans Baldung Grien, Conversion of St. Paul (c. 1505-07)
Courtesy of the National Gallery of Art

Fig. 4 Hans Baldung Grien, Conversion of St. Paul (c. 1515-16)
Courtesy of the National Gallery of Art

*Fig. 5 Caravaggio, The Conversion of St. Paul (1601)
Cerasi Chapel, Manta Maria del Popolo, Rome*

275

Fig. 6 Michelangelo, The Conversion of St. Paul (1545-49)
Vatican Palace, Cappella Paolina

most be an illustration of Donne's poem [Fig. 2], although I am not suggesting that Donne had it in mind.

Even as the speaker affirms that his "memory" looks towards these things while he rides with his back toward the cross, Donne's wit shifts that reassuring recognition into a plea, bargaining for God's corrective fire to burn away his physical and spiritual "deformity" so that the divine image might be seen in his own face. Although there is no specific reference to St. Paul's conversion in the poem (and, indeed, Terry Sherwood argues that "Donne's primary interest is not in the sudden conversion of Paul" [159]), the situation of riding on horseback to business and the plea that his deformities be burned away, recall the pictorial representation of Paul's experience familiar in the Renaissance through such woodcuts as those from Hans Baldung Grien [1505-1507 and 1515-1516 (Fig. 3 and 4)] and such paintings as Caravaggio's of St. Paul's conversion [1600-1601, Fig. 5]. Most of these depictions show Paul as he falls with his horse, witnessing Christ's manifestation in a shatteringly bright vision. Others, like Caravaggio's [Fig. 5] show him having fallen from his horse. In all versions, the horse is a major motif, placing Paul on horseback riding to Damascus to persecute Christians when he sees the vision of Christ.

Scripture does not specify that Paul was on horseback, and the Byzantine convention was to depict him on foot. Leo Steinberg, in describing the convention of the toppled horseman that Michelangelo "shunned" [Fig. 6], observes:

> Western art, since the twelfth century, represented him [Paul] mounted, as befits a great personage visualized in the age of chivalry . . . this motif, orginally antique, was adapted from illustrated manuscripts of the *Psychomachia* of Prudentius. . . . the rider unhorsed—Pride riding before the fall—represents *Superbia*, the first of the mortal sins, overthrown by *Humilitas*. And it was in this form that Paul's Conversion became most familiar to the fifteenth century: an elderly bearded rider, under a shower of hailstones, tumbling head first from his horse. (26)

Moreover, in each of these pictorial versions the horse is a major focal point of the experience, both of St. Paul and of the viewer. Given the associations between horse/body and rider/soul, this dominant visual figure of the horse, either bare of rider or rearing and falling under the power of the vision, suggests the catastrophic upheaval of the previous world of "Saul" and the moment of the spiritual change which then governs the life of "Paul."

With an awareness of such a moment's power that echoes these representations of St. Paul's conversion (intentional or not), Donne's speaker in "Goodfriday, 1613. Riding Westward" asks God to grant him a physical conversion in burning off his "rusts" and "deformity" so that his spirit can control the horse and its rider to turn and face God.

In each of these poems Donne builds upon awareness of traditional associations between horse and rider as body and soul, although each poem presents a different version of the rider and of the horse. In " Satyre I" the soul and body demonstrate a divisiveness that undermines all efforts to make the horse and rider appear harmoniously unified: they fail the training program. In "Natures lay Ideot" the lustful rider discovers that, although he has skillfully trained his horse, he has failed to alter the nature of the animal. The horse, as Donne points out in a later sermon, will "admit any Rider, any burden, without discretion or difference, without debatement or consideration" (9: 379). "Goodfriday, 1613. Riding Westward," however, demonstrates the potential for horse and rider, through submission and control, to be shaped by divine force into an harmonious image, unifying body and soul.

Notes

¹ J. Halliwell-Phillips (24) takes the 1593 date attached to ms. Harl. 5110 as accurate, and this leads him to his remark that Donne's reference to Banks and his horse is "the earliest." John T. Shawcross, however, points out that this date has been placed on the ms. in a later hand, and that this poem is probably of a later date, 1597 or 1598.

² In addition to his note on "horse," 17, n. 80, "a performing horse (called Morocco, from its supposed origin) exhibited by a showman named Banks during the 1590s," Shawcross says that there is some question concerning the addition of the "elephant and ape" to Banks' act in 1594, although Sir John Davies, in "In Dacum" (published with Marlowe's undated *Ovid's Elegies*), talks of all three animals as controlled by three different performers. See also, W. Milgate, ed. (117 and 127, n. 81), who cites other contemporary references to the elephant and ape,

notably by Ben Jonson, Joseph Hall, and Thomas Nashe.

[3] The two primary positions in the "debate" over the poem are readings that find the two "characters" of the poem to represent the body and soul and the readings that find the poem's speaker to be the object of his own satire. John T. Shawcross sees the five satires as a group which "pillory five universal dilemmas besetting man," the dilemma of " Satyre I" being "the opposing concerns of body and soul" dramatized as "a kind of debate between man's body ('thou') and his soul ('I')" ("All Attest" 252-254). John R. Lauritsen agrees and asserts that Shawcross's observation is generally applicable "to the *Satyres* as a group and to much of Donne's love poetry as well" (120). S. F. Johnson as well takes the poem "to be a modernized version of the traditional debate of body and soul" dramatized by the "protagonist, 'I,' . . . as sober John Donne, and the antagonist, 'thou' and 'he,' as wild Jack Donne."

Radically opposite are readings such as that put forward by Wilbur Sanders (34-36) who insists that the "satirist whose fat, phlegmatic complacency" and "comic exasperation" make him equal with the "humorist" as object of the poem's satire. Barbara L. Parker and J. Max Patrick similarly find that "both characters are satirized," but that the speaker "remains the primary butt and focus of the satire" (10, 13). Finding Donne's mocking of the speaker "not unsympathetic" ("The Mocking Voices" 38), Carol Marks Sicherman also thinks that the speaker "manifests, and betrays himself by, inconstancy and inconsistency" (39).

In a similar vein but with a theological emphasis and using Donne's sermons to support his reading, James S. Baumlin finds that because the speaker is unable to "distinguish between comic folly and 'tragical vice' [Dryden's term], Horace's ethical relativism is no longer possible for a satirist with a Christian conscience" (67-76). Baumlin agrees with M. Thomas Hester's suggestion that the poem is "a comic study in failure, a witty dramatization of the radical and seemingly irremedial gap between the intentions of the satirist and the obduracy of his *adversarius*" (17), but he ignores Hester's following counter that "nevertheless, the speaker's failure to reform his foolish companion does not mean that his own attitude and conduct in the company of the fop are themselves satirized in the poem" (17).

N. J. C. Andreasen defends the speaker, whose "personality" reappears (she says) with the same voice in each of the five satires, and sees the conflict between the protagonist, who "stands for simplicity, peaceful contemplation, and the constancy which they possess and produce," and the antagonist, who stands for "fashion, lechery, and social-climbing, and the inconstancy which they possess and produce," as satirizing one aspect of society: "the opportunism and lechery of a young rake" ("Theme" 415). Shawcross views Andreasen's reading as "not only circumscribed but essentially wrong" ("All Attest" 271, n. 14) because he reads the satires as exposing "five basic universal problems" that "propose no real solutions, for all taken together say that such dilemmas find their root in man and his nature"(269).

[4] See Milgate's note (125). Another document, not so well known as Jonson's or Hall's or Nashe's comments, may also shed some light on the "politique" nature of these animals. Brice Harris comments at the end of his facsimile edition of Richard Niccols' *The Beggers Ape* (1627) that the author was "one of the 'most ingenious persons' at Oxford" and continued after his graduation in 1606 "to study and imitate Spenser's poetry." The poem was apparently composed c. 1607 although not published until eleven years after the author's death. In the dialogue of the poem the Ox replies to the fox that if merit were to have her due then "the noble *Horse*" would be rewarded for his unstinting valor against the Eagle and the Dragon (Sig. D 4). A bit later "the noble *Elephant*, who as he stood / From his sweet mouth powr'd forth a fluent flood / Of honied eloquence" inveighed against the cozenage of the Ape and the Fox at court (Sig. E 2). Harris says that the allegorical equivalent for the Horse is the Lord Admiral, the Earl of Nottingham, and for the Elephant, Thomas Sackville, Earl of Dorset. The Ape Harris identifies as the same Ape in Spenser's *Mother Hubberd's Tale* who had its tail cut, that is, Sir Robert Cecil. My point in citing this little poem and its interpreter is to suggest that Donne may have had in mind senses of the word "politique" other than simply the performing trained animals when he described the horse, the elephant and the ape. As Hester (26-28) points out, the three animals were frequent subjects of emblem writers of the period.

[5] Gervase Markham titles chapter 5 of the eighth book of his treatise on horsemanship: "How a Horse may be taught to doe any tricke, done by Bankes his Curtall."

[6] In the pamphlet, *Maroccus Extaticus, or Bankes Bay Horse in a Trance* (1595), the title page shows the horse upright on his haunches with a stick in his mouth and Banks standing on the other side of a pair of dice with his trainer's stick uplifted. [See Fig. 1]

[7] For example, Halliwell-Phillips entitles his essay, "The Dancing Horse." William Cavendish, Duke of Newcastle, in his 1667 English version of *A New Method* 157-158, disdains this way of teaching a horse "tricks": "*Seeing* is all the *Art* when they Teach Horses *Tricks*, and *Gambals*, like *Bankes's* Horse; and though the Ignorant Admire them, yet those Persons shall never Teach a Horse to Go Well in the *Mannage*. There are many Things in the *Sense of Feeling*, which are to be Done with so great *Art*, *Witt*, and *Judgement*, and require so great Experience of the several *Dispositions* of Horses, that it is not every *Mans Case* to be an *Horse-man*, as it is to make a Dogg or a Horse *Dance*: But I am Contented to let the Ignorant Talk, and Think what they will, for I am not Concerned with their Folly."

[8] I am grateful to Frances M. Malpezzi (25) for pointing to this passage.

[9] In equine nomenclature, a "colt" becomes a "steed" after three years just as a "filly" becomes a "mare" after the same time of training.

[10] I do not agree with N. J. C. Andreasen (*John Donne: Conservative Revolutionary* 107), who states that "The lover identifies his philosophy and personality in the first three words of the poem: he is 'Natures lay Ideot'," although my point is that the poem's ironic recognitions lead the reader, at the end of the poem, to return to the first line with an awareness that these three words apply equally well to the speaker as to the woman he has shaped and trained. There is an ambiguous reference built into the placement of this descriptive tag. Syntactically "Natures lay Ideot" could modify the next word "I" as well as the "thee" whom he taught. But the ambiguity, I would argue, becomes clear *after* the reader has read the poem rather than at the beginning.

[11] See A. B. Chambers for a discussion of beliefs in spherical revolution and their relation to Donne's hypothesis.

[12] Donald M. Friedman points out that "Donne is revaluing not only the traditional, identifiable *content* of the spherical analogy, but the habit of mind that finds such verbal structures to be satisfying representations of experience and its moral meaning" and that "the poem enacts a discovery of the inadequacy of such paltering mechanics of the mind . . . by transcending the concept-making skills of the intellect" (421). Patrick F. O'Connell sees the rejection of the "opening equation of the Ptolemaic system with a lack of harmony" as a prelude to accepting a Christ-centered heleocentric or Copernican universe (19). Carol Marks Sicherman says that Donne's "intellectual swagger" has an "obscurantist intention" which succeeds with most modern readers, and "more important, he succeeds in distracting himself from this problem" (Discoveries" 72). I am struck with the similarity between the beginning and ending of Donne's poem and Vogel's discussion of Boethius' distinction between reason and intelligence: "Reason finds its object on a lower plain [sic] in sensible things, known in their universal aspect by discursive reasoning. In the highest point of the mind (*acies mentis*) intelligence attains its primary object–the vision of God" (51).

[13] Frances Malpezzi develops a similar argument (but, as she points out, with a different conclusion) and cites some striking parallels with Donne's use of the horse image in two of his sermons (4: 152-153 and 9: 385). The latter sermon Donne bases upon the text "Psal. 32.9. Be not as the horse, or the mule, who have no understanding; whose mouth must be held in with bit and bridle, lest they come neere unto thee."

Works Cited

Andreasen, N. J. C. "Theme and Structure in Donne's *Satyres.*" *Essential Articles for the Study of John Donne's Poetry.* Ed. John R. Roberts. Hamden, CT: Archon Books, 1975. 411-23.

_____. *John Donne: Conservative Revolutionary.* Princeton: Princeton UP, 1967.

Atkins, Sidney H. "Mr. Banks and His Horse." *N&Q* 167 (1934): 39-44.

Baumlin, James S. *John Donne and the Rhetorics of Renaissance Discourse.* Columbia: U of Missouri P, 1991.

Blundeville, Thomas. *The Foure Chiefest Offices belonging to Horsemanship.* Rpt. London: Peter Short, 1597.

Cavendish, William, Duke of Newcastle. *A New Method.* London: Tho. Milbourn, 1667.

Chambers, A. B. "Goodfriday, 1613. Riding Westward: The Poem and the Tradition." *ELH* 28 (1961): 31-53.

Friedman, Donald M. "Memory and the Art of Salvation in Donne's Good Friday Poem." *ELR* 3 (1973): 418-42.

Furness, Horace Howard, ed. *Love's Labour's Lost.* New Variorum ed. New York: American Scholar Publications, 1966.

Goldberg, Jonathan. "Donne's Journey East: Aspects of a Seventeenth-Century Trope." *SP* 68 (1971): 470-83.

Hackforth, R. Commentary. *Plato's Phaedrus.* New York: Bobbs-Merrill, 1952.

Halliwell-Phillips, J. *Memoranda on Love's Labour's Lost, King John, Othello, and on Romeo and Juliet.* London: James Evan Adlard, 1879.

Harris, Brice, ed. *The Beggers Ape* (1627) [Richard Niccols]. New York: Scholars' Facsimiles and Reprints, 1941.

Hartwig, Joan. "Horses and Women in The Taming of the Shrew." *HLQ* 45 (1982): 285-94.

Hester, M. Thomas. *"Kinde Pitty and Brave Scorn": John Donne's "Satyres".* Durham: Duke UP, 1982.

Johnson, S. F. "Donne's SATIRES, I." *Explicator* 11 (June 1953): item 53.

Lauritsen, John R. "Donne's *Satyres*: The Drama of Self-Discovery." *SP* 16 (1976): 117-30.

Lewis, Marjorie D. "The *Adversarius* Talks Back: 'The Canonization' and *Satire I.*" *New Essays on Donne.* Ed. Gary Stringer. Salzburg: U of Salzburg, 1977. 1-25.

Malpezzi, Frances M. "'As I Ride': The Beast and His Burden in Donne's 'Goodfriday'." *Religion and Literature* 24 (1992): 23-31.

Markham, Gervase. *Cavelarice.* London: Edward White, 1607.

Milgate, W., ed. *John Donne: The Satires, Epigrams and Verse Letters.* Oxford:

Clarendon P, 1967.

O'Connell, Patrick F. "'Restore Thine Image': Structure and Theme in Donne's 'Goodfriday'." *JDJ* 4 (1985): 13-28.

Parker, Barbara L. and J. Max Patrick. "Two Hollow Men: The Pretentious Wooer and the Wayward Bridegroom of Donne's ' Satyre I.'" *Seventeenth-Century News* 33 (1975): 10-14.

Plato's Phaedrus. Trans. R. Hackforth. New York: Bobbs-Merrill, 1952.

Rimbault, E. F., ed. *Maroccus Extaticus, or Bankes Bay Horse in a Trance (1595)*. London: Percy Society, 1843.

Rowland, Beryl. "The Horse and Rider Figure in Chaucer's Works." *UTQ* 35 (1966): 246-59.

Sanders, Wilbur. *John Donne's Poetry*. Cambridge: Cambridge UP,1971.

Shakespeare, William. *The Complete Works*. Ed. Alfred Harbage. Baltimore, MD: Penguin Books, 1979.

Shawcross, John T. "'All Attest His Writs Canonical': The Texts, Meaning and Evaluation of Donne's Satires." *Just So Much Honor: Essays Commemorating the Four-Hundredth Anniversary of the Birth of John Donne*. Ed. Peter Amadeus Fiore. University Park: Pennsylvania State UP, 1972. 245-72.

Sherwood, Terry G. *Fulfilling the Circle: A Study of John Donne's Thought*. Toronto: U of Toronto P, 1984.

Sicherman, Carol Marks. "The Mocking Voices of Donne and Marvell." *Bucknell R* 17 (1969): 32-46.

_____. "Donne's Discoveries." SEL 11 (1971): 69-88.

Sidney, Sir Philip. *The Poems of Sir Philip Sidney*. Ed. William A. Ringler, Jr. Oxford: Clarendon P, 1962.

Steinberg, Leo. *Michelangelo's Last Paintings*. New York: Oxford UP, 1975.

Vogel, Sister Mary Ursula. *Some Aspects of the Horse and Rider Analogy in "The Debate between the Body and the Soul"*. Washington, DC: Catholic U of America P, 1948.

Donne's "Goodfriday, 1613. Riding Westward" and Augustine's Psychology of Time

Helen B. Brooks

> Now that [man] has the capacity for it, you teach him
> to see the Trinity of the Unity and the Unity of the
> Trinity . . . So man is renewed in the knowledge of God,
> after the image of Him that created him.
> —St. Augustine, *Confessions* (XIII: 22)

In his seminal study of the relation between religious meditation and poetry in the sixteenth and seventeenth centuries, Louis Martz finds that although "poetry and meditation are by no means synonymous," there nevertheless is "a middle ground of the creative mind in which the two arts meet to form a poetry of meditation" (21-22). His argument proceeds on the structural parallel between the meditative exercise and the imaginative strategies employed by the religious poets in their efforts to attain a personal relationship with God.

Early in his book, Martz calls attention to the essentially three-fold structure of religious meditation as outlined in the influential sixteenth century treatise on meditation, the *Spiritual Exercises* of St. Ignatius Loyola: the composition of scene, its analysis, and the closing colloquy with God (or Christ or the Virgin Mary). Each part of the meditation was understood to draw on the corresponding power of the soul, namely, memory (or seeing in the imagination the scene of one's sins or of events from the life of Christ); understanding (or attention to and analysis of the truth of the subject of meditation); and will (or the movement of affection toward conformity with that which the understanding has embraced and submitted to the will). With the integration of its three principal faculties, the reformed soul moves in an unbroken progression to colloquy with God.[1] But a further and significant correspondence exists between the powers of the soul and the Trinity. Saint Bernard's *Meditations* provides one of the clearest statements on the soul-Trinity relationship:

> The minde is the Image of God, in which are these three things, *Memory, Understanding,* and *Will,* or *Love.* Wee attribute to the *Memory,* all which wee know, although we thinke not of it. Wee attribute to the *Understanding,* all which we finde to bee true in thinking, which wee also commit unto *Memory.*
>
> By *Memory,* wee are like to the Father, by *Understanding* to the Sonne, by *Will* to the holy Ghost.[2]

Donne likewise views the memory as the site of the *imago Dei*:

> As God, one *God* created us, so wee have a soul, *one soul,* that represents, and is some image of that one God; As the three Persons of the *Trinity* created us, so we have, in our one soul, a *threefold impression* of that image, and as Saint *Bernard* calls it, *A trinity from the Trinity,* in those *three faculties* of the soul, the *Vnderstanding,* the *Will,* and the *Memory.* (*Sermons* 2: 72-73)[3]

And therefore, through the integration of the three powers of the soul, centered on their proper object of devotion, one can "come to know and feel in himself the operation of the higher Trinity," or a "presentness" analogous to divine immutability (Martz 35). Thus a properly executed meditation, as Martz emphasizes, will issue in a seamless flowing together of all its parts, and by extension, of the three corresponding powers of the soul:

> all . . . parts of a given exercise will, when properly performed, flow into one inseparable, inevitable sequence. (37)

Studies of religious poetry owe an immense debt to Martz's formulations, but, to my knowledge, the mechanism by which such integration of parts—and by extension, of the soul's faculties—takes place has been absent from interpretations of meditative poetry in general and of Donne's poetry in particular. If a successful meditation eventuates in the flowing together of its three principal stages into a unified and timeless sequence, then it becomes crucial to our understanding of those poems which conform to the Ignatian model to inquire into the cast of mind necessary to the integration of memory, understanding, and will. Donne's poem "Goodfriday, 1613. Riding Westward" provides us with at least one possible answer. In its unbroken movement from misdirected love to direct colloquy with Christ the poem fully conforms to the true aim of the meditative exercise.[4]

The study that follows accounts for the internal cohesion of "Goodfriday—that is, the way in which the three parts coalesce to form a timeless imaginative experience—by way of Augustine's conception of time. Donne's Augustinianism has been demonstrated in numerous studies, and striking parallels exist here as well between the poem's unifying element—its attempt to evoke an enduring image upon which the mind can focus itself—and the psychology of time Augustine develops in the concluding chapters of the *Confessions* and employs in the structuring of the book itself.[5] Both Augustine and Donne held to a Christocentric theology in which redemption depends on renewal of the defaced, salvific image of God within, with the faculty of memory the "instrument of self-knowledge, which is in turn the key to the knowledge of God" (Quinn 283).[6] Terry Sherwood rightly emphasizes Donne's concern with the protracted form of conversion, or *conversio*, rather than with the "sudden conversion of Paul" (159). For both Augustine (as we find in the *Confesssions*) and Donne, human existence is a life-long struggle to free oneself from the ravages of time, that is, from the transitory, worldly distractions that repeatedly fail to satisfy the soul's unmitigated longing for union with God. "Goodfriday, 1613. Riding Westward" articulates that ongoing struggle.

In the absence of an Augustinian interpretive framework, earlier studies of the poem have focussed primarily on its three-part Ignatian meditative structure. While such studies have elucidated much about the course of the speaker's thoughts, inquiry into that which *binds* the three parts of the poem into a seamless and timeless whole yields further insight into the nature of the speaker's religious imagination. Augustine's conception of time and its relation to the faculties of the human soul provides an illuminating framework for the way the poem—and the speaker—achieves its true meditative aim: the coalescence of the soul's faculties with its true object of desire: the timeless image of God.

In his discussion of the relationship between time and memory in the *Confessions*, Augustine explains time as a kind of distention, or extension, of the soul (*distentio animi*) as it responds to passing perceptions, making time a subjective rather than objective phenomenon.[7] Time manifests itself, according to Augustine, not as distinct units of past, present, and future, but rather as time passing:

> how can . . . the past and the future, *be*, when the past no longer *is* and the future is not yet? As for the present, if it were always present and never moved on to become the past, it would not be time but eternity. (XI.14)

Since the past no longer *is* and the future is *not yet*, neither the past nor the future possesses being. Augustine thus concludes: "we cannot rightly say that time *is*, except by reason of its impending state of *not being*" (X1.14). The reason for this experience of "time," Augustine maintains, is that human attention is nearly always fixed on transitory things, and therefore one's perceptions move unceasingly toward "the past" and thus toward non-existence. In other words, because what humans conceive of as "the past" derives from its inability to remain "present" to consciousness, Augustine regards time as inextricably related to the content of consciousness:

> It seems to me, then, that time is merely an extension, though of what it is an extension I do not know. I begin to wonder whether it is an extension of the mind itself. (XI.26)

Although Augustine effectively challenges the objective existence of time, he nevertheless concedes the necessity for speaking of three "times" since "some such different times do exist in the mind, but nowhere else that [he] can see" (XI.20), providing we understand that they do not exist as distinct units of time:

> It might be correct to say that there are three times, present of past things, a present of present things, and present of future things . . . The present of past things is the memory; the present of present things is direct perception; and the present of future things is expectation. (XI.20)

The crucial point here, and for the unifying element in Donne's poem "Goodfriday," is that of the three functions of the mind—memory, attention, and expectation—the mind's faculty of "attention" (*adtendit*) alone persists in a continuous "present" as it processes, or "understands" both the ongoing remembrance of the past and the expectation of the future (XI.28).[8] For "it is not future time that is long, but a long future is a long expectation of the future; and past time is not long, because it does not exist, but a long past is a long remembrance of the past" (XI.28). And yet the mind's *experience* of the present lacks duration, fixed as the mind most often is on transitory, or worldly objects. The subjectivity of time, then, is engendered by what we later shall see Augustine describe as the human preoccupation with worldly "distractions," which, because they lack duration, forever flow into the "past," or non-existence. In recognizing time as a subjective construct, Augustine vows: "I must not allow my mind to insist that time is something objective. I must not let it thwart me because of all the different notions and impressions that are lodged in it" (XI.27).

Since for Augustine it is in the mind that we "measure" time, and since what it has measured moves into the past and thus into non-existence, the mind nevertheless must measure something which remains fixed in the memory (XI.28). That "something" Augustine identifies as the "impression" (*affectionem*) which remains in the memory once the thing itself has moved into non-existence (XI.27). But whereas transitory objects of attention move into non-existence, or the "past," God remains an enduring presence in Augustine's soul, and in particular within his memory, which for both Augustine and Donne, is clearly the superior faculty.[9] From the time that he first learned of God, Whom he equates with Truth, Augustine maintains that he has not forgotten Him: "[He has] always been present in my memory, and it is there that I find [Him] whenever I am reminded of [Him] and find delight in [Him]" (X.24). For Augustine repeatedly conceives of God as the unchangeable, timeless Being toward Whom the soul naturally inclines as it seeks its perfection: "But my hunger and thirst were not even for the greatest of your works, but for you, my God, because you are Truth itself *with whom there can be no change, no swerving from your course*" (III.6).

Here we see Augustine positing as the soul's end its incarnation into the continuous and suffusing present of the *imago Dei* lodged in its memory, the only object of attention that does not pass into non-existence. Were the soul in the presence of its true object of attention, it would gather together its faculties into a renewal of the indwelling, but defaced triune image of God, since "only things which cannot coexist follow one another" (Gilson 195). This, however, is not Platonic recollection of the past. Gilson explains the difference:

> [For Augustine], we discover truth not in memories deposited previ-

> ously in the soul, but in the divine light which is constantly present there. . . . To see things in God's light implies, not Platonic memory of the past, but Augustinian memory of the present, and this is something altogether different. (82)

Memory therefore should not be conceived of as merely a repository of the "past," for "memory is involved even in the briefest of our sensations. . . . [It is the] 'light of the intervals of time,' [making successive events], which would disintegrate without it, coexist in the light of consciousness" (Gilson 64).[10] Donne maintains in fact that "the art of *salvation*, is but the art of *memory*" (*Sermons* 2: 73).

Robert Jordan sees in Augustine's view of time rich possibilities for the soul to grow into conformity with Christ, possibilities upon which Donne appears to have drawn in "Goodfriday":

> man's escape from temporality or his victory over it is possible because he is capable of entering into a relation with the eternal which results in something that is, in one sense, the same as and, in another sense, different from the eternal, since analogy is the relational similarity of different things, a likeness of unlike things. (269-70)

Whereas God is Pure Actuality, and thus immutable, man, because of his double nature, "exists at all only in so far as [he] participates in the act whereby God exists" (Jordan 271). The human act analogous to the act whereby God exists becomes possible through a mystical-like operation of the three powers of the soul, regarded as consubstantial with the Trinity. Gilson explains how this mental disposition is possible:

> It is possible . . . for the three divisions of time to coincide even though the present moment—and it alone is real—is in itself indivisible; but this is possible only because of the soul. To see this more clearly we must look upon the soul's present as an attention which is directed both towards that which is yet to be (through anticipation), and towards that which is no more (through memory). This attention is continuous: it is, so to speak, the point of transition from something anticipated to something remembered. (195)

The implication is that were it no longer distracted, the soul would lovingly and eternally contemplate its divine essence, the *imago Dei*. Seeing that his own life has been wasted in repeated "distractions,"

Augustine thus vows to devote himself

> only to God's single purpose, *forgetting what I have left behind. I look*
> forward, not to what lies ahead of me in this life and will surely pass
> away, but to my eternal goal. I am intent upon this one purpose, not
> distracted by other aims, and *with this goal in view I press on, eager for the*
> *prize, God's heavenly summons. Then I shall listen to the sound of your praises*
> and *gaze at your beauty* ever present, never future, never past. (XI.29)

Even in the writing of the *Confessions*, Augustine longs for the gift to
seize and hold steady the minds of his readers so that they too might
"glimpse the splendour of eternity which is for ever still" (XI.11). Thus the
primary task before humans is to arrest the passing into non-existence of
that which occupies the soul's attention by focusing the mind's eye (*mens*)
on the only *unchanging* object of attention, namely, the *imago Dei* in Whose
likeness the soul is created, but which has been obscured through the
soul's transitory preoccupations.

As a meditation on the Crucifixion, Donne's "Goodfriday" verbalizes
such an experience. Here, the unity of the speaker's meditative experi-
ence derives from an act of *distentio* in which the soul's attention, though
looking to both the "past" (the historical Crucifixion) and the "future"
(the salvation of the soul), is all the while fixed on the timeless signifi-
cance of the historical Crucifixion as it recurs in time, and here specifically
on Good Friday, 1613. In keeping with Augustine's psychology of time,
Donne provides two skillfully-wrought transitions, making possible a
seamless movement of consciousness through the formal stages of medi-
tation. The first transition occurs within lines 11-14:

> There I should see a Sunne, by rising set,
> And by that setting endlesse day beget;
> But that Christ on this Crosse, did rise and fall,
> Sinne had eternally benighted all.[11]

The four lines drawn from the speaker's memory of Christ on the cross
bridge the Ignatian "composition of scene" (1-14) as it occurs on "this
day," and its analysis (by the understanding) (13-35) *in the present*. The
second transition occurs within lines 33-36:

> Though these things, as I ride, be from mine eye,
> They'are present yet unto my memory
> For that looks towards them; and thou look'st towards mee
> O Saviour, as thou hang'st upon the tree.

Within this final transition, the analysis of Christ's Passion is joined to the closing colloquy with Christ (35-42), the third principal stage of an Ignatian meditation, which looks forward to the absolute redemption of the soul.

Turning to the opening fourteen lines of "Goodfriday," we find the speaker composing by similitude that to which he aspires, namely, the proper "devotion" toward which the soul naturally inclines:

> Let mans Soule be a Spheare, and then, in this,
> The'intelligence that moves, devotion is,
> And as the other Spheares, by being growne
> Subject to forraigne motions, lose their owne,
> And being by others hurried every day,
> Scarce in a yeare their naturall forme obey:
> Pleasure or businesse, so, our Soules admit
> For their first mover, and are whirld by it.
> Hence is't, that I am carryed towards the West
> This day, when my Soules forme bends toward the East. (1-10)

The poem thus begins with the hortatory "Let man's Soule be a Spheare," creating a sense of expectancy as well as the imaginative association of the soul's form with the geometric figure of the sphere, a three-dimensional surface, all points of which are equidistant from a fixed point. We should not overlook an implicit connection here between the form of the sphere and the timeless form of the Trinity as the in-forming principle of the tripartite soul.[12] That the soul is at that moment imaginatively a sphere is signified by the demonstrative pronoun "this" at the end of the first line and by the comparison of the soul with the "other Spheares," or the heavenly spheres. Then, with the introduction of the second half of the opening simile with the words "so, our Soules" (7), the speaker—and we as readers—are whisked off to the timeless world of the spheres. Thus, the transmutation of time (and space) develops concurrently with the evolving meditation.

Suddenly, however, the meditation centers on the "I" of the single speaker, who apparently is traveling in two directions at once: "Hence is't, that I am carryed towards the West" (9).[13] The significance of the word

"Hence" also should not be overlooked. Like many words in Donne's poetry, "Hence" slips in unobtrusively, but it carries considerable imaginative weight in that it provides for the smooth projection of the meditating soul onto the imagined scene. The word "Hence" has, in this context, two possible meanings. Superficially, it means "therefore," or "as a result." But it has a second and more time-present connotation, namely, "from now," and we see once again Donne's attraction to the multivalency of language. The words "This day," which open the next line (10), further reinforce the growing immediacy of the meditative experience. Line 10, which carries the soul in an opposite, but related direction, continues in the present tense as the "Soules forme bends toward the East," and thus toward Christ as its natural and proper object of devotion.

With the imagination firmly identified with the soul-as-sphere at the close of line 10, and thus the smooth transition to "Christ on this Crosse," the primary stage of meditation—the composition of scene—becomes the focus of the soul's attention. The unbroken transition from the composition of scene to its analysis by the understanding hinges on Donne's judicious use of the word "There" at the beginning of line 11:

> This day, when my Soules forme bends toward the East.
> There I should see a Sunne, by rising set,
> And by that setting endlesse day beget;
> But that Christ on this Crosse, did rise and fall,
> Sinne had eternally benighted all. (10-14)

With the word "There," the devotional self is transported to the scene of the Crucifixion. The coalescence of the two meditative stages (11-14) simultaneously imparts increased duration, or extension, to the soul's faculty of attention as it contemplates *in the present* the image of the Crucifixion drawn from the memory.

The identity of the "I" in "Goodfriday," however, is more complicated. If the soul's form "bends" naturally towards the East, and therefore towards God (11), then it can be argued that the "I" that opens line 11 ("There I should see a Sunne, by rising set") is the soul's intelligence, or "naturall forme" witnessing in the mind's eye the vivid and concrete presence of "this Crosse" (13).[14] The "I" of line 11 therefore must be looking in two directions: toward the East—and Christ—as well as toward the West—and death. Indeed the opening lines support the view that Donne's speaker has arrived at a state of self-understanding such that he acknowledges his divided soul, namely, the self engaged in devotion and the self focussed on business and pleasure (9-10). By the close of the poem, however, the speaker finds it necessary to turn his back *eastward* toward Christ to receive corrections (37-38), reflecting both his physical and spiritual reorientation in the course of his meditation on Christ's Passion and death. But the paradox of the Crucifixion is in fact the conjunction of the two: life in the midst of death. This reading of line 11 differs from that of Professor Martz and others who understand the speaker to be "refusing to perform the devotion proper to the day" (54).

It seems that some of the difficulty of interpretation stems from the way the meditation turns on two ways of seeing. Moreover, Donne here and elsewhere in "Goodfriday" seems to be playing physical and inner sight against each other. For example, later in the poem, Donne distinguishes the two modes of seeing by use of the words "I" (the mind's "eye," or *mens*) and "eye" (physically seeing): "though these things, as I ride, be from mine eye" (33). For as the speaker makes clear: "Who sees Gods face, that is selfe life, must dye" (17). The ultimate reformation of the soul is not of this world, but the speaker does come to "see," by way of the timeless meditation, that even "Though these things, as I ride, be from mine eye / They're present yet unto my memory" (33-34).

That the "I" of the devotional self and the "I" of the worldly self are inextricably related follows from the intrinsic nature of the human soul. Augustine struggles with the same conflicting motions:

> All these different desires are good, yet they are in conflict with each other until he chooses a single course to which the will may apply itself as a single whole, so that it is no longer split into several different wills.
>
> The same is true when the higher part of our nature aspires after eternal bliss while our lower self is held back by the love of temporal pleasure. It is the same soul that wills both, but it wills neither of them with the full force of the will. So it is wrenched in two and suffers great trials, because while truth teaches it to prefer one course, habit prevents it from relinquishing the other. (VIII.10)

As a consequence of the Fall, the soul possesses dual but inseparable motions: toward the East and things eternal and toward the West and things temporal.[15] The attention is there, at Golgotha, and yet the fallen soul, traveling both Eastward and Westward, is unable wholly to see Christ face to face. Because of these conflicting impulses, the soul experiences its own temporality, that is, its trajectory away from that toward which it simultaneously—and naturally—bends. Although Golgotha is not physically before Donne's speaker, its timeless significance is eventually perceived as "present yet" (34) in the speaker's memory, the repository of the *imago Dei* now becoming consubstantial with the reformed powers of the soul in meditation.

The analysis in the present of the historical Crucifixion *within the crucible of the speaker's growing self-knowledge* (13-35) continues the timeless meditation. Lines 11-12 move the consciousness of the speaker from the composition of scene to conjecture about what it would be like to see (physically) Christ on the cross:

> There I should see a Sunne, by rising set,
> And by that setting endlesse day beget;
> But that Christ on this Crosse, did rise and fall,
> Sinne had eternally benighted all.
> Yet dare I'almost be glad, I do not see
> That spectacle of too much weight for mee.
> Who sees Gods face, that is selfe life, must dye;
> What a death were it then to see God dye?
> It made his owne Lieutenant Nature shrinke,
> It made his footstoole crack, and the Sunne winke
> Could I behold those hands which span the Poles,
> And tune all spheares at once, peirc'd with those holes?
> Could I behold that endlesse height which is
> Zenith to us, and to'our Antipodes,
> Humbled below us? or that blood which is
> The seat of all our Soules, if not of his,
> Make durt of dust, or that flesh which was worne
> By God, for his apparell, rag'd, and torne?
> If on these things I durst not looke, durst I
> Upon his miserable mother cast mine eye
> Who was Gods partner here, and furnish'd thus
> Halfe of that Sacrifice, which ransom'd us?
> Though these things, as I ride, be from mine eye,
> They'are present yet unto my memory. [11-34]

With line 21, the meditating speaker, out of a deepening sense of his own sinfulness, humbly approaches the Crucifixion scene, questioning his ability to "behold" the crucified Christ. Although the word "could" in the same line implies a conditional present, the references to "those hands," "those holes," "that height," and "that blood" clearly are uttered out of the vivid present of the soul's faculty of attention. The word "behold," implying a sense of wonder, or awe, further reflects the speaker's growing affection for God.

Thus the memory *in the present* of Christ's Crucifixion and of its "ransoming" of man for all time effects the soul's progressive regeneration and its communion with the incarnating Christ. In so doing, the poem radically affirms the timeless truth of the historical Crucifixion, as it continues to be a present redemptive reality within the speaker's meditative soul. For while wondering if he "could," literally speaking, see the painful details of Christ's death, the speaker *is* seeing them (with the combined faculties of the soul) in their eternal spiritual significance. In light of the present study, Professor Paul Stanwood has called my attention to lines 21-22, which occupy the exact center of the poem, and to the way in which the "hands which span the Poles" (of the world and of the cross) divide the poem in a crucifix-like configuration, thereby providing a kind of emblematic image on which the meditating soul focuses itself. Thus in true Augustinian terms, memory and understanding combine to resurrect the *imago Dei* both within and as an outward and visible linguistic sign of Christ's "presentness."

Simultaneously, then, the speaker witnesses the collapsing of space and time in the timeless and universal truth of the Crucifixion. With lines 23-24, space—transformed by the fulfillment of time—now extends from "that endlesse height"—the historical Crucifixion—down "to us," here in this place. At this point, the entire section of analysis (13-35) issues from and bears the marks of the sustained present-mindedness of the speaker's understanding as it looks toward the East and the salvific paradox of Christ's Crucifixion and Resurrection. The poem explicitly affirms as much in its view of Christ's "Sacrifice" as begetting "endlesse day" (12). Whereas at the poem's outset, the speaker seems psychologically and emotionally distanced from the Crucifixion scene, by the close of its analysis, the understanding has moved from the historical Crucifixion to seeing—and addressing—Christ as the soul's indwelling spirit (36).[16] The speaker thus comes to acknowledge his own sinfulness in the recognition of Christ's perfect obedience and sacrifice for human sinfulness for all time (32).

Having uttered twenty-two lines of words "whirling" between past and future, while all the time centered on the Crucifixion scene, the speaker next utters three lines firmly in the present, lines which bridge the analysis to the colloquy with Christ:

Though these things, as I ride, be from mine eye,
They are present yet unto my memory,
For that looks toward them; and thou look'st towards mee. (33-35)

True to Augustine's notion that God is ever-present in the memory
(X.24), the repentant speaker affirms in these three lines that the sub-
stance of all that has gone before in the meditation is "present yet" to the
soul's attention. Unlike the passing into non-existence of temporal objects
of thought, meditation on the Passion of Christ, the central paradox of
Christianity, formalizes the Trinity within. Hence the uninterrupted tran-
sition (33-36) into the third and final stage of the meditation, the speaker's
colloquy with Christ (33-42), is continuous from the analysis:

Though these things, as I ride, be from mine eye
They'are present yet unto my memory
For that looks towards them; and thou look'st towards mee
O Saviour, as thou hang'st upon the tree;
I turne my backe to thee, but to receive
Corrections, till thy mercies bid thee leave.
O thinke mee worth thine anger, punish mee,
Burne off my rust, and my deformity,
Restore thine Image, so much, by thy grace,
That thou may'st know mee, and I'll turne my face. (33-42)

The unbroken movement from "thou look'st towards me" to "O Sav-
iour" (35-36) is a brilliant coalescence of the understanding with the
affections, or will, the third of the soul's faculties. For in the joining of
"mee" and "O Saviour," the poem incarnates the inspirited soul of the
speaker in an unmediated colloquy with Christ. And once again, the
speaker's words—bearing the imprint of the *logos* of the soul—approach
their ontological significance. With the Truth of the Crucifixion grasped
by the soul in its eternal present, the whirling between Christ's historical
Crucifixion and the present subsides, and the lines become more even
and smooth.

At this point in the meditation, the speaker, rather than being "carryed"
towards the West by a misdirected will, as he is in the beginning, now seeks
"corrections" by way of the purifying fire of God's Love (37-38). This state-
ment is remarkably similar to one that Augustine makes in the *Confessions*
while lamenting his inability to follow undeviatingly the will of God:

> My thoughts, the intimate life of my soul, are torn this way and that in the havoc of change. And so it will be until I am purified and melted by the fire of your love and fused into one with you. (XI.29)

Donne's speaker likewise petitions Christ to "burne off" the "rusts" and "deformity" (40) of a divided and corrupt will.[17] These corrections, in conjunction with the imputation of Grace, will prepare him ultimately to see God face to face.

Here, in the closing words of the meditation, the speaker's soul arrives at a moment of arrested motion, as he stands imaginatively in the presence of Christ hanging upon the tree (36).[18] The word "turne," which Donne uses twice in this phase of the meditation, possesses a significance often overlooked in studies of the poem. "Turn," in biblical terms, is most often associated with repentance and conversion, or *conversio*. In the Old Testament, Alan Richardson explains, "the idea of repentance is often expressed by such words as 'turn,' 'return.'" Of most influence, "in the use of these words in a religious sense," Richardson adds, "is that of subjects who had rebelled coming back to serve their rightful king, or of a faithless wife returning to her husband, or of those who had been seduced by the baals . . . returning to the worship of Jehovah" (191). Within this context, "'turning' means much more than a mere change of mind, though it includes this; it represents a reorientation of one's whole life and personality . . . a forsaking of sin and a turning to righteousness" (191). The final statement of the poem, "and I'll turne my face," likewise looks forward with greater assurance—and willfulness—towards God now that the understanding has disclosed to the affections a glimpse of their ultimate goal.[19] When the soul enjoys the full restoration of the image of God (41-42), Christ surely will be the first to "know" (42), or recognize, it as His own.[20] The speaker's closing direct colloquy with Christ, the desired end of the soul's meditation, likewise conforms to Augustine's belief not only in the human capacity to apprehend the *imago Dei* within, but also in God's image as the soul's singularly true object of attention. In a sermon, Donne urges the same:

> Place the affection . . . upon the right object, God, and I have, in some measure, done that which this directed, (Taught you the fear of the Lord) if I send you away in either disposition, Timorous, or amorous . . . the love of God begins in fear, and the fear of God ends in love; and that love can never end, for God is love. (4: 113)

The closing lines of "Goodfriday" often are read as signifying a falling short of the speaker's union with God's image, but a brief look at Donne's Reformation theology provides some clarification on the point. Ontologically speaking, fallen human nature cannot become immutable. The residual tension within the poem's future-oriented closing lines attests to that fact, namely, to the recognition of the lifelong dependency on Christ's saving Grace, a dependency that Protestant thinking had greatly intensified. Shuger, however, explains Donne's theology as "absolutist," in the sense that he repeatedly acknowledges the Christian paradox of the demand for obedience and the inability to be wholly obedient—or, as Shuger describes it, "one must be and cannot be perfect" (188). The effect of this dilemma, for Donne, is the experience of guilt and the consequent need to undergo the suffering that will bring about the right relationship between himself and God. But the experience of guilt here "is not paralyzing but creative insofar as it forces the sinner to seek God's face" (Shuger 188).[21] Shuger argues therefore that "such guilt is not simply the prelude to a *conversio* but almost an intrinsically desirable condition," for as one of Donne's sermons emphasizes "'he that stinks most in his owne . . . is the best perfume to Gods nostrils' *Sermons*, 7: 229-31" (180). Furthermore, the experience of such guilt is to be taken as a sign of divine grace, that is, of being able to perceive one's own sinfulness. The fear of God's power, the demand for perfect obedience and the inability to comply, the ensuing guilt, and the needed punishment, together bring the self into the consciousness of divine dependency.

Against the background of the absolutism of Reformation thought, the meditative state at the end of "Goodfriday" may be read, then, not as a falling short of union with God, but as a sign of the sinful soul's gift of grace and progress toward that day when the soul will stand face to face with God. The growing conformity of the speaker's soul with the image of Christ's suffering through the powers of meditation reinforces this view and what Donne claims elsewhere, namely, that such human suffering serves as an ongoing "'re-crucifixion'":

> God would have us doe it [recall the death of Christ] over again. . . . All being guilty of Christs death, there lies an obligation upon us all, to fulfill his sufferings. And this is the *generality* of afflictions, as we consider them in their own nature. (*Sermons* 10: 161-79)[22]

Elsewhere Donne writes that not until "'I am come to that conformity with my Saviour, as to *fulfill his sufferings in my flesh* . . . then I am crucified with him, carried up to his Crosse . . . and wash off all my former unchast looks'"(*Sermons* 2: 300).[23] The speaker here in "Goodfriday" likewise recognizes that "Who sees Gods face, that is selfe life, must dye; / What a death were it then to see God dye" (17-18).[24]

Donne's speaker does, it seems, bear signs of a contractual relationship between the individual and God, that is, the "obligation" to "fulfill [Christ's] sufferings" in order to merit God's promise of redemption. Donne writes, "*If you obey you shall live, if you rebell you shall die*" (*Sermons* 7: 210).[25] But Donne's speaker appears to fall short of the totalizing conversion experience that Augustine recounts in his *Confessions*, culminating in Book VIII.12. Human nature being what it is, for Donne, the contractual relationship is not without its uncertainties.

But both Augustine and Donne's speaker nonetheless share in protracted conversions in which the will is slowly but surely brought into alignment with the will of God. And thus both also create narratives that capture the timelessness of their individual spiritual journeys. Augustine's is embodied in the tripartite structure of his spiritual autobiography: Books I-IX focus on his past sins; Book X addresses the present,converted state of his soul; and Books XI-XIII look to the future. But the whole of the narrative is uttered out of and informed by the present, converted state of his soul, imparting to the *Confessions* its overall sense of timelessness. Donne's poem, as the present study has attempted to show, is likewise organized around the present-mindedness of the soul's faculty of "attention," in conformity with the meditative experience itself. Dennis Quinn's valuable study of Christian eloquence supports the notion that Augustine—and later Donne—regarded the religious text as an instrument of spirituality, that is, as "a means of 'manifesting Christ'(*Sermons* II, 253-54)" (282). The formative principle, it seems, for both Augustine and Donne, is to enlist the reader in the production of meaning. By this I mean that by granting his or her own temporality to the text, the reader at once mediates and spiritually grasps the words—that is, in their *totality of significance*—as a timeless image in which memory, understanding and will are consubstantial with the *imago Dei*.

And so the speaker's initial expectation in "Goodfriday" becomes increasingly a present, inner reality. For the divine immutability toward which the soul's "forme" unceasingly extends itself not only surfaces as the poem's discursive text, but also inscribes itself on the meditative consciousness. In view of the poem's Augustinian bearings, all parts of "Goodfriday," it is proposed here, "flow into one inseparable, inevitable sequence" through the convergence of the soul's faculties with the timeless significance of Christ's redemptive Crucifixion. The poem thus succeeds not only in capturing the redemptive experience of the soul's meditation on the Passion of Christ, but also in evoking in the reader a corresponding modality of mind as the requisite human matrix in which this timeless image repeatedly comes to life.

Notes

[1] See Martz (27, 34-36). Martz points out that multiple variations on the Ignatian model are possible. St. Ignatius describes the "First Exercise" in the *Spiritual Exercises* as "a meditation on the first, second and third sin employing the three powers of the soul. After the prepartory prayer and two preludes it contains three principal points and a colloquy" (25). Shawcross provides important distinctions among Catholic, Protestant, and Anglican meditative paradigms in his essay "Some Colonial American Poetry and George Herbert." Such distinctions are important to understanding the influence of the Reformation on devotional poetry and its heightened emphasis on the individual's direct relationship to God.

[2] Cited in Martz 36. See also Klinck 13-27. Klinck cites Donne's sermon preached at Lincoln's Inn on Trinity Sunday, 1620, in which Donne draws the familiar correspondence between the soul's faculties and the Trinity:

> It is a lovely and religious thing, to finde out *Vestigia Trinitatis*, Impressions of the Trinity, in as many things as we can . . . Let us theefore, with *S. Bernard*, consider *Trinitatem Creatricem*, and *Trinitatem Createm*, a Creating, and a Created Trinity; a Trinity, which the Trinity in Heaven, Father, and Son, and Holy Ghost, hath created in our soules, Reason, Memory, and Will . . . (13)

[3] In *De Trinitate*, Augustine describes a similar "likeness" between the faculties of the soul and the Trinity (XV.xxiii). Achsah Guibbory points out that "Donne's association of the three faculties with the three persons of the Trinity differs from Augustine's: he finds the understanding an image of the Father, the will the

image of the Son, and memory the image of the Holy Ghost (*Sermons* 9: 84)" (261 n.3).

[4] An Ignatian meditation on the timeless truth of the Crucifixion scene, "Goodfriday" is described by Martz as "expressing the state of devotion which results from the integration of the threefold image of God: memory, understanding, will" (56). Martz and others have pointed to Donne's early exposure to the Jesuits, particularly to his uncle, Jasper Heywood, who was a Jesuit missionary in England, and who most likely would have influenced Donne's thinking along Ignatian lines. See Martz (54-56) for his reading of "Goodfriday, 1613."

[5] Martz, along with other scholars, calls attention to Augustine's own mastery of meditation; see Martz, esp. 113 and 247.

[6] Debora Shuger does not see Donne's theology as "uniformly Christocentric" in the sense of the identification between the soul and Christ as the avenue to salvation. Instead, she contends that Donne also depicts Christ "in the context of absolutist power relations as often as those of paradox and participation" (187). Shuger cites an early sermon of Donne's at Lincoln's Inn in support of her view: "'by Christs taking my sins, I am made a *servant of my God . . . a vassall, a Tributary* debtor to God'" (187). Tanner cites both C.A. Patrides and G.F. Waller, who identify Augustine as "the most important influence on sixteenth- and seventeenth-century conceptions of time, . . . an age newly interested in time as a philosophical concept" (132).

[7] *Confessions*, tr. R. S. Pine-Coffin, XI.26. Unless otherwise indicated, all quotations are from this edition. Tanner's study of *Macbeth* illustrates Shakespeare's deployment of an Augustinian conception of time.

[8] See Augustine's account of his reading of a psalm, *Confessions*, XI.28. In *De Trinitate*, Augustine describes the faculty of "understanding" as being "formed from the memory by the attention of thought" (*Intentionem cogitationis*)(XV.23). Freccero also points out that a unifying mode of consciousness "is what Augustine called 'attention,' evenly balanced between memory and expectation—a *logos* binding together an identity in the past with a will to the future" (198).

[9] Masselink (57) also acknowledges Donne's debt to Augustine, but draws attention to the added influence of the Aristotelian-Thomistic tradition on Donne's thinking.

[10] See also Waddington (96-122) on memory, and a sermon of Donne's on Plato and the role of memory (*Sermons* 2: 74; cited in Guibbory 268-69).

[11] The title and date of the poem vary in manuscript traditions, making the "time" of the poem even less historically specific. See Shawcross, ed., *Complete Poetry* (488) and Gardner, ed., *John Donne: The Divine Poems* (98). The title in the Dobell Manuscript reads "A Meditation upon Good ffriday. 1613." As Shawcross (366) indicates, according to one manuscript, Donne was riding to visit Sir

Edward Herbert in Wales on April 2, 1613.

[12] Severance's study of "Goodfriday" offers a richly detailed analysis of the relationship between the poem's formal shape and numerology.

[13] O'Connell (15-16) points out that Donne's use of the word "carryed" (9) reflects the speaker's initial passivity.

[14] Shawcross's commentary on this line indicates that "intelligence" refers to "the angel supposed to move and direct each of the ten spheres of the created (Ptolemaic) universe. Motion is imparted to each inner sphere by the *primum mobile* (the first mover, 1.8)" (*Complete Poetry* 366).

[15] In her commentary on Dante's *Purgatorio* XVII, Dorothy Sayers clarifies the distinction between the conflicting impulses of the soul, or that between the soul's natural and rational loves: "the *natural* love is the unselfconscious instinct, which itself is wholly free from blame; the *rational* is that which has the conscious assent of the will, and may err by 'faulty aim' (love perverted), 'too much zeal' (love excessive) or 'lack thereof' (love defective)' (201, l. 93). Love therefore is the root of all action, whether virtuous or sinful (201, ll. 103-5). Lines 6 and 10 in "Goodfriday" allude to a similar notion.

[16] Sicherman (78) sees in "Goodfriday" and other of Donne's poems a recurring pattern of development: "confident opening, a middle in which initial certainties give way gradually to new perceptions, and a conclusion manifesting a clear and profoundly rooted assurance." Glaser's study attributes much of the poem's conflict to Donne's break with Rome (the East) and his forging of a new Protestant (the West) religious identity.

[17] See also Sherwood 164-65 and Glaser 173-74 on Donne's use of the metaphor of "rusts" in the poem.

[18] On Donne's use of "tree" (36), see Sullivan 1-8.

[19] Richardson points out that "though the Gk. word *metanoein* is often used for 'repent,' in its NT usage it implies much more than a mere 'change of mind'; it involves a whole reorientation of the personality, a 'conversion.' The word 'convert' is rare in EVV [both the Authorized Version and the Revised Version], and RV usually perfers the literal form, 'turn again' (*epistrephein*, to turn). The word 'conversion' occurs in EVV only in Acts 15.3, 'the conversion of the Gentiles'" (192). Evans (13) cites Donne on this point:

> It is one of Saint Augustines definitions of sinne, *Conversio ad creaturam*, that it is a turning, a withdrawing of man to the creature. And every such turning to the creature . . . is downward in respect of him, whom he was made by, and should direct himselfe to. (*Sermons* II, 5).

Sherwood (159) also stresses that "the soul repeatedly turns away from God, then repeatedly is turned back by repentance." Sherwood (159) cites a supporting statement from one of Donne's sermons: "In one word, (one word will not do it, but in two words) it [repentance] is *Aversio*, and *Conversio*: it is a turning from our sins, and a returning to our God" (*Sermons* 7: 162). Donne calls attention to a similar view of sin held by Augustine: "'It is one of Saint *Augustines* definitions of *sinne, Conversio ad creaturam*, that is a turning, a withdrawing of man to the creature'" (*Sermons* 2: 132; cited in Sherwood 160).

[20] Chambers's study of time in Donne's poetry comments on the future-oriented ending of the poem ("'La Corona': Philolsophic, Sacred, and Poetic Uses of Time" (158-59). See also Chambers's "'Goodfriday, 1613. Riding Westward': The Poem and the Tradition."

[21] Although Shuger does not take up Donne's "Goodfriday" poem, her commentary on Donne's sermons is strikingly pertinent to the present study. Friedman's study of "Goodfriday" also makes clear Donne's Reformation sensibility (see esp. 442). See also studies by Lewalski and Halewood.

[22] Cited in Shuger 188. In a sermon preached on April 30, 1615, Donne shares Augustine's belief in the providential trajectory of evil whereby the effects of sinfulness are converted to good ends: "God allows the consequences of sin to work upon us, bringing us sickenss, tribulation, affliction, but takes control of things, so that 'all this is but to improve us'" (cited in Evans 20). Sherwood (164) also emphasizes, in his analysis of "Goodfriday," the soul's growing desire "to conform to the crucified God." Sherwood explains the desire as the soul's recognition of the need for "corrective suffering." Sherwood also explains Donne's use of the word "anger" in the context of Christ's "mercies" (l. 38) as a "correcting anger" (162).

[23] The spiritual exercises of St. Ignatius also have as their primary focus the reformation of the exercitant's "conscious." See, for example, 15-23 in *The Spiritual Exercises of St. Ignatius*. See also Low's study, esp. 71-74, in which Low finds the ending of "Goodfriday" to be consistent with the Ignatian mediation, that is, in which the speaker has made a "conscious effort of the will" in inwardly "pretending to be something and then becoming it" (74).

[24] On the soul's growing desire to conform to the crucified Christ, see Malpezzi 27-28.

[25] Cited in Shuger 177. See n. 1 of the present study on the influence of Reformation thought on devotional paradigms and in particular on the heightened concern with the individual's relationship to God.

Works Cited

Augustine, Saint. *Confessions*. Trans. R. S. Pine-Coffin. New York: Dorset P, 1961.

_____. *Confessions*. Trans. Rex Warner. New York: New American Library, 1963.

_____. *The Trinity*. Trans. Stephen McKenna, G.SS.R. Washington DC.: Catholic U of America P, 1963.

Chambers, A. B. "'Goodfriday, 1613. Riding Westward'. The Poem and the Tradition." *ELH* 28 (1961): 31-53.

_____. "'La Corona': Philosophic, Sacred, and Poetic Uses of Time." *New Essays on Donne*. Ed. Gary A. Stringer. Salzburg: Institut for Englische Sprache and Literature, 1977. 140-72.

Dante Alighieri. *Purgatory*. Vol. 2. *The Comedy of Dante Alighieri*. Trans. Dorothy L. Sayers. Baltimore: Penguin Books, 1955.

Evans, Gillian R. "John Donne and the Augustinian Paradox of Sin." *RES* 33 (1982): 1-22.

Freccero, John. "Cosmology and Rhetoric." *Disorder and Order*. Ed. Paisley Livingston. Saratoga CA: Anma Libri, 1984. 190-98.

Friedman, Donald M. "Memory and the Art of Salvation in Donne's Good Friday Poem." *ELR* 3 (1973): 418-42.

Gardner, Helen, ed. *John Donne: The Divine Poems*. Oxford: Clarendon P, 1978.

Gilson, Etienne. *The Christian Philosophy of Saint Augustine*. Trans. L. E. M. Lynch. London: Victor Gollancz, 1961.

Glaser, Joe. "'Goodfriday, 1613': A Soul's Form." *College Literature* 13.2 (1986): 168-76.

Guibbory, Achsah. "John Donne and Memory as 'the Art of *Salvation*.'" *HLQ* (Autumn 1980): 261-73.

Halewood, William H. *The Poetry of Grace*. New Haven: Yale UP, 1970.

Jordan, Robert. "Time and Contingency in St. Augustine." *Augustine: A Collection of Critical Essays*. Ed. R. A. Markus. New York: Anchor Books, 1972. 255-79.

Klinck, Dennis R. "*Vestigia Trinitatis* in Man and His Works in the English Renaissance." *JHI* 42 (1981): 13-27.

Lewalski, Barbara Kiefer. *Prostestant Poetics and the Seventeenth-Century Religious Lyric*. Princeton: Princeton UP, 1979.

Low, Anthony. *Love's Architecture: Devotional Modes in Seventeenth-Century English Poetry*. New York: New York UP, 1978.

Loyola, Saint Ignatius. *The Spiritual Exercises of St. Ignatius*. Trans. Louis J. Puhl, S. J. Westminster MD: Newman P, 1957.

Malpezzi, Frances M. "'As I Ride': The Beast and His Burden in Donne's 'Goodfriday.'" *Religion and Literature* 24.1 (Spring 1992): 23-31.

Martz, Louis L. *The Poetry of Meditation*. New Haven: Yale UP, 1954.

Masselink, Noralyn. "Donne's Epistemology and the Appeal to Memory." *JDJ* 8 (1989): 57-88.

O'Connell, Patrick F. "'Restore Thine Image': Structure and Theme in Donne's 'Goodfriday.'" *JDJ* 4 (1985): 13-28.

Quinn, Dennis. "Donne's Christian Eloquence." *ELH* 27 (1960): 276-97.

Richardson, Alan. *A Theological Word Book of the Bible*. London: SCM P, 1950.

Severance, Sibyl Lutz. "Soul, Sphere, and Structure in 'Goodfriday, 1613. Riding Westward.'" *SP* 84 (1987): 24-41.

Shawcross, John T. "Some Colonial American Poetry and George Herbert." *Early American Literature* 23 (1988): 28-51.

Sherwood, Terry G. *Fulfilling the Circle: A Study of Donne's Thought*. Tornoto: U of Toronto P, 1984.

Shuger, Debora Kuller. *Habits of Thought in the English Renaissance*. Berkeley: U of California P, 1990.

Sicherman, Carol. "Donne's Discoveries." *SEL* 11 (1971): 69-88.

Sullivan, David M. "Riders to the West: 'Goodfriday, 1613.'" *JDJ* 6 (1987): 1-8.

Tanner, John S. "The Syllables of Time: An Augustinian Context for *Macbeth* 5.5." *JRMMRA* 8 (1987): 131-146.

Waddington, Raymond B. "Shakespeare's Sonnet 15 and the Art of Memory." *The Rhetoric of Renaissance Poetry*. Ed. Thomas O. Sloan and Raymond B. Waddington. Berkeley: U of California P, 1974. 96-122.

Wrestling with God:
John Donne at Prayer

Jeffrey Johnson

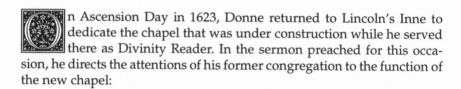n Ascension Day in 1623, Donne returned to Lincoln's Inne to dedicate the chapel that was under construction while he served there as Divinity Reader. In the sermon preached for this occasion, he directs the attentions of his former congregation to the function of the new chapel:

> it is a frivolous contention, whether *Churches* be for *preaching*, or for *praying*. But if *Consecration* be a kind of *Christning* of the *Church*, and that at the *Christning* it have a name, wee know what name *God* hath appoynted for his House, *Domus mea, Domus orationis vocabitur. My house shall bee called the House of Prayer.* (*Sermons* 4: 373)

Donne often quotes in his *Sermons* this passage from Isaiah 56:7 in order, as he does here, to remind his hearers how God himself describes the Church, the members of which congregate, as Donne states, for "no other Service, but Common prayer" (*Sermons* 4: 374).

In many ways, the fundamental religious struggle for Donne derives from his understanding of the Church. Reacting to the difficulties Donne experienced in his personal life in converting to Anglicanism, as well as the inquiries he raises in such works as "Show me deare Christ" and " Satyre III," many critics have analyzed his conflicts primarily in an attempt to identify his sectarian allegiance. In an article that discusses

Donne's life at Mitcham from 1607-10, those years which R. C. Bald describes as "the most disturbed and anxious years of Donne's life" (235), Dennis Flynn argues that although Donne began, during these years, to perceive himself as "an Anglican with reservations," he still "could not fully accept Anglicanism as long as he felt a deep division between his private religious feelings and the institutional religion to which he subscribed" (185, 186). Citing letters that Donne wrote to Goodyere during this period, Flynn insists that Donne's "private habits of prayer continued to reflect his Catholic background" and that throughout this period in his life Donne "emphasizes the value of a private devotion as opposed to the public ritual of his church" (187, 188).

Richard Strier, reacting to Stachniewski's attempt to read the *Divine Poems* as consistently Calvinistic, argues that "the pain and confusion in many of the 'Holy Sonnets' is not that of the convinced Calvinist but rather that of a person who would like to be a convinced Calvinist but who is both unable to be so and unable to admit that he is unable to be so" (361). According to Strier, Donne's irresolution concerning the Anglican Church and his relation to it surfaces in the *Holy Sonnets* because of his inability to rest in the comfort afforded by the doctrine of predestination. Finally, John Carey reduces the issue by simply labeling Donne an apostate. Interpreting Donne's life and faith exclusively as a betrayal of his Catholic upbringing, Carey states that "though Donne eventually came to accept Anglicanism, he could never believe that he had found in the Church of England the one true church outside which salvation was impossible" (15).

As valuable as these biographical discussions are for furthering our understanding of the psychological nuances of Donne's personal struggles, they must be weighed against the theological necessity Donne himself feels for being identified within the common body of Christ, specifically through the Church's defining act within the world, prayer. In fact, Donne's published statements about prayer, especially those found in the *Sermons*, consistently reiterate the efficacy of communal prayer:

> In a Sermon, God speaks to the Congregation, but he answers onely that soule, that hath been with him at Prayers before. A man may pray in the street, in the fields, in a fayre; but it is a more acceptable and more effectuall prayer, when we shut our doores, and observe our stationary houres for private prayer in our Chamber; and in our Chamber, when we pray upon our knees, then in our beds. But the greatest power of all, is in the publique prayer of the Congregation. (*Sermons* 7: 311–28 Jan. 1626/27)

Within this context, in which one's devotional life finds its highest potential within common prayer, Donne identifies what he refers to in several sermons as "St. Augustine's Holy Circle," which is "to pray, that we may heare Sermons profitably, and to heare Sermons that we learn to pray acceptably" (*Sermons* 9: 194–Easter 1630). What one discovers in reading the *Sermons* is that for Donne it is prayer, and specifically public prayer, that defines the Christian life, for common prayer is an activity so central to Christianity that it transcends sectarian allegiances. As a result, Donne pursued a definitional, rather than dogmatic, understanding of prayer which was idiosyncratic, blending quite orthodox teachings with his own highly stylized devotional practice.

In his Second Prebend sermon, explaining that all that is undertaken wisely and well is accomplished by following a pattern, Donne raises the question with his congregation at St. Paul's, "If [God] aske me an Idea of my prayers, shall I not be able to say, It is that which my particular necessities, that which the forme prescribed by thy Son, that which the care, and piety of the Church, in conceiving fit prayers, hath imprinted in me?" (*Sermons* 8: 61–29 Jan. 1625/26). It is within this three-part pattern– the teachings of the Church, the model of Christ, and the particular needs of the self–that Donne couches his discussions of prayer.

The teachings of the Christian Church (whether Catholic or Protestant) are in accord with respect to the primary purpose and significance of prayer. Donne acknowledges, in a sermon on Luke 23: 24, the relative lack of controversy surrounding prayer, stating that "Of all the conduits and conveyances of Gods graces to us, none hath been so little subject to cavillations, as this of prayer," and further that "Almost every meanes between God and man, suffers some adulteratings and disguises: But prayer least" (*Sermons* 5: 232—undated). In spite of some minor areas of disagreement, namely praying for the dead and praying to saints,[1] Catholic and Protestant theologians alike consistently identify prayer as the chief act of religion and as the highest service to God.

Aquinas, in accordance with earlier Church Fathers, explains that because all things showing honor to God belong to religion, prayer itself is an act of religion since through it the believer subjects him or herself to God by confessing dependence upon the Creator (see also Article 3).[2] Aquinas further contends that, as an act belonging to the will, prayer "is the chief of the acts of religion, since by it religion directs man's intellect to God" (Article 3). As a result, Aquinas repeatedly defines prayer as "*the raising up of the mind to God*" (Article 1), as an action in which "we unveil our mind in His presence" (Article 1) and, thereby, "*surrender ourselves to*

God and unite ourselves to Him" (Article 1).

Anglican dogma propounds a similar understanding of prayer to that of Roman Catholicism. Hooker, in particular, first raises the question, "Is not the name of prayer usual to signify even all the service that ever we do unto God?" (V.xxiii),[3] and then continues, "And that for no other cause, as I suppose, but to shew that there is in religion no acceptable duty which devout invocation of the name of God doth not either presuppose or infer" (V.xxiii). Hooker describes prayer as "the sending of Angels upward," as the act of acknowledging God "our sovereign good," and as a "concurrence with him in desiring that wherewith his very nature doth most delight" (V.xxiii). Prayer is, according to this Anglican apologist, a "holy and religious duty of service towards God" (V.xxiv). It is a duty with respect to the love God has extended to us, and it is a service accounted more worthy when accomplished as a common body.

Donne's sermon on Psalm 32: 6 discusses the duty of prayer not only as a public act, but also as a surrendering of the mind, and therefore the will, to God. Donne delineates in his exegesis that prayer is the duty of every godly person who desires to be more godly; that the object of prayer is God alone, for as Donne states, "God alone can heare, and God alone can give" (*Sermons* 9: 328–undated); that the subject of prayer, according to the model provided by David in the Psalms, is the confession of and forgiveness for one's sins, which is the better accomplished through the prayers "recommended to us by the Church, then to extemporall prayers of others, or of our owne effusion" (*Sermons* 9: 328–undated); and that, finally, the time for prayer is now and always, whether in time of calamity or of prosperity, for any time one may "seeke him with a whole heart, seeke him as a Principall" (*Sermons* 9: 328–undated). Yet in urging his congregation to this central duty, Donne never forgets that charity is the wellspring of prayer since devout petitions motivated by charity bring people into community with one another. Prefacing his comments on this subject by stating, "True love and charity is to doe the most that we can, all that we can for the good of others" (*Sermons* 5: 278–undated), Donne entreats his listeners:

> And something there is which every man may doe; There are Armies, in the levying whereof, every man is an absolute Prince, and needs no Commission, there are Forces, in which every man is his owne Muster-master, The force which we spoke of before, out of *Tertullian*, the force of prayer; . . . Charity is to doe all to all; and the poorest of us all can doe this to any. (*Sermons* 5: 279–undated)

Prayer is the act of religion that defines the believer's relationship with God, for as Donne states, "When we leave praying, God leaves us" (*Sermons* 8: 339–20 Feb. 1628/29). Thus, in praying Donne believes God manifests himself within us through our words. Prayer is incarnational in this respect. Prayerful utterances, according to Donne, are as "lineaments and apparel upon our Devotions" (*Sermons* 8: 338); they are a manifestation of God, who himself came to us as the Word made flesh.

It should not be surprising that so much of what Donne says about prayer, in the *Sermons* specifically, occurs within the context of the Psalms. Of the eleven sermons in which prayer is the central focus, only two use verses as sermon texts that are not from the Psalms, and six of the eleven are homilies upon Psalm 6.[4] This connection between the Psalms and prayer reflects the 1559 Prayer Book, which orders the Psalter so that it is read in its entirety each month during the course of the morning and evening prayers.[5]

Beyond the teaching and tradition of the Church, Donne also looks to the example of prayer found in Jesus Christ. The most obvious place to begin is the Lord's Prayer. As a priest in the Church of England, Donne was well-acquainted with the prominence of this prayer in the Anglican liturgy. The Lord's Prayer, as prescribed in the Prayer Book, was recited aloud following the general confession of sin by the congregation and the priest's statement of absolution during morning prayers. It is also the Lord's Prayer that was proclaimed at the opening not only of the evening prayers, but also of the service of Holy Communion.

Donne's own statements in the *Sermons* concerning the Lord's Prayer are rather conventional, and they are often included within passages that comment upon other formulaic statements of faith and doctrine, such as the Ten Commandments and the Apostles' Creed. One of the few instances in which Donne discusses the particulars of the Lord's Prayer appears in his sermon on Psalm 6:2-3. The context for the reference centers upon Donne's insistence that no matter how imperfect or weak our prayers might be, "yet still if it be a prayer, it hath a *Quia*, a Reason, upon which it is grounded," for "that prayer is very farre from faith, which is not made so much as with reason" (*Sermons* 5: 345—undated). Donne then illustrates this idea by noting that within the Lord's Prayer the injunctions "Thy Kingdom come" and "Hallowed be thy name" and the requests for daily bread and forgiveness of sins are grounded upon the reasons that "God hath a Kindome here," that he desires "to be glorified by us," and that the ability to provide sustenance and forgiveness are "in his power," respectively (*Sermons* 5: 345-46).

In spite of its obvious applications as a model of and for devout petition, the Lord's Prayer is not the prayer of Christ's to which Donne most often calls attention in the *Sermons*. Instead, it is Christ's entreaty in the garden of Gethsemane, where he pleads three times to be spared from crucifixion and in his agony sweats drops of blood (Mt. 26:36-46; Lk. 22:39-46), that Donne refers to with regularity in his preaching. On several occasions this prayer serves as an example of the need to be persistent in prayer, "to repeat often the same prayer in the same words," for as Donne notes, "Our Saviour did so; he prayed a third time, and in the same words" (*Sermons* 5: 286–undated). Christ's prayer in Gethsemane is also used in a sermon on the final three verses of Psalm 6 to illustrate two important principles in prayer. Donne begins the third part of the sermon by explaining that the Old Testament definition for clean animals was that they have a divided hoof and that they chew the cud, and by analogy he suggests that all resolutions made in prayer must have similar marks:

> they must divide the hoofe, they must make a double impression, they must be directed upon Gods glory, and upon our good, and they must passe a rumination, a chawing of the cud, a second examination, whether that prayer were so conditioned or no. (*Sermons* 6: 52–Spring 1623)

Alluding then to the incident in Gethsemane, Donne notes, "Christ brought his own Prayer, *Si possibile, If it be possible &c.* through such a rumination, *Veruntamen, yet not my will &c.*" (*Sermons* 6: 52).

Most commonly, however, Donne refers to Christ's prayer in the garden as an example of one who in the midst of his affliction seeks earnestly for release, but who ultimately relinquishes himself, as Christ did, in humble conformity to God's will. In concluding his Lincoln's Inne sermon on Psalm 38:9 ("Lord all my desire is before thee, and my groaning is not hid from thee"), Donne applies the verse "to Christs prayer in his Agony in the garden" (*Sermons* 2: 161–undated) and reiterates that our prayers for deliverance from our sufferings are accomplished in God's time and not in ours. Further, in the final paragraph of his final sermon, *Deaths Duell*, Donne alludes again to this prayer of Christ's, as he urges his listeners to a humble reconciliation with God:

> In that *time* and in those *prayers* was [Christ's] *agony* and *bloody sweat*. I will *hope* that thou didst *pray*; but not *every ordinary* and *customary prayer*, but *prayer actually* accompanied with *shedding of teares*, and *dispositively* in a readines to *shed blood* for *his glory* in *necessary cases*, puts thee into a

conformity with him. (*Sermons* 10: 246)

It is within this struggle of the believer to conform the will with God's that Donne finally understands and defines prayer.

Donne's orthodox views of prayer, especially in relation to the teachings of the Church and the models of Christ, do not negate his personal struggles with regard to the act of prayer as a central expression of Christian faith. The "particular necessities" of Donne's idea of prayer, therefore, include reconciling the duty of prayer with the unavoidable distractions Christians experience, and the importunity God himself urges with Donne's own inclination toward what he calls "impudency."

In a sermon preached on Candlemas Day, Donne asserts to his congregation that they have two great debts to God–the first is the debt of glory and praise and the second is prayer–and then explains by way of a paradox, "we grow best out of debt, by growing farther in debt; by praying for more, we pay our former debt" (*Sermons* 4: 309–1622/23).[6] In the same sermon Donne comments further that "God will not be paid, with money of our owne coyning, (with sudden, extemporall, inconsiderate prayer)," but rather, Donne insists, "with currant money, that beares the Kings Image, and inscription; The Church of God, by his Ordinance, hath set his stampe, upon a Liturgie and Service, for his house" (*Sermons* 4: 310). The economic terms employed in these passages are common to the New Testament, and in using them Donne is attempting to illustrate the obligation believers have to God and to one another because of Christ.

The duty to pray, in particular, stems from the implications Donne perceives in identifying the Church as the body of Christ, who is the Word made flesh. In a Lenten sermon at Whitehall, Donne preaches, "God came to us *in verbo*, In the word," and then urges, "Let us, that are Christians, go to God so, too" (*Sermons* 8: 338–20 Feb. 1628/29), and in his fifth Prebend sermon he reiterates, "Christ is *Verbum*, *The Word*, and that excludes silence . . . *Dicite*, *Say*, sayes *David*, Delight to speake of God, and with God, and for God; *Dicite*, say something" (*Sermons* 8: 119—Nov. or Dec. 1627). For Donne the words of prayer are, as Herbert describes them in "Prayer" (I), "Gods breath in man returning to his birth" (line 2). Prayer is the palpable connection between God and his people, and their collective breathing "unto the nostrils of God *a savour of rest*" (*Sermons* 8: 197–5 April 1628) manifests God's Church in the world.

In spite of the acute sense of duty to prayer that Donne espouses throughout the *Sermons*, there arise distractions of slumber, of deviation, of vain repetition, of ignorance, of negligence and error, and of wanton-

ness and misinterpretation (cf. *Sermons* 10: 56-57–All Saints' Day 1623?).
The distractions are those related to the limitations and corruptions of the
flesh, so that Donne always imagines prayer as the struggle of the body
and soul. In this context, prayer itself is understood as a typological
expression of the Incarnation, as the Word is recreated through the words
of prayer in order to reestablish the relationship of God and his creatures
that has been severed because of original sin.

One of the more memorable passages concerning the distractions to
prayer appears in the funeral sermon preached for Sir William Cokayne,
in which Donne delineates a variety of distractions with particular poi-
gnancy:

> But when we consider with a religious seriousnesse the manifold weak-
> nesses of the strongest devotions in time of Prayer, it is a sad consider-
> ation. I throw my selfe downe in my Chamber, and I call in, and invite
> God, and his Angels thither, and when they are there, I neglect God and
> his Angels, for the noise of a Flie, for the ratling of a Coach, for the
> whining of a doore; I talke on, in the same posture of praying; Eyes lifted
> up; knees bowed downe; as though I prayed to God; and, if God, or his
> Angels should aske me, when I thought last of God in that prayer, I
> cannot tell: Something I finde that I had forgot what I was about, but
> when I began to forget it, I cannot tell. A memory of yesterdays plea-
> sures, a feare of to morrows dangers, a straw under my knee, a noise in
> mine eare, a light in mine eye, an any thing, a nothing, a fancy, a
> Chimera in my braine, troubles me in my prayer. (*Sermons* 7: 264-65–12
> Dec. 1626)

These distractions cause one to forget. The struggle here is the struggle to
remember, to recall the promises of God and the mercies of God. In fact,
one of the functions of structured and repeated prayers in the liturgy of
the Church, whether Protestant or Catholic, is to arouse the memory. As
he concludes his sermon on Psalm 6:2-3, Donne states, "*Pray*, and *Stay*, are
two blessed Monosyllables; To ascend to God, To attend Gods descent to
us, is the motion, and the Rest of a Christian" (*Sermons* 5: 363–undated).
Within this context, it is clear that the benefit of prayer is for those who
pray, for those who thereby complete the double motion of the relation-
ship between the divine and the human; and the purpose of prayer is to
remind the faithful of the preeminence of attaining God's rest.[7]

Because of the human propensity to forget and, therefore, to become
susceptible to sin, Donne pleads for steadfastness in prayer. Again, in the

sermon preached for the funeral of Sir William Cokayne, Donne reminds those present of the biblical precedent for importunity in prayer as he calls to mind the parable of the person seeking bread at midnight (Lk. 11:5-8), the parable of the unjust judge and the persistent widow (Lk. 18:1-6), and the account of the woman from Canaan who pleaded with Christ to heal her daughter (Mt. 15:21-28), concluding, "It is not enough to have prayed once; Christ does not onely excuse, but enjoine Importunity" (*Sermons* 7: 269—12 Dec. 1626).

Beyond persistence, however, Donne expresses the need to pursue what he calls a "religious impudency," as he asserts in the opening paragraph of his sermon on Psalm 6:4-5:

> Prayer hath the nature of Impudency; Wee threaten God in Prayer; . . . And God suffers this Impudency, and more. Prayer hath the nature of Violence; In the publique Prayers of the Congregation, we besiege God, saies *Tertullian*, and we take God Prisoner, and bring God to our Conditions; and God is glad to be straitned by us in that siege. (*Sermons* 5: 364—undated)

In the *Sermons* Donne is fond of the metaphor so commonly found in his religious verse of prayer as warfare, in which one engages God in violent struggle. Nevertheless, Donne always describes the battle not as one enacted against God, but with God; it is a contest God himself encourages. By way of illustrating his point that one may confront God in prayer boldly, and even brazenly, Donne notes that God "grudges not to be chidden and disputed with, by Job" (6:4, 12), nor to be "directed and counselled by *Jonas*" (4:2, 9), nor to be "threatned and neglected by *Moses*" (Ex. 32:32). Furthermore, "Prayer is the way," Donne insists, "which God hath given us to batter Heaven," whether in the public congregation where "we besiege God with our prayers," or in our private chambers where "we wrastle with him hand to hand" (*Sermons* 5: 223–undated). In fact, Donne contends that unless a prayer is undertaken with reason, "with a serious purpose to pray," such prayers "are but false fires without shot, they batter not heaven" (*Sermons* 5: 345–undated).

While a number of critics have discussed Donne's religious verse, and especially the *Holy Sonnets*, as prayerful utterances, only a few have explored the rhetorical implications of this connection. Heather Asals analyzes "The Grammar of Redemption" in the *Holy Sonnets* as an imitation of "God's primary idiom, imperative command, and his secondary idiom, the hortatory 'let'" (134) and concludes that these poems are "essentially explorations in and examinations of the possibilities of language as reflections of God's promises in his Word" (136). In a recent article centering upon Donne's "holy importunitie" and "pious impudencie,"[8] Raymond-Jean Frontain argues that "the *Holy Sonnets* seem scripted to produce a divine reply that would at least resolve the speaker's uncertainty about his condition, if not actually provoke God to intervene and extend to the speaker the prevenient grace he so desperately desires" (99). The orthodoxy of this prayerful struggle in Donne's religious verse, to procure the assurance of salvation, not only echoes the language of the Psalms, but also suggests a public dimension for these poems as devotional models. In an article in which he notes that "as prayers, both the Penitential Psalms and the 'Holy Sonnets' primarily adopt the dramatic pose of the sinner addressing God directly" (209), Roman Dubinski concludes by asserting the plausibility "that in sending his 'Holy Sonnets' to his friends, Donne would expect them to complement the Penitential Psalms as part of their evening penitential devotions" (215). In spite of the rather private implications of Donne's *Holy Sonnets*, at least the first six were sent in 1609 to the Earl of Dorset with a dedicatory sonnet. In addition, Donne's two poetic examples of liturgical prayer, "La Corona" (1607) and "A Litanie" (1608), both reflect devotional intentions; the former was most likely sent with a letter and prefatory sonnet to Lady Magdalen Herbert,[9] and the latter was intended, as Donne himself specifies in a letter to Goodyere, "for lesser Chappels, which are my friends" (*Letters* 33).[10] The nature of the spiritual struggle Donne dramatizes in the *Divine Poems* stems from his orthodox, yet nonetheless troubling, recognition both of his own sinfulness and his dependence upon God, who alone can forgive.

Although this tension defines the prayerful action of the *Holy Sonnets*, it is within his religious occasional verse that Donne resolves his struggle, but nowhere more successfully than in the hymns, in which Donne couches his private concerns in a distinctly public genre. In particular, the imperatives found throughout the three hymns culminate in an expressed conformity to the body of Christ. Following the first two stanzas which question the extent of God's forgiveness, "A Hymne to God the Father" (1623) concludes as Donne insists that God continue to confirm his election: "Sweare by thy selfe, that at my death thy Sunne / Shall shine as it shines now, and heretofore" (15-16). The resolution, "Thou haste done, / I have no more" (17-18), occurs in response to this promise that Donne has been fully incorporated–past, present, and future–within the light of Christ. In "Hymne to God my God, in my sicknesse" (1623 or 1631),

Donne resolves his command "Looke Lord, and finde both *Adams* met in me" (23) specifically within the crucified body of Christ. The final stanza implores God to receive him in Christ's "purple wrapp'd" (26) and to be given not Christ's crown of thorns but "his other Crowne" (27). The reason for this petition is that Donne, in his sickness, accepts that salvation is possible only to the extent that he realizes the sufferings of his own body in terms of Christ's. Finally, in "A Hymne to Christ, at the Authors last going into Germany" (1619), Donne reads the occasion of his journey as an emblem for his relationship with Christ, which he defines in the final sentence of the poem: "Churches are best for Prayer, that have least light: / To see God only, I goe out of sight: / And to scape stormy dayes, I chuse an Everlasting night" (26-28). As he struggles in this poem to divorce himself from the false mistresses of his youth (fame, wit, and hope) and know only "th'Eternall root of true Love" (14), the defiant and sinful individuality of Donne disappears from sight as he conforms himself, through the "religious impudency" of his prayer, to Christ's body, the Church.

The *Sermons* illustrate in the character of Jacob one of Donne's favorite biblical types for the impudent behavior dramatized in the religious verse. In the second part of his sermon on Genesis 18: 25 ("Shall not the judge of all the earth do right?"), Donne states his general point "That God admits, even expostulation, from his servants" and then alludes to the account of Jacob wrestling with God (Gen. 32: 24-28), noting, "God would have gone from *Iacob* when he *wrestled*, and *Iacob would not let him go*, and that prevailed with God" (*Sermons* 3: 145—Trinity Sunday 1620). Further in the same paragraph, following other examples of Old Testament figures who confronted, rebuked, and even chided God, Donne contrasts the reaction of Jehovah to this behavior with that of earthly rulers:

> what Prince would not (and justly) conceive an indignation against such a petitioner? which of us that heard him, would not pronounce him to be mad, to ease him of a heavier imputation? And yet our long suffering, and our patient God, (must we say, our humble and obedient God?) endures all this. (*Sermons* 3: 146)

The point here is that God not only encourages this type of effrontery in prayer, but also rewards it. After all, Jacob secures a blessing from God, which is highlighted by God's renaming of Jacob ("supplanter") as Israel ("God strives").

Even though Jacob's contest with God is the model of "religious impudency" in prayer, Donne consistently reiterates that such brazen approaches must be undertaken above all else for the glory of God. Referring again to this wrestling match, Donne cautions, "Yea, God was so far, from giving [Jacob] present meanes of deliverance, that he made him worse able to deliver himselfe, he wrastled with him, and lam'd him" (*Sermons* 3: 199–7 Jan. 1620). Jacob struggled with God and prevailed, but it came at a price; it involved a sacrifice. While Donne urges believers to strive aggressively to procure God's favor, he never overlooks the fact that the goal of prayer is reconciliation with God and His Church, which involves an acknowledgement of Christ as "a stone of rest and security to our selves" (*Sermons* 2: 186–21 Feb. 1618/19), as well as a true and sorrowful confession of our sins. Jacob's being lamed by God is the emblem for this humble intent in approaching God. Certainly for Donne, prayer is a warring with God, and yet, as he explains in another paradox, "warre is a degree of peace, as it is the way of peace; and these colluctations and wrestlings with God, bring a man to peace with him" (*Sermons* 2: 186). John Booty's discussion of the 1559 Prayer Book complements this pattern for approaching God that Donne finds in the example of Jacob, noting that "the rhythm of penitence and praise, penitence rising to praise, praise falling back into penitence and then rising again to praise, [is] the rhythm of the Christian life," and that, in fact, "all of the Prayer Book can be regarded in terms of this repetition of penitence and praise" (379). While Donne adds his own idiosyncratic and personal "impudency" to this pattern, the pattern itself is entirely orthodox.

None of Donne's published prayers illustrates his ideas as completely as the twenty-three that appear in his *Devotions* (1624). Sharon Cadman Seelig has recently focused upon the last sentences of the final prayer in the *Devotions*, questioning what readers are to make of Donne's seemingly divided self. In the concluding sentence, in particular, Seelig describes that the very structure of the statement expresses not affirmation for his return to health, but anxiety concerning the possibility of a relapse. Such a concern is "not a sudden failure of nerve" or "an inability to accept good fortune" (104), but rather, as Seelig concludes, an understanding that

> to be lowered here is to be raised in heaven, to see that what in human terms is a victory, a return to health, is in theological terms a postponement of the goal, and that fear of relapsing, contrary to our first impression of the matter, may be taken as a sign of hope and of health.(112)

As this statement makes clear, Donne imagines prayer and the Christian life as a contest between human weakness and divine faithfulness, as a coming to terms with one's own propensity to sin in relation to the grace and mercy of God. Because he is acutely aware of the temptations of the flesh and the failings of the will, Donne not only relies upon, but also demands God's own promises of mercy. In fact, Donne believes it necessary and appropriate both to remind and to bind God to such promises as a way to guarantee them. Referring directly to the first half of his text from Psalm 90:14 ("O satisfy us early with thy mercy"), Donne explains that "this is a Prayer of limitation even upon God himselfe, That our way may be his, and that his way may be the way of *mercy*" (*Sermons* 5: 274—undated).

The "religious impudency" Donne exhibits throughout the *Devotions* is clearly illustrated in the final lines of the tenth prayer as he recalls God's nature and limits Him in terms of it:

> And since sinne in the nature of it, retaines still so much of the author of it, that it is a *Serpent*, insensibly insinuating it selfe, into my *Soule*, let thy *brazen Serpent*, (the contemplation of thy *Sonne* crucified for me) be evermore present to me, for my recovery against the sting of the first *Serpent*; That so, as I have a *Lyon* against a *Lyon*, The *Lyon of the Tribe of Judah*, against that *Lyon, that seekes whom hee may devoure*, so I may have a *Serpent* against a *Serpent*, the *Wisedome of the Serpent*, against the *Malice of the Serpent*, And, both against that *Lyon*, and *Serpent*, forcible, and subtill tentations, Thy *Dove* with thy *Olive*, and thy *Arke*, *Humilitie*, and *Peace*, and *Reconciliation* to thee, by the *ordinances* of thy *Church. Amen.* (55)

As he struggles in this prayer with his own sinful nature, Donne commissions God to employ His serpent and His lion against those of Satan. Donne wrestles with God in this way, not to usurp Him, but in order, as Jacob did, to extract His blessing. Donne's impudency toward God is tempered, however, as he is lamed by the memory of his fallen nature. Nevertheless, only by means of humbling himself and remembering who he is in relation to God is Donne able to find peace and reconciliation.

The thirteenth prayer of the *Devotions* models all the elements Donne finds necessary for addressing God. Before examining the prayer, however, a brief overview of this section of the *Devotions* is necessary, the English heading for which reads, "The Sickness declares the infection and malignity thereof by spots." The thirteenth meditation opens as Donne espouses that the human condition consists more of misery than of happiness, and that while "All men call *Misery, Misery*," yet "*Happinesse* changes the name, by the taste of man" (67). As Donne then contemplates the spots that have appeared on his body, he cannot decide whether they portend ill or good, and then concludes the meditation by stating that happiness can only be understood in comparison to misery, that he must suffer in order to receive and appreciate healing.

In the expostulation Donne offers himself to God as a sacrifice, but he immediately laments that his self-offering will be unacceptable since it is a spotted, and thereby impure, one. Quickly shifting his argument yet again, Donne questions why his spottedness should disqualify his sacrifice and keep him from God. In a brilliantly witty passage Donne remembers the promises of God and turns them to his own advantage: his body, spotted as it may be, is not only the dwelling place of Christ, but also the temple of the Holy Spirit; Christ himself, "who hath al our stains, & deformities in him" (69), is spotted; and the spouse of Christ, the Church, is itself tainted in that "every particular *soule* in that *Church* is full of staines, and spots" (69). Donne concludes, therefore, that the only spots, the only deformities upon the body and the soul, that God despises are the ones we try to hide from Him. As a result, Donne urges his readers to confess and repent of their sins, for, as he writes, "When I open my *spotts*, I doe but present him with that which is *His*, and till I do so, I detaine, & withhold *his right*" (70). It is only by presenting our spotted selves to God that we may be reconciled to Him and incorporated fully within the body of Christ.

The thirteenth prayer, which plays upon the paradox of sickness and health addressed in the meditation and expostulation, opens by acknowledging the sovereignty of God and by binding God to His mercy:

> O eternall, and most gratious *God*, who as thou givest all for *nothing*, if we consider any precedent Merit in us, so giv'st *Nothing*, for *Nothing*, if we consider the *acknowledgement*, & *thankefullnesse*, which thou lookest for, after, accept my humble thankes, both for thy *Mercy*, and for this particular *Mercie*, that in thy *Judgement* I can discerne thy *Mercie*, and find *comfort* in thy *corrections*. (70)

In humbling himself to God by acknowledging his own weakness, Donne insists, nevertheless, on reminding God of His divinity so that, as Donne states in a wonderful example of chiasmus, "in thy *Judgement* I can discerne thy *Mercie*, and find *comfort* in thy *corrections*." This opening sentence, as well as the remainder of the prayer, portrays Donne as a type of Jacob, in whom affliction becomes the sign and seal of God's blessing. It is by means of God's touching Donne, as it were, on the thigh and laming him that Donne is assured of his reconciliation to God and his fellowship within the Church:

> I know, O *Lord*, the ordinary *discomfort* that accompanies that phrase, *That the house is visited*, And that, *that thy markes, and thy tokens are upon the patient*; But what a wretched, and disconsolate *Hermitage* is that *House*, which is not *visited* by thee, and what a *Wayve*, and *Stray* is that *Man*, that hath not thy *Markes* upon him? These heates, O *Lord*, which thou hast broght upon this *body*, are but thy chafing of the *wax*, that thou mightest *seale* me to thee; These *spots* are but the *letters*, in which thou hast written thine owne *Name*, and conveyed thy selfe to mee; whether for a *present possession*, by taking me now, or for a future *reversion*, by glorifying thy selfe in my stay here, I limit not, I condition not, I choose not, I wish not, no more then the house, or land that passeth by any *Civill* conveyance.(70)

Donne reminds God, and thereby comforts himself, that his body and soul belong to God and that his present spotted condition is a visible sign of his election. Suffering within the body and in imitation of Christ's suffering conforms one to Christ. As a result, Donne insists that God has an obligation to claim his diseased body since it is actually a part of the body of God's own Son. Prayer thirteen concludes by affirming Donne's desire to conform himself to his Lord:

> Onely be thou ever present to me, O *my God*, and this *bed-chamber*, & thy bed-chamber shal be all one roome, and the closing of these bodily *Eyes* here, and the opening of the *Eyes* of my *Soule*, there, all one *Act*. (70)

Donne's plea in this petition is not exclusively self-interested; throughout the *Devotions* Donne holds himself up as an example of the corporate body of Christ.

In his discussions of the *Devotions*, Terry Sherwood writes that Donne's "double consciousness of self and its shared awareness of community precludes a separation of the self from its Calling in the Body" (185). Prayer brings the individual into community, not only with God, but also with the Church, both Militant and Triumphant. As Donne meditates in his *Devotions* upon the tolling of a bell, he speaks to God in the seventeenth prayer concerning one who has recently died:

When thy *Sonne* cried out upon the *Crosse, My God, my God, Why hast thou forsaken me?* he spake not so much in his *owne Person*, as in the person of the *Church*, and of his afflicted *members*, who in deep distresses might feare thy *forsaking.* This *patient*, O most blessed *God*, is one of them; . . . unite *him & us* in one *Communion of Saints.* Amen. (90)

In this prayer Donne cannot imagine himself and his own fears and sufferings except in the communal context of Christ's passion and his afflicted body, the Church, which Donne particularizes here in the death of the individual for whom he prays.

In defining the central place of prayer in the Christian life, Donne availed himself of a wide spectrum of theological sources, for he was well aware that prayer had not in fact given rise to significant partisan debate either in the Reformation or in the Christian tradition as a whole. Further, Donne reads in New Testament accounts of Christ at prayer a model not only for persistence in making his requests known to God, but also for conforming himself to God by humbly submitting to His will. It is, finally, within these orthodox contexts that Donne argues for "religious impudency" in prayer, the body of Christ wrestling with God to secure its divine blessing. The mannered use of paradox and typological analogy as figures for the act of prayer, mannerisms which themselves define Donne's style, sit comfortably alongside traditional teachings about the centrality of prayer and its constitutive function for the Christian community. Donne could therefore remain, as usual, at his most public when he was at his most private, as illustrated in the hymns and the *Devotions*, in which the prayers stemming from Donne's personal suffering also articulate the petitions of and for the common body of Christ.

Notes

I am grateful to College Misericordia for the Summer Grant I received in support of my research. I wish also to thank my colleague W. Scott Blanchard whose insights were invaluable. I provide in parentheses sermon dates whenever these are available, should the reader wish to consider the consistency of Donne's views in terms of chronology.

¹ For Donne's views against praying for the dead, see *Sermons* 7, 6; and for an engaging discussion of Donne's ideas concerning praying to saints, see Dubinski's reading of "A Litanie."

² All references to Aquinas's *Summa* are from Question 83 of the Second Part of the Second Part (Pt. II-II), and are cited in the text by article number.

³ All references to Hooker are from his *Of the Laws of Ecclesiastical Polity* and are cited in the text by book and chapter numbers.

⁴ The eleven sermons, cited here by volume and sermon number from the Potter and Simpson edition, use the following texts: Luke 23:24 (5: 12—undated); I Corinthians 15:29 (7: 6—21 May 1626); Psalm 6:1 (5: 16—undated); Psalm 6:2-3 (5: 17—undated); Psalm 6:4-5 (5: 18, 19—undated); Psalm 6:6-7 (8: 8—5 April 1628); Psalm 6:8-10 (6: 1—Spring 1623); Psalm 32:6 (9: 14—undated); Psalm 38:9 (2: 6—undated, Lincoln's Inne); and Psalm 90:14 (5: 14—undated, St. Paul's).

⁵ See Booty's edition of the Prayer Book (24), which contains "The Table for the Order of the Psalms to Be Said at Morning and Evening Prayer."

⁶ Concerning this Candlemas Day sermon, Potter and Simpson note that "the text occurs in the Epistle for the Fourth Sunday after Epiphany, and it seems therefore that the sermon must belong to 1616/17 or 1622/23, those being the only years during Donne's ministry in which the Fourth Sunday after Epiphany fell on February 2. Of the two dates, 1622/23 is much more likely" (4: 38-39).

⁷ Describing the ascent of the mind in prayer, Donne writes that

> *S. Bernard* makes certaine gradations, and steps, and ascensions of the soule in prayer, and intimates thus much, That by the grace of Gods Spirit inanimating and quickning him, (without which grace he can have no motion at all) a sinner may come *Ad supplicationes*, which is *S. Pauls* first step, To supplications, . . . He may come *Ad orationes*, which are *Oris rationes*, The particular expressing of his necessities, with his mouth; . . . he may come farther; *Ad Intercessiones*, to an Intercession, . . . And to a farther step then these, which the Apostle may intend in that last, *Ad gratiarum actiones*, to a continuall Thanksgiving. (*Sermons* 5: 341—undated)

⁸ These phrases appear in the opening lines of the tenth expostulation of Donne's *Devotions*, in which he alludes to the sister of Gregory of Nazianzus, Saint Gorgonia, who prayed to God in this manner. Although Donne then states, "I dare not doe so" (52), his tenth prayer, as I explain below, is a witty example of "religious impudency."

⁹ See Gardner's commentary on this prefatory sonnet (55-56) and also the explanatory note in Shawcross's edition (408).

¹⁰ Later in this same letter, Donne expresses with delight his belief that "A Litanie" avoids the sectarian controversy surrounding praying to saints: "That by which it will deserve best acceptation, is, That neither the Roman Church need call it defective, because it abhors not the particular mention of the blessed Triumphers in heaven; nor the Reformed can discreetly accuse it, of attributing more then a rectified devotion ought to doe" (34).

Works Cited

Aquinas, St. Thomas. "Of Prayer." *Summa Theologica*. Vol. 2 New York: Benziger Brothers, 1947. 1537-52.

Asals, Heather. "John Donne and the Grammar of Redemption." *English Studies in Canada* 5 (1979): 125-39.

Bald, R. C. *John Donne: A Life*. New York: Oxford U P, 1970.

Booty, John, ed. *The Book of Common Prayer, 1559*. Charlottesville: U P of Virginia, 1976.

Carey, John. *John Donne: Life, Mind and Art*. London: Faber and Faber, 1981.

Donne, John. *The Divine Poems of John Donne*. Ed. Helen Gardner. Oxford: Clarendon P, 1952.

_____. *Letters to Severall Persons of Honour (1651)*. Ed. M.Thomas Hester. Delmar, NY: Scholars' Facsimiles, 1977.

Dubinski, Roman R. "Donne's 'A Litanie' and the Saints." *Christianity & Literature* 41 (Autumn 1991): 5-26.

_____. "Donne's Holy Sonnets and the Seven Penitential Psalms." *Ren / Ref* 10 (1986): 201-16.

Flynn, Dennis. "Donne's Catholicism: II." *Recusant History* 13 (1976): 178-95.

Frontain, Raymond-Jean. "'With Holy Importunitie, with a Pious Impudencie': John Donne's Attempts to Provoke Election."*JRMMRA* 13 (1992): 85-102.

Hooker, Richard. *The Works of Richard Hooker*. Vol. 1. Oxford: Oxford U P, 1850.

Seelig, Sharon Cadman. "In Sickness and In Health: Donne's *Devotions upon Emergent Occasions*." *JDJ* 8 (1989): 103-13.

Sherwood, Terry. *Fulfilling the Circle: A Study of John Donne's Thought*. Toronto: U of Toronto P, 1984.

Stachniewski, John. "John Donne: The Despair of the 'Holy Sonnets.'" *ELH* 48 (1981): 677-705. Rpt. *The Persecutory Imagination: English Puritanism and the Literature of Religious Despair*. Oxford: Clarendon P, 1991.

Strier, Richard. "John Donne Awry and Squint: The 'Holy Sonnets,' 1608-1610." *MP* 86 (1989): 357-84.

Literary "Things Indifferent": The Shared Augustinianism of Donne's Devotions and Bunyan's Grace Abounding

Mary Arshagouni Papazian

n her influential essay "Donne and Bunyan," Joan Webber accounted for the differences between John Donne's *Devotions Upon Emergent Occasions* (1624) and John Bunyan's *Grace Abounding to the Chief of Sinners* (1666) as works reflecting respectively "the styles of two faiths," Anglican and Puritan. This view of a literary dichotomy between Anglicanism and Puritanism has dominated subsequent readings of Donne's and Bunyan's works. Yet at the same time, Webber noted the troubling similarities between the two, that "both books end on a note of uncertainty," that "the religious needs of the two men were somewhat similar," and, perhaps most significantly, that "had circumstances been different, their roles might have been reversed" (490). Webber rightly sensed that the difference between the two compositions is perhaps more purely literary, or possibly political, than theological. Others have also shared this vague feeling that the differences might not reflect two faiths. In the conclusion of a book on Donne's theology, Paul R. Sellin suggests in passing that Webber "is far too narrow to begin by assuming that Donne's spiritual exercises 'could only have been the creation of a dedicated Anglican theologian.'" "The differences between works like Donne's *Devotions* and Bunyan's *Grace Abounding*," he muses, "may prove as attributable to kind or age as to church or subscribed faith" (50). This important idea that the two compositions are not so dissimilar in theology deserves a thorough investigation.

I would like to suggest that the heretofore standard distinctions between the *Devotions* and *Grace Abounding*, particularly those of genre (meditation vs. autobiography) and style (figurative vs. plain), are neither necessarily related to Donne's and Bunyan's theology, nor do they need to be explained as reflections of two different faiths. Rather, I would argue, the genre and style, to the extent that they are actually different, should be seen as the literary equivalents of religious *adiaphora* (or "things indifferent"), that is, church practices not necessarily related to the issue of salvation. Donne and Bunyan, though they indeed disagreed on questions of church discipline and ceremonies, can be shown to share an essential Reformed Augustinian theology, that emerges from Augustine's *Confessions* and late anti-Pelagian works, which permeated and united various parts of the Protestant movement and indeed their two works. Consequently, as I shall argue, the *Devotions* and *Grace Abounding* do not represent two separate, opposing, and ultimately incompatible faiths, but rather two manifestations of the same spirit divided only by time, genre, and style.

After examining the concept of "things indifferent," the reluctance of many Donne scholars to embrace Donne's indebtedness to Augustine, and Webber's argument of opposition, I will discuss both Donne's *Devotions* and Bunyan's *Grace Abounding* in the context of Augustinian theology. This analysis should reorient our understanding of Donne's religious imagination generally by placing Donne squarely in the context of the broad Reformation traditions, including that of the nonconformists, which dominated Renaissance England. More specifically, this reevaluation will enable us both to read the *Devotions* in terms other than the traditional one which restrictively places it with such reflective meditational compositions as St. Ignatius Loyola's *Spiritual Exercises* and to expose the work also as a spiritual autobiography in an acknowledged tradition. This approach will allow us to recognize Donne's spiritual affinity with Bunyan and the inconsequentiality of their two different, and non-defining, styles.

An analysis of the concept of *adiaphora* in sixteenth and seventeenth century Protestantism suggests to us that there may be problems with the traditional assumptions that lie behind our customary postulation of opposition between Anglican and Puritan. Calvin explains *adiaphora*, "things indifferent," in his *Institutes*: "The third part of Christian freedom lies in this: regarding outward things that are of themselves 'indifferent,' we are not bound before God by any religious obligation preventing us from sometimes using them and other times not using them, indifferently" (3:19:7). Indeed, although Calvin instituted a strict, almost oppressive, form of religious governance in Geneva, he readily accepted the view that one must distinguish between religion and politics, doctrine and discipline, things essential and things indifferent. This distinction between things indifferent and things essential, for example, as Peter Lake explains, allowed Calvin to support "the lawfulness of government by bishops," although it was not to his personal taste (3).[1]

Furthermore, church historians in recent years have made us aware of the complexities of religious belief and practice in pre-Civil War England and have stressed the need to move beyond a simple Anglican/Puritan dichotomy to arrive at a better understanding of the religious orientation and practice in the English Renaissance.[2] These historians further reveal that the established Episcopal Church of England under James I was essentially "Calvinist," particularly with regard to questions of predestination and the workings of divine grace.[3] The understanding that the Church of England was actually consistent in doctrine with the Reformed churches on the Continent, despite differences in matters of ceremonies and discipline, was evident as early as the Elizabethan settlement. As Edmund Grindal, then Bishop of London and later Archbishop of Canterbury, says in a 1566 letter to the noted Protestant reformer, Heinrich Bullinger, in Zurich:

> We, who are now bishops, on our first return, and before we entered on our ministry, contended long and earnestly for the removal of those things [vestments and liturgy] that have occasioned the present dispute; but as we were unable to prevail, either with the queen or the parliament, we judged it best, after a consultation on the subject, *not to desert our churches for the sake of a few ceremonies, and those not unlawful in themselves, especially since the pure doctrine of the gospel remained in all its integrity and freedom; in which, even to this day, . . . we most fully agree with your churches, and with the confession [Helvetic Confession] you have lately set forth* [italics added].[4]

Thus, in pre-Laudian times, it was possible for Calvinists to conform to the discipline of the Church of England without fear of being in error, because the Church of England itself was essentially Calvinist in doctrine.[5]

The union under James I in 1603 of the episcopalian British church and the presbyterian Scottish church offers a striking example of the importance of the concept of *adiaphora* in seventeenth century England. While the two churches might at first glance seem antagonistic because of contrary attitudes toward church government and ceremonies, these differences were understood by contemporaries as mere conventions rather than theological issues, as "things indifferent" rather than "things essential." Raised a Calvinist and dedicated to Calvinist principles, King James desired an episcopacy for political, not doctrinal, reasons. Moreover, at the Hampton Court Conference in 1604, James's interest lay in bringing moderate "Puritans" (Calvinists who believed in a presbyterian form of church government) into the fold by reminding them that, as Calvin himself had said, such matters of church government and discipline were "things indifferent."[6] In short, James does not argue with the doctrine of salvation (*soteriology*) of the Puritans within his realm, but rather demands conformity in practice, a matter of "indifference." As he explains in the revised preface to the 1603 edition of his *Basilikon Doron*,

> I protest upon mine honour, I mean it not generally of all preachers or others, that like better of the single form of policy in our church [of Scotland], than of the many ceremonies in the church of England; that are persuaded that their bishops smell of a papal supremacy, that the surplice, the cornered cap and such like are the outward badges of popish errors. No, I am so far from being contentious in these things *(which for my own part I ever esteemed as indifferent)* as I do equally love and *honour the learned and grave men of either of these opinions* [italics added].[7]

Furthermore, in a 1604 treatise by Robert Pont, *Of the Union of Britayne*, the character, Polyhistor, refutes the statement that "in many pointes of religion the English and Scottish agree not," thusly:

> It is a wicked slander. They agree in doctrine, and their difference in some matters of discipline empeacheth not so their religion but that their may be a sweet harmony in their kingedomes and unity in their churches. *For where the fundamentall doctrine is (as the worship of one God, a true invocation of Christe's name, an assurance of salvation by Him onely, the right administration of the sacraments, baptisme and the supper of the Lord) although in matters and discipline their be not found in all an equality and like perfection, to such an assemblie the faithfull never douted to joyne themselves* [italics added] (7).

As present church historians demonstrate, and contemporary seventeenth-century commentators avowed, English Episcopalian "Calvinism" and Scottish Presbyterian "Calvinism" do, in fact, share an essential theology, particularly with regard to predestination, grace, and the importance of Scripture.

While most Protestants accepted among themselves an essential core of common theology, and were divided fundamentally only by "things indifferent," we should be reminded that they all strongly and vehemently rejected and opposed the contemporary theology of the Roman Catholic church. For example, while all Christians shared the concept of the fall of Adam, original sin, the sacrifice of Christ as a propitiator, and the need for salvation, the Roman Catholic church held, among other things, that salvation was possible through works as well as faith, that the authority of the church equalled that of scripture, that scripture could be validly interpreted only by the Church, that the pope was the head of the "universal" church, that purgatory was an intermediate stage for imperfect souls, that there were seven sacraments, and that the Saints and the Virgin Mary were to be venerated. Reformed churches in England and on the Continent, to the contrary, believed that salvation was possible through faith alone, that all authority rested in scripture, that only baptism and the eucharist were to be considered sacraments, and that God, through his own goodness, mercy, and unbounded grace—and not through any human acts or merit—chose to raise up only an elect to salvation. Hence, conforming protestant episcopalians like Donne and nonconforming protestant presbyterians like Bunyan might disagree on ceremonies and church discipline, but could rightly agree on the more weighty matters of soteriology. (Of course radical protestant sects, with which we do not deal in this essay, held to all varieties of religious beliefs and practices.)

This "Reformed soteriology" so typical of Calvinism and so antithetical to Papism, derives both from Augustine's *Confessions* and his late anti-Pelagian treatises. It was the venerable Augustine who not only embellished the Roman Catholic tradition, but who also provided a foundation for Protestantism. As Diarmaid MacCulloch explains, "overarching all Calvin's theological ideas, as with Augustine, Luther and the earlier Swiss reformers before him, was his constant emphasis on the incomparable majesty of God and the total 'fallen-ness' of humankind, on which ideas he erected the most comprehensive picture of salvation which the Reformation had so far produced" (73-74).

Learned readers have long recognized Donne's indebtedness to Augustine, though generally in the misleading context of the forgoing Anglican/Puritan dichotomy. As early as 1640, Izaak Walton remarked that in Donne "the English Church had gained a second S. Augustine," a figure who, like Augustine, had survived the recklessness of youth to become unparalleled in "learning and holinesse" (sig. B2). In the present century, George Potter and Evelyn Simpson, the modern editors of Donne's sermons, suggest that Donne not only resembled Augustine in the pattern of his life, but that his thought, more importantly, owed much to Augustine's views. In their words, Donne's "quotations cover almost the whole field of Augustine's thought" and "deal with such immense subjects as the Nature of God, the Creation of the Universe, the relation between soul and body, the fall of Adam and its consequences, original sin, the saving work of Christ in all its aspects, death and immortality, and the authority of Scripture" (10: 354-358).

Although Augustine influences Donne's theology in almost every way imaginable, readers of Donne's *Devotions* have been reluctant to come to terms with the strongly Reformed dimension of his Augustinianism, particularly his emphasis on what I shall call "things essential": authority of Scripture, original sin, predestination, the perseverance of the saints, grace, and eventual salvation through faith, not works. In my view, the essentials of Augustine's soteriology, coupled with Augustine's attempt at self-understanding through self-negation, submission to God's will, and total dependence on God's mercy rather than man's reason or actions, expressed movingly in his *Confessions*, offers us an important backdrop for interpreting the emotions and concerns that Donne displays in his *Devotions*, concerns and conclusions that also permeate the great work of Puritan spiritual autobiography, Bunyan's *Grace Abounding*.

Although the significance of the late Augustine for the Reformation has been long recognized,[8] most readers of Donne—from Potter and Simpson forward—have felt uncomfortable in confronting the reality of Augustine's influence in Donne's works.[9] There are two reasons, I think, for this lack of sanction. First, there is much in Augustinian theology that jars those who, like Webber, insist on a rigid post-Laudian Anglican/ Puritan dichotomy in their approach and thus would rather read Donne as a *via media* Anglican or even Anglo/Catholic. For example, although Potter and Simpson agree that Donne "owed much of value to Augustine," they "wonder whether Augustine's influence on him was altogether healthy," for, as they complain, this influence caused Donne to place "too much emphasis on sin and its punishment," to "meditate too long on human guilt and frailty," and, consequently, to "distort the Christian message" (10: 357-58). Regardless of individual sensibilities and personal views of "the Christian message," we must openly embrace the reality that original sin, predestination, human weakness, and the individual's search for evidence of election and salvation were fundamental concerns not only of the late Augustine but also of the broader Reformation tradition, including both conforming Anglicanism and nonconforming Presbyterianism. Indeed, we must not forget that Protestantism's embrace of a conception of man as completely dependent on God's mercy for salvation, a view which has its roots in St. Paul's *Epistles* and Augustine's late anti-Pelagian works, defines a fundamental divide between Roman Catholicism and all forms of Protestantism.

The second reason for this reticence to deal with late Augustinianism in the "reformed" Anglican tradition may arise from the wide influence of Louis Martz's seminal work, *The Poetry of Meditation* (1954). Following Martz, most modern commentators on Donne's *Devotions* have dealt with his work solely in the tradition of meditative writings, while Augustine's *Confessions* and Bunyan's *Grace Abounding*, to the contrary, are generally discussed in the context of autobiography and the development of the novel.[10] In the Martz tradition, Webber opines that "the chief obvious difference between *Grace Abounding* and the *Devotions* is that one is literally autobiographical and the other is not," and "autobiography. . . is a Puritan, not an Anglican habit" (503). N. H. Keeble, in his study of nonconformity in the later seventeenth century, at first glance seems to agree with Webber. He states that *"Grace Abounding* is but one of a large number of introspective and autobiographical nonconformist works intended by their authors for publication" and avers that "Episcopalians did not write spiritual autobiographies." Yet, even though Keeble, like Webber, links spiritual autobiography with nonconformity, he later correctly states that as the Restoration progressed, "this continuing bias [of nonconformists to write spiritual autobiographies] became increasingly unfashionable" (209). In other words, as the seventeenth century drew to a close, introspective autobiography became unfashionable not only for Episcopalians, as it had been even earlier, but also for nonconformists. Accordingly, it is clear that spiritual autobiography was not a defining characteristic of nonconformity, but rather was merely a style of the times, a question of fashion, not faith, a literary "thing indifferent."

Furthermore, the spiritual autobiography in the Christian tradition, not to be confused with the secular autobiography that emerged in modern times, begins perhaps as far back as Hezekiah (Isaiah 38:9-22) in the Old Testament and St. Peter (Acts 11:5-17) and St. Paul (Acts 22:1-21)[11] in the New Testament, and certainly finds its most complete expression in the Roman Catholic St. Augustine, who wrote around 397 CE. Since this literary genre is hallowed both by scripture and the Roman Catholic church, it is available to all subsequent Christian writers. Thus, the generic literary distinction between Anglican and Puritan made by Martz and Webber must be critically analyzed. No one doubts that Donne makes use of principles of meditation in his work, since he even calls the first section of each devotion a "meditation." Meditation, however, is but one element of the whole. To read the *Devotions* only as such is to miss other, perhaps more important, dimensions.[12]

Are Donne's *Devotions* and Bunyan's *Grace Abounding*, two different genres, the products of two faiths, as Webber has maintained, or can both, in fact, be read in light of the same recognized tradition of spiritual autobiography? Kate Frost, in her recent study of the *Devotions*, correctly defines the characteristics of early spiritual autobiography thusly:

> It focuses, through the examination of an individual soul, upon the place of that soul in the schema of Eternity and upon the ways in which God can work in any soul to produce Christian conviction, for its author hopes that sins similar to his own will be acknowledged by the reader, who will be vicariously purified by the author's sufferings. (28)

Both the *Devotions* and *Grace Abounding* are united by common themes characteristic of the tradition of spiritual autobiography. Both begin with personal experience, cite scripture, struggle with the problems of sin, punishment, grace, and salvation, and ultimately direct their concern to an external reader. Moreover, both describe a seemingly never-ending series of afflictions which generate from within them deep introspection and an emotional outpouring as they seek to understand God's purpose. In these central elements, both works derive much, as we shall show later, from a shared Reformed Augustinian heritage and from Augustine's own *Confessions*.

Evidence within the *Devotions* itself suggests that Donne may well have thought of his work in terms of the spiritual autobiographical tradition, for he consciously places it in the tradition of Hezekiah's autobiographical meditations when he reminds Prince Charles in his dedicatory letter opening the *Devotions* that "Ezechiah *writt the* Meditations *of his* Sicknesse, *after his* Sicknesse" (3).[13] Furthermore, Frost describes Donne's work as a "masterpiece in the tradition of self-scrutiny" (14) that "pertains more to autobiography than to devotion" (15). She also asserts that it "may have an identifiable place within an earlier tradition" of spiritual autobiography (22). Read in this light, the ultimate purpose of the *Devotions* is "pious edification" and "moral instruction," and not simply "paramount self-interest" in the modern sense (Frost 16). This emphasis on the work as an exemplum helps explain why the *Devotions* was one of the few works that Donne had published during his lifetime. As Frost reminds us, spiritual autobiographies, though seemingly very private, were really always written for publication, for edification (21), a characteristic that holds true for the works of Augustine, Donne and Bunyan. In other words, this self-scrutiny had an important and necessary public purpose: to gain awareness of the "Human Condition," to use Donne's term, something that can speak to all readers of the work. According to Frost, "for the Christian, the painful process of self-scrutiny led to a perception of himself as the image of fallen Adam and of redeeming Christ, an identification best perceived in times of adversity" (35-36). Indeed, "As Augustine is Paul, so Donne can be both Augustine and Paul. All Christians, remade in the image of Christ, speak as one" (Frost 37). In this, Donne and Bunyan share with St. Paul and Augustine in a casting off of the old Adam, rebirth in the new Adam, and the putting on of Christ that characterizes both the Christian life and the spiritual autobiography. Moreover, as Donne's third expostulation shows, "through chastisement, the Christian is led to recognize his true identity: He is child of God, fallen with Adam but risen in Christ" (Frost 59). In short, like Augustine in the *Confessions*, "in the *Devotions* [Donne] attempts by intense self-analysis to purge his soul of sin and distraction, of whatever does not belong to the image of God implanted at creation, dimmed by the fall of Adam, and restored at baptism. Once discovered, the image of God within the self creates a new, more general sense of selfhood" (Frost 75). It is a process that Donne offers to his readers as a model. For example, as I have shown elsewhere, the actual Latin headnotes to the final two devotions in Donne's work address the reader in just this way. Strung together, they can be translated thus, "May the coals fueling the disease be thy care and study [O Reader]; and [may] the fear of backsliding [be thy care and study]" (204), a turning outward that encourages not only Donne's persona to utilize the steps of the disease outlined in the Latin headnotes as a "school text," but just as important, all readers are instructed to do so as well so that they may be "promoted to a higher School of Divinity" and "raised to the uppermost mansion" (Papazian 206).

For Donne's persona, the course of the sickness forms the narrative structure to the *Devotions*. The progression and remission of his illness reminds him of the "saving cycle" of Christ, as it challenges his rational (though not scientific) mind to understand and gain new insights into God's mysterious ways and saving grace. It teaches him yet again, in microcosm, as Augustine and Bunyan's lives do in macrocosm, that "man believes, suffers, considers" while "God attends, corrects, assures" (Sherwood 180). In short, the *Devotions* is not a mere mystical meditation, but rather a rational, considered, highly structured attempt to understand in this microcosm of life's cycle the saving cycle of grace so well defined in Augustine's late anti-Pelagian theology. In Sherwood's words, "The present must contain the past and the future; it must distil the whole generic pattern in the moment. But the present is personal as well as generic; and the *Devotions* follows the events of Donne's illness, leaving Donne, as an exercise in his own salvation, to scrutinize how each event exists within the generic pattern" (177).

Webber raises two additional arguments. She maintains, first, that "in *Grace Abounding*, we are shown Bunyan [as] the 'I'-in-process, and [that] his feelings are clearly rendered through the interpreter-Bunyan of many years later." She concludes that "thus we are immediately made aware of the passage of time in a completely different way from that in which we experience it in the *Devotions*" (504). She highlights the distinction between the focus on a particular experience, as in the *Devotions*, and on an entire life, as in the *Confessions* and *Grace Abounding*. Yet, both the *Devotions* and *Grace Abounding*, works of approximately similar length, offer within them autobiographical details of their author's life. While Donne focuses on a concentrated, specific experience, that of his fall into sickness in late 1623 and ultimate recovery, Bunyan's narrative, like Augustine's, stretches over his entire life. But rather than see these as distinctly different efforts, both can instead be seen in the overarching context of the "saving patterns of Creation" (Sherwood 182), Donne's in microcosm and Bunyan's in macrocosm. Because "the fulfilled moment can express a whole life and its potential" (Sherwood 176), the experience described in the *Devotions* can be considered a microcosm of a life, the entirety of which becomes Bunyan's subject in *Grace Abounding*.

More specifically, Webber argues that in the *Devotions* "Donne too proceeds through a spiritual-physical crisis, but he indicates periods of time nowhere, and any forward movement is highly qualified by several structural devices implied by his word '*stationes*,' or 'stations,' which describes his alternative to chronological time" (506). Boyd Berry, in his comparison of Donne's *Devotions* and Bunyan's *Grace Abounding* (referring to both Donne and Bunyan as "spiritual hypochondriacs" [197]), maintains, contrary to Webber, that it is *Grace Abounding* which is characterized by constant circularity, while the *Devotions* has a clear, linear structure. In his words, "Each of the twenty-three devotions is a self-contained, tripartite unit, yet the whole progresses linearly through the

chronological stages of Donne's sickness and the Latin poem which serves
as a table of contents and which the *Devotions* explicate at length. . . . The
Devotions are so completely rooted in the progress of the fever over time
that the linear quality could never be eradicated" (193). I have also shown
elsewhere, contrary to Webber's view of Donne's Latin *Stationes* as static,
that the Latin headnotes do, in fact, outline progressive stages of Donne's
sickness, and frame a chronology, indeed an almost day-by-day sequence
of events.[14] Moreover, Berry argues that while "both Donne and Bunyan
suggest the circularity of divine vision by repeating linear movements,
citing Scripture and constructing miniature biblical histories which trace
out a problem from beginning to end," Bunyan "more obviously repeats
himself and his constant problem" (198). Thus, Berry believes, in com-
plete opposition to Webber, that Donne's *Devotions* presents a more con-
vincing linear progress than does Bunyan's *Grace Abounding*. I would
argue that linear and circular patterns characterize both works and that
the difference between focusing on a specific experience in Donne's case,
and an entire life pattern in Bunyan's, in seeking the ways of God, do not
in any way imply that they are the products of "two faiths."

Finally, Webber argues, "Donne's prose is analytical, psychological,
subjective, meditative, private, self-centered, and literary [a figurative
style]" and "Bunyan's prose is reportorial, straightforward, apparently
objective, taking place in public, and inviting the reader to see him as an
instrument of use rather than an object of contemplation [a plain style]"
(527-528). Although Webber makes much of the differences between the
"figurative style" Donne employs in the *Devotions* and Bunyan's funda-
mental use of the "plain style" in *Grace Abounding*, this distinction, even if
defensible, is not a determinate of creed or faith. Both the "grand style" (a
highly figurative style) and the "plain style" can be found in the Scrip-
tures, the works of Augustine, and in the writings of John Calvin, all
fundamental to the protestant milieu which influenced both Donne and
Bunyan. According to Debra Shuger, the Christian "grand style reflects
the revival of Augustinianism in the Renaissance and with it a defence of
emotion as inseparable from Christian inwardness" (8), which could be
expressed in any scriptural style, grand or relatively plain. Calvin, a true
son of the Christian humanist tradition, agreeing with Augustine's prac-
tice, believed that true spiritual emotion could be expressed in a variety of
scriptural "styles," for although Calvin believed in the importance of
rhetoric and persuasion, and emphasized the eloquence of scripture, he
recognized and esteemed scripture's use of both plain and figurative
styles. In the words of William Bouwsma, Calvin's most recent biogra-

pher, "Like earlier commentators in the tradition of Augustine's *De Doctrina Christiana,* . . . Calvin regularly identified metaphor, allegory, personification, metonymy, synecdoche, and other tropes . . . Calvin, in short, recognized that full appreciation of the Bible depends on reading it as literature," and not necessarily as literature employing only the plain style (122-123). Roger Pooley reminds us that for Bunyan, too, the Bible sanctions the use of both the plain and the figurative style. In Pooley's words, "Bunyan's style veers between the openness of plain declaration and the mysterious suggestiveness of allegory, and he can find biblical source and warrant for both" (98). One might say that the actual differences in style, the works of two different writers, reflect not faith but temperament: Donne's was the product of an aristocratic milieu and the university, while Bunyan's was the product of an emerging middle class. Berry correctly locates the differences between Donne and Bunyan in questions of "sensibilities and styles" (194), things I have called "indifferent," rather than in theology or faith.

As I have argued, it is too subjective to lament Augustine's influence on Donne or to insist on an historically imprecise opposition between "Anglican" and "Puritan" styles, between Donne, as representative of the former, and Bunyan, as representative of the latter, and their respective works consequently as the "expressions of two faiths." I would like now to consider both works in the context of Augustinian theology in order to illustrate more fully their shared literary, religious, and psychological dimensions.

In Augustine, self-abnegation and the affirmation of the majesty of God is essential to salvation. As Augustine explains in his *De Doctrina Christiana,* "because man fell through pride, [God] has applied humility to cure him" (37). Indeed, humility is not simply *one* possible "cure" for human sinfulness; it is the *only* "cure" (41). In his treatise *De Correptione et Gratia,* Augustine presents his essential, anti-Pelagian, theology of salvation, accepted, as we shall demonstrate, by both Donne and Bunyan:

> . . . all these do not stand apart from that mass which, we know, was sentenced to the loss of God; all of them, by reason of one, fell under condemnation. And they are singled out *not* [italics added] by their own merits, but by the grace of the Mediator; . . . As for those who by the bounty of divine grace are singled out of that original body of the lost, there is no doubt that the opportunity to hear the Gospel is arranged for them; and, when they hear, they believe, and persevere unto the end in the faith which worketh by charity; and, if ever they go off the track,

they are chastised by *admonitions* [italics added];. . . and some, too, having received grace at various ages, are withdrawn from the dangers of this life by a swift death. All these things are done in them by Him who made them vessels of mercy, and who also chose them in His Son before the foundation of the world by a gracious choice. (259-260)

According to Augustine, Adam's fall results in the inability of even the godly to perform acts of goodness without Divine help, nor are they saved from condemnation "by their own merits." Consequently, without God's merciful saving grace, all individuals are nothing more then lumps of the *massa damnata*, destined to eternal suffering. One loss of identity leads to eternal suffering, the other through grace to eternal joy. Furthermore, Augustine adds in the *De Correptione*, "for such who love Him"— that is, for the elect, whose very identity that separates them from the *massa damnata* comes from God—"God makes all things work together unto good—absolutely all things, even to this extent, that if some of them swerve and stray from the path, He makes their very wanderings contribute to their good, because they come back wiser and more humble" (274). In short, because man can do good only through God's grace, and because God will chastise His own, "the man of God who takes pride is to take pride in the Lord, not only because he has obtained mercy, with the result that he hath faith, but also because his faith does not fail" (C & G 293). It is a process, as the *Confessions* testify, in which Augustine himself was engaged.

Writing the *Confessions* led Augustine to express this clear doctrine of sin, grace, and predestination, the theological views to which sons of the Reformation such as Donne and Bunyan later responded. In the *Confessions* Augustine offers what is generally considered the first "spiritual history," an autobiographical narrative in which he describes his conversion from a wild, doubting, at times licentious, youth, to a thoughtful and devoted son of God. In the course of his reflections on sinfulness and human frailty, Augustine recognizes that even the ability to turn to God and ask for mercy derives from God; for, he cries, "Who will grant unto me that Thou wilt come into my heart and inebriate it, so that I may forget my evils and embrace my one good, Thee?" (I:5:7). In recognizing that the "Who" can only be God, Augustine comes to understand as well that his only recourse is to turn to God in impassioned pleas, yearning for the time "When I shall cleave to Thee with all my being." Only then, Augustine exclaims, will sorrow and toil . . . no longer exist for me. . . . Thou art the Physician, I am a sick man; Thou art merciful, I am a miserable man. Is not 'the life of man upon earth a trial?' Who would want troubles and hardships? Thou dost command that they be endured, not loved. No man loves what he endures, even though he loves to endure. (X:28:297-298)

This lament reveals that Augustine realizes that his salvation depends on his acceptance of his sinfulness and his total dependence on God's mercy, and that he yearns for that time when he will "have nothing to endure." Peace, ultimately, comes only through death, for only then will the godly succeed in abandoning his prideful human self and be received in the merciful arms of the Lord. Ironically, the search for humility leads one almost inevitably to greater focus on the self, magnifying self-centeredness, the initial cause of Adam's fall and man's damnation. Thus, paradoxically, the godly man is unable to achieve by deliberation that perfect humility in this life which he seeks. Anxiety results from the dichotomy. This paradox, this dichotomy, this anxiety, is especially apparent in the writing of a spiritual autobiography in which the central concern is the annihilation of the self by self-examination.

While the *Confessions* moves along a clearly defined narrative line, there is an undercurrent of cycle and oscillation, between hope and despair, as Augustine turns constantly to God in his quest for self-knowledge, a search that is characterized, as we have seen, by impassioned outbursts, questionings, and self-examination. Both Donne's *Devotions* and Bunyan's *Grace Abounding* can be seen in similar terms, for they too are characterized by self-examination, impassioned outbursts, and questionings of God. In all three works, we see the central personae similarly undergo a series of spiritual vacillations that focus on man's weakness and sinfulness, the necessity of throwing himself on God's mercy and committing himself to His care, and the grace of God which brings salvation.

Donne's *Devotions Upon Emergent Occasions* was occasioned by his near fatal illness in late November, early December 1623, and written during a month-long convalescence. The *Devotions* begins with "Stationes," a Latin verse serving as a table-of-contents, the phrases of which are repeated as Latin headnotes to the twenty-three devotions. The "Stationes" provide an outline of the progress of the illness, its treatment, and Donne's final recovery. They define the skeletal structure of the work—that is, the "occasions" to which the devotions proper respond. Each "devotion," in turn, is divided into a Meditation, Expostulation, and Prayer. The devotions offer the impassioned responses of Donne's persona to the step-by-step course of his illness.

A reading of the *Devotions* in the context of Donne's Augustinianism gives us new insights into Donne's religious vision.[15] As in Augustine's *Confessions*, Donne's persona, an inheritor of Adam's sin, recognizes that his sinfulness will not end as long as he remains alive, occasioning a great spiritual struggle. The persona's struggle with the problem of man's inherent frailty is evident from the very onslaught of the sickness. "We study *Health*," he cries in the opening meditation,

> and we deliberate upon our *meats*, and *drink*, and *Ayre*, and *exercises*, and we hew, and wee polish every stone, that goes to that building; . . . But in a minute a Cannon batters all, overthrowes all, demolishes all; a *Sicknes* unprevented for all our diligence . . . summons us, seizes us, possesses us, destroyes us in an instant. O miserable condition of Man. (7)

This early response to his sickness causes Donne's persona, like Augustine before him, to reflect immediately on his inevitable weakness as a son of Adam, a concern that nearly overwhelms him throughout the first phase of his disease. Yet, also like Augustine, Donne's persona constantly turns to God during his sickness, as he seeks to place himself in God's care and comes to understand the meaning of his suffering. Though he wonders "why is there not alwayes a *pulse* in my *Soule*, to beat at the approch of a tentation to sinne" and complains that "I go, I run, I flie into the wayes of tentation, which I might shun" (Expostulation 1, 8), God, however, is not far off. Indeed, in the first prayer he can already turn to God for comfort, for he has a premonition of his election. "O eternall, and most gracious *God*," he begins,

> enable me by thy *grace*, to looke forward to mine end, and to looke backward to, to the considerations of thy mercies afforded mee from the beginning; that so by that practise of considering thy mercy, in my beginning in this world, when thou plantedst me in the *Christian Church*, and thy mercy in the beginning in the other world, when thou writest me in the *Booke of life*, in my *Election*, I may come to a holy consideration of thy *mercy*, in the beginning of all my actions here. . . . Thy voice received, in the beginning of a sicknesse, of a sinne, is true health. (10)

Though initially distraught at his fall into sickness, the persona is not brought to despair by his suffering. Rather, through the process of self-examination and humbling himself before God, he comes to recognize the benefits of affliction and to understand that God will make this "wandering contribute to [his] good" (Augustine's words). It is a process that moves continuously from lamentation on his sinfulness and human condition to hope, as he places himself in God's care, a movement that mirrors the meditation, expostulation, and prayer divisions of each devotion.

In the second devotion, for example, after deploring how quickly the illness fell upon him, and how it robbed him of his physical powers, and fearing that the illness resulted from God's anger, he is able to petition God in the prayer to "Interpret thine owne worke, and call this sicknes, correction, and not anger, & there is soundnes in my flesh" (14). In the third devotion, after lamenting man's smallness in comparison to heaven, he struggles successfully to turn this sickness to an examination of himself in relation to God. "I come unto thee, *O God, my God*," he cries,

> I come unto thee, (so as I can come, I come to thee, by imbracing thy comming to me) . . . ; That which way soever I turne, I may turne to thee; And as I feele thy hand upon all my body, so I may find it upon all my bedde, and see all my *corrections*, and all my *refreshings* to flow from one, and the same, and all, from thy hand. (18)

As he lies in his bed unable to rise—a symbol of total dependence, a helpless man in the presence of Augustine's great Physician—and imagines that his death fast approaches, Donne's persona struggles to submit to God's unfathomable will. It is a struggle, in fact, that infuses the first half of the *Devotions*. Finally, however, he recognizes, as had Augustine before him, that he has no power within himself to act in any way that can be considered good, an acceptance that allows him now to see his sickness as a correction from God, not a punishment. "I may be saved," he cries in the ninth expostulation, "thogh not by my book, mine own *conscience*, nor by thy other *books*, yet by thy *first*, the book of *life*, thy *decree for my election*, and by thy *last*, the book of the *Lamb*, and the shedding of his blood upon me" (49). By the seventeenth devotion, he is able to see affliction as a gift from God, a treasure rather than suffering. "*Affliction* is a *treasure*," he asserts as he lies in his bed listening to the nearby church bells toll for the death of his neighbor, "and scarce any Man hath *enough* of it. No Man hath *affliction* enough, that is not matured, and ripened by it, and made fit for *God* by that *affliction*" (87).

As a consequence of this understanding of the benefits of affliction in bringing him closer to God through submission, Donne's persona comes to yearn not for physical recovery, which would result in continued struggle with the self, but rather for death and salvation through God's mercy. Only death to this life, abandonment of the self, and total affirmation of the goodness of God, as recognized by Augustine, can lead to true and eternal peace. Awareness of this Augustinian paradox, that death to one's physical self leads to life everlasting, allows us to recognize an ironic twist in the *Devotions*—that the moment of spiritual and emotional peace does not coincide with that of physical recovery described in the nineteenth devotion; rather, it is the moment of imagined death. Recognizing the negative effect of physical life, he laments in the eighteenth prayer, "I was *borne dead*, and from the first laying of these *mud-walls* in my *conception*, they have *moldred* away, and the whole course of *life* is but an *active death*" (96). Donne's persona is ready, eager, and even thankful as he anticipates his final dissolution—a loss of self—and looks forward in Prayer 18 to the moment when:

> *time* may bee swallowed up in *Eternitie*, and *hope* swallowed in *possession*, and *ends* swallowed in *infinitenesse*, and *all men* ordained to *salvation* in *body* and *soule*, be *one intire* and *everlasting sacrifice* to thee, where thou mayest receive *delight* from them, and they *glorie* from thee, for evermore. (97)

He does not die, however, but instead proceeds to recover his physical health. But physical recovery—the renewal of self-identity—brings not joy and peace, as most readers would expect, but rather anxiety at the fear of relapsing into sin. Consequently, the work closes not on a note of peace, but rather with a discomforting recognition that as long as he remains a man of dust and ashes, his struggle with humility, self-annihilation, and the contradictory demands of self and God will continue. His final prayer is not a prayer of thanksgiving for having recovered from sickness. Rather, it is an expression of his desire to become one of those who yearns to be, in Augustine's words, "withdrawn from the dangers of this life by a swift death." The conclusion of the work thus remains open-ended and the earthly linear narrative part of a never-ending cycle, for the anxiety brought on by awareness of sin will continue until death, particularly as the persona, despite his desire to please God, becomes more aware of the great gap between "well-knowing" and "well-doing."

Bunyan, the seventeenth-century tinker who became a nonconformist minister, modeled his *Grace Abounding to the Chief of Sinners* as a spiritual autobiography. Writing in 1666, midway through his eleven-year imprisonment for nonconformity, Bunyan offers a straightforward narrative of his life in which he traces his transformation from a profane blasphemer to a new man remade in Jesus Christ. The narrative is divided into 339 brief sections and includes "Grace Abounding," "A Brief Account of the Author's Call to the Work of the Ministry" and "A Brief Account of the Author's Imprisonment." It begins in despair and guilt as Bunyan reflects on his early years, as did Augustine, and moves toward hope and joy, as Bunyan, on reflection, begins to understand the workings of God in his life, but with constant oscillation between despair and hope, as in Donne.

Despite differences with Donne on questions of church government, the use of ceremonies, and conformity to other "things indifferent" that spring from a post-Laudian, post-Civil War experience, Bunyan's *Grace Abounding* nevertheless shares with Donne and Augustine a similar overwhelming concern with abnegation of the self and a wonder and appreciation of God's grace and mercy.[16] Influenced strongly by Luther and Calvin, and particularly Luther's *Galatians*, Bunyan also considers man a sinful creature, tainted by Adam's fall, who similarly must humble himself in the face of God's undeserved yet boundless mercy in election. Although Bunyan probably did not read Augustine directly, as had Donne, nevertheless, Augustine lies behind the Reformation theology that Bunyan inherited, particularly as filtered through Luther. As Dayton Haskin aptly reminds us,

> Luther cannot be accorded all the credit for creating the introspective conscience that Bunyan inherited. He only rescued a suppressed tendency in Western spirituality, an introspective strain that had lain dormant for centuries, but which had received its definitive formulation in the first great autobiography, Augustine's *Confessions*. It was Augustine who stimulated wide interest in interior illumination, and Augustine who first wrote with the introspective question in mind, how am I saved? (309)

The steps toward realization of his elect status that Bunyan undergoes echo Augustine's, while his doubts and conflicts following his calling also bring to mind the reactions and emotions of Donne's elect persona.[17]

Like Augustine and Donne, Bunyan's self is troubled with introspective questions throughout the work. He describes his early years thusly, in language that echoes Augustine in the *Confessions*: "Yea, such prevalency had the lusts and fruits of the flesh in this poor soul of mine, that had not a miracle of precious grace prevented, I had . . . perished" (section 9). At the same time, Bunyan recognizes in section 12, in lines that remind us of the ability of Donne's persona to turn to God even from the first prayer of the *Devotions*, that "God did not utterly leave me, but followed me still, not now with convictions, but with judgments; yet, such as were mixed with mercy." Questions of introspection, particularly with regard to his salvation, begin to haunt him as he wonders "Whether I was elected?" and whether "the day of grace should now be past and gone?" (section 57). Such election, though, as Augustine and Donne had both recognized, comes not from any good in man but rather from the merciful hands of God. As Bunyan confesses in section 59,

> With this scripture [Rom. 9.16] I could not tell what to do; for I evidently saw, that unless the great God, of His infinite grace and bounty, had voluntarily chosen me to be a vessel of mercy, though I should desire, and long and labour until my heart did break, no good could come of it.

Yet despite the comforts of God's word, Bunyan, too, is profoundly aware of his unworthiness. As he cries out prior to his first sense of assurance of God's grace, "my original and inward pollution, that, that was my plague and my affliction" (section 84). Like Donne's persona, Bunyan also finds himself relapsing into sin despite assurances of his election, a process that leads him to oscillate continually between feelings of doubt and feelings of assurance. After fearing that he is reprobate, for example, he finds comfort in faith, only to fall again into doubt and suffering. The endless cycle is recounted in brief in section 92:

> Now was my heart filled full of comfort and hope, and now I could believe that my sins should be forgiven me; . . . Well, I would I had a pen and ink here, I would write this down before I go any farther, for surely I will not forget this forty years hence; but alas! within less than forty days, I began to question all again; which made me begin to question all still.

This repetition of the experience and its narration in the work is reminiscent of the underlying cyclical repetitiveness of experience, if not narration, in both Augustine and Donne. The tension, again, involves a wavering between fear and joy. And, again like Augustine and Donne, Bunyan finds his persona yearning for that peace which only death can bring the elect. As he cries out in *Grace Abounding*, after suffering endless oscillation between assurance and doubt,

128. Now had I an evidence, as I thought, of my salvation from heaven, ... before, I lay continually trembling at the mouth of hell, now methought I was got so far therefrom that I could not, when I looked back, scarce discern it; and oh! thought I, that I were fourscore years old now, that I might die quickly, that my soul might be gone to rest.

And again, much later in the work, after fearing that he had committed the "Unpardonable Sin," another moment of peace leads him to yearn for death:

259 . . . Now was I got on high; I saw myself within the arms of Grace and Mercy; and though I was before afraid to think of a dying hour, yet now I cried, Let me die; now death was lovely and beautiful in my sight; for I saw we shall never live indeed till we be gone to the other World. (80-81)

Fearing the loss of "Grace and Mercy" if he remains in this earthly, sinful world, Bunyan's persona, like Donne's and Augustine's, longs to "be gone to the other world." Inasmuch as this tension between assurance and doubt lies at the heart of Augustine's theology and *Confessions*, it serves as an important connection between the emotional experience in Augustine, Donne, and Bunyan.[18]

Leopold Damrosch has recently asserted that, "although it is some-times alleged that *Grace Abounding* presents a coherent novelistic narra-tive, it is equally possible to complain . . . that the work is repetitive and evades the whole problem of authorial control." Yet, as Damrosch says, this allegation misses the point. Rather "[repetition] is just what Bunyan intended, uninterested as he is in inventing the novel: he perceived his life as a continual oscillation of moods, not as a shapely structure, and oscillation itself becomes his theme" (140).[19] Whether termed Augustin-ian, Reformed Augustinian, Protestant, Anglican, Calvinist, Episcopalian Calvinist, Puritan, Presbyterian, Conformist, or Nonconformist, this spiri-tual vacillation, complete dependence on God, and ultimate assurance of His mercy is the same among them. But while Augustine concludes with a momentary union of the self with God—one reminiscent of Donne's persona at the conclusion of Prayer 18—Donne and Bunyan must con-tinue the fight in this world, at the same time recognizing that true peace, unqualified assurance of election, and a true conclusion to a seemingly endless narrative cycle, whether of an extended illness or the process of life, comes only with death. This underlying concern with sinfulness, human frailty, dependence on God, election, salvation, and the attendant emotions of personal struggle marks the essential similarities between these works, similarities that elements of literary "indifference," such as genre and style, and even disagreement by their authors on matters of theological "indifference," such as church discipline and conformity to ceremonies, need, and should, not obscure. Donne's *Devotions upon Emergent Occasions* and Bunyan's *Grace Abounding to the Chief of Sinners*, for all their differences in some particulars, do not reflect respectively, "the styles of two faiths," Anglican and Puritan.

Notes

[1] See Bouwsma (204) and Vander Molen, "Anglican Against Puritan" (45-57). Professor Vander Molen demonstrates how Calvin's view that matters of church discipline and the use of ceremonies were things indifferent can be seen in his response to the dispute between the congregations of English exiles in Frankfurt and Strasbourg in 1554-55. Despite his own views on church government, in this controversy Calvin supported the Strasbourg congregation led by Richard Cox (Vander Molen's Anglicans) rather than the John Knox led Frankfurt delegation (Vander Molen's Puritans), for although Calvin "did not like many of the ceremonies, he still indicated that he found 'no manifest impiety'" (53).

[2] Compare Greaves. See also Lake, *Anglicans and Puritans?* (25-42 and 159-160), who bases the distinction between Anglican and Puritan not on matters of soteriology, but rather on two distinct positions of the relationship between the visible and invisible church; and Christianson, who carefully re-examines the "controversy [that] still ranges over the boundaries and validity of such terms as 'Anglican' and—especially—'Puritan'" (463).

[3] Some recent studies include Kendall, *Calvin and English Calvinism to 1649*; Collinson, *The Religion of Protestants*; Tyacke, *Anti-Calvinists*; and Clausen, *Calvinism in the Anglican Hierarchy*.

[4] *Zurich Letters, 1558-1579* (Cambridge: Parker Society, 1842), 169, as qtd. in Clausen 15. Compare Lake, *Anglicans and Puritans?* (159-160).

[5] See Tyacke's "Puritanism, Arminianism, and Counter-Revolution" (119-143) and *Anti-Calvinists*, for an excellent analysis of the ways in which the rise of Laud's Arminian party effectively destroyed the Elizabethan and Jacobean compromise and led to a polarization in the English Church that would soon erupt into Civil War.

[6] See Collinson, "The Jacobean Religious Settlement" (28-29 and 46-51). Professor Collinson reminds us that James "was a professing Calvinist himself" and that unity in the Church of England brought together all Protestants, whether Episcopalian or Puritan. At the same time, such a union was impossible between Protestants and Papists because of their disagreement on fundamental questions. Episcopalians and Puritans were divided not by questions of fundamentals, but rather by questions of things indifferent.

[7] McIlwain (7-8). Compare Fincham and Lake (170-207), who demonstrate that King James, at the time he took over the crown of England and developed an ecclesiastical policy that would combine the interests of English Protestants and Scottish Presbyterians, felt that both churches, and both strains within the English church, shared an essential theology that derives from Augustine's late anti-Pelagian works as filtered through Calvin, Bucer, and Peter Martyr, though they may differ with regard to questions of the ceremonies and discipline.

[8] See Placher (115). Compare Tulloch (8, 20, 40-43), who acknowledges that the founders of the Reformation on the Continent and in England were greatly influenced by Augustine, particularly his views on predestination and scripture, despite Tulloch's own distaste of its exaggerations. Latourette (753) reminds us that Calvin was influenced greatly by Augustine's doctrine of predestination and primacy of scripture. Kendall (53-54) reminds us that William Perkins, generally described as the most important Puritan of his day, is often stereotyped as a Puritan, a practice that "tends to overlook the fact that he saw himself as being in the mainstream of the Church of England, which he often defended." According to Kendall, in an attack on the Papists and the separatists, Perkins appealed to the Church Fathers. In his words, "Augustine heads the list in order of frequency of quotation (no less than 588 references, either by name or work cited), followed by Chrysostom (with 129)." These numbers correspond to the citations from Donne's sermons that Potter and Simpson compile.

[9] Some attention has been given to the importance of Augustine for reading Donne's divine poems. See Evans and Grant. Steinmetz (13-16) rightly reminds us that in a sense, every western theologian is Augustinian in one way or another. Consequently, we must define carefully the meaning of "Augustinian." The argument in this essay focuses on the late Augustine of the anti-Pelagian controversy to which the Churches of the Reformation, including in England, turned in their response to Rome. This includes works by Augustine such as *De Correptione*

et Gratia, De Praedestinatione Sanctorum, and *De Dono Perseverantiae.*

[10] See Van Laan, Cox, and Morrissey for readings of Donne's *Devotions* in traditions of meditation. Compare Frost (6-14), who analyzes the limitations of the meditation argument for a complete reading of the *Devotions.* Hawkins, in *Archetypes of Conversion,* provides an example of the tendency to read Augustine and Bunyan in the tradition of autobiography.

[11] Frost (28) incorrectly identifies the passage in Acts 11 as St. Paul's autobiography. In fact, it is St. Peter's account of his vision from heaven. St. Paul's account of his conversion occurs in Acts 22: 1-21.

[12] A similar argument can be made against reading Bunyan's *Grace Abounding* simply as autobiography: It is too limiting a view of a complex work. Beal's evaluation of the work as a Pauline epistle, for example, shows one of its multiple dimensions.

[13] See Frost (47-53 and 63-76) for a detailed analysis of possible parallells between the Hezekiah story in Isaiah 38 and Donne's *Devotions.*

[14] See my essay on "The Latin 'Stationes.'"

[15] Though my argument in this essay does not rest on an argument of consistency, but rather on whether the *Devotions* itself reflects Reformed Augustinian theology, nevertheless there is no reason to doubt that this same vision can be shown to characterize Donne's divine poems, particularly his *Holy Sonnets.*

[16] Rivers reminds us that Bunyan defended the "religion of grace (the descendant of Reformation protestantism)" as reflected in works such as Arthur Dent's *The Plaine Mans Path-way to Heaven* (1601) and Lewis Bayly's *The Practise of Pietie* (1612), against the "religion of reason (usually termed by contemporaries 'latitudinarian' . . . and by modern historians 'Anglican rationalism' or 'moralism')," a shift that "involved by the end of the century the virtual eclipse of Calvinism" (45). Bunyan's denouncement of Anglicanism is of an "Anglicanism" moving toward Latitudinarianism that developed in the 1660's and 1670's, not the pre-Laudian "Anglicanism" with which he shared a fundamental Augustinian and Calvinist theology and view of man.

[17] See my article, "Donne, Election, and the *Devotions,*" in which I consider both Donne's views on election as expressed in his sermons and the elect status of his speaker in the *Devotions.*

[18] Compare Hawkins, "The Double-Conversion," who reads the repetition in the narrative of *Grace Abounding* as representative of a gradual process of conversion that "is supported by the Calvinism of the times" (263). She goes on to say, "that these problems are orthodox Calvinist problems goes without saying" (261) and that "if one does not know the Calvinist doctrinal superstructure, the inner sense of the spiritual pilgrimage is lost" (262). Moreover, this double-conversion pattern "is a way of punctuating as it extends the conversion process, so that the

elect of God, in Calvin's words, 'may employ their whole life in the exercise of repentance, and know that this warfare will be terminated only by death,'" a pattern that we have seen as well in the works of Augustine and Donne (272).

[19] Compare Hawkins, "The Double-Conversion," who argues that "the structural diffuseness which we find in the autobiography is not a product of faulty craftsmanship but a literary counterpart to the theological anxiety which underlies *lysis* [or gradual] conversion" (273).

Works Cited

Augustine, St. *Confessions*. Trans. Vernon J. Bourke. *The Fathers of the Church* series. Vol. 5. New York: Cima Publishing, 1953.

——————. *De Correptione et Gratia*. Trans. John C. Murray. *The Fathers of the Church* series. Vol. 4. New York: Cima Publishing, 1947.

——————. *De Doctrina Christiana*. Trans. John J. Gavigan. *The Fathers of the Church* series. Vol. 4. New York: Cima Publishing, 1947.

Beal, Rebecca S. "*Grace Abounding to the Chief of Sinners*: John Bunyan's Pauline Epistle." *SEL* 21 (1981): 147-160.

Berry, Boyd M. *Process of Speech: Puritan Religious Writing & Paradise Lost*. Baltimore: Johns Hopkins U P, 1976.

Bouwsma, William J. *John Calvin: A Sixteenth-Century Portrait*. New York: Oxford U P, 1988.

Bunyan, John. *Grace Abounding to the Chief of Sinners*. Ed. Roger Sharrock. Oxford: Clarendon P, 1962.

Calvin, John. *The Institutes of the Christian Religion*. Ed. John T. McNeil. Trans. Ford Lewis Battles. Philadelphia: Westminster P, 1967.

Christianson, Paul. "Reformers and the Church of England under Elizabeth I and the Early Stuarts." *J of Ecclesiastical History* 31 (1980): 463-482.

Clausen, Sara Jean. *Calvinism in the Anglican Hierarchy, 1603-1643: Four Episcopal Examples*. Dissertation: Vanderbilt U, 1989.

Collinson, Patrick. "The Jacobean Religious Settlement: The Hampton Court Conference." *Before the English Civil War*. Ed. H. Tomlinson. New York: St. Martin's P, 1983. 27-51.

——————. *The Religion of Protestants: The Church in English Society 1559-1625*. Oxford: Clarendon P, 1982.

Cox, Gerald H. "Donne's *Devotions*: A Meditative Sequence on Repentance." *Harvard Theological R* 66 (1973): 331-351.

Damrosch, Leopold, Jr. *God's Plot and Man's Stories: Studies in the Fictional Imagination from Milton to Fielding*. Chicago: U of Chicago P, 1985.

Evans, Gillian R. "John Donne and the Augustinian Paradox of Sin." *Renaissance English Studies* 33 (1982): 1-22.

Fincham, Kenneth, and Peter Lake. "The Ecclesiastical Policy of King James I." *J of British Studies* 24 (April 1985): 170-207.

Frost, Kate. *Holy Delight: Typology, Numerology, and Autobiography in Donne's Devotions Upon Emergent Occasions.* Princeton: Princeton U P, 1990.

Grant, Patrick. "Augustinian Spirituality and the *Holy Sonnets* of John Donne." *ELH* 38 (1977): 542-561.

Greaves, Richard. "The Puritan-Nonconformist Tradition in England, 1560-1700: Historiographical Refections." *Albion* 17.4 (Winter 1985): 449-486.

Haskin, Dayton. "Bunyan, Luther, and the Struggle with Belatedness in *Grace Abounding.*" *UTQ* 50 (1981): 300-313.

Hawkins, Anne H. *Archetypes of Conversion: The Autobiographies of Augustine, Bunyan, and Merton.* Lewisburg PA: Bucknell U P, 1985.

_____. "The Double-Conversion in Bunyan's *Grace Abounding.*" *PQ* 61 (Summer 1982): 259-276.

Keeble, N.H. *The Literary Culture of Nonconformity in Later Seventeenth-Century England.* Athens: U of Georgia P, 1987.

Kendall, R.T. *Calvin and English Calvinism to 1649.* Oxford: Oxford U P, 1979.

Lake, Peter. *Anglicans and Puritans?: Presbyterianism and English Conformist Thought from Whitgift to Hooker.* London: Unwin Hyman, 1988.

Latourette, Kenneth Scott. *A History of Christianity.* Rev. ed. Vol. 2. New York: Harper and Row, 1973.

MacCulloch, Diarmaid. *The Later Reformation in England: 1547-1603.* New York: St. Martin's P, 1990.

Martz, Louis. *The Poetry of Meditation: A Study in English Religious Literature of the Seventeenth Century.* New Haven: Yale U P, 1954.

McIlwain, C. H. ed. *The Political Works of James I.* Cambridge: Harvard U P, 1918.

Morrissey, Thomas J. "The Self and the Meditative Tradition in Donne's *Devotions.*" *Notre Dame English J* 13 (1980): 29-49.

Papazian, Mary Arshagouni. "Donne, Election, and the *Devotions.*" *HLQ* 55 (Winter 1992): 603-619.

_____. "The Latin 'Stationes' in John Donne's *Devotions Upon Emergent Occasions.*" *MP* 89 (Nov. 1991): 196-210.

Placher, William. *A History of Christianity: An Introduction.* Philadelphia: Westminster P, 1983.

Pont, Robert. *Of the Union of Britayne* (1604). Rpt. in Bruce R. Galloway and Brian P. Levack, eds. *The Jacobean Union: Six tracts of 1604.* Edinburgh: Clark Constable, 1985.

Pooley, Roger. "Plain and Simple: Bunyan and Style." *John Bunyan: Conventicle and Parnassus.* Ed. N. H. Keeble. Oxford: Clarendon P, 1988. 91-110.

Rivers, Isabel. "Grace, Holiness, and the Pursuit of Happiness: Bunyan and Restoration Latitudinarianism." *John Bunyan: Conventicle and Parnassus.* Ed. N. H. Keeble. Oxford: Clarendon P, 1988. 45-68.

Sellin, Paul R. *John Donne and 'Calvinist' Views of Grace.* Amsterdam: VU Boekhandel, 1983.

Sherwood, Terry G. *Fulfilling the Circle: A Study of John Donne's Thought.* Toronto: U of Toronto P, 1984.

Shuger, Debra. *Sacred Rhetoric: The Christian Grand Style in the English Renaissance.* Princeton: Princeton U P, 1988.

Steinmetz, David. *Luther and Staupitz: An Essay in the Intellectual Origins of the Protestant Reformation.* Durham: Duke U P, 1980.

Tulloch, John. *Rational Theology and Christian Philosophy in England in the Seventeenth Century.* Vol. 1. Edinburgh and London: William Blackwood, 1872.

Tyacke, Nicholas. *Anti-Calvinists: The Rise of English Arminianism c.1590-1640.* Oxford: Clarendon P, 1987.

_____. "Puritanism, Arminianism, and Counter-Revolution." *The Origins of the English Civil War.* Ed. Conrad Russell. New York: MacMillan P, 1973. 119-143.

Vander Molen, Ronald J. "Anglican Against Puritan: Ideological Origins during the Marian Exile." *Church History* 42 (1973): 45-57.

Van Laan, Thomas. "John Donne's *Devotions* and the Jesuit Spiritual Exercises." *SP* 60 (1963): 191-202.

Walton, Izaak. *The Life and Death of Dr. Donne.* In *LXXX Sermons.* London: M. Flesher for R. Royston, 1640.

Webber, Joan. "Donne and Bunyan: The Styles of Two Faiths." 1968. Rpt. *Seventeenth-Century Prose: Modern Essays in Criticism.* Ed. Stanley Fish. New York: Oxford U P, 1971. 489-532.

"Saint Pauls Puritan": John Donne's "Puritan" Imagination in the Sermons

Daniel W. Doerksen

hough John Donne was not a Puritan, some of his most distinctive passages in the *Sermons* are marked by what may properly be called a "puritan" imagination.[1] Knowing what the Church of England in his time was actually like helps explain why this should be so. At the height of the Jacobean years, particularly, a significant number of Puritans conformed and were welcomed into prominent positions, where they could and did influence their fellow churchmen. George R. Potter and Evelyn M. Simpson, in their otherwise excellent edition of the *Sermons*, are seriously mistaken in asserting that Donne "disliked the Puritans, and disagreed sharply with many of their doctrines and opinions." In fact these editors immediately try to explain why the *Sermons* do not bear out their assertion, suggesting that Donne "by both instinct and conscious strategy" was "following the taste and the popular expectation of his times" (1: 113). Potter and Simpson labored under a different view of the Church of England than the one now emerging; it is becoming evident that Donne in his attitude toward Puritanism is not a mere time-server, but someone who identifies fully with the official position of the Jacobean church, including its acceptance of conforming Puritans.

In recent years church historians have been giving a progressively more distinct picture of the early seventeenth-century Church of England. The old views, which grouped John Donne rather unquestioningly with Hooker, Andrewes, and Laud, have become more and more untenable. There is now good reason to believe that Donne belongs with the mainstream of the Jacobean church (which in spite of Peter White's recent book can still be called "moderate Calvinist"[2]), while Andrewes and Laud are part of a small minority that had little influence until after 1625, when their party formed an alliance with Charles I that gave them increasing power.[3] Although Donne eventually came under pressure when Laud himself became his immediate superior as Bishop of London, he can be clearly differentiated from the rather Laudian Andrewes: to apply the terminology used in Kenneth Fincham's recent book on the Jacobean bishops (248-93), Donne was a "preaching pastor," while Andrewes was a "custodian of order."[4]

Following the lead of Richard Hooker, who said that a bare reading of scripture or of a homily could take the place of a sermon, Lancelot Andrewes and William Laud, both accomplished preachers themselves, minimized the importance of sermons and decried the popularity of the "preachers of God's word." By contrast, Donne repeatedly paired preaching with the sacraments as essentials of the church (for example, 3: 302, 372; 4: 105, 149), and on one occasion even ventured a slant aspersion on the Homilies: "God hath delivered us in a great measure . . . from this penury in preaching, we need not preach others Sermons, nor feed upon cold meat, in Homilies" (3: 338).[5] In such matters Donne was more like the moderate Puritans than like their most vigorous opponents, the Laudians. And while Hooker, Andrewes, and Land sought to replace the Calvinist, word-centered peity with one that was sacrament-centered (Lake, *Anglicans and Puritans* 173), Donne publicly espoused the position of the Puritans and the moderate conformists that church *doctrine* (as in the Thirty-Nine Articles) is more important than outward forms of worship—even in a 1627 Paul's Cross sermon defending the latter (7: 433). At a time when the Laudians became preoccupied with external uniformity in worship, Donne and the moderates, including moderate Puritans, continued to care most about the *spiritual* well-being of people in the church.

Donne was undoubtedly a conformist,[6] but he conformed to a non-Laudian church that welcomed those Puritans (a significant number) willing to conform either completely or to an acceptable level as specified by King James (Fincham and Lake). Almost no Puritans separated from the Church of England during Donne's time. Conforming Puritans, including scholarly heads of colleges at the universities like Samuel Ward and Richard Sibbes, and arguably even archbishops (George Abbot, Matthew Hutton) and bishops, such as Donne's friends Thomas Morton and John King,[7] were an influential part of the church, with a significant impact on their fellow churchmen. Further examples of special interest to students of Donne are Thomas Gataker and John Preston, who (respectively) preceded and succeeded Donne as lecturer in divinity at Lincoln's Inn.

It is true that in keeping with the stance of the Jacobean church Donne speaks out against "singularity," against holding conventicles forbidden by the Canons of 1604, and against *extreme* positions on predestination. It is probably for such reasons that some readers of Donne, not fully aware of the degree of moderate or conforming puritanism in England, have assumed that Donne "hated the Puritans." However, it is significant that unlike Robert Sanderson, another Calvinist churchman (Lake, "Sanderson" 91-95), Donne does not label any of these nonconformist stances or actions "puritan." In fact Donne deliberately, on principle, avoids name-calling directed against members of his own church, declaring: "truly it is a lamentable thing, when ceremoniall things in matter of discipline, or problematicall things in matter of doctrine, come so farre, as to separate us from one another, in giving ill names to one another. . . . God will not . . . accept any thing for an act of zeal to himself, that violates charity towards our brethren" (2: 111).

Though not a Puritan himself, Donne could get along well with *conforming* Puritans, and even shared some of their views and attitudes. Those who want a full understanding of the mature Donne of the *Sermons* need to recognize that this man had more than a family kinship with his father-in-law Sir George More, a conforming Puritan active in Parliament. As R. C. Bald notes, Donne and More came to be on good terms, despite the disastrous way in which their family relationship began. Even after Anne's death, the wealthy More continued to make the equivalent of dowry payments, and still later Donne helped More out with a loan (426, 513-14). It may not be common knowledge that More, a generous contributor to Bodley's library at Oxford and a man trusted by King James (Bald 129, 313), was a Puritan; Bald certainly does not identify him as such. Nevertheless he is listed as one in Cliffe's study of puritan gentry because he patronized puritan clergy and because of his activities in Parliament, where he spoke repeatedly in favor of legislation against public vices. On one occasion More defended a bill which was criticized as savoring "the spirrit [sic] of a Puritan" (59, 41-42). Donne identified publicly with views of his father-in-law when, within a year of its promulgation by King James, he ironically critiqued the Book of Sports in a sermon (2: 189), in a passage quoted below.

Donne was also a close friend of Dr. Thomas Mountford, of the chapters at Westminster Abbey and St. Paul's Cathedral, a member of the Jacobean church establishment. As rector of St. Martin-in-the-Fields, the parish church of Magdalen Herbert and her family, Mountford repeatedly chose puritan (and other anti-Laudian) lecturers for his church, beginning with Robert Hill. Thomas Gataker, Donne's predecessor as reader in divinity at Lincoln's Inn, preached occasionally at St. Martin's.[8] In 1623 the Puritan Thomas Adams dedicated one of his works, a Paul's Cross sermon called *The Barren Tree*, "To the Reuerend and learned Doctor Donne, Dean of St. *Pauls*, together with the Prebend Residentiaries of the same Church, my very *good Patrons* . . . in humble acknowledgement of your fauours" (A3r-v).

But cordial relationships can exist between people of considerably varying views. Donne's connections certainly tend to show that he did not simply "hate the Puritans," but for evidence of his actual attitudes we must go to his writings. Though Donne regularly avoids labelling his fellow church members "puritan," he is well aware of the term, and both early and late in his preaching career makes some noteworthy comments about people so identified. The third sermon in the Potter and Simpson edition, preached at Paul's Cross in 1616/17, sets out well the position of Donne and his church (before Laud's ascendancy) with regard to Puritans. The text is Proverbs 22: 11, "He that loveth pureness of heart, for the grace of his lips, the king shall be his friend." In talking of the pureness appropriate to a good subject, Donne specifies two kinds of bad puritanism, one of which he interestingly manages to attach to the *Roman* church, while more briefly identifying objectionable *"puritans among our selves"* with those who refuse the Lord's Prayer (1: 187). King James, of course, also wrote on the Lord's Prayer, the repetition of which in the English liturgy had been of concern to some, but by no means all, Puritans.[9] For both kinds of objectionable puritanism, Donne recommends *conferring* to remove "just scruples," but failing that, action to limit the harm such "false puritans" might do.

Donne goes on to talk of a "third sort of Puritans," of whom he and his church approve: "Saint *Pauls* Puritan, Pure in Heart, pure in Hand, pure in Conscience" (1: 188, 189). He speaks of *imagining* them because, although there are such people, Donne is saying that they are wrongly being labelled with what is still at this time generally a pejorative name. The term, he suggests, is being used as a bogeyman to

> make men afraid of the zeal of the glory of God, make men hard, and insensible of those wounds that are inflicted upon Christ Jesus, in blas-

phemous oaths, . . . make men ashamed to put a difference between *the Sabbath* and an ordinary day, and so, at last make sin an indifferent matter. (1: 188)

The concerns expressed here, about swearing and non-observance of the sabbath (unlike George Herbert, Donne repeatedly uses the term "sabbath," here and elsewhere), were those of *conforming* Puritans, who accepted church ritual and episcopacy.

Donne's passage recalls what Richard Baxter said about his father (a contemporary of Donne's), who

> never scrupled Common Prayer or Ceremonies, nor spake against Bishops, nor ever so much as prayed but by a book or form, being not even acquainted then with any that did otherwise. But only for reading Scripture when the rest were dancing on the Lord's Day, and for praying (by a form out of the end of the Common Prayer Book) in his house, and for reproving drunkards and swearers, and for talking sometimes a few words of Scripture and the life to come, he was reviled commonly by the name of Puritan, Precisian, and hypocrite; and so were the godly conformable ministers that lived anywhere in the country near us . . . (Baxter 1.3)[10]

Undoubtedly there were such people, called "Puritans" although they did not welcome the term. In fact, Donne elsewhere corroborates Baxter's assertion: "Let a man be zealous, and fervent in reprehension of sin, and there flies out an arrow [of affliction], that gives him the wound of a *Puritan*" (2: 58). Here Donne may have been thinking of his own father-in-law, Sir George More—or even of himself, as Potter and Simpson suggest (2: 20). Donne is saying that such people should be (and, officially, *are*) welcome in the English Church: "The Church of God encourages them, and assists them in that sanctity . . . and professes that she prefers . . . in her prayers, one Christian truly fervent and zealous, before millions of Lukewarme" (1: 188).

Of course, Donne includes cautions against hypocrisy and against disobedience to lawful authority, as well as against the illusion that one can attain perfection in this life (a view he ascribes to some Romanists). But with these provisos, he goes on to make a remarkable assertion, which should not be written off as empty or merely rhetorical:

> if their purity consist in studying and practising the most available

means to sanctification, and in obedience to lawful authority established according to Gods Ordinance, and in acquiescence in fundamental doctrines, believed in the ancient Church to be necessary to salvation, If they love the peace of conscience, and the peace of *Sion* [i.e., of the visible church], . . . I say, let me live the life of a *Puritan*, let the zeal of the house of God consume me, let a holy life, and an humble obedience to the Law, testifie my reverence to God in his Church, and in his Magistrate: For, this is Saint *Pauls Puritan*, To have *a pure heart* . . . And then to have *pure hands* . . . And to have *pure consciences*. . . . (1: 188)[11]

Along with Sir George More and the likes of Baxter's father, Donne strongly feels the attraction of the Puritan objectives.

Historian Peter Lake calls attention to the positive features of puritanism that formed a common bond between conforming and nonconforming members of the brotherhood. Indeed, presbyterianism and concern about liturgy were peripheral to the *core* of puritanism, which Lake describes as "evangelical" and "pietistic." Consequently, as Lake says, "The removal of presbyterianism from the practical agenda [toward the end of Elizabeth's reign] . . . simply allowed puritan divines to give their undivided attention to their role as preaching ministers and practical pastors. Yet such activities had always stood at the centre of their lives" (*Moderate Puritans* 284-85). How close this brings them to Donne can be seen in Potter and Simpson's correct assertion that "Donne is first and foremost an evangelical preacher" (10: 295); he himself says that "A preachers end is . . . a gathering of soules to God" (7: 329).[12] In some matters of highest concern to both Donne and the conforming Puritans, there is *no* difference between them.

Near the end of his life, in 1629/30, Donne again affirmed that he would be willing to be called by terms of disapproval such as "papist" and "puritan" if that were a consequence of striving after holiness of life:

So, if when I startle and am affected at a blasphemous oath, as at a wound upon my Saviour, if when I avoyd the conversation of those men, that prophane the Lords day, any other will say to me, This is Puritanicall, Puritans do this, It is a blessed Protestation, and no man is the lesse a Protestant, nor the worse a Protestant for making it, Men and Brethren, I am a Puritan, that is, I wil endeavour to be pure, as my Father in heaven is pure, as far as any Puritan. (9: 166)[13]

Taking this statement in the context of Donne's *Sermons* as a whole, I am not claiming Donne is even a conforming Puritan, because he is happier with the rituals of the English church than conforming Puritans were. But unlike Hooker, Andrewes, and Laud, Donne is a *moderate* conformist who is content to be associated with conforming puritanism, in part because he participates with it in the "word-centered piety" that Hooker and the Laudians sought to replace.

Donne's share in some essentials of the Puritan outlook is an intellectual position, but it affects his imagination. This is an aspect of "unified sensibility" in Donne which T. S. Eliot does not recognize as such, or welcome, when in his essay on Andrewes he speaks of Donne as "a little of the religious spellbinder, the Reverend Billy Sunday of his time" (182). Unlike Andrewes, Eliot feels, Donne lacks spiritual control and discipline. I suggest that it is actually Donne's "puritan" imagination that upsets Eliot, because the modern high-churchman prefers his own kind in Andrewes.

It is apparently the lively, quotable parts of Donne's sermons that Eliot considers inferior to the writings of Andrewes (181). What smacks to him of "emotional orgy" (182) is like what W. Fraser Mitchell calls the "vivid— one might almost say lurid—imagery" of the Puritan preachers (197). Unless one has very narrow tastes, there is no need to speak pejoratively of such passages in Donne. They belong, in part, to a tradition going back to the Old Testament prophets, in which Jesus also participated when, for example, he denounced the scribes and Pharisees for straining at a gnat and swallowing a camel, or for being whited sepulchers, beautiful outside, but full of dead men's bones (Matt. 23: 24, 27). When Donne the preacher warns of falling *out of* the hands of the living God, or when he dares the atheist to test his atheism in the dead of night, he is not losing control of his pen or his life, nor engaging in cheap sensationalism, but deliberately challenging his listener or reader with the same kind of intensity that one may find in Isaiah 1:1-20 or the conclusion of Ezekiel 18.

In an important article on "Imagination and Affections in John Donne's Preaching," Paul W. Harland writes that Donne "preached his sermons conscious that he must engage the senses in order to restore them" (36). Donne regarded it as "the preacher's responsibility to stimulate the imagination" (39) in fitting and purposeful ways. Interestingly, Harland finds a parallel to Donne's approach in Richard Sibbes, whom he recognizes as "One of the most perceptive and imaginative Puritan preachers of the time" (39). Sibbes wrote, "Whilst the soul is joined with the body, it hath not only a necessary but a holy use of imagination, and of sensible things whereupon our imagination worketh. What is the use of the sacraments but to help our souls by our senses, and our faith by imagination? As the soul receives much hurt from imagination, so it may have much good thereby" (I.185).

Elements in Donne's sermons at times warrant a comparison to those of "silver-tongued" Henry Smith, the Puritan lecturer active two decades earlier in St. Clement Danes (Donne's parish from 1612 to 1621). Fraser Mitchell says Smith at times "allowed his mind to dwell on a subject with pleasurable expatiation," and "could treat of practical things, especially spiritual conditions, with insight and vividness. This is a typical Puritan note," he says, "and, except in the case of Donne, is almost wholly absent from Anglo-Catholic preaching" (211). One such passage in Donne is the following:

> as a spider builds always where he knows there is most access and haunt of flies, so the Devil that hath cast these light cobwebs into thy heart, knows that that heart is made of vanities and levities; and he that gathers into his treasure whatsoever thou wast'st out of thine, how negligent soever thou be, he keeps thy reckoning exactly, and will produce against thee at last as many lascivious glaunces as shall make up an Adultery, as many covetous wishes as shall make up a Robery, as many angry words as shall make up a Murder; and thou shalt have dropt and crumbled away thy soul, with as much irrecoverableness, as if thou hadst poured it out all at once[.] (1: 195)

Here, and in similar passages, Donne dwells on a subject in an "expatiation" that is aesthetically "pleasurable," and at the same time both practically and spiritually acute. The mixed images are held together by the realization that seemingly unimportant things can gradually add up to something serious: "light cobwebs" turn into a death trap, and the dropping and crumbling of bits of the soul into a total expending. Giving strength behind the seemingly fanciful assertions about "lascivious glaunces" and "angry words" are Christ's stern warnings in the Sermon on the Mount about committing adultery in one's heart, and about harboring or expressing murderous thoughts (Matt. 5: 27-28, 21-22).

Fraser Mitchell notes that London Puritan preachers like Smith and Thomas Adams had a "full-blooded relish for a variegated life which characterised the dramatists and pamphleteers" of the Elizabethan age; they were "accustomed to appeal to citizens of the type depicted in the plays of Jonson and Dekker, or to young benchers of the Inns of Court, whose experience of life (in many instances) may well have been as riotous and dissolute as that described by Donne in his early poems" (198). The Elizabethan and Jacobean public, suggests William Haller, flocked to Puritan sermons for some of the same reasons that drew them to the theaters. The godly preachers, knowing that their public "took a livelier interest in sin itself than in its categories, in the psychology of spiritual struggle than in the abstract analysis of moral behavior," "set out to describe the warfare of the spirit, to portray the drama of the inner life, to expound the psychology of sin and redemption" (32-33).[14]

Donne's "puritan" imagination often reveals itself in a witty probing into the nature of besetting sins, one which exemplifies (to use Sidney's phrase) "delightful teaching." As Harland notes, Donne uses what he sees as St. Paul's approach, "That is, to proceed by the understanding, to the affections, and so to the conscience of those that hear him, by such means of perswasion, as are most appliable to them, to whom he then speaks" (8: 160, cited in Harland, "Imagination" 43). Repeatedly Donne's pastoral concern to promote "a holy life" expresses itself creatively, as in the following passage about the lengths to which human waywardness will go (a passage that has a kind of parallel in Henry Smith[15]):

> Though we grumble, not out of remorse of *conscience*, but out of a bodily wearinesse of the sinne, yet wee proceed in it. How often men goe to *Westminster*, how often to the *Exchange*, called by unjust suits or called by corrupt bargaines to those places, when their ease, or their health perswades them to stay at home? How many go to forbidden beds, then when they had rather stay at home, if they were not afraid of an unkind interpretation? . . . Every way, that is out of the way, wearies us; . . . we goe to bed to night, weary of our sinfull labours, and we will rise freshly to morrow, to the same sinfull labours again. (2: 133-34)

The insight is a biblical one, arising out of his text (Ps. 38:4) but made "appliable" for Donne's hearers (in this case the lawyers of Lincoln's Inn), by the specific place names, and doubtless confirmed by experience. Along with the ironic humor there is the ring of truth. Imagination is what brings the message home, penetrating the human barriers of defensiveness; for of course the effective rhetoric is purposeful.

Even Potter and Simpson are willing, albeit reluctantly, to admit that the Puritans were not "mere killjoys," that "They were inspired by a passionate earnestness which saw life as a preparation for eternity"; they likewise concede that "Donne too was passionately earnest, and sometimes . . . expressed himself much as a Puritan might have done" (4: 15).

Donne's "zeal for the glory of God" can reveal itself in a Puritan-like refusal to allow for mere dabbling in Christianity:

> [Christ] hath been in a pilgrimage towards thee long, coming towards thee, perchance 50, perchance 60 years; and how far is he got into thee yet? Is he yet come to thine eyes? Have they made *Jobs* Covenant, that they will not look upon a Maid; yet he is not come into thine ear? still thou hast an itching ear, delighting in the libellous defamation of other men. . . . Art thou rectified in that sense? yet voluptuousness in thy tast, or inordinateness in thy other senses keep him out in those. . . . Christ Jesus is in thy mouth, but in . . . blasphemies . . . He may be come to the skirts, to the borders, to an outward show in thine actions, and yet not be come into the land, into thy heart. (1: 308)

The persistent and climaxing "expatiation," dealing with spiritual yet practical matters, like that which Mitchell finds in Henry Smith, is marked by both "insight and vividness."

Similarly zealous and demanding is Donne's protest against a merely civil religion in 1618/19, which (in the emphasized words) dares even to challenge ironically King James's Book of Sports, within a year of its issue:

> if we will say . . . we will admit Christ, but we will not admit him to reign over us, to be King; if he will be content with a Consulship, with a Collegueship, that he and the world may joyn in the government, that we may give the week to the world, and the Sabbath to him, that we may give the day of the Sabbath to him, and the night to our licentiousnesse, *that of the day we may give the forenoon to him, and the afternoon to our pleasures*, if this will serve Christ, we are content to admit him, but . . . we will none of that absolute power, that whether we eat or drink, or whatsoever we doe, we must be troubled to thinke on him, and respect his glory in every thing. (2: 189; emphasis added)

Donne's insistence on full commitment (reminiscent of the concern for purity that earned nicknames for Baxter's father) is imaginatively enlivened by his parallels to earthly government.

Because the Puritans insisted on taking even little details of life seriously (they were also called "precisians," and their attention to minutiae in diaries is notorious), it is appropriate to recognize the Puritan element in Donne's famous description of the "weaknesses of the strongest devotions in time of Prayer," where he comments on how "the noise of a Flie, . . . the ratling of a Coach, . . . the whining of a doore" can distract a would-be worshipper (7: 264-65). Perhaps more obviously displaying "puritan" imagination is Donne's invitation to self-analysis:

> we understand the frame of mans body, better when we see him naked, than apparrelled, . . . and better by seeing him cut up, than by seeing him do any exercise alive. . . . Let every one of us therefore dissect and cut up himself, and consider what he was before God raised him friends to bring those abilities, and good parts, which he had, into knowledge, and into use, and into employment; what he was before he had by education, and study, and industry, imprinted those abilities in his soul; what he was before that soul was infused into him, capable of such education; what he was, when he was but in the list, and catalogue of creatures, and might have been left in the state of a worm, or a plant, or a stone; what he was, when he was not so far, but onely in the vast and unexpressible, and unimaginable depth, of nothing at all. (1: 273)

Here again Donne is using St. Paul's method, proceeding from the understanding to the affections, and then to the conscience. The "Calvinism" in the ensuing lines, Donne's manifest adherence to the predestinarian teaching of Article XVII of his church,[16] helps mark this as a "Puritan" rather than Ignatian exercise.

One could easily multiply examples of Donne's "Puritan" imagination in the *Sermons*. His terrible and splendid passage on falling "out of the hands of living God," carefully nuanced to give recognition to God's present mercy, is perhaps the most wonderful (if most terrifying). But Donne can also write engagingly and imaginatively of joy and heaven:

> Howling is the noyse of hell, singing the voyce of heaven; Sadnesse the damp of Hell, Rejoycing the serenity of Heaven. And he that hath not this joy here, lacks one of the best pieces of his evidence for the joyes of heaven; and hath neglected or refused that Earnest, by which God uses to binde his bargaine, that true joy in this world shall flow into the joy of Heaven, as a River flowes into the Sea. . . . As my soule shall not goe towards Heaven, but goe by Heaven to Heaven, to the Heaven of Heavens, So the true joy of a good soule in this world is the very joy of Heaven; and we goe thither, not that being without joy, we might have joy infused into us, but that as Christ sayes, *Our joy might be full*, perfected, sealed with an everlastingness[.] (7: 70-71)

The tone of this passage is similar to that to be found in some writings of the conforming puritan Richard Sibbes, especially in his book *A Glance of Heaven: or A Precious Taste of a Glorious Feast*, where he writes, inter alia, "there is nothing in heaven but God's children have a taste of it before they come there in some measure" (4.167). Izaak Walton, Donne's first biographer, perhaps echoed Donne when he wrote about Sibbes that

> Of this blest man, let this just praise be given,
> Heaven was in him, before he was in heaven.[17]

Thus, far from *hating* the Puritans, as has often been claimed, Donne unlike Andrewes and Laud identified fully with the Jacobean church attitude of welcoming Puritans who conformed to the church, of whom there were a significant number. Like many other conformist churchmen, including leading bishops, Donne shared with the Puritans their evangelical vision, their concern for a wholehearted and practical Christianity, and their view of preaching as a chief means of propagating the gospel. Like Sibbes Donne regarded appeals to the imagination as a vital means of stirring the hearers of a sermon. It is only appropriate to recognize that in some important respects both the imaginative impulse and some of its fine outworkings in Donne's *Sermons* are "Puritan"—characteristic of "Saint *Pauls* Puritan."

Notes

[1] Since the word "Puritan" can mean many things, in this essay I will take my chief application of it from Donne's definition as it emerges in his sermons.

[2] See my review of Peter White's *Predestination, Policy and Polemic*. White challenges the by-now new standard views of Nicholas Tyacke, but his focus on predestination as a supposedly *central* teaching of Calvin or his followers, and his equation of Calvinism with extreme Calvinism (in spite of his occasional recognition that Calvin and English Calvinists could be moderate) limit the effect of his challenge.

Daniel W. Doerksen

[3] Historians I have in mind here include Peter Lake and Kenneth Fincham; see Lake, *Moderate Puritans*; "Calvinism and the English Church"; *Anglicans and Puritans?*; Fincham and Lake, "Ecclesiastical Policy"; Fincham, *Prelate as Pastor.* These build on important earlier work: Charles and Katherine George, *Protestant Mind*; Collinson, *Religion of Protestants*; and Nicholas Tyacke, *Anti-Calvinists.* Most of these books do not deal directly with Donne; Tyacke classes him as an Arminian on the basis of two passages dated 1627 and 1629 which cite scripture against *extreme* Calvinist attitudes. For Donne's part in the new picture, see Norbrook, esp. 19-25; also my book manuscript now being considered for publication, "Conforming to the Word: Herbert, Donne, and the English Church before Laud."

[4] Fincham does not simply equate the two categories with non-Laudians and Laudians, respectively, but his study recognizes a tendency toward such a correlation. See also my article forthcoming in *PQ:* "Preaching Pastor versus Custodian of Order: Donne, Andrewes, and the Jacobean Church."

[5] These remarks were made at Lincoln's Inn. Yet a few years later, as new Dean of St. Paul's, Donne recognized in a sermon that the Homilies were officially sanctioned by the Thirty-Nine Articles (Article XXXV), and defended them (4: 206-07).

[6] The term "Anglican" is unhelpful for Donne's time; never used until 1635, it has accumulated anachronistic implications, especially since the time of the Oxford movement in the nineteenth century.

[7] For Hutton see Peter Lake, "Matthew Hutton—A Puritan Bishop?"; for Morton, see Norbrook (20).

[8] For Robert Hill, see *DNB.* I deal at some length with St. Martin-in-the-Fields, the church of Magdalen Herbert and her family from 1601 until well into the 1620s, in "Conforming to the Word."

[9] Richard Sibbes, for example, commended the prayers of the Church of England as "religiously performed" in a letter written to persuade a fellow Puritan to conform and not separate from the church (I, cxv).

[10] Similarly Lucy Hutchinson wrote that

> whoever was zealous for God's glory or worship, could not endure blasphemous oathes, ribald conversation, prophane scoffes, sabbath breach, derision of the word of God, and the like; whoever could endure a sermon, modest habitt or conversation, or aniething that was good, all these were Puritanes; and if Puritanes, then . . . seditious factious hipocrites, ambitious disturbers of the publick peace . . . , according to the Court account. (Hutchinson 44)

[11] In my book manuscript, cited above, I discuss at length the importance of church doctrine, centering on the *Thirty-Nine Articles*, as a unifying force binding together the whole church, but especially the Calvinistic moderate majority in the church leadership, consisting of moderate conformists and moderate puritans. Donne fully shared in that doctrinal consensus, including the predestinarian teaching of Article XVII.

[12] See also Donne's sermon (4: 10) to the Virginia Company.

[13] This is one of a number of passages in which Donne makes it clear that he and his church consider themselves unambiguously Protestant. See my article, "Recharting the *Via Media* of Spenser and Herbert."

[14] As Louis Martz has noted, self-examination was encouraged in all branches of the church from the late Middle Ages on, so that the puritan emphasis on it should not be seen in isolation (119, 121 and passim). It is, however, ironic that while justifiably calling attention to continental influences, Martz failed even to mention some germane English works, such as John Downame's *Christian Warfare* or the writings of Richard Sibbes.

[15] And this is the whole progress of sin . . . The more he sinneth, the more he searcheth to sin . . . As soon as he hath that he desireth, he hath not that he desireth. When he hath left fighting, he goeth to fighting again. Yet a little and a little more, and so we flit from one sin to another. While I preach, you hear iniquity engender within you, and [it] will break forth as soon as you are gone. (Cited in Emerson 126)

[16] There is more about Donne's views on predestination in the chapters on "Doctrine" and "Donne" in my book manuscript, "Conforming to the Word." See also Paul Sellin.

[17] Grosart, *Works of Richard Sibbes*, 1.xx. In his will Walton gave "To my son Izaak . . . Doctor Sibbes his Soul's Conflict, and to my daughter his Bruised Reed, desiring them to read them so as to be well acquainted with them." In his immediately previous sentence, Walton left to his son-in-law Doctor Hawkins "Doctor *Donne's* Sermons, which I have heard preached, and read with much content." Walton (certainly a Laudian partisan but not necessarily a very discerning judge) apparently saw no ideological divide between the sermons of Donne and those of Sibbes. Grosart cites the will from Izaak Walton, *The Compleat Angler*, ed. Major, 4th ed (1844), pp. xlii-xlvi.

Works Cited

Adams, Thomas. *The Barren Tree*. London: 1623.

Bald, R. C. *John Donne: A Life*. Oxford: Oxford UP, 1970.

Baxter, Richard. *Reliquae Baxterianae*. Ed. M. Sylvester. London, 1696.

Cliffe, J. T. *The Puritan Gentry: The Great Puritan Families of Early Stuart England*. London: Routledge, 1984.

Collinson, Patrick. *The Religion of Protestants: The Church in English Society, 1559-1625*. Oxford: Clarendon P, 1982.

Doerksen, Daniel W. "Recharting the *Via Media* of Spenser and Herbert," *Ren/Ref* n.s. 8 (Aug. 1984): 215-25.

_____. Review of Peter White, *Predestination, Policy, and Polemic: Conflict and Consensus in the English Church from the Reformation to the Civil War*. *Seventeenth-Century News* 51, 3-4 (Fall-Winter 1993): 54-55.

Eliot, T. S. *Selected Prose*. Ed. Frank Kermode. London: Faber & Faber, 1975.

Emerson, Everett H. *English Puritanism from John Hooper to John Milton*. Durham NC: Duke U P, 1968.

Fincham, Kenneth, and Peter Lake, "The Ecclesiastical Policy of King James I." *J of British Studies* 24, 2 (Apr. 1985): 182-86.

Fincham, Kenneth. *Prelate as Pastor: The Episcopate of James I* Oxford: Clarendon P, 1990.

George, Charles and Katherine. *The Protestant Mind of the English Reformation 1570-1640*. Princeton: Princeton U P, 1961.

Grosart, Alexander B., ed. *Works of Richard Sibbes*. 7 vols. 1862-64. Rpt. Edinburgh: Banner of Truth Trust, 1977-82.

Haller, William. *The Rise of Puritanism*. 1938. Rpt. New York: Harper, 1957.

Harland, Paul W. "Imagination and Affections in John Donne's Preaching." *JDJ* 6 (1987): 33-50.

Hutchinson, Lucy. *Memoirs of the Life of Colonel Hutchinson*. Ed. J. Sutherland. London: Oxford U P, 1973.

Lake, Peter. *Anglicans and Puritans?: Presbyterianism and English Conformist Thought from Whitgift to Hooker*. London: Unwin Hyman, 1988.

_____. "Calvinism and the English Church 1570-1635." *Past and Present* 114 (1987): 32-76.

_____. "Matthew Hutton—A Puritan Bishop?" *History* 64 (1979): 182-204.

_____. *Moderate Puritans and the Elizabethan Church*. Cambridge: Cambridge U P, 1982.

_____. "Serving God and the Times: The Calvinist Conformity of Robert Sanderson." *J of British Studies* 27 (1988): 81-116.

Martz, Louis. *The Poetry of Meditation*. Rev. ed. New Haven: Yale U P, 1962.

Mitchell, W. Fraser. *English Pulpit Oratory from Andrewes to Tillotson: A Study of its Literary Aspects*. 1932. Rpt. New York: Russell & Russell, 1962.

Norbrook, David. "The Monarchy of Wit and the Republic of Letters." *Soliciting Interpretation: Literary Theory and Seventeenth-Century English Poetry*. Ed. Elizabeth D. Harvey and Katharine Eisaman Maus. Chicago: U of Chicago P, 1990.

Sellin, Paul. *So Doth, So Is Religion: John Donne and Diplomatic Contexts in the Reformed Netherlands, 1619-1620*. Columbia: U of Missouri P, 1988.

Sibbes, Richard. *Works*. Ed. A. B. Grosart. 7 vols. 1862-64.

Tyacke, Nicholas. *Anti-Calvinists: The Rise of English Arminianism c.1590-1640*. Oxford: Clarendon P, 1987.

White, Peter. *Predestination, Policy and Polemic: Conflict and Consensus in the English Church from the Reformation to the Civil War*. Cambridge: Cambridge U P, 1992.

Donne's Earliest Sermons and the Penitential Tradition

P. G. Stanwood

f his 160 extant sermons, Donne preached on the Psalms thirty-four times, and twenty-one of these sermons are on the penitential psalms. They thus form the largest group of related texts in his canon: on Psalm 6, six sermons; on Psalm 32, eight sermons; on Psalm 38, six sermons; and one sermon on Psalm 51. Donne did not leave any sermons on the final three penitential psalms, that is, Psalms 102, 130, and 143; but that may mean only that he did not save those sermons or trouble to revise them for publication.

I wish to advance three points: First, Donne probably preached a series on the penitential psalms, of which we possess only about one-half of the whole course; second, Donne preached these sermons at the beginning of his career, at Lincoln's Inn, as early as 1616 and likely before the beginning of his travel with Doncaster in May 1619; third, Donne's sermons on the penitential psalms belong to a literary and devotional tradition, and his preaching on these texts represents a particular form of Christian verbal art, of a specific and predictable kind; for he is not simply preaching on the penitential psalms as he might preach on other texts. We shall, finally, glimpse the shape of a further point, that is, Donne preached in a style that did not markedly change or "develop" over the period of his ordained ministry, but which he had clearly laid out in his *Essayes in Divinity*, probably composed in the time shortly before his ordination in early 1615, though published posthumously in 1651, and which the sermons on the penitential psalms also reflect.[1]

Donne's preaching on the Psalms extends over a career of many years, from Lincoln's Inn to St. Paul's, where as prebend for Chiswick he had preached on his "appointed" Psalms 62, 63, 64, 65, and 66, and where he had given his last sermon (in 1631) on a text from Psalm 68:20: "And unto God the Lord belong the issues of death." In the first of his prebend sermons, dated May 8, 1625, Donne begins by a consideration of "the dignity of the Booke of Psalmes," agreeing with St. Basil "That if all the other bookes of Scripture could perish, there remained enough in the booke of Psalmes for the supply of all."[2] In introducing this prebend sermon on Psalm 62: 9, Donne speaks of the variety and kinds of psalms, noting especially two liturgically organized sections of the psalter: the fifteen psalms following Psalm 119 are distinguished as "graduals" (or "ascents"), that is, Psalms 120-134; and additionally "hath there beene a particular dignity ascribed to those seven Psalmes, which we have ever called the *Penitentiall Psalmes*; Of which S. *Augustine* had so much respect, as that he commanded them to be written in a great Letter, and hung about the curtaines of his Death-bed within, that hee might give up the ghost in contemplation, and meditation of those seven Psalmes" (6: 293)— a scene, as Janel Mueller remarks, which is analogous to (though very different from) Izaak Walton's account of Donne's deathbed meditations on the portrait of himself in his shroud (Mueller 194).[3]

But Evelyn M. Simpson is troubled by Donne's interest in Augustine and in the penitential psalms: "we may perhaps wonder whether Augustine's influence on him was altogether healthy. A modern reader cannot help feeling that an undue number of Donne's sermons are devoted to four of the Penitential Psalms . . . and that in many other sermons there is too much emphasis on sin and its punishment" (10: 357-58). Simpson continues:

> The sermons which he based on [the penitential psalms] are for the most part tedious, and we could well have dispensed with at least half of them. However beautiful the *Psalms* may be as a manual of devotion, they do not and could not anticipate the whole Gospel. Christ came to bring salvation to men, to give them light and life and forgiveness. Therefore the Christian should have a repentance deeper than any of the Jewish psalmists could feel, but he should also have a joy and assurance which they knew only in part. To meditate too long on human guilt and frailty, as Donne is apt to do, is to distort the Christian message, and in this distortion Augustine, with his emphasis on original sin and his

> description of humanity as a *massa damnata* (a phrase which Donne quotes several times), must have had a share. (10: 358)

I think that Donne does not distort the Christian message, but he realizes more profoundly than many late twentieth-century readers the wretchedness of humanity. In their desire to display a supposed development of character and style, Simpson (and her co-editor George R. Potter) are quick to disparage Donne's dark solemnity but eager to celebrate his triumphant moods. They believe that Donne's preaching may be defined by one of three periods:

> During the early years of his ministry and whilst he held the readership at Lincoln's Inn, his sermons were apt to be severely logical, without much rhetorical ornament, and his imagery was largely, though not exclusively, drawn from his knowledge of the law. During the first few years of his life as Dean of St. Paul's he preached the majority of his finest sermons. Logic still has a place, and gives backbone to his discourses, but he has become a great orator, who uses every rhetorical device at his command. His style is rich and flexible, and is ornamented by imagery drawn from nature and from a wide experience of life. In the final stage, during the last years as Dean of St. Paul's, we see Donne becoming an old man, given to constant repetition, but still the orator, capable of magnificent perorations, and of passages of sustained beauty. (8: 33-34)

But such a tendentious account does not properly reflect Donne's pastoral and homiletic experience, and the division of his career into different periods may be quite misleading.

Some while ago I reported the discovery of a commonplace book kept by one John Burley who heard Donne preach two sermons in October 1625 at Chelsea and took notes of them (Stanwood, "Sermon Notes"). The first sermon Burley heard was on Psalm 6: 4-5, which was printed as two sermons on the same text in *LXXX Sermons* (1640), nos. 52-53, part of the series of six sermons on this first of the penitential psalms, a series which continues in the folio edition with eight sermons on Psalm 32, the second of the penitential psalms, then one sermon on Psalm 51, followed by the five prebend sermons on Psalms 62-66. With two exceptions, Potter and Simpson group these undated sermons on Psalm 6 among Donne's early work, for they seem obviously connected, with one often referring to distinctions made in another.[4]

But Burley heard Donne preach on Psalm 6 in 1625, at a time when we know that Donne had left London, presumably on account of the plague, and at one of the times when he explicitly says that he was revising his sermons.[5] The likelihood is that Donne was reusing an old Lincoln's Inn sermon for a different congregation. Preaching more than once from the same notes, generally at widely spaced intervals and for various occasions was common practice in Donne's time—as it probably remains to this day.[6] We may infer this conclusion from Burley's report of the sermon on the Psalm, and have our judgment confirmed by his notes on the sermon on Colossians 1: 24, which appeared in *Fifty Sermons* (1649), no. 16, as one of several preached at Lincoln's Inn. Potter and Simpson are thus content to give this sermon an early date, that is, sometime between October 1616 and February 1622, when Donne was Reader of Divinity (3: 33-34). There is no reason to doubt that Donne did indeed preach on Colossians 1: 24 at Lincoln's Inn, nor is there any reason to suppose that he did not also preach the same sermon many years later to a different auditory.

Yet how are we to regard the sermon on Psalm 6: 6-7, which was "Preached to the King at White-hall, upon the occasion of the Fast, April 5, 1628"? Although it appeared as part of the series on Psalm 6 in *LXXX Sermons*, the heading is surely correct, and Potter and Simpson reasonably accept the date and put the sermon amongst Donne's late work, in their volume 8 (no. 8), calling the sermon "not a great one, but it has passages of eloquence, and it was adequate for the occasion" (8: 20). But I agree with I. A. Shapiro that the sermon was not composed specially for this time; for the first sixty-four lines (in Potter and Simpson's edition) and the final forty lines are all that make the sermon distinctive for this occasion. Without these lines, the text fits perfectly in terms of theme and style with the other sermons on Psalm 6, and Donne could have been confident in any case that what he repeated in 1628—perhaps eleven years later and in an entirely different context—would not be remembered.[7]

A similar case can be made for the final sermon on Psalm 6: 8-10, which Potter and Simpson also removed from its logical place in the series that occurs in *LXXX Sermons*. A reference in the sermon to a "flat Map upon a round body" (6: 1-2 and 59) coincides with a similar remark in a letter to Sir Tobie Matthew of 1623; yet Potter and Simpson admit that the sermon has "some slight connection" with most of the other sermons on Psalm 6. The probability of Donne's recasting all of his sermons on this Psalm at some time after his first preaching of them must be seriously entertained.

The series of five sermons preached on Psalm 38, the third of the penitential psalms, appeared in *Fifty Sermons* (1649), nos. 19-23, a sixth and final sermon in the sequence (on verse 9) being circulated only in manuscript during the seventeenth century. This fact may be due, as Potter and Simpson say, to an oversight by Donne's son, who edited the first printed collections of the sermons; or Donne's commendation of auricular confession (2: 160) may have been thought too unsettling for the time, yet Donne's advice "that sick persons shall make a speciall confession, yf they feele their consciences troubled with any weighty matter" simply recalls the commendation in the Book of Common Prayer preceding the Holy Communion. But of course Donne had preached a whole sermon principally on the Sacrament of Penance, in the third of his sermons on Psalm 32, and while this sermon appeared in *LXXX Sermons* nine years earlier, Donne's views on the subject must have been well known, and so the reminder in this later sermon should not have caused much notice; indeed, his point of view is familiar and entirely consistent with the reformed emphasis on pastoral consolation as opposed to discipline.[8] The sermon, in any event, clearly belongs to a series on Psalm 38, the first five of this series being plainly headed "at Lincoln's Inn."

If we may assume that the sermons on Psalms 6 and 38 belong to the Lincoln's Inn years, then we should reasonably suppose that the undated eight-sermon series on Psalm 32 and the single sermon on Psalm 51 belong also to this period. They appear in sequence, following the sermons on Psalm 6, in *LXXX Sermons*, nos. 56-64. For whatever reasons, the younger Donne decided to put the group on Psalm 38 in a different volume, yet all of these sermons share a common interest in explicating the penitential psalms, one of the most familiar of devotional works, a point which the liturgically and sacramentally oriented John Donne could not possibly miss.

In their confusing attempt to date the series of sermons on Psalm 32, Potter and Simpson recognize that Donne "followed the Fathers and the whole Christian Church in interpreting the Psalms in a Christian sense. For him as for St. Augustine the Book of Psalms foreshadowed both the sufferings and the glorification of Christ" (9: 38). Donne's editors, however, say that his "sermons on the Penitential Psalms will never have many readers. Their justification is their place in the normal rhythm of the Church's year, which Donne accepted and observed" (9: 38).[9] His editors see Donne's preaching on these psalms as dutiful, but required by the "somewhat monotonous" exigencies of the dull parts of the Christian year. However, it is hard to imagine that Donne saw his preaching in these terms; rather, he would have seen his exposition of the psalms, particularly the seven penitential psalms, as contributing to an already rich and traditional literature of psalmic commentary.

Donne was obviously reflecting a particular and popular interest in the penitential psalms and seemingly (to our taste) emphasizing too much the misery of mankind and its need for repentance. But this is an obvious concern of many reformers: Luther's earliest published work is a commentary on the seven penitential psalms (1517, rev. 1525). Melancthon, Calvin, and others, including numerous Roman Catholic exegetes such as Cajetan, Lorinus, and Bellarmine, wrote commentaries on these and the other psalms, to all of whom, along with Augustine in the *Enarrationes in Psalmos*, Donne is indebted. The seven penitential psalms became a traditional feature in office books and liturgies from the time of Cassiodorus onwards, the medieval church also referring each of these psalms to one of the seven deadly sins, the saying of the appropriate Psalm being held to act as a deterrent to the sin.[10]

These seven psalms, like the whole of the Psalter, had traditionally been regarded as "the songs of David," all being ascribed to the same author. The penitential psalms were generally seen as the personal expression of David's sorrow for his own wickedness, his adultery with Bathsheba and his contrivance in the death of her husband Uriah (2 Sam. 11-12). The preface that introduces the penitential psalms in one of the earliest English primers of 1538, and frequently reprinted in later primers, summarizes the conventional understanding:

> Hereafter foloweth the seven penitentiall psalmes. Why that these. vii. psalmes folowynge are called penitentiall, and be chiefely noted aboue other, the common opinion and mynde of many wryters is and hath ben, that the kynge and prophete David compuncte and stryken with hartie repentaunce of his greuous adulterie committed with Bersabe, & the detestable murther of Urie her husbande, beinge his knyght and seruaunt (after he was admonyshed by Nathan, the prophete of god) shulde make them specially to declare his inwarde sorowe, and depe contrition that he toke for the same: but wheter it were done upon that occasion or not, that I referre to the judgement of other, because that in the psalter they stande not together orderly: yet this is very certayne, that they may well and of good congruence be called penitentiall, for so moche as penaunce in them is so diligently, often, and manifestly treated, repeted, and commended, as in the selfe psalmes is easely perceyued.[11]

These early primers frequently show David kneeling before an altar, or else depict him looking from his balcony at the naked Bathsheba in her bath. We are thus urged to think that these psalms are literally about David though typologically aimed at the penitent sinner. Donne understands the penitential psalms in precisely these terms, for he says, in the first of his sermons on Psalm 38, "For thine arrowes stick fast in me, and thy hand presseth me sore" (verse 2): "These *Psalmes* were made, not onely to vent *Davids* present holy passion, but to serve the Church of God, to the worlds end. And therefore, change the person, and wee shall finde a whole quiver of arrows. Extend this *Man*, to all *Mankind*; carry *Davids* History up to *Adams* History, and consider us in that state, which wee inherit from *him*, and we shall see *arrows* fly about our ears" (2: 55). This is but one example of many instances in Donne's sermons on the penitential psalms that characterizes his interpretation of them.[12]

In the sixteenth century, there were numerous translations, adaptations, or treatises of "the seven psalms," including those by St. John Fisher (1509), Sir Thomas Wyatt (1549), Thomas Becon (*c.* 1567), William Hunnis (1583), William Byrd (1589), Richard Verstegan (1601), and (putatively) Edmund Spenser.[13] Donne himself wrote "*Upon the translation of the Psalmes by Sir* Philip Sydney, *and the Countesse of Pembroke his Sister*," praising the Psalms generally as having "The highest matter in the noblest forme" (line 11). Sir Richard Baker (1568-1645), Donne's close friend from Oxford days, who, on account of debt, spent his last years in the Fleet prison, quite naturally turned to the penitential psalms as a consolatory source and an appropriate subject for his own commentary.[14] Such devotional writing, besides treatises and courses of sermons on the penitential psalms in particular, or on penitence more generally are common enough in this period almost to form a kind of genre of penitence and self-examination, a mode of weeping and misery over fallen humanity and the desolation of Jerusalem's children.[15] Donne's sermons on the penitential psalms belong to this genre.

In bringing together all twenty-one of Donne's sermons on the penitential psalms, we are able to recover a natural sequence bound by chronology as well as theme, mood, and exegetical discipline. With respect to this last concern, we can begin to recognize the difficulty of dating Donne's sermons through any supposed development in his beliefs or in his homiletic style. Donne's ideas were well formulated by 1615. Potter and Simpson, who try to make sense out of the opposite case, indeed recognize that "occasional echoes from the *Essays* can be found throughout the sermons, even in those of Donne's last years" (5: 30 and n. 73); and Dennis Quinn, who accepts 1628 as the date of the sermon on Psalm 6:6-7 notes that it is "a lecture rather than a sermon" (Quinn, "Donne's Christian Eloquence" 296).[16] These confusions emanate from an old-fashioned desire to force development and growth on a writer who is already mature; but we all know from Gardner's arrangement of the *Songs and Sonets* that such instinctive critical editing is highly arbitrary and illusive. Do any of us now date Donne's poetry according to the imputed sophistication of form and idea? The situation with the sermons is similar. Since Donne's method of rhetorical analysis and exposition hardly changes from sermon to sermon—the text at hand being the primary determinant of the discourse—then our first task is to study the sermons as whole expressions, not as documents for mapping the growth of the preacher's mind, or for signposting the personal issues of his heart, or for signaling what we might now call "his spiritual pilgrimage." But Donne did leave us with a group of sermons obviously addressed to the themes of the penitential psalms; and we may profitably study them by recalling the course and the time for which they were designed.

Now let us reflect once more on Donne's evident fascination with St. Augustine's writing and experience. Donne's attraction to the penitential psalms may be explained by a cultural and exegetical tradition in which Augustine is a central but not single influence. Why, then, should Augustine, of all the Fathers, have touched Donne's thought so deeply? Because of his obvious genius, his immensely varied and extraordinarily productive career, and his long life (354-430), which bridges antiquity and the beginning of a new age, Augustine naturally affected every subsequent movement of the church. His name came to be attached to almost any tendency of thought, as the authority *par excellence*; in the Middle Ages and later, commentators appeal to Augustine, finding some saying of his that supports even contradictory ideas. Such authority is different from real influence, which is more difficult to describe; surely the many references Donne makes to him neither provide the structure for a systematic theology nor even the adequate intimation of one. Augustine's theological teaching must therefore be carefully distinguished from the "Augustinianism" current in the Reformation period, with which Donne is often identified.

We have seen that Evelyn Simpson accuses Donne of following the supposed example of Augustine by too much emphasizing sin and its punishment, with the numerous sermons on the penitential psalms one egregious result of that indebtedness. Yet the real Augustine's theology of grace defined in the anti-Pelagian writings is much more complex than Simpson and more recent critics readily admit.[17] It is an oversimplification of subtle arguments to say that Augustine so emphasized divine grace that he reduced humanity to abjection. The truth is that Donne's religious imagination moves readily between the heaviness of sin, on the one hand, and the *pondus gloriæ*, the weight of glory, on the other. Donne himself clarifies this point in the first of his sermons on the Penitential Psalm 32, perhaps also pointing to Augustine's measured, or at least ambivalent sense: "Our first errors are out of Levity, and S. *Augustin* hath taught us a proper ballast and waight for that, *Amor Dei pondus animæ*, The love of God would carry us evenly, and steadily, if we would embarke that" (9: 258). This weight carries a burden, as the word requires, and that is "the sin of the whole World; And that sinne is *forgiven.*" Donne's intention in this sermon is characteristic of his homiletic design elsewhere, and that is to celebrate the general pardon of all transgressions through the Atonement of Christ. Let us be exalted in this joy, in such a regeneration, he urges, where "the Sun shall set, and have a to morrows resurrection" (9: 273).[18]

Notes

[1] *Essayes in Divinity* was another of Donne's works, published long after his death, edited by his son. We have depended upon the younger Donne's prefatory comments "To the Reader" in order to date the composition of the work: "they were the voluntary sacrifices of severall hours, when he had many debates betwixt God and himself, whether he were worthy, and competently learned to enter into Holy Orders." In her modern edition, Evelyn M. Simpson argues for late 1614 or early 1615, an inference that depends largely upon the reliability of Donne's son. But I think that we should approach his testimony with some skepticism. Firstly, his remarks seem not necessarily to accord with the theological or exegetical content of the work; secondly, Donne might have begun the *Essayes* long before 1615 and continued to work on the book, which seems unfinished, for many years. Finally, Simpson's early dating of the *Essayes in Divinity* because of style probably cannot be justified. See the "Introduction" to her edition, and also the "Bibliographical Note" that follows.

[2] See *Sermons* 6: 292. The reference to Basil occurs in *Homilia in Psalmum primum*, Antwerp, 1568, 62A. I am indebted to Janel Mueller for this note and for her commentary in her edition of *Donne's Prebend Sermons*.

[3] Donne imaginatively reconstructs the details that Possidius gives in his life of Augustine. He writes: "Nam sibi jusserat Psalmos Davidicos, qui sunt paucissimi de poenitentia, scribi, ipsosque quaterniones jacens in lecto contra parietem positos diebus suae infirmitatis intuebatur, et legebat, et jugiter ac ubertim flebat" (*Vita S. Augustini*, in *Patrologia Latina* 32.31.63-64).

[4] Donne's *LXXX Sermons* is divided into sections according to subject in a way that is common for sermon collections of this time. There are sermons "On the Nativity," "On the Purification," and so on, with a further section of "Sermons Preached upon the Penitentiall Psalmes" (sigs. 2V4-3K2), which includes the fifteen sermons on Psalm 6, 32, and 51 (nos. 50-64); only one of these is dated, sermon 54, on Psalm 6: 6-7 "Preached to the King at White-Hall, upon the occasion of the Fast, April 5. 1628," but this is probably a reworking of an earlier version, as I argue above. The prebend sermons are given in a separately identified section.

[5] Donne wrote to Thomas Roe from Chelsea, where he was staying with Sir John and Lady Danvers, on November 25, 1625: "I have revised as many of my sermons as I had kept any note of, and I have written out a great many, and hope to do more. . . . " See *The Life and Letters of John Donne* 2: 225, and Bald 479-81.

[6] See esp. Brown, and also Potter and Simpson's comments, *Sermons* 10: 408-09.

[7] Shapiro writes: "If the development of Donne's thought and theology after he took orders is to be inferred correctly from his sermons, an accurate chronology of those must be established. We must regard with caution those to which Donne attached a particular date" ("Sermon Dates" 56). While I agree with the last statement, I am extremely doubtful, as I argue in the present essay, that Donne's beliefs changed in any important way during the years of his ordained ministry.

[8] In preaching on Psalm 32: 5, Donne obviously wished to open the significance of the text: "I acknowledged my sin unto thee, and mine iniquity have I not hid. I said, I will confess my trangressions unto the Lord, and thou forgavest the iniquity of my sin." Donne understood this Psalm as part of David's own repentance, and he applies it also to his own audience. He is not interested in the details of sacramental confession, but agrees with the Reformation emphasis (of Luther and others) on God's unconditional offer of forgiveness and the free gift of grace to all who believe in absolution, whatever the process leading to it. See Tentler 360.

[9] But what is meant by "the normal rhythm of the Church's year"? The seasons of Advent and Lent are traditional times of special penitence; but the penitential psalms are used liturgically in the English church only on Ash Wednesday when

the Book of Common Prayer appoints them as Proper Psalms, the first three at Morning Prayer, Psalm 51 at the Commination, and the last three at Evensong.

[10] Thus Psalm 6 is *contra iram* (anger); Psalm 32, *contra superbiam* (pride); Psalm 38, *contra gulam* (gluttony); Psalm 51, *contra luxuriam* (lechery); Psalm 102, *contra avaritiam* (avarice); Psalm 130, *contra invidiam* (envy); Psalm 143, *contra acediam* (sloth). Influenced by Augustine's *Enarrationes*, Cassiodorus (*c*. 485-*c*. 580) wrote his *Complexiones in Psalmos*, in which he associates the seven psalms with the seven "remissions of sin" set forth in the gospels, that is, baptism, martyrdom, almsgiving, conversion, charity, forgiveness, and penitence ("Quos non credas incassum ad septenarium numerum fuisse perductos, quando et majores nostri septem modis peccata nobis dimitti posse dixerunt: primo per baptismam; secundo per passionem martyrii; tertio per eleemosynam; quarto per hoc quod remittimus peccata fratribus nostris; quinto cum converterit quis peccatorem ab errore viae suae; sexto per abundantiam charitatis; septimo per poenitentiam": see Cassiodorus's exposition of Psalm 6, in *Patrologia Latina* 70.60). By order of Innocent III (1160-1216), the penitential psalms were to be prayed in Lent. See Oesterley ch. 13, "The Psalms in the Christian Church"; Deissler and B. Fischer 2: 822-23. On the development and forms of the Divine Office, see Butterworth; and Christopher Wordsworth and Henry Littlehales.

[11] See *Thys prymer in Englyshe and in Laten* (STC 16006), described in Hoskins 138.

[12] Dubinski suggests that Donne reflects in the Holy Sonnets the concerns and the "development" of the penitential psalms: "The spiritual situation of the Penitential Psalms forms the basis for Donne's improvisation in the 'Holy Sonnets,' but the improvisations are in a new key affected by the typological transference of the psalmist's situation to that of an early seventeenth-century Protestant" (208).

[13] William Ponsonby attributes to Spenser *The seven Psalmes* in "The Printer to the Gentle Reader" in his edition of the *Complaints. Containing sundrie small Poemes of the Worlds Vanitie* (London, 1591). See Zim, esp. ch. 1, "'Holy Davids divine Poeme'" and the appendix. These psalms in particular and the Book of Psalms in general have attracted commentators and expositors over the centuries. Colish reviews patristic and medieval exegetes; Snaith demonstrates the persistence of the appeal of these psalms.

[14] See *Meditations and Disquisitions, upon The Seven psalmes of David, commonly called the Penitentiall Psalmes* (1640), ed. A. B. Grosart, 1882; and Bald 43, 72: "Richard Baker, the future chronicler, matriculated from Hart Hall on the same day as the Donne brothers, and was for a time [Henry] Wotton's 'chamber-fellow'" (43).

[15] In addition to the works already mentioned, see such examples as the

following: Sir Anthony Cope (d. 1551), *A godly meditacion upon. xx. select and chosen Psalmes* (1547): Richard Stock (1594?-1626), *The Doctrine and Use of Repentance* (1610); Archibald Simson (1564?-1628), *A Sacred Septenarie, or, A Godly and Fruitful Exposition on the Seven Psalmes of Repentance* (1623); Sir John Hayward (1564?-1627), *Davids Teares* (1636). There are many sermons on penitence, such as Lancelot Andrewes's Lenten homilies, concerning which see Lossky, ch. 4, "Lent."

Stevens studies Donne's sermons on the penitential psalms in the light of their long tradition in Christian meditation and penitential discipline, quite properly treating these sermons as a common group; but he does not attempt to date them or to relate them to Donne's homiletic career.

[16] Quinn remarks elsewhere that "A roughly chronological reading of the whole body of sermons convinces me . . . that Donne's methods of exegesis did not change radically during his fifteen years as a preacher, although one can easily discern a growth of power and complexity in Donne's interpretation of his texts" ("John Donne's Sermons" 241-42).

[17] See for example Grant, who uses the term "Augustinianism" very loosely to denote a putative traditional piety modified by such doctrines as predestination. It is difficult to reconstruct what Augustine was actually writing from Grant's tendentious account.

[18] Donne may be remembering Augustine's *Confessionum libri tredecim* (*Confessions*): "Pondus meum amor meus; eo feror, quocumque feror" (*Corpus Christianorum* 13.9.16-17). In his second prebend sermon, preached on Psalm 63: 7, "Because thou hast been my helpe, therefore in the shadow of thy wings will I rejoyce," Donne appeeals to 2 Corinthians 4: 17, *Pondus Gloriæ, An exceeding waight of eternall glory*, around which he organizes the whole discourse, with burdensomeness on one side and "joy super-invested in glory," on the other (*Sermons* 7: 51-71, esp. 55 and 71). I am generally indebted to my colleague Mark Vessey for helpful advice about Donne's use of patristic sources.

Works Cited

Andrewes, Lancelot. *Works*. Ed. J. P. Wilson and James Bliss. Library of Anglo-Catholic Theology. 11 vols. Oxford: John Henry Parker, 1841-54.

Bald, R. C. *John Donne: A Life*. Oxford: Clarendon P, 1970.

Brown, David D. "The Text of John Tillotson's Sermons." *The Library* 13 (1958): 18-36.

Butterworth, Charles C. *The English Primers, 1529-1545: Their Publication and Connection with the English Bible and the Reformation in England*. Philadelphia: U of Pennsylvania P, 1953.

Colish, Marcia L. *"Psalterium Scholasticorum*: Peter Lombard and the Emergence of Scholastic Psalms Exegesis." *Speculum* 67 (1992): 531-48.

Corpus Christianorum. Series Latina 27. Ed. Lucas Verheijen. Turnhout: Brepols, 1981.

Deissler, A. and B. Fischer. "Busspsalmen." *Lexikon für Theologie und Kirche*. 10 vols. Freiburg: Herder, 1957-65. 2: 822-23.

Donne, John. *The Elegies and The Songs and Sonnets*. Ed. Helen Gardner. Oxford: Clarendon P, 1965.

——————. *Essays in Divinity*. Ed. Evelyn M. Simpson. Oxford: Clarendon P, 1952.

——————. *The Life and Letters of John Donne*. Ed. Edmund Gosse. 2 vols. 1889. Gloucester MA: Peter Smith, 1959.

Dubinski, Roman. "Donne's Holy Sonnets and the Seven Penitential Psalms." *Ren/Ref* n.s. 10 (1986): 201-16.

Grant, Patrick. *The Transformation of Sin: Studies in Donne, Herbert, Vaughan, and Traherne*. Montreal: McGill-Queen's UP, 1974.

Hoskins, Edgar. *Horae Beatae Mariae Virginis or Sarum and York Primers*. London: Longmans, Green, 1901.

Lossky, Nicholas. *Lancelot Andrewes The Preacher (1555-1626): The Origins of the Mystical Theology of the Church of England*. Trans. Andrew Louth. Oxford: Clarendon P, 1991.

Mueller, Janel M., ed. *Donne's Prebend Sermons*. Cambridge MA: Harvard UP, 1971.

Oesterley, W. O. E. *The Psalms: Translated with Text-Critical and Exegetical Notes*. London: SPCK, 1939.

Patrologiae cursus completus, bibliotheca omnium SS. patrum, doctorum, scriptorumque ecclesiasticorum. Series Latina. Ed. J. P. Migne et al. 221 vols. Paris, 1844-1903.

Quinn, Dennis B. "Donne's Christian Eloquence." *ELH* 27 (1960): 276-97.

——————. "John Donne's Principles of Biblical Exegesis." *JEGP* 61 (1962): 313-29.

——————. "John Donne's Sermons on the Psalms and Traditions of Biblical Exegesis." Diss. U of Wisconsin, 1958.

Shapiro, I. A. Correspondence. *RES* 30 (1979): 194.

——————. "Donne's Sermon Dates." *RES* 31 (1980): 54-56.

Snaith, Norman. *The Seven Psalms*. London: Epworth P, 1964.

Stanwood, P. G. "John Donne's Sermon Notes." *RES* 29 (1978): 313-17.

——————. *The Sempiternal Season: Studies in Seventeenth-Century Devotional Writing*. Seventeenth-Century Texts and Studies, 3. New York: Peter Lang, 1992. (Reprints "John Donne's Sermon Notes.")

Stevens, Timothy Scott. "Things That Belong to the Way: John Donne's Sermons on the Penitential Psalms." Diss. Northwestern U, 1990.

Tentler, Thomas N. *Sin and Confession on the Eve of the Reformation*. Princeton NJ: Princeton UP, 1977.

Wordsworth, Christopher, and Henry Littlehales. *The Old Service Books of the English Church*. London: Methuen, 1904.

Zim, Rivkah. *English Metrical Psalms: Poetry as Praise and Prayer 1535-1601*. Cambridge: Cambridge UP, 1987.

Donne's Sermons and
the Absolutist Politics
of Quotation

Jeanne Shami

onne's religious imagination was formed in his youth, but flour-
ished in the historical and political circumstances that prevailed
during a crucial period in the reign of the Stuart monarchs:
1615-1631. Both of these facts are important in assessing Donne's position
on many of the controversial issues of these years: the challenge to Cal-
vinist orthodoxy in the Church of England by the Arminian (or
Anti-Calvinist) ecclesiastical leaders; the challenges both institutional
and personal to the authority of the monarch to levy taxes without
parliament, to imprison without cause, and to make war without consul-
tation; the challenges by writers and public figures of all sorts to the
monarch's right and ability to censor public media such as the pulpit,
printed books, and the stage; the powerful cultural impediments to the
subject's right to offer responsible counsel.

The extent to which Donne's Catholicism modulated into the voice of
the Anglican divine of the 1620s is not the subject of this essay, although it
seems reasonable to say that Donne never completely rejected the religion
into which he was born.[1] He did, however, most certainly reject its
post-Tridentine corruptions and political aspirations.[2] What Donne re-
tained from his personal and cultural ties to the recusant tradition, and
from his education at Lincoln's Inn, was a family tradition of responsible
counsel embodied in his great-uncle Sir Thomas More, and a casuistical
discourse which enabled him to adjust the imperatives of his conscience

to the laws of political authority.[3]

Donne's place within the ecclesiastical establishment first as Reader at Lincoln's Inn and then as Dean of St. Paul's was a powerful one, despite the prevailing conditions of censorship, and despite his public responsibilities to preach and exemplify political obedience. The centrality of Donne's London parish, the fact that he was not a Bishop (and thus more directly answerable to the Court), and the fact, in a time when positions were hardening, that Donne was not clearly aligned with any political faction were all conditions that enhanced the influence of his pulpit messages.

This paper, then, addresses itself to two related problems: the increasingly popular view of Donne's religious politics as absolutist, and the politics driving the modern critical use of Donne's sermons as evidence to prove this view. From the outset, I wish to challenge the opinion that Donne as preacher merely echoed and publicized Divine Right propaganda. The received view is that the political content of the sermons is little more than a display of outward conformity to an absolutist system which Donne may (or may not) have supported personally, but which he promoted enthusiastically and without reservation from the pulpit. Such a view grossly oversimplifies Donne's complex relationship with the court and is based on an interpretive method and style of argument that have never been adequately analyzed.[4] Labelling (and consequently dismissing) Donne as a royalist propagandist, in fact, distorts our understanding of Donne's political position.

It is important, therefore, to challenge the paradigm of Donne as royalist puppet, and to work instead toward a view which recognizes the complexity of Donne's political attitudes and which places Donne among others who remained politically "obedient" while still offering political advice to the Court. Donne's sermons reveal that he can more usefully be characterized as one of the major participants in a theological "middle group" comprising men such as Archbishop Abbott, Joseph Hall, Thomas Gataker, and John Williams.[5] These ecclesiastical leaders were proponents of moderate resistance to absolutism in both Church and State, but recognized that their power to offer counsel or to effect change was inextricably (and uncomfortably) tied to their authorized positions within the ecclesiastical hierarchy. These were leaders who chose to work within existing political structures rather than tearing down the temple, and who participated daily in the spiritual and political life of their time. Although seldom acknowledged, the influence of these moderate counsellors, reforming by inches rather than cataclysmically, was profound.

The title of my paper takes me first to a larger problem, however, and one that helps to explain why Donne's sermons have been consistently misinterpreted by modern readers as univocally absolutist. That issue is the politics motivating the use of Donne's sermons by literary critics. One must begin by noting, however, that the sermons have largely been ignored by Donne critics. Since 1982 when John R. Roberts drew attention to the fact that readers of Donne's poetry were still concentrating their efforts on less than half the canon, readers have been alerted to an imbalance in Donne criticism (Roberts 62). Readers of Donne's prose have reason to feel this imbalance more acutely (Shawcross 10). Despite the lip-service paid to the importance of the sermons, Donne criticism is still focused on a mere fraction of a fraction of his total output. Readers approach the sermons with the aid of Troy Reeves' *Index* to argue casually from the sermons to the poems, to Donne's life, and now that it is popular, to Donne's politics. In fact, critics who profoundly mistrust the literal in poetry and appreciate the witty complexity of Donne's poetic strategies, find nothing anomalous in reading the sermons literally, believing that Donne's beliefs are here straightforwardly expressed. In so doing, they reduce the sermons to a reference text which will reify Donne's beliefs and render them uninterpretable. Clearly the danger of misinterpretation was something Donne feared even in his day and to which he alluded frequently both in letters and sermons (Patterson, "Misinterpretable Donne"). Preachers who were "misinterpreted" were silenced, called in before the Star Chamber and High Commission courts, or ignored. But no interpretation has become the norm in the twentieth century, the direct consequence of an ahistorical and essentially unscholarly approach to the evidence of the sermons.

Consider first the question of arguing within the sermons, that is, making reasonable generalizations about them as a whole. It should go without saying, for example, that sermons preached during the reign of James cannot be read through the same historical lens as those preached under Charles. Despite this historical situation, readers of Donne consistently refer to "the sermons" as if 1625 had never occurred. As recently as 1991, in fact, a critic can claim that "The Donne who backs first James I and then Charles I over religious policy is, at the same time, backing their [absolutist] models of kingship and rule" (Parfitt 121).[6]

A similar difficulty emerges when readers use the sermons to determine Donne's religious alignments, or to make sense of his views on a controversial issue. They cannot afford to ignore or quote selectively among Donne's apparently contradictory statements in order to find consistency in his views. In fact, it is only by doing precisely this that Horton Davies can group Donne exclusively among the metaphysical Arminians (195-203), or that Lewalski (*Protestant Poetics* 17) and Sellin can find in Donne a consistently Calvinist theology. It cannot be said too often that Donne's views on any subject are complex and elusive. To cite just one example, consider Donne's remarks on the value of opinion, a word which did not carry the casual connotations in the Renaissance that it does for many modern readers, and which always meant more than ungrounded relativity of viewpoint (Woolf 33-35). Donne's comments on opinion can be marshalled to support almost any position (Shami, "Donne on Discretion" 65-66 n.20). To prove that opinion undermines faith, a reader could cite a January 1620 sermon in which Donne argues that opinions can leave the auditory "unsatisfyed, and unsetled" (2: 320). To prove that opinion is a valuable moral measure for forming conscience, a reader can cite a November 1626 sermon: "They that rest in the testimony of their owne consciences, and contemne the opinion of other men, . . . They deale weakly, and improvidently for themselves, in that they assist not their consciences, with more witnesses, And they deale cruelly towards others, in that they provide not for their edification, by the knowledge and manifestation of their good works" (7: 250). But readers looking for an equivocal comment, one that is more versatile in its applications, can consider the following: "when the soule considers the things of this world, . . . She rests upon such things as she is not sure are true, but such as she sees, are ordinarily received and accepted for truths: so that the end of her knowledge is not Truth, but opinion, and the way, not Inquisition, but ease" (6: 76). Opinion seems inferior to truth in this passage, and yet the way to Truth is "Inquisition," a word that would surely have resonated negatively for Donne's audience in the light of Counter-reformation attempts by the Roman Church, particularly in Spain, to control the consciences of Europe. These three passages taken together show Donne moving uneasily between public and private moral standards. But readers of Donne's poetry would surely object if I were to confirm my sense that Donne believes that opinion is a good, although imperfect, measure of truth by quoting these lines from *Metempsychosis*: "Ther's nothing simply good, nor ill alone, / Of every quality comparison, / The onely measure is, and judge, opinion" (lines 518-20).

My point is that to make sense of any of these statements, context is all. But rarely are the sermons seen as issuing from any specific context—generic, historical, theological, political, or cultural. Too often they become a Scripture which any poor devil looking for a publication can quote to her own purposes—usually by lifting passages, at will, from anywhere, with the aid of the *Index*—and using them to create a collage of comments that supposedly represents Donne's "mature" views. At its best, such a practice allows critics to develop a thesis which brings many diverse and seemingly contradictory comments into some sensible relation. At its worst, this means that for the sake of an argument, readers pillage the sermons for a quotation that will confirm their view. As A.B. Chambers noted wryly in a review essay on recent Donne scholarship, "merely to quote is to establish a point" (110).[7]

Arguing from the sermons to Donne's poems, his life, or his political beliefs, however, is much more difficult. Generally, the sermons are read as authoritative reference texts, a body of material which can be appropriated literally by readers to provide glosses on Donne's poetry and earlier writings, to confirm a biographical profile, or to support generalizations about Donne's beliefs. Inherent in such appropriations are at least three faulty assumptions. One is that the sermons are straightforward, unequivocal, and easily understood. No one would say this explicitly, but in fact, readers do not "interpret" the language of the sermons as they do the poetry. A second assumption is that the sermons can be taken as a whole. For the purposes of quotation, chronology and occasion are irrelevant. It is not unusual for critics to quote freely across the full range of sermons to support a thesis about what Donne supposedly "believes." A third assumption is that fragments of sermon text, taken out of context, are sufficient to prove a point. A corollary of this view is that many fragments, taken out of context, are more persuasive than only one.

A consequence of these first three assumptions is the powerful though unarticulated view that the sermons are less significant than the poems or ideas they are selected to illustrate. That is, they are less valuable as cultural performances, connected inevitably to audiences, occasions, or an author, but ironically more valuable in their utilitarian function as "authorities" or glosses. Few people read the sermons, yet the weakest argument acquires credibility when supported by quotations from them. In other words, the sermons are often seen as means to other ends, rather than as the end of legitimate scholarly inquiry. This is a view enhanced by the fact that most readers of the sermons come to them via anthologies, or more perniciously, through the *Index*, a blunt instrument that dulls responses, determines topics of worthwhile inquiry, and threatens to become a substitute for reading the sermons themselves.[8]

The interpretive problems raised by these assumptions fall into at least three categories:

1) The first is the question of how to interpret the biographical data of the sermons. Many critics use the sermons, like the verse letters, as sources of direct biographical information.[9] But the practice raises as many questions as it answers. To what extent, for example, can one assume that the "I" of Donne's sermons is literally Donne? Marotti (204), following Carey's lead, assumes that Donne is reflecting upon his own flattery in a sermon in which he says "when men of high degree doe not performe the duties of their places, then they are a lie of their owne making; And when I over-magnifie them in their place, flatter them, humor them, ascribe more to them, expect more from them, rely more upon them, then I should, then they are a lie of my making" (6:306-7). Tempting as such an identification might be to someone who comes to the sermons with a particular view of Donne's character or his politics, it doesn't hold as a methodology of criticism. How would such a practice help to elucidate the following passage where the "I" is cast in the role of the hearer, as he often is in the sermons? "Discredit a mans life, and you disgrace his Preaching: . . . for . . . if I believe the Preacher to be an ill man, I shall not be much the better for his good Sermons" (7: 151). Or shall we take Donne literally when he says: "I have nothing to plead with *God*, but onely his owne promises . . . I cannot plead descent; *My mother was an Hittite*" (8: 72)?[10]

Too eager an attempt to find Donne in the confessional attitude can only detract from the strength which invests these moments of first-person meditation, a strength which derives from the carefully controlled vulnerability which Donne allows them to manifest. Donne writes: "for whatsoever the Preacher can say of Gods mercy in Christ Jesus to any man, all that belongs to me, for no man hath received more of that, then I may doe; And whatsoever the Preacher can say of sinne, all the way, all that belongs to me, for no man hath ever done any sin, which I should not have done, if God had left me to my selfe, and to mine own perversenesse towards sin, and to mine own insatiablenesse in sin" (5: 41). The temptation, often unresisted, with such a passage is to interpret it as autobiographical evidence of Donne's own sinfulness. The fault is in part Donne's who attempts to achieve "nearness" with his congregation by attributing to the "I" of the sermons the most extreme weaknesses.

The problem is augmented by the dramatic turn of speech of such passages which reinforces the impression that Donne, like Paul, is the chief of sinners. However, his explanation of how Paul's words must be interpreted illuminates the way in which he intended his hearers to respond to his own words. Donne says that the accusation is not to be taken literally, but as an expression of humility and thanksgiving that God would see fit to rescue even him from his sins. Ultimately, Donne concludes, "This is the conclusion for every humble christian, no man is a greater sinner then I was, and I am not sure but that I may fall to be worse then ever I was, except I husband and imploy the Talents of Gods Graces better then I have done" (1: 318). Davies, however, labels this an "autobiographical text," conceding only that if it is, it has a clear application to the congregation (475). Nor does it help to flatten the personal edge by recourse to the typical or symbolic "I" to whom all the biblical texts can be applied and in which the pattern of salvation is manifested.[11] Clearly, any analysis of this practice will have to measure biographical, rhetorical, and cultural factors across a wide range of texts before concluding that Donne is confessing to a sinful and misspent youth.

2) A second class of misinterpretations results from difficulties of access to the large and complex body of material which constitutes Donne's sermons. The usual approach to the sermons is synecdochal, the use of fragments to represent the whole, whether these fragments are selected by reference to the *Index* to Donne's *Sermons*, or whether they depend on the pre-selection of "significant" texts by earlier critics.

The evolution of a tradition of scholarship which finds Donne's politics to be "absolutist" relies on just such a synecdochal approach. Consequently its claims are largely unsubstantiated, but have been immensely popular for all that. One of the founding claims of John Carey's *John Donne: Life, Mind, and Art* is that Donne was most fascinated by God's attribute of power as something that somehow compensated for his own political powerlessness. As Carey expresses it: "when Donne entered the Church he found in God, and in his own position as God's spokesman, a final and fully adequate expression of his power lust. If we ask what positive quality Donne most consistently reverences in the sermons, the answer is neither beauty, nor life, nor love, but power. His God is a heavenly powerhouse, with all circuits ablaze . . . Further . . . it is God's destructive power that Donne particularly relishes dwelling on . . . It is God as killer and pulverizer that Donne celebrates" (122-123). The proof for such provocative claims, however, hides in terse, enigmatic footnotes, the *arcana imperii* or mysteries of state of sermon scholarship for most readers who don't have their ten volumes of Potter and Simpson handy when they are evaluating an argument. The sheer number of these quotations, taken from across the entire range of the *Sermons*, is persuasive. No one objects that the words of the sermons themselves are seldom quoted. And should this disregard for the words and their contexts pose a problem, Carey dismisses it by rejecting the possibility that historical context is significant. To do so, however, he must substitute one of his own assumptions (that is, that Donne was always the same) for one he is anxious to refute (that is, that Donne's views changed throughout his career). "It's often assumed," he says, "that early and late Donne, poet and preacher, were different people. Donne, as he grew older, wanted to believe this, and talked as if he did, which is how the illusion got about" (10). This assertion leaves Carey free to quote from the entire body of the sermons, without having to justify his procedure.[12]

But it is a procedure and a focus that even someone armed only with the *Index* might challenge. Even a cursory glance at the *Index* under "GOD: Attributes of" (3: 82) would have sent him to 204 places that mention God's Mercy as compared to 41 that mention "Power" (3: 83). One of these quotations actually celebrates the power of God to *comfort*, "a power to erect and settle a tottering, a dejected soule, an overthrowne, a bruised, a broken, a troden, a ground, a battered, an evaporated, an annihilated spirit" (3: 270). A glance at all of Donne's sermons would have sent Carey to sermons that consider the Son's attribute of Wisdom, and the Spirit's attribute of Goodness to balance the focus on Power attributed to the Father.[13] In fact, a glance at sermons by other preachers of the period would have shown him that the power of the Lord of Hosts was a common homiletic refrain of the early Stuart period, particularly among Puritan preachers, who had little hope for present political and theological victory but who were confident in the final victory of Christ over Antichrist.[14] It might even have led him to the conclusion that Donne is "oppositional" rather than "absolutist."

3) A third interpretive difficulty is generated by readers of the sermons when fragments from the sermons are taken completely out of their historical, occasional, and rhetorical contexts. Carey, for example, cites disparagingly a passage in which Donne defines his calling as a preacher by distinguishing between the extraordinary commission of the Prophets and the present-day ordinary function of the minister (114). Donne writes that it is sometimes impertinent and even seditious to compare these two vocations, rejecting the conclusion that since "The Prophets would chide the King openly, and threaten the Kings publiquely, and proclaime the fault of the Kings in the eares of the people confidently, authoritatively, therefore the Minister may and must do so" (2: 303). Donne argues by analogy to the justice system that "no man will thinke that the Justices in their Sessions, or the Judges in their Circuits may proceed to executions, without due tryall by a course of Law, because Marshals, in time of

rebellion and other necessities, may doe so, because the one hath but an ordinary, the other an extraordinary Commission" (2: 303-4). Carey concludes that the distinction between Prophet and Minister is another example of Donne's cowardly rationalizations (113-115). He does this without any reference to Donne's other comments on the Law and its processes as the foundation of the State in his sermons, or to the specific occasion of this sermon and its peculiar textual transmission. In fact, the sermon from which this quotation is taken was preached on December 19, 1619, at The Hague, while Donne was on the continent as chaplain to Doncaster's embassy. Donne rewrote the sermon eleven years later while visiting his daughter at Aubrey Hatch in Essex, at which time he revised his short notes, and as he describes it, "digested them into these two [sermons]" (2: 269). It is hard to imagine the complexities of interpretation that Carey has consigned to a footnote. How, for example, do we construe a statement made to a foreign congregation in 1619, recorded in note form, and expanded for publication eleven years later, although never delivered as a sermon to an English congregation? Even Carey would have to admit that 1630 was not 1619, either politically or theologically, although the liberties claimed by Charles in the name of martial law would have made Donne's distinction between lawful due process and illegal claims for privilege more pertinent in 1630. What drew Donne to return to this sermon in 1630, and what does he mean when he says that he "digested" his notes into two sermons? These questions obviously interfere with Carey's main point about Donne's relations to power.[15]

When a sermon fragment is used to illuminate a poem, the conclusion can be even more tenuous. On the basis of a quotation from the sermons taken completely out of context, Marotti suggests that Donne's verse letters to women record the tension between his "natural urges" and the proper social decorum of the situation, which demanded a "desexing of the man/woman relationship" (214). Marotti argues that since Donne believed physicality to be essential to human love, he could not be comfortable with a more sublimated form of the affection. This statement may be partially true, but the quotation Marotti uses to support his claim is taken from a sermon in which Donne is discussing not the instability of one's moral integrity when confronted with women, as Marotti implies, but the fragility of one's reputation (214 and 337n.165). The sermon uses the example of the Platonic but scandalous devotion of Paula for Jerome to make Donne's point that "a familiar and assiduous conversation with women will hardly be without tentation and scandal" (1: 201). But to whom? The sermon makes it quite clear that their spiritually intimate relationship was not a scandal to Jerome or Paula, but to those who observed it, not only their enemies, but even their friends and supporters who "loved Religion well" (1: 201) and were inclined to believe the best of the situation. The problem Donne is dealing with is the problem of reputation rather than conscience, with the giving of scandal rather than with the morality of illicit love. Upon examination, Marotti's supporting quotation about Jerome and Paula has no bearing at all on the poem he is discussing and is hardly axiomatic, as Marotti asserts, of the tension between Donne's appetites and the decorum of the complimentary love lyrics (214).

While it is fruitless to attribute motives to readers of Donne's sermons, it is impossible to ignore the effects of the fragmentary and uncontextualized approach which has become the practice among critics. I have already mentioned the problems of access to the sermons; but one aspect of the problem which needs more attention is the political effect of this method of quotation. It isn't difficult to discern, for example, that nearly all of the references to the "I" of the sermons have as their project the confirmation of Donne's grasping, egotistical nature. Similarly, many of the fragments which supposedly represent the "whole" Donne seem to be selected deliberately to prove a thesis which a fuller quotation could not support. As with so many other areas of scholarly endeavour, the forces of political correctness feel justified in aggressively labelling Donne as "absolutist" and by definition, therefore, unacceptable.[16] And if his own words, fully cited, will not support such a label, then it seems acceptable to "quote" them until they do. The result is that Donne's so-called absolutist politics are overshadowed by the equally absolutist, but now politically correct, attitudes of Donne's twentieth-century readers.

The trend in quotation that I am describing can best be illustrated from Shuger's recently published chapter on Donne's sermons. Shuger takes "Measure God by earthly Princes" as the epigraph to the section of her essay analyzing how Donne uses the analogy between God and King. No specific reference is provided for the quotation, merely "Donne, *Sermons*." In fact, the reference in the sermon from which it is taken qualifies, if it does not negate, the absolutist meaning Shuger intends and epitomizes the misinterpretability of isolated quotations from the sermons. Donne continues the analogy in parentheses: "Measure God by earthly Princes; (for we may measure the world by a Barly corne)" (5: 371), nullifying Shuger's claim about the extraordinary degree to which Donne stresses the analogy between God and Kings to glorify Kings. Clearly, the parenthetical material undercuts the epigraph's imperative, revealing a complex irony that Shuger's quotation masks.

Similarly, in a paragraph discussing Donne's habit of depicting divine/human interaction as analogous to seventeenth-century absolute monarchy, Shuger focuses on the highly politicized language in which Donne speaks of God's unrevealed decrees. Donne associates these, she notes, with royal prerogative and absolute power, implying that there exists a reserve of power behind the ordinary lawful operations of the monarch (or divinity) that can neither be questioned nor limited. To prove this point, Shuger cites many passages from the sermons, concluding with a pastiche of comments in a single sentence: "it is not merely unnecessary to probe God's secrets, but 'Libell' to publish them, 'an injury to God, and against his Crowne'" (167, quoting from *Sermons* 4:78-81). Donne's own words are much more ambivalent, however, and reveal a concern for decorum and audience, for the "fit" place in which to discuss controversial matters, specifically the doctrine of Election, which Donne saw as a doctrine which perplexed the consciences of weak men or offered contentious men the delights of disputation. Donne says:

> Those men who will needs be of Gods Cabinet Counsell, and pronounce what God did first, what was his first Decree, and the first clause in that Decree, those men who will needs know, and then publish Gods secrets, (And, by the way, that, which sometimes it may concerne us to know, yet it may be a Libell to publish it) Those mysteries, which, for the opposing and countermining stubborne, and perverse Heresies, it may concerne us, in Councels and Synods, and other fit places, to argue, and to cleare, it may be an injury to God, and against his Crowne, and Dignity, in breaking the peace of the Church, to publish and divulge to every popular auditory, and every itching eare, and thereby perplexe the consciences of weak men, or offer contentious men, that which is their foo, and delight, disputation. (4: 305)

Donne's wording is far more tentative than Shuger's (it "may" be a libel; it "may" be an injury to God), suggesting in fact that the error is not in questioning and knowing, but in publishing what we know, particularly in public sermons where the abilities of the congregation to discern the subtle points of controversy might not be sufficient to render that place fit to argue and clear points of mysterious doctrine.

It is time to cast aside both the "absolutist" approach to quoting Donne, as well as the "absolutist" model of his politics, and search for a model that more judiciously represents Donne's attitude to authority within the specific cultural and rhetorical contexts in which the sermons were preached. This model must take into account that Donne feared misinterpretation and had to devise a language by which he was free to speak according to his conscience and still fulfill his responsibility of counsel to the King, a responsibility which he felt was being mishandled publicly by the King's outspoken critics and undermined privately in the "bed of whisperers."[17] Donne survived in such misinterpretable circumstances because he developed a casuistical discourse inspired by the traditions of both legal interpretation and biblical exegesis in which he was experienced. The conjunction of these interpretive languages made Donne's literal sense a particularly flexible medium through which he adjusted to the dangers of misinterpretation and to his responsibilities of religious and political counsel.[18]

The casuistical thrust of legal discourse is inherent in the fact that, as a general rule, legal discourse proposes for its audience a hostile listener or interpreter (Crystal and Davy 193). It is constructed on the premise that the author must choose words which even the most unsympathetic listener cannot turn against him, and is acutely aware of the literal sense which his words convey. In the sermons, Donne characteristically uses language that will discharge his reponsibilities of counsel without putting him within the "vast reach of th'huge statute lawes" (*Satyre* II, 112). More positively, legal discourse channels stories and events that are technically outside the law into legally relevant forms. In so doing, legal discourse establishes a story's terms of reference, tells readers what the story is "about" from the point of view of the law, and so offers the possibility of resolution to conflicts. In his sermons, Donne uses this aspect of legal discourse to create a framework within which his audience can resolve cases of conscience with some degree of certainty.[19] He does this by treating the Bible as a whole as a formal contract, a digest of legal precedents and concepts pertaining to salvation within which human actions find their moral meaning. And although no single precedent can be extracted from the Bible as a rule for action, the process of comparison of texts yields certain patterns for salvation.

Biblical exegesis on the other hand has as its main goal the ethical and moral reform of the listener. Its aim is what Donne calls "nearness," the recognition by the audience that the preacher "speaks to my conscience, as though he had been behinde the hangings when I sinned, and as though he had read the book of the day of Judgement already" (3: 142).[20] However, as some preachers discovered, this act of penetrating the consciences of the congregation was politically and legally dangerous. The

High Commission reports cite the unfortunate, but typical, case of one Vicars who was punished for coming "too near" describing an actual member of his congregation in a sermon. He was charged for holding "that it was lawfull for a minister to preach soe particularly that his auditors might knowe what and whome he meant, but yet to do it so covertly that noe legall advantage might be taken against him" (Gardiner, *Reports* 199). Clearly, Donne and Vicars were following the same exegetical principle, although Donne was demonstrably more skilful in choosing words whose "literal and ordinary" sense was less open to hostile interpretation.[21]

The problem with literal and uncontextualized readings of Donne's sermons which fail to take into account his use of casuistical discourse is that they clearly misinterpet Donne's positions on a variety of theological and political subjects. Such readings produce Donne the Puritan and Donne the Arminian without assessing how and why the sermons allow for such extremes in interpretation. The language of power and submission which readers often quote to prove Donne's absolutism, for example, can just as easily, and without distortion, focus attention on Donne's efforts to mediate between the competing claims of obedience to law and conscientious interpretation of it, or to use Donne's terms from a 1622 sermon, "passive obedience" energized by "active discretion," the mother and father of all virtues (4: 49). It is clear that in the 1620s Donne found it increasingly difficult to fulfill his responsibilities of counsel, to speak his mind. But in contrast to the more conventional distinction between active and passive obedience,[22] Donne chooses to focus on "discretion" as the complement, perhaps even as the corrective, to obedience. Donne's variation on the formula seems to suggest that "discretion" is another kind of obedience, but at the same time to signal that it is a more strenuous, indeed a more discerning kind of obedience, one which requires balance and poise between the two elements of the equation. Donne's sermons manifest this balance by establishing a casuistical middle ground among many of the controversies and conflicting allegiances of the period, a locus of moderate counsel which proponents of Donne's absolutist politics are uncomfortable examining, and this despite the fact that recent historical research has made it clear that the simple categories of power and submission, authority and resistance, Royalist and Parliamentarian just don't hold.[23]

Fundamental to Donne's casuistry, and one of his most profound challenges to absolutist prerogative in the sermons, is the belief that human actions operate with reference to some clearly articulated law:

Divine Law as evidenced in Scriptures, natural law, or human and posi-
tive law.[24] God's word is His contract with men, a faithful saying, an
everlasting covenant. As Donne reiterates throughout his sermons, "he
hath made a conditionall contract with us, so as that if we performe our
part, he will performe his, and not otherwise" (1: 297). "Gods ordinary
working is by Nature, these causes must produce these effects; and that is
his common Law; He goes sometimes above that, by Prerogative, and that
is by miracle, and sometimes below that, as by custome, and that is
fortune, that is contingency" (3: 229). Working within Divine Law through
the agency of human law is preferable to the alternative, which is chaos,
or simply submission to a clearer but less interpretable law (such as
martial law, or the law of arms which the Jews that prosecuted the
judgment against Christ, or which invasive armies, pour upon nations
[8:344]).

Not surprisingly, Donne's sermons typically demonstrate a legal un-
derstanding of the relationship between God and men. Donne reiterates
in the sermons that God operates by the laws He has published in the
Bible and that on the issue of our salvation we will all be tried and judged
with reference to these laws. "The *Scripture* is a Judge, by which God
himself will be tryed. As the Law is our Judge, and the Judge does but
declare what is Law, so the Scripture is our Judge, and God proceeds with
us according to those promises and Judgements, which he hath laid down
in the Scripture" (8: 281). In a 1629 sermon, Donne states clearly that "the
Mysterie of Godlinesse is without controversie; and godliness is, to be-
lieve that God hath given us a Law, and to live according to that Law" (8:
345). And as the refrain to this sermon reiterates "All, upon all sides, is
still referred to Law. And where there is no law against thee (as there is
not to him that is in Christ; and he is in Christ, who hath endeavoured the
keeping, or repented the breaking of the Law) God will never proceed to
execution by any secret purpose never notified, never manifested" (8:
348).

Proponents of the view that Donne's politics are absolutist are troubled
by the fact that occasionally, certain aspects of moral law, which Donne
calls God's *arcana imperii* (like His miracles), are marked off as areas not
subject to human understanding. They find his acknowledgement of
mysteries of state, like his acknowledgement of the King's prerogative,
distressingly undemocratic. Such a reaction, while understandable, how-
ever, is profoundly unhistorical; even challengers of the King's preroga-
tive in the 1620s disputed its abuses rather than its existence. What should
be emphasized is that Donne's typical stress as a preacher is on God's

published laws, and the judgments that proceed from them.[25] In fact, it is clear that while Donne accepts the reality of the *arcana*, he does not believe that earthly princes have handled them well. "Princes," Donne says, "glory *in Arcanis*, that they have secrets which no man shall know, and, God knowes, they have hearts which they know not themselves; Thoughts and purposes indigested fall upon them and surprise them. It is so in naturall, in morall, in civill things; we are ignorant of more things then we know" (8: 255-56). Donne proceeds, in fact, not by stressing the absolutist analogy between Kings and God, but by contrasting the secretiveness and lack of self-knowledge of earthly Kings with God's openness. Unlike earthly Princes, "God hath suffered man to see *Arcana imperii*, The secrets of his State, how he governs; He governs by Precedent . . . He does as he did before" (5: 365). Donne frequently contrasts God's direct manner of dealing with men with the methods of Roman Catholicism, particularly those used by Jesuits. Jesuits, Donne says, would be disadvantaged if cases were judged by laws which were known before. But the Kingdom of God, he avers, is not a tyranny. God proposes conditions, and governs by His word, by His law, whereas the Roman Church expunges and interlines articles of Faith upon Reason of State and emergent occasions (3: 125-29). Some earthly princes, the Roman Church, in fact sin itself, do not govern by law, but tyrannically, and are in opposition to the "Law" in the heart which cannot be eluded. Donne cites Chrysostom who says that, in contrast to God, "sin doth not govern us by a rule, by a Law, but tyrannically, impetuously, and tempestuously" (5: 202).

Donne's sermon defending James's *Directions to Preachers* is paradigmatic of the processes by which Donne's casuistry operates (Shami, "Kings" 15-18). It shows how Donne could find freedom to act according to conscience even within the absolute limitations outlined by the King. Literally, these royal directions severely limited commentary on the deep religious points of predestination, election, and reprobation. More to the point, no preacher was allowed to limit the "power, prerogative, and jurisdiction, authority, or duty of soveraign Princes" (Kenyon 146), although strictly speaking, Donne himself was not under any new constraints since the *Directions* excluded Bishops and Deans. Donne, however, speaks as one to whom the *Directions* apply, defending them precisely because the application of the principles has not been spelled out too explicitly. Although Donne was obviously uncomfortable delivering the sermon (Patterson, *Censorship* 99; Chamberlain 451), he found space to interpret the *Directions* as conducive to peace and order rather than to repression, and in so interpreting them, defused their interpretive power.[26]

The peace which is intended, he says, is "not to shuffle religions together, and make it all one which you chuse, but a peace with persons, an abstinence from contumelies, and revilings" (4: 196). Donne is careful not to be specific, either about what is allowed or what is forbidden, but suggests that "discreet and religious" preachers will find enough, even within these limits, for controversy. Donne concludes that "heere is no abating of Sermons, but a direction of the Preacher to preach usefully, and to edification" (4: 209). It is the attitude of obedience and the generosity of his interpretation of the King's motives on this occasion that gives Donne the greatest flexibility and power in applying these directions. In fact, this interpretive "generosity" was itself a kind of critique, challenging James to be at his best, but allowing Donne to keep preaching when less astute preachers were foolishly martyring themselves into silence.[27] Furthermore, Donne demonstrates through his choice of text and his use of biblical and patristic sources how to preach according to both conscience and the King's intention.[28]

Politically, this sermon takes its ground against disorderly preaching by analogy with orderly forms of government and by contrast with the practices of the Roman Church. Donne says that "*Parliaments* determine in *Lawes*, *Iudges* in *Decrees*, wee [Preachers] in *Orders*" (4: 198). But in the Roman Church the most disorderly men are those in orders. He says that they are "so out of all Order, that they are within Rule of no temporall Law, within jurisdiction of no Civill Magistrate, no secular Judge. They may kill *Kings*, and yet can be no *Traytors*" (4: 198).

Donne's generous interpretation of James's published instructions allowed him to take certain kinds of political initiatives in his texts and interpretations. In a sermon preached on the anniversary of the Gunpowder Plot, November 5, 1622, only two months after defending James's *Directions*, Donne shows what he could do when left "more to mine own liberty" (SP/14/134/59). Donne's "liberty" seems to refer, at least in part, to his choice of text and it is significant that he chooses a disputed text, one which the Council of Trent places outside the scriptural canon, as his text for the day. Another aspect of this liberty is that the text can be spoken either historically, of the death of the good King Josiah, or prophetically, of the bad king Zedekiah, of the Jews' Calendar and the Papists'. And since Donne chooses to dwell on the conflict of interpretation, the sermon becomes a flexible medium for interpretation which does not fix upon either of these alternatives but plays between them. On the surface, at least, this sermon should have been acceptable to James. Its underlying premise and overt political message is that all Kings, even bad Kings, must be preserved—a doctrine which James had expounded with an admirable instinct for self-preservation in his writings (James I, *The Trew Law* 60). Donne's argument is that good or ill, Kings are "to be lamented, when they fall into dangers, and . . . preserved by all means, by *Prayer* from them who are private persons, by *counsell* from them, who have that great honour and that great charge, to be near them in that kinde, and by *support* and *supply*, from all, of all sorts, from falling into such dangers" (4: 239).

Even such pious and politically correct statements, however, were fraught with danger in 1622. Only a year later, "old Dr. White" was placed under house arrest for praying for the preservation of the King (Chamberlain 473). The mention of "supply" also seems safe in its absolutist suggestion that recalcitrant Parliaments should vote sufficient subsidies to maintain the King. In November 1622, however, the word "supply" would have drawn audience attention to the fact that James had dissolved Parliament earlier that year because he did not want to have a vote on supply made conditional on his waging war with Spain, especially since he was still hoping for peace through a marriage alliance. The notion that "supply" would preserve the King from danger could very well have been interpreted as criticism of James's passive foreign policy.

What is particularly challenging in this sermon, though, is Donne's parallel application of the text to both good and bad Kings, an application which he presents in the sermon as a problem of interpretation for his audience. Although he insists that present application can only be made to the good King, Josiah, he notes parenthetically that the text is more ordinarily and more probably held by the expositors to apply to the bad King. And although he assures his audience, and the King, that the case of the bad King Zedekiah is merely hypothetical, and that it reinforces the case for preserving the good King, the comparison and its obvious application to the present dissatisfaction in the kingdom would have been only too apparent to the audience at Paul's Cross.

Donne's approach to the subject of the sermon is twofold. He has much to say about the duties of a people to a bad King, but does so in the context of a direct attack on the political theology of the Papists who have made treason an article of religion. Donne's application of the text complicates the discourse of absolutism noted by readers in this sermon not only by calling attention to the conventions of interpretation by which Kings are to be judged, but by his advice to his hearers as to their own religious responsibilities. With the *Directions* only three months old, Donne confronts openly the political threat posed by Roman Catholicism, a topic expressly limited by the *Directions*, at the same time as he engages directly with popular dissatisfaction with the King. Donne's conclusions may seem absolutist, but the process by which he reaches these reveals his ambivalence towards current political developments.

A starting point for Donne is that either historically or prophetically, Jeremy looks upon the Kingdom through the glass of the King, not imagining that he could pretend the weal of one without the other. Donne sanctions here their intimate relationship by comparing the King to the husband, the head, and the soul of the kingdom. "Greater Treasons, and Seditions, and Rebellions have never been set on foote," he says, "then upon colour, and pretence, of a care of the State, and of the good of the Kingdome" (4: 245). But the discussion of the evil King which follows indicates much about the political atmosphere within which the sermon was delivered, complicated by the conventions appropriate to the anniversary for celebrating the King and denouncing Catholic treachery.

Donne begins by saying that to judge a King as evil requires a "large comprehension" (4: 249); it requires an understanding of the King's office, his actions, and those of other princes. What follows is an odd extenuation of royal policy which suggests that perhaps the connection with Zedekiah is not far off. Donne is not simply saying that a King may appear to be evil but be truly good when all is known (a safe and "absolutist" attitude to interpretation). What he is arguing instead is that despite weaknesses (and there are weaknesses on all sides), a bad monarch is better than no monarch. Accordingly, part of what people are critical of in James is defended as necessary political policy. However, Donne offers some rather pointed criticism, couched in hypothetical terms, as he defends the Prince's craftiness, falseness, and departure from the exact rule of his duty. "Many times [not sometimes] a Prince departs from the exact rule of his duty, not out of his own indisposition to truth, and clearnesse, but to countermine underminers." Just as God, who is not froward by nature, can be made so with the froward, so "with crafty neighbours, a Prince will be crafty, and perchance false with the false" (4: 249). This is to put the best possible interpretation on James's refusal to consult on his Spanish foreign policy but does not disguise the fact that James's actions at this time require interpretation. The best Donne can do is to urge private men not to call Kings ill hastily, even when they "pretermit in some things, the present benefit of their Subjects, and confer favours upon others" (4: 250). Such judgments Donne identifies with the Papist adversaries who believe, among other things, that "that King that vexes his Subjects, That that King that gives himselfe to *intemperate hunt-*

ing [one of James' most prominent weaknesses] (for in that very particular they instance) that in such cases, (and they multiply these cases infinitely) Kings are in their mercy, and subject to their censures, and corrections" (4: 250). He contrasts this method of censure with the proper one, in which secret actions are left to God's judgments (4: 250).

In the event of evident bad actions, Donne must offer certain necessary fictions to his hearers in order to channel their interpretations, but it is significant that these are presented as constructions rather than as truths.[29] Accordingly, if the King's breath or power be at any time soured in the passage, so that his good intentions are ill executed by inferior ministers, this must not be imputed to him. "Princes," he says, "purpose some things for ease to the people . . . and if they prove grievances, they tooke their putrefaction in the way . . . The thing was good in the roote, and the ill cannot be removed in an instant" (4: 251). Our duty is not only to avoid speaking ill of the King, but to speak well of him. "And in those things [and there are such things, obviously], which will not admit a good interpretation, we must be apt to remove the perversenesse and obliquity of the act from him, who is the first mover to those who are *inferiour instruments*" (4: 252). But though Princes, unlike God, do not so much as act in particular actions, and are thus excusable, Donne expresses the limits of this fiction: Princes are inexcusable, "at least, for any cooperation in the evill of the action, though not for countenancing, and authorising an evill instrument; but that is another case" (4: 253).

On the issue of prayer for the King, the sermon is equally complex. Donne says that the prayer that God would keep the King and the Prince in the true religion is always good and useful. But his hearers must be careful to draw the line between prayer and libel at the point at which their publicly uttered wishes take on political meaning. Donne says that "when that prayer is accompanied with circumstances, as though the King and the Prince were declining from that Religion, then even the prayer it selfe is libellous, and seditious" (4: 253). The implication, surely, is that such circumstances do exist, and that the warning is political as much as moral. The paragraph ends with a strong, unusually insistent first-person testimony of Donne's belief in James's constancy in religion, answering again to real fears that he was "submitting us to that Idolatry, and superstition, which did heretofore oppresse us" (4: 254). The intensity of the assertions, the ethical appeal embodied in the repetition of his certainty that he has "not been stupefied in this point" (4: 254), and the frank addressing of the immediate religious concerns of his hearers speak to the kinds of interpretation Donne is urging upon his audience. They must "interpret fairly, and loially, his proceedings," "these ways, which his wisdome hath chosen for the procuring of peace," despite external testimony to the contrary (4: 254). This call to fair interpretation can be construed as absolutist mystification but rings much more with the notes of patience than of self-delusion. Donne is calling attention to the saving fictions by which his hearers can ride out this storm, these abuses, and maintain their political safety.

Crucial to Donne's political theology in this sermon is his assertion that the souls of his hearers are not the King's. Conscience is liberty. And he frames this assertion as James's imagined answer to Donne's question on this point. "I know," Donne says, "he would bee the first man, that would say, *No, No*; your souls are not mine, so" (4: 255). That is, their lives are his, but not their souls. However, as James must answer for their souls, they are his. They appertain to his care and account. "And therefore, though you owe no obedience to any power under heaven, so as to decline you from the true God, or the true worship of that God, and the fundamentall things thereof, yet in those things, which are, in their nature but circumstantiall, and may therefore, according to times, and places, and persons, admit alterations, in those things, though they bee things appertaining to Religion, submit your selves to his directions" (4: 255-6). The repetition of "in those things" cautions Donne's audience to obey only in such matters.

These pleas for obedience in indifferent matters also contrast such actions with those of Papist conspirators who for an ill breath think it good physic to cut off the head, or to suffocate, strangle, or murder that man. These men are responsible for contrary defamations against James: first that he persecuted their religion and now that he has left his own. The plea is overtly political: "Not onely upon your Allegiance to God, but upon your Allegiance to the King, be good: No Prince can have a better guard, then Subjects truly religious" (4: 261). And this requires a daily withdrawing from sin, not a Sunday zeal. In an obvious reference to the prohibition against Sunday afternoon sermons instituted with James's *Directions*, Donne reminds his hearers that they are not starved for want of an afternoon sermon if they cleanse their hearts all week. More important, subjects must value their Prince so that those ambassadors who watch for the destruction of this Israel may be disappointed. Donne cautions his hearers not to play into the hands of the foreign ambassadors by challenging the *Directions* openly. He says that "even *Ambassadors* themselves may be misled to an undervalue of the Prince, by rumours, and by disloyal, and by negligent speaches, from the Subject" (4: 262).

Loyalty is as much an element of the common safety as obedience.

Donne's final paragraph addresses his hearers directly, advising them what they can do even if they are dissatisfied with James's religion. He says "Let not a mis-grounded, and disloyall imagination of coolness in him, cool you, in your own families" (4: 263). And in a clear allusion to recent relaxation of the penal laws, Donne warns family leaders not to be indifferent to Papists, as if Papist and Protestant were but several callings. Though Donne allows the Prince the liberty to open and close the doors of the kingdom "as God shall put into his minde," however, he does not think that this means a relaxing of religious vigilance in the households of the nation. Their responsibility remains despite the new lenience towards Papists. "A Thief that is let out of New-gate is not therefore let into thy house; A Priest that is let out of prison, is not therefore let into thy house neither: still it may be felony, to harbour him, though there were mercy in letting him out" (4: 263).

We know that James demanded a copy of the sermon.[30] Perhaps his purpose was to see whether Donne had contravened the *Directions* and not whether it warranted publication, as Donne suggested in a letter. The sermon, however, was neither censured nor published. James apparently countenanced such criticism, perhaps because to take offence would have confirmed the public impression of his guilt, perhaps because he believed that such hypothetical criticism of "our, not Zedekiah, but Josiah" was a small price to be paid to avoid more direct challenges.

Donne's sermons provide ample evidence of his respect for the letter of the law coupled with an anti-absolutist determination to interpret it flexibly. This approach is well-illustrated in the sermons mentioned above, but I would like to turn to a less well-known sermon preached on January 1, 1624/25, the Feast of the Circumcision, on Abraham's circumcision at the age of 99. Donne's selection of text is unusual, and yet both theologically and politically apt. Abraham's circumcision and its symbolic significance as the mark of the Covenant are appropriate to the feast day. Yet Donne turns Abraham's apparently straightforward consent to the rite in Genesis into a particular case of conscience focused on the issue of obedience.

The call to obedience in this sermon is qualified in typically Donnean ways. For one thing, Donne distinguishes casuistically in the sermon between absolute obedience to men, which requires dispute, resistance, and even suffering on occasion, and obedience to God, which demands that we become "speechless and thoughtless." It is these latter words that Donne's "absolutist" critics quote; however, as with the application of precedent in legal interpretation, the key is in knowing which kind of obedience is applicable to any case, and the implication is that "blind" obedience is never intended. Similarly, Donne offers us a rule: only God knows why he commands a thing; our part is to obey. But, characteristically, Donne concedes that the example is different from the rule.[31] Sometimes, he says, good and godly men reason and dispute against God's commands. Furthermore, Donne suggests, Abraham might legitimately have disputed with God, if any man had taken the liberty. He might have argued, Donne says, that God's promise to him needed no seal, but knew that obedience was better than wit or disputation.

Donne complicates conventional absolutist interpretations, then, by characterizing the text as a case of conscience and by encoding within it Abraham's imagined expostulations (that is, that this seal was frivolous, obscene, incommodious, and needless). Circumcision, he concedes early, is a misinterpretable sign. But Donne raises questions not to domesticate them through some Foucauldian "escape-valve" theory of the way authority controls resistance but to offer them as reasonable, and therefore legitimate, objections to the letter of the law. In framing the example as a test of obedience, and in allowing fully a quarter of his time to the voice of Abraham's expostulation, Donne both legitimates and expresses the limits of resistance in a context where the idea of resistance was not even suggested in his biblical source.

In the light of historical circumstances preceding the sermon's delivery, the interpretation of the sermon becomes even more problematical. In the final weeks of December, 1624, King James once again issued proclamations ordering relaxation of the penal laws against recusants in anticipation of the marriage between Charles and Henriette Marie of France (Gardiner, *History* 278-9). This was not the first time James had done so. But, after the outburst of popular relief at the failure of the Spanish match a year before, the penal laws had been tightened up again and attacks on Catholicism had crept back into sermons. The terrible uncertainty resulting from James's new efforts to appease Catholics worried many who felt that this laxity would be detrimental to continued reform in the Church. This fear of idolatry was compounded by the fear of sedition. Penal laws had been seen for some time as a means of identifying and suppressing potential threats to national religious and political security. Now, the security provided by these laws was being abandoned once more for what many saw as political concessions that would drive England even closer to the brink of Idolatry. For most Churchmen, the French match was only marginally preferable to the infamous Spanish match (Cogswell 278-81).

Donne's attitude to these recent events is difficult to assess; it is likely that he understood the penal laws as they stood *before* the December 1624 proclamation as the political price agreed upon for the liberty of conscientious resistance. And it is reasonable to think that, in keeping with his view of the function of laws generally, Donne saw the penal laws as an effective means of allowing and yet containing such resistance. As Donne observes: "The *Lawe* is my *Suretie* to the *State*, that I shall pay my Obedience, And the *Lawe* is the States *Suretie* to mee, that I shall enjoy my Protection" (6: 253). The place to dispute the Law is "In those *Councells,* where *Lawes* are made" (6: 259).

It is interesting to speculate, then, on how this debate over the relaxation of penal laws can help to put in context this sermon on Abraham's obedience to the misinterpretable and apparently incommodious law of circumcision. Historically, of course, circumcision was a sign to Jews of their covenant with God, a form of continuous renewal which emphasized the responsibility of every family to affirm their identity as the people of God (Van Seters 291-93). Donne's stress on circumcision as a legal and moral constraint on idolatry, then, brings the sermon directly into the discussion of the consequences of the Charles's impending marriage. As Donne expresses it:

> In this rebellious part, is the root of all sinne, and therefore did that part need this stigmaticall marke of Circumcision, to be imprinted upon it. Besides, (for the Jewes in particular) they were a Nation prone to *Idolatry*, and most, upon this occasion, if they mingled themselves with Women of other Nations: And therefore, . . . God would be at the cost even of a *Sacrament*, . . . to defend them thereby against dangerous alliances, which might turn their hearts from *God; God* imprinted a marke in that part, to keep them still in mind of that law, which forbade them *foraigne Marriages*, or any company of *strange Women* . . . And *God* foresaw that extreme Idolatry, that grosse Idolatry, which that Nation would come to . . . (6: 192)

The warning of the idolatry that would ensue if the law of circumcision were not obeyed needs to be interpreted in relation to the circumstances of the proposed French marriage. Equally important is Donne's application of the lessons learned from obedience to legal circumcision to the circumcision of the heart. Donne points out that for Abraham circumcision was a legal sign, one which in Donne's time needs to be replaced with a spiritual one. The same is true, of course, of the penal laws: as the legally enforced signs of conformity, instituted to prevent "grosse idola-try," they must now be replaced by a spiritual conformity. The time is now right for a spiritual renovation among outwardly conforming Christians, perhaps even recusants. This situation reinforces Donne's comments else-where about the value of hypocrisy; as a prelude to conformity and as a way of giving good example it is acceptable, even if the heart is not entirely conformed. Donne's comments on conscience in the sermon reinforce such a view. According to Donne an annual repentance is not enough. And he makes this point in provocatively antiabsolutist lan-guage which suggests that his hearers must challenge the prerogative of their sins. Sedition, he argues, is not in questioning our conscience, not in disputing the "prerogative" of our sins, but in not questioning, in not disputing, in allowing our consciences to become dusty or cobwebbed. Through this discourse of resistance, Donne challenges his audience to think the unthinkable: "we dare not," he says satirically, "dispute the prerogative of our sinne, but we come to thinke it a kinde of sedition, a kinde of innovation, and a troubling of the state, if we begin to question our Conscience, or change that security of sinne which we sleepe in, and thinke it an easier Reformation to repent a sinne once a year, at *Easter*, when we must needs Receive, then to watch a sinne every Day" (6: 196). The point is, surely, that the prerogative of conscience justifies disturbing our "state." In the end, Donne identifies the uncircumcised with idola-tors, those who have been too timid to trouble their consciences with seditious questioning and who have defined obedience as conformity to annual communion.

What seems clear is that Donne's casuistical thinking responds in changing ways to the increasing royal stress on the legality of prerogative government by stressing the prerogative of the conscience in applying laws, both divine and human, to difficult moral decisions, including the question of obedience. But it is not the prerogative of conscience so much as the publicly authorized vocation of minister as "conscience" of the Church that gives Donne freedom to speak. From the pulpit, he argued quite explicitly that although the King had to be obeyed in matters of spiritual and secular discipline, preachers spoke authoritatively on mat-ters of doctrine (Shami, "Kings" 14-15). Suffice it to say that Donne circumscribed the authority of human rulers within the boundaries of divine law and individual conscience in his sermons.

Throughout his career, then, Donne was obedient (although not thereby absolutist), insofar as he could discern the rules of allowable discourse. For his audience, many of them lawyers, Privy Councillors, and Parliamentarians, obedience meant rejecting rumour and the bed of whisperers as the means of offering counsel, even when more direct means were proving ineffective. For Donne, this problem of unlawful counsel and criticism was serious enough for several of his sermons to challenge his audiences to criticize judicially, and openly, within the authorized conventions of discourse.

Donne's sermons must be taken seriously as political statements by a person of considerable experience and discretion. Authorized to bring men to God by drawing their sins near to their consciences, he manages, despite the threats of censorship, to offer advice that is both principled and yet acceptable to both James and Charles. Donne's obedience, in the end, is not the "blind" obedience which he himself disparaged as the practice of the "Church of Rome" (2: 105), but an active challenge to both King and congregation to resolve grievances openly, charitably, and flexibly—within the law. His moderation in a time of bitter intolerance should be judged more realistically by his twentieth-century critics who enjoy rights of speech and publication unprecedented in human history. If Donne's politics are "absolutist" it is important for critics to explain how they are and to find evidence not only in the sermons but in their contexts. If the sermons cannot support this interpretive model, perhaps critics will have to be satisfied with a more complicated but no doubt more realistic interpretation of Donne's relations to the structures of authority in his society. Donne's political casuistry allowed him to develop a language of obedience which resists the "absolutist" label and which served as a model of the kind of counsel available to one trying to adjust the law of conscience to the laws of political authority.

Notes

[1] In a letter to Sir Robert Karre, dated 1627, Donne thanks Karre for remembering him to the King, adding "My Tenets are always, for the preservation of the Religion I was born in, and the peace of the State, and the rectifying of the

Conscience; in these I shall walke, and as I have from you a new seal thereof, in this Letter, so I had ever evidence in mine own observation, that these ways were truly, as they are justly, acceptable in his Majesties eare" (Letters 306-7). There seems to be no good reason to treat Donne's comments about "the Religion" metaphorically, or to assume that he must be referring to his spiritual birth into the Protestant religion. The phrase "the Religion I was born in" could just as likely refer to the "old Catholicism" of his family tradition. See the articles by Flynn and Haigh in list of works cited.

[2] This can be seen primarily in Donne's attacks on the political prerogative of the Pope in his sermons. See especially 3: 350; 7: 124-26.

[3] The influence of Donne's Catholicism on his life and work has been debated by Bald, Chanoff, Carey, Hester, and most persuasively by Flynn.

[4] This view is advanced most plainly by Bald, Carey, Gleason, Goldberg, Marotti, Parfitt, Shuger.

[5] Historians are more reluctant than literary critics to label Donne politically. Prest, for example, identifies the avowedly Puritan preachers at Lincoln's Inn between 1600 and 1640, but says simply that Donne could not be so described (197). Historical work on the effects of patronage relationships on political faction provides several models for talking about such a complex middle ground. See especially the work by Cust, Thompson, Fincham, Lake, Collinson, and Cogswell. Most recently, essays by Norbrook and Patterson ("John Donne, Kingsman") have suggested that the "absolutist" model applied to Donne needs to be qualified and reconsidered. However, neither essay ventures far into the sermons.

[6] A notable exception to this approach is the article by Gifford.

[7] In *Biathanatos*, Donne satirizes weak interpreters of Scripture on just this question of quoting out of context. He writes: "If any small place of Scripture, misappeare to them to be of vse, for iustifying any opinion of theyrs, then (as the Word of God hath that precious Nature of Gold, that a litle quantity thereof, by reason of a faithfull tenacity and ductilenes, will be brought to couer 10000 tymes as much of any other Mettall) they extend it so farre, and labor, and beat it to such a thinnesse, as it is scarse any longer the Word of God, onely to giue theyr other Reasons, a litle tincture and colour of Gold, though they haue lost all the weight and estimation" (110). My own analogy is more pedestrian. Approaching the *Sermons* through the *Index* is analogous to exploring London by tube. Like users of the underground, users of the *Index* pop up unexpectedly and without orientation at key points on the map, but have no idea how they got there, or where they are in relation to other important locations. The distances and relationships between places are distorted, and certainly the texture of the experience is profoundly different. My advice is to explore the sermons on foot.

[8] On the reliability of the *Index* to Donne's Sermons see the review by Shami.

[9] Published comments, for example, on lines 39-42 of "The Calme" are almost uniform in attributing to Donne "a rotten state," "hope of gaine" and the desire to be released from "the queasie paine / Of being belov'd, and loving" as his motives for embarking on the Essex expedition. Few make mention of the "thirst / Of honour."

[10] The words are Ezekiel's; however, they have an interesting autobiographical resonance if one remembers Donne's Catholic mother, who lived with him even while he was Dean of St. Paul's, and if one interprets the statement ironically to refer to Donne's complex religious background.

[11] See works by Lewalski (*Donne's Anniversaries*), Lecomte, and Carrithers. For a more complex view see the essay by Sister Geraldine Thompson.

[12] The notion of a Donne fascinated by the power of God has proved attractive to critics. It reappears in Arthur Marotti's study, *John Donne: Coterie Poet*, as an assertion that "The sudden serious interest in fathers and depiction of paternal deity reveal Donne's preoccupation with powerful authority and his relationship to it. John Carey has observed that Donne's primary emphasis in his later *Sermons* is upon God's power, rather than His love: 'It is Power that does all' [*Sermons*, 8: 128]" (254). Carey's proof has been reduced to six words of Donne's embedded in Marotti's text, and a footnote to Carey's pages 122-125 noted above. When Parfitt wants to make the same point he quotes one passage from Donne on "God's Ordinance of preaching [which] batters the soule," footnotes Carey, and adds Carey's interpretation, that "the power is at the service of orthodoxy against 'innovation.' As preacher Donne achieves the status for which he had been looking for many years; becomes a kind of monarch, almost a god" (105).

This notion that Donne relishes the violent destructiveness of the God of Power is accepted and elaborated extensively in a chapter on Donne in Debora Shuger's *Habits of Thought*. On the basis of footnotes to Carey's footnotes and isolated comments taken from the sermons at large, Shuger claims that "Donne's theology is 'absolutist' not by implication or inference but quite literally and explicitly. The sermons insist on the analogy between God and king and further-more locate the point of contact in power . . . freedom from law, and the distant fearfulness of majesty. Moreover, . . . Donne presses the absolutist qualities of divinity in order to generate terror, insecurity, and guilt. God is the utterly absolute monarch a Stuart could only dream of being" (169). Carey has been apotheosized in this passage in a move that is rhetorically satisfying, perhaps, but begs every question worth asking.

[13] See particularly the articles by Klinck and Nicholls and *Sermons* 3: 327-28, 5: 87-8, 6: 266, and 4: 102. In fact, we have four of a series of six sermons which Donne preached on the Trinity. *Sermons* 3: 12 and 3: 13 are devoted to God the Father; *Sermons* 3: 14 and 3: 15 are devoted to Christ the Son. The sermons on the

Holy Ghost, projected as part of the series [3: 257, 274], are not extant.

[14] See, for example, a series of sermons by Gilbert Primrose, *The Righteous Mans Evils, and the Lords Deliverances*. London, 1625.

[15] For a full discussion of this sermon in its historical context of the Doncaster Embassy in 1619 see Sellin 109-134.

[16] Shuger comments at one point that "To the extent that we cannot but perceive 'oppressive systems' as bad and liberation as good, we are confused by a spirituality based on the duplication of political relations of domination and submission, one valorizing obedience, guilt, and fear" (162). She also admits that the "psychocultural significance" of what she labels "absolutist theology" has become "opaque" to our age which "equates power with oppression and oppression with all that is evil — slavery, sexism, feudalism, colonialism" (161). It is clear that this opacity is exacerbated by her method of selective quotation.

[17] The point is handled in detail in an unpublished essay by Shami ("Gossip").

[18] Gray and Shami consider Donne's use of the *Devotions* to fulfill his responsibility of counsel to Prince Charles, to whom the work is dedicated.

[19] Certainty in law was definitely a goal of lawyers as well as theologians (especially those concerned with proving Election). See White 20; Lakoff 140. In both contexts it was difficult to achieve.

[20] The importance of this concept for Donne is discussed in Shami, "Donne on Discretion" 49-54.

[21] The golden rule for both biblical and legal exegesis was to interpret the literal sense according to the intention. In legal terms the "grammatical and ordinary sense of the words is to be adhered to unless that would lead to some absurdity or some repugnace or inconsistency with the rest of the instrument, in which case the grammatical and ordinary sense of the words may be modified so as to avoid that absurdity and inconsistency, but no further" (Crystal and Davy 215). Donne also is aware that "The literall sense is always to be preserved; but the literall sense is not alwayes to be discerned: for the literall sense is not alwayes that, which the very Letter and Grammer of the place presents ... But the literall sense of every place, is the principall intention of the Holy Ghost, in that place" (6: 62). This latter statement may seem to contradict Donne's statement in *Biathanatos* that the intention of the law may be altered by circumstances and that occasionally a conscience "well temper'd, and dispassion'd" can determine that a Law is no longer binding (47). Clearly, the "principall intention" of the Holy Ghost is difficult to determine and leaves room for the spirit rather than the letter of the law to guide the conscience, rather than a strictly historical sense of the intention of the lawgiver.

[22] See for example John Denison, *A checke to curiosity; and the safest service* (London, 1624); Thomas Barnes, *Cure for the Comfortles* ... (London, 1624); Elias

Petley, *The Royal Receipt* (London, 1623); James Ussher, *A Briefe Declaration of the Universalitie of the Church of Christ* . . . (London, 1624).

[23] See especially Sharpe, Cust, and Cogswell.

[24] See Bullough. This article is a work which repays closer attention. These are also Donne's divisions in *Biathanatos*, one of his most heavily casuistical works.

[25] Shuger takes up this point (178-180), but dismisses too easily the importance of the language of contract law in Donne's sermons. She says that "Donne sets the standard of obedience so high that no one can perform his part of the bargain" (178).

[26] See Norbrook (22) on why Donne might have been selected for the task.

[27] See Cogswell 27-29; Davies; Godfrey 7-14.

[28] This point has been developed in an unpublished paper by Donna Achtzehner, " 'that I have spoken as his Majestie intended': Ambiguity and Communication in Two Sermons of John Donne."

[29] In her paper on Donne's sermons, Achtzehner (2-3) comments on the impact of delivery on a preacher's audience, citing specifically the comments of Chamberlain on Donne's Sept. 15 sermon defending James's *Directions* and on the well-known comment by Tom Tell-Troath on the importance of the choice of texts and body language in communicating the full message of the sermon.

[30] This sermon, corrected in Donne's hand, has recently been discovered by Jeanne Shami. A full discussion of the significance of this discovery is forthcoming in *English Manuscript Studies* 5 (1994).

[31] For discussions of Donne's use of example, see Shami, "Donne's Protestant Casuistry," and Masselink. For extended discussion of Donne's casuistical use of examples see works by Slights and Brown.

Works Cited

Achtzehner, Donna. " 'that I have spoken as his Majestie intended': Ambiguity and Communication in Two Sermons of John Donne." Unpublished paper, 1993.

Bald, R.C. *John Donne: A Life*. Oxford: Clarendon P, 1970.

Brown, Meg Lota. " 'In that the world's contracted thus': John Donne and Renaissance Casuistry." Diss. Berkeley, 1987. Ann Arbor: UMI, 1987. 8726152.

Bullough, Geoffrey. "Donne the Man of Law." *Just So Much Honour*. Ed. Peter Amadeus Fiore. University Park: Pennsylvania State U P, 1972. 57-94.

Carey, John. *John Donne: Life, Mind and Art*. London: Faber and Faber, 1981.

Carrithers, Gale. *Donne at Sermons: A Christian Existential World*. Albany: State U of New York P, 1972.

Chamberlain, John. *The Letters of John Chamberlain*. Ed. Norman E. McClure. Vol. 2 Philadelphia: American Philosophical Society, 1939. 2 vols.

Chambers, A. B. "Will the Real John Donne Please Rise?" *JDJ* 4.1 (1985): 109-120.

Chanoff, David. "Donne's Anglicanism." *Recusant History* 15 (1980): 154-167.

Cogswell, Thomas. *The Blessed Revolution: English Politics and the Coming of War, 1621-1624*. Cambridge: Cambridge U P, 1989.

Collinson, Patrick. *The Religion of Protestants: The Church in English Society 1559-1625*. Oxford: Clarendon P, 1982.

Crystal, David and Derek Davy. *Investigating English Style*. London: Longmans, 1969.

Cust, Richard. *The Forced Loan and English Politics, 1626-1628*. Oxford: Clarendon P, 1987.

Davies, Godfrey. "English Political Sermons, 1603-1640." *HLQ* 3 (1939-40): 1-22.

Davies, Horton. *Like Angels From A Cloud: The English Metaphysical Preachers 1588-1645*. San Marino: Huntington Library, 1986.

Donne, John. *Biathanatos*. Ed. Ernest W. Sullivan II. Newark: U of Delaware P, 1984.

_____. *Letters to Severall Persons of Honour (1651)*. Introduction by M. Thomas Hester. Delmar NY: Scholars' Facsimiles & Reprints, 1977.

Fincham, Kenneth. *Prelate as Pastor: The Episcopate of James I*. Oxford: Clarendon P, 1990.

Fincham, Kenneth and Peter Lake. "The Ecclesiastical Policy of James I." *J of British Studies* 24 (1985): 169-207.

Flynn, Dennis. "Donne's Catholicism: I." *Recusant History* 13 (1975): 1-17.

_____. "Donne's Catholicism: II." *Recusant History* 13 (1976): 178-195.

_____. "Donne the Survivor." *The Eagle and the Dove: Reassessing John Donne*. Ed. Claude Summers and Ted-Larry Pebworth. Columbia: U of Missouri P, 1986. 15-24.

_____. "The 'Annales School' and the Catholicism of Donne's Family." *JDJ* 2.2 (1983): 1-9.

Gardiner, Samuel Rawson. *The History of England from the Accession of James I, to the Outbreak of the Civil War 1603-1642*. Vol. 5. London: Longmans, Green, 1883-84. 10 vols.

_____, ed. *Reports of Cases in the Courts of Star Chamber and High Commission*. Camden Society. New series. 1886.

Gifford, William. "Time and Place in Donne's Sermons." *PMLA* 82 (1967): 388-98.

Gleason, John B. "Dr. Donne in the Courts of Kings: A Glimpse from Marginalia." *JEGP* 69 (1970): 599-612.

Goldberg, Jonathan. *James I and the Politics of Literature: Jonson, Shakespeare, Donne and their Contemporaries*. Baltimore: Johns Hopkins U P, 1983.

Gray, Dave, and Jeanne Shami. "Political Advice in Donne's *Devotions*: 'No Man is an Island.'" *MLQ* 50.4 (1989): 337-356.

Haigh, Christopher. "The Fall of the Church or the Rise of a Sect?" *Historical J* 21 (1978): 181-86.

_____. "The Continuity of Catholicism in the English Reformation." *Past and Present* 93 (1981): 37-69.

_____. "From Monopoly to Minority: Catholicism in Early Modern England." *Transactions of the Royal Historical Society*, 5th ser. 31 (1981): 129-47.

Heatherington, Madelon E. "'Decency' and 'Zeal' in the Sermons of John Donne." *TSLL* (1967): 307-16.

Herrup, Cynthia. *The Common Peace: Participation and the Criminal Law in Seventeenth-Century England*. Cambridge: Cambridge U P, 1987.

Hester, M. Thomas. *'Kinde Pitty and Brave Scorn': John Donne's Satyres*. Durham: Duke U P, 1982.

_____. "Reading Donne's Prerogative." Response to a paper delivered by Jeanne Shami at the International Medieval Institute, Kalamazoo MI, May 4, 1989. 1-7.

_____. "'this cannot be said': A Preface to the Reader of Donne's Lyrics." *Christianity and Literature* 39.4 (1990): 365-385.

James I. "The Trew Law of Free Monarchies." *The Political Works of James I*. Ed. C. H. McIlwain. New York: Russell & Russell, 1965. 53-70.

Kenyon, J. P. Ed. *The Stuart Constitution 1603-1688: Documents and Commentary*. Cambridge: Cambridge U P, 1966.

Klinck, Dennis. "John Donne's 'knottie Trinitie.'" *Renascence* 33.4 (1981): 240-55.

_____. " *Vestigia Trinitas* in Man and his Works in the English Renaissance." *JHI* 42.1 (1981): 13-27.

Lake, Peter. *Anglicans and Puritans?: Presbyterianism and English Conformist Thought from Whitgift to Hooker*. London: Unwin Hyman, 1988.

Lakoff, Robin Tolmach. *Talking Power: The Politics of Language*. New York: Harper Collins, 1990.

Lecomte, Edward. *Grace to a Witty Sinner: A Life of Donne*. New York: Walker, 1965.

Lewalski, Barbara K. *Donne's Anniversaries and the Poetry of Praise: The Creation of a Symbolic Mode*. Princeton: Princeton U P, 1973.

_____. *Protestant Poetics and the Seventeenth-Century Religious Lyric*. Princeton: Princeton U P, 1979.

Marotti, Arthur. *John Donne: Coterie Poet*. Madison: U of Wisconsin P, 1986.

Masselink, Noralynn Jean. "Example and Rule in Donne." Diss: U of Illinois, 1987. Ann Arbor: UMI, 1987. 8803129.

Mueller, William. *John Donne: Preacher*. Princeton: Princeton U P, 1962.

Nicholls, David. "Divine Analogy: The Theological Politics of John Donne."

Political Studies 32 (1984): 570-80.

Norbrook, David. "The Monarchy of Wit and the Republic of Letters: Donne's Politics." *Soliciting Interpretation: Literary Theory and Seventeenth-Century English Poetry*. Ed. Elizabeth D. Harvey and Katherine E. Maus. Chicago: U of Chicago P, 1990. 3-36.

Parfitt, George. *John Donne: A Literary Life*. Basingstoke: Macmillan, 1989.

Patterson, Annabel. "All Donne." *Soliciting Interpretation: Literary Theory and Seventeenth-Century English Poetry*. Ed. Elizabeth D. Harvey and Katherine E. Maus. Chicago: U of Chicago P, 1990. 37-67.

_____. "John Donne, Kingsman?" *The Mental World of the Jacobean Court*. Ed. Linda Levy Peck. Cambridge: Cambridge U P, 1991. 251-272.

_____. "Misinterpretable Donne: The Testimony of the Letters." *JDJ* 1 (1982): 39-53.

Prest, Wilfred R. *The Inns of Court Under Elizabeth I and the Early Stuarts, 1590-1640*. Totowa NJ: Rowman and Littlefield, 1972.

Reeves, Troy D. *Index to the Sermons of John Donne*. 3 vols. Salzburg: Institut fur Anglistik und Amerikanistik, 1981.

Roberts, John R. "John Donne's Poetry: An Assessment of Modern Criticism." *JDJ* 1 (1982): 55-67.

Sellin, Paul. *'So Doth, So Is Religion': John Donne and Diplomatic Contexts in the Reformed Netherlands, 1619-20*. Columbia: U of Missouri P, 1989.

Shami, Jeanne. "Donne on Discretion." *ELH* 47 (1980): 48-66.

_____. "Donne's Protestant Casuistry: Cases of Conscience in the Sermons." *SP* 80.1 (1983): 53-66.

_____. "Gossip, Scandal, and the 'bed of whisperers': Donne and the Laws of Homiletic Counsel." Unpublished essay, 1993.

_____. " 'Kings and Desperate Men': John Donne Preaches at Court." *JDJ* 6.1 (1987): 9-23.

_____. Review of Troy D. Reeves. *Index to the Sermons of John Donne*. *Ren/Ref* 8.1 (1984): 59-62.

Sharpe, Kevin. "Introduction: Parliamentary History 1603-1629: In or out of Perspective?" *Faction and Parliament: Essays on Early Stuart History*. Ed. Kevin Sharpe. London: Methuen, 1978. 1-42.

Shawcross, John T. "Donne as Religionist: The 1980s." Response to three papers on Donne and Religion at the International Medieval Institute, Kalamazoo MI, May 10, 1990. 1-10.

Shuger, Debora K. *Habits of Thought in the English Renaissance: Religion, Politics and the Dominant Culture*. Berkeley: U of California P, 1990.

Slights, Camille Wells. *The Casuistical Tradition In Shakespeare, Donne, Herbert, and Milton*. Princeton: Princeton U P, 1981.

Thompson, Christopher. "The Origins of the Politics of the Parliamentary Middle Group." *Transactions of the Royal Historical Society*, 5th ser. 22 (1972): 71-86.

Thompson, Sister Mary Geraldine. " 'Writs Canonicall': The High Word and the Humble in the Sermons of John Donne." *Familiar Colloquy: Essays Presented to Arthur Edward Barker*. Ed. Patricia Bruckmann. Ottawa: Oberon P, 1978. 55-67.

Tyacke, Nicholas. *Anti-Calvinists: The Rise of English Arminianism, c. 1590-1640.* Oxford: Oxford Historical Monographs, 1987.

Van Seters, John. *Abraham in History and Tradition.* New Haven: Yale U P, 1975.

Wall, John, and Terry Burgin. " 'This Sermon . . . Upon the Gun-Powder Day': The Book of Homilies of 1547 and Donne's Sermon in Commemoration of Guy Fawkes Day, 1622." *South Atlantic R* 49.2 (1984): 19-30.

Webber, Joan. *Contrary Music: The Prose Style of John Donne.* Madison: U of Wisconsin P, 1962.

White, Stephen D. *Sir Edward Coke and 'The Grievances of the Commonwealth.' 1621-1628.* Chapel Hill: U of North Carolina P, 1979.

Woolf, D. R. *The Idea of History in Early Stuart England: Erudition, Ideology, and 'The Light of Truth' from the Accession of James I to the Civil War.* Toronto: U of Toronto P, 1990.

Wright, Nancy E. "The Figura of the Martyr in John Donne's Sermons." *ELH* 56.2 (1989): 293-309.

Coda

"To his dear name addrest":
In Honor of John T. Shawcross

It is appropriate that essays addressing the highly mercurial topic of Donne's religious beliefs and the essentially religious nature of his imagination should be gathered in celebration of the rich career of John T. Shawcross.

"Rare poems ask rare friends," Ben Jonson noted when sending manuscript copies of "Mr. Donne's Satires" to Lucy, Countess of Bedford, and in John Shawcross the poems have had the rarest of friends. For, as Ted-Larry Pebworth concludes in his survey of the place of Shawcross's influential 1967 edition of Donne's *Complete Poetry* in the history of Donne's text, few editors have written as frankly about the ultimate instability of Donne's text, or worked as hard to establish as fair a text as possible. And, as John R. Roberts points out in his analysis of Shawcross's contributions to our understanding of Donne's poetry, few commentators have brought such an extraordinarily wide range of reading to bear upon the examination of Donne's meaning, particularly in matters biblical and theological.

What is more, as Pebworth and Roberts are preempted from saying by the somewhat arbitrary division of labor imposed upon them by the editors of this volume, few scholars in the field have proven as generous as John Shawcross in their encouragement of the work of others, particularly that of younger scholars. A founding member of the John Donne Society, he was elected its second president and has been one of the animating forces of its annual conference, informally commenting upon drafts of papers, formally responding to panel presentations, and generously volunteering the bibliographic information needed to secure a point of interpretation in preparing a conference paper for publication. In February 1994 he received the Donne Society's first lifetime achievement award. He has made of the seventeenth-century studies community in general, and of the Donne studies community in particular, a circle of friends such as the one that Donne attempted to create through his extraordinary verse epistles.

In short, John Shawcross has served as a sphere of influence or planetary intelligence as powerful and as gracious as any that Donne himself could have imagined. By the essays that make up this volume his friends and colleagues have attempted to celebrate—as Ben Jonson did that "reverend head," William Camden—a man at whom one can only marvel and exclaim: "What name, what skill, what faith hast thou in things!"

John T. Shawcross:
Editor of John Donne

Ted-Larry Pebworth

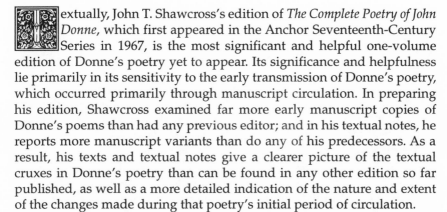

extually, John T. Shawcross's edition of *The Complete Poetry of John Donne*, which first appeared in the Anchor Seventeenth-Century Series in 1967, is the most significant and helpful one-volume edition of Donne's poetry yet to appear. Its significance and helpfulness lie primarily in its sensitivity to the early transmission of Donne's poetry, which occurred primarily through manuscript circulation. In preparing his edition, Shawcross examined far more early manuscript copies of Donne's poems than had any previous editor; and in his textual notes, he reports more manuscript variants than do any of his predecessors. As a result, his texts and textual notes give a clearer picture of the textual cruxes in Donne's poetry than can be found in any other edition so far published, as well as a more detailed indication of the nature and extent of the changes made during that poetry's initial period of circulation.

To appreciate fully the significance of Shawcross's attention to the manuscript readings of Donne's poems, one needs to recall the details of their early transmission. Unlike his contemporary Ben Jonson, who collected and oversaw the publication of his poems, Donne seems to have had a sincere dread of print publication, at least of poetry. Although he apparently had no problem with the idea of a gentleman's publishing prose works, at least those of a serious sort, he considered the printing of poetry—indeed, any manifestation of appearing to be a professional poet—both demeaning to his dignity and potentially offensive to his aristocratic patrons. In 1609, Donne wrote in a letter to his friend Henry

Goodyer that he sought to pursue "a graver course, then of a Poet, into which (that I may also keep my dignity) I would not seem to relapse" (*Letters* 103). Aside from a few commendatory and elegiac pieces included in the books of others, the only authorized printings of Donne's poems during his lifetime are the *Anniversaries* with their accompanying "Funerall Elegie" (1611, 1612). And in a letter to George Gerrard (or Garrard) dated 14 April 1612, Donne lamented those printings as lapses in gentlemanly conduct, characterizing his decision to allow his poems to be printed as a kind of fall from grace: "Of my Anniversaries, the fault that I acknowledge in my self, is to have descended to print any thing in verse, which though it have excuse even in our times, by men who professe, and practise much gravitie; yet I confesse I wonder how I declined to it, and do not pardon my self" (*Letters* 238).

Two years later, when he was pressured by the Earl of Somerset to print a collection of poems before entering holy orders, Donne expressed a fear that such a general publication might offend his longtime patroness, the Countess of Bedford, and vowed his determination to restrict the proposed book's distribution. Writing on 20 December 1614 to Goodyer, who had introduced him to the countess and who frequently acted as their go-between, Donne remarked, "One thing more I must tell you; but so softly, that I am loath to hear my self: and so softly, that if that good Lady were in the room, with you and this Letter, she might not hear. It is, that I am brought to a necessity of printing my Poems, and addressing them to my L. Chamberlain. This I mean to do forthwith; not for much publique view, but at mine own cost, a few Copies" (*Letters* 196-97). Although a collection of his poetry seemed fated to be set in type, Donne clearly intended to treat the distribution of its copies as one would that of manuscripts, not offering them in large numbers for sale to the vulgar, but giving them in limited numbers to members of an intimate coterie of friends, patrons, and prospective patrons. Apparently Donne managed to avoid printing his poems altogether, for no publication from 1615 is known. During the rest of his life, his poetry apparently continued to exist and circulate almost exclusively in manuscript. From the surviving manuscript evidence, moreover, it is clear that many of the original recipients of his poems either made additional copies themselves or had copies made by scribes of various levels of competency for further distribution, and so continued—and complicated—their transmission.

A putatively complete collection of Donne's poetry was first published in 1633, two years after the poet's death, as *Poems, by J.D. with Elegies on the Authors Death* (*STC* 7045). Very little is known of the circumstances surrounding this publication, but from internal evidence, we may draw certain conclusions. The book presents an incomplete canon; it includes poems not of Donne's authorship; its ordering of the poems is more than a little chaotic; and a comparison of its versions of the few poems printed during Donne's lifetime presumably with his cooperation (notably the *Anniversaries* and the elegy on the death of Prince Henry) with their original printings shows the texts printed in the 1633 *Poems* to be nonauthorial. Most likely, then, the first collection of Donne's poems was not set from an autograph manuscript collection, or indeed from any single manuscript collection, but from multiple manuscript sources of varying textual authority as they happened to come into the compiler's or printer's hands.

The second edition of *Poems*, which appeared in 1635 (*STC* 7046), expanded the collection's contents with the addition of both authentic and nonauthentic pieces, rearranged the poems along broad generic lines, and introduced new textual variants from at least one additional manuscript source. Each successive seventeenth-century edition reprinted, with inevitable corruptions, the contents of the preceding edition; and the final seventeenth-century edition (1669, *Wing STC* D 1871), published some 38 years after Donne's death, added a few more poems to the canon.

For the next two hundred years, this final seventeenth-century edition served as the basis for all complete editions of Donne's poetry (1719, 1779, 1793, 1810, and 1855). Indeed, these five purported "editions" of the eighteenth and early nineteenth centuries were essentially reprints of the 1669 collection with little or no editorial intervention. The first attempt at a critical scholarly edition occurred late in the nineteenth century, made by that indefatigable editor of late Renaissance literature, the Reverend A.B. Grosart. For his 1872-73 Fuller Worthies Library edition of *The Complete Poems of John Donne*, Grosart determined to go behind the early printed editions to such seventeenth-century manuscripts containing Donne poems as he could locate. His impulse was a good one, but his methods left much to be desired. Working before most of the surviving manuscript sources had been identified or catalogued, he had less than a comprehensive view of their extent and nature and of the problems they present; and as a consequence, he was indiscriminate in their use and created from them a bibliographically indefensible patchwork of texts.

Probably because Grosart produced such unsatisfactory texts, his emphasis on the importance of manuscripts in the editing of Donne did not prevail. When James Russell Lowell prepared the 1895 Grolier Club edition of *The Poems of John Donne*, he returned to seventeenth-century printings for his copy-texts, but not exclusively to the corrupt 1669 edition. Instead, he chose the first collected printing of each poem, in effect basing the bulk of his edition on the 1633 *Poems*, with the texts of 1635 and 1669 printings used only for those poems that first appeared in them. A year later, E.K. Chambers based his Muses Library edition of the *Poems* on "the principal seventeenth-century editions, those of 1633, 1635, 1650, and 1669," remarking, "No one of these is of supreme authority, and therefore I have had no choice but to be eclectic" (1:[v]).

At this point in the history of Donne's poetical texts, there entered the magisterial figure of Herbert J.C. Grierson, against whose monumental edition all subsequent editors of Donne's poetry have had to react. Grierson's own edition (1912) was itself prepared in reaction to the efforts of Grosart, Lowell, and Chambers. Grierson found Grosart and Chambers to be too unsystematic in their eclecticism, while he determined that Lowell was sound in his principle for selecting copy-texts but misleading and even distortive of meaning in his silent emendations of punctuation (2:cxii-cxiv). In other words, Grierson, like all before him except Grosart, put his faith in the posthumous seventeenth-century printings, not in the early manuscripts. Satisfying himself first on aesthetic grounds that the 1633 edition of *Poems* was textually superior to the subsequent seventeenth-century editions (1:iii-iv), he then proceeded, ostensibly through the use of accepted bibliographical tests, to determine that the 1633 printing "is, taken all over, far and away superior to any other single edition, and, I may add at once, to any *single* manuscript" (2:cxv-cxvi). He thus relegated the manuscript evidence to a secondary role, to be used only as a corrective and then only when the 1633 text was manifestly in error. In practice, he was strongly disinclined to find that first collected printing in error. He even reproduced 1633's corrupt texts of the *Anniversaries* and the elegy on Prince Henry while being fully aware of the earlier, presumably authorized—and therefore more authoritative—printings of those poems.

To his credit, Grierson did examine—in person or by proxy—and collate some 37 early manuscript collections of Donne's poetry, though he did so selectively, only at points he predetermined as being textual cruxes; and in his textual notes he did report—though unsystematically and frequently inaccurately—some manuscript readings at those highly selective points of crux. He persisted, however, in treating the first collected printing as if it had Donne's imprimatur, judging the value of the early manuscripts by how closely they conformed to the readings in the 1633 *Poems*. Issued between the gold-stamped dark blue covers of an "authoritative" Oxford edition, Grierson's text of Donne's poetry—despite its manifest faults in both approach and execution—has exerted enormous influence on all subsequent editors.

The next editor of Donne's poems, John Hayward, consulted 26 manuscripts in the preparation of his 1929 edition of the *Complete Poetry and Selected Prose* (all but two of them already reflected in Grierson's edition) and he made a few more emendations from manuscripts than did his predecessor, but his texts and his attitude that the manuscripts "must be regarded as tributaries to the chief source—the edition of 1633" (xxi) in large measure duplicate Grierson's. His textual notes, on the other hand, are even more selective and less helpful than Grierson's, since he typically uses such terms as "the MSS," "the best MSS," and "most of the MSS" to designate the sources of his emendations and the few variants that he records. The one improvement over Grierson's edition is that Hayward used the first printing of the elegy on the death of Prince Henry (in the third edition of Joshua Sylvester's *Lachrymæ Lachrymarum*, 1613) as copy-text for that particular poem. The major significance of the Hayward text is historical: it was reprinted by Modern Library in 1952, without Hayward's notes but with a new introduction by Charles M. Coffin, and as a consequence was for many years the chief text by which Americans were introduced to Donne's poetry.

The last complete edition of Donne's poetry before Shawcross's is that prepared by Roger Bennett and published in 1942. It is marred by the unwise decision to modernize spelling and punctuation, which obscures some of the subtleties of the original orthography, and by an incomplete study of the manuscripts. Because of the war then raging in Europe, Bennett was unable to consult manuscripts in British repositories and so had to rely exclusively on American-owned manuscripts. Bennett did have respect for the early manuscripts, however; and he incorporated their readings much more liberally than did Grierson or Hayward and even used manuscripts as copy-texts for over 30 of the poems. Moreover, Bennett is the first editor of Donne to use the initial independent printings of the *Anniversaries* and "A Funerall Elegie" (1611, 1612) as the copy-texts for those important poems.

Although Bennett's is the last scholarly edition of Donne's complete poetic canon to be published before Shawcross's in the 25 years between 1942 and 1967, the Donne canon was treated piecemeal by its scholarly editors. There were three influential critical editions of portions of the canon issued in the two decades prior to Shawcross's *Complete Poetry*: Helen Gardner's edition of *The Divine Poems* (1952), Frank Manley's edition of the *Anniversaries* (1963), and Gardner's edition of *The Elegies and The Songs and Sonnets* (1965); and there was an *editio minor* of the *Songs and Sonets* by Theodore Redpath that appeared in 1956. Besides fragmenting the canon, all but one of these editions is seriously flawed.

Redpath's edition of the *Songs and Sonets* is a textbook rather than a scholarly edition, but it has had considerable influence on Donne studies, especially in Great Britain. It shares the shortcomings of Bennett's edition of the *Complete Poems*, namely, modernizing spelling and punctuation, while departing from the early printed texts verbally less frequently than Bennett had done.

Manley's edition of the *Anniversaries* is basically sound. Working with poems printed during Donne's lifetime, presumably with his cooperation, Manley based his texts on collations of all known copies of the first printings and emended their readings conservatively. The only faults are one verbal error in the reading text itself and errors and omissions in his list of press variants.

The most ambitious of the four editions, and the ones making the largest textual claims are the two Oxford volumes prepared by Helen Gardner. The shortcomings in Gardner's approach and practice are too numerous to comment on here in detail (see Pebworth "Manuscript Poems" passim), but a few deserve mention. Most generally, she collated far too few manuscript sources to justify definitive claims; and she made sweeping, largely unsupported—and unsupportable—generalizations about those few that she did collate. For example, at a time when over 100 early manuscripts containing Donne poems were known to exist, she collated only 31 for *The Divine Poems* and 43 for *The Elegies and The Songs and Sonnets* (with 23 manuscripts used in both editions, for a total of 51 in all). Moreover, she continued—and rigidified—Grierson's method of grouping and assessing manuscripts according to their agreement or lack of agreement with the early printings. In addition, for far too many of the poems, she created bibliographically indefensible eclectic texts based on aesthetic considerations rather than on sound objective evidence, while reporting too few manuscript variants to allow the reader to test her textual decisions. Perhaps most shockingly, she excluded (without sufficient explanation for her action) "Sapho to Philaenis," "The Expostulation," "His Parting from Her," "Variety," "Sonnet: The Token," and "Self Love" from the canon, printing them as dubia.

It is against this background of conflicting critical and textbook editions that John Shawcross prepared *The Complete Poetry of John Donne*. Reversing the trend of more than two decades, he determined to edit the

entire canon, to see Donne's poetry whole; and unlike most of his prede-
cessors—including Grierson, Hayward, and Gardner—he began not with
a preconception about the relative value of the textual sources, but with
an open-minded attempt "to examine and collate all known printed and
manuscript sources" (xxi). He not only compared the texts in the seven
seventeenth-century editions and issues of *Poems, by J.D.*, all of which had
been consulted by Donne's twentieth-century editors, but also collated 27
seventeenth- and early eighteenth-century publications containing indi-
vidual poems (listed on 420-22), many of which had never been used
before in preparing an edition of Donne. In addition, he consulted 159
early manuscripts containing Donne poems (listed on 422-27), nearly four
times the number of manuscript sources alluded to by Grierson or
Hayward, and more than three times the number reported by Gardner.
From that extensive study of what was then all of the known manuscript
and early printed sources of Donne's poems, Shawcross determined that
the "posthumous printing of most of the poems seems to have been based
on a manuscript or manuscripts that were not superior to some of the
extant manuscripts and only somewhat superior to others. Indeed, some
manuscripts seem closer to Donne than the probably editorialized print-
ings" (xxi). This insight constitutes a major advance in understanding the
state of Donne's texts.

In editorial theory and practice, Shawcross followed his twen-
tieth-century precedessors. Like them, he used early printings as copy-texts
for most of the poems, emending them with verbals from selected manu-
script sources to create eclectic texts. But unlike the Oxford editors, he laid
no claim—given the state of the artifacts—to establishing a bibliographi-
cally definitive text, and he freely admitted that his textual decisions were
"somewhat subjectively based" (xxi). Most importantly, however, through
his historical collations, which he admits are not complete but which are
in fact much fuller than those in any previous edition, Shawcross makes
his readers aware of more variants in wording in the early sources than
had ever before been reported. For example, whereas Gardner reports
only nine verbal variants in the manuscripts and early printings of "A
Hymne to God the Father," Shawcross reports twelve; and whereas
Gardner reports ten verbal variants in the early sources of "The
Autumnall," Shawcross reports 23. Many of the variants first recorded in
Shawcross's edition are of considerable interest and value, contributing
much to our understanding of Donne's poetry and its early transmission.

Finally, in the matter of canon, Shawcross restores—on good artifactual
authority—poems rejected by Gardner; and he adds, for the first time in

an edition of Donne, the English epigram "Faustus" (165), which he himself discovered in an important manuscript, as well as the Latin epigram addressed to Joseph Scaliger (166), first noticed by Geoffrey Keynes (275).

Shawcross's edition is enhanced by three very helpful lists: a chronological schedule of the composition of Donne's poems, giving both inferential and conjectural dates and such evidence as has been presented for that dating (411-17); an index of textual differences between his and Gardner's editions of the Elegies, Songs and Sonets, and Divine Poems, indicating the reasons for those differences (493-99); and a table of short forms of titles to be used with the Combs and Sullens concordance to Donne's English poems (501-504). Praise is also due to the learned and provocative commentary contained in Shawcross's notes and glosses, an important element of his edition treated at length by John R. Roberts elsewhere in this collection of essays. An especially refreshing aspect of Shawcross's commentary is his restoration of Donne's eroticism, which had been platonized virtually out of existence by Grierson and Gardner.

Shawcross's edition of *The Complete Poetry of John Donne* is an impressive work. Honest and disarmingly modest in its refusal to claim definitiveness in its texts, it nonetheless reflects a depth and breadth of objective textual investigation never before attempted by an editor of Donne's poetry. Its textual decisions made by a scholar/critic of profound learning and discriminating taste, a mark of its achievement is that it has not been bettered in the years since it appeared.

Wesley Milgate completed the four-volume Oxford edition of Donne's poetry under the watchful eye of Helen Gardner, upon whose principles and pronouncements he relied heavily. He published *John Donne: The Satires, Epigrams and Verse Letters* in 1967 (the same year that Shawcross's *Complete Poetry* appeared) and *John Donne: The Epithalamions, Anniversaries and Epicedes* in 1978. Like Gardner, Milgate collated far too few manuscript sources and reported far too few variants for his two volumes to be as useful as Shawcross's one-volume edition.

In 1971, A.J. Smith published *John Donne: The Complete English Poems*. Although its professed aim is "to provide a text which is closely faithful to the early versions without being archaic" ([13]), it wisely does not "pretend to a scientific definitiveness" (14). Useful for its commentary, Smith's edition is textually indefensible. It represents no systematic study of the early sources on the part of its editor; it merely modernizes the spelling of texts in the early printings. Smith gives very few variant readings from early sources in the notes, and then usually identifies them only as being from a "MS" or from "the MSS." Its most egregious fault, however, is its ordering of the *Songs and Sonets*. Because those poems are ordered differently in the early artifacts, Smith adopts what he calls a "neutral order," that is, he arranges the poems alphabetically by title ([353]). What results is the placing of poems next to poems that they appear next to in no early artifact of Donne's poetry and the consequent breaking up of what can be determined bibliographically as probable small sequences of poems within the larger collection. Donne's own ordering of the *Songs and Sonets* (if he ever conceived of the poems as a sequence) may not be reflected in any early artifact, but Smith's solution—actually more deliberately "random" than in any way "neutral"—misleads more than it clarifies.

C.A. Patrides' edition of *The Complete English Poems of John Donne* in the Everyman's Library series (1985) is deliberately regressive in its texts. Following the dictates not only of Grierson, but also of George Williamson (whose many considerable strengths did not include textual criticism), Patrides uses as copy-text for most of the poems their earliest printings and resists—on bibliographically unconvincing grounds—almost all emendation of them, even those made by Grierson (1-5; see also Patrides "John Donne Methodized" passim). The Patrides edition is valuable for its learned and witty commentary and for its extensive secondary bibliography, but its texts are among the most unsatisfactory of any recent edition of Donne's poetry and are further marred by inattentive proofreading.

Finally, there is the Oxford Authors *John Donne*, edited by John Carey (1990), which includes most of the English poetry as well as selected prose works. Textually, this volume is the least defensible modern edition of Donne. Carey apparently made no comprehensive textual study of the early artifacts containing Donne's poetry. Instead, he modernized the spelling of the texts in the Gardner and Milgate Oxford editions and "restored" to them "readings from the seventeenth century editions, particularly the 1633 edition of Donne's poems, where Donne's editors have discarded them" (xxxix). In addition to producing this textual hodgepodge, Carey, while admitting that "not all" of Donne's works "can be dated exactly"—an understatement worthy of Anglo-Saxon poetry—nevertheless arranged the poems "in the chronological order of their composition, as far as possible," in order to allow "a clear sense of Donne's development, as writer and thinker" ([xxxviii]). Given the extreme difficulty of dating most of Donne's individual poems, such an arrangement can only be highly conjectural at best, based primarily on Carey's own, questionable "sense of Donne's development." It obfuscates far more than it illuminates.

Placed against these three editions of Donne's poetry that have been published since 1967, Shawcross's edition of *The Complete Poetry* is luminous in its textual scholarship and exemplary in its good sense. Regrettably, however, this excellent edition is currently out of print and hence unavailable for classroom use.

The prevailing theory of editing Renaissance coterie poetry such as Donne's has changed over the last decade. Aided by the computer, we can now with relative ease and a high degree of accuracy collate—down to the last punctuation mark—all known early copies of individual poems, a task of formidable if not impossible size and complexity during the 1960s with a poet such as Donne. As a result of these detailed collations, we have come to distrust posthumous printings as authoritative and to rely instead on manuscript sources produced closer to the time of a poem's composition by copyists within the author's milieu. Moreover, we have begun to realize that the synthetic or eclectic text often misrepresents the text and textual history of poetry that was designed for manuscript circulation. Textual theorists now conclude that an edition should present edited, though unsynthetic, documentary texts, that is, texts correcting any slips or obvious errors in the copy-text, and texts made to conform to print conventions, but not texts conflating two or more early sources.

For the past twelve years, a small committee of textual scholars has been engaged in preparing just such documentary texts for *The Variorum Edition of the Poetry of John Donne*, a multivolume work to be issued over the next decade by Indiana University Press. In the early years of the Variorum project, John Shawcross was a member of that textual committee, and his knowledge of the sources of Donne's texts and his contributions to the discussions of the problems encountered in assessing texts were invaluable to his colleagues on the committee. Because of the press of numerous other projects and obligations, however, he thought it best a few years ago to withdraw from participation in the work of the textual committee, though he remains an active and valuable member of the Variorum Advisory Board. The Variorum project will ultimately produce an edition of Donne's poetry that is quite different from John Shawcross's, but it will owe an inestimable debt to his pioneering work with the manuscripts, and it will accomplish its tasks with his always generous good will and encouragement.

Works Cited

Bennett, Roger E., ed. *The Complete Poems of John Donne*. Chicago: Packard, 1942.

Chambers, E.K., ed. *The Poems of John Donne*. The Muses Library. 2 vols. London: Lawrence & Bullen, 1896.

Combs, Homer Carroll, and Zay Rusk Sullens. *A Concordance to the English Poems of John Donne*. Chicago: Packard, 1940.

Donne, John. *Letters to Severall Persons of Honour (1651): A Facsimile Reproduction*. Intro. M. Thomas Hester. Delmar, NY: Scholars' Facsimiles & Reprints, 1977.

Gardner, Helen, ed. *John Donne: The Divine Poems*. Oxford: Clarendon P, 1952.

_____, ed. *John Donne: The Elegies and The Songs and Sonnets*. Oxford: Clarendon P, 1965.

Grierson, Herbert J.C., ed. *The Poems of John Donne*. 2 vols. London: Oxford UP, 1912.

Grosart, Alexander B., ed. *The Complete Poems of John Donne*. 2 vols. The Fuller Worthies Library. London: for private circulation, 1872-73.

Hayward, John, ed. *John Donne, Dean of St. Paul's: Complete Poetry and Selected Prose*. Bloomsbury: Nonesuch P, 1929.

Keynes, Geoffrey. *A Bibliography of Dr. John Donne*. Fourth ed. Oxford: Clarendon P, 1973.

Lowell, James Russell, ed. *The Poems of John Donne*. Intro. Charles Eliot Norton. 2 vols. New York: Grolier Club, 1895.

Manley, Frank, ed. *John Donne: The Anniversaries*. Baltimore: Johns Hopkins U P, 1963.

Milgate, W., ed. *John Donne: The Epithalamions, Anniversaries and Epicedes*. Oxford: Clarendon P, 1978.

_____, ed. *John Donne: The Satires, Epigrams and Verse Letters*. Oxford: Clarendon P, 1967.

Patrides, C. A., ed. *The Complete English Poems of John Donne*. Everyman's Library. London: Dent, 1985.

_____. "John Donne Methodized: Or, How to Improve Donne's Impossible Text with the Assistance of his Several Editors." *MP* 82 (1985): 365-73.

Pebworth, Ted-Larry. "Manuscript Poems and Print Assumptions: Donne and His Modern Editors." *JDJ* 3.1 (1984): 1-21.

Redpath, Theodore, ed. *The Songs and Sonets of John Donne*. London: Methuen, 1956.

Smith, A.J., ed. *John Donne: The Complete English Poems*. Penguin English Poets. Harmondsworth: Penguin, 1971.

Williamson, George. "Textual Difficulties in the Interpretation of Donne's Poetry." *MP* 38 (1940): 37-72.

John T. Shawcross:
Critic of John Donne

John R. Roberts

o view the extensive bibliography of John Shawcross in its entirety is to wonder whether there is, in fact, more than one John Shawcross. And indeed there is: there is Shawcross the Spenserian, Shawcross the Miltonist, Shawcross the textual editor, Shawcross the bibliographer, even Shawcross the Joycean, to name but a few. I wish to focus exclusively on Shawcross the critic of John Donne's poetry and prose.

As of 1991, Shawcross has published twenty-one essays on Donne, as well as a major edition of Donne's poetry and several very important reviews of books concerned primarily with Donne. If I were asked, however, to select the one work on Donne that is Shawcross's most important contribution to Donnean studies, I should without a moment's hesitation point to his very fine edition, *The Complete Poetry of John Donne*, which first appeared in 1967, was reprinted in 1968, and reissued in 1971. Although unfortunately now out-of-print, this edition presents the best text we have of Donne's poems to date and is unquestionably the most useful for teaching Donne to both undergraduate and graduate students. In addition to providing a good text of the poems, the Shawcross edition includes a very useful biographical table, a succinct discussion of Donne's canon, a chronology of the poems "as well as it can currently be established" (xxi), a very detailed textual introduction and notes, a perceptive and balanced critical introduction to the poems, a number of poems on Donne in praise of his poetry that appeared in the early editions, a helpful selective bibliography of critical studies of the poems, a table for use with the Combs and Sullens' *A Concordance to the English Poems of John Donne* (1940), and some examples of musical renditions of poems by several of Donne's contemporaries.

For readers of Donne's poetry, perhaps the most important critical contribution Shawcross makes in his edition is the very detailed glosses and explanatory notes that accompany each of the poems, notes that, in his words, "illuminate for the reader Donne's frequently involved syntax, his alchemical, scientific, sexual, and religious imagery, and his archaic language or allusive material" (xxi). Shawcross, however, very wisely warns readers that they "must recognize that annotations are never conclusive: beyond supplying information, the notes try to hint at additional meanings and levels of interpretation which the reader should explore for himself" (xxi). The notes and glosses, however, are so numerous and helpful that later editors of Donne's poems are clearly indebted to Shawcross's edition, although some do not acknowledge the debt as fully as they should.

In the general introduction to the edition, Shawcross comments on what will become his central credo concerning Donne's poems, ideas that are more fully explored and developed in his many reviews, notes, and essays that followed the publication of the edition. For instance, Shawcross decries the fact that "too often critical writing—and the way in which critical problems are posed—reflect the narrowness and prejudgment of the critic" (xix), and he cites two examples to illustrate his point. The first is the insistence of some critics to see a dichotomy between "Jack Donne the rake" and "Dr. John Donne, Dean of St. Paul's," a myth that Donne himself helped create and that Walton accepted in order to present Donne in his biographical account as a modern St. Augustine. A second critical fault that Shawcross highlights in his introduction is the tendency of critics to generalize on the nature of Donne's art based on a consideration of only a handful of the love poems that are totally detached from other genres and other themes. In other words, Shawcross argues that an understanding of the complexities of Donne's poetry demands that critics abandon the old clichés about both Donne the man and Donne the poet and that the poems be read as poems, not as versified biography or philosophy. At the same time, however, Shawcross insists that, *when appropriate*, a solid historical and/or biographical grounding of the poems serves to contribute to a fuller understanding of them. Throughout his edition Shawcross's major concerns are with *text* and *context*, and these two interests inform almost all of his subsequent work on Donne.

Before the appearance of his very valuable edition, Shawcross published three short, but very perceptive essays on Donne's poetry. The first is a persuasive explication of "A Lecture upon the Shadow" (1964), in which he stresses how a correct understanding of the direction the lovers walk (west) clears up several ambiguities in the poem. He also suggests that there are possible biographical interpretations of the poem that would date it as having been written in 1601. He thinks that the poem was perhaps addressed to Ann More and that in it Donne is reminding her that love that is concealed, like theirs, is imperfect. The second essay is an explanation of "A Nocturnall upon S. Lucies Day" (1965), in which Shawcross dates that often misunderstood poem as probably written on or about December 12, 1617, and also suggests that it too most likely was addressed to Donne's wife. The third is an examination of the Hawthornden MSS of William Drummond (1967) that contain new information on Donne's epigrams, epicedes, and obsequies and that report an anecdote about Donne's life found in a letter to Sir Robert Carr. Each of these early essays presages some of the main features of Shawcross's later critical work—his vast knowledge of texts, both those of Donne as well as Donne's contemporaries; his belief that certain poems can be better understood when seen in their historical and/or generic contexts; his interest in biography and in the dating of the poems when this kind of information is truly relevant for a clearer interpretation of individual poems; his conviction that Donne intends to communicate with his readers and that, therefore, the intentionality of the poems, when it can be determined, contributes to a fuller appreciation of them; and his warning that the titles of Donne's poems, for the most part, should not be used in critical interpretations of them because they are often the work of a copyist or an editor. In these essays, as in his later work, Shawcross demonstrates his very extensive knowledge of nearly all aspects of the seventeenth century, of the craft of poetry, and of textual criticism; yet he never engages in what I would call "intellectual acrobatics": his focus is on a better understanding of Donne's poems, not on an exhibition of himself or a dazzling demonstration of his critical and scholarly talents.

In the year following the publication of his edition of the complete poems, Shawcross edited, with an introduction and notes, an early nineteenth-century biography of Donne by Mark Noble, which among other things, shows that Donne had a "more ordinary and generalized reputation and reading public than we have been led to believe" (4); a year later, he edited, with Ronald David Emma, an anthology, *Seventeenth-Century*

English Poetry (1969), in which one finds selections from Donne's poems with annotations and glosses.

In the early 1970's Shawcross remained actively engaged in Donne studies and published three items—a very detailed, but very unfavorable, review of Judah Stampfer's *John Donne and the Metaphysical Gesture*; a long essay on the texts and the meaning of the *Satyres*; and an address on Donne's poetry delivered at the sixty-second annual dinner of the Poetry Society of America. Although Shawcross has been and still is very generous with his time and very supportive of scholars in seventeenth-century studies, sharing his ideas and knowledge especially with young persons in the profession, his review of Stampfer's book indicates that he has little patience with shoddy, inaccurate, and wrongheaded work and also shows how much he values careful and thorough scholarship as well as clarity of expression, both hallmarks of his own work. The review begins this way: "This book should not have been published; it should not even have been written. There is nothing in it of significance; it is totally lacking in value; and it is too often wrong" (301). Thereafter in the review, with a spirit of scholarly objectivity, Shawcross explains in great detail (over five pages) what he finds wrong with the book, amassing numerous examples of inaccuracies and mistakes, incomprehensible phraseology, and faulty conclusions.

In 1972 Shawcross's masterful essay, "'All Attest His Writs Canonical': The Texts, Meaning and Evaluation of Donne's Satires," appeared in *Just So Much Honor: Essays Commemorating the Four-Hundredth Anniversary of the Birth of John Donne*, edited by Peter Amadeus Fiore. Again in this essay Shawcross exhibits his comprehensive knowledge of the text of Donne's poems, his concern about locating the poems within their proper tradition, and his keen critical intelligence and good judgment. He discusses in detail the ordering of the *Satyres* and the importance of that ordering in interpreting them; the problem of dating them; the subject matter, prosody, and stylistic features of the poems; and their possible biographical dimensions. He argues that all five of the poems were likely written in 1597-98 while Donne was in the employment of Egerton, and he shows how they depict "a full range of deadly sin" (262). The essay is one of the most comprehensive and engaging studies of the *Satyres* in print, and better than any of his work up to this time, shows how well Shawcross effectively combines textual scholarship with critical analysis—his most significant contribution to Donne studies in general.

The address that Shawcross delivered in New York at the sixty-second annual dinner of The Poetry Society of America in May 1972 was subsequently published in the society's bulletin. In his address, Shawcross evaluates the present state of interest in Donne's poetry and suggests that, "while the scholars' factory continues and students sometimes become enamored of him, I am not sure that Donne is the critics' darling anymore or the poetic influence he was earlier in our own century" (9), and he further laments that "critical" books on Donne "are unfortunately spotty and inadequate, with only one or two exceptions." He insists that there is a need for "more literary assessment" of Donne's poems, "more analysis of his craft, more joy in sheer reading pleasure than now appears." In short, Shawcross holds that "we have to read Donne's poetry as poetry" (11); and he suggests that there are three reasons why many scholars misread Donne: (1) some insist on viewing too many of the poems as autobiography, failing to recognize the subtle uses of personae and rhetorical strategies; (2) others often view Donne's poems as little more than versified philosophy; and (3) still others are too concerned about applying labels—such as "metaphysical" or "poems in the private mode"—to the kind of poems that Donne wrote.

For nearly eight years—from 1972 to 1980, Shawcross published nothing on Donne; and by simply looking at his bibliography, one might conclude that he himself lost interest in Donne for a while. However, that is not the case; for during those years Shawcross, although heavily burdened with administrative responsibilites, worked diligently on a book-length study of Donne that he recently returned to and hopes to complete in the not-too-distant future. The volume, which takes its working title "John Donne: Accessories to This Name" from "A Valediction of my name, in the window" (14), will examine all important matters to be encompassed by a reader in reading and interpreting both Donne's poetry and prose.

In the 1980's, Shawcross published eight essays and three reviews of books on Donne. Those essays written at the beginning of the decade are rather random in subject matter and seem to be things he "came across" while pursuing other interests. In "The Book Index: Plutarch's *Moralia* and John Donne" (1980), "A Note on the Eighteenth Century's Knowledge of John Donne" (1982), and "The Source of an Epigram by John Donne" (1983), he presents interesting and very scholarly information about relatively limited aspects of Donne's poetry and reputation. However, his lengthy review articles of Helen Peters's edition of *John Donne: Paradoxes and Problems* (1981) and of John Carey's *John Donne: Life, Mind and Art* (1982), as well as his less detailed review of my *John Donne: An Annotated Bibliography of Modern Criticism, 1968-1978* (1983), focus again on central issues in Donne studies. Shawcross's review of Peters's edition reflects, once more, his extensive knowledge of textual criticism and specifically his thorough knowledge of the manuscripts and early editions of Donne's poetry and prose. He thinks Peters's edition is seriously flawed, and he says so in no uncertain terms: This edition "is not a straightforward, cleanly cut, easily useable or useful edition of prose by a major author, although it is one we are going to be stuck with." He calls for an entirely new edition, "not just a correction of all the errors [in Peters's edition] for some new printing" (52); but he adds that he thinks it unlikely anyone will undertake the job in the near future. His evaluation of Carey's book is also fundamentally negative, as indicated by the title of the review, "Annihilating the Poet in Donne" (1982). Shawcross complains that the major defect in the book is that Carey "does not offer a view of Donne the poet because he does not treat the poetry as poetry but ultimately only as versified biography" (269), a point of view that many other reviewers of the book have echoed. Fortunately, for me at least, Shawcross liked my annotated bibliography of Donne criticism for the years 1968-1978 (1983), and very kindly praised its accuracy and completeness, its clear and usable format, its various indices, the objective annotations, and its useful cross-references.

From 1983 to the present Shawcross has done some of his best work on Donne, much of it resulting, at least in part, from his very active membership on the textual committee for the forthcoming variorum edition of Donne's poetry, for which he served as editor-in-chief from 1981 to 1990. He is one of the four textual editors for the first volume in the series, Volume 6: *The Anniversaries, Obsequies, and Epicedes* (expected in 1994 from Indiana U P). At the present time Shawcross remains active on the Advisory Board of the edition and, although no longer taking an active role in the actual editing of the variorum text, is frequently consulted by the present textual editors as they continue to prepare the projected next nine volumes.

At least seven of Shawcross's most recent, and most provocative, essays deal with showing how textual decisions made by editors can drastically influence critical interpretations of Donne's poems. In "A Consideration of the Title-Names in the Poetry of Donne and Yeats" (1983) Shawcross again, with numerous additional examples, warns readers not to base critical interpretations of Donne's poems on their titles, many of which do not come from Donne himself but from some copyist or early editor; and he points out how titles often "delimit and even diminish our reading" of a poem. For instance, if one reads Donne's epigram that begins "Both rob'd of aire" without the title, the poem appears to be a "witty comment on love and lovemaking"; but, if one reads the assigned title, "Hero and Leander," he is directed to see the poem as a rendering of the story of the two famous lovers, "not some generalized witty social comment" (160). Later on, in "But Is It Donne's? The Problem of Titles on His Poems" (1988), Shawcross returns to the issue of titles—this time in even greater detail. He argues that a title "will direct the reader to read in a certain way, to look for certain narrative or attitudinal elements, and, unfortunately at times, to miss certain implications which just don't fit the title" (146). If a poem is not titled, but referred to only by its first line, he argues, "perhaps the reader will discover things in a poem otherwise obscured and will surely avoid readings which are otherwise extrinsic to that text" (149). Shawcross maintains that his guideline for giving titles to Donne's poems would be (1) "to ascertain what might have been Donne's title (there may be few beyond the generic and verse letter forms)"; (2) "to accept well-known titles if they do not conflict with the substance of the poem and are obvious possibilities (like 'The Flea')"; (3) "a kind of combination of the two others, to employ a well-known title that might have been Donne's but without whatever questionable additions might have accrued (like 'A Valediction')"; and (4) "to omit titles and give only a short form of the first line (definitely not to make up titles like 'Recusancy')" (as Helen Gardner does in her edition of the love poems) (148).

In "A Text of John Donne's Poems: Unsatisfactory Compromise" (1983) Shawcross comments on other problems editors confront in editing Donne's poems, such as how to resolve conflicting and/or different texts in various manuscripts and early printed editions, how to order the poems within a generic category, how to order genres in a single volume edition, and how to resolve the question of classification by genre for certain poems. The ways in which editors resolve these issues, Shawcross argues, will obviously affect critical interpretations of the poems. Because of the complexity and uncertainty of these issues, Shawcross maintains that any editor of Donne, after weighing as objectively as possible all the available evidence, is going to be forced nonetheless "to step in and make sense of a line, is going to have to interfere" and, "whatever textual conclusion is made, it is going to be an unsatisfactory compromise for some readers" (16). For instance, in line 29 of the holograph verse letter to Lady Carey and Mrs. Riche, the only poem we have in Donne's own hand, it is impossible to say with certainty that the next to last letter in the word "Religions" is an *n* and not a *u*, even though all other known texts of the poem have "Religions," not "Religious." An editor must decide which word to print, and inevitably some readers will be dissatisfied with his choice. Also, in "'What do you read?' 'Words'—Ah, But Are They Donne's?" (1988), Shawcross argues the need for "a defensible text" of Donne's poems—"defensible if not certain; if not assuredly the author's, at least defensible" (23), and he insists that "the overriding concern in establishing a defensible text is the contextual base which emerges for that text and every part of it—word, comma, spelling, capitalization, stanzaic shape, and so forth" (27). He shows once again that the textual editor cannot rely only on the evidence he discovers from a careful examination of manuscripts and early editions, which are often contradictory or at least inconclusive, but he must also make subjective decisions based on the poet's craft and on the belief that the poet is a "continuing presence in his work" (26). In other words, the editor must make choices on a contextual basis and not simply on the "authority" of manuscripts and early editions.

Shawcross in "The Making of the Variorum Text of the *Anniversaries*" (1984) specifically outlines some of the basic problems and questions that arose as he worked with the other textual editors on this volume of the edition, such as the problem of choosing a copy-text, of formatting, and of specific readings of individual lines—issues which, at the time Shawcross was writing, had not been resolved entirely by the textual committee.

In "The Arrangement and Order of John Donne's Poems" (1986) Shawcross continues to demonstrate very convincingly how textual criticism is closely allied with "literary" criticism or interpretation. In this essay he describes the collections of Donne's poems in manuscript and in print and comments on the importance of generic grouping and its effects. His main purpose, however, is "to indicate the importance of generic arrangement and order for our reading of a poem and of a group of poems" and "to re-view the reliability of arrangement and order of Donne's poems specifically" (121).

In his most recent essay on textual scholarship, "Scholarly Editions: Composite Editorial Principles of Single Copy-Texts, Multiple Copy-Texts, Edited Copy-Texts" (1988), Shawcross comments on three of Donne's poems—"The Lier," Holy Sonnet: "This is my playes last scene," and "The Flea"—as examples of textual cruxes that must be resolved by the scholarly editor. Shawcross believes that, although consistency in spellings, punctuation, capitalization, italicization, and so forth may be acceptable in semipopular or popular editions of a poet's work, the same kind of consistency should not be imposed on scholarly editions; therefore, he advances for discussion a new editorial principle. Basically

Shawcross argues that for a poet like Donne, where there is almost no holograph material, editorial "interference" is often required. He maintains, in fact, that for a scholarly edition of a poet's corpus, such as the forthcoming variorum edition, "an editor must consider individually each piece of writing and all its contexts; must decide the most accurate presentation of the text and the history of the text; and must therefore at times seem inconsistent in what is being done." He continues, "Treatment of some texts will offer a simple text with notes and variants" (e.g., "The Lier"); "some texts will offer a single text with editorial interference, discussion, notes, and variants" (e.g., Holy Sonnet: "This is my playes last scene"); "and some texts will be offered in multiple versions with discussion, notes, and variants" (e.g., "The Flea") (311).

In addition to focusing his attention in the 1980's on textual aspects of Donne's poems, Shawcross wrote on a wide range of other issues as well. For example, in 1985, in "Opulence and Iron Pokers: Coleridge and Donne," he explains Coleridge's understanding, appreciation, and admiration of Donne's art and attempts to dispel old clichés that critics continue to harbor about Donne's poetry, such as the meaning of "metaphysical" when applied to it, the notion that Donne's prosody is faulty, and the mistaken notion that in the eighteenth century Donne's poetry was almost forgotten. In "On Some Early References to John Donne" (1988), Shawcross again attacks the cliché that Donne's poetry was little known before the nineteenth century. He points out that A. J. Smith's *Critical Heritage of John Donne* (1975) "has provided evidence to question the implications of that belief" (115) and notes that since 1975 additional allusions, imitations, and brief discussions have been discovered. To this ever-growing list Shawcross himself adds six more unrecorded early references to Donne. In "The Concept of *Sermo* in Donne and Herbert" (1987), Shawcross demonstrates how the medieval concept of *sermo*—"a conversation and a joining together of ideas, presented to lead the auditor into a heartfelt and thoughtful experience—underlies some of the poetry of both Donne and Herbert, providing a somewhat different avenue into our understanding of those poems and our appreciation of their form, structure, and imagistic components" (205).

Throughout Shawcross's criticism of Donne there is an emphasis on the necessity of locating the poem in its proper context while, at the same time, there is also the warning that the "primary context" is the text itself. Biography, historical information, philosophical ideas, and other considerations can be useful sometimes, he argues, but they can also mislead the reader if they are only partially accurate or wrongly imposed on a poem.

In "Poetry, Personal and Impersonal" (1986), Shawcross shows that the critical discussion on some of Donne's poems "provides excellent examples of indefensible biographical or philosophical interpretations" (53), pointing out, for instance, how the reference to Mary Magdalen in "The Relique," which some critics have assumed must be an allusion to Magdalen Herbert, and how the title "Twickenham Garden," the residence of Lucy, Countess of Bedford, have led critics to gross misinterpretations of those poems. He argues that there is, in fact, a "pre-text" before the actual text and insists that, when we read Donne, "we should remember the way in which he has interwoven biographical details into the poems, the way in which they may inform us of biographical—or more usually ideational or psychological—matters, and the way in which they may represent an imaginative and artistic artifact without significantly direct biographical overtones." He adds, "An author does write out of himself—his experiences and his thoughts and his total being; but a major factor in the evaluation of a piece of literature is the execution of the work itself and the result of that execution (the literary artifact), not what we have learned about the author" (66).

Somewhat along similar lines, in "Literary Revisionism and A Case for Genre" (1985), which in revised form appears as the first chapter in his *Intentionality and the New Traditionalism: Some Liminal Means to Literary Revisionism* (1991), Shawcross challenges "modish literary criticism," especially deconstructionism and flawed reader-response theories, and argues for the authorial presence in poems, maintaining that the very existence of a poem or other piece of literature implies that the author had some kind of "intent" when the piece was written. Shawcross, in fact, identifies three "texts"—"the text, the reader's text, the author's text"— and argues that the job of the literary critic is "to render all three texts in all their relationships" (415). He comments specially on the importance of genre, which "predicates an author and authorial presence, and in turn implies meaning for the reader" (426). He uses Donne's poetry in this essay as an illustration of his viewpoint.

In the 1990's Shawcross continues to write on the text and contexts of Donne's poems, as evidenced by his favorable review of *The First and Second Dalhousie Manuscripts: Poems and Prose by John Donne and Others, A Facsimile Edition*, edited by Ernest W. Sullivan, II (1991), and by his very interesting essay "Donne's `Aire and Angels': Text and Context" (1990). This most recent essay again addresses the issue of how both text and context influence interpretation. Shawcross points out that "the position of a poem alongside other poems may be meaningful, to the reader at least, even if not so intentionally arranged by an author. For as the reader moves from one poem—its subject, treatment, attitude, effect, language—to another, various comparisons or contrasts or developments of these poetic elements may be experienced, and thus its 'context' rather than its being read in isolation may offer meaning." He also argues, as he has for so many years, that "what text is read, and the instabilities of that text, will predicate its interpretive possibilities" (34). He shows that the ambiguities of "Aire and Angels" are "underscored by not only its imagery but also its positioning among the Songs and Sonets" (37).

Shawcross's scholarly publications on Donne are not simply a reshuffling of what is already known but are original and thought-provoking contributions to our understanding of the poet. His masterful command of the textual history of the poems and his vast knowledge of the historical, political, and social contexts in which they were written, combined with his very keen critical insights and clear prose style, make his work a joy to read. Also, as surely is already apparent, much of Shawcross's work on Donne has important and obvious implications for the reading of other poets as well, for it addresses general literary and textual issues that need to be taken into account when one reads any Renaissance poet.

If John Donne were alive today, I think he would say, "John, thou hast done very well indeed."

Bibliography of Publications Primarily Concerned With John Donne by John T. Shawcross

"Donne's 'A Lecture upon the Shadow.'" *ELN* 1 (1964): 187-88.
"Donne's 'A Nocturnall upon S. Lucies Day.'" *Explicator* 23 (1965): Item 56.
"John Donne and Drummond's Manuscripts." *ANQ* 5 (1967): 104-05.
The Complete Poetry of John Donne (editor). Garden City: Doubleday/Anchor Books, 1967. Rpt. New York: New York U P, 1968; and London: U of London P, 1968. Reissued 1971.
"An Early-Nineteenth Century Life of John Donne: An Edition with Notes and

Commentary." *J of the Rutgers U Library* 32 (1968): 1-32.

Seventeenth-Century English Poetry (edited with Ronald David Emma). Philadelphia: J. B. Lippincott, 1969.

Review of Judah Stampfer's *John Donne and the Metaphysical Gesture. JEGP* 70 (1971): 301-06.

"All Attest His Writs Canonical: The Texts, Meaning and Evaluation of Donne's Satires." *Just So Much Honor: Essays Commemorating the Four-Hundredth Anniversary of the Birth of John Donne.* Ed. Peter Amadeus Fiore. University Park: Pennsylvania State U P, 1972. 245-72.

["John Donne"]. *The Poetry Society of America Bulletin* (May 1972): 9-14. (Address to The Poetry Society of America at its sixty-second annual dinner)

"The Book Index: Plutarch's *Moralia* and John Donne." *JRMMRA* 1 (1980): 53-62.

Review article of *John Donne: Paradoxes and Problems*, ed. Helen Peters. *Analytical and Enumerative Bibliography* 5 (1981): 46-53.

"A Note on the Eighteenth Century's Knowledge of John Donne." *Kentucky R* 3 (1982): 68-73.

"Annihilating the Poet in Donne" (review of John Carey's *John Donne: Life, Mind and Art*). *Review* 4 (1982): 265-73.

Review of John R. Roberts's *John Donne: An Annotated Bibliography of Modern Criticism, 1968-1978. Analytical and Enumerative Bibliography* 7 (1983): 156-58.

"A Consideration of Title-Names in the Poetry of Donne and Yeats." *Names: J of the American Names Society* 31 (1983): 159-66.

"A Text of John Donne's Poems: Unsatisfactory Compromise." *JDJ* 2 (1983): 1-19.

"The Source of an Epigram by John Donne." *ELN* 21 (1983): 23-24.

"The Making of the Variorum Text of the *Anniversaries*." *JDJ* 3 (1984): 63-72.

"Opulence and Iron Pokers: Coleridge and Donne." *JDJ* 4 (1985): 201-24.

"Literary Revisionism and A Case for Genre." *Genre* 18 (1985): 413-34. (Revised as "Introduction: Literary Revisionism: Definitions and Devices." *Intentionality and the New Traditionalism: Some Liminal Means to Literary Revisionism.* University Park: Pennsylvania State U P, 1991. 1-19).

"Poetry, Personal and Impersonal: The Case of Donne." *The Eagle and the Dove: Reassessing John Donne.* Ed. Claude J. Summers and Ted-Larry Pebworth. Columbia: U of Missouri P, 1986. 53-66.

"The Arrangement and Order of John Donne's Poems." *Poems in Their Places: The Intertexuality and Order of Poetic Collections.* Ed. Neil Fraistat. Chapel Hill: U of North Carolina P, 1986. 119-63.

"'What do you read?' 'Words'—Ah, But Are They Donne's?" *The Donne Dalhousie Discovery.* Ed. Ernest W. Sullivan, II, and David J. Murrah. Lubbock: The Friends of the University Library/Southwest Collections, Texas Tech U, 1987. 21-31.

"The Concept of *Sermo* in Donne and Herbert." *JDJ* 6 (1987): 203-12.

"But Is It Donne's? The Problem of Titles on His Poems." *JDJ* 7 (1988): 141-49.

"Scholarly Editions: Composite Editorial Principles of Single Copy-Texts, Multiple Copy-Texts, Edited Copy-Texts." *TEXT* 4 (1988): 297-317.

"On Some Early References to John Donne." *JDJ* 7 (1988): 115-17.

"Donne's 'Aire and Angels': Text and Context." *JDJ* 9 (1990): 33-41.

Review of *The First and Second Dalhousie Manuscripts: Poems and Prose by John Donne and Others: A Facsimile Edition*, edited by Ernest W. Sullivan, II. *ANQ* 4 (1991): 39-41.

Intentionality and the New Traditionalism: Some Liminal Means to Literary Revisionism. University Park: Pennsylvania State U P, 1991.

Contributors

HELEN B. BROOKS was appointed to Humanities Special Programs at Stanford University following completion of her doctorate at Stanford in 1980. She teaches courses in Renaissance intellectual and cultural history, Shakespeare, English Renaissance poetry, and critical theory. Her publications include studies of Donne and of John Davies of Hereford. She is completing a publication on covenant theology and the poetry of John Donne.

CATHERINE CRESWELL recently defended a doctoral dissertation in English at the State University of New York at Buffalo. She has presented several papers on Donne and is currently completing a book manuscript on the constitution of subjectivity in Donne's poetry and religious writing.

THERESA M. DI PASQUALE is an assistant professor of English at Florida International University. Her articles on Donne's lyrics appear in *Renaissance Discourses of Desire*, ed. Claude Summers and Ted-Larry Pebworth, and in the *John Donne Journal*. She is currently completing a book on the sacramental poetics of the *Songs and Sonets*.

DANIEL W. DOERKSEN, a professor of English at the University of New Brunswick, Fredericton, Canada, has published articles on George Herbert and Edmund Spenser, and is a Contributing Editor of the *Divine Poems* volumes in the *Donne Variorum*. He has completed a book manuscript, "George Herbert's Church: Conforming to the Word," and is at work on a study of Donne's *Sermons*.

DENNIS FLYNN is a professor of English and department chair at Bentley College. The author of several essays on Donne, he is a Contributing Editor for the *Donne Variorum* project, and is working on a biography of Donne. A book-length study of Donne and the ancient Catholic nobility is forthcoming from Indiana University Press.

RAYMOND-JEAN FRONTAIN (co-editor) is an associate professor of English at the University of Central Arkansas, and the editor of three collections of essays tracing biblically-inspired literary traditions. A Contributing Editor of the *Divine Poems* volumes in the *Donne Variorum*, he is presently researching the biblical models for Donne's *Anniversaries*.

KATE G. FROST, an associate professor of English at the University of Texas in Austin, is the author of *Holy Delight: Typology, Numerology, and Autobiography in John Donne's "Devotions upon Emergent Occasions."* At present she is engaged on a critical edition of the *Devotions*, as well as on a lengthy study of the 1595 Donne Lothian portrait.

PAUL W. HARLAND teaches Renaissance and twentieth-century literature at Augustana University College in Camrose, Alberta, where he is an associate professor. He has published articles on Donne's homiletic personae and on Donne's view of the imagination and affections.

JOAN HARTWIG, a professor of English at the University of Kentucky in Lexington, is the author of *Shakespeare's Tragicomic Vision* and *Shakespeare's Analogical Scene: Parody as Structural Syntax*, as well as several articles on Andrew Marvell. A founding member of the John Donne Society Conference, she has read papers at their annual meetings. Her essay included here is part of a longer study on the significance of the horse in English Renaissance literature.

M. THOMAS HESTER is a professor of English at North Carolina State University and a founding editor of the *John Donne Journal*. He is the author of *Kinde Pitty and Brave Scorn: Donne's Satyres*, and the editor of *Dictionary of Literary Biography: British Seventeenth-Century Nondramatic Poets* (3 vols.), *John Donne: Selected Prose* (forthcoming), and the *Satyres* volume in the *Donne Variorum Edition*. A past president of the John Donne Society, he is presently working on a book to be titled "Donne and the Politics of Wit," and with Ernest Sullivan is collaborating on an edition of Donne's prose letters.

JEFFREY JOHNSON is an assistant professor of English at College Misericordia and the author of articles on Vaughan and Herbert. In addition to a forthcoming article that examines the sermon and hymn marking Donne's "last going into Germany," he is a Contributing Editor of the *Epigrams, Epithalamia, Epitaphs, and Inscriptions* volume in the *Donne Variorum*.

GEORGE KLAWITTER is an associate professor of English at Saint Edward's University, Austin, Texas, and a Contributing Editor for the *Donne Variorum*, his responsibilities being the criticism published on the *Songs and Sonets* between 1920 and 1939. His publications include articles in both medieval and Renaissance studies, and an edition of Richard Barnfield's poems. His book-length study of Donne's narrators is forthcoming from Peter Lang.

JOY L. LINSLEY is the Cullen Foundation Professor of English at the University of Saint Thomas in Houston. Although she has worked primarily with the English Romantic poets and is associate editor of the six-volume *Journal of Thomas Moore*, she has been a student of John Donne for many years.

FRANCES M. MALPEZZI (co-editor), a professor of English at Arkansas State University, has published essays on Du Bartas, Sylvester, Spenser, Donne, Herbert, Herrick, and Vaughan. She has focused on the religious imagination of Donne in essays appearing in the *American Benedictine Review, South Central Review, Religion & Literature,* and *Renascence.*

MARY ARSHAGOUNI PAPAZIAN is an associate professor of English at Oakland University in Rochester, Michigan. She has published articles on Donne in *Modern Philology, Renaissance and Reformation, Huntington Library Quarterly,* and elsewhere. A Contributing Editor of the *Songs and Sonets* volumes in the *John Donne Variorum*, she is presently at work on a book on Donne's Augustinianism and attitudes towards affliction in the *Devotions* and *Divine Poems.*

TED-LARRY PEBWORTH is William E. Stirton Professor in the Humanities and Professor of English at the University of Michigan in Dearborn, where he co-organizes (with Claude J. Summers) the Biennial Renaissance Conference series. A past president of the John Donne Society of America, he is a textual editor and a member of the Advisory Board of the *Donne Variorum*. He is the author, co-author, or co-editor of twelve books on seventeenth-century literature, and has published numerous textual and critical articles.

ALLEN RAMSEY teaches Renaissance studies, Shakespeare, and compositon at Central Missouri State University, where he is a professor of English. His essays on Renaissance literature, modern drama, and rhetoric have appeared in *Studies in the Humanities, Publications of the Arkansas Philological Association, The Midwest Quarterly, Rhetoric Society Quarterly,* and *Faulkner Journal.*

Contributors

JOHN R. ROBERTS is a professor of English at the University of Missouri at Columbia. He has published two annotated bibliographies of modern critical studies of Donne, annotated bibliographies of critical studies on Herbert and Crashaw, and essays on Southwell, Donne, Herbert, and Crashaw. The inaugural president of the John Donne Society, he is both a member of the Advisory Board and General Editor of the commentary for the *Donne Variorum Edition.*

JOSHUA SCODEL, an associate professor of English at the University of Chicago, is the author of *The English Poetic Epitaph: Commemoration and Conflict from Jonson to Wordsworth*, which includes a chapter on Donne's funerary poetics, and of an essay in *Modern Philology* on Donne's use of the mean. He is currently at work on a book-length study of moderation and excess in early modern England, in which Donne will be a central figure.

JEANNE SHAMI is an associate professor of English at the University of Regina in Saskatchewan, Canada, where she has taught since 1977. Her scholarly work focuses on Jacobean and Caroline sermons in general, and on Donne's sermons in particular. She is currently completing a book on the impact of James's *Directions to Preachers* on sermons 1621-25, and is Commentary Editor of the *Verse Letters* volume in the *Donne Variorum Edition.*

P. G. STANWOOD is a professor of English and former director of graduate studies in English at the University of British Columbia, Vancouver. A member of the executive committee of the John Donne Society, he is the author of *The Sempiternal Season: Studies in Seventeenth-Century Devotional Writing*, and with Heather Ross Asals *of John Donne and the Theology of Language.*

JULIE YEN received her Ph.D. from Brown University and is currently an assistant professor of English at California State University, Sacramento. A Contributing Editor of the *Satyres* volume in the *Donne Variorum*, she has written on Donne's poetry and on Aurelian Townshend, and is currently working on a book-length study of Donne's poetry and early prose.

Index
of
The Works of John Donne

SATIRES 8, 429

SONGS AND SONETS ix, 3, 5, 7, 373, 420

VERSE LETTERS 432